LINCOLN ARCHAEOLOGICAL STUDIES No. 2
GENERAL EDITORS: MICHAEL J. JONES AND ALAN VINCE

The Archaeology of Wigford and the Brayford Pool

Kate Steane
with Margaret J. Darling, Jenny Mann,
Alan Vince and Jane Young

Oxbow Books

Lincoln Archaeological Studies are published by
Oxbow Books, Park End Place, Oxford OX1 1HN

ISBN 1 84217 021 X

A CIP record for this book is available from The British Library.

This book is available direct from

Oxbow Books, Park End Place, Oxford OX1 1HN
(Phone: 01865–241249; Fax: 01865–794449)

and

The David Brown Book Company
PO Box 511, Oakville, CT 06779, USA
(Phone: 860–945–9329; Fax: 860–945–9468)

or from our website

www.oxbowbooks.com

Printed in Great Britain at
The Short Run Press
Exeter

Contents

Preface and Acknowledgements

The name of 'Wigford' is derived from that of the medieval suburb, probably originating in the early 10th century, and applies to that part of Lincoln City south of the river and southwards for about a mile to the St. Catherines area and South Common. Although Wigford contained the city's two surviving Saxo-Norman churches, the remarkable 12th century St Mary's Guildhall, and an extensive area of waterfront, and moreover had yielded several discoveries of Roman buildings and burials, no formal archaeological investigations took place before 1972.

This was the first year of operation of the Lincoln Archaeological Trust, and it was a hectic time for rescue archaeology, with many redevelopment schemes planned in the commercial part of the city. The need for a new multi-storey car park between Lucy Tower Street and Brayford Wharf North occasioned the first excavation in Lincoln to be directed solely at medieval occupation – the extended City Wall (lt72) – for this site lay under water in the Roman period. Not far away to the south-east, construction of a large new office building between High Street and the Brayford Pool involved the destruction of both the Holmes Grainwarehouse and, further east, of 181–3 High Street (hg72). This site was situated opposite the early church of St Mary le Wigford, which still retains its builder's dedicatory inscription, a reused Roman tombstone. Here a pioneering trench was excavated adjacent to the High Street to test for the survival of archaeological deposits in this part of the town, where little effort had been made previously to investigate sites in advance of redevelopment. The site proved to be extremely productive, and actually got more interesting as the work progressed, with evidence for structures going back to the 10th–11th centuries, thereby corroborating a pre-conquest origin for the medieval suburb; then, after a break in the sequence, more deposits belonging to all four centuries of the Roman period and possibly occupation a century earlier - for the first time in the city.

Thus, the rich potential of the whole area was clearly demonstrated. Over the next fifteen years, as reported in this volume, and since, some of that potential has been fulfilled. Already published is the excavation of the church of St Mark from 1976 (Gilmour and Stocker 1986) and a comprehensive survey of St Mary's Guildhall from 1982 (Stocker 1991). The investigation of the Roman commercial suburb over several subsequent years has shown that it extended for at least a kilometre and has yielded remains of at least eighteen traders' houses to date. Lincoln is now a well-quoted example of Roman suburban occupation. While the commercial highpoint appears to have been the late 3rd century, the earliest levels beneath the houses have produced evidence for various types of land use, in one case as a 1st century cemetery, not devoted solely to the army but definitely Roman in nature.

In the meantime, the city was also making its own contribution to the emerging discipline of waterfront archaeology, with further structures revealed to the east of Brayford Pool at Dickinson's Mill (1972–3), the new Lincolnshire Echo building on Brayford Wharf East (1982), and St Benedicts Square (1985). An important element of the work in the 1980s was a number of environmental studies, again a developing aspect of research which has been thoroughly worthwhile; there is useful evidence here on the surrounding fauna and flora and the nature of the river. Although not reported on here, subsequent investigations on Waterside North (1987–91) have added considerably both to knowledge of the riverfront downstream of Brayford Pool, and of some more environmental aspects (e.g., Dobney et al, 1996). Related to this has been analysis of O.D. levels and of the occurrence of peat deposits, which has helped elucidate the early topography of the Wigford area.

Brief accounts of all of the excavations appeared in the Annual Reports of the then Trust. Longer accounts, although still in interim form, were published of those sites investigated up to 1980 (Colyer 1975; Jones (ed), 1981). More considered analyses include not only those on St Marks Church and St Mary's Guildhall, mentioned above, but also that on the late Iron Age and Early Roman levels at 181–3 High Street (Darling and Jones 1988). Several other detailed accounts had been drafted by 1987, when English Heritage recommended a change in publication policy, with the result that no further major reports have appeared from 1991 until after the archive had been computerised, and an assessment made of the significance of the material so that decisions could be made about how to publish the rest of the material. The current publications project was also generously funded by English Heritage. This volume represents both a significant experi-ment, and, we hope, a considerable advance in publishing detailed results, a process which has already begun (Vince (ed), 1993; Dobney et al, 1996; Jones (ed), 1999) and which will continue largely through the medium of this series.

It is to be hoped that the benefits of the integrated analytical approach adopted by the Lincoln post excavation team, which toiled for several years on this mass of material, will be apparent, and that the discoveries made in Lincoln since the foundation of the Lincoln Unit in 1972 will thereby achieve the recognition which they deserve.

Acknowledgements

Those who took part in the excavations are too numerous to mention here. Individual site directors and supervisors are thanked in the introductory sections of the appropriate site report.

The current integrated project was developed with the advice of Dr Michael Parker-Pearson, then an Inspector of Ancient Monuments with English Heritage and Tim Williams of English Heritage's Archaeology Division. Their colleague, Dr G J Wainwright, agreed to provide substantial funding. Christopher Scull of the Archaeology Division, and Malcolm Cooper and Andrew Brown, Inspectors of Ancient Monuments, have also provided much support subsequently. Alan Vince, who coordinated the necessary assessment documents, was in daily charge of the project from its inception until he left to take up a post with the University of York in October 1995. Since that date, Kate Steane has borne much of the burden of preparing the site narratives, along lines recommended by the academic reader, Steve Roskams of the University of York, who has devoted much time then and since to ensuring that the presentation of information followed a logical and standard format. J E Mann and M J Jones have read the whole revised text, the first-named particularly with regard to the integration of finds and pottery data, the second both as a copy-edit and to ensure that the academic statements were clear.

Various specialists within the Unit have been involved closely, some over a period of several years. They are listed on the title page, but the contributions of Margaret Darling and Barbara Precious (Roman pottery), Jenny Mann (non-ceramic finds) and Jane Young (post-Roman pottery) have been fundamental. Other experts have also prepared accounts of artefacts (see also bibliography). They include Petra Adams and Julian Henderson (medieval and later glass); Marion Archibald (medieval coins and tokens); Neil Berridge, K Siddiqui (analysis of soapstone fragments); Mark Blackburn (Anglo-Saxon coins); Anthea Boylston, Charlotte Roberts, and R Wiggins (human remains); J Carrott, Alan Hall, M Issitt, Harry Kenward, Brian Irving, Frances Large, and Annie Milles (biological remains); Keith Dobney, Debbie Jaques, and Sally Scott (animal and fish bones); Hilary Cool, Jenny Price and Sally Cottam (Roman glass); John Davies (Roman coins); Charles French (molluscs); Rowena Gale, Carole Morris, Maisie Taylor (wood); Joanna Bird (Samian pottery), Brenda Dickinson (Samian stamps) and Katherine Hartley (mortaria stamps); Lucy Bown and Judy O'Neill also contributed to the work on the post-Roman pottery; Theo Hofso (Roman sandal); M Hutchinson (stone analysis); David King (medieval window glass); Carole Long (Roman wall-plaster); Glenys Lloyd Morgan (mirror); Don Mackreth (Roman brooches); Jackie McKinley (cremations); Katherine Holman and John McKinnell (rune); Lisa Moffett (environmental samples – plants, fish scale); David Moore (stone artefact geology); Ruth Morgan (dendrochronology); Quita Mould (leather objects); C Nicholson (parasite eggs); David Peacock and David Williams (amphorae and marble petrology); James Rackham (animal bones); Neil Roberts (diatoms); Fiona Roe (stone objects); T P Taylor (soil analysis); Penelope Walton Rogers (textiles); Tony Wilkinson (sediments and environmental coordinator). Radio carbon dates were provided by the Harwell Low Level Measurements Laboratory through the good offices of English Heritage's Ancient Monuments Laboratory, and by Beta Analytic Inc.

M J Jones
City Archaeologist, Lincoln,
and former Director, City of Lincoln Archaeology Unit

Summaries

This volume describes the results of almost twenty years of excavations in the below hill area of the City of Lincoln, analysed as part of a major project funded by English Heritage and Lincoln City Council. The sites excavated between 1972 and 1987 included several on the banks of the Brayford Pool and the River Witham, as well as others fronting the High Street in what was an important Roman and Medieval suburb. The Report explains the procedures used to computerise and integrate the stratigraphical, artefactual, and environmental data in order to provide integrated accounts of the sequence at each site. Stratigraphic contexts were grouped at two levels, the second involving Land Use Blocks (LUBs). Line drawings have been digitised as part of the process of computerising the data, which is also being made available in archive form.

Separate chapters introduce the volume, and discuss the main results, while an appendix explains the rationale of the archive system. A full bibliography is presented.

This part of the city contains the earliest evidence for occupation of the settlement, dating to a century or so before the Roman arrival. During the Roman legionary period (c AD 50–80) there was associated occupation close to the river, and a burial ground further south, close to the junction of the two important military routes, Ermine Street and the Fosse Way. The street frontage was further developed, after extensive drainage and landfill operations in the 2nd century, as a commercial zone, with traders' houses extending for several hundred metres to the south of the river-crossing. The waterfront was consolidated and saw some reclamation. There is little evidence as yet for occupation of the suburb between c. AD 400 and c. AD 900, but the suburb of Wigford (lit. 'The roadside beyond the river') was established by the early 10th century at the latest, and several parishes were in being well before the Norman Conquest. Remains of domestic, ecclesiastical, and commercial structures were discovered, and the waterfront was further exploited for fishing and for wharfage. This was clearly a flourishing part of the city, and even in spite of the economic decline of the late medieval period the Carmelite friary and nearby ceramic industry appear buoyant. The High Street frontage remained built up throughout, until a revival from the 18th century.

The report is the first of several monographs covering the results of excavations in the 1970s and 1980s, to be published in this series. Apart from four volumes of site reports, there will be separate corpora of Roman and of Medieval pottery, Roman glass, and Post-medieval artefacts, and a major Synthesis.

Zusammenfassung

Dieser Band beschreibt die Resultate der fast zwanzigjährigen Ausgrabungen am Fuße des Hügels der Stadt Lincoln, die, fundiert als Teil eines Hauptprojektes von der Organisation 'English Heritage' und der Stadt Lincoln selbst durchgeführt und analysiert wurden. Die zwischen 1972 und 1987 freigelegten Fundstätten beinhalten mehrere Uferteile des Brayford Pool und des Witham, sowie auch Teile des Bereiches der High Street, der ein bedeutsamer römischer und mittelalterlicher Vorort war. Der Bericht dokumentiert die Verfahrensweisen, die zur Integration und Computerisierung der stratigraphischen sowie den Kunst- und Umweltdaten benutzt wurden, um die Zusammenfassungen der Darstellungen der Sequenzen von jeder Ausgrabungsstätte verfügbar zu machen. Die stratigraphischen Inhalte wurden nach zwei Richtlinien gruppiert, die zweite verwendete 'Land Use Blocks' (LUBs). Federzeichnungen wurden digitalisiert als Teil des Verfahrens, um die Daten zu computerisieren, die ebenfalls in Archivform verfügbar gemacht wurden.

Getrennte Kapitel formieren das Vorwort des Bandes und erörtern die Hauptresultate, während ein Anhang das Grundprinzip des Archiv Systems erklärt. Der Band beinhaltet ein vollständiges Literaturverzeichnis.

Dieser Teil der Stadt enthält die frühesten Belege für die Gründung einer Niederlassung, die ungefähr auf ein Jahrhundert vor der Ankunft der Römer zurückgeführt werden kann. Man geht davon aus, daß in der römischen Legionärszeit (c. AD 50–80) eine Besiedlung in der Nähe des Flusses erfolgte und eine Begräbnisstätte weiter südlich, in der Nähe der Kreuzung zweier bedeutender militärischer Wege, der Ermine Street und dem Fosse Way, angelegt wurde. Die Straßenfassade wurde nach ausgiebiger Dränage und Landgewinnung im zweiten Jahrhundert weiter als Handelszone mit Kaufmannshäusern, die sich mehrere hundert Meter südlich bis zur Einmündung des Flusses Witham in den Brayford Pool erstreckten, ausgebaut. Der Uferbezirk wurde befestigt und urbar gemacht. Es gibt bis heute wenig Belege für eine Besiedlung dieses Vorortes zwischen c. AD 400 – c. AD 900, der Vorort Wigford hingegen (wörtlich: 'der Wegrand jenseits des Flusses') wurde spätestens im frühen 10. Jahrhundert errichtet, und mehrere Gemeinden existierten tatsächlich vor der normannischen Eroberung. Überreste von häuslichen, kirchlichen und kaufmännischen Strukturen wurden entdeckt, und man baute den Uferbezirk für Fischerei und Schiffsverkehr mit Löschgelegenheiten aus. Dieses war eindeutig ein schwunghafter und gedeihender Teil der Stadt, und sogar in Anbetracht des wirtschaftlichen Verfalls in der spätmittelalterlichen Zeitspanne schienen die Karmeliter Orden und die nahegelegene Keramik Industrie aufzublühen. Die bebaute High Street Fassade blieb weiterhin bis zu einer Erneuerung im 18. Jahrhundert in ihrer Form bestehen.

Der Bericht ist die erste von mehreren in dieser Serie veröffentlichten Monographien, die die Resultate der Ausgrabungen in den 70iger und 80iger Jahren dokumentiert. Abgesehen von vier Bänden mit Ausgrabungsstätten-Berichten gibt es eine unabhängige Corpora über römische und mittelalterliche Töpferei, römisches Glas, spätmittelalterliche Kunstgegenstände und eine übergreifende Synthese.

Résumé

Ce volume représente les résultats de presque vingt ans de fouilles dans la région en aval de la colline de la ville de Lincoln, analysés dans le cadre d'un projet exceptionnel financé par le Patrimoine Anglais (English Heritage) et le conseil municipal de Lincoln (Lincoln City Council). Les sites fouillés entre 1972 et 1987 parmi lesquels plusieurs sur les rives de l'étang de Brayford et de la rivière de Witham, ainsi que d'autres exposant la rue principale (High Street) dans ce qui était un important faubourg médiéval. Le rapport explique les règles de procédure utilisées pour informatiser et incorporer les données stratigraphiquelles, environnementales aussi celles se rapportant à l'objet façonné ou artefact, de façon à fournir des résultats intégrés de la séquence dans chaque site. Les contextes stratigraphiques étaient groupés à deux niveaux, le second nécessitant des 'blocs de terrain utilisés' (Land Use Blocks) ou LUBs. Des dessins au trait ont été digitalisés dans le cadre du processus d'informatisation des données qui est également disponible sous forme d'archives.

Des chapitres séparés introduisent le volume et examinent les résultats principaux pendant qu'un appendice explique le raisonnement du système des archives. Une bibliographie complète est soumise.

Cette partie de la ville contient la toute première évidence de l'occupation de la colonisation datant plus ou moins d'un siècle avant l'arrivée des Romains. Durant la période légionnaire romaine (c. AD 50–80) il y avait une occupation adaptée proche de la rivière et un cimetière plus loin au sud proche de la jonction des deux importantes routes militaires, Ermine Street et le Fosse Way. La route en bordure de la rivière fut davantage développé après de considérables systèmes de fossés et d'enfouissement des déchets au deuxième siècle en tant que zone commerciale avec des établissements commerçants s'étendant sur plusieurs centaines de mètres jusqu'au sud de la traversée de la rivière. Le bord de l'eau fut consolidé et asséché. Il y a très peu d'évidence jusque là de l'occupation du faubourg entre c AD 400 et c AD 900, mais le faubourg de Wigford (littéralement: la route au delà de la rivière) était établi au plus tard au début du dixième siècle, et plusieurs paroisses existaient bien avant la conquète des Normands. Des vestiges de structures domestiques, écclésiastiques et commerciales étaient découverts et le bord de l'eau était davantage exploité pour la pêche et les quais. C'était clairement une partie florissante de la ville et même en dépis du déclin économique de la dernière période médiévale, la confrèrerie Carmélite et à proximité l'industrie céramique apparaîent soutenues. L'alignement de la grande rue (High Street) est restée tout le temps une agglomération jusqu' à son renouvellement au dix-huitième siècle.

Le rapport est le premier parmi plusieurs monographies couvrant les résultats de fouilles dans les années 1970 et 1980, a être publié dans cette série. Mis à part quatre volumes de rapports sur le site, il y aura des recueils séparés sur la poterie romaine et médiévale, sur le verre romain, des objets façonnés post-moyennageux, et une synthèse majeure.

1. Introduction to Wigford and the Brayford Pool

Kate Steane

The geography and history of Wigford (Figs. 1.1 and 1.2)

The glacial gap through the Jurassic limestone ridge now provides a valley through which the River Witham finds a course to the sea. To the west of the ridge (the 'Lincoln Edge'), the Witham flows northwards, meeting the River Till, flowing from the west, at the Brayford Pool before cutting east and thence towards Boston and the Wash. The suburb of Wigford is situated on low lying land between the sharp ascent of the ridge to the north – the core of the historic city – and the terraces and equivalent scarp to the south. To the east, Wigford was bounded by marshy ground, since drained by the artificial Sincil Dyke (Fig. 1.2).

In this Introduction, an account is presented of existing knowledge of the history and archaeology of Wigford and the Brayford Pool before the excavations of 1972. At the time, nothing was known of its prehistory, and so the arrival of the Roman army represented the first historic event. Roads were built by the army – both Ermine Street and the Fosse Way, which met before crossing the river. By AD 80 the tribal lands of the Corieltauvi were considered to be sufficiently pacified, and the legions had moved on, although it is possible that a caretaker garrison remained in occupation until the foundation of the *colonia*. The dating of the *colonia's* foundation to the Flavian period (AD 69–96) is given by a stone erected at Mainz by a citizen of Lincoln, most likely between AD 85 and AD 95; the only contemporary evidence of Roman activity in Wigford formerly consisted of a cemetery (see m82). The Roman suburb which succeeded the cemetery was unknown before the 1970s; it lay so far to the south of the walled *colonia* that remains of a building on Monson Street had been interpreted as a semi-rural villa.

Lincoln revived as a town in the Late Saxon/ Anglo-Scandinavian period. By the mid 10th century it had developed into one – and probably the largest – of the five boroughs of the East Midlands. Little was known about Wigford's part in that development except that being on a waterway with access to the sea, it must have been important. Cameron (1985, 45–6, partly following Hill 1948, 35, and Gelling) argues that the name Wigford is derived from the old English 'wic', meaning 'hamlet' or 'street', sometimes used at a former Roman site. Vince (in Jones and Vince forthcoming) now suggests that Wigford was of Anglo-Scandinavian origin in terms of both its name and its reoccupation. This settlement, by the ford, lay to the east of Brayford, from the Old English 'brad', meaning 'broad' (Cameron, *op cit*, 17–18). It had been previously referred to as the 'broadmere' (*ibid*), and is presumed to be of natural origin. It was certainly far more extensive before the modern period.

By the Norman conquest Lincoln was a thriving market town. The Witham was bridged by 1160 – the structure still exists on High Street. At this date the city was still of national importance. Its commercial success was based partly on the wool trade and as a cloth-making centre. The wealth of Wigford in the medieval period is well documented, and survives to some extent in the urban landscape. The two surviving Saxo-Norman churches are situated here, St Mary le Wigford and St Peter at Gowts. In the medieval period, there were twelve parishes, five with churches on the east side of the road and seven on the west (Hill 1948, 147; Gilmour and Stocker 1986, 1–4). The construction of a major building complex, perhaps the town house of Henry II, took place in the mid–late 12th century (smg82; Stocker 1991). Analysis of the remains has introduced a new perspective. There is historical evidence for other significant buildings in the suburb, no longer standing, the origins of which may also belong to the early medieval period (Hill 1948, 165–8). It had some status

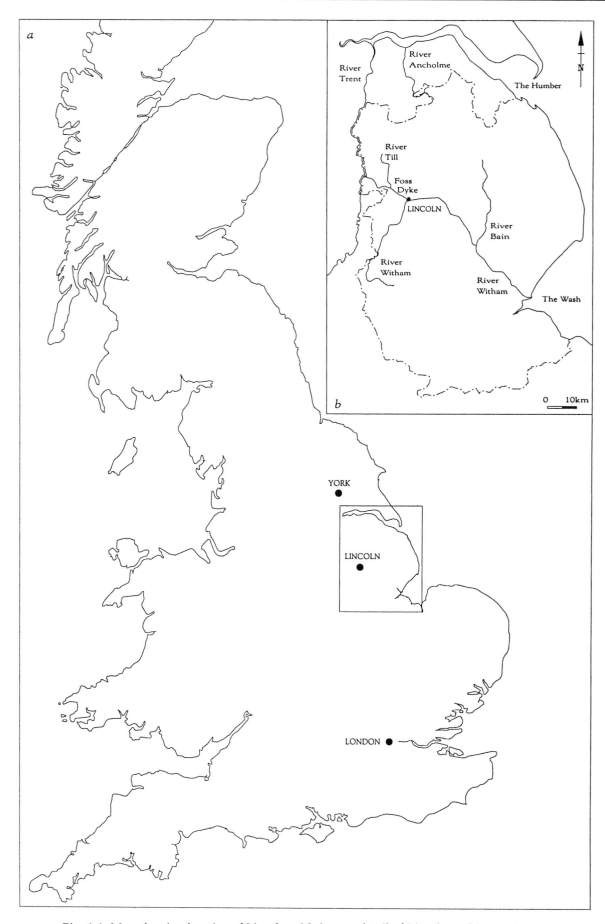

Fig. 1.1 Map showing location of Lincoln with inset – detail of Lincoln and its environs.

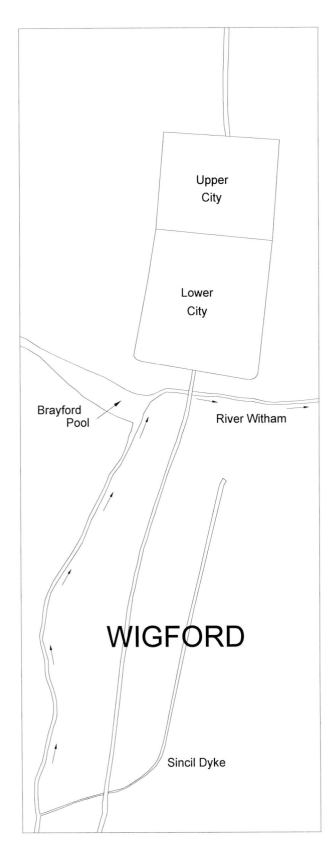

Fig. 1.2 Location map of Wigford.

– the first mayor, Adam, lived here *c*1210, and there were other wealthy people in the 12th and 13th centuries (*op cit*, 168–9, 234, 385–6). At the end of the 12th century the 'king's bar' is first referred to (*op cit*, 162), the first mention of the Bargates; there were two gates out of Wigford to the south, one along the former Fosse Way, the other perhaps on the line of Ermine Street. These two gates and the short wall between them are the only known defences of Wigford, other than the waterways. Repairs may have been made to the defences after the battle of Lincoln in 1217 which affirmed the accession of the young Henry III. The Lincoln house of the Carmelite Friars, which lay south of St. Marks Church, was founded by 1269 and expanded in 1280 (*op cit*, 150; z86).

By the 15th century it was a different story. The parish churches of Wigford, along with those from the rest of the city, were in serious decline. Returns for 1428 showed no more than 10 inhabitants for the parishes of St Michael and St Andrew in Wigford (*op cit*, 287). In the 16th century Leland noted one church in Wigford in complete ruin. In 1549, the parishes were re-organised; in Wigford, St Margaret and part of Holy Cross were added to St Botolph while Holy Trinity, St Edward, St Andrew and the remainder of Holy Cross became part of St Peter at Gowts. The site of the Friary was added to St Mark; part of St John went to St Mary le Wigford, and the rest to St Benedict. Speed's map of 1610 shows houses confined largely to the frontages of the High Street; documents show that gardens extended from the houses to the river to the west, and to Sincil Dyke on the east.

The Marrat map of 1817 also indicates a mainly ribbon development; his 1848 edition and Padley's of 1851 reveal the arrival of the railways, with the pattern of occupation complicated by both the Midland and Great Northern. The areas between the road and the river now began to be infilled with buildings. In the north-east part there was more development; the Corn Exchange and the New Market. Further east, beyond the suburb, Oxford Street, Pelham Street and Melville Street linked Wigford to Lincoln's eastern riverside. To the south, Monson Street became the first of the Victorian terraced streets which were to dominate Wigford by the turn of the century, and in so doing also revealed funerary remains from the 1st century AD.

In summary, the area covered by the sites reported on here was, before 1972, poorly known in terms of its early topography and the first millennium and a half of its occupation. The excavations beginning in that year accordingly had the potential to examine the origins of settlement and the early landcape; the nature and extent of the suburb in the Roman-Medieval periods, and the date of gaps in occupation and of reoccupation (eg, did Lincoln possess a Mid-Saxon trading focus here?); and archaeological evidence for the apparent late medieval decline. The whole subject of the (changing) position and nature of the waterfront, together with related artefactual and ecofactual data, was at the time becoming a major component of urban research. Moreover, there might be benefits from evidence for economic activity and social status and differentiation.

Excavations (Fig. 1.3)

The sites published here were excavated between 1972 and 1987. They are normally referred to in the text by their codes, and that practice is also followed in this section. The development of the High Street frontage occasioned the excavations at hg72, sm76,

z86 and ze87. These offered an opportunity to investigate building (near-)frontages of Roman and later date as well as the pre-urban landuse of the area. Excavation to the east of the High Street was undertaken before re-development at m82 and before car park surfacing at cs73. In the north-west part of the suburb work was necessitated at dm72, bwe82 and sb85 by commercial re-development schemes. One excavation, ws82, was little more than a pipe trench watching brief. To the north of the Brayford Pool lt72 and bwn75 were investigated in advance of a multi-storey car park and supermarket construction. The work at smg82 was undertaken as part of a restoration programme. Every excavation varied in the extent and depth of stratigraphy uncovered, and each had a different period emphasis.

A number of individuals, sometimes more than

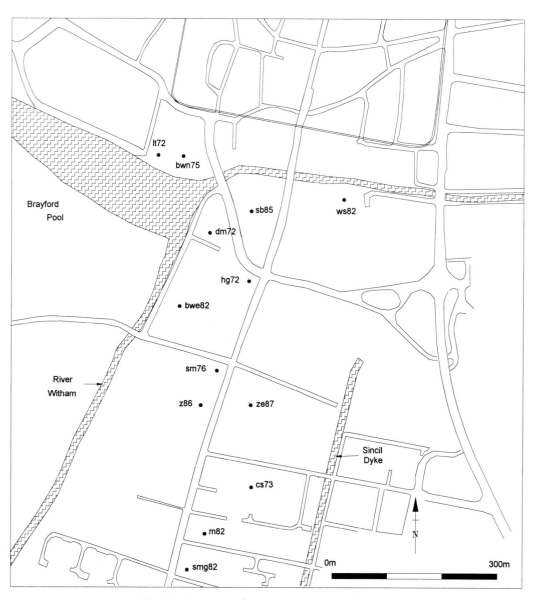

Fig. 1.3 Location of sites excavated in Wigford.

one per site, were involved in the direction of the excavations, including Kevin Camidge (z86), Prince Chitwood (ze87) Christina Colyer (sm76), Lisa Donel (ze87), Brian Gilmour (bwe82, lt72 and sm76), Chris Guy (sb85), Michael Jones (bwn75, hg72 and sm76), Robert Jones (bwn75 and dm72), John Magilton (m82 and smg82), Timothy Marshall (cs73 and hg72), Malcolm Otter (hg72, z86 and ze87), Colin Palmer Brown (smg82), Andrew Snell (z86) and Geoff Tann (ws82). These site directors worked successively for the Lincoln Archaeological Trust (1972–84) and the Trust for Lincolnshire Archaeology Lincoln office (1984–8). In 1988 the City of Lincoln Archaeological Unit was established. Christina Colyer was overall Trust director 1972–78; Mr Jones succeeded her in the post.

Funding for the excavations almost invariably came from more than one source. The Department of the Environment or later, English Heritage, contributed towards the funding of most of the sites (cs73, m82, smg82, dm72, hg72, ws82, z86, sm76 and ze87). The Manpower Services Commission provided excavation teams for several (m82, smg82, ws82, z86, sm76 and ze87). The Lincoln County Borough Council, later Lincoln City Council, contributed directly towards excavations, in some cases as developer, and in others not (cs73, bwn75, dm72, hg72, lt72, sb85 and ze87). Other developers helped to fund excavations; bwe82 was funded entirely by the Lincolnshire Publishing Company; the work at z86 was partly funded by British Rail and Anglian Water; at ze87 the Home Office contributed towards the costs. A private individual made a contribution to the cost of sb85.

Previous publications for most of the sites included interim papers in the annual report of the Lincoln Archaeological Trust (1972–84) or the Trust for Lincolnshire Archaeology (1985–8). The archaeology of the standing structure and contemporary deposits at St Mary's Guildhall (smg82) has been analysed and published in full (Stocker 1991); there has been no further interpretation since. The published excavation report on the post-Roman sequence at St Mark's Church (Gilmour and Stocker 1986) has, however, been subjected to scrutiny based on the stratigraphic analysis (see sm76). The earliest phases of the excavation at Holmes Grainwarehouse (hg72) and the pre-Roman Belgic pottery from that site have also been reconsidered (cf Darling and Jones 1988).

Archiving and post excavation analysis

In 1988 English Heritage commissioned the City of Lincoln Archaeology Unit to undertake the Lincoln Archaeological Archive Project over a three-year period to computerise the existing records for sites excavated in the above period; this project was managed by Alan Vince. The records were listed in detail, suitable for permanent curation, while their computerisation is also intended to facilitate future research and decision-making (see Appendix 1 for details).

In 1991, the potential of the sites (1972–1987) was assessed and a research design for the analysis and publication of their excavations was presented to English Heritage (Vince (ed) 1991); among the publications proposed was the present volume. The subsequent analysis provided sufficient material for a seminar to be held in 1994 to present the findings to all the specialists involved on the project and to take on board feedback from them. A first draft of the report text was submitted to English Heritage in 1994. English Heritage subsequently commissioned alterations and a more systematic and formalised structure, on the recommendation of S. P. Roskams of the University of York, the academic adviser. Kate Steane has coordinated the major reordering of the stratigraphic data in line with these recommendations. Michael J Jones, the Unit Director, had meanwhile replaced Alan Vince as project manager in 1996 following the latter's appointment to a post elsewhere.

The Stratigraphic framework: rationale

Each site narrative is an attempt to present an interpretation of what took place through time backed by an integrated analysis of the evidence. The primary framework is stratigraphic; within this framework the pottery and other finds have specific context-related contributions with regard to dating, site formation processes, and functions.

The stratigraphic framework has been built up using the context records made on site to form a matrix. The contexts, set into the matrix, have been arranged into context groups (cgs); each cg represents a discrete event in the narrative of the site. The cgs have been further grouped into **Land Use Blocks** (LUBs); each LUB represents an area of land having a particular function for a specific length of time. The move from contexts to cgs, and to LUBs indicates a hierarchical shift, from recorded fact to interpretation, and from detail to a more general understanding of what was happening on the site. Here the cgs are the lowest element of the interpretative hierarchy presented in the text.

The LUBs are presented chronologically by period and each site has a LUB diagram, so that the whole sequence of LUBs can be viewed at a glance. Because it is near to the top of the interpretation hierarchy, the LUB depends on the stability of the context group structure and this in turn depends on the strength of the dating evidence.

Within the text each Period (see below, Fig. 1.5) has a LUB summary, so that it is possible to move through the text from period to period in order to gain an outline summary of each site sequence.

Structure of this publication

The organisation of this volume originated from the initial authorship of the first drafts of the site narratives written as part of the Archive Project between 1989 and 1990. The volume begins with the sites analysed by Paul Miles (cs73, m82 and smg82), followed by those examined by Chris Guy (bwe82, bwn75, dm72, hg72, lt72, sb85 and ws82), and those by Kate Steane (z86 and part of sm76). In 1994 Lisa Donel produced a report on ze87, a site which originally had not formed part of the project; it was included at a late stage, and some of the normal post excavation processes have not been undertaken for this site. Hence the site has only been included here because of its contribution to the global picture.

Each site narrative is made up of three parts: an introduction, an interpretation of the sequence of events from the excavated evidence, and finally a discussion of various aspects of the discoveries.

Site introductions

Each introduction includes information about when, where, why and how the excavation was undertaken, who supervised the work, and which organisation funded it. Previous published work on the site is listed here.

For each site, the outline post-excavation stratigraphic hierarchy is set out; this includes the number of contexts from each site, the number of context groups (cgs), the number of unstratified contexts, and the number of land use blocks (LUBs). For each site there is an introduction to the material evidence uncovered during excavation. Numbers of combined stratified and unstratified Roman and post Roman pottery, registered finds, building material fragments, animal bone fragments and burials are mentioned; these are grouped into a table here to give an idea of the quantities involved (Fig. 1.4). The presence or absence of organic material is noted. All those who have contributed in any way to the narratives are acknowledged either by name or by reference to their reports.

Sequence of events

Each excavation report is structured using the period categories below (Fig. 1.5). This framework was based on our ability to recognise and date phases of activity on a regular basis: major historical events generally did not leave recognisable stratigraphic traces on a site. The list could perhaps be criticised on the grounds that it does not draw a distinction between the legionary period and the early *colonia* – it was partly based on the general periods of Roman occupation at London – but the change in occupation is not as easily recognised from the artefactual evidence at Lincoln as might be assumed.

The term 'Ultimate Roman' has been used to describe features which seal or cut through late Roman deposits and are earlier than Late Saxon features but contain no artefacts which indicate they are of that date.

Each site has been interpreted as a sequence of LUBs (see above for explanation); each LUB within a

site	Rpot	post Rpot	regist finds	bm frags	animal bfrags	burials
cs73	348	30	11	–	70	–
m82	2674	93	185	276	1492	4 cremations
smg82	3968	1270	471	1885	784	5 inhumations
bwe82	2144	498	206	263	1167	–
bwn75	–	–	–	–	–	–
dm72	285	490	26	115	375	–
hg72	9213	2101	786	428	3654	1 inhumation
lt72	47	1230	269	664	1257	–
sb85	1522	1821	212	638	2160	–
ws82	22	85	19	239	261	–
z86	4354	3816	942	2562	7215	12 inhumations
sm76	18948	2370	3025	10915	7521	636 inhumations
ze87	212 samian	8825	478	un-quant	5628	4 inhumations

Fig. 1.4 Finds recovered from Wigford sites: numbers of Roman and post Roman pottery sherds, registered finds, building material fragments, animal bone fragments and number of human burials.

period	date range
Iron Age	>mid 1st century AD
Early Roman	mid 1st–early 2nd century
Mid Roman	early 2nd–mid 3rd century
Late Roman	mid 3rd–late 4th century
Very Late Roman	late 4th–very late 4th century
Ultimate Roman	late 4th–late 9th century
Early Anglo-Saxon	5th–late 7th century
Mid Saxon	late 7th–late 9th century
Late Saxon	
(Anglo-Scandinavian)	late 9th–late 10th century
Saxo-Norman	early 11th – early/mid 12th century
Early Medieval	early/mid 12th–early/mid 13th century
High Medieval	early/mid 13th–mid 14th century
Late Medieval	mid 14th–end 15th century
Post-Medieval	beginning 16th–early 18th century
Modern	mid 18th–20th century

Fig. 1.5 Period terms used in this volume.

site has a LUB number (from either 0 or 1 onwards). For each site a two dimensional LUB diagram has been prepared, illustrating the changing land use. Such diagrams have been used to great effect in both London and Norwich (Davies, B 1992 and Shepherd 1993). In this volume LUBs were not normally created unless there was positive excavation evidence; the exception was when a LUB was needed to clarify the LUB sequence (eg LUB 15, hg72).

Each LUB is described in the text and illustrated with plans, sections and photographs by context group (cg). The cg is the lowest stratigraphic unit used in the narratives and each site has its own cg sequence (cg1 to whatever); context codes (letters or numbers) are not mentioned in the text except as part of a registered find reference (eg a late Saxon iron knife blade (64) <41> from cg26, LUB 11 sb85; here the bracketed code (64) is the context). Although it makes for a rather inelegant prose style, every cg number used in the interpretation of each site is mentioned in the site text; the one exception is smg82 where 48 cgs from LUB 30 onwards are not mentioned because these are fully discussed as contexts in Stocker 1991. For each site there is a concordance of cg numbers linked with associated LUB numbers which can be used for quick reference from the cg number to the LUB number (eg, when moving from sections to text).

The interpretation and dating of the LUBs arises from a dynamic dialectic between an understanding of the stratigraphic sequence and site formation processes together with an analysis of the pottery and other finds. Pottery, in particular, sometimes provides evidence for site formation processes and where appropriate this information is included in the text. Site formation is described and discussed by cg within the LUB framework. To enable the reader to understand the sequence clearly, when a

cg is first described, whatever was earlier in the sequence is also mentioned, whether this was the limit of excavation or previous cgs. Whenever a cg is mentioned outside its LUB, then its associated LUB number is attached; in order to work back from plans and sections where cgs are numbered without their LUB numbers, then it is possible to look up this information in the appropriate table. Residual material is rarely mentioned in the text unless there are conclusions to be drawn from it. Where there is a possibility that deposits were contaminated, the presence of intrusive material is noted.

Roman pottery evidence is presented where it dates the Roman sequence; numbers of sherds from the relevant cg are quoted together with the justification for the dating. Detailed information on Roman pottery was provided by Margaret Darling and Barbara Precious before the reader stage of the post-excavation process. As part of the process of following the reader's advice, edited and selected Roman pottery data has since been transferred from the earlier draft. Kate Steane, as coordinator of the site narratives, has undertaken this work and is responsible for the text relating to dating. In some cases this has led to gaps in the explanation of Roman pottery dating in the text (for example sm76, LUBs 2, 4, 8 and 16); further detail is available in the relevant Roman pottery archive, together with the Roman pottery corpus whose publication is in preparation (Darling and Precious forthcoming). The Roman pottery codes used in the text are listed and explained in Appendix 2.

Post Roman pottery dating evidence is presented in the text by Jane Young; key dating groups are mentioned together with sherd counts where appropriate. It is necessary to refer to the Saxon and medieval corpus (Young et al, forthcoming) for information on the dated ceramic horizons, and to find out what is in each assemblage readers should refer back to the archive. In some cases, post-Roman fabric codes are referred to in the text; these are explained in Appendix 3. In some cases, the dating of post-Roman stratigraphy relies on the tile.

Registered finds (and building materials) are rarely presented as key dating evidence and only selectively used for interpretative purposes, the criteria used resting on the relationship between artefact and deposit as outlined by Roskams (1992, 27–8). Finds contemporary with and functionally connected to their cg (Roskams Type A) are always discussed in the text; those that are broadly contemporary with but not functionally related to their cg (Roskams Type B) are noted only where they are deemed relevant to the site narrative or to the site discussion. Finds that are intrusive or residual but locally derived (Roskams Type C) and those that are residual and imported on to the site (Roskams Type D) are occasionally discussed where it is considered appropriate. The same criteria are used for bulk finds, including building materials.

Remains of buildings found on each site have been given a structure number during post-excavation analysis for ease of reference in the texts. Although some attempt was initially made for these to be numbered sequentially through the site, subsequent work has often meant that structure numbers do not reflect the site chronology and must be considered as random labelling (eg Structure 13, hg72 is not the 13th structure on the site). The numbering of buildings inevitably rouses debate concerning its definition, and whether mere traces of possible structural activity count. Structure numbering in these volumes has tended to be inclusive, rather than exclusive, and groups of features indicating some evidence of undefined buildings have been called Structural Features and numbered as if they were a building (eg, Structural Features 2, hg72). Substantial alterations of buildings probably within existing walls have been given the same structure number, but a different phase (eg Structure 13.2, LUB 18 hg72). Different rooms in the same building have been given alphabetic codes (eg Structure 3B, LUB 6 hg72). Finally there are building phases by room (eg, Structure 4C.3, LUB 17 hg72).

The site-by-site computer archive for stratigraphy, pottery and other finds is the foundation on which the narratives have been built. Together with this archive are numerous specialist reports (the 'research archive'), whose conclusions have contributed to a deeper understanding of the sites. Information about animal bone is included where it adds to an understanding of the site narrative. Animal bone assemblages have been examined by cg, but numbers of bone for each cg have not been given, merely broad descriptions: very small (under 30), small (30–100), moderate (100–200) or large (over 200). In turn both the archive and specialist reports link with the stratigraphic site records and the rest of the recorded material evidence; at this level, it is the context which is the key that unites the site elements. The archive holds a concordance between context and grouped context numbers for each site.

Each site narrative has therefore been produced by assessing the available information in terms of how appropriate it is in adding to an understanding of the site sequence and site formation processes and using that information in a selective way. The full archive from which this material has been drawn is to be made available via the Lincoln City and County Museum for future research.

The Figures illustrating the site narratives

The illustrations for each site are listed by site in the same sequence, location plan/s first, followed by LUB diagram/s, phase plans, section/s, photographs, finds drawings (where appropriate) and diagrams. The figure numbers appropriate to a LUB are mentioned at each LUB heading, and sometimes again in the text. All plans and sections were drawn with CAD and all are annotated with cg numbers.

Each site has a site location plan (scale 1:1,250) and most show the location of individual site trenches or areas, together with the location of the section drawings published here (except small sites cs73 and ws82, where section locations are marked on the 1:1,250 plans). Every site has a LUB diagram, and a sequence of phase plans which include one or more LUBs; the phase plan figure numbers are noted on the LUB diagrams, as well as in the text. The phase plans mostly provide outline information only and usually much more detail is available in the archive.

For a detailed understanding of the plans it is necessary to refer to Fig. 1.6, for a list of encoded line conventions and hatch patterns; walls are indicated in most cases with a hatch pattern, but occasionally stones have been picked out when the line of the wall was unclear (eg, Fig. 7.6). Most of the phase plans illustrate specific features (walls, pits, ditches, etc), rather than layers (dumps, surfaces, etc); this partly stems from the lack of on-site single context planning but was also an attempt to disentangle the complexity of the sequences by illustrating events which scored or had some strong impact on the land. Where possible, features are projected; occasionally intrusive features are represented with the appropriate delineation, where this enhances the understanding of the sequence. Often features will appear on more than one plan; this generally but not always indicates continuity of function, rather than uncertainty regarding phasing. The plans illustrate what is being discussed in the text.

For most sites one or more section has been illustrated to give some idea of the depth and complexity of the deposits; only for sb85 is no section available owing to the pressures under which that site was recorded. The reliability of the sections is generally excellent, but in some cases there are layers which are not shown on the sections when theoretically they should be – it is possible that the excavator did not observe these layers or made a decision not to include them as being too slight to be significant, or perhaps amalgamated layers during the drawing process.

The location of the published sections is indicated on the area location plans, or in two cases (cs73 and ws82) on the site location plans. LUBs are not shown on the section-drawings; they remain annotated only by context group. Stones in walls are identified,

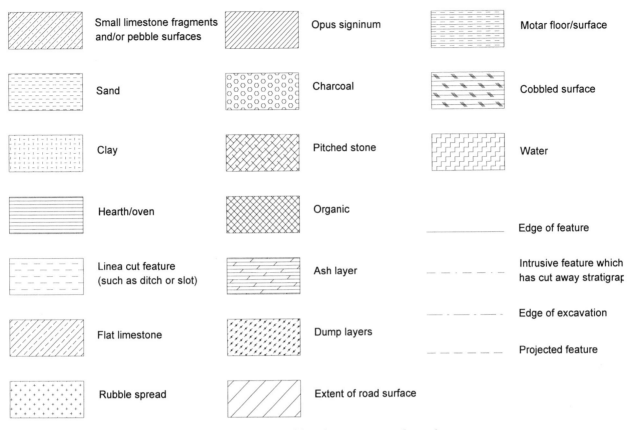

Small limestone fragments and/or pebble surfaces	Opus signinum	Motar floor/surface
Sand	Charcoal	Cobbled surface
Clay	Pitched stone	Water
Hearth/oven	Organic	Edge of feature
Linea cut feature (such as ditch or slot)	Ash layer	Intrusive feature which has cut away stratigrap
Flat limestone	Dump layers	Edge of excavation
Rubble spread	Extent of road surface	Projected feature

Fig. 1.6 Key to lines and hatch patterns used on plans.

but for clarity of sequence no other type of layer or feature has been depicted or annotated in the published sections. Where available a datum level is marked on the sections, mostly at 5m OD (4m for the ze87 section).

All of the site reports are also illustrated with photographs. Other diagrams, such as radio carbon date lists and finds drawings, are included where appropriate.

Site discussions

The format of the site discussions varies from site to site depending on the characteristics of each site. For some sites, the structure of the discussion is constrained by the limited stratigraphic sequence (cs73 and ws82), or by the paucity of evidence (bwn75); for others, the discussion of the site is necessarily extensive owing to the depth and complexity of the deposits and significance of the finds (hg72, sb85, z86, and particularly sm76).

Three of the sites (smg82, hg72 and sm76) have already been partially published (Stocker 1991, Darling and Jones 1988, and Gilmour and Stocker 1986); where alternative interpretations have been suggested by the analysis undertaken for this project, an explanation is provided at the beginning of the discussion (hg72, sm76).

For some of the sites there is also a general discussion of topographical development (m82, dm72, hg72, sb85, z86, sm76, and ze87); for some sites attention is directed to dominant elements of the topography, such as the road (smg82 and z86) or the river/Brayford Pool (smg82, bwe82, lt72, ws82 and z86). Roman buildings are discussed in varying detail (m82, smg82, hg72, z86, sm76 and ze87), as are some of the more extensively excavated post-Roman buildings examined in the site narratives (hg72, z86 and sm76), and other post-Roman structures (such as the south-west extension of the city wall and Lucy Tower, lt72).

Pottery is not discussed separately from the site narratives and in sections referring, for example, to function, but a discussion of the whole assemblage from Wigford is included in the General Discussion. Some of the discussion on Roman pottery is based on information gleaned from plotdate analysis. This is a recent technique for examining Roman pottery, developed by Margaret Darling with Barbara Precious (see Darling 1999, 56–7, Table 5) to examine the dated content of groups of pottery. This works from the archive measure of sherd count and filters the

pottery in the individual group, LUB, or groups of
LUBs, through a file which assigns dates based on
the fabric and vessel type. The resulting raw values
are then spread across the period, and plotted either
as raw sherd count values or, more usually for
comparisons between groups of disparate sizes, as
percentages (using a program kindly adapted by
Paul Tyers). When combined with analyses of the
pottery for fabrics and functions, this is a useful
tool for assessing groups and their relationships.
Presentation of such detail in the present volume is
confined to the General Discussion (below). Details
for each site are available in the archive (although
these were prepared before some re-phasing took
place).

The post Roman pottery is similarly discussed
generally for the whole of Wigford.

Registered finds do not figure prominently in the
site narratives but are often referred to in the discussions and in some cases have whole sections
dedicated to one or a group of finds (m82, dm72,
hg72, lt72, sb85, z86, and sm76), sometimes related
to a specific activity (eg, the finds from the cremation burials at m82). The animal bone from a site
is only discussed where clear conclusions could be
drawn, and then under function rather than as an
assemblage.

There is only minimal citing of stratigraphic
parallels in the narrative discussions; there has not
been an opportunity to search the literature deeply
for similar material. Any parallels are drawn from
within the volume.

By comparing the LUB diagrams across the sites
in Wigford, it is possible to obtain a good impression
of the changing nature of occupation and land use
through time. A general discussion of Wigford can
be found after the individual site reports.

Bibliography

A consolidated bibliography is presented using a
Harvard-based reference system. The large number
of unpublished CLAU archive reports is referred to
in the texts by author and date, in the manner of
published reports, so that specific archive reports
may be consulted on demand. In the bibliography,
the unpublished nature of these reports is made
clear. The format and abbreviations used are those
recommended by the CBA.

The archive

The paper, digital, and artefactual archive is to be
made available for further research.

The primary site excavation archive (both paper
and artefactual) is all accessible by context. In order
to compare the archive with the text published here,
it is necessary to turn the context data into cg
information. This is achieved by using the context to
cg concordance files which are part of the computerised, or digital, archive (termed **phasing** files). The
digital archive contains such types of documentation
relating to the various post excavation processes on
which this report is based. Included with each excavation archive are the external specialist reports (part
of the Research Archive). A more detailed explanation of the archive can be found in Appendix 1.

Finds reports

The finds reports refer to context codes and cgs,
and some also to LUBs. To locate a find within the
site framework is possible with the aid of a cg
number, by consulting the relevant site cg to LUB
table in this volume, and by tracing details of the cg
within its LUB in the text.

2. Chaplin Street 1973 (cs73)

Introduction

Excavations were carried out in 1973, on the north side of Chaplin Street (Fig. 2.1), in order to investigate the underlying stratigraphy in advance of the area being sealed by a car-park. The excavation was supervised by Timothy Marshall for the Lincoln Archaeological Trust. Funding was provided by Lincoln County Borough Council and the Department of the Environment.

Layers down to the presumed natural sand were excavated by machine in one trench (Fig. 2.1). Surviving cut features were hand-dug, and the sections were probed for dating evidence for higher layers (Fig. 2.8). The site context codes were not adhered to rigorously and so pottery dating is therefore a little tenuous; most ditch-fill contexts, in particular, also include subsided later material. Of the 71 contexts, 68 were interpreted as 24 context groups (cg1–25,

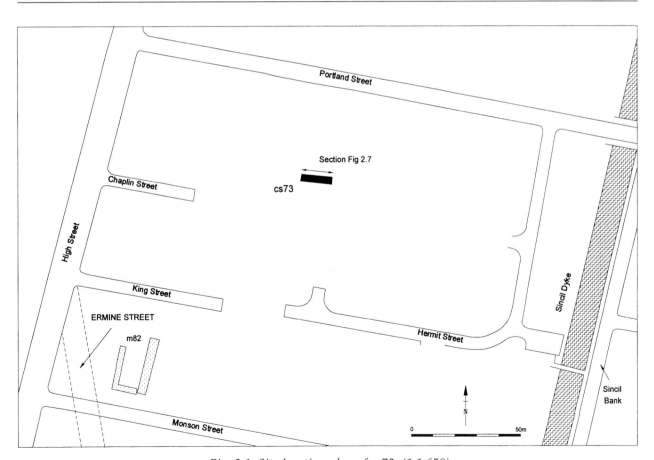

Fig. 2.1 Site location plan of cs73. (1:1,650)

with cg16 unused) and 3 were deemed as being unstratified. The contexts groups are discussed below as 12 land-use blocks, LUBs 1–12 (Fig. 2.10) which are all from the one trench (Fig. 2.2).

There was an assemblage of Roman sherds (348 sherds) including mortaria (Hartley 1973); there was little post Roman pottery (30 sherds). Eleven registered finds were recovered during the course of the excavation; these do not aid the interpretation or add to the dating evidence. However, mention of them can be found in archive reports (Roman glass: Price and Cottam 1993a; bone finds: Rackham 1994; coins: Archibald 1994). Four fragments of Roman tile were found. Soil samples and some animal bone (70 fragments) were also recovered, but were not considered to be worth further analysis. There were some fragments of human bone (Boylston and Roberts 1994).

Post-excavation stratigraphic analysis was undertaken by Paul Miles and later by Kate Steane. Maggi Darling worked on the Roman pottery; Jane Young examined the post-Roman pottery. Jane Cowgill and Jen Mann examined the registered finds. Paul Miles and Zoe Rawlings digitized the plans.

Interpretation of the sequence of events

Natural

Natural sand **LUB 1** was exposed along the length of the excavation trench.

LUB 1 Natural (Fig. 2.7)
At the limit of excavation natural sand cg5 was found at OD 4.65 m.

Mid Roman

Cutting the natural sand cg5 (LUB 1) was a north–south gully **LUB 2**. To the east of the site cutting layers **LUB 3** which filled the gully (LUB 2) was a north–south ditch **LUB 4**. The one dated sherd of pottery recovered from the ditch suggests a possible date around the late 2nd to early 3rd centuries. A

clayey layer **LUB 5** sealed ditch cg3 (LUB 4); this was associated with possible 3rd century pottery. Through this horizon were cut a north–south ditch and a gully **LUB 6**; pottery sherds with a possible date of mid 3rd century or later were associated with them. These features were themselves sealed by a clay layer **LUB 7**; also associated with pottery of a similar date. Gully cg25 cut LUB 7, possibly associated with a posthole **LUB 8**; no pottery was associated with these features.

LUB 2 Gully (Figs. 2.3, 2.7 and 2.9)
Cutting the natural sand cg5 (LUB 1) was north–south gully cg2; it was flat-bottomed (1.30m wide and 0.20m deep) with a primary fill of sand.

LUB 3 Sandy layer (Fig. 2.7)
Sandy layers cg6 sealed natural cg5 (LUB 1) and

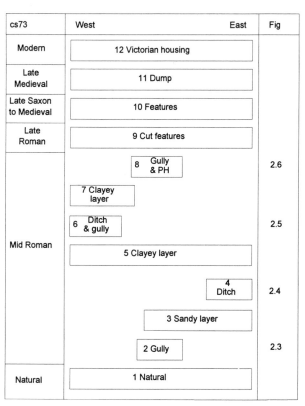

cs73	West	East	Fig
Modern	12 Victorian housing		
Late Medieval	11 Dump		
Late Saxon to Medieval	10 Features		
Late Roman	9 Cut features		
Mid Roman	8 Gully & PH		2.6
	7 Clayey layer		
	6 Ditch & gully		2.5
	5 Clayey layer		
		4 Ditch	2.4
	3 Sandy layer		
	2 Gully		2.3
Natural	1 Natural		

Fig. 2.2 LUB diagram of cs73.

0   5m

Fig. 2.3 Gully: LUB 2. (1:100)

filled the gully cg2 (LUB 3). There was no pottery or finds associated with these layers.

LUB 4 Ditch (Figs. 2.4 and 2.7)

Ditch cg3 was a broad v-shaped feature running north–south (2.6m wide and 0.60m deep), cutting through sand cg6 (LUB 3). The primary fill was a thin layer of yellow clay; over this was a layer of heavy "sticky" black peat with lenses of yellow and brown sand. Two Roman sherds were found in ditch cg3, one a SAMCG rim from a decorated form of Hadrianic date, which might indicate deposition from around the late 2nd and early 3rd centuries.

LUB 5 Clayey layer (Fig. 2.7)

Brown peaty clay layer with black silt cg7 sealed sand cg6 (LUB 3) and ditch cg3 (LUB 4), extending over much of the site. The 20 sherds from cg7 provide little strong dating evidence; apart from a SAMEG, Dr 37, of mid to late Antonine date, other sherds suggested a possible 3rd-century date.

LUB 6 Ditch and gully (Figs. 2.5, 2.7 and 2.9)

Cutting clay horizon cg7 (LUB 5) was a north–south, v-sectioned feature cg1 (2m wide and 0.55m deep) with a gully in the base (0.12m deep). The lowest fill of this possible ditch was of mixed yellow and beige light silty material – primary silting over which was yellow sand with brown clay lenses sealed by mixed "sticky" black peaty material, possibly indicating the main period of use; this was sealed by clayey layers. Ditch cg1 produced eight

Roman sherds, including a DWSH body sherd from a jar, indicating a probable date of mid 3rd century or later; the samian ware was of Hadrianic or Antonine and early to mid Antonine in date.

Sealing cg7, to the west of the site, was a yellow sandy layer with silt lenses cg8. This layer may have represented the upcast from ditch cg1. It was cut by gully cg4 which was flat bottomed (0.60m wide by 0.30m deep). It was filled by a thin layer of black-brown clayey silt overlain by a thicker layer of brown yellow fairly uniform sandy silt. Only 2 sherds came from ditch cg4, one resembling a bowl from the Rookery Lane kiln, possibly of 3rd-century date.

LUB 7 Clay layer

The ditch cg1 and gully cg4 (LUB 6) was sealed by bright yellow sand interleaved with sticky grey-black material which was more a brown-green in places cg9; pottery from cg9 (17 sherds) included a wide mouthed bowl type which was largely responsible for dating the small assemblage probably to the mid 3rd century.

LUB 8 Gully and post-hole Fig. 2.6

Gully cg2 (LUB 2) was re-cut by gully cg25, which cut layers cg9 (LUB 7). The posthole or small pit cg10 which cut cg7 (LUB 5) may relate to this activity; the pit was filled with animal bone. There was also a mound of bright yellow sand with some clayey patches cg17 which sealed cg7 (LUB 5). No pottery was associated with these features.

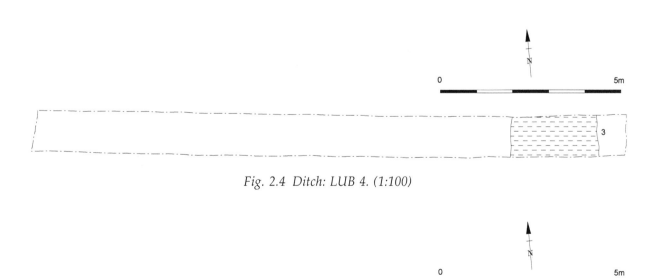

Fig. 2.4 Ditch: LUB 4. (1:100)

Fig. 2.5 Ditch and gully: LUB 6. (1:100)

Late Roman

Overlying the site was a sandy silt layer **LUB 9** with much mid 3rd-century pottery and some mid to later 3rd-century pottery but also a few intrusive post-Roman sherds.

LUB 9 Layers (Fig. 2.7)

Layers of grey black silt cg11 with charcoal and lenses of dark green or grey green sandy silt cg11 sealed cg9 (LUB 7), cg10 and cg17 (LUB 8). These layers produced the largest group of pottery from the site (246

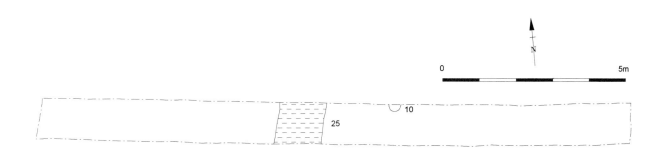

Fig. 2.6 Gully and posthole: LUB 8. (1:100)

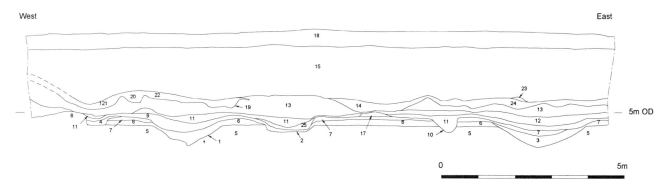

Fig. 2.7 Section from west to east across the north side of the trench illustrating the stratigraphic sequence from LUBs 1–12. (1:100)

Fig. 2.8 Looking west along the trench: general view.

sherds), and one context (AS) produced a notable quantity of joining sherds and near complete profiles. Dating for cg11 comes mainly from NVCC, particularly a BKFOF and a probable handled flask, and from DWSH, GREY Dales ware jars and BWM of Rookery Lane kiln type. These, supplemented by a SAMEG, Dr 30, of *c* AD 180–260, indicate a mid 3rd-century date. Apart from sherd links between component contexts, sherds of the same EMED amphorae as in layer cg7 (LUB 5) occurred and sherds of a GREY cooking pot were found both in this group and cg9 (LUB 7) indicating disturbance of earlier layers.

Overlying layers cg11 to the east of the site were green grey gritty layers cg12 with animal bone and lenses of black silt. This was sealed by a thick green grey gritty sandy layer cg13.

Layers cg12 and cg13 both contained sherds of the same Roman pottery vessel suggesting either disturbance or contemporaneous formation. The 26 sherds from cg12 included Hadrianic to early Antonine Samian, but DWSH, a GREY funnel necked beaker and a NVCC probable flagon or jug suggested a mid–late 3rd century date. Pottery from layer cg13 (21 sherds), was dated again by DWSH and a probable NVCC flagon or jug, supplemented by a BB1 cooking pot of mid-3rd century type; the only samian sherd was SAMEG of late 2nd- to 3rd-century date.

It would seem that the site was abandoned in the late Roman period, but disturbed by later activity. Layer cg11 produced three post-Roman sherds; one is of late Saxon or Saxo-Norman date and two are of late medieval date. Layer cg12 produced one sherd of LKT dating to the 10th century. Three fragments of human bone from the left lower leg of an adult were found in cg11 (Boylston and Roberts 1994).

Late Saxon to Medieval

LUB 9 was cut by several features **LUB 10** possibly indicating activity during the medieval period, but the only pottery recovered to suggest this was intrusive into LUB 9.

LUB 10 Features (Fig. 2.7)
A number of features cg19, cg20 and cg21 cutting cg13 (LUB 9) were only recorded in section; these were sealed by heavy black grey clay cg22. Also cutting cg13 (LUB 9) was a feature cg14 with a fill of thick black grey clay. To the east of the site was a layer cg24 (not described) sealing cg13 (LUB 9), over which was a north–south strip of brown loam cg23 with much red ash (seen in both north and south sections). There were no finds recorded from this LUB; interpretation of the date of these features is suggested by the intrusive finds from LUB 9.

Fig. 2.9 Looking west across gulley cg2 in the foreground, and into ditch cg1: LUBs 2 and 6.

Late medieval

Sealing LUB 10 was a thick dump **LUB 11**, associated with late medieval pottery.

LUB 11 Dump (Fig. 2.7)
Overlying cg22, cg14 and cg23 (LUB 10) was a 1.4m thick undifferentiated soil layer cg15.

Pottery from this LUB (10 post-Roman sherds from cg15) includes a jar/pipkin and a dripping pan dating to the medieval or late medieval period together with several earlier sherds.

Modern

Sealing LUB 11 was Victorian building disturbance **LUB 12**.

LUB 12 Victorian building (Fig. 2.7)
Dump cg15 (LUB 11) was directly overlain by Victorian building disturbance cg18, relating to the construction of Victorian terraced housing.

Discussion of cs73

Roman activity

All the features encountered ran roughly parallel to
Ermine Street, which lay about 100m to the west of
the site. Certainly this area represents marginal land,
as there was no apparent activity here in either the
early Roman or very late Roman periods. These mid
Roman features might have marked the boundary
between properties which would have fronted the
street and marshy land to the east; it may be that
this was the only period during which properties
were developed to the west of the site. In the mid
Roman period there was much construction activity
in the suburb to the south of the walled *colonia*. We
have clear evidence of construction taking place
during this period to the south of cs72 at m82, and
to the north at ze87. To the north-east of cs73 was
probably marsh as also to the east of ze87.

A shallow gully (LUB 2), was succeeded by a ditch
(LUB 4) and subsequently a ditch and a gully (LUB
6). Another shallow gully and a posthole (LUB 8)
belonged to the subsequent phase. Interleaving the
cutting of these features were a sandy layer (LUB 3)
and clayey layers (LUBs 5 and 7) with some brown-
green material (LUB 7). Ultimately sealing the
features were layers of black silt with lenses of green
sandy silt (LUB 9). The presence of dark silt layers
suggests that the features at times may have held
water, and the green colour perhaps indicates
stagnation or sewage. The ditches most probably
would have been used for drainage but perhaps they
also operated as an open sewer, silting up and
overflowing; it may be that they were the source of
the dark silty material. Although the gullies appeared
to operate independently of the ditches, in that they
were not always active at the same time, they too
were sealed by dark silty material. They do not
appear to represent wall foundation trenches, as no
trace of building material was recovered; nor do they
seem to indicate fence foundations – there was no
indication of postholes. The most likely interpretation
is that the gullies were used in a similar way to the
ditches. From the pottery it seems possible that they
were in use between the late 2nd and late 3rd
centuries. Of the datable types of pottery, there are
no 1st-century vessels, and if widely dated vessels
are excluded, 58% of the pottery lies in the 2nd

cg/LUB	cg/LUB	cg/LUB	cg/LUB	cg/LUB
1/6	6/3	11/9	16/–	21/10
2/2	7/5	12/9	17/8	22/10
3/4	8/6	13/9	18/12	23/10
4/6	9/8	14/10	19/10	24/10
5/1	10/8	15/11	20/10	25/8

*Fig. 2.10 Concordance of cg numbers with LUB numbers
for cs73.*

century, declining to 25% in the 3rd century, and
16% in the later 3rd century, at which point it lies
well below all other Wigford sites except hg72.

In the mid Roman period there was much construction activity in the suburb to the south of the
walled *colonia* and it may be that these ditches and
gullies were part of the process either of preparation
in the form of drainage, or provided services for the
new buildings in the form of water provision and/or
cess removal. We have clear evidence of construction
taking place during this period to the south of cs73 at
m82, and to the north at ze87. To the north-east of
cs73 was probably marsh, as also to the east of ze87.

The layers (LUB 9) sealing the features contained
pottery which was mid to late 3rd century which
might suggest that the sequence of activity continued
with a flooding of the area with grey black silt with
lenses of green silt. But the near complete profiles
and joining sherds within this material suggest the
dumping of rubbish, rubbish which also seems to
have intruded into earlier LUBs (LUBs 5 and 7). The
area then seems to have been abandoned, and not
occupied again until the late Saxon period at the
earliest.

Post-Roman activity

Intrusive late Saxon and medieval sherds indicate
some reworking of the layers (LUB 9); these layers
were cut by several features recorded in section
(LUB 10). There is not enough evidence to interpret
these. The whole site was sealed by a thick late
medieval dump (LUB 11). The reason for this dump
may have been related to the creation of orchards
or gardens developed during this period. Over the
dump the Victorian houses (LUB 12) were built.
Chaplin Street was laid out between 1867 and 1876.

3. Monson Street 1982 (m82)

Introduction

In May 1982, planning permission was granted for the erection of a new building for the General and Municipal Workers' Union on the site of nos 2 and 3 Monson Street, which lay on the north side of the road close to its junction with High Street (Fig. 3.1).

Excavations, in advance of redevelopment, took place in June and July 1982, partly in response to discoveries of Roman buildings made earlier in the year beneath St Mary's Guildhall 60m to the south,

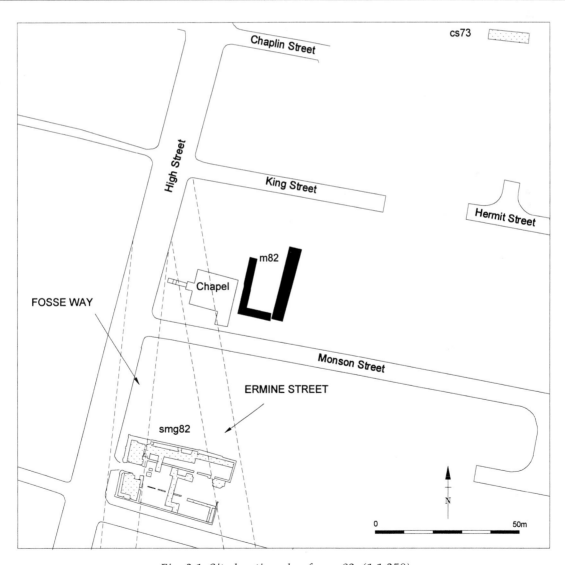

Fig. 3.1 Site location plan for ms82. (1:1,250)

and also because mid 19th-century finds of tomb-stones had indicated a legionary cemetery in the area (Trollope 1860, 18). The other noteworthy 19th-century discovery in Monson Street was a poly-chrome mosaic pavement, the central roundel of which was missing; the remainder comprised an 8-pointed flower with a guilloche border set in a square of plain white and red stripes. A newspaper report (Stamford Mercury, 15 Aug 1845) described it as having been near the Unitarian Chapel, 3 feet below the surface of High Street, but it can be located more precisely to the area of no 2 Monson Street (Richmond 1946, 46). This Roman structure became known as the Monson Street 'villa'; at the time there was no awareness of the actual extent of suburban occupation.

The excavations were directed by John Magilton for the Lincoln Archaeological Trust. There were several constraints on the area available for examination in 1982. Backfilled stone-lined Victorian cellars occupied the street frontage at the southern end of the site, and could not be emptied for safety reasons. To the east, it was not possible to excavate close to the Hop Pole Inn because of the danger of subsidence and, at the request of the architects, no digging was done on the actual site of the proposed new building for the same reason. A lack of both time and resources imposed further constraints. Funding was provided, in part, by the Department of the Environment. Part of the team was provided through a Job Creation Scheme sponsored by the Manpower Services Commission.

The area first examined was L-shaped, consisting of an east–west trench 2 m wide and 9 m long, parallel to the back wall of the Victorian cellars, and a trench of similar width roughly 15 m long at right angles to it, close to the western boundary of the site. Both were excavated by machine to the top of Roman levels (no later deposits were apparent), and then totally excavated by hand. It was hoped that the western trench would locate the line of the Roman road earlier examined beneath the "Norman House" at St Mary's Guildhall (Trench VI: q.v.), but this was not found and must lie further west, beneath the Unitarian Chapel at the junction of High Street and Monson Street. Upon completion of the first two trenches, a third trench was excavated near to the eastern edge of the site and parallel to and about 3 m away from the Hop Pole Inn, principally to confirm the alignment of Roman houses discovered in the first trenches and, if possible, to determine their eastern extent. Owing to lack of time, only the uppermost Roman levels were revealed, and no excavation of Roman deposits was possible.

An interim report was published (Magilton 1982). Interim discussions of the cemetery (Magilton 1983b), the Roman houses (Magilton 1983a), and

some of the finds (Mann 1982b) were also published.

Of the 205 contexts 193 were interpreted as 121 context groups (cg1–127 but cg81, cg82, cg84, cg85, cg86 and cg123 were not used) and 12 were deemed as being unstratified. The context groups are discussed below as 20 land-use blocks, LUBs 0–19 (Fig. 3.23). The LUB diagram is split into three areas from south to north (Figs. 3.2 and 3.3), corresponding to the later lane and building to the south (Area 1) and the building plots of the two later strip buildings to the north (Areas 2 and 3). In Area 1 there are natural (LUB 0), Roman (LUBs 1–4, 6–9, 11–12, 17–18) and late Saxon to modern LUBs (LUB 19). In Area 2 there are natural (LUB 0), Roman (LUBs 1, 3–4, 7–8, 10, 13–14 and 18) and late Saxon to modern LUBs (LUB 19). In Area 3 there are natural (LUB 0), Roman (LUBs 1, 5, 7–8, 10, 15–16 and 18) and late Saxon to modern LUBs (LUB 19).

A total of 2,674 sherds of Roman pottery was recovered from the site, peaking in the mid–late 1st and later 3rd centuries. There were only 93 post Roman sherds. The registered finds numbered 185; several finds were examined by specialists including a Roman brooch (Mackreth 1993), a Roman mirror (Lloyd-Morgan 1982), Roman glass (Price and Cottam 1993b), bone objects (Rackham 1994), stone objects (Roe 1994) and a hone (Moore 1991). Some building material was recovered (276 fragments), a large proportion of which was Roman plaster fragments and pieces of Roman tile (stone identification:

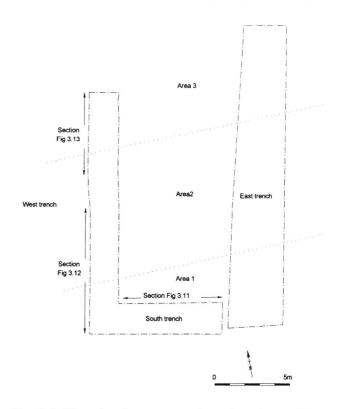

Fig. 3.2 Plan showing areas and sections for ms82.
(1:244)

Roe 1994). A small proportion of the entire animal bone assemblage (total of 1,492 fragments) from Monson Street was examined as part of the post excavation project, and all dated to the Roman period (Dobney *et al* 1994d); an earlier assessment report on the animal bone was undertaken by Sally Scott (Scott 1987), who also carried out a comparative study of the Roman bone assemblages from Monson St and St. Mary's Guildhall (Scott 1986a). Selected soil samples were assessed and a report on the charred plant remains was produced (Moffett 1993). There were 4 cremations (McKinley 1993).

Post-excavation stratigraphic analysis was undertaken by John Magilton and Paul Miles with additional work by Kate Steane. Maggi Darling worked on the Roman pottery; Jane Young examined the post-Roman pottery. Jane Cowgill and Jen Mann worked on the registered finds, and Jen Mann with Rick Kemp, on the building materials. Paul Miles and Zoe Rawlings digitized the plans and Dave Watt drew the finds illustrations.

Interpretation of the sequence of events

Natural

Natural sand **LUB 0** was sealed by what appeared to be an old ground surface **LUB 1**, which rose gently to the west and south; there was no dating evidence for the ground surface.

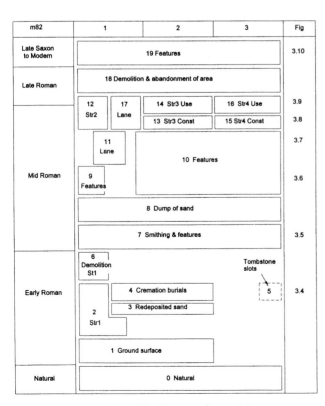

Fig. 3.3 LUB diagram for ms82.

LUB 0 Natural (Fig. 3.12)
Natural yellow sand cg1 was recovered at the limit of excavation in Areas 1, 2 and 3; this was found below 4.80 OD on the site.

LUB 1 Ground surface (Fig. 3.12)
The top of natural cg1 (LUB 0) appears to have been marked by a leached-out grey-white band cg119, at around 4.80m OD but sloping up to west and south; probably the result of podsolisation of an old ground surface (unplanned). There was no dating evidence.

Early Roman

A stone-founded building, Structure 1, **LUB 2** had been erected. Sand was deposited over the rest of the site **LUB 3**. Into it at least four cremation burials had been cut **LUB 4**, and possibly two tombstones slots **LUB 5**. These elements all formed part of an early Roman cemetery; pottery from LUBs 3 and 4 dated from the mid to late 1st century, with sherds from LUB 4 possibly continuing into the early 2nd-century period. With the abandonment of the cemetery came the demolition of Structure 1 **LUB 6**; the pottery was either residual or dated the end of the cemetery within the mid-to-late 1st century, possibly confined to the legionary period.

LUB 2 Structure 1 (Figs. 3.4, 3.11 and 3.14)
The podsolised grey layer (LUB 1) was overlain in Area 1 by a layer of redeposited yellow sand cg73, over which was a construction surface of light yellowish brown mortar and limestone chips cg3 (unplanned). Probably associated with this surface were the mortared stone wall foundations cg2, cut into the natural sand, of a building aligned roughly east–west, probably at right angles to Ermine Street (see Fig. 3.1). Only the north-east corner of the building lay within the limits of the excavation; part of the north wall cg2 (at least 6.6m long) and the north-east corner with a gap possibly indicating a doorway. The foundations were composed of irregular pieces of limestone rubble bonded with yellow-brown mortar in a construction trench about 0.6m wide and originally about 0.4m deep, although the upper part of the foundations had been robbed. No floor levels survived within the building. To the north of and abutting the building was a gully cg5 (0.55m across and of unrecorded depth) which cut cg119 (LUB 1); it had a fill of light greyish-brown sand with bone and much mortar rubble. Gully cg5 may have been associated with rainwater drainage during the life of the building.

Although no pottery or other finds survive from this building or associated layers it seems from overlying stratigraphy that the building was constructed during the second half of the 1st century. A stone building of this early period is most unusual; it is possible that it was a mausoleum associated with the cemetery or a temple.

LUB 3 Redeposited sand
(Figs. 3.11, 3.12 and 3.13)
Partly sealing construction layer cg3 (LUB 2), in Area 1, were layers of redeposited sand cg4 (0.20m thick); in Area 2 the ground surface cg119 (LUB 1) was sealed by redeposited sand cg17 (0.20m thick). These layers seem to represent the laying out of a cemetery around Structure 1; some of the sand may have been redeposited from the construction trenches of Structure 1 (LUB 2). Pottery from cg4 (15 sherds) including an unidentifiable samian stamp of Neronian or early Flavian date, and at least two early rusticated jars are stratigraphically the earliest pot from the site, dated to the mid to late 1st century.

LUB 4 Cremation burials
(Figs. 3.4, 3.12, 3.15 and 3.19)
In Areas 1 and 2, were four cremation burials. Immediately to the north in Area 2, cutting cg17 (LUB 3) was a pit cg18 (1.20m wide and 0.60m deep). The fill of cg18 consisted of soft grey-brown sand 0.4m thick sealed by narrow bands of charcoal. Nearly all associated finds lay in the upper half of the pit. The cremated bones (235.3g) were contained in a rusticated jar which rested upright in the bottom of the pit and was sealed by a lid (Figs. 3.15 and 3.19 No 1). The jar was in LEG fabric and the style of rustication was that of early vessels; it was covered by a CR lid. Both the jar and the lid fit a mid to late 1st century date. It is particularly interesting that the cremated bones were of a young juvenile, 5–7 years, as the jar type and fabric is typical of the legionary period in Lincoln. Together with the cremated bones the jar held five nails, two of which were hobnails, five melted glass blobs and three fragments of tubular unguent bottles, all heat distorted.

North of cg18 in Area 2, cutting cg17 (LUB 3) was pit cg16 (1.20m wide and 0.60m deep) which contained cremated bones; the 157.4g recovered from cg16 represents only a maximum of 9.8% of the total weight of bone expected from an adult cremation burial (McKinley 1994). The bone represented the remains of an adult, possibly female. Two fillings were distinguished within the pit, both of mottled sand; all of the finds came from the lower layer but pottery was not recovered from either fill. Cremation burial cg16 included cremated chicken bone, five nails, one complete glass unguent bottle (Fig. 3.19 No 3) and a fragment from another, both heat-distorted, as well as a severely heat-blistered copper alloy mirror (Fig. 3.19, No 4). An environmental sample taken from cg16 (for charred plant remains) contained much poorly preserved charcoal which

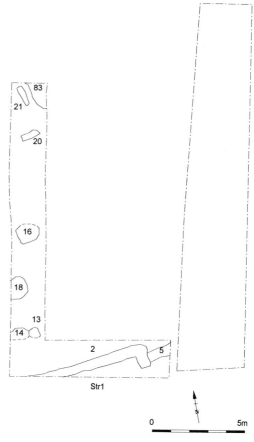

Fig. 3.4 Mausoleum and cemetery: LUBs 3, 4 and 5.
(1:200)

appears to be pyre debris, but also includes cremated bone (Moffett 1993).

Cutting cg4 in Area 1 (LUB 3) was a bowl-shaped cut cg13 (0.75m wide) which represented the remains of a cremation burial; it had a fill of yellow and grey sand with charcoal and small quantities of cremated human bone (3.8g), the remains of a juvenile/subadult. There were also four nails, two of which were hobnails, one complete tubular glass unguent bottle (151) <118> (Fig. 3.19 No 2) and a heat-distorted fragment of another. The only pottery in the grave filling was a sherd from a flagon; it is unlikely to have been a container for the cremated remains, although it could have been part of the grave furniture.

Just to the west of and possibly cutting cg13 was a bowl-shaped cut cg14 (min 0.80m wide); it too represented the remains of a cremation burial and had a fill of yellow and grey sand with charcoal, together with a small quantity of cremated human bone (12g), the remains of an individual of unknown age, as well as a fragment of cremated pig/sheep bone, five nails (four of which were hobnails), and four pieces of glass: a melted glass blob, an unguent bottle and single fragments of a square or rectangular bottle and a cup.

The eight sherds from cg14 included sherds from two GREY jars, one with linear rustication, and the other being the same as a jar in cg15 (LUB 7), both of which could fit a later 1st century or 2nd century date. This dating is echoed by the samian, a Neronian–early Flavian Dr 29 rim, and a Curle 11 rim of Flavian to Flavian–Trajanic date. Since this feature was cut by pit cg15 (LUB 7), it is uncertain to which context the jar rim belonged. Since a pit (cg15) had disturbed the top of this feature, the later material could be intrusive.

In Area 3 there was a pit cg83 which cut cg119 (LUB 1); this may have been part of a cremation burial, most of which lay beyond the excavation. Pit cg83 was a shallow feature at least 1.9m across, filled with pale brown sand flecked with charcoal.

LUB 5 Grave marker slots?
(Figs. 3.4 and 3.16)

In Area 3 were two features which cut into natural sand (LUB 0). These comprised two narrow straight-sided slots, cg20 and cg21 (Fig. 3.16) which cut cg119 (LUB 1). The slots, which lay roughly at right angles to one another, were each a little over a metre long, a maximum of about 0.5m deep and 0.2m wide, although cg20 had partly collapsed at the top and thus appeared slightly wider than cg21. Both slots had been straight sided, but in both the base of the slot sloped, cg20 varying in depth from 0.25m on the west to 0.5 m on the east, and cg21 from 0.3m on the north to 0.56m on the south. The fill in both cases was pale brown sand.

These two features may represent the remaining depths of foundation slots for tombstones, the stones themselves having been slighted in antiquity, after the area went out of use as a cemetery. There were no associated finds, but it seems possible that these slots were contemporary with the cemetery to the south; alternatively, they could have dated earlier as they cut natural. The finds from the cemetery and their context are discussed in more detail below.

LUB 6 Demolition and robbing of Structure 1
(Fig. 3.11)

The robber trench cg6 cut through sand cg4 (LUB 3), removed stone from the walls of Structure 1, and was sealed by rubble cg7. This appears to mark the end of the use of the site as a cemetery.

The robber trench cg6 and rubble cg7 produced 24 sherds of mid to late 1st-century date, including a LEG fabric cup copying a pre-Flavian Lyon form, of which further sherds occurred in cg11; the sole samian sherd was a Flavian Dr 27 rim fragment. It is also possible that this represents residual material as pottery from cremation burials cg13 and cg14 (LUB 4) may have dated to between the late 1st and early 2nd centuries (although this may equally have

been intrusive from cg15, LUB 7). If the use of the cemetery was confined to the legionary period, there followed a gap of several decades before the site was used again.

Mid Roman

Sealing and cutting the cemetery makeup LUB 3 and cemetery features LUB 4 were a number of features indicating activity, including smithing, after the cemetery went out of use **LUB 7**; pottery indicates that this activity took place between the early and mid 2nd centuries. It was subsequently sealed by a dump of redeposited sand **LUB 8**, containing pottery probably dating to the mid 2nd century. The dump was cut by a north–south slot and gully **LUB 9** in Area 1, as well as other less regular cut features in Areas 1, 2 and 3 **LUB 10**; mid to late 2nd century pottery was found in these features. Apparently later than LUB 9, but on a similar north–south alignment was a north–south lane **LUB 11**; pottery from the lane dated between the late 2nd century and into the 3rd. These remains probably indicate slight timber structures aligned on to Ermine Street to the west.

Sometime between the early 3rd and the mid 3rd century the area became a building site; in Area 1, a 'strip building' (trader's house), Structure 2, was erected on a roughtly east–west alignment, parallel to Ermine Street **LUB 12**. In Area 2 a similar building, Structure 3, was constructed **LUB 13** and went into use **LUB 14**; pottery dates construction to the mid 3rd century and the occupation of the buildings from the mid 3rd century into the 4th century. In Area 4, Structure 4 was built **LUB 15** and inhabited **LUB 16**; its construction did not produce any pottery but it was stratigraphically later than LUB 10 and possibly contemporary with LUB 13; pottery from its use dated to the mid 3rd century or later. Between Structures 2 and 3 there was an east–west lane **LUB 17**, dated by pottery to around the mid 3rd century or later.

LUB 7 Smithing and contemporary cut features
(Figs. 3.5 and 3.11.)

A thick laminated deposit of hammerscale cg19 sealed the upper fill of cremation burial cg16 (LUB 4) in Area 2: this type of deposit, in such quantity, is normally found only *in situ* on a floor very close to where iron smithing has taken place (G McDonnell, pers comm); it may have been the remnant of a much more widespread deposit, surviving only where it had subsided into the cremation burial pit. This would imply that there had been a smithing workshop here, and that some truncation of deposits had subsequently occurred. There was no associated slag amongst the soil sample and none is recorded slag amongst the soil sample and none is recorded from the deposit. Most of the sample consisted of plate scale although some spheroidal scale was also present.

In the south-west corner of the site, cutting cremation burials cg13 and cg14 (LUB 4) was a pit cg15; the finds (glass, nails and a copper alloy fragment) from cg15 were possibly derived from the cremation burials.

In Area 1, against the south section, posthole cg10 cut cg7 (LUB 6), and was cut by a small postpit or posthole cg11 which in turn was cut by another such feature cg12. Cutting sand cg4 (LUB 3), to the north of these postholes, was part of a gully cg8 aligned north-west to south-east and a pit cg9 (not planned).

The features cg8, cg9, cg11, cg12 and cg15 produced 161 sherds, mostly from cg15 (96 sherds), dating up to early to mid 2nd century; BB1 first occurs here, in cg9 and cg12. Pottery from cg15 contained no BB1 or BB type vessels, and the samian extended only to the Trajanic period in date, but produced a PART type beaker with a small oval dimple; on ceramic grounds, therefore, this pit could pre-date cg9 and cg12, particularly cg12 where 10 of the 24 sherds were BB1.

Just to the north-east of pit cg15, sealing cg4 (LUB 3) were layers of sandy clay with burnt material cg31 (unplanned), possibly cut by small oval pit cg94. Pottery from cg31 (23 sherds) gave a date of mid to late 2nd century; the samian was of Hadrianic or Antonine date. Recognised in section, cutting cg4 (LUB 3) but not otherwise recorded, were four cut features in Area 1, cg77, cg78, cg79 and cg80 (Fig. 3.11.).

In Area 3 cutting slot cg21 (LUB 4) was a possible pit cg22, to the north of which was a gully cg23 aligned south-west to north-east. Shallow east–west gullies cg23 and pit cg22 produced 42 and seven sherds respectively (including five sherds SAMSG), of 1st-century date, none being conclusively 2nd century.

LUB 8 Dump of sand
(Figs. 3.11, 3.12 and 3.13)
In Area 1, sealing cut feature cg80 (LUB 7), gully cg5 (LUB 2) and rubble cg7 (LUB 6), was a layer of sand cg76 (up to 0.4m thick). In Areas 1 and 2 sealing gully cg8, pits cg9 and cg15, as well as cut features cg77, cg78, cg79 and cg12 (all LUB 7), was a layer of greyish brown sand cg75 with charcoal, limestone chips and mortar flecks. Part of a 'hearth bottom' was recovered from cg75 (it weighed 223gm, and was 35mm high and 72mm wide), together with a small quantity of slag and hammerscale; this material had probably been disturbed from underlying deposits (LUB 7). In Area 2, sealing cremation burial

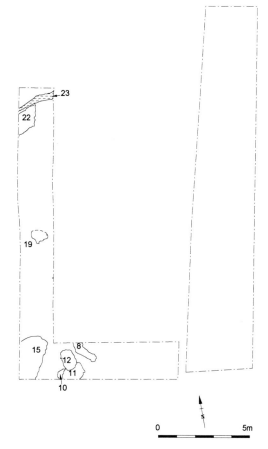

Fig. 3.5 Features: LUB 7. (1:200)

cg18 (LUB 4) and hammerscale deposit cg19 (LUB 7), was sand cg74 (0.20m thick). In Area 3, sealing cg22 and cg23 (LUB 7), were layers of yellow and grey sand cg34 (0.40m thick).

All these sand dumps (cg34, cg74 cg75, cg76) were probably part of the same event. Pottery from dump cg34 (42 sherds altogether) contained BB1, but on body sherds alone, only an early to mid 2nd-century date is feasible; there was a single samian sherd of Flavian–Trajanic date. Pottery from dump cg75 (66 sherds) was the largest group and included BB1 and GREY BB types, and the SAMCG included a Dr 31 of Antonine date. Dumps cg74 and cg76 produced only six and eight sherds, cg74 being indeterminate 1st–2nd century, while cg76 included an unusual GREY BFBH with lattice decoration.

LUB 9 Cut features (Fig. 3.6.)
Cutting sand cg76 (LUB 8), in Area 1, was a substantial north–south slot cg25 (0.40m across and 0.80m deep); to the west of this was a north–south gully cg26 (1m across and 0.40m deep). The gully cg26 was cut by a small pit or posthole cg29 and posthole cg27. These may have represented boundary markings or drainage or both. The pottery from slot

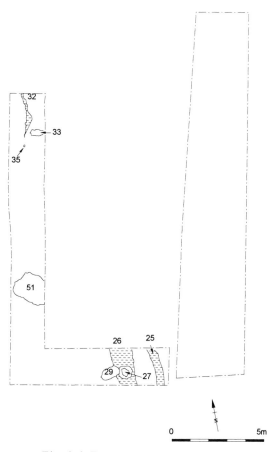

Fig. 3.6 Features: LUBs 9 and 10. (1:200)

cg25, gully cg26 and pit cg29 (75 sherds), broadly dated to the mid to late 2nd century as indicated by a BB1 bowl sherd from cg29; a SAMCG Dr 37 sherd from cg29 is dated *c* AD 130–165.

LUB 10 Features
(Figs. 3.6, 3.12, 3.13, 3.20 and 3.21)
In the south-west corner of Area 1, a posthole cg30 (unplanned but recorded in section, Fig. 3.12) cut cg75 (LUB 8); it was sealed by a patch of light yellow-brown clay and mortar cg42. In Area 2, sand cg74 (LUB 8) was cut by shallow, irregular pit cg51 with pottery of mid to late 2nd century. In Area 3, cutting sand cg34 (LUB 8), was a north–south gully cg32, pit cg33 and stakehole cg35.

The pottery from pits cg51 and cg33 only contained 16 sherds and included a fragment of a GREY ring/vessel support from cg51 (with further fragments from slot cg55 LUB 14).

Bands of sand, clay and limestone rubble cg48 sealed gully cg32, pit cg33 and stakehole cg35. Over rubble cg48 was a layer of dark sand with limestone rubble cg91. Pottery from rubble cg48 and cg91 (104 sherds) gave an early to mid 3rd-century date on the basis of BB1 and GREY cooking pot rims and

NVCC beaker sherds; no Dales ware was present.

Rubble cg48 was cut by a posthole cg89 (unplanned), over which was a layer of soft silt cg90, cut by posthole cg88 (unplanned but recorded in section Fig. 3.13). Pottery from layer cg90 (28 sherds) included the first appearance of DWSH which, together with a GREY folded funnel necked beaker and NVCC beakers, suggests a mid 3rd-century date; a samian Dr 31 of mid–late Antonine date was also found.

The layers cg90 and the posthole cg88 were sealed by a thin layer of ash and charcoal cg56 into which had been cut two postholes cg57 and cg58, as well as an oval pit cg59, 0.6m long. An unusual assemblage of finds (Figs. 3.20 and 3.21) was recovered from this pit. A complete iron tripod ((54) <11> Fig. 3.20 No 1) was found inverted and sitting at the bottom of the pit; one leg appears to have been bent prior to burial. Another large iron object, probably part of a triangular tripod ((54) <223>; Fig. 3.21), had been placed between the feet of the inverted tripod, and was almost certainly deposited after it had been broken; complete tripods are uncommon finds and the form of the latter is rare in Britain, although it can be paralleled in Germany (pers comm W H Manning). The pit also contained a bar of iron ((54) <221> Fig. 3.20 No 2) which is slightly angled in the centre and has shaped terminals which suggest possible use as a double-ended spoon or spatula. The bones of a two- to three-month-old piglet were also placed in the pit. The presence of a large part of the skeleton may indicate some sort of ritual activity (Dobney *et al* 1994d) but the bones do not seem to be articulated, from the evidence of the photographs. The relationship of these bones and the ?spoon/spatula to the other items is not known. Two nails, two fragmentary cow bones and a single grey ware body sherd were the only other finds recovered. During conservation it was noted that considerable amounts of charcoal and some bone were incorporated in the corrosion products. Within some of the deeper cracks in the objects appeared to be plant roots which may have accelerated the speed of corrosion. The unusual nature of the assemblage suggests that it may have some particular significance, perhaps as a votive offering (pers comm W H Manning). It is difficult to determine whether the significance lies in the composition of the assemblage, which appears to be related to heating (?cooking), or whether the iron, in this instance, is attributed with some magical powers.

LUB 11 North–south lane (Fig. 3.7 and Fig. 3.11)
Sealing possible posthole cg29 (LUB 9) in Area 1, was a dump of yellow sand cg28, the makeup for limestone rubble, cobbles and pebbles which had been rammed between the larger stones to produce a hard, level surface cg36. Layers cg24 and cg93

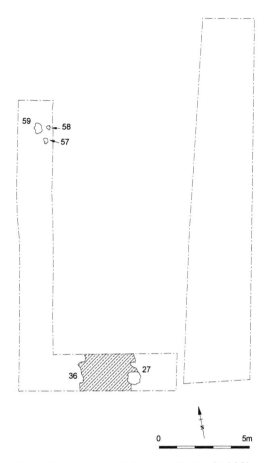

Fig. 3.7 *North–south lane: LUB 11. (1:200)*

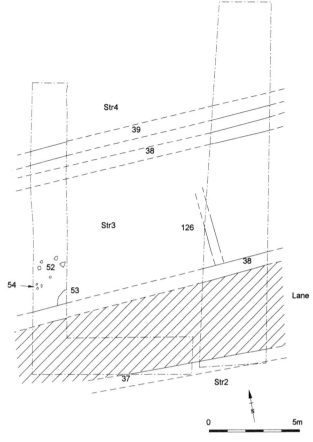

Fig. 3.8 *Structures 2, 3 and 4 with lane: LUBs 12, 13, 15 and 17. (1:200)*

were stratigraphically isolated, but probably part of the same surface. The lane appeared to run north–south along the line of the earlier gully cg26 (LUB 9); the lane surface had partially sealed post-hole cg27 (LUB 9) allowing the post to continue in use. Both the alignment and the continued use of the post suggest that this lane surface merely represented a continuation of an existing feature.

Pottery from cg28 (31 sherds) included a NVCC thick-walled base to a closed form which suggests a 3rd-century date; the samian extended to the Antonine period. There were sherd joins from cg28 with cg11 (LUB 7) and cg75 (LUB 8) suggesting some disturbance of earlier material. The only other pottery (5 sherds) from LUB 11 came from cg24, and were indeterminate, although a sherd from a SAMEG bowl gives an overall date range of c AD 150–250.

LUB 12 Structure 2 (Fig. 3.8)
In the south-east part of Area 1 was evidence of a possible "strip building" running roughly east–west. The mortared limestone foundations of wall cg37 (0.60m wide) cut through lane cg36 (LUB 11);

this wall probably represented the north wall of the building. The wall was constructed of mortared roughly-faced blocks of limestone on pitched foundations of smaller pieces of limestone rubble.

There was no pottery dating. Stratigraphically this building dates between LUBs 9 and 18, ie, between the early 3rd and 4th centuries.

LUB 13 Construction of Structure 3
(Figs. 3.8, 3.12, 3.13, 3.16, 3.17 and 3.18)
In Area 2, walls cg38 of mortared limestone with stone rubble foundations cut into sand cg74 (LUB 8). The building was a little over 5m wide internally and of undetermined length, its extent from east to west being more than 13.5m. The external walls (0.60m wide) were constructed of roughly-faced limestone rubble, of which a maximum of four courses survived, bonded with yellow-brown sandy mortar which, with some smaller pieces of rubble, formed the wall core. Its width was 0.6m. Part of a narrower internal north–south wall cg126 was located in the east trench; it would have apparently abutted walls cg38 (no other relationships were recorded). About 3m to the east there appeared to

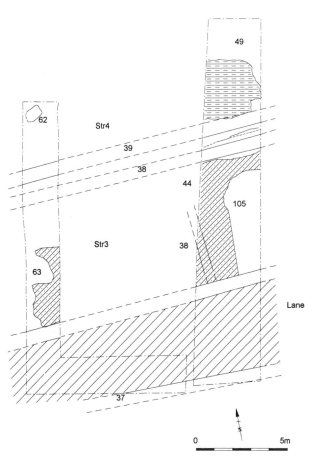

Fig. 3.9 Use of structures: LUBs 14 and 16. (1:200)

had accumulated; it contained a Kentish Ragstone hone and a spindlewhorl made from a samian body sherd, reshaped into a disc with smooth ground edges and with a central perforation. Close to the south wall, sealing cg64 was a deposit of limestone rubble and mortar cg66.

Sealing cg66 and cg87 was a layer of yellow-brown sand cg92; sealing cg92 and cg65 was a brown deposit cg67, sealed by clay floors cg68 with charcoal flecks, pebbles, mortar flecks, limestone and tile chips, which was cut by stake-holes cg125.

At the east end of the building, circumstances allowed the excavation only of various layers making up cg44, to the east of the robbed internal wall cg126 (LUB 13). The upper layer consisted of reddish-yellow clay which included patches of mortar and pebbles, together with fragments of tile and limestone. It sealed an area of large pieces of limestone rubble, and was perhaps levelling or make-up for a floor surface.

The pottery from cg63 (49 sherds, many of indeterminate dating and one post-Roman sherd) dated to the mid 3rd century due to the presence of DWSH. Pottery from cg66 (25 sherds not closely datable) probably dated to the mid 3rd century, possibly into the 4th century on the basis of NVCC painted BKFB. The pottery from layers cg92, cg65 and cg67 (62 largely indeterminate sherds with few fine wares) could be loosely dated from the mid 3rd to 4th centuries. Silt cg64 and clay floor cg68 had only eight and five sherds respectively which were undiagnostic.

LUB 15 Construction of Structure 4
(Figs. 3.8 and 3.13)
Walls cg39 cut sand cg34 (LUB 8). The south wall was best preserved in the west trench. Its foundations consisted of three courses of pitched limestone rubble, on top of which four mortared courses survived. The width of the wall, represented by the uppermost course of limestone blocks, was about 0.85m, the courses below being offset from the foundations which were about 1.10m wide. In the east trench, the only part of the wall to survive robbing was a layer of mortar which sealed the pitched foundations. Neither portion of the wall was removed during excavation.

Structure 4 was more than 13.4m long and more than 5.3 m wide internally. Its southern wall was located in the west and east trenches, but the limits of the building lay beyond the area of excavations. There was no pottery dating. Stratigraphically the construction dates between LUBs 10 and 16, ie, between the early-to-mid and mid 3rd centuries.

LUB 16 Structure 4: Use
(Figs. 3.9, 3.13 and 3.18)
Sealing postholes cg57, cg58 and pit cg59 (LUB 10)

have been another internal north–south wall, but this was totally robbed away by robber trench cg105 (LUB 18; see Fig. 3.9).

Sealing cg74 (LUB 8) was a thin layer of sandy clay and charcoal cg46 over which was a layer of brownish yellow sand cg47. Both these layers abutted the foundations of wall cg38, overlying the chamfered offset of the wall, suggesting that the foundations had already been constructed. Cutting sand cg47 were postholes cg52 and cg54 and a small pit cg53.

The pottery from cg38 (28 sherds) dated to the mid 3rd century on the presence of DWSH and late NVCC beaker sherds.

LUB 14 Use of Structure 3
(Figs. 3.9, 3.12 and 3.13)
The earliest identified floor at the west end of the building was a layer of rough limestone rubble paving cg63 which sealed pit cg53 and postholes cg54 (both LUB 13); the paving was cut by posthole cg87 (unplanned; but seen in section Fig. 3.13) together with slot cg55. To the north of, and partly sealing the paving cg63, was brown silt cg65. Over the paving but not the postholes, brown silt cg64

was a dump of sandy material cg60 of variable thickness (between 0.15m and 0.25m thick), possibly associated with the construction of the building. Makeup layer cg60 was sealed by cg61, a thin ashy deposit, sealed by clay layers, part of which which was extensively burnt; there were three thin limestone slabs in the north-west corner of the trench which may indicate that the next floor surface had been paved, or which may have been part of a hearth surround.

At the north end of the trench, partly cut into floors cg61, was a subrectangular hearth cg62 (0.7m wide and more than 0.75m long), its west end cut away by a later pit (cg111, LUB 19). It consisted of small pieces of limestone rubble set in clay on a foundation of five larger pieces of rubble in yellow-brown silt.

In the east trench, an area of coarse mortar cg49 roughly 3m square sealed the construction trench of the south wall of the building cg39 (LUB 15). It had been carefully laid on a bedding of pitched limestone rubble but was poorly preserved and friable when excavated. No earlier layers were investigated in this area.

Pottery from the makeup and floors (156 sherds) mostly came from cg60 (142 sherds), many of which appeared to be residual mid to late 2nd-century material, but dated by DWSH, GREY cooking pot and late NVCC to the mid 3rd century or later.

LUB 17 The lane (Figs. 3.8, 3.11 and 3.17)
Separating Structures 2 and 3 was a lane about 3.6m wide. This was investigated mainly in the southern trench; the uppermost surface was located in the southern part of the east trench, but circumstances did not permit any record, other than photographic, to be made.

Sealing both the earlier lane cg36 (LUB 11) and the construction trench of wall cg38 (LUB 13) was a layer of mainly redeposited natural sand, usually about 0.25m thick but deeper in places where the first lane had subsided into earlier features, which provided the makeup for cobbled lane cg40. A layer of dark yellowish-brown sand and silt separated this lane surface from its successor cg124, which was composed predominantly of worn limestone cobbles. To the east of the site only the surface cg41 was exposed (it was not excavated).

Pottery from cg40 (246 sherds), many of which were notably abraded, showed a notable paucity of fine wares. Only a single sherd possibly of LCOA would suggest a date much after the mid 3rd century, and some of the pottery was residual from the 2nd and 3rd centuries.

Late Roman

The use of at least Structures 3 (LUB 14) and 4 (LUB 16), and probably 2 continued at least into the late 3rd century, as did the lane between Structures 2 and 3 (LUB 17). It is possible that the paucity of 4th-century pottery indicates that the buildings were abandoned and robbed during that century **LUB 18**.

LUB 18 Demolition and abandonment of area (Figs. 3.9, 3.11 and 3.18)
Rubbly layers cg45 in the gap between Structure 3 and Structure 4, in the western trench, were probably demolition material. The original record states that much tile was present, mostly ceramic but including some stone slates. Pottery from cg45 consisted of 40 sherds of which 26 came from a single GREY cookpot of mid 3rd-century type. Similar demolition material cg50 was recovered in the east trench; this deposit produced 20 sherds, dated to the mid 3rd century with a possible continuation into the 4th century.

Sealing layers cg44 (LUB 14), and rubble cg45, as well as the levelled north wall of Structure 3 and the south wall of building 4, was a mixture of yellow-brown mortar and sand cg69 with limestone rubble and pebbles, tile chips, painted plaster and clay. In the original site records 'wall collapse' was suggested. A noticeable quantity of stone slate, mostly of Collyweston slate and others of Coal Measures Sandstone (Roe 1994), was found in this destruction material. The pottery from cg69 (26 sherds) was probably mid 3rd century or later; the possibility of a 4th-century date is only based on the presence of HADOX and MHAD sherds from closed vessels.

Sealing lane surface cg124 (LUB 17) was a brown silty deposit with limestone cg70 up to 0.2m deep together with a layer of sandy clay with mortar and limestone chips and fragments cg43. The majority of the artefacts from cg70 probably had a structural function and probably derive from the buildings; these include iron nails and an iron bolt (29)<63>. Both cg43 and cg70 contained a notable quantity of ceramic tiles and stone slates, a sample of the latter being identified as Coal Measures Sandstone (Roe 1994). A large assemblage of animal bone from cg70 was dominated by equal numbers of cattle and caprovids. Other species included horse, pig, dog, cat, red deer, domestic fowl, and goose (Dobney *et al* 1994d).

Layer cg70 produced the largest pottery group from the site (644 sherds), giving a mid to late 4th-century date (10 intrusive post-Roman sherds are noted) based on late BB1, DWSH JDLS? and JLS, late GREY including a BIBF, probable LCOA including a JLS, late NVCC including a FDN and late fabrics. This group contained many small sherds, but also some medium–large with minimum abrasion; most would fit a late 3rd-century running into 4th-century dating. Ten samian sherds occurred in cg70, eight of which were SAMEG of late 2nd- to 3rd-century date.

Pottery from layer cg43 (38 sherds) dated mid 3rd to 4th centuries and included SAMEG possibly of 3rd-century date; the preponderance of GREY body sherds (24 sherds) limits the dating, although a GREY funnel neck beaker and the presence of a MONV mortarium may suggest it is slipping into the 4th century.

Cutting layers cg69 was a north–south trench cg105; it was probably a robber trench (drawn on Fig. 3.9 to locate wall). An unusual pottery object ((201) <181> (Fig. 3.22), possibly a fragment from a household god, came from trench cg105 (see discussion for further details).

It would seem that the site was abandoned possibly by the early 4th century with cg70 perhaps representing an abandonment deposit with mid to late 4th-century material. Several post-Roman sherds occur intrusively in Roman deposits cg70 and cg105 (eight post-Roman sherds) suggesting some later reworking.

Late Saxon to Modern

The site was subsequently characterised by cut features **LUB 19** indicative of pits and robbing, wells and a cellar.

*LUB 19: Post-Roman occupation
and robbing features (Figs. 3.10 and 3.11)*
Cut through the floors cg61 (LUB 16), was an irregular T-shaped feature cg110, straight-sided and about 0.3m deep, filled with dark brown sand and clay, pebbles, and small pieces of limestone. Although this contained one post-Roman sherd, it may have been a contaminated Roman feature.

Floors cg49 (LUB 16) were disturbed by a pit cg112 curved in shape, a large square pit cg113 and

pit cg116. Pit cg113 contained pottery (32 post-Roman sherds) which formed a cohesive group dating to the 14th century. Pit cg116 and demolition layers cg69 were cut by a robber trench cg118 of the

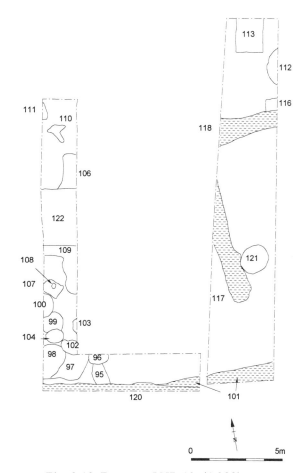

Fig. 3.10 Features: LUB 19. (1:200)

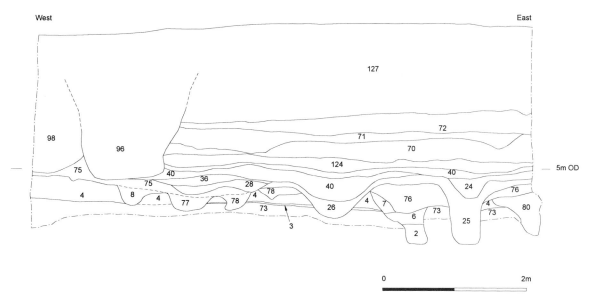

Fig. 3.11 Section west to east, north of the south trench illustrating the stratigraphy in area 1, LUBs 1–19. (1:50)

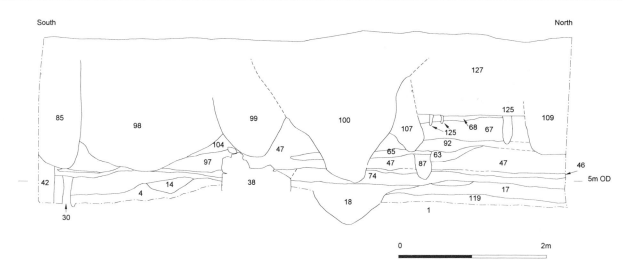

Fig. 3.12 *Section from south to north, along the southern part of the west side of the west trench, illustrating the stratigraphy in areas 1 and 2, LUBs 1–19. (1:50)*

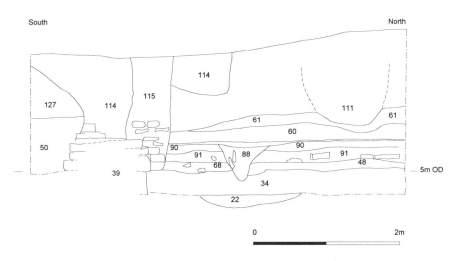

Fig. 3.13 *Section from south to north, along the northern part of the west side of the west trench, illustrating the stratigraphy in areas 2 and 3, LUBs 7–19. (1:50)*

east–west wall of Structure 4 (LUB 15). Cutting cg69 (LUB 18) was a robber trench cg117 of a north–south wall (LUB 15).

The demolition material over the lane surface cg70 (LUB 18) was sealed by a spread of rubble cg71. These were sealed by layers of grey clay cg72; sealing these layers together with stakeholes cg125 (LUB 14) were undescribed layers cg127 (removed mechanically).

Cutting layers cg127 was the small pit cg107, itself cut by posthole cg108; pits cg109 and cg111 together with gully cg95 also cut layers cg127. Cutting into the Roman stratigraphy from undescribed layers cg127 was pit cg97, which was in turn cut by pit cg98. Pit cg98 was itself cut by pits cg99, cg96 and cg102. Pit cg99 was cut by pit cg100 and pit cg104; pit cg98 was cut by pit cg102.

The north wall of Structure 2 (LUB 12) was robbed by trench cg101, which cut through cg72. The south wall of Structure 3 (LUB 13) was partially cut by pit cg103. The south wall of Structure 4 (LUB 15) and rubble cg50 (LUB 18) were cut by pit cg106, which in turn was cut by Victorian cess pit cg122; the cess pit also cut pit cg109.

Pit cg98 was cut by the construction trench for the post-medieval cellar cg120. Well pit cg114 cut through layers cg127 and well cg115 was constructed of unmortared limestone.

Robber trench cg105 (LUB 18) was cut by a well cg121 of medieval or later date.

Much of the early pitting and foundation robbing seems to have taken place during the early to late 11th century. There was also some later medieval pitting (including cg113), with wells cg121 and

Fig. 3.15 Cremation pit cg18 looking west.

which diverged from the Fosse Way at the point where the drier ground began. Small groups of pottery came from LUBs 4, 5 and 6, mostly dating to the mid to late 1st century.

The cemetery seems to have gone out of use by the early 2nd century at the latest (and may have been confined to the legionary period), when smithing (LUB 7) took place. The commercially favourable location of the road junction provided an opportune site for smithing, which seems to have taken place directly over the remains of the cemetery, suggesting a response to demand, rather than advance planning, in the early days of the colonia.

Possibly indicating more planned use of the land was a dump of redeposited sand (LUB 8) which was cut by a north–south slot and gully (LUB 9), suggesting a boundary or structure, about 20m to the east of Ermine Street, and parallel to it. These cut features seem to have silted up and were replaced by a north–south lane (LUB 11) which ran parallel to Ermine Street. To its rear there are only slight traces of activity (LUB 10), which also related to the Ermine Street frontage, in the mid to late 2nd century. Pottery from LUBs 7, 8, 9 and 10 all contained high percentages of 1st-century pottery, with LUBs 9 and 10 having the latest content. The dating of the samian and coarse ware coincided for all four of these LUBs.

In the first part of the 3rd century the area was built over, and although the alignments remained the same, the whole pattern of the site changed. Buildings were constructed which clearly fronted on to Ermine Street. The dominant influence of Ermine Street, rather than the Fosse Way was also echoed to the south (smg82). Traces of three traders' houses were uncovered (LUBs 12–16), together with a lane (LUB 17) leading east from Ermine Street. The lane between Structures 2 and 3 was about 3.6m wide.

This arrangement lasted at least until the late 3rd

Fig. 3.14 Foundations of early stone structure cg2, looking east.

cg115 either being medieval or post-medieval and the cellar cg120 being post-medieval or modern.

Discussion of m82

Topography

The natural sand at 4.80m OD was found at a relatively high level, which made it dry enough for use as a cemetery (LUBs 2–5), rather than being marshy (cf: z86; sm76, bwe82). The site is significant in that it lies about 25m to the south of the postulated junction between Ermine Street and the Fosse Way (Fig. 3.1). In the 1st century the site lay well to the south of any occupation to the south of the main river crossing (it is more than 450m from hg72); the island here was used for structures associated with the army's presence. The cemetery then occupied the first dry ground to the south of the southern channel of the river noted in the area of St. Marks, and appears to have been set out in relation to Ermine Street

Fig. 3.16 Cemetery-period slots cg20 and cg21, looking north.

Fig. 3.17 South-west corner of excavation, looking east: south wall of Structure 3 cg38, and lane surface cg40.

Fig. 3.18 East trench looking south: north wall of Structure 3, robbed south wall of Structure 4, mortar floor of Structure 4 cg49.

century. There is very little evidence for the late 4th century, the tail for that period being largely composed of fabrics and vessel types with long date-ranges. The similarity of the overall dating profiles from m82 and the adjacent smg82 may indicate a lessening of activity in this area of the suburb in the latest period. Building debris covered the abandoned site. There may have been some reworking of the site, but no definite re-occupation until the 11th century, when this part of Wigford seems to have become populated again.

The cremation burials LUB 4; bone and other finds

The cremation burials were examined (McKinley 1993) and finds were recovered from four of the possible five cremation burials. Since the fills of the pits were not sieved, it is uncertain how complete a bone assemblage was recovered. The charcoal was not kept from most of the burials. so it is not known if any carbonised foodstuffs (with the exception of the dates in cg18 and cg16) were deposited with the burials.

The human bone assemblage from the cremation burials LUB 4

The fill of each cremation burial was passed through a stack of sieves of 10, 5 and 2mm mesh size (McKinley 1993). The weight of bone collected from each sieve, together with the maximum fragment sizes for skull and long bone, illustrates the degree of bone fragmentation (McKinley 1989). The identifiable bone was then separated for further examination, being divided into the categories of skull, axial, upper and lower limb. This may illustrate any deliberate bias in the skeletal elements collected for burial (McKinley 1989). Age was assessed from the stage of tooth development and eruption (Van Beek 1983), the stage of ossification and epiphyseal bone fusion (Gray 1977; McMinn and Hutchings 1985), and the general degree of degenerative changes to the bone. Sex was assessed from the sexually dimorphic traits of the skeleton (Bass 1987), including maximum cranial vault thickness '1a' according to Gejvall (Gejvall 1981). Further details are available in the archive (McKinley 1993).

A minimum of four individuals were identified; a young juvenile (5–7 years old) in cg18, an adult (>18 years old) in cg16, a juvenile/subadult (5–18 years old) in cg13 and an individual of unknown age in cg14. With the exception of cg18, the cremation burials were substantially disturbed, especially cg13 and cg14, which probably accounts for the very small quantities of bone recovered from the latter two. The undisturbed cremation burial cg18 suggests good recovery of bone from the pyre for burial, although it is difficult to assess proportions for this juvenile burial (50%+).

Cremation appears to have been efficient, with most of the bone being light, brittle and white in colour. Several bones (particularly the foot bones) did show black-grey spongiosa indicative of incomplete oxidation (McKinley 1989 and 1994b). The bones showed no indication of deliberate fragmentation, the vast majority of those from the undisturbed cremation burial being in excess of 10mm (*ibid*). There was no apparent bias in bones collected for burial.

The inclusion of pyre debris (wood ash) in the pit of cg16 might be taken to suggest relatively close proximity of the pyre site to the burial, but, in view of the sandy nature of the soil, the paucity of any fuel ash slag would suggest the pyre sites were not in the immediate vicinity. However, this may be a problem of identification and retrieval (see above).

Two cremation burials contained fragments of

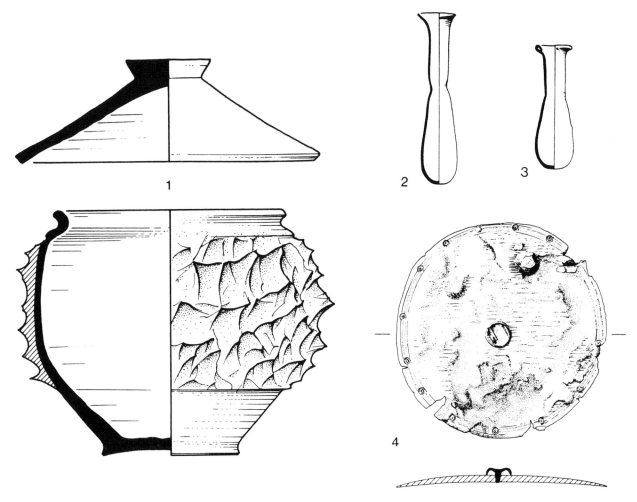

Fig. 3.19 Finds from the cremation burials. 1: cremation jar from cg18; 2: glass unguent bottle from cg13; 3: glass unguent bottle and 4: copper alloy mirror from cg16. Scale: no 1 – 1:4, nos 2–4 – 1:2.

cremated animal bone, chicken in cg16 and imma-ture pig/sheep in cg14. The inclusion of animal bone in cremation burials of this date is not unusual (Philpott 1991, 428–9); about 14% of the cremations from Baldock (McKinley forthcoming b, McKinley forthcoming c), and about 48% of those from St. Stephens cemetery, St Albans (McKinley forth-coming a), contained cremated animal bone, the commonly occurring species being domestic fowl, pig, and sheep.

Other finds from the cremation burials LUB 4
(Fig. 3.19)
The location of the finds within the pit fills was not recorded. The only complete ceramic vessel was the rusticated 'legionary' ware urn with covering cream ware lid from cg18 (Fig. 3.19 No 1). Other ceramic vessels were only represented by stray sherds.

The most common finds from the cremation burials are the iron nails (from cg13, cg14 and cg18). The presence of hobnails in each of these suggests that shoes may have been put on to the pyre, either

worn by the corpse or included amongst the funeral offerings. The presence of hob nails in cg14 perhaps indicates that the cremation burial was not that of an infant.

All the cremation burials contained tubular glass unguent bottles and it is possible that several more fragments are represented by some of the melted blobs. Such vessels were produced as containers for small quantities of oils, perfumes, or cosmetics, which are thought to have been used to anoint the corpse before or after cremation (Philpott 1991, 118). These oils and ointments may well have been expensive commodities and are likely to have been far more valuable than their glass containers. Two of the vessels are complete, although in fragments; (151)<118> (Fig. 3.19 No 2), from cg13, is typical of the standard form of tubular unguent bottle, most common during the second and third quarters of the 1st century, and found in 1st-century funerary contexts elsewhere in Britain as at Colchester (May 1930, 254–73, nos 7, 29, 30, 44, 56 and 72). The other, (128)<80> (Fig. 3.19 No 3), from cg16, is shorter and

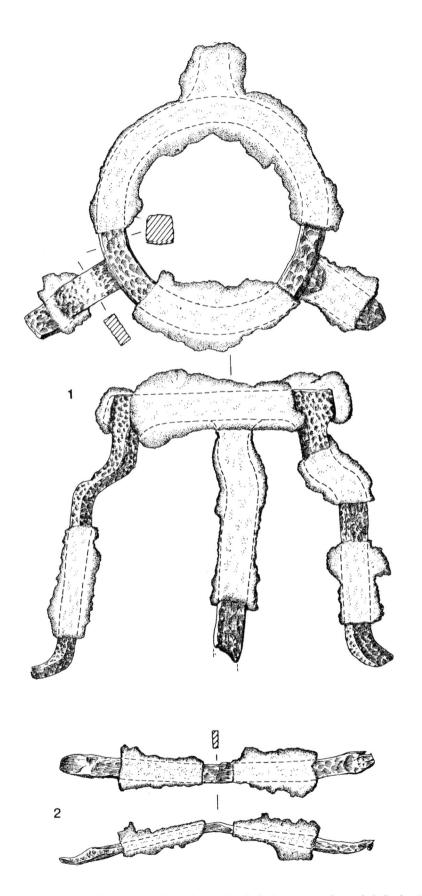

Fig. 3.20 Finds from pit cg59. 1: iron tripod, 2: iron spoon/spatula? Scale: 1:2.

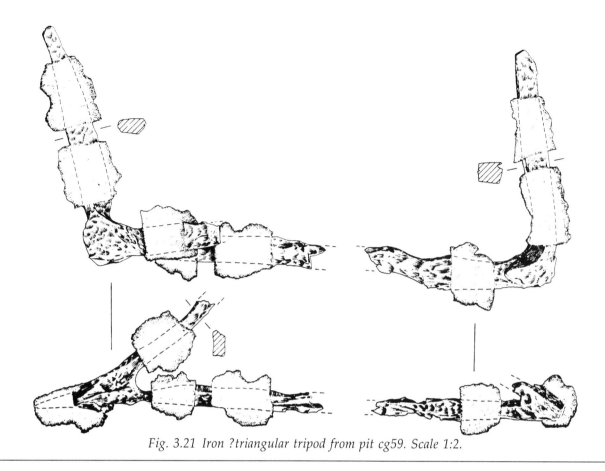

Fig. 3.21 Iron ?triangular tripod from pit cg59. Scale 1:2.

wider, with an unevenly rolled-in rim edge, and is a less common form (Price *et al* forthcoming). These, and most of the other fragments and melted blobs, are of blue-green glass but a fragment from a pale yellow unguent bottle came from cg16, while melted lumps of the same colour were found in cg13 and cg18; unguent bottles of this colour occur far less commonly than those of blue-green glass.

Most of the unguent bottles appear to have been melted during cremation of the body, suggesting that they had been placed with the body, or thrown on to the pyre during cremation, or had been close to the source of heat. All but one of the melted lumps and one of the vessel fragments from cg18 have cremated bone adhering, whereas most of the remaining fragments from some of the other burials are merely distorted by heat. These may have been put onto the pyre but fell off early in the cremation process, or perhaps were distorted by close contact with the hot bones. Burials cg13 and cg16 contained melted lumps but also produced fragments which seem to have had no close contact with heat. This variation in condition suggests that some unguent bottles may have been reserved as accompanying grave goods when the cremation was finally placed in the ground, thus remaining untouched by heat. Interestingly, only one of the five fragments of the complete unguent bottle from cg16 has been distorted by heat, and this appears to have happened after breakage.

None of the other glass vessel fragments could be certainly identified as cinerary urns although a single fragment from a square or rectangular bottle was found within the disturbed cremation burial cg14, and part of a cylindrical bottle was found in the fill of intrusive pit cg22 (LUB 6); both vessel forms were sometimes reused as containers for cremation ashes. Neither of the two bottle fragments shows any evidence of heat-distortion: it is thus possible that they formed the cinerary containers, but this seems unlikely considering how little of the vessels was recovered. One other glass vessel fragment (157) <151> was found in cg14; this is a rim fragment from a Claudio-Neronian drinking cup with horizontal wheel-cut decoration, possibly a cylindrical 'Hofheim' cup or a tall beaker.

The mirror found in cg16 (128) <83> (Fig. 3.19 No 4) is in poor condition. The disc had been cast and decorated with inscribed concentric circles on both sides, and on the back with an evenly spaced band of punched ring-and-dot motifs. The central stud was in an extreme state of deterioration. Both sides had been silvered or tinned. Lloyd-Morgan (Lloyd-Morgan 1982) suggests that it is a pre-

Flavian type, but that it may have remained in use by its owners for some time. During conservation it was noted that one surface had become severely blistered while the reverse contained localised deposits of what appeared to be microscopic glassy vitreous waste. This evidence, alongside the fact that the object is severely cracked and crazed, suggests that it may have been subject to fairly intense heat, perhaps from the pyre.

The presence of the glass vessels, especially the unguent bottles, in a 1st-century cemetery site suggests that considerable resources were being devoted to the burial rite, perhaps at the expense of members of the legion; this interpretation is reinforced by the quantity of tombstones that have been found in the area. The tubular unguent vessels are likely to have had expensive and possibly exotic contents and these would have been affordable to only a very small percentage of the population. The fact that the funeral offerings had been burnt would also indicate that these were Romanised individuals although the presence of animal bones might also indicate native influence. (Philpott 1991, 118).

Tombstones in the Monson Street area

The evidence of possible tombstone slots (LUB 5) and the 19th-century evidence for tombstones in the area confirms the use of this area as an early Roman cemetery.

A tombstone was found in 1849 on the site later occupied by no 2 Monson Street (*RIB* 258; Trollope 1860, 17–18), later excavated in 1982. It was discovered "7 feet" below the ground surface, and had been broken and thrown into a hole below the original natural surface. The dedication, to *Titus Valerius Pudens*, a soldier of the 2nd legion *Adiutrix* who had originated from *Savaria*, a Claudian colony in Upper Pannonia, was probably erected in AD 76.

On the south side of Monson Street, opposite no 2, two further tombstones were found (*RIB* 249, 253), one erected to a soldier of the 2nd legion Adiutrix and the other to a freedman and set up by his heir, a veteran of the 14th legion Gemina (Trollope 1860). Two other tombstones thought to have come from this area, and perhaps also found in 1849, were to a soldier of the 9th legion (*RIB* 260) and to a woman called Fortuna (*RIB* 264). About 60m to the south, on the east side of High Street at the back of St Mary's Guildhall, Stukeley recorded a further tombstone (*RIB* 267), and about 140m south of Monson Street, on the south side of St Peter-at-Gowt's churchyard, a tombstone to a soldier of the 9th legion (*RIB* 254) had been discovered around 1800. On the west side of High Street, at its junction with Princess Street (formerly Salthouse Lane) a further tombstone to a 9th legion soldier was discovered in 1865 (*RIB* 255).

As well as tombstones, a number of burials were recorded in Monson Street in the 19th century. In 1855 a pinkish mica-dusted urn was found and three years later two urns containing ashes, a flagon, and four glass phials were discovered together with possible building foundations and an area of charcoal and soot, perhaps a pyre-site (Trollope 1860). At least six inhumations, unlikely to be earlier than the second century, are also known, each accompanied by a pottery vessel (Trollope 1860, 16). Other burials were found to the south, in the Gowts Bridge area (Richmond 1946).

Roman Traders' Houses; structures and fittings

The construction of stone-founded buildings (LUBs 12, 13 and 15) on the site appears to have been part of a planned development in the area (see also smg82) between the early and mid 3rd century. Structure 3 (LUBs 13 and 14) was over 5m wide internally and over 13.5m in length, possibly up to 35m long, if it lay gable-end at Ermine Street. Structures 2 and 4 were probably of similar dimensions, but not enough of them was excavated.

Little survived to indicate the nature of occupation; there were very few artefacts from the site and the majority were probably structural. This may be explained by the fact that only areas internal to the buildings were excavated and by the depth of the removal of overlying deposits during the machining. Painted plaster occurred in quantity only at the eastern end of the buildings (the domestic quarters?), mainly in the probable robber trench cg105 (LUB 18), perhaps representing robbing of the internal partition in Structure 3. The use of stone roofing materials, of both Coal Measures Sandstone and Collyweston slate, may imply a degree of wealth; although these were found within the rubble over and between Structures 3 and 4 (cg45 and cg69 LUB 18) as well as in later layers over the lane (cg70 LUB 18 and cg72 LUB 19), it is possible that only one of the buildings used stone in preference (or possibly in addition to) ceramic roof tile.

Well-laid floors in Structure 3 and Structure 4 were restricted to the eastern end which, being furthest from the road, was probably the domestic area. The paving in the western part of Structure 3, which lay close to the postulated line of Ermine Street, was similar to that found at St Mary's Guildhall, where the northern building, facing on to the west side of Ermine Street, had two layers of limestone paving. If the tripartite division into shop, workshop, and living quarters proposed for other houses (sm76) is also true for the Monson Street buildings, the central (workshop) areas would have been in the unexcavated area between the west and east trenches, although there was some evidence

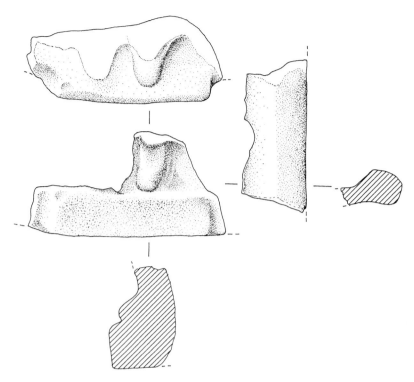

Fig. 3.22 Ceramic object from cg105. Scale 1:2.

for non-domestic activity at the west end of the northernmost building Structure 4.

It is conceivable that the polychrome mosaic pavement found in Monson Street and illustrated by Trollope in the 19th century (Trollope 1860) came from a house similar to those revealed by excavation in 1982. Although no stratified tesserae were recovered during the excavations (only two unstratified pieces were found), such a floor would not be out of place in a wealthy trader's house of the 4th century.

Approximately 10.7k of painted plaster was attributed to robber trench cg105 (LUB 18); the plaster is likely to have come either from the internal wall that this trench removed or a nearby internal wall of Structure 3. The fragments are relatively large, while the colours generally are poorly preserved, possibly indicating that the plaster is from the lower part of a wall which had been exposed to the elements following the decay/destruction of the building (a few pieces with straw or reed impressions on the reverse could possibly be from a ceiling or internal wall). The paint is of rough-and-ready workmanship (brush strokes are frequently visible); little can be said of the decorative scheme employed although some fragments suggest panelled and possibly geometric ornament. More than a third of the plaster was painted plain white, and two fragments appear to represent green foliage on a white ground. Several pieces show clear evidence of redecoration.

Household god? (Fig. 3.22)

Part of an unusual pottery object (201) <181> (Fig. 3.22) came from robber trench cg105 (LUB 18) and another fragment from cg70 (LUB 18): there were joining sherds between the two context groups. This appears to be an object possibly from a household shrine, a pottery figure of a household god or *lar* set in a plaque. All that remains is a fragment of the base with one foot and the scar of a second, plus a non-joining fragment, probably from the side.

cg/LUB	cg/LUB	cg/LUB	cg/LUB	cg/LUB	cg/LUB	cg/LUB	cg/LUB
1/0	17/1	33/10	49/16	65/14	81/–	97/19	112/19
2/2	18/4	34/8	50/18	66/14	82/–	98/19	114/19
3/2	19/7	35/10	51/10	67/14	83/4	99/19	115/19
4/3	20/5	36/11	52/13	68/14	84/–	100/19	116/19
5/2	21/5	37/12	53/13	69/18	85/–	101/19	117/19
6/6	22/7	38/13	54/10	70/18	86/–	102/19	118/19
7/6	23/7	39/15	55/14	71/19	87/14	103/19	119/1
8/7	24/11	40/17	56/10	72/19	88/10	104/19	120/19
9/7	25/9	41/17	57/10	73/2	89/10	105/18	121/19
10/7	26/9	42/10	58/10	74/8	90/10	106/19	122/19
11/7	27/9	43/18	59/10	75/8	91/10	107/19	123/–
12/7	28/11	44/14	60/16	76/8	92/14	108/19	124/17
13/4	29/9	45/18	61/16	77/7	93/11	109/19	125/14
14/4	30/10	46/13	62/16	78/7	94/7	110/19	126/13
15/7	31/7	47/13	63/14	79/7	95/19	111/19	127/19
16/4	32/10	48/10	64/14	80/7	96/19		

Fig. 3.23 Concordance of cg numbers with LUB numbers for ms82.

4. St Mary's Guildhall 1981–4 (smg82)

Introduction

The Norman and later buildings forming St Mary's Guildhall, also known locally as John of Gaunt's Stables, lie on the east side of the High Street in Wigford, c 800m south of the walled city (Fig. 4.1). For much of the 20th century they had been occupied by a building firm and maintenance of the fabric had been neglected, but in July 1981 Lincoln Civic Trust obtained the lease from the City Council with the intention of restoring and adapting the structure.

The only part of the Norman building to survive above ground is the central archway and northern half of the west range, facing High Street (Fig. 4.17). The southern half of this range had been rebuilt in the post-medieval period on Norman foundations, and incorporates many architectural fragments of

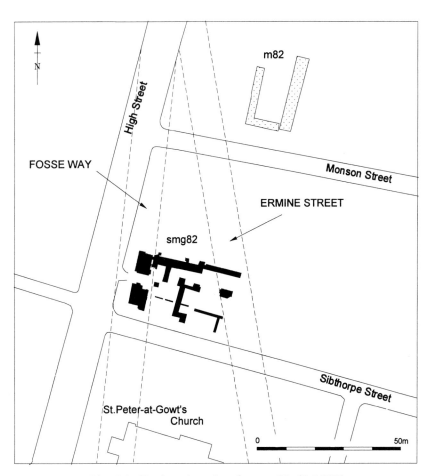

Fig. 4.1 Site location plan for smg82. (1:1,250)

Norman date, as does the south gable wall, rebuilt for a second time in *c* 1895. The south range, facing Sibthorp Street, is contemporary with the rebuilt gable, and also incorporates reused architectural fragments.

The north range of the Guildhall, attached to the east wall of the Norman part of the west range, has two elements. At the eastern end lies the so-called Norman House, a two-storey structure which utilises several Norman and later architectural features, and this is linked to the west range by a single storey building which also contains much reused stonework. A courtyard about 8 m wide separates the north and south ranges. It formerly contained several insubstantial timber structures, removed as part of the restoration programme.

In view of the extensive restoration programme envisaged by the Civic Trust, it was decided that a comprehensive survey of the fabric should be undertaken before details were again obscured. A small trial trench under the direction of Geoff Tann was dug in 1981 to assess the survival and depth of deposits. Work on the standing building, supervised by David Stocker, started late in 1981, when accretions of bricks and plaster were removed from the Norman part of the Guildhall to expose the original stonework. Interior wall elevations were drawn at a scale of 1:10, and exterior walls were recorded photogrammetrically. The many architectural fragments incorporated in later walls were also drawn and photographed.

Limited excavation was undertaken from February to June 1982 to reveal the original plan of the Guildhall; this was supervised by John Magilton, for the Lincoln Archaeological Trust. Further small-scale work, supervised by Colin Palmer-Brown, was undertaken in the summer of 1983 and in the autumn of 1984, on both occasions in response to a threat to Roman levels which arose during the programme of restoration. Part of the funding for the period 1982–1984 was provided by the Department of the Environment, and, for 1984, by its successor English Heritage. Some of the team was provided through a Community Programme sponsored by the Manpower Services Commission.

Substantial foundations were uncovered of a Norman north range, shorter and wider than the present buildings, but no Norman structures lay beneath the modern south range. It was also decided to investigate earlier levels, partly because of a limited threat from new service trenches, but principally as a research excavation to establish the date and nature of Roman occupation in this part of Lincoln.

The areas which could be examined (Fig. 4.2) were

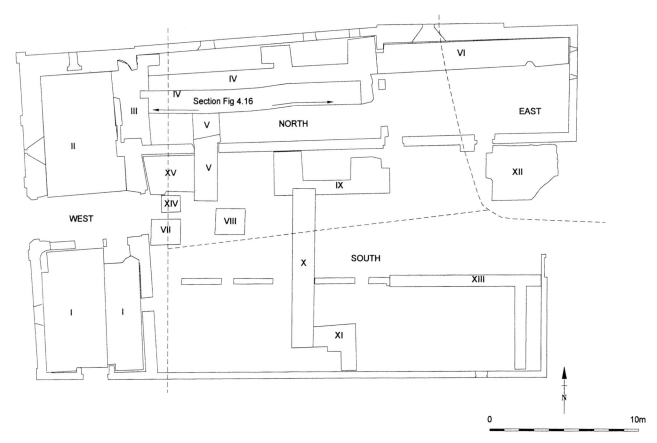

Fig. 4.2 Plan showing areas (north, south, east and west), trenches and section for smg82. (1:247)

constrained by the need to keep clear of the walls of standing buildings, in particular the south wall of the north range and of the "Norman House" which leans outwards at an alarming angle. The whole interior of the Norman west range was examined, the northern part and half of the southern part in 1982 and the remainder in 1984. A long trench was dug in the centre of the north range (Trench IV) and against the north wall of the "Norman House" (Trench VI) although, for safety reasons, the latter could not be excavated to any depth.

Work in the modern south range was restricted to a north–south trench extending through a doorway into the courtyard (Trench X/XI). The trial Trench (VII) had been dug in the centre of the courtyard; this, and most subsequent work in the courtyard, was too shallow to reach Roman deposits. Salvage work in 1983 in the eastern part of the south range, in the base of modern foundation trenches, revealed a Roman wall and other features (Trench XIII).

In addition to the problem of standing buildings was the need to excavate for the most part by artificial light. Portable gas lamps were first used, later replaced by fluorescent lights. Neither was ideal, and this led to difficulties with interpreting the post-Roman levels in particular, where pits could barely be distinguished from the dark loamy material through which they had been cut.

Interim reports were published (Jones 1981c; Magilton and Stocker 1982). Interim discussions on the Roman houses (Magilton 1983a) and some of the finds (Mann 1982b) were also published. The archaeology of the standing structure and contemporary deposits and finds has been analysed and published in full (Cowgill 1991; Stocker 1991; Vince 1991; Young 1991). A single Norman silver penny from the site has also been published (Blackburn et al 1983).

The site was discussed in Popular Archaeology (Jones 1982). Of the 820 contexts, 795 of them were grouped into 314 context groups and 25 were deemed unstratified. The context groups run from cg1 to cg321 but exclude some numbers which were unused (cg23, cg46, cg54, cg103, cg145, cg230, cg319) and others which were allotted to published contexts (cg44–5; cg55–62; cg66–86; cg114–121; cg123–9; cg131–4; cg136; cg138–9; cg144; cg205–10; cg220–4; cg226–7; cg229; cg233; cg259–260). The 242 Roman to early medieval context groups (517 contexts) discussed here are interpreted as 32 land-use blocks (LUBs 0 to LUB 32; Fig. 4.24); the 72 post Roman context groups (378 contexts) have been archived as belonging to 11 LUBs (LUBs 34–43; Fig. 4.24).

The trench numbers I–XII used in this report were those applied in post-excavation work, and are the same as those used in the report on the standing structure (Stocker 1991). Extra trench numbers – XIII–XV – have been assigned in order to enhance the presentation of the stratigraphic sequence. The LUB diagram (Fig. 4.3) is subdivided into four areas, which correspond broadly to the layout of the standing buildings, and thus to the areas available for excavation, but also reflect the topography. The Western Area (Trenches I, II, III, within the West Range of the standing building, together with the west parts of trenches IV, VII, XIV and XV) corresponds with the area of excavated Fosse Way road surfaces. Discussed here, in this area, there were natural (LUB 0), Roman (LUBs 1, 17 and 22) and late Saxon LUBs (LUBs 30 and 32). The Northern Area (Trench IV and the western part of Trench VI) lay within the north range of the standing building, with other trenches outside (Trench VII, VIII, IX, XIV, XV and the north part of X) and a trench between the two (Trench V); this area represents the Roman activity to the north of the site. LUBS dealt with are as follows: natural (LUB 0), early Roman (LUBs 4 and 6), mid Roman (LUBs 10–16, 18, 19 and 21), late Roman (LUBs 24–25), very late Roman (LUBs 26–29) and late Saxon to early medieval LUBs (LUBs 31–2). The Southern Area includes the remaining trenches (Trench XI, XIII and the southern part of Trench X), and, for LUBS, natural (LUB 0), early Roman (LUBs 3 and 5), mid Roman (LUBs 7–9, 19 and 21), late Roman (LUBs 23 and 25) and late Saxon to early medieval LUBs (LUBs 31–2). The Eastern Area (Trench XII, and the eastern end of Trench VI) corresponds to the area of the presumed Ermine Street surfaces: natural (LUB 0), Roman (LUB 2) and late Saxon to early medieval LUBs (LUBs 31–2).

The pottery from the site was made up of 3,968 Roman pottery sherds and 1,270 post-Roman pottery sherds. The accessioned finds (471) include nails, coal, and slag samples. The majority of the finds were either stone architectural fragments from the building, ironwork and glass, much of the latter surviving in a blocked window. A detailed catalogue of the architectural fragments and a discussion of the medieval window glass have been published (King 1991). Roman glass from the site was also more recently examined (Price and Cottam 1993e). The metal finds are generally in a poor condition with little actual metal surviving; these include Roman coins (Davies 1987) and a Roman brooch (Mackreth 1993). There were worked bone finds (Rackham 1994) and stone finds (hones: Moore 1991; other worked stone finds: Roe 1994). All the organic finds were found in blocked features uncovered during restoration of the standing building and are all post 18th century in date; included are finds of wood (Morris 1994; Gale 1992) and leather (Mould 1993). The very small assemblages of finds from the long narrow trenches mean that it is difficult to interpret the long structural sequence uncovered. The low level of lighting would have affected the quality of retrieval

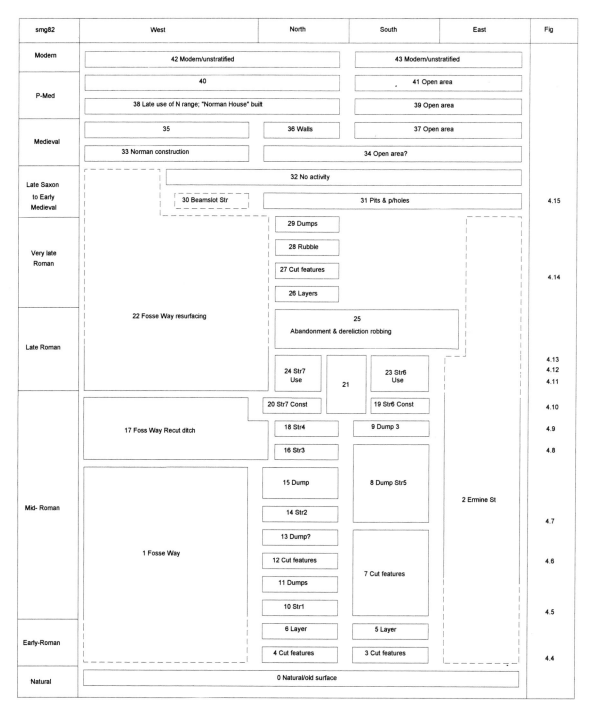

smg82	West	North	South	East	Fig

Fig. 4.3 LUB diagram for smg82.

in the indoor areas, and evidence from the context records suggests that some material, most noticeably slag and perhaps coal, was not rigorously recovered. A large quantity of building material fragments (1,885) was recorded from the excavations, most (1,010) of which is post-Roman tile. An assemblage of animal bones (784) was recovered; the 1994 assessment was carried out by K Dobney, A Milles, B Irving and D Jaques of the York Environmental Unit (Dobney *et al* 1994g). An assessment report of

selected samples of animal bone had been produced previously by S Scott (Scott 1987), who also produced a comparative study of the Roman animal bone assemblages from Monson Street and St. Mary's Guildhall (Scott 1986a), and a report on 16th-century cattle horn core assemblages (Scott 1986b). Three environmental samples were taken, but none was considered worthy of full analysis (Moffett 1993). The five Roman infant burials have also been identified (Boylston and Roberts 1994).

Much of this report is based on a draft report written in 1986 by the excavator, John Magilton, and developed in the light of stratigraphic analysis undertaken by Paul Miles between 1989 and 1994. Barbara Precious worked on the Roman pottery; Jane Young examined the pottery from the post-Roman to the post-medieval periods and Rick Kemp worked on the early modern pottery. Jane Cowgill and Jen Mann analysed the registered finds and the building materials were examined by Jen Mann and Rick Kemp. Paul Miles and Zoe Rawlings digitized the plans.

Interpretation of the sequence of events

Natural

At the limit of excavations natural sand was uncovered **LUB 1**.

LUB 0 Natural sand

Natural white sand cg1 was found at 4.59m OD in Trench I, at 4.70m in Trench IV, and at *c* 4.80m OD in Trench X/XI; the natural sand sloped very gently to the south and west. In Trench I, natural sand was sealed by iron panning. The upper part of "natural" was recorded as podsolised, probably representing the pre-Roman ground surface. No finds were recovered from the sand and gravel.

Early Roman

The metalling of the Fosse Way **LUB 1** was found at the west side of the site and that of Ermine Street **LUB 2** on the east. The earliest pottery dating for the Fosse Way came from a secondary road side ditch cg16 (LUB 17), dated to between the early to mid 2nd century, which suggests that the first ditch cg3 might have dated to the 1st century. The lack of dating evidence from this road reflects both the paucity of any dating evidence on the surfaces, together with the lack of extensive area excavation. Ermine Street, however, was only excavated down to the early to mid 3rd century; there was evidence for a depth of 0.55m of earlier road surfaces which probably dated back to the 1st century.

There were a number of cut features either predating the roads, or lying between them, both in the southern part of the site **LUB 3** and the northern **LUB 4**. They were sealed by sand **LUB 5** and **LUB 6** which was tenuously dated by pottery to between the late 1st and early 2nd centuries.

LUB 1 The Fosse Way (Figs. 4.4–7, 4.16 and 4.18)

This road was examined at several points. Almost the whole of the road in Trenches I, II, and III was exposed, and its eastern edge was exposed in Trenches IV and VII. At the limit of excavation a metalled surface cg225, probably the Roman road, was seen in Trench XV.

In Trench I the road surfaces were revealed by a deep pit cut in order to provide a sewer pipe channel as part of the conversion programme. Sealing natural sand cg1 (LUB 0) was redeposited sand cg36 (0.25m thick), possibly levelling material for the earliest road cg237. This may have derived from the excavation of roadside ditches, traces of which were recovered from both Trench IV and Trench VII. Cutting natural in Trench IV was a roadside ditch cg3 running north–south along the eastern edge of the Fosse Way; its rounded base was cut to a depth of *c* 0.3m below natural sand cg1, but no pottery was recovered from its fill.

Road surface cg237 consisted of limestone rubble and occasional pieces of mortar in a matrix of fine grey sand; this may have been a surface in its own right, or simply make-up for surface cg238, pebbles in orange-brown mortar. Sealing cg238 was a layer of orange-brown gritty sand in the western part of the trench, sealed by a layer of yellow sand, limestone chippings and large pebbles cg239. Over cg239 was a layer of gritty sand sealed by possible surface cg240 of sand, limestone chippings and large pebbles. Sealing cg240 was soft clean yellow sand over which was a layer of limestone brash, orange-brown sand, and pebbles cg241; this was sealed by soft sand with stones, sealed by pebbles bonded by orange mortar cg242. Sealing cg242 was compact gritty orange sand, sealed by mortar-bonded pebbles cg243; the mortar was yellow in places and red-brown in others. Sealing cg243 was a surface of very tightly-packed cobbles strongly bonded by mortar cg244, over which were several deposits cg245: grey sand mixed with pebbles was sealed by a compact layer of yellow/brown clay sand with mortar flecks, limestone blocks and chippings. Deposits cg245 may represent further road surfaces. Over cg245 was orange/brown sand with small pebbles, possibly make-up for cobbles, pebbles bonded by mortar and large rounded stones cg37. All these surfaces together only produced three sherds of pottery dating to the 3rd to 4th centuries.

There was an enigmatic shallow cut cg38 in cg37, which probably represented some form of surface damage. It was sealed by a make-up layer of sandy clay, pebbles, limestone chippings, set with large rounded cobbles cg39. This layer reversed the camber of the previous road surfaces, so that surface water would have drained towards the centre of the road: perhaps a central drain was provided. Sealing cg39 was the final surviving surface of cobbles and pebbles cg246; this was overlain by cg247, a layer of yellow-green sandy soil with limestone chippings and small pebbles which probably represented road silt. Cut-

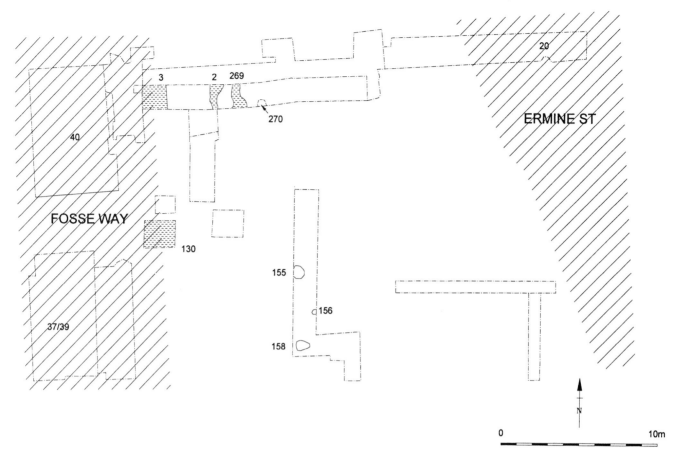

Fig. 4.4 The Fosse Way and Ermine Street with cut features between them: LUBs 1, 2, 3 and 4. (1:235)

ting road surface cg39 was a small posthole cg41. This was sealed by deposits cg42 of green/grey sandy soil and clay with large limestone blocks. Over these were further deposits cg63; these consisted of sandy light brown soil with pebbles and limestone chippings, over which were clay and ash.

In Trench II, surfaces cg40 were excavated only until a relatively intact surface could be exposed for preservation and display. This was of pebbles and some limestone cobbles set in hard brownish-yellow mortar, with the underlying make-up of large limestone rubble blocks exposed to wear in many places. This surface was a minimum of 4.65m wide, and several wheel ruts, generally about 0.15m wide, were identified as silt-filled depressions in the surface. These were best preserved at the northern end of the area, where four roughly parallel ruts *c* 0.75m apart were detected (Fig. 4.18). These imply that carts with an axle length of *c* 1.5m were in general use.

LUB 2 Ermine Street (Figs. 4.4–13 and 4.19)
As the road was seen only in a trench less than 2m wide (Trench VI), its alignment cannot be determined with accuracy. Natural sand exposed in the north range lay at 4.7m OD, so a road build-up of some

0.55m is likely to have preceded the excavated surfaces; earlier road surfaces could be seen to have extended further west. The full depth of these later surfaces was some 0.8m, giving a probable build-up totalling 1.35m during the whole Roman period.

The road surface cg20, at the limit of excavation, postdated Structure 7 (LUB 20); two stones sealed the foundations of the east wall cg21. The surface consisted of gravel with occasional cobbles and small limestone rubble at 5.25m OD. The road sloped slightly towards the east where there was a central stone-lined drain cg261, which lay about 3.5m east of wall cg21 (LUB 20 Fig. 4.19); it was about 0.2m wide and an earlier surface formed its base. The drain had probably been stone-capped, but evidence was lacking due to the construction of a later drain cg267 on the same line.

Surface cg20 was sealed by surface cg262 consisting of large cobbles and some gravel; over this was makeup of sandy clay sealed by surface cg263 which was similar to cg262, though employing smaller cobbles and less gravel. Over cg263 was a makeup layer of green sandy clay; this was sealed by surface cg264 which consisted of limestone rubble over which was rammed gravel. Over surface cg264 was another surface cg265: this consisted of green sandy clay, limestone rubble and rammed gravel. In turn this was sealed by another surface cg266: green sandy clay make-up sealed by limestone rubble, gravel and sand. A possible rut was noted in surface cg266.

By the time surface cg265 was laid down, the central drain cg261 had become blocked and was perhaps too deep to be adequately cleaned out due to the build-up of surfaces. A new drain cg267 was constructed on the same line as the early drain, possibly at the same time as resurfacing cg266. Sealing cg266 was green sandy clay make-up sealed by surface cg268 of pebbles, limestone rubble and a little sand.

Very few finds were recovered from within or beneath the surfaces, but the adjoining building to the west, Structure 7, constructed at the same time as the stone drain cg261 was installed, was dated to the early to mid 3rd century by the pottery. Pottery from the make-up for surface cg263 suggests a 3rd or early 4th-century date.

*LUB 3 Cut features in southern part of site
(Trenches X/XI; Figs. 4.4 and Figs. 4.20–21)*
At the southern end of Trench X cutting cg1 (LUB 0) was an irregular pit cg158 filled with yellow-brown sand, measuring 0.96m by 0.66m and about 0.25m deep. To the north, also cutting cg1 (LUB 0) was a small shallow pit cg156 filled with olive-brown sand and clay flecked with charcoal. Just south-east of this was a small pit cg157 (unplanned), with a yellow-brown sand fill, together with one sherd of undatable Roman pottery. Near the centre of Trench X was a further shallow pit cg155 cutting cg1 (LUB 0) with a maximum diameter of 0.95m.

It seems probable that these features date to the early Roman period; they were sealed by LUB 5 which contained one sherd of pottery dating to between the 1st and early 2nd centuries.

*LUB 4 Cut features in northern part of site
(Trenches IV and VI; Figs. 4.4 and 4.16)*
In Trench IV a ditch or gully cg2 cut sand cg1 (LUB 0) and lay 3 metres east of ditch cg3 (LUB 2); it was irregular, with a fill that was indistinguishable from the overlying layer cg4 (LUB 6). About a metre further east was an irregular gully cg269 cutting cg1 (LUB 0); the fill was slightly darker than the overlying layer. A small pit or posthole cg270 also cut cg1 (LUB 0).

In Trench V, a feature cg271 cut sand cg1 (LUB 0), but was not excavated or planned; its upper filling was indistinguishable from overlying layer cg4 (LUB 6). It may have been the southern edge of a pit or an east–west gully. Also cutting sand cg1 (LUB 0) was a north–south feature cg272 (unplanned).

No pottery or registered finds were recovered from any of these features; as the overlying LUB

dated from the late 1st century, the features were earlier, but probably only just earlier and contemporary with LUB 3.

LUB 5 Layer (Trenches X/XI)
Sealing cg155, cg156, cg157 and cg158 (LUB 3) was a layer of light yellowish-brown sand, cg159 which covered most of Trenches X and XI to a depth of 0.3m. This material only contained one sherd of pottery dating between the 1st and early 2nd centuries.

*LUB 6 Layer sealing early cut features
(Trench IV)*
Features of LUB 4 were sealed by a layer of sand, occasional pebbles, and limestone fragments cg4 in the western part of Trench IV; the equivalent layer cg5 in the eastern end of the trench was not excavated, although its top was revealed. Layer cg4 was of variable thickness, from a maximum of over 0.4m at the western end of the trench to less than 0.2m towards the centre. Its deposition may have been connected with the construction of an early surface of the Fosse Way to the west, possibly the primary surface. These layers were perhaps equivalent to sand dump cg159 (LUB 5) in southern Trenches X/XI. This LUB was tenuously dated by pottery to between the late 1st and early 2nd centuries.

Mid Roman

In the southern part of the site, LUB 5 was cut by several features **LUB 7** which were difficult to interpret; they contained early to mid 2nd-century pottery. These were cut by pits and the traces of a possible earth-fast timber structure **LUB 8**, Structure 5. Sealing the remains of this were dumps **LUB 9** with pottery dating to the early 3rd century.

In the northern area LUB 6 was cut by features and a possible timber-framed structure **LUB 10**, Structure 1. Over these were dumps **LUB 11** which were cut by further features **LUB 12**, themselves sealed by a dump **LUB 13**. This sequence of events was dated by scanty pottery to between the early and mid 2nd century.

Cutting into LUB 13 were traces of a timber structure **LUB 14**, Structure 2, sealed by sand **LUB 15** which provided the make-up for a subsequent timber building **LUB 16**, Structure 3. LUBs 14–16 may have dated into the late 2nd century; pottery dating between the early and late 2nd century was recovered from LUB 16, but there was no dating evidence from LUBs 14 and 15.

The Fosse Way (LUB 1) has pottery evidence for its use during this period; the roadside ditch silted up in the mid to late 2nd century. The roadside ditch **LUB 17** of the Fosse Way cut dump LUB 15.

LUB 16 was succeeded by a further structure, possibly stone-founded with a timber superstructure **LUB 18**, Structure 4, dated by the pottery to the early 3rd century.

The stone-founded walls of Structure 6 **LUB 19**, to the south of the site, cut LUB 9; it represented a strip-building fronting Ermine Street and backing on to the Fosse Way. To the north of the site was another structure, another stone-founded strip-building **LUB 20**, Structure 7. Between the two strip-buildings was a gap **LUB 21** which was possibly used as a lane. The stratigraphic sequence suggests that the construction of both Structures 6 and 7 took place between the early to mid 3rd century.

The metalling of the Fosse Way **LUB 22** sealed the walls of Structure 7; the camber of the road altered, presumably tilting the run-off into a central drain. This alteration of the road took place in the early to mid 3rd century. The excavated surfaces of Ermine Street (LUB 2) date from the early to mid 3rd century, although there was an indication of earlier surfaces. They too exhibited a central drain, rather than roadside ditches.

LUB 7 Cut features (Trenches X/XI; Fig. 4.5)
At the southern end of Trench X was a steep-sided east–west linear feature cg167 cutting cg159 (LUB 5) which had large limestone slabs in its fill, one of which stood upright against its northern edge, in a matrix of dark brown silt flecked with charcoal and limestone chippings. About 0.3m to the north a small subrectangular vertical-sided pit cg168 cut cg159 (LUB 5); it was about 0.5m across, filled with pale brown sand.

An L-shaped ditch or gully cg161 about 0.5m deep cut cg159 (LUB 5), possibly the north-east corner of a feature. Its basal filling was a layer of charcoal and ash with limestone chippings about 100mm thick which was sealed by a thicker layer of brown sand with charcoal flecks and limestone chips. West of it lay an area predominantly of charcoal cg316, very likely the base of a bonfire from which the charcoal and ash in the base of cg161 were perhaps derived. The junction between charcoal cg316 and gully cg161 was cut by a narrow, shallow east–west gully cg163. To the west of gully cg163, cutting cg159 (LUB 5) was a pit cg160 at least 0.85 m across.

North of cg161 a further ditch cg162 cut cg159 (LUB 5); it was filled with brown sand, limestone chippings and charcoal. Its alignment was roughly east–west and it was *c* 0.55m deep, with a wide U-shaped profile. To the north and south of the ditch two small, shallow pits cg166 and cg164 cut cg159 (LUB 5), while further north, in the north-west corner of the trench, a larger pit cg165 also cut cg159 (LUB 5); it was about *c* 0.35m deep filled with yellow-brown sand, clay, and limestone fragments.

Cutting cg159 (LUB 5) in the northern part of the trench was a pit or ditch cg170 with bands of charcoal and limestone chips in its fill.

Sequences of up to three intercutting features were found, but no clear subdivision of use could be suggested, as the interpretation of these features, seen in a trench only *c* 1.5 m wide, is difficult. Although the northernmost of the linear features cg162 has a profile appropriate to a ditch, cg167 and cg161 (to a lesser extent) are steep-sided, and would not have maintained this profile for any length of time in the soft material through which they had been dug unless infilling had occurred fairly quickly. From the material in its filling, cg167 may have been a robbed wall. This seems unlikely at such an early date, despite the presence of a 1st-century stone-founded structure at the Monson Street site (m82, this volume). Perhaps it was a palisade trench in which undetected vertical timbers were held upright by packing stones, although the trench seems unduly wide for this purpose. Cg161 could be part of the same feature as cg167, forming an enclosure 5.4m across and of undetermined extent from east to west. Cg161, however, seems to have been open when the ?bonfire cg316 west of it was in use.

A characteristic of the fillings of several of these early features is the presence of limestone chippings. As there is no clear evidence of masonry buildings in the vicinity, their source is problematic unless they represent road surfacing material, perhaps associated with the Fosse Way to the west and Ermine Street to the east.

Features cg167 and cg163 contain pottery dating to the early to mid 2nd century, and cg161 produced undiagnostic sherds (1st to 3rd) which stratigraphically have to date before the early to mid 2nd century (below cg175, LUB 8). But the rest of the scanty pottery from LUB 7 was residual, perhaps confirming a 1st-century date for the underlying features (LUB 3). A sherd join between cg166 and the overlying cg186 (LUB 22), and a tentative link between cg167 and the overlying wall cg178 of Structure 5 (LUB 8) suggest that either these features were open for a period of time, or, more likely, that earlier material was redistributed during the construction of the later structures.

LUB 8 Pits and possible Structure 5
(Trenches X/XI; Figs. 4.7–8)
Near the centre of Trench X, post-pit cg178 cut both features cg160 and cg161 (LUB 7); it was 1.25m in diameter and limestone rubble packing supported a central post, which rested on a padstone. Smaller postholes cg169, cutting pit cg168 (LUB 7) and cg174, cutting feature cg162 (LUB 7) may have been associated with the same structure. A large postpit

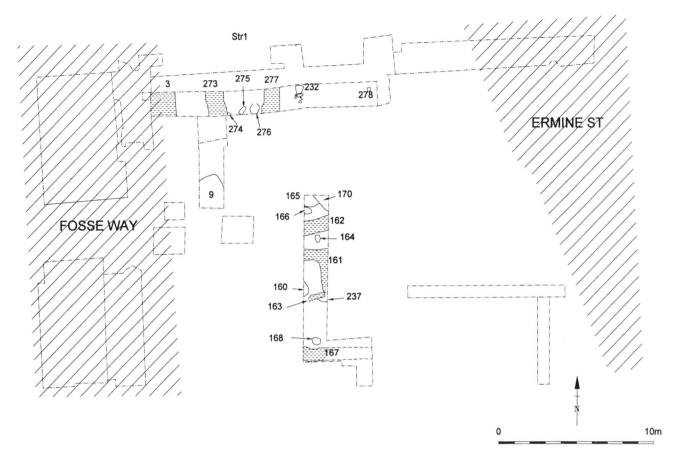

Fig. 4.5 The Fosse Way and Ermine Street with cut features and structure 1: LUBs 1, 2, 7 and 10. (1:235)

cg177 cut cg161 (LUB 7). Although the postholes may have formed part of a structure, no floors could be identified. Cg178 would have contained a post more than 0.3m in diameter, which would imply a very substantial building, Structure 5.

A large shallow pit cg171 cut cg163 (LUB 7), extending across the width of the trench and filled with dark brown silty sand. Shallow pit cg175 and small pit cg176 are of similar phase since both cut cg161 (LUB 7). The edge of a feature cg173 of undetermined nature cut cg162 (LUB 7) at the eastern edge of the excavation.

At the northern end of Trench X was the burial of an infant cg172, of approximately 39 weeks' gestational age (ie, approximately full term; Boylston and Roberts 1994); this burial was sealed by dump cg179 (LUB 9), but there was no record of what it cut.

Dating material was fairly scanty, but the features may be ascribed broadly to the mid to late 2nd, perhaps extending into the early 3rd century as suggested by the stratigraphic sequence. A sherd join between cg170 (LUB 7) and cg179 (LUB 9) together with a tentative link between cg178 and cg167 (LUB 7) demonstrates the disturbed nature of some of this material.

LUB 9 Dumps
Features of LUBs 7 and 8 were sealed by a dump cg179 of dark yellow-brown sandy loam and clay flecked with charcoal about 0.3m thick which occurred throughout Trench X.

A moderate quantity of pottery was recovered from cg179 (170 sherds), most of which consisted of rather abraded sherds. There was clearly a high amount of residual pottery, indicated by the presence of Trajanic, Hadrianic, early Antonine and Antonine SAMCG – the latest sherds of which came from a decorated Dr37 bowl dated *c* AD 150–180. However, the presence of cornice-rimmed beakers in NVCC suggests that the dump probably accumulated during the early 3rd century.

LUB 10 Features and Structure 1
(Trenches IV/VI; Figs. 4.5, 4.16 and 4.22)
Cutting cg4 (LUB 6) in Trench IV was a north–south linear feature cg273 about 1.35m wide (Fig. 4.22); its shallow base had a step in it, and the thin basal layer was mainly of charcoal, from which a piece of slag (broken "hearth bottom" weighing 597gms) was recovered, but the upper filling was barely distinguishable from the sealing layer cg7 (LUB 11).

An irregular, shallow feature cg274 lay alongside its eastern edge.

Further east were two features which cut cg4 (LUB 6): a rectangular slot 0.42m long and 0.17 m wide cg275, its sides packed with limestone rubble, adjacent to an oval posthole cg276, with flat limestone slabs in the base and rubble on edge around its sides. These lay west of another north–south linear feature cg277 with a steep western edge and a more gradual slope to the east, the base of which was packed with small slabs of limestone laid horizontally. Its upper filling was mainly dark brown clay, some of it burnt, and patches of silt. There was also a shallow scoop with a dark sand fill cg6 (unplanned). Cutting cg5 (LUB 6) was a posthole cg278.

To the east of Trench IV, east of linear feature cg277, sealing cg5 (LUB 6) were traces of limestone flags cg232, probably the remains of a surface between cg277 and cg278.

In Trench V, at its southern end, cutting cg4 (LUB 6) was a large pit cg9 with fill cg150: its basal fill was of very black silty sand and over this were sand and pebbles.

The eastern linear feature cg277 may represent the west wall of a structure, initially paved with small pieces of limestone rubble set in clay cg232. The wall itself may have been timber framed, its horizontal sill resting on the rubble fill of cg277. Postholes cg275 and cg276 could have formed part of an external porch. The linear feature cg273 to the west may have been a shallow boundary or drainage ditch parallel to and 3m east of the Fosse Way.

Dating evidence for LUB 10 consists of very small amounts of pottery dating to the late 1st to the early 2nd century with only two sherds – a single sherd of GREY with acute lattice decoration from linear feature cg273, which may be BB1, and a SAMCG Dr18/31 from scoop fill cg6 – dating from the early to mid 2nd century.

LUB 11 Dumps (Trenches IV/VI; Fig. 4.16)

In Trench IV, sealing features cg6, cg273, cg274, cg275, cg276 and cg277 (LUB 10) was a layer of silts and sand cg7, variously of brown, grey-brown, or red-brown, which varied in thickness from less than 0.05m at the western edge of the trench to about 0.20m at the eastern end. Over flagstones cg232 (LUB 10) were rubble and flags cg8, over which were white clay and sand cg13.

In the western half of Trench IV, pit cg9 (LUB 10) and sand cg7 were sealed by a mixed sandy layer with flecks of charcoal and iron-staining, stone chips and small pebbles cg10 (0.15m thick to the west).

These layers may represent demolition debris over the remains of Structure 1. The small group of pottery from LUB 11 largely consists of later 1st- to early 2nd-century pottery, but one sherd – a definite

sherd from a BB1 dish or bowl, suggests an early to mid 2nd-century date for layer cg10. Layer cg7 produced a silver *denarius* of Vitellius (409) <382>, minted AD69 (an issue which occurs rarely as a site find) and showing wear which is consistent with continued use into the 2nd century.

LUB 12 Cut features
(Trenches IV/VI; Figs. 4.6 and 4.16)

A shallow oval depression cg11 in cg10 (LUB 11) directly overlay the earlier ditch cg273 (LUB 9) and was probably created by subsidence into the ditch; its only fill was the overall sealing layer cg12 (LUB 13), which reinforces this suggestion. To the north, mostly lying beyond the limits of excavation, cutting cg10 (LUB 11) was a pit cg279 in which two layers were distinguished; it was c 1.3m wide at the side of the trench and 0.4m deep, the basal layer consisting of charcoal-flecked brown sand and limestone rubble sealed by yellow-brown sand. West of these pits, cutting cg10 (LUB 11) was a small shallow, irregular feature cg280, its only filling the overlying layer cg12 (LUB 13).

The single sherd of pottery from these features did not provide useful dating evidence. LUB 12 is dated by its place in the stratigraphic sequence to the early to mid 2nd century.

LUB 13 Dump (Trenches IV/VI; Fig. 4.16)

Sealing the features in LUB 12 and the dumps to the east of the trench (LUB 11) was a layer of grey-brown sand cg12, generally 0.15 to 0.2m deep, throughout Trench IV.

Much of the pottery (40 sherds in total) from cg12 appears to be residual, of late 1st- to early 2nd-century date. Given that the underlying features date at the earliest to the early 2nd century, a sherd of a SAMLM dish, Dr 18/31, dated to c AD100–120 (296), was either residual or was in use much later than the date of manufacture. The end date for this vessel accords well with the associated coarse wares which include a GREY cooking pot with lattice decoration dated to the early to mid 2nd century.

LUB 14 Possible building, Structure 2
(Figs. 4.7 and 4.16)

At the eastern end of Trench IV sealing cg12 (LUB 13) was a hearth cg148 consisting of a small area of clay, two tiles, and limestone rubble. This had been partly cut away by a large pit cg147. Pit cg147 measured about 2.6m from east to west, and was more than 0.9 m from north to south, extending beyond the limits of excavation. Its greatest depth was c 0.5 m, and its filling was of soft brown silty soil in the base, sealed by sand, clay, limestone rubble, and pebbles.

The pottery from cg147 consists of two un-

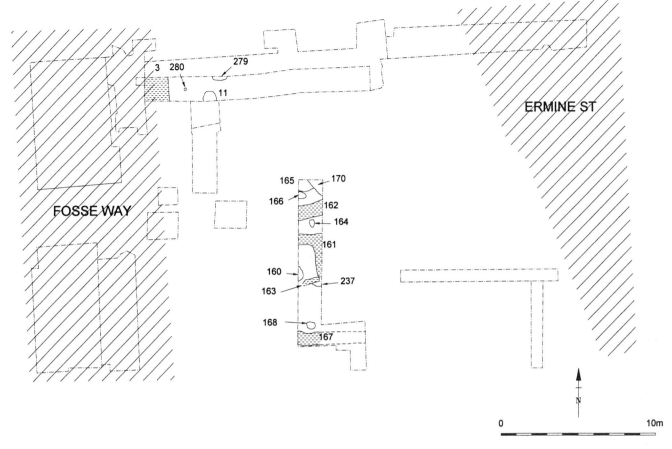

Fig. 4.6 The Fosse Way and Ermine Street with Structure 5? and cut features: LUBs 1, 2, 8 and 12. (1:235)

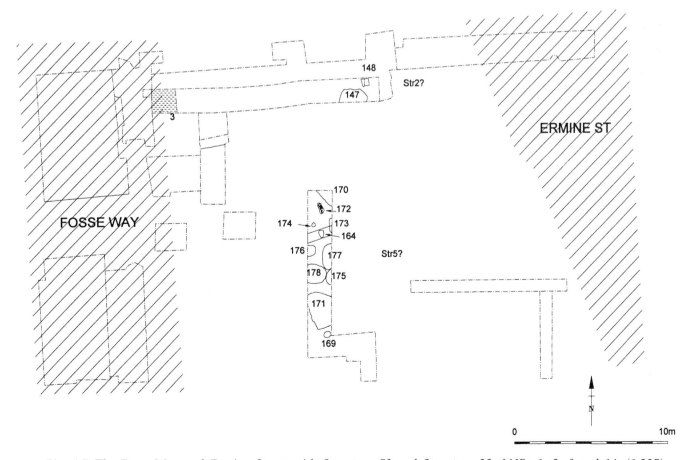

Fig. 4.7 The Fosse Way and Ermine Street with Structure 5? and Structure 2?: LUBs 1, 2, 8 and 14. (1:235)

diagnostic sherds of broad 1st- to 2nd-century date. LUB 14, therefore, is dated by its place in the stratigraphic sequence to between the early and late 2nd century.

LUB 15 Dump layer (Trenches IV/VI; Fig. 4.16)
Sealing hearth cg148 and pit cg147 (LUB 14) was a layer of sand, varying in colour from yellow-brown to dark brown, with occasional areas of pebbles and silt cg14.

In common with much of the material from the underlying layers, cg14 (25 sherds in total) contains some residual material, including SAMSG dated to *c* AD80–100, whilst the majority of the pottery is of an early to mid 2nd-century date. An *as* of Antoninus Pius (401) <377> from this layer was too badly corroded to be more closely dated than to his reign (AD 138–161); even so it provides a *tpq* of *c* AD138 for this context which fits well with the date of *c* AD120–160 for a SAMCG Dr37. However, the associated coarse wares included an expanded-rimmed GREY bowl which generally dates from the later 2nd to perhaps the 3rd century. A sherd link with LUB 18 suggests that this layer was disturbed by later activity. Stratigraphically this LUB dates to between the early and late 2nd centuries.

LUB 16 Possible building, Structure 3
(Trench IV; Figs. 4.8 and 4.16)
Cutting though cg14 (LUB 15) was a flue cg15 aligned north–south and about 0.3m wide. It had been constructed in a much wider trench, the base and sides of which had been lined with pink clay containing pieces of limestone rubble. The walls of the flue consisted of a thin layer of yellow material, probably a much finer clay which had been made friable by heat. In its base was a shallow layer of fine brown sand containing occasional large flecks of charcoal which was sealed by a mixed clay layer comprising the main filling. The function of the flue, which had been partly cut away by later features, is uncertain. An industrial function is possible, but there were no finds to indicate its nature.

Seven postholes cg17, cg281 (with postpipe cg282), cg283, cg284, cg285, cg286 and cg287 cut through cg14 (LUB 15). Posthole cg283 contained a single limestone slab, interpreted as a padstone, in the base and in cg281 the post had been packed with limestone rubble; in posthole cg286 was a fragment of Millstone Grit quern (277) <320>, also possible packing. Possibly associated with these was a decayed mortar floor cg200. These postholes possibly relate to a structure fronting Fosse Way. At the east end of Trench IV, over cg14 (LUB 15) was a possible hearth cg201.

The small group of pottery from cg17 (13 sherds) produced samian dating from the early to later 2nd century and associated coarse wares of a similar date. Therefore the dating for cg17 rests on the mid to later 2nd- or possibly early 3rd-century date provided by the underlying layers cg14 (see above LUB 15). Pottery joins between cg200, and cg14 (LUB 15), emphasise the close link between the posthole fills and the underlying sand.

LUB 17 The Fosse Way: recut ditch (Fig. 4.9)
At the western end of Trench IV, a roadside ditch cg16 cut through sand cg14 (LUB 15); it was more than 2m wide and 1m deep, and although on its eastern edge the ditch had a near-vertical side, its base was rounded. It replaced an earlier roadside ditch cg3 (LUB 1). Three silt/sand fills were distinguished, the middle and upper possibly representing accumulation after the ditch had been recut. The lower fills of cg16 produced small quantities (19 sherds) of the earliest pottery from the Fosse Way sequence which included samian dated to the Neronian and Neronian-Flavian period; however, the associated coarsewares are probably early 2nd century in date, in particular some sherds of GREY that are similar to BB. The overlying fill produced a definite sherd of BB1 cooking pot placing this layer into the early to mid 2nd century – probably the Hadrianic period *c* AD120–140.

At the limit of excavation in Trench VII was a north–south ditch cg130, *c* 0.95m wide and at least 0.25m deep, filled with and sealed by a layer of clean orange sand. The presence of samian dated to the Antonine period places the ditch fill into the mid to late 2nd century. The associated coarsewares formed a small assemblage (63 sherds) and included several complete profiles confirming that it was a rubbish deposit. They fit well within a mid to late 2nd-century date range, in particular a BB1 flanged dish with lattice decoration. Ditch cg130 is likely to be the equivalent of the ditch cg16.

LUB 18 Structure 4 (Figs. 4.9 and 4.16)
In Trench IV, a narrow wall cg149 cut across the fill of flue cg15 (LUB 16); it was constructed of limestone rubble *c* 0.35m across, of which only one course survived. It was aligned north-north-west by south-south-east (parallel to Ermine Street).

Compact white clay floor cg18 extended across much of the west end of Trench IV, on both sides of wall cg149 and over the whole of Trench V. To the east of wall cg149 was a thin layer of charcoal cg202 which extended over clay floor cg18. Cutting charcoal spread cg202 immediately east of the wall was a posthole cg203. The narrow wall cg149 probably represented an internal division, as there was evidence for activity on both sides.

Cutting floor cg18 to the west of Trench IV was a shallow pit cg204 (1.2m by at least 2.0m); its fills contained large amount of charcoal and ash sealed

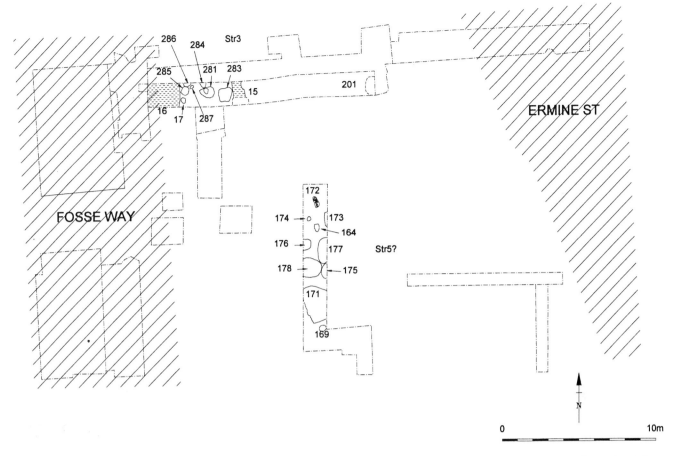

Fig. 4.8 The Fosse Way and Ermine Street with Structure 5? and Structure 3: LUBs 2, 8, 16 and 17. (1:235)

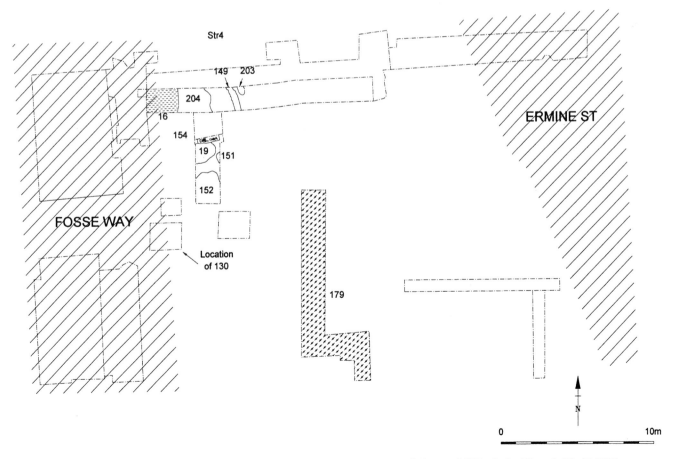

Fig. 4.9 The Fosse Way and Ermine Street with Structure 4 and dump: LUBs 2, 9, 17 and 18. (1:235)

by a thicker layer of charcoal and clay, the uppermost filling being predominantly of limestone rubble. In the top fill of pit cg204 was a cream ware object (237) <385> which may be part of a vessel or perhaps some type of stand, possibly industrial; the object is very fragmentary and difficult to interpret.

Pit cg204 produced a GREY folded beaker from its lowest fill, a form which is more common in the 3rd, perhaps mid 3rd, century; in the next fill was a SAMEG Dr33, which is more precisely dated from the late 2nd to mid 3rd century. Unfortunately, the highest fill within pit cg204 produced largely undiagnostic pottery broadly dating from the mid to the late 2nd century. In summary, although the group is very small (27 sherds), it appears that pit cg204 was the latest datable feature, early–mid 3rd century in date.

Also cutting floor cg18 was the flue of an oven cg19 (Trench V), the chamber of which must have lain west of the trench. The flue, roughly 0.5m wide, had been constructed in a pit or trench up to 1.3m across. The sides and base had been built of clay-bonded limestone rubble lined with a thin layer of clay. Its principal filling was of light red burnt clay presumably derived from the destruction of its superstructure.

South of the oven was a large hollow cg152 in cg18, the result of slumping into an earlier pit cg9 (LUB 10) which seems to have collected domestic debris. To the east of the oven, cutting cg18, was a pit cg151 of undetermined function.

An east–west trench cg153, cutting cg18 just south of the line of the later stone wall of Structure 7 (LUB 20), may have represented the remains of a timber wall, but this was not clear. It was perhaps as likely to have been the lower, under-excavated part of trench cg154. This feature, 1.4m long, contained several infant burials, lying with heads to the west. The burials were thought on excavation to represent two individuals, but in fact one represents at least three infants, two of 39 weeks and one of 40 weeks gestational age. The other burial is that of an infant of approximately 37 weeks; all were approximately full-term perinatal deaths (Boylston and Roberts 1994).

Structure 4 is dated between the late 2nd and mid 3rd centuries by pottery from cg204; this feature dates to the early 3rd century or even the mid 3rd century.

LUB 19 Structure 6 (Fig. 4.10)

The stone-founded walls cg180 of the southern building Structure 6 cut cg179 (LUB 9); the north wall was located about 3m from the northern end of Trench X where four courses of roughly faced limestone survived, the top three courses being bonded with mortar and the bottom course with yellow clay which sealed shallow-pitched limestone foundations. The southern wall was located initially at the southern end of Trench XI, where only the pitched foundations survived, and glimpsed again in Trench XIII where the wall was 0.5m wide and bonded with hard orange-yellow mortar. The pottery evidence for the wall construction cg180 is too small (5 sherds) to provide more than a probable 3rd-century date; the dating for the construction of Structure 6 to between the early and mid 3rd century comes from its place in the stratigraphic sequence.

LUB 20 Northern stone building, Structure 7 (Figs. 4.10, 4.16 and 4.23)

In Trenches IV and V, sealing cg18 and cg204 (both LUB 18) was a mixed layer of dirty sand and limestone rubble cg22, probably make-up for the construction of Structure 7. Cutting hollow cg152 (LUB 18) were stone-founded walls cg21. The robbed west and south walls of Structure 7 were revealed in Trenches IV and V, and the east wall foundations were revealed in Trenches VI. The south-west corner of the building was noted during salvage recording in Trench XIV, and this second point provided a clear indication of the alignment of the western wall. As the north wall was not found, dimensions can only be estimated. The south wall was *c* 20m long, and the building was at least 7.5m wide.

The west wall cg21 (later robbed: cg90 and cg91 LUB 25) of the building had been up to 0.9m wide. Although the south wall had also been completely robbed within the area of excavation, its foundations consisted of mortared limestone rubble in a trench *c* 0.6m wide. The south face of the wall, revealed in 1983 in Trench XIV, extended for 1.3m west of Trench V to the south-west corner of the building. It was of coursed limestone rubble, standing 0.5 m high. The east wall in Trench VI was 0.6m wide, constructed of mortar-bonded limestone rubble. Only part of its first course survived, and was not removed during excavation, but underlying foundations of pitched limestone rubble could be seen where the wall itself had been destroyed.

The dating for the construction of Structure 7 to between the early and mid 3rd century comes from its place in the stratigraphic sequence.

LUB 21 Area between Structures 6 and 7 (Fig. 4.10–13)

To the south of the wall cg21 (LUB 20) and north of wall cg180 (LUB 19), a dump layer cg181 immediately overlay dump cg179 (LUB 9). It appeared to have built up against the wall cg180 (LUB 19).

Layer cg181 produced a large group of mid to late 3rd-century material (one of the largest pottery assemblages from the site – 168 sherds). It is composed of relatively homogeneous forms of at least a mid 3rd- to a possible later 3rd-century date.

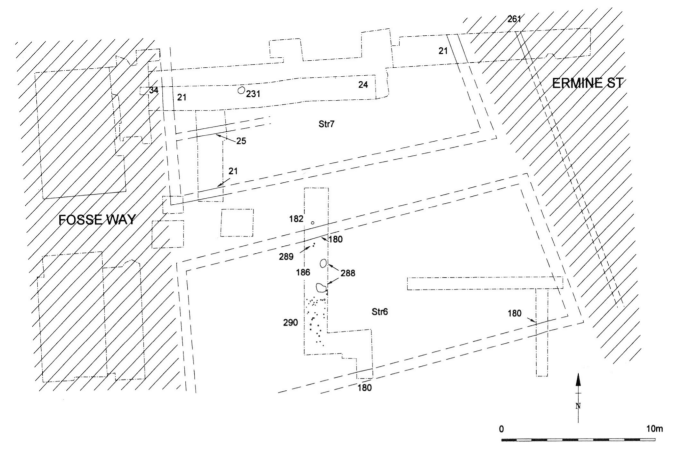

Fig. 4.10 The Fosse Way and Ermine Street with Structures 6 and 7: LUBs 2, 19, 20, 21 and 22. (1:235)

A single post hole cg182 cut into dump cg181, and may perhaps have been a scaffold support. Overlying the posthole was a layer of mortar cg183 (unplanned) which may have been an external feature, possibly a lane surface; this layer produced a small group (12 sherds) including a cooking pot in BB1 with a rim type (Gillam 1976, 76–9) dating to the mid to late 3rd century.

LUB 22 Fosse Way: resurfacing
(Figs. 4.10–13 and 4.16)
The fill of ditch cg16 (LUB 17) in Trench IV was cut by the foundation trench for the west wall cg21 (LUB 20) of the first stone building, Structure 7, and sealed by a series of road surfaces cg34 which had accumulated against the wall. The earliest of these was of compact pebbles, limestone cobbles, and hard grey-brown yellow mortar which incorporated tile fragments, and sealed a thick mortar base. It was sealed by a similar surface more than 0.15m thick. The next surface was of larger limestone cobbles and compacted pebbles in a hard brown-yellow mortar, and the final surface was of compacted pebbles and decayed mortar. The total depth of the four road surfaces sealing the ditch was *c* 0.6m.

Sealing fill of ditch cg130 (LUB 17) in Trench XIV was a thin layer of limestone rubble set in sand and mortar capped by a surface of pebbles and flat, well-worn stones cg248. Pottery from layers cg248 (62 sherds in total) broadly date to the 3rd century, possibly the mid 3rd, based on the presence of a NVCC beaker and a MOMH hammer-headed mortarium. In surface cg248 was a shallow pit cg249; pottery from this pit (19 sherds) included more definitive mid 3rd-century types including folded beakers in NVCC. Pit cg249 was perhaps a pothole which was sealed by a make-up layer of pebbles and mortar beneath a second metalled surface cg250; sherd joins between cg248 and cg249 suggest that the activities were related. This was composed of small, worn slabs of limestone, interspersed with gravel, and contained mid to late 3rd-century pottery. It was sealed by a third surface composed of a sparse gravel layer set in yellow-brown sand and clay cg251. A layer of brown sandy soil cg252 sealed cg251. Pottery from surface cg250 and layer cg252 produced very small groups of pottery (9 sherds in total) but included a mid to late 3rd-century type, a BFB in BB1.

At the limit of excavation in Trench VII was sand

cg135; this was sealed by thin layers of light grey-brown sand with charcoal flecks, a layer of burnt clay and a metalled surface of closely-packed small stones set in mortar cg253. Over this were thin layers of charcoal, ash and clay cg254 sealed by blocks of stone and mortar cg255; over cg255 were further thin ash deposits cg256. Pottery from Trench VII dated from the mid 3rd extending into the 4th centuries.

Late Roman

The roads (LUBs 2 and 22) continued in use during the late Roman period. The latest pottery associated with Ermine Street dated to the 3rd century, perhaps into the 4th. However despite the lack of positive dating evidence it would seem probable that, as principal arteries to the south and south-west, both roads continued in use until at least the end of the 4th century.

The occupation of Structures 6 **LUB 23** and 7 **LUB 24** continued from the mid-Roman period, as did the use of the space between them (LUB 21). There was pottery evidence from Structure 6 for activity continuing from the mid 3rd century into the 4th century; Structure 7 has pottery dating as late as the early to mid 4th century.

The structures were subsequently demolished and the area seems to have gone through a period of abandonment, when the structures were robbed **LUB 25**; this took place according to the pottery in the mid to late 4th century.

LUB 23 Use of Structure 6 (Figs. 4.11–13)
Immediately overlying dump layer cg179 (LUB 9), and with a vertical interface against the southern face of the north wall cg180, was a band of laminated clay floors cg185 variously of red, yellow, and dark grey clay, about 0.1m thick. This was traced across much of Trench X, although it did not survive towards the south wall cg180. A very small quantity of pottery came from cg185 (35 sherds), some of which may be residual as indicated by a tentative sherd link with underlying LUB 9 (cg179); a stamp from a SAMCG bowl, Dr31, is dated *c* AD160–200 but the associated coarse wares fall into a mid 3rd-century date range, including a BKFO in GREY. The lower layers of floors cg185 were cut by pit cg184, and the uppermost lens sealed pit cg184.

Sealing floors cg185 was a thin layer of brownish-yellow clay with sand and charcoal flecks cg186. Pottery from cg186 (23 sherds) contains some re-deposited material as there is a join between this layer and pit (LUB 7). This is further attested by sherds of residual SAMSG and SAMCG samian with dates ranging from the Flavian/Trajanic to the Antonine periods. The associated coarse wares

broadly date to the 3rd century but must be at least early to mid 3rd century based on the evidence discussed above.

Clay/sand floor cg186 was cut by postholes cg288, and many stakeholes cg289 and cg290. Partially sealing floor cg186 were traces of further clay floors cg291, which were cut by pit or posthole cg293 and stakeholes cg292.

To the north of the trench, sealing cg293 was charcoal cg188. Over this was an area of light red clay cg294, possibly a hearth, sealed by a large number of thin layers of grey clay with charcoal flecking cg295, over which was a layer of yellow-brown clay and sand cg297. This was cut by a sub-rectangular post-pit cg296 with large packing stones and a post-pipe. Sealing the post-pit was a layer of grey flecked ash/clay deposit with some charcoal flecks cg298. Cutting cg298 was an irregular pit cg47 close to the north wall surrounded by many stake-holes cg235 (unplanned). The pit was about 0.3m deep, with a bowl-shaped base, and was filled with green-brown soil from which objects and metal fragments, mainly of copper alloy, were recovered. Small-scale copper working, based on melting down old pieces of jewellery and other scrap metal, seems to be indicated. The 109gms of copper alloy waste includes large pieces of sheet and casting waste. No slag was recovered but its presence was suggested by the context records. Amongst the waste was a complete crossbow brooch ((2075)<241>, which was possibly due to be melted down for reuse; the brooch probably dates to the second half of the 3rd century (Mackreth 1993). Pottery from cg188 stratigraphically up to cg47 forms a large group of mainly homo-geneous pottery types (109 sherds) dating to the mid to the later 3rd century, with minimal residual material. The pit cg47 produced 45 sherds of a similar date.

To the south of the trench were traces of clay and sand floors cg187 which sealed cut features cg288 and cg290 and floor cg291. Pottery from floors cg187 (45 sherds), overlying cg186 in the sequence of floors, is more precisely dated to the mid 3rd century by a BB1 grooved flanged dish, a castor box lid in NVCC and a DWSH jar. However, there is some residual material in the form of SAMCG dated to the Antonine period.

Cutting floors cg187 was a roughly square cut posthole cg301 with stone packing and a fill of ashy silt. Probably contemporary with this posthole were many thin layers cg303 sealing cg187. Sealing both the posthole cg301 and the thin layers cg303 was a lens of ashy clay cg302 which had sunk into the depression of the posthole. Sealing layers cg303 was an extensive floor of pinky-red fired clay cg304; in this layer was a shallow depression with silt cg305. The floor cg304 and depression cg305 were sealed by

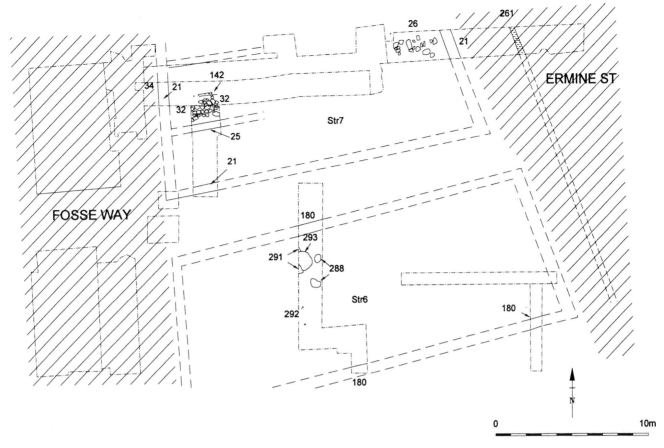

Fig. 4.11 The Fosse Way and Ermine Street with Structures 6 and 7: LUBs 2, 21, 22, 23 and 24. (1:235)

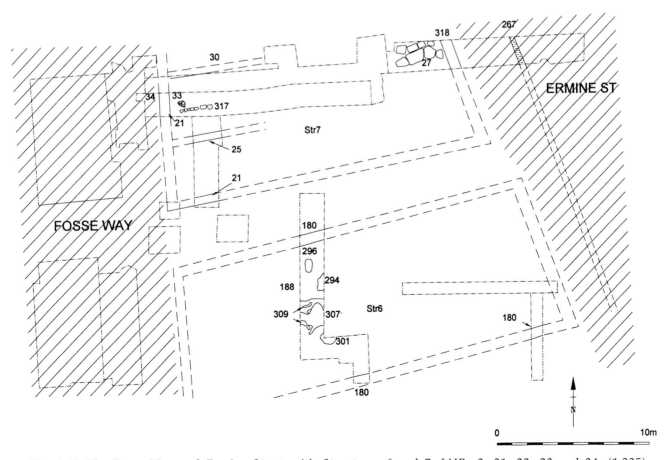

Fig. 4.12 The Fosse Way and Ermine Street with Structures 6 and 7: LUBs 2, 21, 22, 23 and 24. (1:235)

brown/grey sandy silt cg306. Over this was grey flecked ashy clay cg307 cut by posthole cg310. Clay cg307 was sealed by a patchy layer of orange clay with brown sandy silt cg308. Over this were the remains of a creamy/white clay floor cg309. Cutting cg309 was a straight-sided rectangular posthole cg311. Sealing cg311 was a green-brown layer cg51, which contained slag pieces and blobs of copper-alloy waste and a lead ?alloy bowl ((2037)<187>); the bowl had been originally cast, but when excavated it was reportedly found in pieces spread randomly over a small area. The fragments were too corroded to determine whether it had been cut up on purpose. There was also a piece of iron that may have been used as a tool ((2037)<176>). These artefacts perhaps suggest metalworking, possibly associated with pit cg47 to the north. A 4th-century date for the latest activity cg51 is provided by the presence of a GREY BFBH from a small group of pottery (20 sherds) from context (2039). There is an absence of later 4th-century fabrics and forms. Late Saxon pottery is also present (8 sherds) and might represent contamination by overlying post-Roman activity.

To the far south of the trench was a small irregular-shaped fragment of clay/sand mortar cg299, possibly flooring remains (there was no record of what it sealed).

LUB 24 Use of Structure 7
(Figs. 4.11–13, 4.16 and 4.23)
Sealing limestone rubble cg22 (LUB 20) were patches of clay, varying from white to red cg24; there were traces of a mortar surface in places and also small pebbles. Partly over clay cg24 the excavation records note "a large quantity of white-painted wall plaster" cg312. Less than 6k of this plaster was recovered; the fragments are mostly very small in size and in some cases only the upper skim survives, perhaps suggesting that it represents redeposited building debris.

Cutting cg24 was an internal partition wall cg25, *c* 3.5m north of the outer wall of the building. It was *c* 0.4 m wide, and composed of mortared limestone rubble, roughly coursed, standing to a maximum height of 0.5m. The narrowness of the wall and its lack of foundations both suggest that it acted as a sill wall for a wooden partition. Limestone paving cg32 butted the partition wall cg25 to the south; within it was found a *follis* of Constantine I, issued in AD319 but showing some wear. The paving cg32 was bounded to the north by a narrow slot cg142 containing four stake-holes; this slot apparently presented the limit of paving cg32. The paving cg32 was sealed by a layer of grey clay cg321.

To the north of wall cg25, sealing fallen plaster cg312 and also clay floors cg24 in the western part of Structure 7, were thin layers of brown soil cg313

which was in one place sealed by the remains of limestone paving cg32. From cg313 the remains of a ceramic lamp-holder were recovered. Sealing soil cg313 were white clay cg314 and layers of orange sandy material cg315 cut by posthole cg231, irregular shallow pit cg35 and pit cg236. Sealing floors cg315 was a layer of white clay cg29 (unplanned).

Floor cg29 is dated to the 3rd century or later by a coin broadly dating from the 3rd to the 4th century. This agrees well with the associated pottery (25 sherds) which contains SAMEG of a late 2nd- to 3rd-century date, whilst sherds of a NVCC castor box and lid refine the date for this feature to at least the mid 3rd century. Floor cg29 also contained a large iron knife/cleaver with a curved back ((208) <376>).

Cutting floor cg29 was an east–west wall cg30 of unmortared limestone. It was seen only in the side of Trench IV, and for safety reasons could not be fully investigated; the portion revealed was nearly 2.0m long and four courses survived, standing to a height of 0.35m. The wall had been robbed to the west of this portion, and also probably to the east, where the masonry had partially subsided into a possible robber trench.

Sealing clay layer cg314 was a dark brown silty soil cg320; on this was a linear feature of thin limestone ashlars cg317 aligned roughly east–west, probably the foundation for a partition wall foundation at the west end of the building. Over cg29 and cg320 and butting against walls cg30 and cg317 were shallow bands of hard dark brown soil cg31 (unplanned) separated by ash or mortar traces.

These layers cg31 produced the largest pottery assemblage from the site (230 sherds) with little residual material; the pottery assemblage includes a GREY BFBH together with two disc-necked flagons in GREY and NVCC wares which are more commonly dated to the 4th century. An absence of very late 4th-century material such as LCOA and SPIR suggests a date from the early to the mid 4th century for these layers.

Cutting soil cg31 was posthole cg33, which contained a roughly square post-pipe tapering toward its base (Post-pipe 0.07m across, 0.10m deep); the limestone in its fill may have been packing.

To the east of Structure 7, at the limit of excavation, were worn limestone rubble and slabs cg26, sealed by limestone paving slabs set in brown sandy clay and mortar cg27 (Fig. 4.23). The slabs were bounded by worn rubble cg318, which overlay the wall cg21 at this point, perhaps indicating a new doorway. These floors were presumably designed for heavy-duty use at the eastern frontage of the building, fronting on to Ermine Street. Over floor cg318 was a thin layer of burnt clay cg28.

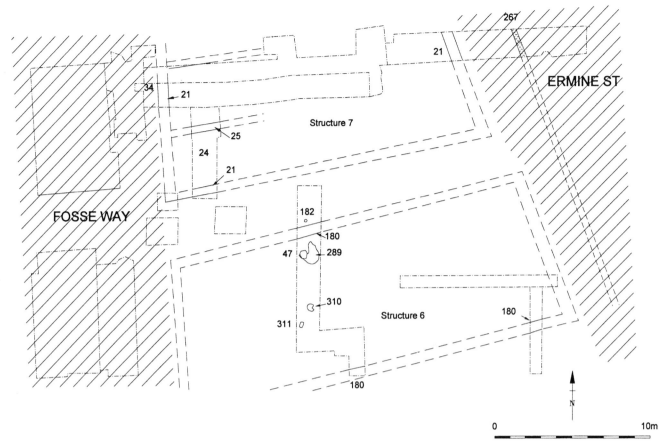

Fig. 4.13 The Fosse Way and Ermine Street with Structures 6 and 7: LUBs 2, 21, 22, 23 and 24. (1:235)

LUB 25 Abandonment, dereliction and robbing (Fig. 4.16)

Over the levelled wall cg180 (LUB 19) were limestone blocks and mortar cg137. Sealing pit cg47 (LUB 23) was wall collapse cg49 with mid to late 4th-century pottery. Over this was sandy loam cg52 with large amounts of green/brown inclusions, probably the result of vegetation; it contained a large group of pottery (334 Roman sherds and 17 post-Roman sherds) dating to the late 4th century, but with no very late Roman fabrics and forms, together with a moderately-sized assemblage of animal bone (Dobney *et al* 1994g) suggesting domestic waste. In the south-east corner of Trench X was demolition material and ash cg300 (there is no record of what they sealed).

Cutting cg31 (LUB 24) were robber trenches cg90 and cg91 of wall cg21, and pit cg89; robber trenches cg90 and cg91 contained 27 sherds of pottery broadly dated to the 4th century. Cutting cg90 was pit cg143. Over cg28 (LUB 24) was a layer of silty soil cg92; pottery from this layer (4 sherds) included a GREY BFBH which dates the small group to the mid to late 4th century.

Cutting road surface cg268 (LUB 2) was pit cg95

which was sealed by limestone rubble and mortar cg93. Sealing cg183 (LUB 21) was a general spread of red tile cg48 with pottery (56 sherds) including a GREY BFBH which dates the group to the mid to late 4th century.

The deposits in LUB 25 included not only late 4th-century pottery, but also small groups of intrusive post-Roman pottery, dating between the late Saxon and late medieval period.

Very late Roman

During the very late 4th century there was further activity on the site. There were a number of dumps and possible surfaces **LUB 26** cut by a ditch **LUB 27**; over this were traces of rubble dumping **LUB 28**, sealed by further dumps **LUB 29**. All this late Roman activity was associated with very late 4th-century pottery.

LUB 26 Layers: dumps and surfaces? (Fig. 4.16)

Limestone blocks and mortar cg137 (LUB 25) were sealed by pit cg140 which contained six sherds of Roman pottery dating to the late and very late 4th century.

Sealing cg31 (LUB 24) was a black deposit cg88 *c* 0.20m thick. Over cg92 (LUB 25) was dark brown silty soil cg146 *c* 0.80m thick. Pottery from cg88 and cg146 (224 sherds in total) dated to the very late 4th century by the presence of GREY BIBF and double lid-seated jars in LCOA and DWSH. Layer cg88 also contained a moderately-sized assemblage of animal bone indicating domestic waste (Dobney *et al* 1994g).

Sealing cg88 and cg146 was a surface or floor of mottled clayey/ashy material 0.10–15m thick cg96. It spread over a large area of Trench IV, extending west of the line of the Roman frontage sealing the latest road cobbles, at least as far as the west limit of Trench IV. It was not associated with a late survival of the northern Roman building 7 as it sealed pit cg143 (LUB 25) which cut the robber trench of that building. Layer cg96 produced 92 sherds of exclusively Roman pottery dated to the late to very late 4th century merely by the presence of a GREY BIBF.

LUB 27 Cut Features (Fig. 4.14)
Cutting clay layer cg96 (LUB 26) was east–west ditch or gully cg99; it was at least 6m long, up to 0.40m deep and of unknown width (only one side lay within the excavation). Also cutting cg96 (LUB 26) was a "shallow pit" cg100 (unplanned). The Roman pottery from ditch cg99 consisted of 74 sherds, dated to the very late 4th century, by the presence of a JDLS in LCOA and an OXRC carinated bowl; this group also included two intrusive sherds of post-Roman pottery. There was a sherd join between cg99 and earlier stratigraphy cg31 (LUB 24) demonstrating the residual nature of some of the Roman pottery. The pit cg100 produced 11 sherds of Roman and 1 sherd of intrusive post-Roman pottery; a beaker in SPOX dates this small group to the 4th century.

LUB 28 Rubble (Fig. 4.16)
Sealing layer cg96 (LUB 26), gully cg99 (LUB 27) and grey clay cg321 (LUB 24) were areas of small limestone rubble cg87, cg97 and cg101 in the west and east parts of Trench IV; these were probably equivalent to each other. They perhaps represent a crude trampled surface or floor within or outside a building, or a rubble platform for a timber building. Cutting cg101 was a pit cg102 (unplanned).

Rubble cg97 included sherds of very late 4th-century pottery – JDLS in GREY and DWSH – and there were three intrusive sherds of post-Roman pottery; these together with Roman pottery sherd joins with LUB 31 demonstrate the disturbed nature of the rubble, which had been cut into by the later features (LUB 31).

LUB 29 Dumps (Fig. 4.16)
Over cg96 (LUB 26), and sealing cg102 (LUB 28) to the north-west, were layers of earth cg104 at least 0.20m thick. To the north-east of the site earth layer cg108 sealed rubble cg97 (LUB 28). These layers contained very late 4th-century pottery, together with intrusive post-Roman pottery (29 post-Roman sherds in cg104 and 21 in cg108).

Late Saxon to Early medieval

In the south-west part of the site, in the southern part of the Norman west range, were clear traces of a beamslot **LUB 30** which had cut into Ermine Street (LUB 22); although there was no direct dating evidence, both its position in the road and its alignment suggest a late Saxon rather than a late Roman date. In both the northern and southern parts of the site, postholes and pits **LUB 31** cut through the underlying stratigraphy, suggesting occupation on the site through the 10th and 11th centuries as indicated by the pottery. There was, however, no evidence for activity between the late 11th century and mid to late 12th century, **LUB 32**.

LUB 30 Beamslot structure (Fig. 4.15)
A north–south slot cg64 ran almost the full length of Trench I, cutting an earlier slot in almost the same position (both slots are cg64) which cut into road surface cg63 (LUB 22); the latest slot was cut by postholes. They most probably represent the west wall of a building which had encroached on to the Roman road surface. Four probable postpits cg65, to the east of the slots, also cut the road surface cg63, together with a large bowl-shaped pit cg43.

The position and alignment of these features would favour a Saxo-Norman date, but pre-Guildhall layers and the upper Roman road formed a foundation for the construction of the Guildhall (LUB 33+), so that the Roman road (LUB 22) physically appeared directly below layers cg70 (LUB 35). No post-Roman pottery was recovered from these layers; there were a few residual Roman sherds.

LUB 31 Pits and possible post/stake structures (Fig. 4.15)
In Trench VI was a complex sequence of pits and other features: cutting cg267 (LUB 2) was pit cg94; cutting cg28 (LUB 24) was pit cg105; cutting cg95 (LUB 25) were pits cg215 and cg217; pit cg217 was cut by posthole cg219 and pit cg218. Cutting cg268 (LUB 2) was pit cg107 and pit cg216. Cutting cg91 (LUB 25) was pit cg112 (unplanned), sealed by brown soil layer cg113. Stakeholes cg106 also cut cg104 (LUB 29) and pit cg94. Sealing features cg106

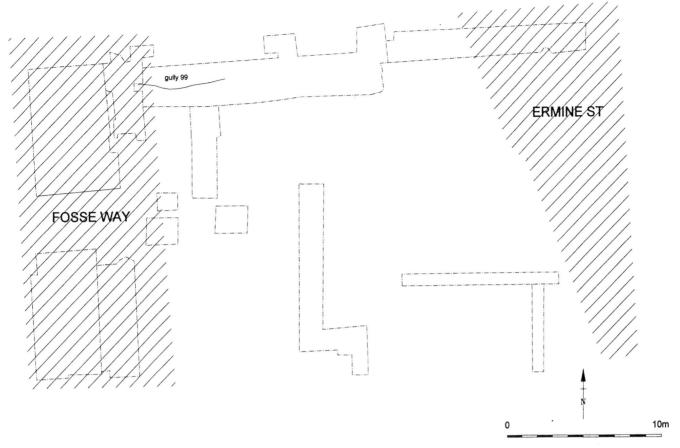

Fig. 4.14 *The Fosse Way and Ermine Street and east-west ditch: LUB 27. (1:235)*

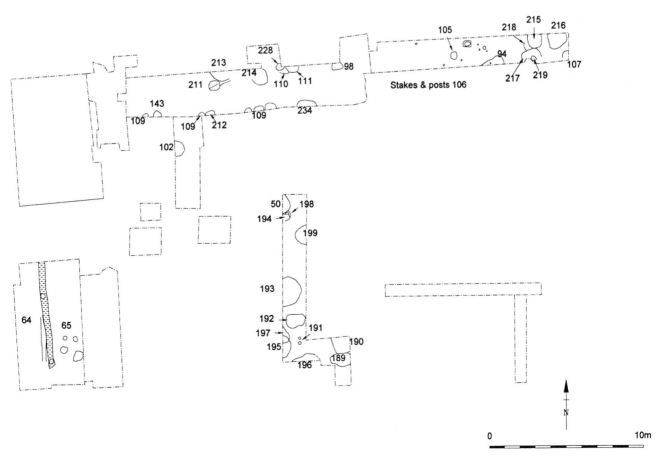

Fig. 4.15 *Beamslot Structure with pits and postholes: LUBs 30 and 31. (1:235)*

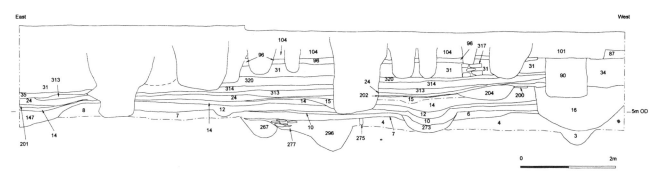

East   West

Fig. 4.16 Section from east to west, to the south side of trench IV, illustrating the stratigraphy in this part of the site from LUBs 4 to 29. The later pits are drawn but not annotated and later layers are not illustrated; both pits and layers have already been published (Stocker 1991) and are not discussed here. (1:80)

Fig. 4.17 West front of standing structure, with St Peter at Gowts church, looking south-east.

was a layer of brown soil with mortar fragments cg122 and a thin layer of mortar with ash cg320. In Trench IV cutting cg104 (LUB 29) were several small pits or postholes cg109, cg211, cg212, cg213 and cg214. Pit cg213 was recorded as cutting Roman levels. Cutting cg97 (LUB 28) was small pit cg110 and pit cg234; cg97 (LUB 28) was sealed by a patch of burnt limestone rubble, clay and sand cg98. Cutting pit cg110 were pits cg228 and cg111.

In Trench X/XI sealing cg52 (LUB 25) was layer cg53, which was cut by pits cg189, cg192, cg193 and

cg195, and stakeholes cg191. The fact that sherds from three of the five post-Roman pottery vessels from pit cg192 are diagnostically early makes it possible to postulate occupation predating the mid 10th century. Sealing pit cg196 was a layer of burnt material cg196; this was in turn cut by pit cg197. Cutting cg48 (LUB 25) was pit cg198 and pit cg199; cutting pit cg189 was pit cg190. Cutting cg198 were pits cg50 and cg194. Pits cg195, cg193 and cg190 could be dated by the pottery to between the late 10th and mid 11th centuries. Pit cg193 contained a

Fig. 4.18 Surface (1039) of western road cg40 (Fosse Way) with wheel ruts. Looking north.

small assemblage of animal bone containing a horncore with evidence of having been chopped (Dobney *et al* 1994g).

Cutting cg256 (LUB 22) in Trench VII was pit cg257 (26 post-Roman sherds), cut by pit cg258 (with no diagnostic material): neither feature was planned.

In Trench IV small pits and postholes cg109, cg143, cg212, cg234 appear to form an east–west alignment, as do similar features cg211, cg214, cg110 and cg111 to the north of them. Perhaps these represent the remains of an earthfast timber structure.

Few of these deposits contained large groups of pottery: cg190 (28 post-Roman sherds), cg192 (15 post-Roman sherds), cg193 (60 post-Roman sherds) and cg195 (91 post-Roman sherds) were most useful. The sherds were mostly small and worn, and do not appear to represent primary rubbish. Although the number of 10th-century wares (LKT and LSH) was quite high, 11th-century material was present in most features.

The 19 intrusive sherds of 10th-century date from LUB 25, four of which definitely belong to the early part of the century and confirm occupation on the site during this period.

LUB 32 *Evidence Truncated?*
There appears to be a gap in the site sequence between the late 11th century and the construction of the Guildhall in the mid to late 12th century: almost no pottery was recovered. Although there was late/post-medieval truncation, it seems unlikely to have removed all traces of activity of this period. The construction of the 12th-century Guildhall may have involved the removal of these deposits.

Medieval to Modern

The post-Roman site sequence has recently been published as a separate monograph (Stocker 1991), and is not repeated in detail here; group context and LUB numbers have been assigned, for archiving purposes. There are no changes of dating since the report was published.

1 and 2: Roman
    (LUBs 1–29)
3: Late Saxon to early medieval
    (LUBs 30–32)
4: Construction of medieval building complex, *c* 1150 to *c* 1170
    (LUBs 33–34)
5: Medieval alterations, late 12th century to *c* 1400
    (LUBs 35–37)
6: Late medieval and early post-medieval repair and re-use, 15th to early 18th centuries
    (LUBs 38–39)
7: Early industrial maltings, early 18th to later 19th centuries
    (LUBs 40–41)
8: Construction of final maltings, later 19th century
    (parts of LUBs 42–43)
9: Modern uses 1896–1982.
    (parts of LUBs 42–43)

Discussion

Chronology of occupation

The date span of the Roman pottery from the site has a very similar profile to that from the adjacent site at Monson Street (m82). Both sites show evidence of early Roman occupation, although there is a slightly higher proportion from m82. Wares dating from *c* AD120–180 are better represented at smg82. Occupation appears to be continuous with the main period

lying in the mid to late 3rd century, but with m82 having proportionally slightly more pottery. Both sites continue into the early to mid 4th century, but it is only smg82 which continues into the very late 4th century.

Fig. 4.20 Southern trench X/XI looking north: earliest features cut into natural sand.

Fig. 4.19 Surface (388) of eastern road cg20 (Ermine Street) with drain (387) looking north.

Fig. 4.21 South range trench X/XI looking east: earliest features cut into natural sand.

Fig. 4.22 Ditch (320) cg6 looking north.

The roads

The relatively high level of the underlying natural sand (4.59–4.80m OD) allowed for early occupation in this area (cf m82, above) close to the convergence of the Fosse Way and Ermine Street.

Although the various metalled surfaces of the Fosse Way (LUBs 1, 17 and 22) were traced, at one point in Trench I, from the natural sand upwards,

the earliest dating evidence for this road was not until the early to mid 2nd century. This dating evidence came, however, from ditch cg16 (LUB 17) which postdated the earlier roadside ditch cg3; the existence of an earlier ditch supports the contention that the road had been in existence in the 1st century (Whitwell 1992, 45), yet there was no direct relationship between ditch cg3 (or cg16; both Trench IV) and the undated earlier road surfaces (Trench I). Metalling cg34 (LUB 22) sealed the ditch cg16; the camber of the road altered, presumably tilting the run-off into a central drain. The layout of the Fosse Way seems to have gone through this alteration in the early to mid 3rd century, at the same time as the erection of the stone-founded buildings (LUBs 18 and 19); the walls of Structure 7 (LUB 20) sealed the ditch cg16, and the metalling abutted its walls.

The early Roman road surfaces of Ermine Street were not excavated, but it has been calculated, using the depth of stratigraphy in a nearby trench, that there was evidence for the existence of 0.55m of road surfaces which pre-dated the early to mid 3rd-century excavated surface (LUB 2). This would agree with interpretations of the road being crucial to the Roman military conquest (Whitwell 1992, 45). The road probably butted against Structure 7 (LUB 20) and had a stone-lined central drain cg261. This evidence, together with that from Ermine Street indicates that in the early to mid 3rd century the layout of both the Fosse Way and Ermine Street underwent great alterations as part of a planned development of the area; stone-founded buildings together with new road surfaces with central drains to match. This planned development emphasizes the greater importance of Ermine Street; both stone-founded buildings lay at right-angles to Ermine Street, not to the Fosse Way. The relative importance of Ermine Street can also be observed on the site at Monson Street (m82).

There is archaeological evidence for the continued existence of the Fosse Way and Ermine Street into the early 4th century. Their use throughout the 4th century can be assumed. But what happened to the roads in the post-Roman period? From the evidence of the site, it would seem that Ermine Street was lost by the late Saxon period, at this point; it had been cut by several pits (LUB 31). But although the more important Roman road had disappeared, the less important one in the Roman period, the Fosse Way, continues to exist to this day, although its line has shifted to the west. There is evidence for encroachment over the eastern edge of the Roman road surface; first an undated but probable Saxo-Norman building (LUB 30) and later the Norman construction of St Mary's Guildhall itself (LUB 33).

During medieval alterations between the 12th and 15th centuries (LUB 35), a deep east–west pit cg71 cut fine black silty soil cg70 within the southern part of the west range of the Guildhall. It was about 0.80m north–south and nearly 3.20m east–west with a wide V-shaped profile from east to west and a slot about 0.45 m wide in the base; the pit was near-vertical on the north and south sides but sloped at approximately 45 degrees on the east and west. It was 1.80m deep and appeared to cut *c* 0.45m below the earliest road visible in its side. It may have been

Fig. 4.23 Flagstone surface cg27 looking north-east.

dug to remove a large upright feature, probably a Roman milestone. The discovery of what may have been the base of the milestone, which was found to have been incorporated into the south-east corner of the medieval Guildhall's west range, reinforces this interpretation. The site lies almost exactly a Roman mile from the centre of the upper city.

The idea that the Guildhall was constructed on a pre-existing street frontage, which had already encroached on to the road surface, is supported by two further facts: the decorative frieze on the west front does not extend around the side of the building; and a few pre-Guildhall pits were found in the area immediately to the rear of the Guildhall – suggesting that this was already a rear area used for rubbish tipping before the Guildhall was constructed (LUB 31).

Occupation between the roads: chronological sequence

The nature of the early activity either between or predating the roads is unclear (LUBs 3 and 4); there were a number of cut features which may have represented early military occupation (cf the early cemetery at m82) or early *colonia* commercial activity.

cg/LUB	cg/LUB	cg/LUB	cg/LUB	cg/LUB	cg/LUB	cg/LUB	cg/LUB	cg/LUB	cg/LUB	cg/LUB	cg/LUB	cg/LUB	cg/LUB
1/0	24/24	47/23	70/35	93/25	116/38	139/43	162/7	185/23	208/38	231/24	254/22	277/10	300/25
2/4	25/24	48/25	71/35	94/31	117/38	140/26	163/7	186/23	209/38	232/10	255/22	278/10	301/23
3/1	26/24	49/25	72/35	95/25	118/36	141/42	164/7	187/23	210/38	233/38	256/22	279/12	302/23
4/6	27/24	50/31	73/35	96/26	119/38	142/24	165/7	188/23	211/31	234/31	257/31	280/12	303/23
5/6	28/24	51/23	74/35	97/28	120/38	143/25	166/7	189/31	212/31	235/23	258/31	281/16	304/23
6/10	29/24	52/25	75/35	98/31	121/38	144/42	167/7	190/31	213/31	236/24	259/43	282/16	305/23
7/11	30/24	53/31	76/35	99/27	122/31	145/–	168/7	191/31	214/31	237/1	260/43	283/16	306/23
8/11	31/24	54/–	77/35	100/27	123/38	146/26	169/8	192/31	215/31	238/1	261/2	284/16	307/23
9/10	32/24	55/37	78/38	101/28	124/38	147/14	170/7	193/31	216/31	239/1	262/2	285/16	308/23
10/11	33/24	56/37	79/38	102/28	125/38	148/14	171/8	194/31	217/31	240/1	263/2	286/16	309/23
11/12	34/22	57/37	80/38	103/–	126/40	149/18	172/8	195/31	218/31	241/1	264/2	287/16	310/23
12/13	35/24	58/43	81/38	104/29	127/40	150/10	173/8	196/31	219/31	242/1	265/2	288/23	311/23
13/11	36/1	59/39	82/38	105/31	128/40	151/18	174/8	197/31	220/38	243/1	266/2	289/23	312/24
14/15	37/1	60/41	83/40	106/31	129/42	152/18	175/8	198/31	221/38	244/1	267/2	290/23	313/24
15/16	38/1	61/43	84/42	107/31	130/17	153/18	176/8	199/31	222/38	245/1	268/2	291/23	314/24
16/17	39/1	62/43	85/42	108/29	131/40	154/18	177/8	200/16	223/38	246/1	269/4	292/23	315/24
17/16	40/1	63/1	86/42	109/31	132/37	155/3	178/8	201/16	224/38	247/1	270/4	293/23	316/7
18/18	41/1	64/30	87/28	110/31	133/39	156/3	179/9	202/18	225/1	248/22	271/4	294/23	317/24
19/18	42/1	65/30	88/26	111/31	134/39	157/3	180/19	203/18	226/38	249/22	272/4	295/23	318/24
20/2	43/30	66/33	89/25	112/31	135/22	158/3	181/21	204/18	227/35	250/22	273/10	296/23	319/–
21/20	44/33	67/33	90/25	113/31	136/43	159/5	182/21	205/38	228/31	251/22	274/10	297/23	320/31
22/20	45/33	68/33	91/25	114/33	137/25	160/7	183/21	206/38	229/38	252/22	275/10	298/23	321/24
23/–	46/–	69/33	92/25	115/36	138/39	161/7	184/23	207/38	230/–	253/22	276/10	299/23	

Fig. 4.24 Concordance of cg numbers with LUB numbers for smg82.

If the 1st-century pottery does indicate contemporary structures, they could even indicate a military base: potentially a significant discovery. The early features were sealed by sand dumps (LUBs 5 and 6) which dated to the late 1st and early 2nd centuries, and were cut by further cut features to the south of the site (LUB 7) and the traces of a possible timber-framed structure (LUB 10), Structure 1 to the north. To the north sealing LUB 10 were dumps LUB 11, cut by more features LUB 12, sealed by a further dump LUB 13. LUB 7 together with LUBs 10–13 all dated from the early to mid 2nd century; the exact nature of the activity on the site is unclear, but there seems to have been continuous use of this area between the two roads during the first part of the 2nd century. This is definitely earlier than that found at Monson Street.

To the south of the site were traces of an earth-fast structure, Structure 5 (LUB 8), cutting LUB 7; to the north, cutting LUB 13, was evidence of another possible structure (LUB 14), Structure 2, which was demolished and sealed by a dump (LUB 15) over which a later (earth-fast) timber structure, Structure 3, was founded (LUB 16). It was later replaced by a successor (LUB 18), Structure 4, with stone-founded walls. It would seem that the northern part of the site was occupied by buildings from the later part of the 2nd century into the 3rd century. There was limited evidence of building plans because of the lack of area excavation, but the evidence that presents itself through the archaeological record suggests that these building were constructed as required, holding a position between the two roads.

In the early to mid 3rd century there was a dramatic change in direction. The road frontages were subjected to planned development. Two structures (LUBs 19 and 20) extended between the two roads. Fronting Ermine Street were Structures 6 and 7, with a space between them (LUB 21). The development may have belonged to the same scheme as that found at Monson Street (m82) to the north.

Structures 6 and 7 were demolished in the late Roman period and the area seems to have gone through a period of abandonment, when the structures were robbed (LUB 25), between the mid to late 4th century. The paucity of 4th-century pottery on the Monson Street site would suggest that the structures there too were demolished and the area abandoned during the 4th century.

There was certainly further activity on the site in the very late 4th century. There were a number of dumps and possible surfaces LUB 26 cut by a ditch LUB 27; over this were traces of rubble dumping LUB 28. The interpretation of this activity is problematic, but evidence for it was not found at Monson Street. Perhaps the activity related to the special position that the site held, situated between the two roads.

The layers and features of LUBs 26–29 at smg82 were probably of very late Roman date although some intrusive post-Roman sherds were present. There are high amounts of residual 3rd-century and earlier Roman pottery from these LUBs, but the pottery peaks in the early to mid 4th century. Very late Roman pottery fabrics (LCOA, OXRC and SPIR), and forms (JDLS and BIBF) are present in varying quantities throughout LUBs 26–29 as well as the post Roman LUB 31. Roman pottery from LUB 29 has a much later emphasis than that from LUBs 26–28, supporting the interpretation that very late Roman activity was occurring sequentially on the site (LUBs 26–29); the assemblage from LUB 31 is again very similar to that from LUB 25, suggesting not only much reworking of the later Roman layers, but an end to the very late Roman activity on the site.

There was no evidence for activity on the site from the very late Roman period to the late Saxon period apart from fragments of middle and late Saxon vessels recovered residually. Ermine Street may not have continued in use, while by the late Saxon period the Fosse Way was certainly in use, but had shifted westwards. Encroaching on to the Roman road, in the south-west part of the site, were traces of a beamslot structure LUB 30 which was probably late Saxon. Over a large area of the site postholes and pits (LUB 31) indicated occupation through the 10th and 11th centuries. Any evidence for activity on the site between the late 11th century and mid to late 12th century LUB 32 may have been removed by subsequent construction work.

Construction of Structures 6 and 7: LUB 19 and 20

No excavation took place on the supposed line of either the west or east walls of Structure 6 (LUB 19). The likely position of the latter has been calculated partly by projecting southwards the estimated line of the eastern road, Ermine Street. Its western frontage was presumably on the same alignment as that of Structure 7. Structure 6 defined by these walls was about 9m wide internally and probably *c* 24m long. As the two roads did not lie parallel to one another, the resulting ground plan was irregular, with the north and south walls lying roughly at right angles to Ermine Street and oblique to the east wall. There was no trace of east–west internal divisions (as in Structure 7), but the width of the structure may suggest that the building was aisled.

The presence of a large quantity of tile in destruction debris cg48 (LUB 25) suggests that Structure 6 had a tiled roof, at least in its later phases.

Dating summary of Structures 6 and 7

The date for the construction of both these stone structures relies on the dating of the underlying stratigraphic deposits. Structure 6 is broadly dated to the early 3rd century or later, and Structure 7 to the early to mid 3rd century. Although both struc-

tures produced small amounts of residual 1st- and 2nd-century wares, plotdate analysis demonstrated that there is a different dating emphasis for the two buildings.

The pottery assemblage suggests that Structure 6 had an earlier emphasis, with a broad peak from the early to the later 3rd century, which may have been the main period of occupation, and tailing off sharply in the early to mid 4th century. In contrast, Structure 7 peaks in the mid to late 3rd century, and finishes strongly in the early to mid 4th century. This is probably a reflection of the large group of pottery from the structure cg31, the later sequence of floors, dated to the early to mid 4th century. There is no late to very late 4th-century pottery from either of the structures (see above).

Structures 6 and 7:
evidence for function and status

Within Structure 6 there were clay floors cut by postholes and stakeholes. There was a significantly high percentage of beakers from Structure 6, which, together with a higher amount of table wares, suggests a relatively high-status assemblage. Liquid holders are also higher in Structure 6 as are kitchen to table wares, suggesting an emphasis towards dining and drinking functions. Relatively high prosperity is also suggested by a base silver finger-ring of typical 3rd-century form; found in the deposit cg140 (LUB 26) overlying the destruction of this building Structure 6, and which may therefore have derived from its occupation.

In the very latest stages of Structure 6, a bowl-shaped pit was associated with small scale copper-working.

Within Structure 7 together with clay floors and post-holes were traces of mortar floors, possible indications of plastered walls, internal partitions and limestone slabbed floors. Structure 7, in contrast with Structure 6, has a marked emphasis towards kitchen wares, with very few drinking vessels, liquid holders or table wares. The cooking vessels are mainly jars in GREY, BB1, together with a high percentage of DWSH. However, this assemblage includes a single, smashed GREY cooking pot, which could distort the statistics. The high percentage may also be a reflection of the date of the latest floors (cg31), which produced the largest pottery assemblage from the site, dated to the early to mid 4th century. Nevertheless, the results suggest that Structure 7 may well have been an area where food was prepared and cooked. From one of the clay floors in Structure 7 (cg 29, LUB 24) a large knife/cleaver was recovered, possibly further confirmation of food preparation.

5. Brayford Wharf East 1982 (bwe82)

Introduction

Between late March and early May of 1982, excavations were carried out on the site of a former malthouse prior to the development of the site for new offices for the Lincolnshire Echo. The site was directed by Brian Gilmour for the Lincoln Archaeological Trust and funded by the developers, the Lincolnshire Publishing Company.

From subsoil tests and the information shown on the Ordnance Survey Geological Sheet, analysed by Tony Wilkinson (who served as the site environmental coordinator), it was hoped that the excavation would produce evidence of waterfront activity from the Roman period onwards. The site lay to the east of the present course of the River Witham, c 50m south of the point where it opens out into the Brayford Pool (Fig. 5.1). A narrow east–west trench, 2.5m wide by 55m long, was dug within the area previously occupied by the basement of the 19th-century malthouse. For purposes of stability, the trench was dug in four successive sections across the site, partly by hand and partly by machine. The north section of each trench was drawn and some north–south sections were also recorded. Plans were drawn of intrusions and structures. The floor of the malt-house lay one metre below the ground surface; construction

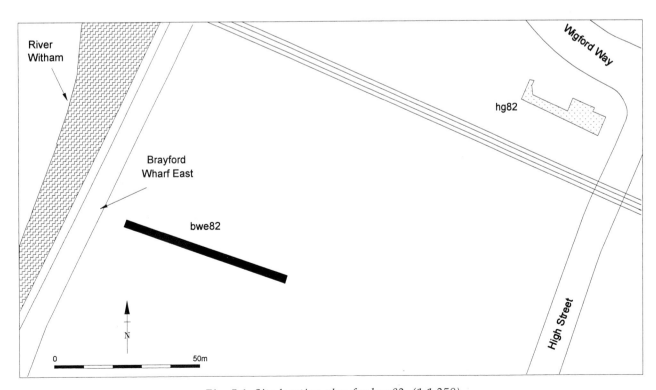

Fig. 5.1 Site location plan for bwe82. (1:1,250)

of the basement had thus largely removed any levels post-dating the 16th century. From a depth of 0.75m below the floor level the ground was waterlogged.

An interim account was published in the Trust's Annual Report (Gilmour 1982).

Because the four trenches were dug successively it is not always possible to correlate the layers recorded on the section drawings. This is particularly true of the lower layers, which were only observed in 0.3m square sondages spaced one metre apart at the bottom of the trench. Of the 149 contexts, 142 were interpreted as 77 context groups (cg1–cg82; cg40, cg76, cg77, cg78 and cg79 remaining unused) and 7 were unstratified. The 77 grouped contexts are discussed below as 19 land-use blocks, LUBs 1–19 (Fig. 5.3, 5.17). Of these, LUBs 1–6 were Roman in date, LUBs 7–12; Late Saxon to Saxo-Norman; the various deposits of LUB 13 Early to High Medieval, and the sequence of dumps LUBs 14–17 Early–Late Medieval; LUB 18 was Post-Medieval, and LUB 19 a modern pit. The land-use sequence covers the site as a whole to emphasise the gradual shift of the river to the west (Figs. 5.3); this two-dimensional approach has been made easy because the trench was so narrow. Different sections of the trench are referred to either in terms of their being in the eastern or western parts of the trench, or in relation to the river (cf also Sections, Figs. 5.2, 5.10–11).

The Roman pottery assemblage (2,144 sherds in total) was most unusual in that it was composed of a very large proportion of fine wares, both samian and colour-coated wares; 47.4% of the total pottery from the site is represented by samian and fine wares. This may be compared with sm76, a site with quantities of 3rd-century pottery, where the equivalent is 25.5%; the average for all Wigford sites is 23%. Most of the post-Roman pottery (498 sherds altogether) consisted of small featureless body sherds; groups were generally small and were made up of Lincoln and local wares. A modest quantity of registered small finds (206 finds) was recovered; approximately 25% of this was leather which had been preserved by the anaerobic conditions (Mould 1987 and 1993), as had several pieces of wood (Gale 1992; Morris 1994); some of the wood was examined for radio-carbon dating (by the Low Level Measurements Laboratory, Harwell) and some for tree ring dating (Morgan 1983). There was a similar quantity (27%) of ironwork, but little non-ferrous metal, in conditions ranging from

heavily corroded to well preserved. Roman glass formed a substantial proportion of the remaining finds (Cool and Price 1987b); other materials including bone and stone were relatively sparse (bone: Rackham 1994, stone: Roe 1994, hones: Moore 1991, marble: Peacock and Williams 1992). The Roman coins were identified by John Davies (Davies 1987). A large proportion of the building material (total 263 fragments) from the site were Roman ceramic tiles (stone identification: Roe 1994). Of the total animal bone assemblage (1,167) recovered from the site, only a small proportion was examined (Dobney *et al* 1994a). Samples were taken from some contexts for diatoms (Roberts 1984). Reports have been produced on parasite eggs (Nicholson and Carrott 1993), land and freshwater snails (French 1982; Milles 1993) and charred plant remains (Moffett 1993).

Post-excavation stratigraphic analysis was undertaken by Chris Guy and later by Kate Steane. Maggi Darling worked on the Roman pottery; Jane Young examined the post-Roman pottery. Jen Mann analysed the registered finds and Roman building materials, and Rick Kemp the medieval building materials. Helen Palmer Brown and Zoe Rawlings digitized the plans.

Interpretation of the sequence of events

Mid Roman

During the first part of the 3rd century (as suggested by the pottery) the river had flooded across the whole of the site **LUB 1**; to the east, features associated with bank consolidation cut into the silts **LUB 2**, probably in the mid 3rd century, on the evidence of the pottery.

LUB 1 River silts and peat (Figs. 5.10 and 5.11)
At the western end of the site the lowest layer observed in a machine-dug sondage was a deposit of silty clay, sealed by a layer of fine silt and silty clay mud with reeds overlain by humic silt cg1; these river deposits were recovered between 0.57m OD and 1.61m OD. Seasonal flooding of the broad shallow river is suggested by the earliest deposits found to the east of the site, river sands, with fragments of wood and abundant molluscs cg2; small fragments of fish scale were recovered from the sand (Moffett 1993). Pottery from river sands cg2 (6 sherds)

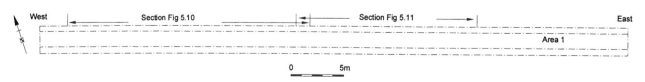

Fig. 5.2 Plan showing areas and sections for bwe82. (1:342)

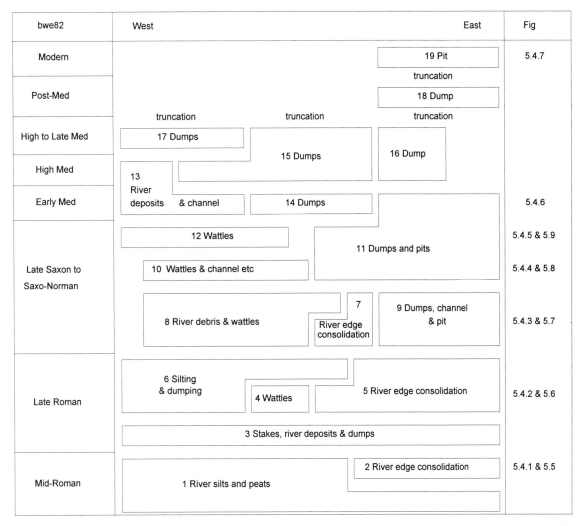

bwe82	West	East	Fig
Modern		19 Pit	5.4.7
		truncation	
Post-Med		18 Dump	
	truncation	truncation	truncation	
High to Late Med	17 Dumps	15 Dumps	16 Dump	
High Med	13 River deposits			
Early Med	deposits & channel	14 Dumps		5.4.6
Late Saxon to Saxo-Norman	12 Wattles	11 Dumps and pits	5.4.5 & 5.9
	10 Wattles & channel etc		5.4.4 & 5.8
	8 River debris & wattles	7 River edge consolidation	9 Dumps, channel & pit	5.4.3 & 5.7
Late Roman	6 Silting & dumping	4 Wattles	5 River edge consolidation	5.4.2 & 5.6
	3 Stakes, river deposits & dumps		
Mid-Roman	1 River silts and peats	2 River edge consolidation	5.4.1 & 5.5

Fig. 5.3 LUB diagram for bwe82.

included a possible South Carlton mortarium, ML2; the remaining GREY sherds included a string base, usually indicative of 3rd- to 4th-century date and here interpreted as 3rd-century on the basis of the overlying dated stratigraphic sequence.

Overlying cg2 were further river sands together with some peat cg3; similar material cg11 overlay cg1; also similar was cg8, the lowest layer observed in the centre of the trench. These three glimpses of river sands with peat cg3, cg11 and cg8 were all thought possibly to form part of the same layer; although there was no pottery from cg11, the pottery from cg3 and cg8 supported this and has subsequently been grouped together. These two context groups produced 19 sherds, including a samian 79R or Lud TgR of late Antonine date, a single GREY undecorated DGR, with a NVCC BKFO and a NVCC BKBARB which had high quality scroll decoration and a rouletted line. Conservatively the date should be early to mid 3rd century.

Also overlying cg2 were further layers of sand interleaved with peat sealed by river debris of twigs cg4 (Fig. 5.11); within cg4 was a rich freshwater assemblage of snails (Milles 1993), as well as fragments of three leather shoes together with four fragments of secondary leather (cobbling?) waste, probably debris thrown into the river to become beached here.

The layers of sand and peat cg4 contained the bulk of the pottery (128 sherds) from this LUB. The samian, at an exceptionally high proportion of 22%, ranged from Hadrian-Antonine to mid–late Antonine, c AD 160–190. NVCC beakers included body sherds from folded types, including BKFOS, the rim of a curved rim folded beaker BKFOC, and a rim from a grooved funnel neck (as RPNV 49/51). A possible NVCC flagon or jug sherd with a cordon at the base of the neck also occurred. The GREY wares contained a narrow-necked jar JNN with a cordon at the base of the neck, a cooking pot of Gillam 1976 type 8 of mid 3rd-century date, an undecorated angular rimmed plain rim dish, and a folded beaker.

There was no DWSH. The date rests largely on the NVCC, which already accounted for 19.6%, and the grooved funnel neck beaker and possible flagon would suggest a mid 3rd-century date.

The molluscan ecology from this LUB confirms that there was a larger flowing body of water with poorer water conditions, representative of occasional seasonal drying out and restricted flow (French 1982).

LUB 2 River edge consolidation
(Figs. 5.4, 5.5 and 5.11)
Cutting sand/peat layers cg4 (LUB 1) was a stake at least 1m long driven into the ground with two horizontal members cg5 (Fig. 5.12). This would have consolidated the bank, which was enhanced by sandy loam cg6 dumped behind the stake, sealing cg4 (LUB 1) and raising the ground surface to 3.75m OD.

The pottery from this LUB (72 sherds) was all recovered from dump cg6. The samian (19.4%) included a SAMEG sherd of late 2nd- to early 3rd-century date. Two unusual vessels occurred, a CR beaker with a frilled cordon and an OX necked bowl with a three-ribbed handle, the fabric nearing SPOX. The date of the GREY cooking pots ranged from the late 2nd to the mid 3rd century or the mid to late 3rd century. NVCC included probably two folded beakers BKFO, a scaled beaker probably of bag-shape type, a probable flagon or jug sherd, and

sherds representing two box lids; the NVCC accounted for a notable 33.3%. MOSL occurs for the first time as a beaker body sherd. A MHAD sherd from a closed form also occurred. There was no DWSH. A mid 3rd-century date is probable.

Late Roman

There was a build-up of riverlain deposits cut by stakes, together with some dumping **LUB 3** with

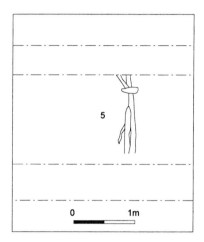

Fig. 5.5 Inset plan of stake with horizontal withies cg5: LUB 2. (1:61)

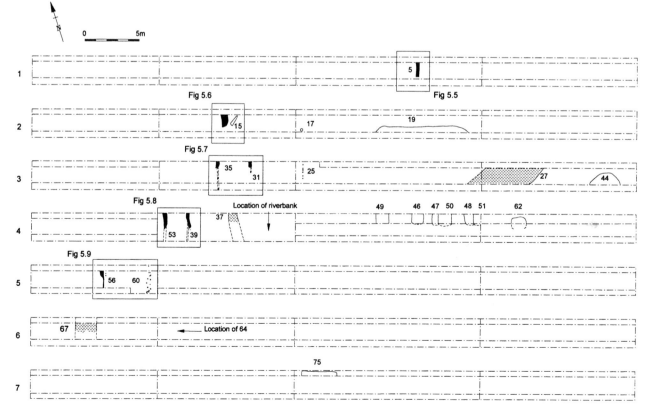

Fig. 5.4 Phase plans 1 to 7. (1:333)

pottery of a mid to late 3rd-century date. Over LUB 3 along the river margin were remains of a wattle structure **LUB 4**, radio-carbon dated to AD260±80. Towards the east the peat was consolidated with dumps retained by timber **LUB 5**; the dumps included some late 3rd-century pottery and some which dated to the 4th century. River silts were deposited towards the west of the site together with some dumping **LUB 6**, and mid to late 4th-century pottery.

LUB 3 Stakes, river deposits and dumps
(Figs. 5.10, 5.11 and 5.13)
Towards the river, sealing cg3 (LUB 1) but creeping over the bank consolidation cg5 (LUB 2), was an accumulation of peat over which branches had collected cg7 (Fig. 5.13). The peat cg7 contained a rich, probably mostly freshwater, assemblage of snails (Milles 1993). Finds from the peat cg7 included fishbone (Moffett 1993) together with some leather

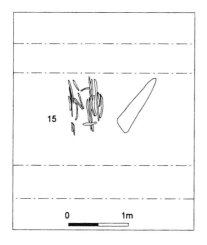

Fig. 5.6 Inset plan of wattles cg15: LUB 4. (1:61)

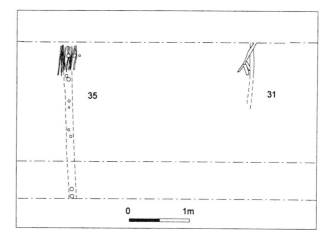

Fig. 5.7 Inset plan of wattles cg31 and cg35: LUB 8. (1:61)

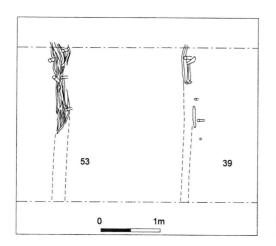

Fig. 5.8 Inset plan of wattles cg39 and cg53: LUB 10. (1:61)

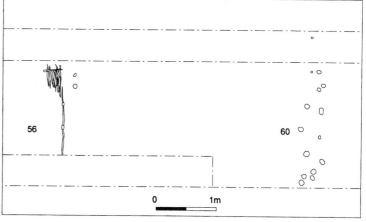

Fig. 5.9 Inset plan of stakes and wattles cg56 and cg60: LUB 12. (1:61)

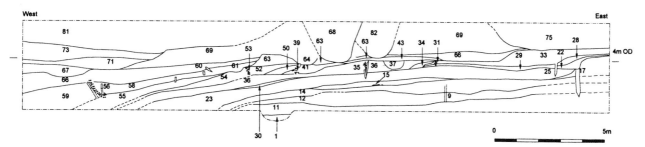

Fig. 5.10 Section from west to east along the north side of areas 3 and 4, illustrating the stratigraphy in these areas from LUB 1 to LUB 19. (1:163)

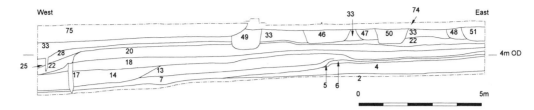

Fig. 5.11 Section from west to east along the north side of area 2, illustrating the stratigraphy in these areas from LUB 1 to LUB 19. (1:150)

(mainly shoe fragments but also including two pieces of possible cobbling waste), glass and a quantity of pottery (226 sherds).

The pottery assemblage was notable for the paucity of jars and cooking pots. The samian included four sherds SAMEG extending to *c* AD 200–260. Two MOMH mortaria occurred, one perhaps of early to mid 3rd-century date. NVCC included folded beakers, including a folded scaled funnel neck beaker (BKFOSF), sherds from two Hunt cups, and seven probable plain-rimmed beakers. Other vessels included flagons or jugs, a box lid, a basal sherd from a bowl or dish, and a rim from a MOSL beaker. GREY wares included a notable group of bowls and dishes, virtually all undecorated, mostly flanged bowls, bowls with triangular and rounded rims (BTR and BG225), a straight sided plain rimmed dish (DPRS) and a rounded rim dish (DG225). Two cooking pot rim fragments were of the Gillam 1976 types 76–9, suggesting a mid to late 3rd-century date. A body sherd with notched decoration appears to be a 3rd-century type. Of less common fabrics, a BB2 grooved rim bowl is a rare occurrence, a body sherd from an OX bowl of samian Dr38 type, and a painted flange of PARC occurred with sherds of a PARC closed vessel with horizontal stripes. An unusual find was a GREY cylindrical object, a ?stand of some type. A mid to late 3rd-century date seems definite; whether the material extends into the 4th century is very debatable and rests upon the NVCC BD sherd, which could be from a mid to late 3rd-century type.

The flow of the river may have been very slow here, possibly impeded by stakes set into the peat cg9, which overlay river sand cg8 (LUB 1), *c* 19m towards the river (not planned; see section Fig. 5.10).

To the east, sealing cg7 was dump cg13 which was interleaved with peat; the dump included gravel, sandy loam, tile and brick, bone, shell and pottery, together with a small quantity of leather and some domestic rubbish. Pottery from dump cg13 (124 sherds) was residual.

Peat, silt and sand cg10 and cg12 were deposited by the river to the west of stakes cg9, sealing earlier river deposits cg8 and cg11 (LUB 1). Pottery from layers cg10 (13 sherds) consisted of 12 sherds from a

Fig. 5.12 Looking west at timber revetment cg5.

single DWSH jar, together with a SAMEG 3rd-century mortarium.

Over dump cg13 was a deposit of sand, silt and peat cg14 and cg16 together with river debris; deposit cg14 contained building debris – tile, painted plaster and structural ironwork – which indicates dumping, together with a little domestic rubbish including several shoe fragments and pottery sherds. The pottery from cg14 (145 sherds) included SAMEG extending to an early to mid 3rd-century date, two mortaria, both from the Nene Valley (one having 33% of the vessel), usually seen more often in 4th-century contexts and DWSH in

Fig. 5.13 River debris cg7, with Roman shoe.

four of the six layers. The range of NVCC beakers was supplemented by sherds from two painted beakers and a funnel neck with a bead. Flagon-type sherds occurred, together with a crude base perhaps more likely to be a jar or wide-mouthed bowl form, and a possible bowl or dish with a chamfer. A MOSL beaker was of the slit-folded type. GREY ware included a flanged bowl with a low bead, a handled jar with a notched rim, a folded beaker, and a probable wide-mouthed bowl. A PART sherd stamped with a demi-rosette (probably from a beaker) occurred residually. Apart from an OX sherd (probably from a sandy copy of a samian Dr 38 bowl), there was also a HADOX hemispherical bowl with rouletting. A BB1 plain-rimmed dish also appeared to be of a later type. Much of the material would fit a mid to late 3rd-century date, but the occasional sherd could suggest that this group ran into the 4th century.

The evidence of the molluscan assemblage suggests the same conditions as in LUB 1 (French 1982).

LUB 4 Wattles (Figs. 5.4, 5.6 and 5.10)
Set into the top of the western end of deposits cg16 (LUB 3) were wattles supported by stakes cg15; the wattles were aligned north–south and had collapsed eastwards. It is possible that cg15 was part of a fishweir. A radio-carbon date for the wattles of AD260 ±80 years was obtained (by the Low Level Measurements Laboratory, Harwell). No pottery or other finds was recovered from this feature.

LUB 5 River edge consolidation
(Figs. 5.4, 5.10 and 5.11)
Sealing sand, peat and silt cg14 (LUB 3) were dumps of sandy loam and sandy clay with fragments of limestone, pottery, bone, and flecks of charcoal cg18, raising the ground surface to 3.93m OD. These dumps contained some building material (tile fragments, mortar and painted plaster), together with a little structural ironwork, but leather was virtually absent.

Pottery from dumps cg18 (194 sherds) had sherd links to earlier flood debris of LUB 3, suggesting a poorly-defined interface between these deposits. The total of 26 sherds of SAMEG extending to the late 2nd to early 3rd century in date represented 51% of all samian, which accounted for 26% of all the pottery. Mortaria occurred only as body sherds from the Nene Valley and Mancetter-Hartshill. NVCC vessels were similar to the earlier contexts, but included for the first time a definite pentice-moulded beaker, a disc-necked flask with two handles and a fragment possibly from a vessel decorated with a face showing as applied ?curls. A beaker base in a reddish fabric was of the later tall variety. Rhenish ware included a MOSL folded beaker with a beaded funnel neck. DWSH occurred only as a single sherd in one context, but a GREY dales ware type jar was also found; also the lid-seated J105 jar. BB1 included a cooking pot of Gillam 1976 type 10, and a bowl with a grooved rim. OX fabrics included a bowl of samian form Dr38, and a rare candlestick. PARC occurred only as sherds from closed forms with horizontal stripes, and MHAD sherds were from a closed form with false cordons. A 4th-century date seems assured from the presence of the pentice-moulded beaker, and the disc-necked flask, although much of the material would fit a mid to late 3rd-century date range.

Dumps cg18 contained a high proportion of possibly high-status finds such as a rare candlestick, an unusual glass jug (53) <240> (Cool and Price 1987b, no 6) and a silver ligula (53) <72>, as well as the quantity of samian. These dumps cg18 also contained intrusive post-Roman material.

At the river edge a wooden pile cg17 was driven into the dumps cg18, part of an attempt to consolidate the bank. The dumps were also cut by a possible beam slot cg19, measuring 6m east–west. Pottery from the fill of the beam slot cg19 (39 sherds) included SAMEG samian of late 2nd- to 3rd-century date, an OX bowl of samian Dr 38 type, an unusual GREY flat-topped jar JFT, a fragment of a later type of BB1 cooking pot, and dales ware, particularly a flanged dish, which would suggest a 4th-century date, possibly mid or perhaps later 4th century.

Dumps cg20 both sealed the fill of slot cg19 and built up the ground surface behind the river edge, raising the ground level to *c* 4.20m OD (Fig. 5.14). There were further dumps cg21 to the east, sealing dump cg6 (LUB 2). Both dumps cg20 and cg21 contained some building debris (tile and plaster with a few iron nails); other finds largely consisted of domestic refuse, mainly vessel glass and pottery. Leather was virtually absent from dumps cg20 and cg21. Evidence of specialised activity is provided from cg20 by a single crucible sherd, and perhaps by a small, possibly part-worked, copper alloy bar (ingot?) (49) <73>.

Pottery from dumps cg20 (32 sherds) contained late 2nd- to early 3rd-century SAMEG, a GREY high beaded bead-and-flange bowl, a NVCC bowl of samian Dr 38 type, and more importantly a rim fragment of a DWSH rounded rim bowl or dish, again suggestive of a mid or perhaps later 4th-century date. Pottery from dumps cg21 (271 sherds) contained 75 sherds of samian (27.7%) including only four sherds of SAMEG extending to a date between the late 2nd and 3rd centuries. There were ribbed oxidised amphora sherds of probably later Roman date. Only two body sherds of DWSH occurred. The only wide-mouthed bowl rim was of the undercut curved type as seen in the Rookery Lane kiln assemblage. A mid 4th-century date is applicable to cg21, although there seemed to be a high residual content. There were two intrusive post-Roman sherds from cg21.

Timber pile cg17 appears to have either rotted away above the water level or to have been truncated and removed. The remains were sealed by layers of sandy loam cg22, which had built up over the area to the east. The western edge of these layers dipped down sharply on the line of bank consolidation cg17, suggesting that this was still the edge of the river. Pottery from cg22 (134 sherds) had a lower samian content than earlier dumps, declining substantially to a mere 6%; the samian extended to a SAMEG Dr 37 of late 2nd- to early 3rd-century date. NVCC represented 24.6%. One of the contexts (46) within cg22 contained pottery which was notably rather fragmented and included an intrusive post-Roman sherd. A mid to late 4th-century date for cg22 is indicated by the NVCC plain-rimmed dish, the shell-tempered bowl, and the late G43 beaker.

The molluscan evidence for this LUB suggests a mixed water condition along the river's edge (French 1982).

LUB 6 Silting and dumping (Fig. 5.10)

Towards the river, west of bank consolidation cg17 (LUB 5), there were extensive deposits of silty sand with bands of peat and debris; sealing cg1 (LUB 1) was cg24; sealing cg15 (LUB 4) was cg80, over which was cg23. These appear to have accumulated in the river channel and reflect varying flow conditions. This material contained pottery (176 sherds) together with other refuse which included fragments of limestone, bone and shell. Building/structural debris occurred in cg23 and cg80 indicating that rubbish was being dumped along the river margin; the pottery assemblage from cg80 suggests some post-Roman contamination. There was a rich freshwater assemblage of snails with a dry land component (Milles 1993). The molluscan evidence also indicates that there were mixed water conditions; a variable flow prone to very shallow and stagnant water conditions which suggests the edge of a river that was going out of active use (French 1982). This is corroborated by the analysis of the plant remains, which indicates a natural vegetation that would be associated with the river shallows and banks, mixed with plants associated with habitats created by human disturbance. Some of the seeds may have come from plants growing upstream. The presence of seeds of garden plants, charred remains, and a few woodland species, ties in with evidence of rubbish dumping (Moffett 1993).

The pottery from this LUB contained a diminished quantity of samian (accounting for only 6.8%),

Fig. 5.14 Roman pile cg17 with dumps cg20, looking north at the section.

but the NVCC is still relatively high at 28.4%. The only mortaria were body sherds from the Nene Valley. A probable North African amphora sherd was noted. Both GREY and BB1 high-beaded bead and flange bowls occurred, but the wide-mouthed bowls were predominantly of the Rookery Lane kiln type, with only one verging on the Swanpool kilns variety. Only three sherds of DWSH occurred, and a single shell-tempered triangular rimmed bowl. There were also some thick flat shell-tempered fragments, not certainly pottery vessels rather than tiles. NVCC included pentice-moulded beakers, painted beakers, a slit-folded beaker and the late G43 type, alongside plain-rimmed dishes, and a rare jar as RPNV 77. Fragments of one or possibly two Rhenish motto beakers also occurred. Swanpool SPOX fabric appeared positively for the first time as bowls copying samian Dr 38 type, a B332 vessel, a D-shaped rim bowl and a sherd from a closed form. Notably there were no late lid-seated jars or the late LCOA fabric (of which only three sherds occur in LUB 11), and no SPIR fabric is recorded from the site. The material indicates a mid to late 4th-century date. There was an intrusive post-Roman sherd in cg80.

Late Saxon to Saxo-Norman

The river edge was consolidated **LUB 7** in the centre of the site, and river debris **LUB 8** built up against it to the west. To the east of the river edge were new dumps, cut by a channel and a pit **LUB 9**. LUBs 7, 8 and 9 contained several late Saxon pottery sherds; the stakes in LUB 7 were radio-carbon dated to AD870 ±70, the wattles cg31 in LUB 8 were dated to AD780 ±80, while the stakes cg35, also in LUB 8, dated to 1000 ±70, and those in LUB 9 to 850 ±70.

By the river, sealing some of the earlier river debris LUB 8, were wattles and a channel **LUB 10**. Further dumping, which was cut by pits **LUB 11**, sealed the earlier bank consolidation LUB 7 and also part of the river debris LUB 8. More wattles **LUB 12** sealed earlier examples LUB 10· to the west of the site. A few sherds from LUBs 10, 11 and 12 suggest a Saxo-Norman date. Stakes from LUB 10 were radio-carbon dated to 1000 ±70.

LUB 7 Riverfront consolidation
(Figs. 5.4, 5.10, 5.11 and 5.15)
The west end of dumps cg22 (LUB 5) was cut by features associated with bank consolidation cg25, aligned north–south. It comprised irregularly spaced stakes at least 0.4m long (Fig. 5.15); a radio-carbon date of AD870±70 years was obtained (by the Low Level Measurements Laboratory, Harwell) from one of the posts. Layers of dark loam and peaty clay cg28, with a surface OD of 4.38m, appear to have

Fig. 5.15 Looking east at timber stakes cg25 of Late Saxon waterfront.

accumulated over several decades behind stakes cg25. The molluscan evidence suggests a significant decrease in variety and abundance of the freshwater snail assemblage; the minor presence of land snails indicates the beginning of change to terrestrial conditions (French 1982).

A small group of late Saxon pottery was recovered from these features (five post-Roman sherds from cg28). It may represent contamination from cg33 (LUB 11) as one vessel has cross-joins. The latest sherds date to the late 10th or 11th centuries.

LUB 8 River debris and wattles
(Figs. 5.4, 5.7 and 5.10)
To the west of bank consolidation cg25 (LUB 7) and sealing it, there was a layer of peat cg29, which sealed a human skull in a very shallow depression in the top of deposits cg23 (LUB 6). No other human bones were found and it seems probable that the skull was derived from river debris that had lodged here. Also sealing deposits cg23 (LUB 6) further west was a thin layer of sand cg30.

Set into the west end of peat cg29, at a distance of 5.4m west of bank consolidation cg25 (LUB 7), were the fragmentary remains of wattles cg31 aligned north–south. Peat cg32 had accumulated in the still

water to the east of the wattles and had silted through them to be sealed by a sandy layer cg34, towards the river. Sandy layer cg34 appeared to have been dumped in order to bank the edge of the river.

Set into deposits cg23 (LUB 6), possibly contemporary with wattles cg31, but 3m to the west, were wattles held in place by upright stakes cg35. Peat cg36, which contained a small quantity of leather, including shoemaking waste, appears to have accumulated to both east and west of these wattles. Interleaved bands of sand and peat cg38 had built up above the peat cg36 against the west side of the wattles cg35, and spilled through to the east side.

The molluscan evidence from the peat to the west of the wattles cg35 suggests that there was an increase in catholic freshwater snails and a decrease in others; this indicates that the vegetation had become choked, leading to stagnating water conditions (French 1982).

A radio-carbon date of 780 ±80 was obtained from wattles cg31, while a date of 1000 ±70 years was obtained (by the Low Level Measurements Laboratory, Harwell) from a sample of the wood from stakes cg35 . The latter date is clearly more in line with other dating evidence. The earlier date may indicate re-used drift wood in the wattle construction. A few post-Roman sherds were recovered from the peat

Fig. 5.16 Looking north-west at north–south wattling cg53.

cg32 (nine post-Roman sherds) and peat and sand cg38 (10 post-Roman sherds), the latest of which dated to the late 10th to 11th centuries.

LUB 9 Dumps with channel and pit
(Fig. 5.4)
Sealing dump cg21 (LUB 5) at the eastern end of the site were dumps of rubble and loam cg26, which raised the ground level to *c* 4.53m OD; there were remarkably few finds within the dumps and little contemporary pottery (19 post-Roman sherds). It did, however, contain quite a high number of residual Roman sherds. The latest sherds dated to the late 10th or 11th centuries.

Dumps cg26 were cut by a channel aligned northeast–southwest cg27, which was *c* 2.5m wide and *c* 0.75m deep with a rounded profile. The lowest fill within the channel was peaty silt, which was cut by a row of stakes, the significance of which is uncertain; the stakes had a radio-carbon date of 850 ±70 (obtained by the Low Level Measurements Laboratory, Harwell). In view of the dating of cg35 above (LUB 8), this early dating could indicate re-use of river debris, but of course is only approximate.

The upper fill of the channel cg27 was peat. The channel may have been dug to drain the area adjacent to the river. The nature of the fills suggests that the water within it was slow moving and that it became clogged with reeds. The molluscan evidence from the channel cg27 suggests mixed water conditions with a slight increase in catholic species; the vegetation would have been choked but still open, with moving water adjacent (French 1982).

Cut through the dumps cg26 (LUB 9) to the east of the channel was a pit cg44, which was filled with sandy clayey loam containing bone; it may have been a pit associated with occupation further to the east. The latest sherds from cg44 (two post-Roman sherds) date to the 10th century.

LUB 10 Wattles, channel and river deposits
(Figs. 5.4, 5.8, 5.10 and 5.16)
Wattles cg35 (LUB 8) were replaced by wattles supported by stakes cg39, also aligned north–south, 3m further west of their predecessor. Stakes cg39 cut into sandy river deposit cg36 (LUB 8); they had a radio-carbon date of 1000 ±70 (obtained by the Low Level Measurements Laboratory, Harwell). Peat cg41 had built up to the east of cg39 and sand/peat layers cg42 built up over it and to the west. Possibly contemporary with wattles cg39 were wattles held between two rows of stakes cg53, 2m to the west

(Fig. 5.16); it is not clear into which deposit they had cut, but it was possibly cg36 (LUB 8). A layer of peat cg52 built up behind the wattles, while sand cg54 accumulated in front, overlying cg36, and filtering through the wattles.

A channel or ditch cg37, roughly parallel to the river, was dug through the sand and peat cg38 (LUB 8), 3–4m east of wattles cg39, possibly to prevent flooding from the river. It was aligned approximately north–south and was 1m wide by 0.35m in depth, with a rounded profile. The ditch cg37 had filled with bands of peat and sand. Sealing peat cg41 and channel cg37 was a layer of sand with lenses of both peat and burnt clayey silt cg43.

Only 8 sherds were recovered from this LUB from cg43; all were Lincoln and local wares of the 11th century.

LUB 11 Dumps and pits
(Figs. 5.4, 5.10 and 5.11)
Sealing peat cg32 (LUB 8), and building up the dry land to the east, were layers of sandy loam and burnt silty clay cg33 with flecks of charcoal, pottery (49 post-Roman sherds), tile and bone, but few other finds. These were probably dumped here to a level of 4.65m OD; the edge of dry land had moved westwards by about 1m.

Pit cg44 and channel fill cg27 (LUB 9) were sealed by a very mixed layer of bands and lenses of burnt sandy material and sandy loam cg45 (136 post-Roman sherds) which contained frequent flecks of charcoal and shell. It was partly dug by machine and includes the fills of pits which were not recognised at the time. However one pit cg62 was identified as cutting cg45 and further west there were several more pits; cg46 (46 post-Roman sherds), cg47 (four post-Roman sherds), cg48 (three post-Roman sherds) and cg49 (10 post-Roman sherds) had been dug into the layers cg33; pit cg50 (15 post-Roman sherds) cut earlier pit cg47, and pit cg51 (11 post-Roman sherds) cut pit cg48. Crucible sherds were found in the fills of pits cg46 and cg62 (28 post-Roman sherds), and within dump cg45, while dump cg33 also produced a potsherd from a vessel that may have been used for industrial purposes. A small assemblage of animal bone was recovered from pit cg46, representing mainly primary butchery waste dumped directly into the pit (Dobney *et al* 1994a).

The post-Roman pottery formed mixed assemblages difficult to assess. It is possible to generalise that the high numbers of SNLS, ST, TORK and LFS indicate an earliest date for activity in the early 11th century. Some of the LFS bowl rims are more usually found in mid 11th- to early/mid 12th-century levels, as are two of the ST lamp rim types. The latest sherd, however, appears to be a LSW1 globular lamp with a spot of glaze; as this type did not normally occur

before the early to mid 12th century, it could be intrusive.

LUB 12 Wattles (Figs. 5.4 and 5.9)
Sealing river sand cg54 (LUB 10) was a layer of peat cg55 with a surface OD of 2.4m. This peat was cut by two north–south lines of stakes supporting wattles cg56 and cg60, 4.2m apart. Sandy peat cg58 built up between the two lines of stakes and peat cg61 built up behind wattles cg60. To the west within the river, sealing river deposit cg24 (LUB 6), a layer of peaty silt cg57 had built up; sealing peat cg58 and silt cg57 was a layer of sand cg59 which built up to the west of wattles cg56; this contained two fragments of leather turnshoe and a small quantity of shoemaking waste.

Only nine sherds of pottery were recovered from this LUB from cg59, the latest of which probably date to between the mid 11th and the mid 12th century.

Early Medieval

River deposits built up to the west of the site, cut by a channel **LUB 13**. Dumping extended westwards towards the river **LUB 14** as well as to the east of the site over LUB 11. There were a few early medieval pottery sherds from LUBs 13 and 14.

LUB 13 River deposits and channel
(Figs. 5.4 and 5.10)
Sealing layers cg59 and peat cg61 (LUB 12) were various water-laid deposits cg66 together with a little river-deposited rubbish. A channel cg67 was cut into the top of cg66; its fill was interleaved bands of peat and silt which also extended further to the west.

The latest pottery (23 post-Roman sherds from cg66 and six post-Roman sherds from cg67) from this LUB is of 'splashed' glaze types from Lincoln and Nottingham, and dates to between the mid 12th century and the early 13th century.

LUB 14 Dumps (Fig. 5.10)
Overlapping cg33 (LUB 11) and sealing cg43 (LUB 10) were mixed bands and lenses of loam and sand cg63 containing flecks of charcoal, bone and shell. These dumps cg63 were cut by a tree root cg64, perhaps the remains of a tree by the edge of the pool. Only two sherds of pottery were recovered from this LUB from cg63. These sherds date to the mid to mid/late 12th century.

High Medieval

During this period the ground was raised with dumps. In the middle of the site extending towards

cg/LUB	cg/LUB	cg/LUB	cg/LUB	cg/LUB	cg/LUB	cg/LUB
1/1	13/3	25/7	37/10	49/11	61/12	72/17
2/1	14/3	26/9	38/8	50/11	62/11	73/17
3/1	15/4	27/9	39/10	51/11	63/14	74/18
4/1	16/3	28/7	40/–	52/10	64/14	75/19
5/2	17/5	29/8	41/10	53/10	65/15	76/–
6/2	18/5	30/8	42/10	54/10	66/13	77/–
7/3	19/5	31/8	43/10	55/12	67/13	78/–
8/1	20/5	32/8	44/9	56/12	68/15	79/–
9/3	21/5	33/11	45/11	57/12	69/15	80/6
10/3	22/5	34/8	46/11	58/12	70/16	81/17
11/1	23/6	35/8	47/11	59/12	71/17	82/15
12/3	24/6	36/8	48/11	60/12		

Fig. 5.17 Concordance of cg numbers with LUB numbers for bwe82.

the west and the river deposits LUB 13 were dumps **LUB 15** with a few sherds of early 13th- to early to mid 14th-century pottery. To the east of the site, sealing dumps LUB 11 were further dumps **LUB 16** with a sherd of 13th-century pottery. The river margin had shifted considerably towards the west of the site.

LUB 15 Dumps (Fig. 5.10)
The tree cg64 (LUB 14) by the river bank was removed by pit cg65; both pit and waterlain deposits were sealed by dumping cg69. The dumps seem to have advanced the river bank *c* 6m to the west, although they did not extend as far west as channel cg67 (LUB 13), which may therefore have continued in use. Cutting the dumps were pits cg68 and cg82. The LUB contained a small group of medieval pottery (two post-Roman sherds from cg68 and 17 from cg69), the latest sherds of which are of LSW2 dating to between the early 13th century and the early/mid 14th century.

LUB 16 Dump
To the east of the site, dump cg70 sealed pit cg62 and layer cg45 (both LUB 11). The pottery assemblage (29 post-Roman sherds) contains mostly residual 10th- and 11th-century material, with one sherd of NOTG dating to the 13th century and one post-medieval sherd of PMX (unidentifiable) which was possibly intrusive.

High Medieval to Late Medieval

During this period the river margin was no longer located within the site, but lay to the west; dumps **LUB 17** with a sherd of pottery dating to the late 15th or early 16th century, sealed the earlier river deposits LUB 13 and the western part of dumps LUB 15.

LUB 17 Dumps (Fig. 5.10)
Dump cg71 overlapped the west end of cg69 (LUB

15) and sealed the channel cg67 (LUB 13) with limestone rubble, tile and sandy loam; its surface was 3.88m OD and it may have extended the area above water by about 4m, but as it lacked height this probably would have only been the case during the summer. Deposits of peat and silt cg72 accumulated to the west and sealed the dump cg71. Dumping cg72 was sealed by dump cg73 and over this were large quantities of sandy loam and stone cg81. The top of these dumps was at 4.85m OD.

Few sherds were recovered from this LUB (four post-Roman sherds from cg71, nine from cg73 and 11 from cg81) . The latest are LLSW and one LSW4 indicating a date of the late 15th or early 16th century.

Post-Medieval

Most of the site had been truncated, leaving evidence for further dumping only on the east **LUB 18**, dated by pottery to between the late 16th and late 18th centuries; a clay tobacco pipe stem suggests a date no earlier than the 17th century.

LUB 18 Dump (Fig. 5.11)
Dump cg70 (LUB 16) had been levelled and the rest of the deposit was sealed by a sandy loam dump cg74 (containing residual Roman and late Saxon finds including 29 post-Roman sherds), which also sealed the truncated late 10th- to 11th-century pits cg46, cg49, cg50 and cg51 (LUB 11). Two sherds of pottery came from this LUB dating anywhere between the late 16th and late 18th centuries. A single clay tobacco pipe stem fragment was recovered, consistent with a mid 17th- or 18th-century date.

Modern

Cut into LUB 18 was a pit **LUB 19** which contained a sherd of modern pottery.

LUB 19 Pit (Figs. 5.4, 5.10 and 5.11)
Cut into dump cg74 (LUB 18) was a large pit cg75, filled with brick rubble and mortar. A single clay tobacco pipe stem fragment was found, consistent with an 18th- or 19th-century date, together with a single modern potsherd.

Discussion

The Roman period

In the pre-Roman and early Roman periods the east bank of the Witham lay at least 75m east of its present position. The river seems to have been generally shallow towards its eastern margin as sand and peat accumulated here during the late 2nd and into the early/mid 3rd centuries, reflecting varying flow conditions.

In the mid 3rd century the river bank was advanced at least 22m westwards by consolidation of the bank with stakes cg5 (LUB 2) and the dumping of building material and domestic refuse behind them. More peat developed in the channel to the west of the bank; this was possibly enhanced by stakes cg9 (LUB 3) which seemed to have broken the flow 19m further west; the actual purpose of the stakes was unclear. There seems to have been no clearly defined river-front through the mid/late 3rd to the early 4th centuries. Wattles cg15 (LUB 4) possibly represented the remains of a fishweir.

Dumps of rubbish and building debris had been used to reclaim land in the mid 4th century. The river bank had been consolidated, but only a single wooden pile cg17 (LUB 5) remained, which had been driven into the dumps creating a bank about 10m west of the mid 3rd-century bank consolidation. It seems to have been part of what had once been a substantial attempt to retain the river edge; the rest of the structure had been robbed or decayed away. Cutting the dumps was a possible beam slot cg19 (LUB 5), perhaps part of a building associated with fishing or river activity. To the west, debris and refuse washed up along the shallow river's edge.

Sources of rubbish used in the dumps

The 3rd-century river margin (LUBs 1–3) appears to have been used as a convenient site for the casual disposal of rubbish, contrasting with what appears to have been a deliberate (organised?) policy of refuse disposal in the mid 4th century (LUB 5). The difference in complexion between these deposits is illustrated by the occurrence of leather – both shoes and cobbling waste (albeit in small quantities) – in the 3rd-century deposits (LUB 3), and its virtual absence from the 4th-century dumps (LUB 5). There is only slight evidence of other specialised activities in the 4th-century dumps, provided by the crucible sherd (12) < 175> from dump cg21 (LUB 5), and the ?part-worked copper-alloy bar/ingot (49) <73> from cg20 (LUB 5), while the glass cube (62) <99> from cg13 (LUB 3) may also have been associated with manufacturing.

Some indication of urban wealth in the 3rd century is provided by a few of the finds, such as the unusual glass jug (53) <240> and the silver ligula (53) <72> from dumps cg18 LUB 5 (reinforced by the quality and quantity of pottery, especially the finewares and samian, see below). It is just possible that the proportion of sandals (18%) among the shoes is indicative of refuse from higher-status establishments, but the assemblage is too small to be certain.

The unusual Roman pottery assemblage can be viewed functionally since samian and fine wares are mostly tableware and drinking vessels. The proportion of a total site assemblage taken by tableware and drinking vessels for the city of Lincoln taken from 26 sites ranges from 14.3% (if extraordinary sites such as bwe82 are excluded) to 15.9%. An average about 14%, regardless of the area of the city, is usual. The figure for bwe82 is 37.8%, and the only other site approaching this level, with 33.3%, is another waterside site, wo89, located on the north bank of the Witham, east of Ermine Street (Donel 1989). The site has the highest percentage of samian from any site in Lincoln. The analysis by source shows the assemblage to be virtually the same as that from sm76 (Fig. 5.18).

Although the date emphasis of the site favours the period of the largest importation of samian, which may account partially for the particularly high proportion of samian, this is stratified with exceptionally large quantities of colour-coated wares, virtually all of which would be dated to the 3rd century in Lincoln. 96% of the samian can be allocated to the period approximately AD140 to the end of importation, peaking at *c* AD180, and is virtually identical to the samian from sm76 (the *c* AD140 start is directly related to vessels dated to the broad Antonine period). Neither site appears to have significant quantities of 2nd-century coarse wares, and the main use of both sites appears to start in the 3rd century. It is accepted that the "life" of samian vessels is longer than that of normal coarse-ware vessels, particularly those used for cooking, and it is conceivable that this life became longer towards the end of importation, when new supplies became scarcer. The dating problem presented here is not confined to this site, but applies also to sm76, and to a lesser extent, to z86 and sb85.

This does not, however, explain the abnormal bias of the assemblage from this site towards samian and fine wares. The consolidation of the river edge seems to have involved the use of material which had originally come from a variety of sources. Nor does it seem possible at present to offer an explanation. More data and studies of fragmentation from similar rubbish-dump sites are necessary. It is perhaps significant that another unusual assemblage from Lincoln derives from a similar dump of rubbish by the Witham (Donel 1989), and this site may aid understanding of such dumps.

Sitecode	CG	EG	SG	sherds
bwe82	80.3	19.3	0.5	400
sm76	81.2	18.0	0.8	1127

Fig 5.18 Comparison of samian from bwe82 and sm76.

The Roman animal bone assemblages were all derived from what are interpreted as waterlain deposits. The presence of butchered elements from the common domesticates suggests that small quantities of noxious waste were being dumped into the river during this period. The preservation and surface integrity indicate waterlogging of the material, although colour appears variable (Dobney *et al* 1994a).

The quantity of bone fragments relative to pot sherds has been recorded. The average proportion of bone at 18% over LUBs 1–6 appears to be slightly low in comparison to similar figures from sm76, where the proportion of bone from levelling deposits averages 27%, with a range of 21–37%. Both bwe82 and sm76 may, however, have lower bone content than usual, since the stratified groups from Z86 indicate a bone content relative to pot of 34%.

Similarly, comparison of the bone content between bwe82 and sb85, both sites being primarily composed of successive dumps, shows the percentage from bwe82 at 17.5% lower than that at sb85 with 27.6%. Both these waterside sites differ substantially from the waterside sites along the Witham, where the percentage of bone fragments to sherds is extremely high and close to 50%. Although the proportions of bone fragments to pottery sherds decline from LUB 1 to LUB 5, they rise abruptly in LUB 6, and the two main groups have the same proportions overall.

The post-Roman period

From the end of the Roman period, the river bank itself seems to have remained fairly static, possibly for some centuries, despite the removal or decay of timbers. In the late Saxon period there was an attempt to consolidate the bank cg25 (LUB 7), only about a metre to the west of the latest Roman bank. Soil cg28 (LUB 7) had developed on the bank while peat formed in the river shallows. At the eastern end of the site there was a wide shallow channel cg27 (LUB 9), probably to drain the area close to the river, and further east than that was a pit cg44 (LUB 9). Both channel and pit suggest an attempt to use the land for occupation.

Lines of wattles supported by stakes (cg31 and cg35 LUB 8; cg39 and cg53 LUB 10; cg56 and cg60 LUB 12) appeared to follow the margins of the river; they may well represent the remains of fishweirs. The wattle lines would appear to have been set in the shallow water of the river margins. To act as fish-traps they would be open at the south and channel the fish northwards with the water current and entrap them where the two lines of wattles closed together (Salisbury 1991). Peats developed in the still water to the east and between the lines of wattles, while sand banks built up in the river shallows to the west.

These three successive sets of wattles were dated approximately by radio-carbon to the 9th century on, but the pottery suggests a later sequence. Each new structure was set further west.

The river margin gradually moved westwards; the build-up of peat appeared to have become consolidated. A channel cg37 (LUB 10) possibly helped to prevent flooding from the river; it was cut some 3m or 4m behind wattles cg39 (LUB 10) sometime in the late 10th to 11th centuries, and was associated with river bank cg34 (LUB 8).

Late 10th- to late 11th-century pits and dumps (LUB 11) contained a small quantity of craft/industrial debris: the small group of crucible sherds (and the LKT jar which may have served some industrial function) from pits cg46 and cg62, and associated dump cg45 (all LUB 11). These may have some connection with possible occupation on the High Street frontage, and the date coincides with a period when crafts and industries appear to be have been flourishing within the town.

From the single large, possibly late Saxon, pit cg46 (LUB 11), several sheep horncores showed evidence of butchery around their bases, perhaps hinting at hornworking activity. This appears to corroborate other finds evidence from the pit which may also relate to craft or industrial processes (Dobney *et al* 1994a). As at Lucy Tower, the water margin again seems to have been used as a convenient dumping place for medieval rubbish, including a small quantity of leather shoes and waste.

By the period between the mid 12th and the late 13th century there were no more pits, but there was evidence for a tree cg64 (LUB 14) along a river bank, which was some 9m to the west of bank cg34 (LUB 8); possibly contemporary with the tree was a north–south channel cg67 (LUB 13) in the river margins, perhaps cut to help prevent flooding.

Further advance of the waterfront occurred in the early to mid 14th to 15th centuries cg73 (LUB 17), while another took place in the 15th to 16th centuries cg81 (LUB 17). The extent of both advances was beyond the limit of excavation. Truncation has removed evidence of later developments, beyond the large modern pit cg75 (LUB 19).

The water level can be inferred from the section (Fig. 5.10). There seems to have been a rapid rise in water level from around 2.5m OD (cg11 LUB 1) in the mid 3rd century to over 3.5m OD (cg23 LUB 6) in the mid to late 4th century. This only gradually rises to just below 4m (cg29 LUB 8) in the late 10th to 11th centuries, with little movement of bank location during this time. Fluctuation in the velocity of the river has left its mark on the stratigraphy. Seasonal flooding was indicated by a meshed debris of twigs, bits of leather and other rubbish; this was often interleaved with sand transported by fast flowing currents, and peat which has built up in times of still water. The bank was occasionally eroded by the swiftness of the river.

Diatoms were present in the majority of the samples analysed, and were dominated in all cases by freshwater, periphytic forms. Virtually no fully marine diatoms were recorded, but salt-tolerant species were represented in varying numbers throughout the samples. This suggests that a weak tidal influence may have been felt as far upstream as the bwe82 site during the Roman and early medieval period (Roberts 1984).

Appendix: Radio-carbon Dating (Fig. 5.19)

Many of the stakes and wattles were sampled for radio-carbon dates; some contexts were fairly well dated by pottery, such as those from cg15 (LUB 4), cg27 (LUB 9) and cg39 (LUB 10). But the radio carbon-dating of stakes cg25 (LUB 7) and possible fishweirs cg31 and cg35 (both LUB 8) indicated that they were late Saxon in origin, rather than Roman, as originally presumed.

LUB	cg	radio-carbon dates
4	cg15	AD260 ± 80
7	cg25	AD870 ± 70
8	cg31	AD780 ± 80
8	cg35	AD1000 ± 70
9	cg27	AD850 ± 70
10	cg39	AD1000 ± 70

Fig 5.19. Radio-carbon dates by grouped context.

These dates are of course to be used with caution, and can only be accepted with confidence by allowing for the standard deviations. Stratigraphically cg31 (LUB 8) is later than cg25 (LUB 7) but it has an earlier radio-carbon date. Wattles cg31 and cg35 (both LUB 8) have been interpreted as being contemporary (as they can be from the stratigraphy) and can be seen as part of the same structure. These possibly suggest the re-use of wood and even the repair of long standing structures. The pottery from loosely associated contexts was dated between the late 10th and late 11th centuries.

6. Brayford Wharf North 1975 (bwn75)

Introduction

Excavations to the north of Brayford Pool were carried out in December 1975 in order to evaluate the site for further investigation, which in the event did not prove possible. The site was formerly occupied by Victorian printing, engineering, and organ building works. It lay within the medieval suburb of Newland, whose name was first mentioned in 1163–6 (Hill 1948, 157; Cameron 1985, 85). The work was undertaken under the supervision, first of Michael Jones and then of Robert Jones, for the Lincoln Archaeological Trust. Funding was provided by Lincoln County Borough Council and the Department of the Environment.

Three trenches were excavated by machine (Figs. 6.1–2). Trenches 1 and 2 were aligned north–south; Trench 1a was an extension to the east at the north end of Trench 1. Some of the major features observed in these trenches were planned and the west section of Trench 1 and the north section of Trench 1a were drawn; this left many contexts unplanned at the time when the trenches were backfilled, a decision taken outside the control of the Trust. Interim accounts were published (Jones and Jones 1976, Jones 1981a).

Of the 198 contexts 194 were interpreted into 88 context groups (cg1–cg99, not using cg25, cg43, cg44, cg46, cg47, cg49, cg70, cg71, cg84 and cg87) and 4 were found to be unstratified. The grouped contexts are discussed below as 32 land-use blocks, (LUBs 1–32; Fig. 6.12). There are 6 areas used in the LUB diagram (Figs. 6.2 and 6.3). Area 1 covers the whole of Trench 2, in which very little was recorded – only part of LUB 22 and the floating LUB 17. Areas 2–6 cover Trench 1, starting in the south with Area 2 and finishing in the north with Area 5; Trench 1a is Area 6. Area 1 includes LUBs 17 and 22; Area 2 includes LUBs 19, 22–4 and 30; Area 3 includes LUBs 13, 16, 18–22, 26–7, 30–31; Area 4 includes LUBs 1, 2, 4–5, 8, 11–16, 18, 25–30 and 32; Area 5 includes LUBs 1, 4–

6, 8–10, 18 and 30; Area 6 includes LUBs 1–4, 7, 18 and 30.

No dating evidence survives the excavation – all finds were lost – but a tentative sequence of events can be established from the drawn sections. Building material was recorded in the context records, but nothing was retained. In view of the lack of dating evidence, the site has been subdivided for post-excavation analysis into sections relating to the sequence and nature of the land-use blocks: river silts and bank consolidation; river silts and stone-founded walls; river silts and riverside activity; waterfront structure and water edge; activity to the north of the water edge; clearance and late activity. Post-excavation stratigraphic analysis was carried out by Chris Guy and later by Kate Steane. Plans and sections were digitized by Helen Palmer Brown and Zoe Rawlings.

Interpretation of the sequence of events

River silts and bank consolidation

At the limit of excavation in Areas 4, 5, and 6 were river silts **LUB 1**; these were cut by two channels **LUB 2**, one in Area 4 and the other in Area 6, possibly associated with flood prevention. In Area 6 the channel LUB 2 was sealed by dumps **LUB 3**. River silting **LUB 4** covered Areas 4 and 5 and even part of 6, sealing LUBs 2 and 3. Cutting through the silts LUB 4 were river-edge features **LUB 5**. In Area 5 there was evidence for bank consolidation **LUB 6**, cutting into LUB 4. To the north of the site in Area 6 were traces of a structure **LUB 7**, sealing both LUB 3 and LUB 4.

LUB 1 River silts (Figs. 6.8 and 6.9)

At the limit of excavation in Area 6 was black clay with much charcoal cg73 (between 4.57m and 4.69m

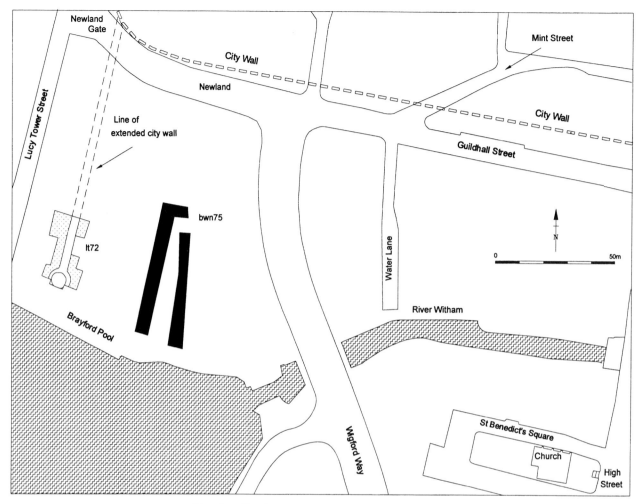

Fig. 6.1 Site location plan for bwn75. (1:1,543)

OD) and layers of sandy silt cg74 (between 4.55m and 4.90m OD). Sealing cg73 and cg74 was a layer of sandy soil with charcoal flecks cg75.

At the bottom of the trench in Area 5, there was a deposit cg1 of sandy silt (between 4.22m and 4.45m OD), which merged with a layer of silt with charcoal flecks (between 4.35m and 4.80m OD). This appeared to have been scooped out by the river, in Area 5, and sealed by silty clay, over which was clayey soil with charcoal flecks, and very fine sand, over which was sandy soil with a few patches of sand and charcoal flecks cg3. These silty sandy layers probably represent river silts.

Also sealing cg1, but in Area 4, was a layer of sandy clay over which, towards its south end, was a thin layer of mixed clay, cg90.

Further south (about 4.6m south of cg1) in Area 4 were layers cg2 (between 3.55m and 4.05m OD); these consisted of a layer of sandy silt, sealed by a deposit of clay, over which were layers of sandy silt (due to the limit of excavation there was no record of what these layers sealed). Sealing cg2 was a layer

of clay with a few charcoal flecks, the northern part of which was sealed by a thin layer of clay cg59. Both cg2 and cg59 probably represent waterlain material.

At the limit of excavation at the south end of Area 4, were layers cg7 (between 4.06m and 4.72m OD); these consisted of a layer of clay which was overlain to the north by a deposit of clay with some charcoal flecks, with a spread of patchy clay above it, and to the south by silt, over which was fine sandy silt with much charcoal and clay. Layers cg7 probably also represent waterlain material.

Waterlain layers visible in the section were only recorded in Areas 4, 5 and 6; presumably any waterlain deposits at this stage in Areas 2 and 3 lay below the excavated levels.

LUB 2 Channels (Fig. 6.9)
Cutting through river silts cg90 and cg59 in Area 4, was a cut with a fill of clay with much charcoal cg4. The feature was 3.75m wide and over 0.43m deep. It may have represented a channel running east–

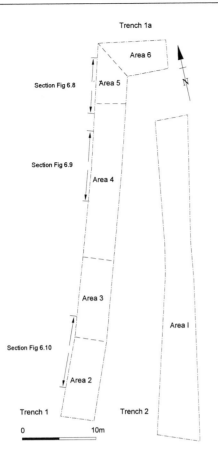

Trench 1a

Area 6

Section Fig 6.8   Area 5

N

Section Fig 6.9

Area 4

Area 3

Area I

Section Fig 6.10

Area 2

Trench 1   Trench 2

0   10m

Fig. 6.2 Plan showing areas and sections for bwn75. (1:500)

west, parallel to the river as a form of flood prevention.

In Area 6 layer cg75 was cut by cg76, a feature with a fill of dark greyish-brown sandy soil with some clay. It would appear to cut diagonally across the site – possibly running north-west to south-east. There was no indication of depth or width. This channel may have been associated with flood prevention or drainage (in advance of development).

LUB 3 Dumps
Sealing cg76 (LUB 2) in Area 6, was a layer of yellow mortar with many stones cg77. Sealing cg77 was a layer of dark greyish soil with charcoal flecks and orange sand cg78.

LUB 4 River silts (Figs. 6.8 and 6.9)
Possible channel cg4 (LUB 2) was sealed by river silts with much charcoal cg56 in Area 4. Over these were sandy layers, including charcoal and clay cg5. This material was probably equivalent to cg57 to the north (which sealed cg90 LUB 1); deposit cg57 included mortar and charcoal. Over it were sand and clay layers cg17.

In Area 6, cutting cg78 (LUB 3), was a scoop cg79 with a fill of dark brown soil with limestone rubble.

Sealing cg79 was a layer of dark brown sandy soil cg81.

LUB 5 Features (Fig. 6.8)
Cutting cg5 and cg17 (LUB 4) in Area 4 was a feature cg6, possibly a gully (0.44m wide and 0.4m deep with a rounded bottom). Further south, cutting cg56 (LUB 4), was another feature cg58, *c* 0.65m wide (but wider at the top) and at least 0.55m deep, with steep sides. At the bottom of the feature was a wooden post cg8 with its top leaning to the south. The fill of the feature was a fine clayey soil with much charcoal. These features may perhaps indicate another move towards river control or they may somehow have been related to fishing or riverside mooring.

LUB 6 Bank consolidation (Fig. 6.8)
Possibly later than the channel cg4 (LUB 2) in Area 5, was what might have been consolidation of the bank. A large post-pit cg14 cut river silts cg3 (LUB 1). Within the post-pit was the ghost of a substantial post (*c* 0.28m wide and at least 0.47m deep). The backfill of the post-pit seemed to have spilled out over layer cg3, as gritty silty soil cg13; this may have happened through river action or may have been part of a dump of material up against the timber.

In Area 5, at the limit of excavation, there was a layer of silt with crushed limestone, a few small stones and charcoal flecks cg93, which might represent dumping associated with the timber bank consolidation.

LUB 7 Structure 1?
In Area 6, cutting cg78 (LUB 3), was a pit or posthole cg82 with a fill of very dark grey clay. Partly sealing cg79 (LUB 4) was limestone rubble set in yellow mortar cg80, over which (and over cg82) was a layer of yellow clay cg83, which was cut by a pit cg85 with a fill of fine sandy soil with mortar.

Stone-founded walls and river silts

Sealing features LUB 5 and the remains of the bank consolidation LUB 6 were dumps **LUB 8**, in preparation for the construction of a substantial stone-founded wall **LUB 9**, the construction of which was followed by further dumps **LUB 10** to the north. Up against the river side of the wall (LUB 9) were possible river silts **LUB 11** in Area 4. Cutting these was another wall **LUB 12**.

Structure 1 (LUB 7) may have continued in use in Area 6 during this phase.

LUB 8 Dumps (Fig. 6.8)
Layer cg13 (LUB 6), in Area 5, was sealed by a fairly gritty soil with a few traces of decayed vegetation

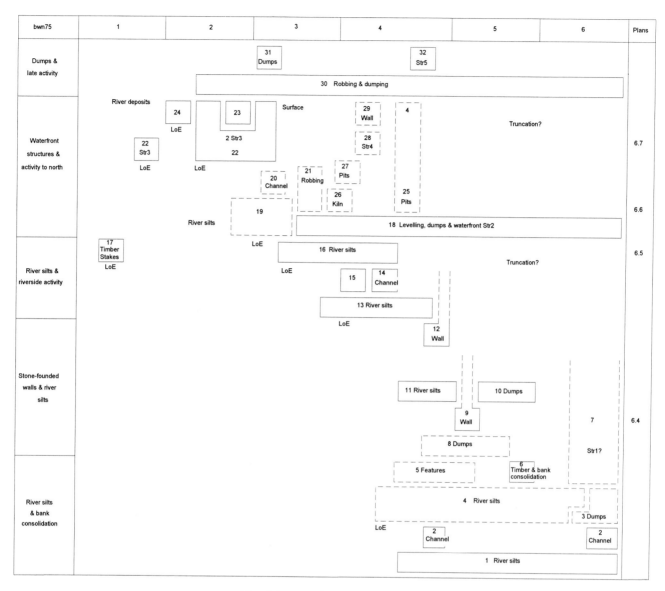

Fig. 6.3 LUB diagram for bwn75.

and charcoal and a thin layer of gritty clay, overlying which was fairly gritty soil with a lens of clay cg15. These layers may represent a build-up of marginal ground as part of river bank consolidation. They may be equivalent to a layer of soil with a few mortar flecks sealed by a layer of mixed clay cg18 in Area 4; this sealed feature cg6 (LUB 5) and layers cg17 (LUB 4).

LUB 9 Wall (Fig. 6.4 and 6.8)
In Area 5, cutting through cg18 to the south and cg15 (both LUB 8) to the north, were substantial stone foundations cg37 (0.4m wide and 0.65m deep) of large stones set in sandy mortar.

It would appear that this wall represented the river edge, the limit of river flooding, with the river to the south and dry land to the north. The wall was

partially planned and apparently turned to the south. This might suggest that perhaps the wall represented part of a jetty complex or even a boathouse, but the interpretation is not clear.

LUB 10 Dumps (Fig. 6.8)
To the north of the stone foundations cg37 in Area 5, and sealing cg15 (LUB 8), was a dump of very compact soil with a few tiles and charcoal flecks sealed by clay cg94; further north in Area 5, dumps of gritty soil with small stones and charcoal flecks cg16 sealed cg13 (LUB 6).

LUB 11 River silts? (Fig. 6.8)
In Area 4, sealing the construction trench of wall cg37 (LUB 9) to the south, were layers of sand with small pebbles, patches of clay and charcoal cg34.

These layers may represent waterlain layers, abutting the wall cg37.

LUB 12 Wall (Fig. 6.9)
About 6m south of wall cg37 in Area 4, cutting through cg34 (LUB 11), were the foundations of another wall cg35; the foundations, 0.4m deep and at least 0.7m north–south, consisted of limestone rubble in clayey soil.

River silts and riverside activity

Up against wall LUB 12 were river silts **LUB 13** (Area 4) in which there was evidence for an east–west channel **LUB 14** and a river-edge pit **LUB 15**. These were sealed by further river silts **LUB 16** which spread over Areas 3 and 4. In Area 1 there was a row of east–west stakes **LUB 17** which may belong to this phase of the site.

LUB 13 River silts (Fig. 6.9)
Sealing feature cg58 (LUB 5) in Area 4 was an extensive layer of fine sandy soil with much charcoal, a spread of slightly clayey soil with lenses of clay and some charcoal and mortar cg10; there was a lens of clay cg60. These layers possibly butted up against wall cg35 (LUB 12); any direct relationship had been removed by later robber trench cg36 (LUB 18).

At the limit of the excavation, to the south of Area 4, was a layer of clay over which was a thin layer of silty clay, which was sealed in turn by a layer of mixed clay cg11. Layers cg11 also probably represent waterlain silts.

To the south of cg11, also in Area 4 and at the limit of excavation, there was a layer with wood traces cg62. This was sealed by a layer of dark brown sandy soil cg65 over which was a layer of mixed clay with gravel which merged with a layer of clay mixed with soil cg19. These dark layers with wood traces suggest flood debris. Immediately to the south of these, at the limit of excavation, was a deposit of black clay cg64, suggestive of a river flood deposit.

LUB 14 Channel
Further south in Area 4, cutting cg10 and cg11 (LUB 13), was a channel cg61 over 2m across. To the north it was cut by postholes cg9 and cg12. It had a fill of silty clay with patches of clay. This may relate to river control or fishing activity.

LUB 15 Riverside pit with burning
Deposits cg64 and cg19 (LUB 13), south of Area 4, were cut by a pit with a fill of clay with extensive traces of burning on the surface cg21.

LUB 16 River silting
Sealing channel cg61 (LUB 14) was a deposit of

mixed clay cg63. Cutting cg63 was a scoop with a bottom fill of sandy clay, over which was a very dark greyish-brown clayey soil sealed by a layer of greyish-brown clay cg20.

Sealing pit cg21 (LUB 15), to the south of Area 4, was very dark brown clay cg66. Probably equivalent to this, in Area 3, was grey-black sandy clay with lenses of white ash cg67 (at the limit of excavation). These deposits suggest marginal river deposits, the river being used as a dumping ground for ash.

LUB 17 Timber stakes (Fig. 6.5)
In Area 1 a row of east–west stakes cg91 was discernible: their stratigraphic context was not recorded. However, it seems possible that the stakes were associated with marginal river deposit cg67 (LUB 16). They may mark the river-front at some period.

Waterfront structures and water edge

Over much of Areas 3, 4, 5 and 6 there was evidence for levelling and dumping, and to the west in Area 3, the construction of a waterfront structure **LUB 18**. To the south of this were river silts **LUB 19**, cut by a channel **LUB 20**. The waterfront structure was robbed **LUB 21**. Replacing it in Area 2 was a substantial waterfront structure **LUB 22** of mortared stone. There were dumps and surfaces within the structure **LUB 23**. To the south there was evidence of river deposits **LUB 24**.

LUB 18 Levelling, dumps and waterfront: Structure 2 (Fig. 6.8 and 6.9)
Over the southern part of Area 5 and most of Area 4, there was a concerted operation involving the levelling of the underlying features, the robbing cg36 of wall cg35 (LUB 13), and a dump of clayey soil cg38 sealing the whole area, including cg36, cg34 (LUB 11), cg94 (LUB 10), cg10 and cg60 (LUB 13). In Areas 5 and 6, dump cg16 and clay cg83 were sealed by an extent of loam cg72.

In Area 3, sealing clay with ash cg67 (LUB 16), was a deposit of sandy clay, sealed by clay with stones cg23. This dump was probably associated with a waterfront structure, only indicated by its robbing (LUB 21).

LUB 19 River silts (Fig. 6.10)
Sealing cg67 (LUB 16), in Area 3, was very dark sandy clay with traces of wood cg22.

In Area 2, at the limit of excavation, was a layer containing charcoal and possible traces of wood cg95, possibly the remains of waterlain material.

LUB 20 Channel? (Fig. 6.10)
Cut through cg22 (LUB 19), to the south of Area 3,

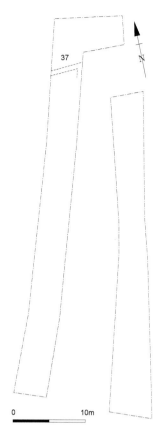

Fig. 6.4 Wall cg37: LUB 9. (1:500)

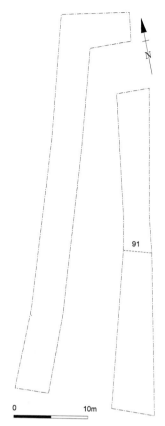

Fig. 6.5 Stake-line cg91: LUB 17. (1:500)

was a pit or channel cg27; it was *c* 1.53m wide at the top, had fairly steep sides and was at least 0.71m deep, the bottom not being observed. It was backfilled with sandy clay with a few fragments of stone, tile and animal bone.

LUB 21 Robbing of Structure 2

Dumps cg23 (LUB 18) in Area 3 were cut by a robber trench cg26; this was 4.6m long and 0.76m deep with vertical sides and a very uneven base. It was filled with clay with limestone rubble and tile.

LUB 22 Waterfront: Structure 3
(Figs. 6.7, 6.10 and 6.11)

To the south of the trench in Areas 1, 2, and 3 was the latest waterfront structure on the site. Fronting the Brayford was an east–west wall cg24 of mortared limestone at the limit of excavation (there was no stratigraphic record of what this wall cut). It was 0.8m wide, at least 1.8m high and at least 15.5m long. From the photographic record it is apparent that there was another east–west mortared limestone wall cg92 (there was no stratigraphic record of what it cut, but it was at least 2.30m long, and of similar width and build to cg24). Between walls cg92 and cg24 was a straight butt joint, which suggests that an

opening on to the river may have existed at one time, and/or that the walls belonged to different properties.

Sealing cg95 (LUB 19) were dumps of mortar and rubble cg99, which lay between east–west wall cg24 and another east–west wall cg98 *c* 5m to the north. This was of mortared limestone, 0.7m wide and at least 4.5m in length, and probably cut cg27 (LUB 20). Set into the dumps cg99 was a stone-lined drain cg97 (*c* 0.13m deep), which ran between the two walls and was integral with each. The walls, drain, and dumps were all part of one construction.

In Area 1, what was an eastwards continuation of the south wall cg24 was sealed by thickening cg89.

LUB 23 Dumps and surfaces within Structure 3
(Fig. 6.10)

The drain cg97 (LUB 22) was sealed by dumps of clayey soil with mortar and fragments of tile and limestone, over which was some extensive burning cg96. Over this were patches of mortar, a layer of soil, a layer of clay, a layer of dark brown soil with much clay and mortar, a thin patchy layer of mortar and crushed limestone and another layer of soil cg45. Over these was a layer of soil, a layer of clay, a layer

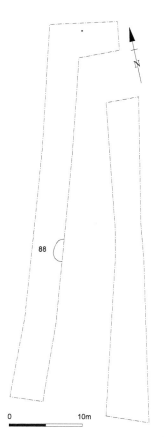

Fig. 6.6 *Kiln or oven cg88: LUB 26. (1:500)*

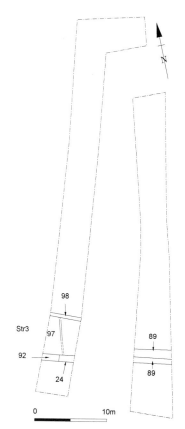

Fig. 6.7 *Waterfront, structure 3 with walls and drain cg24, cg92 and cg89: LUB 22. (1:500)*

of soil with much limestone overlain by a patchy layer of mortar cg48. These layers possibly represent a sequence of make-up dumps and surfaces between the two walls cg24.

LUB 24 River deposits
To the south of Structure 3 (LUB 22), in Area 2 at the limit of excavation, was dark brown soil with charcoal flecks cg51, possibly a river deposit.

Activity to the north of the water's edge

While there was activity along the waterfront (Structures 2 and 3), there were contemporary traces of occupation on the dry land to the north. Cutting dumps LUB 18 were pits LUB 25 in Area 4. In Area 3 there was a kiln or oven **LUB 26**; a layer possibly associated with this was cut by pits **LUB 27**, which in turn were cut by the robbed foundations of a building **LUB 28**. This was cut by the robbed foundations of a later wall **LUB 29**.

LUB 25 Pits (Fig. 6.8 and Fig. 6.9)
Cutting cg38 (LUB 18) in Area 5 was a possible pit cg41 (at least 2.4m wide and more than 0.5m deep), with a fill of mixed clayey soil with fragments of

brick and stone. Cutting cg72 (LUB 18) was another possible pit cg42 (at least 0.34m deep and at least 0.6m north–south), with a fill of gritty clayey soil with some stones.

Cutting cg38 (LUB 18) in Area 4 was a possible pit cg39, 2.18m north–south and 0.28m deep (truncated), with a fill of burnt limestone and clay. It was cut by another possible pit cg40, 3.15m north–south and over 0.17m deep (truncated), with a fill of clay.

LUB 26 Kiln or oven (Fig. 6.6)
Sealing dump cg23 (LUB 18) in Area 3 was a spread of mortar with stones cg68. Possibly associated with this, on the other side of the trench (also in Area 3), were the remains of an oven cg88 at 5.05m OD, probably cutting into dump cg23. There was no description of these remains.

LUB 27 Pits
In Area 3, cutting cg68 (LUB 26), was pit cg28 which was 4.6m long and 0.76m deep with vertical sides; it was filled with clay with limestone rubble and tile. This was cut to the north in Area 4 by pit cg29, 2.05m north–south and 0.54m deep, with a clay fill. Pit cg29 was cut by pit cg69, (0.75m long and 0.31m deep), with a fill of yellow grey clay; it was cut in

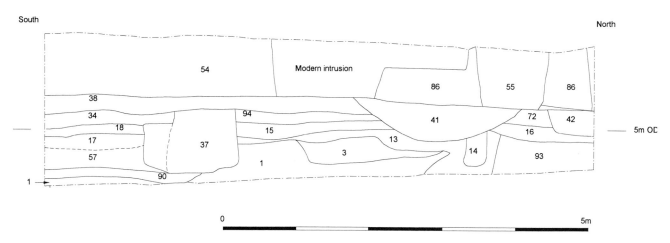

Fig. 6.8 Section of the west side of most of Area 5 (extending into Area 4 to the south) illustrating the stratigraphy here, from LUB 1 to LUB 32. (1:50)

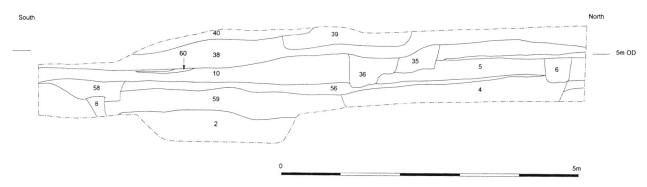

Fig. 6.9 Section of the west side of some of Area 4, illustrating the stratigraphy here, from LUB 1 to LUB 25. (1:62)

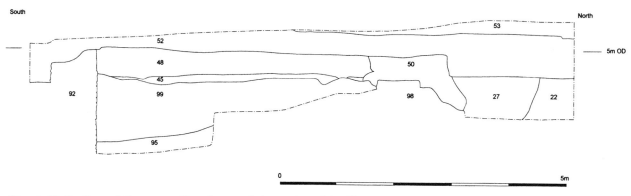

Fig. 6.10 Section of the west side of part of Areas 2 and 3, illustrating the stratigraphy here, from LUB 19 to LUB 31. (1:64)

turn by a pit cg30 containing cinders (0.84m long and 0.21m deep).

LUB 28 Structure 4

Pit cg30 (LUB 27) in Area 4 was sealed by mortar and brick fragments cg31, probably construction debris. Probably cutting cg38 (LUB 18) was a structure of which only the robbed foundations cg32 remained. These were 4.60m north–south and over 0.60m deep. Little of the sides was observed but the bottom was reasonably flat. The fill was of mixed clay and limestone rubble to the south, and soil with sand and charcoal to the north, with mortar with a few brick and tile fragments between.

Fig. 6.11 *Looking south, wall cg92 to the right and wall cg24 to the left; stone-lined drain cg97 along the centre, of one build with wall cg24 to the left and wall cg98 in the foreground.*

LUB 29 Wall and robbing

Robber trench cg32 (LUB 28) was cut by a later wall of which only the robber trench cg33 (0.6m wide and 0.65m deep) survived; it was vertical sided with a flat base. The lower fill was limestone rubble set in mortar, perhaps the remains of the wall. Overlying this there was a fill of clay with limestone rubble. Because of the way the trench was excavated the alignment of this wall is unknown.

Dumps and late activity

Structure 3 (LUB 22) was robbed and sealed by dumping which extended from Areas 2 to 6 **LUB 30**. There were further dumps **LUB 31** in Area 3 and traces of a building in Area 4 **LUB 32**.

LUB 30 Robbing and dumping (Figs. 6.8 and 6.10)

The wall cg98 (LUB 22) was robbed cg50 and it was sealed by dump cg52, which consisted of brick, tile and limestone over which loam had been laid.

cg/LUB	cg/LUB	cg/LUB	cg/LUB	cg/LUB	cg/LUB
1/1	18/8	35/12	52/31	68/26	84/–
2/1	19/13	36/18	53/31	69/27	85/7
3/1	20/16	37/9	54/30	70/–	86/30
4/2	21/15	38/18	55/32	71/–	87/–
5/4	22/19	39/25	56/4	72/18	88/26
6/5	23/18	40/25	57/4	73/1	89/22
7/1	24/22	41/25	58/5	74/1	90/1
8/5	25/–	42/25	59/1	75/1	91/17
9/14	26/21	43/–	60/13	76/2	92/22
10/13	27/20	44/–	61/14	77/3	93/6
11/13	28/27	45/23	62/13	78/3	94/10
12/14	29/27	46/–	63/16	79/4	95/19
13/6	30/27	47/–	64/13	80/7	96/23
14/6	31/28	48/23	65/13	81/4	97/22
15/8	32/28	49/–	66/16	82/7	98/22
16/6	33/29	50/30	67/16	83/7	99/22
17/4	34/11	51/24			

Fig. 6.12 *Concordance of cg numbers with LUB numbers for bwn75.*

In Areas 4 and 5, pit cg40 (LUB 24) and cg38 (LUB 18) were truncated, (together with other archaeological remains of which there is now no trace), and sealed by an extensive and thick deposit of clayey soil with mortar and limestone fragments, sealed by loam layers, over which were further layers of clayey loam with tile fragments, charcoal flecks and small stones and brick fragments cg54. In Area 5 and 6 there were dumps of dark loam and rubble cg86 sealing cg41 (LUB 24) and cg72 (LUB 19).

LUB 31 Dumps (Fig. 6.10)

Above cg52 (LUB 31) in Area 2 there was modern brick rubble with cement and mortar cg53.

LUB 32 Structure 5 (Fig. 6.8)

Cutting dumps cg54 (LUB 31) in Area 5, was evidence for a structure with concrete foundations. Possibly associated with this was trench cg55, (1m wide and 0.8m deep), with a fill of loam.

Discussion of bwn75

At the beginning of the sequence the site was on the edge of the Brayford Pool – c 60m from its present line. The waterfront rose gradually from south to north; this is clear from the LUB diagram which shows the change in phase at the depth limit of excavation. The base of the trench contained evidence of early land use (LUBs 1–4) in Areas 4–6, in contrast to much later use (LUBs 19, 22 and 24) in Areas 1 and 2. The depth of the excavation trench was more or less consistent, indicating that stratigraphic evidence was lost below the limit of excavation in Areas 1, 2 and 3. There was similar loss of later stratigraphy in Areas 5 and 6, due to two episodes which involved levelling, LUBs 18 and 30; on each occasion deposits had been removed in Areas 5 and 6 in an attempt to level the land surface.

The early remains of substantial timber river bank consolidation (LUB 6) in Area 5 could represent Roman construction, replaced later in stone (LUBs 9 and 12). This would mean that the river silts (LUB 13) may represent post-Roman deposits, followed by activity in the Late Saxon period (LUBs 14 and 15) in Area 4. Levelling, dumps and waterfront Structure 2 (LUB 18) may then be medieval, replaced in the late or post-medieval period by Structure 3 (LUB 22). Further levelling (LUB 30) would possibly have occurred in the late post-medieval or early modern period. Dumps (LUB 31) and Structure 5 (LUB 32) appear to be modern.

The waterfront appears to have been advanced southwards from the time of the earliest deposits onwards, partly as a response to rises in river level. Today it lies *c* 15m to the south of the late or post-medieval waterfront Structure 3 (LUB 22), and between 50–60m to the south of possible Roman timber and bank consolidation (LUB 6) and Roman wall (LUB 9). The edge of the Brayford Pool was not at first clearly definable (LUB 1); then there was bank consolidation (LUB 6) in Area 5, later a wall (LUB 9) about 3.5m to the south of LUB 6 in Area 4, and a further wall (LUB 12) about 7m to the south of LUB 9. Later there was Structure 2 (LUB 18) in Area 3, and Structure 3 (LUB 22) in Areas 1 and 2. The purpose of advancing the Pool edge further south was possibly linked with the need to deepen the river for larger boats; the deeper the river was cut, the more narrow its width. This would have been advantageous to water craft; larger boats would be able to tie up in deeper water. Another factor was the need for more land to the north of the river for development, and hence the levelling of the land by the river. The existence of the river-edge structures emphasises the importance of the waterways as a means of transporting goods. It seems possible that Structure 2 (LUB 18) and Structure 3 (LUB 22) both represented substantial quays at which boats moored during the movement of goods.

7. Dickinson's Mill 1972 (dm72)

Introduction

In the winter of 1972–3, an opportunity arose to examine an area to the east of Brayford Pool following demolition of the 19th-century Dickinson's Flour Mill and a further mill to the north. Although a very large area was available, the disturbance caused by the foundations of the mill and the high level of the water table (1.10m below ground surface) meant that the plan for a long east–west trench from the High Street to the Brayford (Trench I) was partially abandoned and another trench was opened up to the north-west (Trench II). The site objectives were to reach Roman levels, examine the medieval occupation, investigate the nature of any structures and locate a waterfront sequence together with any wharfs. The excavation was carried out under the supervision of Robert Jones for the Lincoln Archaeological Trust. Funding was provided by Lincoln County Borough Council and the Department of the Environment. An interim report was published

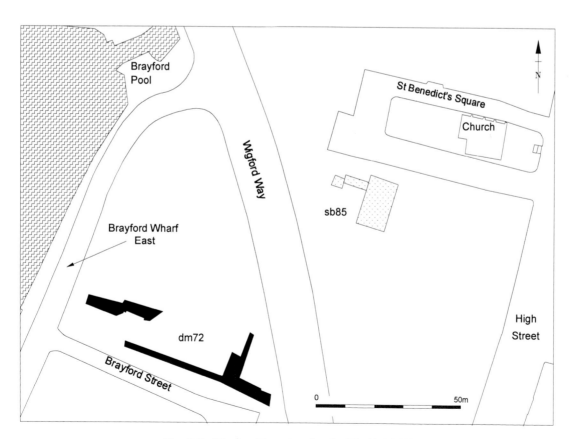

Fig. 7.1 Site location plan for dm72. (1:1,250)

in The Trust's First Annual report (Jones 1973); the site was later included in a report on the sites outside the walled city (Jones 1981b).

The OD heights given in this report are estimates based on an OS spot height and two of the section drawings. The 82 contexts were interpreted as 35 context groups (cg1–cg35). The context groups are discussed below as 18 land-use blocks, LUBs 0–17 (Fig. 7.18). The three areas on the LUB diagram correspond to the west of Trench I, the east of Trench I and Trench II (Figs. 7.2 and 7.3). The site narrative is ordered chronologically, combining the trenches into a single sequence (Fig. 7.3). Trench I covers most of the stratified archaeology, Roman to late Saxon (LUB 0), late Saxon (LUBs 1–5), medieval (LUB 11), post-medieval (LUBs 12–16) and modern (LUB 17). There was further medieval activity in Trench II (LUBs 6–10), and some of modern date (LUB 17).

A total of 285 Roman pottery sherds and 490 post-Roman pottery sherds was recovered from the site; a specialist report on the Roman mortaria was prepared (Hartley 1973). In Trench II, anaerobic conditions had preserved parts of a clinker-built boat reused in the construction of medieval bank consolidation or a wharf (interpreted with advice from P Marsden; see LUB 7), but there were no other finds. Few registered finds were recovered from Trench I (26), doubtless due at least in part to the disturbance of earlier levels by the mill foundations, and to the difficulties of excavation presented by the height of the water table. Material from Trench I included hones (Moore 1991), Roman glass (Cool and Price 1987a), post-medieval glass (Henderson 1988) and bone finds (Rackham 1994); all metalwork was heavily corroded. Most of the building material (115 fragments were recovered) from this site was medieval/post-medieval ceramic tile, including a Dutch tin-glazed example (Downey and Young 1984). A very small assemblage of animal bone (375 fragments) was recovered from the site, the majority of recorded contexts dating to the late Saxon period (Dobney *et al* 1994b). Assessment of selected soil samples was undertaken and a report produced on the land and freshwater snails (Milles 1993) and on the charred plant remains (Moffett 1993).

Post-excavation stratigraphic analysis was carried out by Chris Guy and later by Kate Steane. Maggi Darling worked on the Roman pottery; Jane Young examined the post-Roman pottery. Jen Mann analysed the registered finds and, with Rick Kemp, the building materials. Helen Palmer Brown and Zoe Rawlings digitized the plans and Dave Watt drew the finds illustrations.

Interpretation of the sequence of events

Roman to Late Saxon (Anglo-Scandinavian)

At the limit of excavation in Trench I was a layer of peat **LUB 0**, which on artefactual evidence had probably accumulated during or after the Roman period.

LUB 0 Peat
Peat cg1 was observed at the limit of excavation to the east of Trench I (no OD height available). A

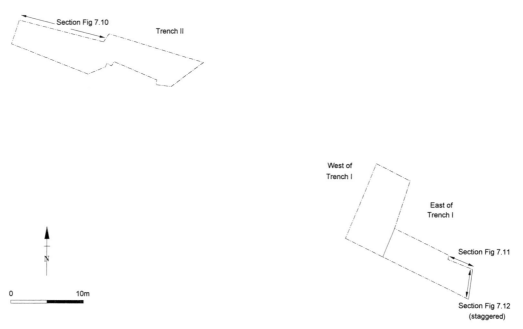

Fig. 7.2 Plan showing trenches and sections for dm72. (1:500)

small piece of lead waste, a fragment of box-flue tile and possible 4th-century pottery were recovered from peat cg1 suggesting that the peat was accumulating in the Roman period or later.

Late Saxon

Over the peat in Trench I were deposits from the river **LUB 1** with pottery which dated them to the second half of the 10th century. This was sealed by an area of hardstanding **LUB 2** of probable 11th-century date as suggested by pottery from adjacent river deposits. Later, there was some evidence for a timber building, Structure 1 **LUB 3**, associated with river dredging **LUB 4**. The traces of the building were sealed by waterlain deposits **LUB 5**. Pottery from LUBs 4 and 5 suggests an 11th-century date.

LUB 1 River silts and peat (Figs. 7.11–12)
Overlying peat cg1 (LUB 0) and extending over the whole of the excavated area of Trench 1 was sand cg2 at 2.3m OD; overlying this at the west end of the trench was peat cg3 sealed by silt cg4. The earliest pottery recovered came from the waterlain deposits of sand cg2 (four post-Roman sherds), peat cg3 (29 post-Roman sherds), and silt cg4 (37 post-Roman sherds). With the exception of one NOTS bowl, one SNX sherd and one intrusive medieval sherd, the pottery is all of Lincoln or local manufacture and dates to the mid to late 10th century.

In cg2 97% of the potsherds were of Roman date

and this fell to 72% in cg3 and 34% in cg4. Most of the post-Roman pottery consisted of medium sized unworn, heavily sooted sherds with little leaching of the shell. Several vessels were represented by more than one sherd and there were cross deposit joins, indicating either contemporary dumping or post-depositional movement of finds. It is impossible to choose between these options on the available evidence.

LUB 2 Hard-standing (Figs. 7.4 and 7.13)
Sealing river silt cg4 (LUB 1) was a make-up layer of sand, clay and gritty soil in which limestone rubble cg5 was set at 2.9m OD. Some of the stones had sunk down into the peat, and it is possible that more than one phase of construction is represented. The extent of the stones was recorded on plan, but not located in section. Pottery from the make-up cg5 (32 post-Roman sherds) consisted of small worn sherds of Lincoln and local shell-tempered wares, the latest being typical of the mid to late 10th century. A few of the sherds of late 9th- to early 10th-century date were obviously residual.

The stones appeared to mark a consolidation of the shore, a "hard-standing", perhaps for boats to be beached on or for access to the Pool. They may have lain at the edge of the pool, as there was an edge where they appear to have been eroded by the river.

Sealing cg4 (LUB 1) to the west of the hard-standing cg5 were silty river deposits cg6. These contained a small group of pottery (13 post-Roman sherds) with the latest sherds dating to the 11th century. This pottery probably gives a better date to the hard-standing cg5.

LUB 3 Structure 1? (Fig. 7.5)
Sealing the stone surface cg5 and the silt cg6 in Trench I were possible traces of a timber building. There was a layer of compact orange soil cg7, possibly a floor, associated with an east–west gully cg35, butted by a north–south running gully cg34. These gullies may represent wall-trenches for a timber building, or might have had a different function.

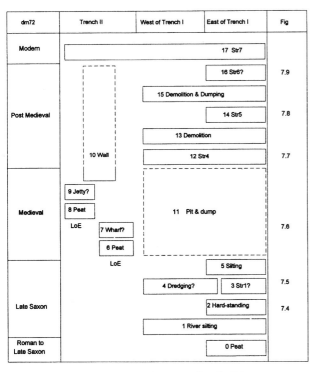

Fig. 7.3 LUB diagram for dm72.

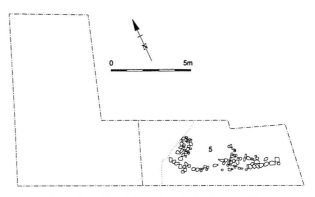

Fig. 7.4 Hardstanding: LUB 2. (1:227)

Since the possible building post-dated silt cg6 it cannot have been constructed before the 11th century. The structure has been interpreted as being contemporary with the possible dredging, LUB 4, and this would indicate a slightly later date for the use of the building but still within the 11th century.

LUB 4 Dumping

Contemporary with the building in Trench I was a series of layers cg10 to the west which may have been the result of dumping. Some of the deposits contained a great deal of shell, and a small amount of pottery (21 post-Roman sherds) and bone. These dumps may have been laid down for reclamation purposes. The latest sherds date to the 11th century. Two vessels are represented by more than one sherd.

LUB 5 Silting

The possible building traces cg7, cg34 and cg35 (all LUB 3) were sealed by silt and sands cg8, possibly waterlain deposits from the river; cg8 contained a small group of mostly residual pottery (20 post-Roman sherds), the latest sherds, in a SNX fabric, may date to the 11th century.

Medieval

In Trench II, towards the river to the west, the earliest deposit uncovered was peat **LUB 6** into which a timber consolidation of the bank or a timber wharf was constructed **LUB 7**. There is no pottery dating for these LUBs, but the fragments of reused boat (LUB 7) were identified as being of medieval construction. This was partially sealed by peat **LUB 8**, which had been cut by the piles for a stone structure, possibly a jetty **LUB 9**. The peat contained pottery sherds dating to the High to late medieval periods and pottery from LUB 9 dated to the late medieval period. The jetty was removed and sealed by a dump, and into it an east–west wall was set **LUB 10**; no dating was associated with this activity, which could have been any time from the late medieval period to the mid 19th century, when the mill was built.

In Trench I the land was raised with dumps **LUB 11** which sealed those in LUB 5. Pottery from the dumps dated to the High to late medieval periods, considerably later than the Saxo-Norman pottery from LUB 5, suggesting either a gap in deposition or some sort of truncation.

LUB 6 River peat

The river margins in Trench II were represented by a build-up of peat cg24 (no OD height was available); there was no dating evidence.

LUB 7 Reclamation and consolidation? or wharf? (*Figs. 7.6, 7.10, 7.14 and 7.15*)

In Trench II cutting the peat cg24 (LUB 6) was a timber structure, either bank consolidation or a wharf cg25 formed of fragments of a clinker-built boat held in position by eight piles on the west side and two tie-beams to the east (the timber had survived due to the anaerobic conditions). Visible in the south section to the east of the planks was a horizontal beam which appears to have tied the construction to the material dumped behind it. A similar beam to the north projected slightly west of the planks and may have acted additionally as an anchor post. A further post can be seen in Section 1 (Fig. 7.10), 3.4m to the west of the structure; this may be part of the same structure. The top of the medieval construction cg25 was at least 3m OD but probably higher.

Peter Marsden, then of the Museum of London, commented (1973) that judging from the location of the diamond-shaped roves (which invariably lay inside medieval boats), from the overlaps of the scarf joints between the individual strakes (which always point to the stern), and from the clinker overlaps between the three strakes represented in this fragment, it is clear that this fragment was from the starboard side of the boat somewhere between the keel and the gunwale. The vessel from which this piece had come was already quite old, for two internal repairs had been made to the middle strake.

An assemblage of freshwater snails was associated with the wharf (Milles 1993). There was no dating evidence associated with this structure but there was medieval or late medieval pottery from the peat cg26 over it.

LUB 8 Peat (*Fig. 7.10*)

A layer of peaty organic material cg26 overlay part of the construction cg25 (LUB 7) to the west of Trench II, suggesting its disuse, and to the east was the limit of excavation; fish-scale was found in this

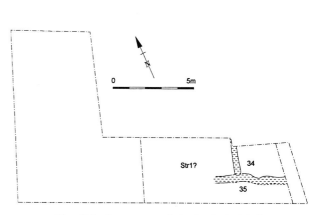

Fig. 7.5 Structure 1?: LUB 3. (1:227)

layer (Moffett 1993). Only seven sherds of post-Roman pottery were recovered, the latest of which can only be broadly dated to between the early 13th and the mid to late 15th centuries.

LUB 9 Jetty? (Figs. 7.10 and 7.16)

In Trench II was an east–west limestone wall set on timber piles cg27 (seen only in the north section, Fig. 7.10) which cut peat cg26 (LUB 8). It was supported on timber piles one of which was 0.10 m in diameter and at least 0.85m long. The limestone blocks which formed the footings were very rotten, possibly because they had been below the water level at 3.5m OD. Set on these footings was a wall of faced blocks, the west end of which was beyond the limit of excavation. It was at least 3.80m long but had been robbed out to the east.

This wall was part of a structure projecting into the Brayford Pool, probably a dock or jetty; it lay further west than the earlier wooden structure cg25 (LUB 7). Pottery from within the footings cg27 (seven post-Roman sherds) suggests that it was built after the mid 14th century to the mid to late 15th century.

LUB 10 East–west wall (Fig. 7.10)

In Trench II the structure cg27 (LUB 9) was robbed cg28; sealing the robber trench was a dump cg29. Into this was set an east–west wall cg30 made of stone blocks. It was at least 2.25m east–west and 0.75m wide. Although the wall cg30 was possibly part of a structure, it seems more likely to have been a boundary in this location.

LUB 11 Pit and dumps? (Figs. 7.11–12)

In Trench I, dump cg8 (LUB 5) was cut by a pit cg9. It was unplanned, as only the bottom of the pit was excavated, suggesting that it may have been cut from higher up. The pit contained a very small assemblage of animal bone with some heavily butchered fragments (Dobney *et al* 1994b). The pit also included a small group of pottery (44 post-Roman sherds) dating to the mid 11th century and an iron knife) of pre-Conquest type. The pottery assemblage contained sherds mainly of contemporary jars and bowls of mid 11th-century date, most represented by several sherds. On the evidence of the finds, the pit was used in the mid 11th century.

The pit was sealed by silty soil cg11 about 1.5m thick, which sealed the whole of Trench I (LUB 5); although much of this layer was removed by machine there were lenses observed within it and it may represent more than one phase of activity. A mixture of material dating from the Roman to the late medieval periods (82 post-Roman sherds) was recovered from cg11. A moderately large animal bone assemblage came from cg11, which consisted mostly of primary butchery waste and possibly some tanning waste (Dobney *et al* 1994b).

Over dumps cg11 were further dumps cg32 varying in thickness, but in places over 1m thick, sealing the whole of Trench I (LUB 5); cg32 contained several lenses suggesting more than one phase of filling had taken place. Dump cg32 produced a small group of pottery (19 post-Roman sherds) possibly dating to the end of the 15th century; fragments of 17th- and 18th-century wine-bottle glass are intrusive, possibly from machining.

Post-Medieval

Sometime in or after the 16th century, Structure 4 was built together with an associated path used by horses **LUB 12**. This was later demolished **LUB 13**, and its demolition deposits contained 17th-century pottery. It was replaced with a building with cellars, Structure 5 **LUB 14**. This in turn was demolished **LUB 15**; the dumping sealing its demolition contained mid to late 17th-century pottery. An ash pit and north–south wall cut the dumps **LUB 16**; these dated any time between the late 17th century to the mid 19th century, when the mill was built.

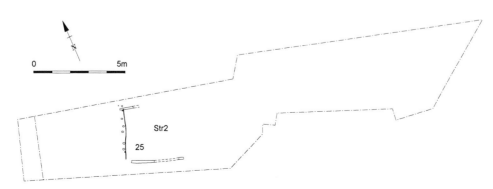

Fig. 7.6 Structure 2: LUB 7. (1:200)

LUB 12 Structure 4 with path
(Figs. 7.7 and 7.11–12)
At the extreme east end of Trench I, cut into dump cg11 (LUB 11) there was a north–south wall of limestone blocks cg13, only seen in the east section of the site (Fig. 7.12). This was at least 1.25m long, and survived to a height of 0.50m (five courses) above an offset course; the width of the wall is unknown. It is not possible to say whether the wall, cg13, was part of a structure or a boundary. It was contemporary and possibly associated with a rough mortar pathway cg12 aligned east–west, stretching across Trench I, and curving to the north at its western end; the pathway had a secondary phase of surface cg31. Iron horseshoe fragments (BB) <Fe5>, (AH) <Fe2> were recovered from both phases of the pathway.

The debris which had formed on the path cg12 contained pottery sherds (seven post-Roman sherds) which dated between the 16th and 18th centuries,

but as the destruction debris (LUB 13) was associated with 17th-century pottery, this gives a stratigraphic *terminus ante quem* for this LUB. To the west of the wall cg13 and to the south-east of the path cg12, was a spread of soil with shells cg17.

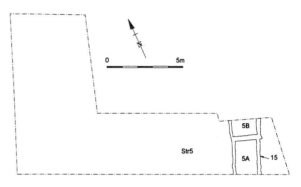

Fig. 7.8 Structure 5 with rooms 5A and 5B. (1:244)

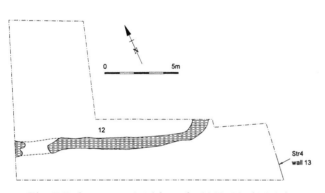

Fig. 7.7 Structure 4 with path: LUB 12. (1:244)

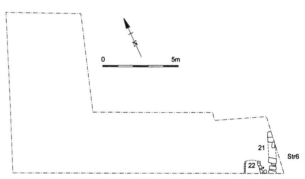

Fig. 7.9 Pit and wall: LUB 16. (1:244)

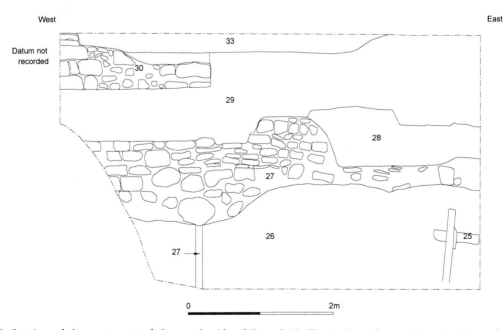

Fig. 7.10 Section of the west part of the north side of Trench II illustrating the stratigraphy here, from LUB 7 to LUB 17. (1:50)

LUB 13 Demolition (Fig. 7.12)
The pathway cg31 (LUB 12) in Trench I went out of use and the building at the east end of the site cg13 (LUB 12) was demolished; these were sealed by demolition material cg14 (43 post-Roman sherds) from which 17th-century pottery was recovered.

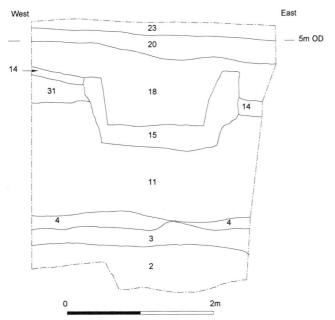

Fig. 7.11 Section of the east part of the north side of the East end of Trench I, illustrating the stratigraphy here, from LUB 1 to LUB 17. (1:50)

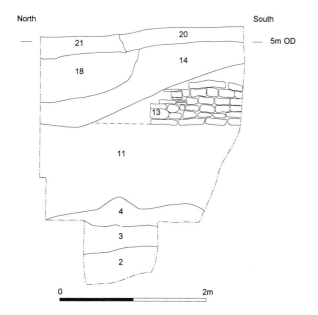

Fig. 7.12 Section of the east side of the East end of Trench I, illustrating the stratigraphy here, from LUB 1 to LUB 16. (1:50)

LUB 14 Structure 5 (Figs. 7.8 and 7.11)
At the east end of Trench I a building with at least two stone-built cellars cg15 (rooms 5A and 5B), aligned north–south, was constructed over demolition deposits cg14 (LUB 13); the floors of these cellars lay at 3.9m OD. Structure 5 must have been constructed in the 17th century or later, since pottery of that date was associated with the LUB 13 demolition.

LUB 15 Demolition and dumping
(Figs. 7.11–12 and 7.17)
The cellars cg15 (LUB 14) were partly robbed cg16 and backfilled with a dump of soil cg18 (up to 1m thick), containing very little building debris but a quantity of pottery (52 post-Roman sherds) and some other finds and bone. This dump was sealed by a levelling layer of similar material cg20 (41 post-Roman sherds), over 1m thick to the west of Trench I. Cutting through layer cg18 was a pit, cg19 (27 post-Roman sherds). There are joins between potsherds from four separate vessels recovered from the dumps cg18 and cg20 and those found in pit cg19, indicating that the dumps cg18 and cg20 derive from the same source.

The latest pottery can be dated to the mid to late 17th century. The latest of several clay pipes from cg20 (AB) <Cp2,3> date to *c* 1640–60 and a clay pipe bowl (AL) <Cp6> from the upper fill of pit cg19 dates to *c* 1650–80. A glass vessel base (AP) <G4> (Fig. 7.17 No2) from the lower fill of pit cg19 is part of a beaker. This is of distinctive pale smokey-brown colour with applied milled strips above the base ring, and is characteristic of a series of beakers (known as *stanenglas* or *keulenglas*) produced in the Low Countries, particularly the Lower Rhineland and Netherlands, during the late 16th to early 17th century (Henderson 1988; Henderson forthcoming).

All three context groups included material that dated to the late 15th to mid 16th centuries. Other high-status finds included several imported LANG and RAER German stoneware jugs, along with a number of cistercian cups. A sherd of blue, green and orange decorated Dutch tin-glazed tile dating to the late 16th to early 17th century was recovered from the lower fill of pit cg19 (Fig. 7.17 No1; Downey and Young 1984, 28–29). The upper fill of pit cg19 contained some intrusive modern glass.

LUB 16 Structure 6? Pit and wall
(Figs. 7.9 and 7.12)
A stone-lined ash pit cg22 and a north–south wall of limestone blocks cg21 were cut through the levelling layer cg20 (LUB 15). The wall was *c* 0.55m wide and at least 3.10m long and only the bottom course or two survived. A clay tobacco pipe stem from the cg22 dated to the 18th century at the earliest, but

given the paucity of finds and loose stratigraphy, it is impossible to date the LUB precisely.

Modern

Dickinson's Flour mill **LUB 17** was erected on the site in the mid 19th century.

LUB 17 Truncation, levelling and mill: Structure 7 (Figs. 7.10–11)
The mill, known later as Dickinson's Flour Mill, cg23 and cg33, was erected over both Trenches I and II, sealing cg21 and cg22 (LUB 16) in Trench I and cg30 (LUB 10) in Trench II.

Discussion

Topography

The LUB diagram clearly demonstrates the change of land-use through time. The influence of the river/pool is visible at the east side of the site in the earliest phases (LUBs 0 and 1). Then there was evidence for the waterfront; a hard-standing was built (LUB 2) probably in the late Saxon period. Other waterside activity included possible dredging (LUB 4) and a riverside structure, Structure 3 (LUB 3). The river again prevailed (LUB 5).

By the Medieval period the waterfront had moved westwards. Land had been reclaimed by dumps (LUB 11), and to the west there was evidence for the Pool (LUB 6) and a possible wharf (LUB 7). Yet further west at a later date, there was evidence for the river

(LUB 8) and a possible jetty (LUB 9) which was later replaced by a wall (LUB 10).

On the land at the east (Trench I) was a series of structures, possibly warehouses (LUBs 12, 14 and

Fig. 7.13 Looking west at hard standing cg5.

Fig. 7.14 Looking north-east; detail of north end of boat fragment with piles on west side, cg25.

16), set back from the Pool, as possibly also represented by the wall of LUB 10 (Trench II).

In the modern period a mill (LUB 17) was constructed over the whole site, indicating that during this period the waterfront was further west – as is clear from contemporary illustrations.

River levels

The silting deposits cg2 in Trench I (LUB 1), dating to the second half of the 10th century, lay at 2.3m OD, which must have been the approximate level of the river, liable to flooding. The 11th-century hard-standing cg5 (LUB 2) was at 2.9m OD and the water level would have been slightly below that. The top of the medieval construction cg25 (LUB 7) was at least 3m OD in height but probably higher. This in itself does not give any clear indication of the water level, but the preservation of the remaining timbers suggests that they had been continuously waterlogged. The footings of the possible jetty cg27 (LUB 9), dating to the late medieval

Fig. 7.15 Detail of reused clinker boat cg25 looking east.

Fig. 7.16 Limestone wall cg27 looking north.

period, were thought to be under water at 3.5m OD. In the early to mid 17th century the floors of the cellars cg15 (LUB 14) of Structure 5, presumably above the water level, were constructed at 3.9m OD.

Waterfronts

The early medieval waterfront (LUB 7) was apparently little more than a consolidated bank or wharf, against which boats could have tied up, but still represents the earliest vertical timber wharf located in the city. It was constructed of re-used timber with earth packed behind the planks; no surface remained. The closest parallel for this wharf is that found in Thoresby College Courtyard, Kings Lynn (Parker 1965), but that was more solidly built with larger piles which were more regularly spaced. Although the Dickinson's Mill construction may not have been very high, perhaps no more than 1m, the shallow draught of contemporary craft would still have allowed them to moor alongside it.

The stone jetty (LUB 9), built between the mid 14th and 15th centuries, does not seem to have been an immediate replacement of the timber wharf. Its existence would suggest that the handling of water-borne goods was carried out here on the east side of the Brayford. The stone jetty would have projected out into the Pool, perhaps to enable vessels of deeper draft to moor along its western side, whilst shallow-draught vessels used the north and south sides. Unfortunately, only the edge of this jetty was within the excavation, so its full extent and details of its infill and surface are unknown.

Buildings

Late Saxon Structure 1 (LUB 3) may have been a building at the water's edge; however, the remains are slight and could represent other activity.

The ground level was raised (by about 1.5m) by the dumping of material during the medieval period (LUB 11). On dump LUB 11, in the early post-medieval period, a possible Structure 4 (LUB 12) was built, which may have been associated with a path used by horses. The structure consisted of a north–south stone wall seen only in section. The most likely interpretation of evidence such as this adjacent to the river suggests the unloading of boats and a warehouse.

After the demolition of Structure 4, a substantial building, Structure 5 (LUB 14), was constructed here in the 17th century, including two stone-built cellars; this building, too, might well have represented a warehouse near the river.

After the demolition of Structure 5, the ground was raised by dumping (LUB 15; about 1m thick).

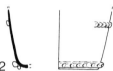

Blue
Yellow-Orange
Green

Fig. 7.17 Finds from pit cg19. 1: Dutch tin-glazed tile, 2: glass beaker base. Scale: no 1 – 1:4, no 2 – 1:2.

cg/LUB	cg/LUB	cg/LUB	cg/LUB	cg/LUB	cg/LUB	cg/LUB
1/0	6/2	11/11	16/15	21/16	26/8	31/12
2/1	7/3	12/12	17/12	22/16	27/9	32/11
3/1	8/5	13/12	18/15	23/17	28/9	33/17
4/1	9/11	14/13	19/15	24/6	29/10	34/3
5/2	10/4	15/14	20/15	25/7	30/10	35/3

Fig. 7.18 Concordance of cg numbers with LUB numbers for dm72.

A late post-medieval ash pit and wall, which might suggest Structure 6? (LUB 16), may have been part of a later replacement to Structure 5, or possibly represented a new use of the site, with the wall forming the rear boundary of a property fronting on the High Street.

Dickinson's Mill, Structure 7 (LUB 17), represents an intensification of use for the site in the mid 19th century. The first reference to a mill on this site was in 1854, leased by John Hartley, although Hartley, Rudgard and Foster had a steam corn mill, possibly on the site in 1844. The mill was sold to Melville in 1863, then to Dickinson in 1869. It was a five-storeyed red brick building with a hipped slate roof (Chambers and Wilson 1972). The mill was demolished in 1971, and the site is now occupied by the southern half of the General Accident Insurance Group/CGU building.

8. Holmes Grainwarehouse (hg72)

Introduction

In the autumn of 1972 redevelopment occasioned a rescue excavation on the site of 181–3 High Street (to the east of Holmes Grainwarehouse). The site was recorded under the supervision of Malcolm Otter, later of Timothy Marshall and, for the last few weeks, after the formation of the Lincoln Archaeological Trust in October, of Michael Jones. Excavation was funded jointly by the Department of the Environment and the Lincoln County Borough Council.

Since the site was in a part of the city not previously investigated, its stratigraphic complexity was unexpected, and pressures of time as well as the limited area excavated (initially 6.5m x 13m, later extended westwards by machine by some 15m), made interpretation difficult. This was compounded by the extent of the disturbance to earlier levels by post-medieval and modern activity. Machines were used to remove the uppermost levels and the western extension to the excavations. During excavation, the stone-lined cellar LUB 44 was revealed by machine work so that only part of the fill was formally excavated; this also explains why some of the pottery vessels were freshly broken but substantially complete. The generally hot and dry conditions of the summer of 1972 doubtless contributed to the difficulty in recognition and interpretation of levels during excavation, particularly those associated with the Late Saxon occupation, together with the lack of experience in excavating features of this period (which had previously gone unrecognised).

The material from this site has been worked on by several people over the years. After organisation of the records by Michael Jones, Colin Palmer-Brown produced a Level III report and a matrix. Context information in some of the original records was not of the fullest detail (eg OD levels), and many of the smaller deposits were not planned, owing to the pressures on resources. The site plans were redrawn following the excavations and some of the original ones discarded. The patchy quality of some of the initial record has affected not only the understanding of the stratigraphic sequence, but also an understanding of the finds in relation to the stratigraphy. The earliest phases, the pre-Roman 'Belgic' pottery, and some of the other early finds have already been published (Darling and Jones 1988) and an interim account of the site has appeared (Jones 1981). The Roman coins have also been also published (Mann & Reece 1983).

In this report, of the 408 contexts, 398 have been interpreted as 207 context groups (cg1–209; cg53 and cg179 are not used) and 10 were deemed unstratified. The context groups are discussed below as 48 land-use blocks, LUBs 1–48 (Fig. 8.37). The site was divided into five areas for the land-use diagram, roughly following the pattern of the archaeology of the early Roman period (Figs. 8.2 and 8.3), so that the western part of the site forms Area 1, the central part of the site has been divided into three, Area 2 to the south, Area 3 to the north and Area 4 in the centre, with Area 5 at the east. This arrangement was not always echoed by the archaeology and has necessitated division of blocks on the land-use diagram in the mid Roman period (LUBs 22–25). Area 1, at the west end of the site, was excavated by machine down to the early–mid Roman levels (LUBs 1, 2, 3 and 7) and the only other information that was retrieved here was either pitting (LUBs 20, 31 and 41) or stone walls (LUB 42). Area 2 contained evidence of occupation from the late Iron Age and throughout the Roman period (LUBs 1, 2, 4, 5, 7, 19, 20, 23, 24, 25, 26, 28 and 29), Late Saxon occupation (LUBs 30, 35, 36, 37 and 39) and medieval activity (LUBs 42, 43, 44 and 45). Area 3, also had evidence of occupation from the Late Iron Age and throughout the Roman period (LUBs 1, 2, 4, 5, 7, 11, 18, 22, 23, 24, 25, 26, 28 and 29), some Late Saxon activity (LUBs 30, 32, 33 and 34)

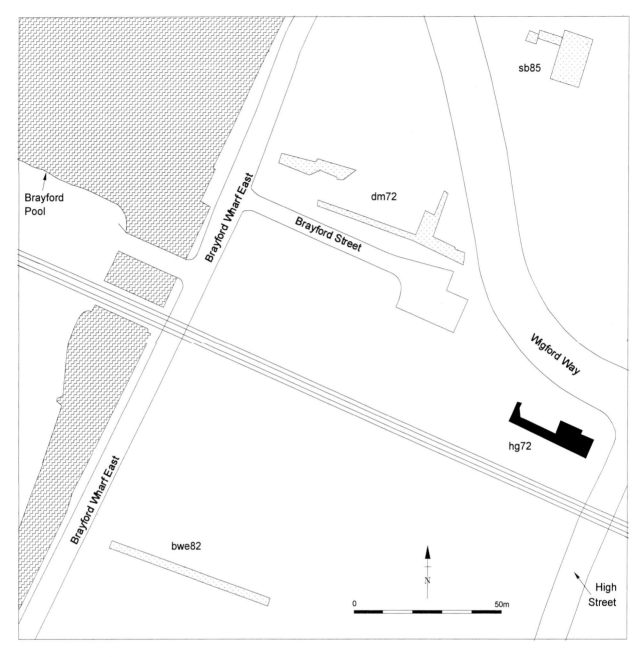

Fig. 8.1 Site location plan for hg72. (1:1,250)

and some medieval activity (LUBs 40, 42 and 43). Area 4, in the central part of the site also showed evidence of occupation from the Late Iron Age and throughout the Roman period (LUBs 1, 2, 4, 5, 7, 8, 9, 12, 13, 15, 16, 20, 22, 23, 24, 25, 26, 28 and 29), Late Saxon refuse (LUBs 30, 38 and 39) and one medieval structure (LUBs 42 and 43). Area 5 showed evidence of occupation from the Late Iron Age and throughout the Roman period (LUBs 1, 3, 4, 5, 6, 7, 9, 10, 13, 14, 16, 17, 20, 21, 24, 25, 26, 27, 28 and 29) but all evidence of the late Saxon and medieval periods had been cut away, and the later stratigraphy here consists of post-medieval and modern activity (LUBs

46, 47 and 48), traces of which were limited to this area.

There were 9,213 sherds of Roman pottery (including that in Iron Age tradition) and 2,101 sherds of post-Roman pottery recovered from the site together with 786 registered finds. Almost three-quarters of the registered finds is metalwork, generally heavily corroded Roman brooches (Mackreth 1993). A large quantity of coins was recovered, virtually all of Roman date; some of these were in such poor condition that they disintegrated completely (Mann and Reece 1983). A substantial proportion (c 20%) of the material is glass (Roman glass:

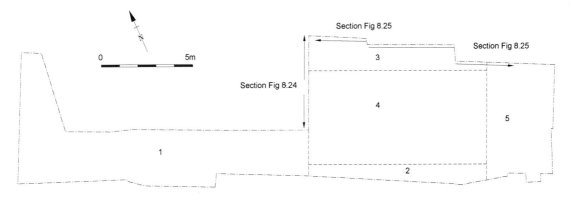

Fig. 8.2 Plan showing areas and sections for hg72. (1:200)

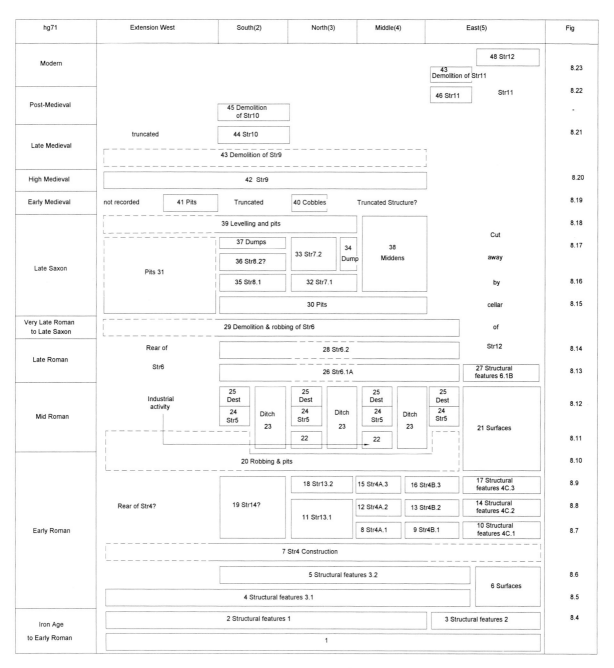

Fig. 8.3 LUB diagram for hg72.

Cool and Price 1986; medieval and post-medieval glass: Henderson 1984b, Adams and Henderson 1995e), with smaller quantities of bone and antler (Rackham 1994), ceramic and stone objects (hones: Moore 1991; other worked stone: Roe 1994), all generally in good condition. Although organics generally did not survive, several small fragments of linen were found (Walton Rogers 1993). The slag collected probably represents only a fraction of that noted during excavation. Some of the accessioned copper alloy and slag was later deemed to be of little use in interpreting the site and was thus discarded; since routine X-raying of copper alloy and slags was not practised, this represents a potential loss of information. Of the building material (428 fragments recovered), most was of Roman tile; non-ceramic building materials (such as stone roofing slates) may not have been retained even if recognised. Fragments of human bone were recovered including fragments of at least one Roman infant (Boylston and Roberts 1994) as well as a moderately large assemblage (3,654 fragments) of animal bone (Dobney *et al* 1994c).

The degree of disturbance on this site, however, has produced an unusually high residuality factor and it is often difficult to distinguish between contemporary and residual material (the majority of the registered finds are either only datable to a general period or are completely undiagnostic; the animal bone is even less diagnostic).

Further post-excavation stratigraphic analysis was undertaken by Chris Guy and later by Kate Steane. Barbara Precious worked on the Roman pottery and Jane Young on the post-Roman pottery. Jen Mann analysed the registered finds and, with Rick Kemp, the building material. Helen Palmer Brown and Zoe Rawlings digitized the plans and Dave Watt drew the finds illustrations.

Interpretation of the sequence of events

Late Iron Age to Early Roman

Disturbed subsoil **LUB 1** indicated activity dating, from the pottery, to the Late Iron Age. In Areas 1–4 postholes, gullies, pits and a hearth **LUB 2** were mostly recorded as being later than LUB 1; they indicated Structural Features 1. In Area 5, postholes and slots **LUB 3** indicate Structural Features 2; a north–south ditch at the western limit of the area might be linked to the construction of Ermine Street. Pottery from LUBs 2 and 3 dated from the late Iron Age to the Roman conquest period, with a diminished amount in Iron Age tradition form LUB 1.

LUB 1 Disturbed subsoil (Figs. 8.24 and 8.25)
The disturbed nature of the sand cg1 suggested that

there had been some activity on the site. The dating of the nine sherds from cg1 is uncertain with such a small assemblage; however, the majority of the native coarsewares appear to belong to the latest Iron Age phase, which could overlap into the Roman period (Darling 1988, 33).

LUB 2 Structural features 1 (Fig. 8.4 and 8.24)
In Areas 1–4 gullies cg2 and cg6 cut subsoil cg1 (LUB 1). Gully cg2 ran north-east to south-west for about 1.5m (about 0.50m deep and 0.50m wide). Gully cg6 ran on a similar alignment to cg2 for about 3.30m (1m wide and 0.50m deep). Cutting cg6 was another gully cg5, also aligned north-east to south-west, but about 1m long (0.20m wide and 0.20m deep). These may have been associated with pit cg4 (only partly excavated) and curving gully cg11, which also cut cg1 (LUB 1). Curving gully cg11 was presumably part of a circular drainage feature around a round structure; the curve of the arc indicated a diameter of about 5–7m. These may have been contemporary with, or may have belonged to a different phase from, postholes cg13 and cg191 cutting cg1 (LUB 1); these postholes appear to form a rectilinear structure, possibly a building. Cutting pit cg4 was a possible hearth cg12 (partly cut away by subsequent activity; 0.60m east–west). It was an area of clay with a slight ridge around the outside of the top; it is not clear if it filled a hole or stood proud of the surface. It may possibly have been a hearth although the site records do not indicate that the clay was burnt.

All these features suggest that there was some form of occupation in Areas 1–4, probably in the form of more than one structure; however, the evidence was difficult to interpret, hence the term "structural features". The pottery (57 sherds), with the exception of one of IAGRB, was all shell-tempered. The sherd of IAGRB came from the backfill of circular gully cg11. Although the structure appears to be Iron Age in date, the backfill could be later, possibly dating to the Roman conquest period.

LUB 3 Structural features 2
(Figs. 8.4, 8.25 and 8.26)
To the east of the site in Area 5, were the traces of apparently parallel shallow slots cg7 and cg20 which cut cg1 (LUB 1). The depth of the slots was about 0.25m; each was about 1m long but probably extended to the north of the trench. There were other cut features cg192 which were also considered to belong to this phase of activity.

Sealing layer cg1 (LUB 1) was silt cg8. Slots cg7 and cg20 were in turn sealed by a thin layer of redeposited sand cg22 (0.03m thick), possibly trample. Cutting silt cg8 and delimiting the extent of the features to the west was a ditch cg9 aligned north–south (about 2.20m wide and 1.10m deep). Sealing

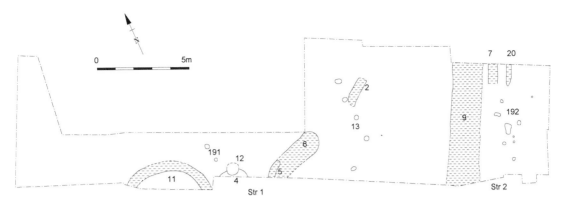

Fig. 8.4 Structural features 1 and 2: LUBs 2 and 3. (1:200)

cg22 was redeposited sand cg23 (0.50m thick in places) which may have represented the remains of upcast from the ditch cg9.

The slots and postholes seem to be divided from activity in LUB 2 by ditch cg9. This ditch ran north–south, as did Ermine Street a few metres to the east. The ditch might be the only evidence that there was a precursor to Ermine Street, or it could be that this ditch was instead linked to conquest activity.

It is not clear what exactly the postholes and slots represent, but they may have been part of a roadside building or buildings, or they may have represented the first of a sequence of roadside activity – possibly booths or stalls.

A small group of pottery (10 sherds), late Iron Age to the Roman conquest period in date, was recovered from slots cg7 and cg20, as well as from silt layer cg8 and cut features cg192. Occupation material cg22 produced 36 sherds of a similar date, but also the first evidence of imported Roman pottery, a dish (PC16) in TN, dated to *c* AD 50–70; however, this may have intruded from cg25 (LUB 6), as joins were found between this group and LUBs 5 and 6 indicating that the lower material had been reworked.

Early Roman

There was evidence for Early Roman occupation in Areas 1–5, but there is no clear evidence for the arrangement of any walls or internal fittings amongst the variety of features and deposits excavated. In Areas 1–4 there were pits, a gully, a slot and posthole, together with possible floors, Structural Features 3.1 **LUB 4** which were apparently abandoned before there were traces of further structural activity in Area 4, an area of collapsed wallplaster, and an east–west slot **LUB 5**, Structural features 3.2. To the east of the site, in Area 5, sealing features in LUB 3 were possible surfaces, perhaps indicating an area to the edge of Ermine Street **LUB 6**. Pottery from LUBs 4 to 6 dates from the middle to the late 1st century.

Subsequently, what appears to have been a gable-ended strip building, Structure 4, was erected **LUB 7**; it had two (4A and 4B) or possibly three (Structure 13) rooms as well as activity along the road (4C), to the east of the building. Pottery from LUB 8 suggests that Structure 4 was probably constructed in the later part of the 1st century.

Room 4A.1, in the western part of Area 4, contained a hearth **LUB 8** and was divided from room 4B.1 **LUB 9**, to the east of Area 4, by a slot; further to the east, in Area 5, there were postholes **LUB 10**, evidence of activity along the roadside – Structural evidence 4C.1. To the north, in Area 3, was a cellar, Structure 13.1 **LUB 11**, which may have been part of Structure 4, or part of a building to the north. Pottery from LUB 8 dated to the later part of the 1st century; that from LUBs 9, 10 and 11 add little to the dating evidence.

The next phase of Structure 4 revealed that Room 4A.2 **LUB 12**, in the western part of Area 4, was not occupied but used as a dumping ground for rubbish. Room 4B.2 **LUB 13**, in the eastern part of Area 4, showed signs of occupation. In Area 5, some sort of roadside activity continued, Structural features 4C.2 **LUB 14**. Pottery from LUBs 12, 13 and 14 dated between the late 1st century and the early 2nd century.

The last phase of Structure 4 showed no evidence of activity in room 4A.3 **LUB 15** to the west of Area 4. Room 4B.3 **LUB 16** to the east of Area 4 appeared to continue in use, possibly as a domestic dwelling. There was further roadside activity, Structural evidence 4C.3 **LUB 17**, including a possible cess pit. In Area 3 there was another sunken feature **LUB 18**, Structure 13.2. LUB 16 relied on stratigraphy, but pottery from LUB 17 dated to the early 2nd century and pottery from LUB 18 indicated an early to mid 2nd-century date.

To the south of Structure 4 was some slight evidence of a building, Structure 14 **LUB 19**, which contained pottery dating to the later 1st and early 2nd centuries as well as one sherd possibly dating between the early to mid 2nd century.

Structures 4, 13 and 14 were abandoned and robbed **LUB 20**; pottery from this LUB dated between the early and mid 2nd century. In Area 5 there was a series of pebble/cobble surfaces **LUB 21**, suggesting that Ermine Street had widened or shifted westwards.

LUB 4 Structural features 3.1
(Figs. 8.5, 8.24 and 8.25)
In Area 4, ditch cg9 (LUB 3) was backfilled cg10, and over its western scarp was sealed by sand with lenses of dark earth cg14, possibly hearth debris and floors. Although pit cg3 cut natural cg1 (LUB 1), it was thought to be later than gully cg11 (LUB 2) because of the date of the pottery from its fill. Pit cg3 was 1.5m across and 0.70m deep.

In Area 1 pit cg3 and cg10 from this LUB, together with cg12 and cg5 (LUB 2), were sealed by clayey material, ash and burnt daub and charcoal cg15, possibly clay floors and hearth debris. From cg15 a socketed iron spearhead <Fe291> (Darling and Jones 1988, fig 11, 7) was recovered. Similar spearheads, with slightly curving asymmetrical shoulders folded over to form an open socket, are known from military sites both in Britain and Germany; flanged variants such as this example occur mainly at Hod Hill (Manning 1985, 165).

Cutting layer cg15 was a gully cg17 (3.6m long, 0.20m deep with a narrow gully along the bottom), postholes cg19 and slot and posthole cg16 (the slot was about 2m long, 0.15m wide and 0.80m deep). Pit cg49 (0.30m deep) cut slot cg11 (LUB 2) and probably also cut cg15. Although post-pit cg18 (0.50m across and 0.50m deep) and postholes cg21 were recorded as cutting cg1 (LUB 1), they too were probably associated with layer cg15 (but here this layer had been cut away by later features).

These features all indicate that there were one or more buildings on the site, but their indeterminate nature means that they are here termed "structural features".

The moderately sized assemblage of Roman pottery (135 sherds) largely consisted of pottery of the late Iron Age to the Roman conquest period tradition (83% of the sherd total). Joins with LUBs 2 and 3 below indicate that some of this material was derived from earlier stratigraphy. Romano-British pottery occurs for the first time in this LUB, but given the large amount of probably residual Iron Age pottery in relation to the small amount of Romanised wares, the dating evidence is minimal, placing it towards the middle of the 1st century or later.

LUB 5 Dumps and Structural Features 3.2
(Figs. 8.6, 8.24 and 8.25)
In Area 4, overlying possible floors cg15 (LUB 4), was a brown deposit with lenses of red, mauve and black cg24 (0.28m thick). A tinned copper-alloy Langton Down brooch (MR) <Ae93> (Mackreth 1993) was found within this material, which also produced a small assemblage of animal bone, mostly primary butchery waste (Dobney *et al* 1994c). The dumping of this noxious waste suggests that there may have been a period of abandonment of Areas 1–4 and the west of Area 5, and that cg24 perhaps indicates dumping.

Cutting into layers cg24 was a north–south slot cg46 (unplanned). Layers cg24 were overlaid by a thin spread of sand cg26, possibly a floor; this was sealed by dark brown sandy layers cg28 and cg29, possibly trample. An area of wallplaster had collapsed on to a patch of mortar of unrecorded extent and location cg32. The wallplaster was lifted but has since suffered considerable damage. However, the remaining plaster is largely white in colour, although a small area appears to have been decorated with red, ochre and black.

The mortar cg32 was possibly cut by an east–

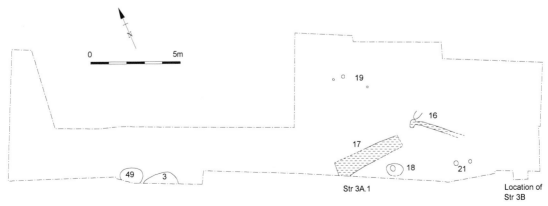

Fig. 8.5 Structural features 3A.1 and 3B: LUBs 4 and 6. (1:200)

west slot cg39 (0.3m deep with a U-shaped profile).

These slots and layers probably all represent the remains of buildings of some sort, subsequent to the those in LUB 4, and so they have been labelled Structural features 3.2; they were all recovered from Area 4, in the central and eastern parts of the site. These appear to be the first definite structures fronting on to the street.

Some of the total pottery assemblage (421 sherds) from this LUB was residual. Several pottery sherd joins with LUB 6, surfaces to the east, support the stratigraphic evidence that the two LUBs were contemporary at least for a while. These structural features produced the first instance of LEG, PINK & RDSL which form *c* 6% of the total number of sherds. The presence of these wares, together with the samian, places this feature within the Neronian period or later.

LUB 6 Surfaces (Figs. 8.5–6 and 8.25)
At the east end of the site, sealing cg22, cg23 and cg192 (LUB 3), was a layer of mixed sand cg25 (0.20m thick), possibly a dump of redeposited natural sand. It was sealed by clay, limestone chippings and mortar cg27, possible surfaces, and thin layers of light and dark sand cg35, also possible surfaces; posthole cg50 (unplanned) cut sand cg35.

These might represent the fringe of Ermine Street. The LUB produced a smaller (127 sherds), but very similar assemblage to that from LUB 5 with some residual pottery. However, most of the samian dates to *c* AD 50–70 and includes a decorated sherd of Dr29 by the potters MASCLUS and NIGER dated AD 50–65 from cg35. The samian, together with some of the coarse wares, suggests LUB 6 dated between the mid and late 1st century, probably associated with the legionary occupation.

LUB 7 Structure 4, construction (Figs. 8.7 and 8.25)
The mortared stone foundations of a wall cg47 (0.76m wide) ran east–west towards the southern part of the site in Areas 1 and 4; it was at least 26m long. Sealing cg29 (LUB 5) was sand make-up cg36; cutting this was pit cg38 which was located in Area 3. It appeared to contain limestone chips and unshaped fragments of limestone and sand, possibly rubbish deposited during and/or after the construction of Structure 4.

The structure associated with wall cg47 probably represents part of a "strip building", of commercial function, gable-ended to Ermine Street. The site was cut, to the east, by the robbing cg111 (LUB 29) of a later north–south wall cg34 (LUB 26), which may have respected the original line of the east wall of Structure 4. There was no pottery associated with

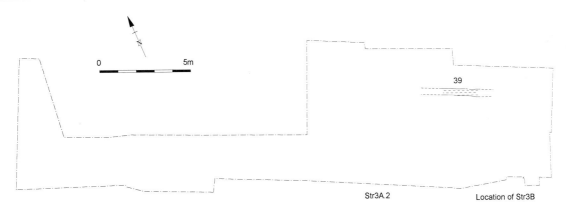

Fig. 8.6 Structural features 3A.2 and 3B: LUBs 5 and 6. (1:200)

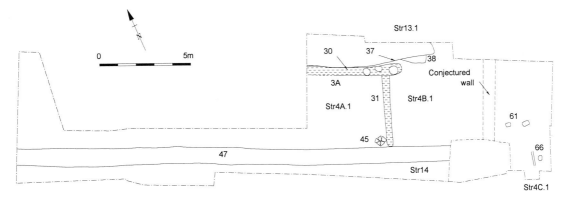

Fig. 8.7 Structure 4, rooms 4A.1 and 4B.1, and area 4C.1 with Structure 13.1 to the north: LUBs 8, 9, 10 and 1.
(1:200)

the construction of wall cg47; the latest date for the pottery from pit cg38 was between the mid and late 1st century but this small group of sherds does not add to the dating evidence. The construction of Structure 4 probably dated to the later 1st century (see LUB 8), possibly after the foundation of the *colonia*.

LUB 8 Room 4A.1 (Figs. 8.7 and 8.27)
Over LUBs 5 and 7, in the western part of Area 4, a hearth cg45 sealed clay floor cg209 and butted the north face of wall cg47. A fragment of human bone was recovered from the clay floor cg209 (Boylston and Roberts 1994). There was an east–west slot cg30 with three postholes along its bottom, which appeared to cut slot cg31 (LUB 9) but was possibly contemporary. The small pottery assemblage from this room (39 sherds) is not large enough to refine the dating other than placing it towards the later 1st century.

LUB 9 Room 4B.1 (Figs. 8.7, 8.24 and 8.25)
A north–south slot cg31 divided room 4A.1 from room 4B.1 (there is no record of what cg31 cut). Sand make-up cg36 (LUB 7) was sealed by a clay floor cg41; also sealing part of cg36 was a patch of green/yellow earth cg42. The small pottery assemblage (22 sherds) is very similar to that from the underlying stratigraphy and adds little to the dating evidence.

LUB 10 Roadside: Structural features 4C.1 (Fig. 8.7)
In Area 5, a strip of clay and a layer of mortar cg51 sealed posthole cg50 and layer cg35; cg51 was cut by two postholes cg61 together with a slot or gully possibly aligned north–south with a small posthole to its east cg66. Sealing surface cg51, and possibly also postholes cg61, were spreads of silty sand, ash and burnt clayey material cg65.

These indeterminate 'structural features' were located between the strip building and the street,

possibly indicating the position of roadside stalls. The small pottery assemblage (27 sherds) is very similar to that from the underlying stratigraphy and adds little to the dating evidence. Samian dated to the mid 1st century was derived from the latest surface cg65.

LUB 11 Cellar 13.1 (Figs. 8.7, 8.8, 8.24 and 8.25)
Pit cg38 (LUB 7) was cut by a sunken feature cg37 in Area 3; it was approximately a metre deep. The presence of horizontal timbers along the bottom of the feature suggests a plank floor raised above the cut of the feature; the sand and daub backfill suggested wall-construction. The sunken feature probably represents a cellar, associated either with a building to the north or with Structure 4 itself. The pottery assemblage (15 sherds) is too small to refine the dating, although a sherd of GREY rusticated ware, which ranges in date from the later 1st to the early 2nd century, may place it towards the end of the 1st century.

LUB 12 Room 4A.2 (Fig. 8.8)
Sandy and ashy spreads cg190 (unplanned) covered the western part of Area 4, sealing hearth cg45 (LUB 8) and slots cg30 and cg31 (LUB 9). From the sand and ash cg190 a very small assemblage of cattle scapulae was recovered; it had been all heavily butchered (Dobney *et al* 1994c). A glass vessel fragment (KE) <G131> recovered from cg190 is part of an unusual polychrome jug, blue-green with opaque white marvered spots, probably of Neronian or early Flavian date (Cool and Price 1988, 42–3; fig 11, 10b).

In the spreads cg190 was a large depression cg44, which contained a moderate assemblage of animal bone suggesting domestic refuse and the dumping of primary butchery waste. A high proportion of the scapula blades showed evidence of hook damage, very similar in characteristics to the assemblage from cg76 LUB 20 (Dobney *et al* 1994c). The animal bone

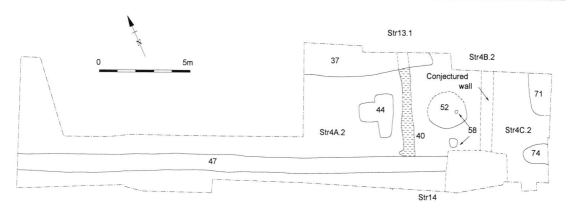

Fig. 8.8 Structure 4, rooms 4A.2 and 4B.2, and area 4C.2 with Structure 13.1 to the north: LUBs 12, 13, 14 and 11. (1:200)

suggests that during this period Room 4A.2 was used to dump rubbish. The coarse wares from the pottery assemblage (171 sherds) include a sherd of GREY with nodular rusticated decoration, which suggests a date ranging from the late 1st to the early 2nd century for this LUB. An *as* of Vespasian, issued AD 71, shows wear consistent with use into the late 1st or early 2nd century. Depression cg44 also contained some intrusive medieval pottery.

LUB 13 Room 4B.2 (Figs. 8.8 and 8.25)
In the east part of Area 4, dividing room 4A.2 from room 4B.2 was a north–south slot cg40 which cut pit cg38 (LUB 7). It was either cut by or cut cg37 (LUB 11); the relationship was unclear. Floor cg41 (LUB 9) was sealed by sandy material cg43. There was a silty layer cg54 (no record of what it sealed). Probably cutting sandy layer cg43 was a circular pit cg52 (relationships not clearly recorded). Sandy layer cg43 and pit cg52 each contained a single coin. Cutting silty layer cg54 and cg43 were three postholes and stake-holes cg58 (one unplanned). These were sealed by several lenses and spreads of clay, sand, burnt clay, burnt sand and ash, cg59 which have been interpreted as clay floors with fire ash. Layers cg59 contained a small quantity of domestic refuse, together with five coins.

Almost all of the seven coins from this room are *asses*, showing varying degrees of wear, including a very worn Claudian copy and three Neronian issues; the two latest coins (from cg59) – an *as* and a *dupondius* – are both of Vespasian issues of AD 71. The presence of these coins suggests commercial activity here.

The moderately-sized pottery assemblage (170 sherds) is similar to that from LUB 12, including the presence of nodular rusticated decoration. Sherd joins between LUBs 12 and 13 suggest that they might be contemporary; the similar date-range from the late 1st to the early 2nd century also supports this interpretation.

LUB 14 Roadside: Structural features 4C.2
(Figs. 8.8 and 8.25)
In Area 5 pit cg71 (0.4m deep) cut cg35 (LUB 6). Over gully and posthole cg66 and ashy layers cg65 (both LUB 10) was a thin sandy layer cg67; this was sealed by many layers of sand, clay and burnt organic material cg68 (0.5m thick) and a dark grey sandy spread cg69. Layer cg67 was cut by pit cg74 (0.15m deep).

The pits along the eastern edge of the excavation, being relatively shallow, might represent damage to the surface along the edge of the road, but they could alternatively indicate evidence of roadside stalls or structures. The layers suggest considerable roadside activity. The undefined nature of the evidence has meant that this LUB again consists of "structural features".

A *tpq* of AD 70 is provided by a sherd of decorated samian dated AD 70–85 from burnt organic layer cg68. The moderately-sized coarse ware assemblage (206 sherds in total) contains similar pottery to that from LUBs 12 and 13. Sherds of GREY with nodular rusticated decoration, a fragment of MOLO with a hooked rim, and a sherd of RC with sand rough-casting suggest a date ranging from the later 1st into the 2nd century.

LUB 15 Room 4A.3 (Fig. 8.9)
There is no evidence for activity during this phase of the room, in the west of Area 4; possibly whatever evidence there was for this phase of the building has been lost owing to material having been cut away and removed from the site before abandonment. Layers cg76 were originally interpreted as belonging to this period, but the pottery from them suggests that they were related to the disuse and demolition of the building (see LUB 20).

LUB 16 Structure 4B.3 (Fig. 8.9)
In the east of Area 4, against south wall cg47, was an east–west slot cg62; this cut layers cg59 (LUB

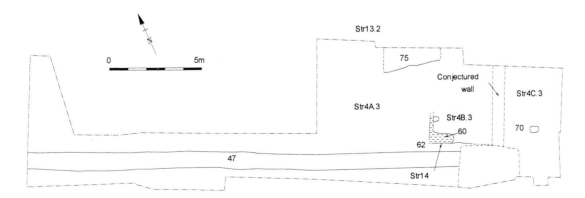

Fig. 8.9 Structure 4, rooms 4A.3 and 4B.3 and area 4C.3 with Structure 13.2 to the north: LUBs 15, 16, 17 and 18. (1:200)

13). Beside slot cg62 was a transverse slot cg60, dividing rooms 4A.3 and 4B.3. Over layers cg59 (LUB 13), and within this room was an ashy fibrous layer, sealed by clay layers cg63, probably floors.

Sealing these layers cg63 were ash spreads with charcoal lenses cg64, containing a little domestic rubbish; the description suggests hearth debris and within the rubbish was a burnt piece of micaceous sandstone (IA) <M59> which may have been used as a rubber, grinder or smoother. Ash spreads cg64 were sealed by a clean sand layer cg80, possibly a new floor surface, over which was a thin ashy spread cg193, hearth debris. This structure must date to the later 1st or early 2nd century on stratigraphic grounds and, although only a small group, the pottery is similar in date to that from earlier LUBs. A single GREY plain-rimmed dish suggests a date for the occupation of the structure ranging towards the early 2nd century.

LUB 17 Roadside: Structural features 4C.3
(Figs. 8.9 and 8.25)
In Area 5, layers cg69 (LUB 14) were cut by a posthole cg70. The layers and posthole were sealed by silty material over which was a thin burnt clay layer cg72. Layers cg68 (LUB 14) were sealed by sandy layers with charcoal flecks cg73, which had been cut by pit cg201 (unplanned); it had a greenish fill and had been backfilled with greenish-brown sand. The fill of pit cg201 suggests that it might have served as a cess-pit.

The indeterminate nature of this LUB means that it is characterised as "structural features", but it probably represents activity fronting along the roadside.

A sherd of decorated samian dated *c* AD 75–95 from sand floor cg73 provides a *tpq c* AD 75 for this activity. There is little to distinguish this moderately sized assemblage (203 sherds) from that of under-lying LUB 14, apart from a sherd of probable LOND/PART type ware which is generally assigned an early 2nd-century date.

LUB 18 Structure 13.2 (Fig. 8.25)
In Area 3, the fill of sunken feature cg37 (LUB 11) had been cut by a later sunken feature cg75; it had steep sides and a flattish bottom, and to the east it cut through floors and layers cg59 (LUB 13). Ashy occupation spreads were found to the west of the feature, which was backfilled with building debris and some domestic refuse.

The pottery from cg75 is similar in content and number of sherds to that from LUB 17 but the presence of a GREY jar, J105, suggests an early to mid 2nd-century date for this LUB. There is some pottery evidence for Structure 13 being part of the same complex and/or contemporary with Structure

4; there are probable sherd links from the recutting of the sunken feature cg75 with LUB 13 and LUB 15. The finds recovered from cg75 are primarily domestic in character; while some are almost certainly rede-posited, others suggest a date into the 2nd century. Amongst these is part of a copper-alloy spoon (IQ) <Ae85> of late 1st- to 2nd-century type. A fragment of human bone was recovered from cg75 (Boylston and Roberts 1994).

Possibly contemporary with cg75 was a pit cg182 with a fill of greenish soil, burnt clay and sand (unplanned; there was no record of what it cut); this may represent a cess-pit.

LUB 19 Structure 14? (Fig. 8.24)
To the south of Structure 4, in Area 2, were layers of clay, sand, mortar and limestone chippings, cg48 which may have been construction debris for east–west wall cg47 (LUB 7); these overlay cg24 (LUB 5). These layers may represent floors to the south of the wall, belonging to a building which shared wall cg47 (LUB 7) as a party wall (similar to the layout at z86).

The increase in the amount of grey wares and the presence of high rather than low relief linear rusti-cated decoration from construction debris cg48 suggest a date towards the later 1st or early 2nd century. A GREY cooking pot of tenuous similarity to BB could date this group to the early to mid 2nd century, but the group is too small (42 sherds) to refine the dating further.

LUB 20 Demolition of Structure 4 and pits
(Figs. 8.10, 8.24 and 8.28)
Pit cg81, which had cut sand layer cg80 (LUB 16) in Area 4, may have been related to demolition activity. In the east part of Area 4, sealing layer cg193 (LUB 16), was a layer of loose, cindery, burnt material cg194 which contained a large quantity of burnt daub with wattle impressions (unplanned). A small sample (FW) <SS34> of this was kept; most of the fragments have wattle impressions on the reverse, and one appears to have been 'keyed' for the application of a surface coat of plaster. Within cg194 was also found the rib of an infant (Boylston and Roberts 1994), probably residual from an earlier infant burial. In Area 2, sealing cg48 (LUB 19), was rubble, charcoal and mortar cg78 (0.60m thick). The north–south wall cg47 in Areas 1 and 4 was thoroughly robbed cg55. Pottery from the robbing activity cg55 includes the first presence on the site of SAMLM dating to *c* AD 100–130.

Three pits also probably date from this period. Pit cg56 in Area 1 cut robber trench cg55 and this pit was cut by cg57. Pit cg208 (unplanned; but recorded in section Fig. 8.24), in Area 2, cut cg48 (LUB 19).

Sealing pit cg44 (LUB 12), in the west part of

Area 4, were layers cg76, greenish silty sand, overlain by ash; over this was a patch of sand and pebbles which in turn was overlain by layers of mixed charcoal, sand and clay, including a spread of charcoal 0.25m thick, over which was a sandy layer with a thin layer of burning on top. There were further layers of sandy silt. None was planned or appeared on a section drawing.

A large assemblage of animal bone from cg76 does not represent what would be considered normal occupation debris, but is most likely to represent dumping of noxious waste in a convenient disused building, possibly during an abandonment phase (Dobney *et al* 1994c). Layers cg76 contained several dozen iron nails, perhaps from the collapse or demolition of timber-framed walls or from floor or roof joists, and five copper-alloy coins. One of these disintegrated before it could be identified, but the other four show a similar range of issues and denominations to those from LUB 13. The layers cg76 suggest abandonment and building collapse, together with noxious animal waste dumping.

The first instance of BB1 from the lowest of the layers cg76 provides a *tpq* of *c* AD 120 for the activity; further BB1 sherds were recovered from later cg76 layers. The forms, body sherds of a cooking pot and probable dish, both with acute lattice decoration, fit into the BB1 repertoire which began to be widely distributed from *c* AD 120 onwards. The presence of MOLO, dated to the 2nd century, a MICA plate and a possible lid, together with a CC beaker similar to those produced at South Carlton, provides further evidence for an early to mid-2nd century date. There was a high proportion of redeposited material and sherd links with LUBs 12, 13 and 16.

The nature of the rubbish dumping cg44 in Room 4A.2 (LUB12), dating to the late 1st to early 2nd century, and the lack of evidence for the use of Room

4A.3 (LUB 15), ie, contemporary activity with Rooms 4B.3 (LUB 16) and Structural features 4C.3 (LUB 17), suggest some continuity of use from LUB 12 through to LUB 20 in Room 4A. The high proportion of redeposited material in cg76, with sherd links to LUBs 13 and 16, suggests that Room 4A.2/3 was being used as a dumping place for clearances of material from Room 4B.2 and 4B.3. This might explain the presence of the coins. There were also sherd links with cg44 (LUB 12), suggesting either a lack of definition between the two deposits or a certain amount of post-depositional disturbance of cg44 (LUB 12).

The total pottery assemblage for cg55, cg78 and cg194 (125 sherds) is similar to that from cg76; in particular, the presence of a few rim sherds of BB1 dates the group to the early to mid 2nd century.

LUB 21 External surfaces (Figs. 8.11 and 8.25)
In Area 5, sealing cg73 (LUB 17), there was a series of surfaces cg100: pebbles mixed with mortar and sand, sealed by a layer of cobbles and sand and pebbles. To the south-east were other traces of a cobbled surface cg196. These surfaces suggest an encroachment of the road; it had either been widened or had been shifted towards the west, or the front part of the property was metalled. The pottery from cg100 is of indeterminate 1st- to 2nd-century date, whereas cobbled surface cg196, although equally mixed in date, produced a grooved rimmed GREY dish with burnished intersecting arcs which probably dates from the mid 2nd century but continues into the later Roman period. The total assemblage is very small, consisting of only 30 sherds.

Mid Roman

There was evidence in Areas 3 and 4 for industrial activity **LUB 22**, possibly defined to the west by a

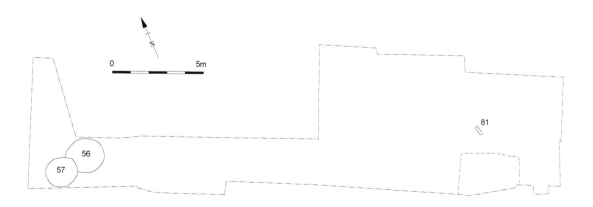

Fig. 8.10 Pits post-dating structure 4: LUB 20. (1:200)

ditch **LUB 23**. Both contained pottery dating from the 2nd century into the 3rd. A circular building, Structure 5 **LUB 24**, in Areas 2, 3, 4 and 5, sealed the industrial features; the ditch LUB 23 was still open while Structure 5 was in use. Pottery from LUB 24 dated the building to the early 3rd century. The road surfaces LUB 21 continued to be used during this period. Structure 5 appears to have been destroyed by fire, and was sealed by material **LUB 25** containing pottery of a similar date to its use.

LUB 22 Industrial activity (Figs. 8.11 and 8.25)
In Area 3 and in the northern part of Area 4, layer cg194 (LUB 20) had been cut by slot cg84, which was in turn cut by a slot with a bowl-shaped hearth cg85. The hearth was cut by a posthole cg86. Cutting cg194 (LUB 20) was posthole cg87 (unplanned); this was sealed by sand cg93, which was cut by a small pit cg94 filled with clay, some of it burnt. The pottery dating evidence from pit cg94 consists of a small number of sherds (4 sherds), including two minute fragments of abraded probable NVCC with scale decoration, one of which was folded and of an indeterminate 3rd-century date. This pottery sherd suggests that the pit may have been open for some time, as it underlay cg96 (LUB 25).

Pit cg77 was recorded as cutting cg44 (LUB 12). Sealing pit cg77 in Area 4 were layers cg82, a spread of charcoal-flecked sand sealed by another layer of sand (unplanned). Within each of these sand layers was found a Kentish Rag hone (IW) <M50>, (HO) <M55> (Moore 1991); both show evidence of wear, while one still shows traces of the rebates characteristic of Roman hone manufacture.

Pit cg77 contained 24 sherds, one of which, from its lower fill, was a thin-walled, finely executed collared flask fragment of an almost black fabric with a very high burnish, probably over a slip, and although containing more particles of fine quartz, it resembles PART. No direct parallels have been found to date but, despite the absence of a rim, the form is reminiscent of late Roman flasks of probable mid–late 3rd, but more commonly regarded as 4th century, in date. There is no direct association with substantially later stratigraphy to account for this possible anomaly. However, the upper fill of pit cg77 had a sherd join with cg82, which also contained a highly polished, thin strap handle in a fabric virtually identical to that of the flask fragment. Layer cg82 contained only 9 sherds, most of which dated to the late 1st or early 2nd century, except this one sherd, a handle which was part of a probable later Roman flask of mid to late 3rd- or, more commonly, 4th-century date.

Sealing the sand layers cg82 was a sequence of surfaces cg83 (unplanned); this consisted of clay, mortar and pebbles, sealed by burnt clay and clay with stones set in it, and over the stones was a localised spread of mortar, clay and pebbles sealed by sandy soil. Within the stones was a redeposited cheese-shaped weight of Lincolnshire Limestone (GU) <M51> (Roe 1994).

Sealing surfaces cg83 was a thick multi-coloured ashy layer cg89. It was sealed by clay floor cg189 which was cut by stone-packed posthole cg91; a similarly packed posthole cg88 cut surfaces cg83.

These features and surfaces suggest some sort of industrial activity. The total pottery assemblage from this LUB consists of 199 sherds. The abundance of early samian reflects the residual nature of this assemblage which is largely composed of pottery dating from the later 1st to the early 2nd century, but also contains a small number of 1st-century fabrics including LYON (cg85). Abrasion of much of the material demonstrates redeposition, and a number of sherd joins between the various activities suggest that they are interrelated. Evidence of burning on pottery types that are not associated with cooking, from cg83 and cg85, could be consistent with the use of the site for industrial activity. Diagnostic pottery which clearly post-dates *c* AD 120 is rare, but appears in cg83 in the form of BB1 cooking pots and dishes

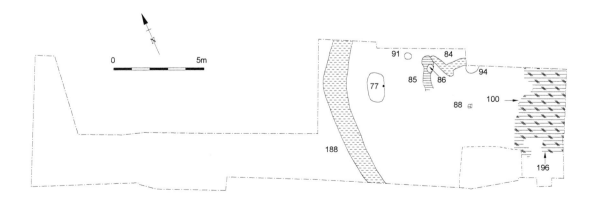

Fig. 8.11 External surfaces to the east with industrial area and ditch to the west: LUBs 21, 22 and 23. (1:200)

dating from the early to mid 2nd to the early 3rd century.

The date for this area of industrial activity must either rest on two sherds from the late 3rd/early 4th centuries (cg77 and cg82), or rely on the bulk of the assemblage and the dates of the overlying stratigraphy. The presence of the overlying stratified pottery which succeeds the bulk of the LUB 22 assemblage does rather suggest that these two anomalous sherds are somehow intrusive in the sequence.

LUB 23 Ditch (Figs. 8.11, 8.12 and 8.25)
To the west of Areas and 3 and 4, a curved ditch cg188 ran round to the west of the features of LUB 22, cutting the robbed remains cg55 (LUB 20) of the east–west wall and the demolition debris cg78 (LUB 20). Most of the pottery from the fill dated from the mid 2nd century but sherds of BB1 cooking pots could extend into the 3rd century.

The ditch was re-cut cg79; its backfill contained a burnt iron-stained layer up to 0.17m thick, the northern end of which contained large quantities of iron slag, small pebbles and ash. Only two small pieces of slag were retained: one (HC) <M52> was identified (by Justine Bayley) as smithing slag and the other (HL) <M49> as fuel-ash slag.

In the lower part of this sequence (HL) the bulk of the pottery, including several examples of RC beakers and one from Colchester(?), suggests a date towards the mid to late 2nd century. But at the top of the sequence (GK) a hooked flanged MOMH mortarium was recovered which is dated to *c* AD 160–250. Given the date of the mortarium, the date of the group could well extend into the 3rd century; the coarse wares fit broadly within this date-range. This could imply that the ditch was backfilled over a period of time. A small amount of the pottery was burnt. There is an absence of SAMEG, DWSH and fabrics in the later Nene Valley repertoire from the total assemblage, which could indicate that the

activity did not extend much beyond the early 3rd century.

LUB 24 Structure 5 (Figs. 8.12, 8.25 and 8.29)
In Areas 2, 3, 4 and 5, sealing the posthole cg91 and pit cg94 (LUB 22), were clay floors cg90 over which was a curved wall cg95, with plaster on its internal face. The stone wall was *c* 0.55m wide, but only survived in places and extended to the north of the site; details of the wall's construction were not recorded. The wall was part of a sub-circular structure with a diameter of between 7 and 8m. The internal plaster on wall cg95 is noted in the excavation records as 'a huge fragment of wallplaster red/pink on white background', commenting also that there were at least two layers of plaster, the earliest extending right down to the level of the clay floor, the later layer stopping some 38 mm short of it. This suggests that the building had been refloored and the wall subsequently replastered.

Floors cg90 were cut by a large posthole or pit cg92. Pit cg92 contained a number of smashed, although not complete vessels.

Two stone-packed postholes cg33 (not planned) cutting cg24 (LUB 5) may have been associated with this building; they had later been truncated and so were isolated from their stratigraphy, but they contained eight sherds of pottery. The samian from posthole cg33 is the first example on the site of SAMCG – a decorated bowl (Dr37) by the QUINTILIANUS group of potters dated to *c* AD 125–150. The presence of later samian as well as a fragment of a probable KOLN beaker with barbotine decoration, probably a hunt cup of late 2nd-, or early 3rd-century date, suggests that it could be related to the period of Structure 5, rather than the earlier industrial period.

The small assemblage from floors cg90 (40 sherds) included fresh sherds of a folded, but undecorated, beaker in a white fabric with a metallic finish of probable Nene Valley origin. Although the sherds were undiagnostic where form is concerned, the

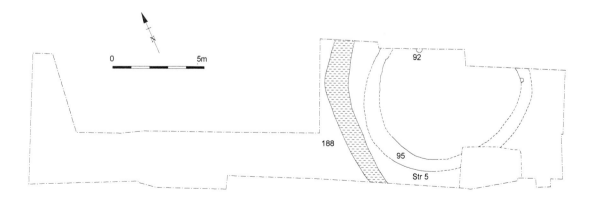

Fig. 8.12 Ditch and Structure 5: LUBs 23 and 24. (1:200)

fabric appears to be part of the earlier rather than later Nene Valley repertoire, dating to the early 3rd century. Pit cg92 (68 sherds) did not contain any diagnostically later pottery.

The date and the reasonably fresh condition of the pottery appear to be in conflict with the evidence of the perhaps intrusive later sherds from the underlying stratigraphy (see cg77 and cg82, LUB 22), which could place the date of this structure well into the 3rd or possibly 4th century.

LUB 25 Demolition of Structure 5 (Fig. 8.25)
Sealing posthole cg92 in Area 3, and over most of Area 4, were layers of burnt material cg96, an extensive layer of charcoal, then charcoal mixed with sand and burnt mortar over which was burnt stone with charcoal. Within this material was an incomplete inhumation of an infant aged about 37 weeks (Boylston and Roberts 1994). There was also a quantity of painted plaster and several dozen nails, with a small quantity of fragmented copper-alloy sheet and strip. One (EZ) <G92> of the two pieces of vessel glass recovered had been distorted by heat. Burnt material cg96 produced a pottery assemblage which contained examples of smashed and burnt (some heavily) pottery. The group, as a whole, is very similar to that from LUB 23 and hence the bulk of the material dates from the late 2nd to early 3rd century. A probable NVCC beaker sherd is likely to date to the 3rd century, whereas fragments of a flagon or jug in NVCC could date to the mid 3rd century. As the assemblage is a large group of 489 sherds, the continued absence of DWSH and later BB1 forms adds credence to an early 3rd-century date. Deposit cg96 was contaminated by a sherd of Late Saxon pottery.

Two further infant bones found within a later surface cg97 (LUB 26) may be from the same inhumation as that from cg96 (LUB 25), suggesting that this had been disturbed, and perhaps accounting for the fragmentary nature of the skeleton (Boylston and Roberts 1994).

Late Roman

There was possibly another building Structure 6.1 **LUB 26** constructed on Ermine Street, in Areas 2, 4 and 5; the cobbles immediately to the west of the wall cg34, however, suggest an external surface. The pottery from LUB 26 indicates a mid 3rd-century date. There was activity **LUB 27** to the east of the building, in Area 5, cutting the earlier road surfaces (LUB 21); pottery dates this activity from the mid 3rd century into the 4th. There was evidence of surfaces within Structure 6.2 **LUB 28** and pottery from these dated from the early through to the late 4th century.

LUB 26 Structure 6.1A (Figs. 8.13, 8.24 and 8.25)
In Area 5, apparently cutting the remains of Structure 5 (LUB 25), were the stone foundations for wall cg34 (relationships were not recorded). It was at least 1.83m north–south and 0.56m wide; no further description was recorded. Sealing ditch fill cg79 (LUB 23) in Area 2 was a layer of sand with some stone and mortar cg195, perhaps deposited to counteract the consolidation of the underlying fills. Overlying cg195 was sandy make-up and a mortar surface cg97, covering Areas 2 and 4, possibly linked to wall cg34. A large group of finds from the make-up, composed largely of iron nails and painted plaster with some domestic rubbish, is closely comparable to that from the underlying destruction levels of Structure 5 (LUB 25).

Sealing the mortar cg97 was gravelly mortar sealed by cobbles; there were two patches cg98 and cg99. Cobbles cg98 were sealed by mixed sand, mortar, ash and clay cg101 (0.50m thick), possibly make-up for cobble surface cg102; this surface was very worn. Building debris – a small quantity of iron nails and painted plaster, together with vessel glass fragments – was found within cobbles cg99. As might be expected, much of the material within the mortar and cobble make-up and surfaces seemed

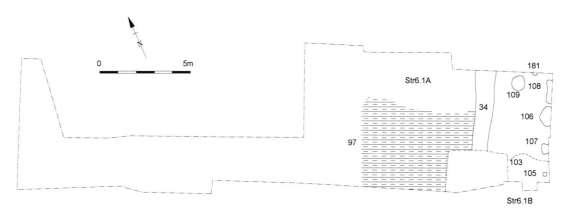

Fig. 8.13 Structure 6.1A and 6.1B: LUBs 26 and 27. (1:200)

to have been disturbed from LUB 25; two infant bones from cg97 suggests redeposition from cg96 (LUB 25). The cobbled surfaces suggest an external area.

The pottery assemblage (6 sherds) from wall cg34 is entirely composed of 1st-century pottery, and is accordingly considered to be residual. Burnt material and the comparative similarity between the pottery from cg195 (95 sherds) and that from ditch fill LUB 23, suggest redeposition. The pottery assemblage from cg97 (457 sherds) is also very similar to the underlying structure (LUB 24), having a number of CR flagons sherds as well as RC beakers that may be derived from the South Carlton kilns. This suggests that some of the material is residual. However, in comparison to the underlying LUB 25, there was a relatively higher occurrence of NVCC, including an identifiable BKFOSF dated to the mid to late 3rd century which provides a mid 3rd-century start date for its deposition. The first incidence of DWSH and obtuse lattice decorated BB1 from the site in the overlying deposit (cg98 – 63 sherds) confirms the date range. Similarly-dated groups were derived from cg101 (84 sherds) and cg102 (11 sherds), but the absence of BFBH and later Roman fabrics suggests that occupation did not extend much beyond the late 3rd century. Layer cg195 and mortar surface cg97 were contaminated by intrusive medieval pottery.

LUB 27 Roadside: Structural features 6.1B
(Figs. 8.13 and 8.25)
In Area 5, to the east of wall cg34 (LUB 26), the cobbles cg100 (LUB 21) were cut by small pits cg108 and cg109, posthole cg181 and slot cg104 (unplanned); slot cg104 was cut by pit cg106. Cobbles cg196 (LUB 21) were cut by pits cg103 and cg107. Posthole cg105 cut pit cg103. Cobbles cg100 (LUB 21) were also sealed by a patch of pebble surface cg110. This was sealed by layers cg202 and cut by a posthole or slot cg203, which was abutted by a cobbled surface cg204. This was sealed by gravelly surface cg205,

over which was a layer of dark green silt cg206. Both the cut feature cg203 and the silt were sealed by sandy make-up cg207. The cobbles probably indicate the edge of the street; the pits and postholes were all probably associated with roadside activity, possibly indicating the position of roadside stalls. Their undefined nature has led them to be labelled "structural features". The stratigraphic sequence was truncated at this point by modern disturbance.

The very small group of pottery from this LUB (31 sherds), of which 10 sherds are exclusively late 1st- to 2nd-century wares, relies on the presence of BKFOS NVCC beakers for a mid 3rd-century date (although these forms continued in use into the 4th century).

LUB 28 Structure 6.2 (Figs. 8.14 and 8.24)
Sealing cobbles cg102 (LUB 26) was sand with pebbles cg112, possibly make-up (0.15m thick). A large group of finds recovered from make-up cg112 was composed largely of structural debris, including several dozen nails and other fragments of iron with some painted plaster, together with domestic refuse, much of it redeposited; also in cg112 was a moderately-sized bone assemblage which also suggested domestic refuse (Dobney *et al* 1994c). The pottery assemblage (633 sherds), although mostly residual as it contains some abraded pottery, includes a number of smashed vessels with near complete profiles; the bulk of the material is mid to late 3rd century in date, but a sherd of a jar in NVGW, RPNV69–70, dated to the 4th century, and a fragment of a large jar in TILE and part of a DWSH lid-seated jar, may date to the early 4th century. There is an absence of BFBH GREY bowls, SPOX, and no very late Roman fabrics such as LCOA, OXRC and SPIR. Make-up cg112 also contained a worn coin of Constantine II, a **Gloria Exercitus** issue of AD 330–5. An early to mid 4th-century date for the group from cg112 is likely. Make-up cg112 was cut by slots cg113 and cg114 and sealed by metalled surfaces

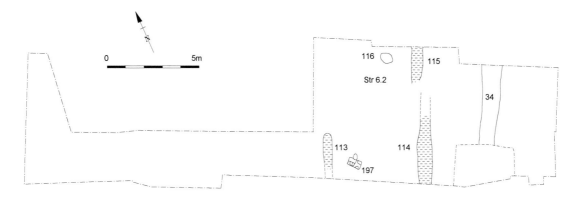

Fig. 8.14 Structure 6.2: LUB 28. (1:200)

cg117, possibly cg118 and mortar/clay floors cg119. Between the slots, in Area 2, may have been a tiled hearth cg197 (there was no written record at all for the hearth, although it was planned as being cut by posts cg134 LUB 35). Cobbles cg99 were cut by possible gully cg115 and pit cg116.

The assemblage from slot cg113 consists of 14 Roman sherds broadly dating to the mid 3rd century or later. However, there was also a sherd of late 9th- to 10th-century medieval pottery implying contamination by later activity. The remaining context groups from LUB 28 (cg114, cg115, cg116, cg117 and cg119) produced pottery very similar in content to that from cg112. The presence of a high number of Cream flagon sherds from cg114 (94 sherds) and cg115 (224 sherds) is reminiscent of the assemblages from underlying LUBs 24 and 26. Although it is possible that make-up layer cg112 consisted of material imported on to the site, the presence of the flagon sherds from cg114 and cg115 suggests that some of the pottery may have been disturbed from underlying layers. Apart from cg119 the total assemblage from these context groups (469 sherds) dates to the mid to late 3rd century. The assemblage (14 sherds) from the latest layer in the sequence of mortar/clay floors cg119, includes two vessels – a JDLS in DWSH and a NVCC BFB – which are commonly dated to the mid to late 4th century.

Very Late Roman to Late Saxon

Structure 6 was demolished and robbed **LUB 29**; this activity was associated with very late 4th-century pottery.

LUB 29 Demolition and robbing of Structure 6 (Figs. 8.24–25)

The Roman wall cg34 (LUB 26) was robbed cg111. In Area 5, overlying gully cg115, pit cg116 and layer cg119 (LUB 28), were sand, limestone chips, mortar and plaster cg120 (0.50m thick). This was sealed by layers of mixed mortar cg121. Both the robbing cg111 and the debris cg121 were sealed by stone rubble and soil cg122 which spread into Areas 3 and 4; this was cut by a scoop cg125 (unplanned) with more rubble and building debris, over which were further layers of rubble and soil cg130, which also sealed gully cg114 (LUB 28), in Areas 2 and 4.

Sealing part of scoop cg125 (LUB 29) was building material cg180. Rubble and loose soil cg145 (no record of what it sealed) was thought to be equivalent to cg130. A deposit of green mortary material cg138 probably belongs to this LUB (no record of what it sealed).

Layers cg120, cg122, cg130 and cg180 contained much redeposited building material, which, as well as rubble and mortar, included ironwork (largely nails), painted plaster and a little window glass, together with some domestic rubbish and a large quantity (68) of Roman coins. Dumps cg122 and cg130 contained small assemblages of animal bone which both suggest domestic refuse (Dobney *et al* 1994c).

In addition to the large amount of residual Roman pottery there was also some of very late 4th-century date. Dumps cg120 contained the first incidence of LCOA ware from the site – a JDLS, of late to very late 4th-century date. Increasing amounts of LCOA came from cg122 and cg130 groups and cg130 produced the first incidence of OXRC and SPIR wares together with GREY BIBF bowls, suggesting that the Roman occupation continued into the very late 4th century.

It is possible that this LUB was at least in part Late Saxon in date, because of the presence of post-Roman pottery (eight sherds from cg120, 81 sherds from cg122, four from cg125, 99 from cg130, seven from cg180 and a single sherd from cg138; this pottery forms about 8% of the sherd count and is itself mixed). The pottery suggests the site was reoccupied by the early to mid 10th century (as indicated by pits LUB 30) as most of the pottery was typical of the 10th century. But there were few other finds from cg122 and cg130 of diagnostically late-Saxon type. Intrusive early to mid 11th-century pottery probably came from later activity (LUBs 39 and 41).

Late Saxon

In Areas 2, 3 and 4 were a number of pits **LUB 30** with pottery dating to the 10th century, and in Area 1 pits **LUB 31** contained pottery dating from the mid 10th century.

In Area 3 were traces of a timber building, Structure 7.1 **LUB 32** associated with pottery dating to the late 10th or early 11th century. Replacing this building was another, Structure 7.2 **LUB 33** associated with early 11th-century pottery. To the north of Area 4 was a dump **LUB 34** containing late 10th- to early 11th-century pottery; it sealed LUB 32, and was contemporary with LUB 33.

In Area 2 was evidence for another timber building, Structure 8.1 **LUB 35**; this cut LUB 30 and contained pottery of a similar date; the next phase of this building, Structure 8.2 **LUB 36** contained early to mid 11th-century pottery. It was sealed by dumps **LUB 37** with early to mid 11th-century pottery.

In Area 4, between the two structures and sealing LUB 30, was a series of dumps, probably middens **LUB 38**; the pottery is contemporary with that from Structures 7 and 8. In Areas 2 and 3, any remains of the structures were sealed by dumps, which were cut by pits **LUB 39**; the pottery dated up to the mid 11th century.

LUB 30 Pits (Figs. 8.15 and 8.24–25)
In Areas 2, 3 and 4 were a number of cut features. A shallow feature cg123 (unplanned) cut the cobbles cg99 (LUB 28), and was filled with clay containing ash and other fire debris; also cutting these cobbles was pit cg127 which had a sand and mussel shell fill. Pit cg129, a pit full of building debris cg135 (unplanned) and an undefined feature cg124 (unplanned), all cut cg120 (LUB 29); pit cg131, which cut layers cg120 and cg130 (LUB 29), had a "sticky" green fill with oyster shells. Two small pits cg132, to the south of Area 4, cut cg130. Pit cg126, with a green mortary material in the fill, cut cg122 (LUB 29) and a pit cg136, with greenish-yellow sand with black material, cut pit cg127. Pit cg139 cut cg138 (LUB 29); it was large and roughly circular with a black "sticky" lower fill below a decayed organic fill; a crucible sherd and an antler fragment from the fill suggest craft and industrial activity in the area (Dobney *et al* 1994c). Later deposits appear to have slumped into pit cg139. Pottery vessels from these pits (three post-Roman sherds from cg126, 19 from cg127, 15 from cg129, 21 from cg131, nine from cg132, six each from cg135 and cg139, 84 from cg136 and three from depression cg123) were mainly heavily-sooted jars and bowls, and a high proportion of these vessels have an internal iron coating indicating that they were intended for use as liquid containers. However, pottery from pit cg136 did not have an internal iron slip.

Most of the pottery dates to the 10th century; the typology of several of the vessels suggested a date for much of the material to before the mid 10th century. Pottery from pit cg136 dates to or from the mid 10th century and those from pit cg132 produced a small group with the latest sherds dating from the late 10th century.

LUB 31 Pits to west of site (Fig. 8.15)
In Area 1, which was largely excavated by machine, there were a number of pits cg184 which could belong to this period (unplanned; no recorded stratigraphic relationships). Recorded as possibly overlying cg49 (LUB 4) was a layer of green-black soil cg160. Pit cg185 (no record of what it cut) had ashy organic fills. Pit cg156 (unplanned) cut cg55 (LUB 20). Pit or pits cg158 and pit cg154 (no recorded stratigraphic relationships) possibly belong to this LUB, together with pit cg155 (no record of what it cut). A pit cg153 (unplanned; no recorded stratigraphic relationships) with a greenish fill was cut by an ash-filled pit cg157.

Although little material was recovered from these pits (a single post-Roman sherd each from cg154 and cg160, three sherds in cg156 and cg157 and two sherds in cg155), sherds were dated to the 10th century, and the pottery from cg155, cg156 and cg157 indicted a date after the mid-10th century. A bone skate (OE) <B30> (Rackham 1994) was found in one of the pits assigned group context cg184, suggesting this feature to be of Late Saxon or later date.

LUB 32 Structure 7.1
(Figs. 8.16, 8.24, 8.25, 8.26 and 8.30)
Sealing pit cg126 (LUB 30) in Area 3 was a spread of ashy layers and lenses of mussel shell cg128, which also filled a gully which formed its southern edge; the gully cut pits cg126 and cg127 (LUB 31). The gully possibly represents evidence for a timber structure. Found within the gully were fragments of a vessel (AF) <P34> with traces of haematite or madder on the interior, possibly used as a dye-pot, and a perforated ceramic disc, perhaps used as a spindlewhorl (AF) <P8>. Gully cg128 was also filled with a large assemblage of pottery (210 post-Roman sherds). Most of the pottery vessels were unglazed, heavily-sooted jars. A high proportion of the shell-tempered wares had decalcified interiors, and two vessels had thick white interior deposits, indicating their use as liquid storage vessels. There were seven vessels with spalled surfaces together with heavy sooting; these may be wasters.

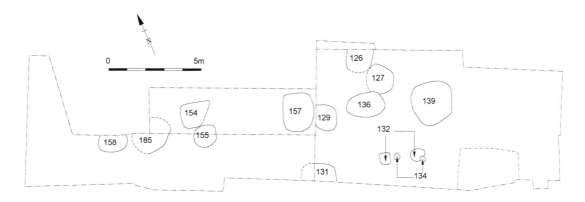

Fig. 8.15 Pits: LUB 30. (1:200)

It seems most likely that the pottery was deposited in the late 10th or very early 11th century; it was mixed with residual earlier 10th-century material.

LUB 33 Structure 7.2 (Fig. 8.17)

In Area 3, sealing the area north of the gully cg128 (LUB 32), was a flat stone surface cg150; over the surface was a layer of ash cg152 (LUB 0.30m thick). It is interesting that no finds at all were recovered from ash layer cg152 or surface cg150. Also sealing the gully was a thick layer of ash cg199 (0.45m thick). Two postholes cg143 cut layer cg199. Layer cg199 contained a small (17 post-Roman sherds) but probably contemporary assemblage of early 11th-century pottery.

LUB 34 Dump (Figs. 8.17 and 8.25)

To the south of Area 3, a "sticky" brown layer, cg144 (0.45m thick), overlay gully cg128 (LUB 32) but had no stratigraphic relationship with deposits of Structure 7.2 (LUB 33). Within it were found two crucible sherds, and a moderate assemblage of animal bone which suggests dumping of primary butchery waste; all five identifiable cattle horncores had been sawn, chopped or exhibited knife marks around their base (Dobney *et al* 1994c).

Dump cg144 contained a large group of material (134 post-Roman sherds) very similar in composition to that from cg128. Some of the material again seems to be of an earlier 10th-century date. Only a few sherds can reliably date the deposition of this dump to the late 10th or early 11th centuries. Fragments of 17th- or 18th-century wine-bottle glass from within dump cg144 were intrusive, presumably from drain cg178 (LUB 48) which had truncated the upper part of the dump.

LUB 35 Structure 8.1 (Fig. 8.16)

In Area 2, sealing pit cg131 was a reddish dark brown deposit cg133 with small stones, which may have been part of the levelling for the construction of this building. Pottery vessels from cg133 are heavily sooted with two vessels having internal iron slips similar to those found on material from the earlier pits. Cutting cg197 (LUB 28), cg132 (LUB 30) and cg133 was a row of postholes cg134 aligned east–west. The pottery from this LUB dates to the late 10th century (25 post-Roman sherds from cg133 and a single sherd from cg134).

LUB 36 Structure 8.2? (Fig. 8.17)

Layers of ash and charcoal (0.15–0.30m thick) cg140 sealed the postholes cg134 (LUB 35) in Area 2 and the south of the gully cg128 (LUB 32), in the northern part of Area 4. This deposit was sealed by a thick clay floor cg141, over which there was a layer of mixed ash cg142 (thickness not recorded but described as varying between thin and thick) which extended to the northern part of Area 4. Layers cg140 (57 post-Roman sherds) and cg142 (24 post-Roman sherds) contained small assemblages of mixed pottery, including a crucible sherd with the latest sherds dating up to the early to mid 11th century.

LUB 37 Dumps over Structure 8.2 (Fig. 8.24)

Layer of stone and dark soil, cg146, sealed cg142 (LUB 36; unplanned) in Areas 2 and 4. An assemblage of animal bone from cg146 suggests domestic refuse (Dobney *et al* 1994c). Within cg146 were found a single crucible sherd and part of a glass 'cake' containing a blob of lead (AD)<G1O>. Layer cg146 also contained a large assemblage of pottery (303 post-Roman sherds) composed mainly of heavily-sooted vessels with decalcified interiors; several also have internal white deposits. One sherd has a possible deposit of madder on the interior. This group is very similar in composition to that from gully cg128 (LUB 32) and dump cg144 (LUB 34). Again, most of the material dates to the 10th century with a smaller number of sherds dating to the 11th century. There are some definite joins back to earlier deposits. The presence of several LFS vessels dates the

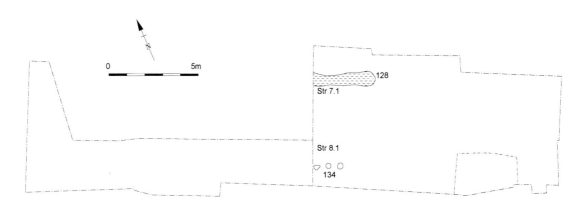

Fig. 8.16 Structures 7.1 and 8.1: LUBs 32 and 35. (1:200)

deposition of the dump to the early to mid 11th century.

LUB 38 Middens (Fig. 8.33)
In Area 4, between Structures 7 and 8, pit cg136 (LUB 30) was sealed by secondary deposits of ash, mussel shell and other debris cg137 and cg147 (both unplanned). Ash cg137 was overlain by dumps of soil cg162 and cg163 (both unplanned), which indicate levelling and/or the raising of the ground surface.

A large group of finds was recovered from dump cg137, particularly the lowermost levels, which had slumped into pit cg136 (LUB 30). A little industrial waste included fragments of fuel-ash, ?iron and smithing slag, one piece of which had fused to a hearth-bottom, together with two crucible sherds and a few small pieces of copper-alloy sheet, strip or waste, including two tapering fragments of copper-alloy strip (AS) <Ae12> and (BA) <Ae50>, possibly unfinished finger-rings. There was also a little structural ironwork and domestic refuse including a copper-alloy strap-end (AH) <Ae5> (Fig. 8.33 No 1) and a small decorated copper-alloy bell (BA) <Ae49> (Fig. 8.33 No2). Only a handful of registered finds came from dump cg147, although these included

another crucible sherd (AB) <P19>, together with an unusual item – a small sherd from a soapstone vessel (AB) <M66>. Moderately sized assemblages of animal bone were examined from cg137 and cg147, which represent a mixture of domestic and primary butchery waste; there was also one human bone fragment (Dobney *et al* 1994c). Most of the pottery vessels (330 post-Roman sherds in cg137, 170 in cg147, six in cg162 and nine in cg163) were heavily-sooted jars and bowls, several with interior white deposits, similar to the material in cg128 (LUB 32), cg144 (LUB 34) and cg146 (LUB 47). Debris cg137 and cg147 contained large assemblages of pottery in which there was a considerable proportion of 10th-century material in association with some from the 11th century. Overall the pottery gives the LUB a latest date between the early to mid 11th century.

LUB 39 Levelling and pits (Figs. 8.18 and 8.24)
To the south (Area 2) and north of the site (Area 3) Structure 7.2 (LUB 33) and dumps (LUB 37) were sealed by levelling. Levelling layer cg146 (LUB 37), in Area 2 was sealed by further levelling layers of ash and stone, cg164. Cut into dump cg147 (LUB 38), in Area 2 was a large pit, cg148; its lower fill was stony while the upper fills were described as

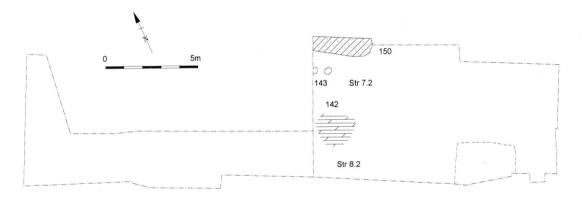

Fig. 8.17 Structures 7.2 and 8.2: LUBs 33 and 36. (1:200)

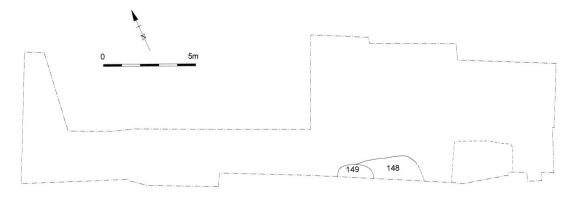

Fig. 8.18 Pits: LUB 39. (1:200)

'sticky'. It was cut by another pit, cg149, filled with fire debris, and containing a ceramic ingot mould (EL) <P28>. Sealing surface cg150 (LUB 33) in Area 3 was dark material with stone cg151.

Levelling cg164 contained a small assemblage of pottery (27 post-Roman sherds), the latest sherds dating to the mid 11th century. Levelling cg151 contained a small group (14 post-Roman sherds) dating to the 11th century. Pits cg148 and cg149 (33 and 39 post-Roman sherds repectively) contained mostly residual 10th-century material with some late 10th- or 11th-century sherds.

Early Medieval

Sealing levelling and pits LUB 39, in Area 3, were cobbles **LUB 40**, dated by their location in the stratigraphic sequence to the early medieval period. In Area 1 were pits **LUB 41** containing a few sherds of 12th-century pottery.

LUB 40 Cobbles (Fig. 8.19)
Sealing levelling deposit cg151 (LUB 39) in Area 3 was a surface, cg172, formed of a spread of small cobbles. These traces of activity probably indicate the presence of another structure on the site, all direct evidence of which had been removed by levelling for Structure 9 (LUB 42). There was no pottery dating, but stratigraphically it belongs to this period.

LUB 41 Pits (Fig. 8.19)
In Area 1, cutting pit cg153 (LUB 31) were at least two pits cg159, excavated as one. A small assemblage of animal bone from cg159 is composed mainly of primary butchery waste and several horncores had been chopped and sawn through their bases (Dobney *et al* 1994c). On the south side of Area 1 was an unplanned pit cg161, possibly part of this group. Sealing pit cg159 was levelling cg186, machined away on top. Cutting earlier pit cg158 (LUB 31) was pit cg187; it too was partly machined away. Pits cg159

(19 post-Roman sherds), cg161 (one post-Roman sherd) and cg187 (30 post-Roman sherds), together with levelling cg186 (26 post-Roman sherds), saw the introduction of 12th-century wares on to the site.

High Medieval

Over Areas 1, 2, 3 and 4 was evidence of a stone-founded building **LUB 42**, whose construction was dated by pottery to between the late 13th and the early to mid 14th century. It probably extended to the east into Area 5, so fronting the High Street, but the front of the building was cut away by later cellarage. It had a minimum of three rooms together with an internal garderobe or fireplace.

LUB 42 Structure 9 (Figs. 8.20 and 8.24)
There was a levelling dump cg175 which contained lenses of clean sand and mixed layers of mixed sand and clay; it sealed cg146 (LUB 39) in Area 2 and cg162 (LUB 38) in Area 4. Sand, clay and limestone chips cg165 sealed cg164 (LUB 39) in Area 2, and mixed sandy spread cg173 sealed the cobbles cg172 (LUB 40) in Area 3. Integral with the construction layers cg165 and cg173 were the stone wall foundations cg166 of a building aligned east–west which probably fronted on the High Street and extended about 24m back from it. Both the north and south walls had substantial foundations (0.84m wide) constructed with pitched stones; those for the southern wall had one or two offsets on its north side. The north–south distance between the walls was 4.75m. The building had two internal north–south dividing walls cg167, creating at least three rooms. The east wall was 0.89m wide at its base and had facing stones to the east and west with a rubble core. The wall to the west was 0.66m wide and was composed of small stones. Both internal walls cg167 sealed the offsets on the north side of the south wall cg166.

To the east of the building was a stone-lined pit cg168, possibly the base of a garderobe. The pit was

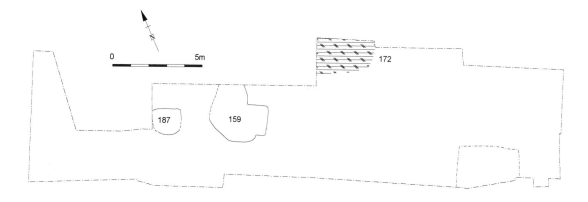

Fig. 8.19 Cobbles and pits: LUBs 40 and 41. (1:200)

1.37m north–south by at least 0.76m east–west. It was constructed of stone bonded with crumbly mortar and was only faced internally. Running to the north, and of the same build, was the north–south wall cg166. It was sealed by dark soil cg174 (four post-Roman sherds). There was some building debris cg171 (no recorded relationships) containing eight post-Roman sherds inside the building.

That levelling layer cg165 was associated with the construction of Structure 9 is supported by the fact that it has sherds of the same vessel as foundations cg166. Both cg165 (28 post-Roman sherds) and cg166 (27 post-Roman sherds) contain similar assemblages of 14th-century pottery. The internal walls cg167 (seven post-Roman sherds) and dark soil cg174 (four post-Roman sherds) associated with Structure 9 also contain sherds dating to the late 13th or 14th century. The pottery indicates that the construction of Structure 9 probably dates to between the late 13th and the early/mid 14th century.

Late Medieval

Structure 9 was demolished **LUB 43**, leaving no remains of internal flooring or other occupation material.

Another building was constructed on the site, Structure 10. The only evidence surviving of this was a stone-lined cellar **LUB 44**, constructed sometime before the late 15th century; it contained some finds of considerable interest (see discussion). The cellar was found where Areas 2, 4 and 5 met, but the building to which it belonged probably covered the whole site.

LUB 43 Demolition of Structure 9

The robber trench cg183 of the walls cg166 (LUB 42) was filled with rubble. Fill cg183 contained three sherds of 14th- to 15th-century pottery.

LUB 44 Structure 10
(Figs. 8.21, 8.31, 8.34 and 8.35)

Another building was constructed, but the only evidence for this was a stone-lined cellar cg169, possibly a cold cellar, cutting through cg146 (LUB 37) in part of Areas 2, 4 and 5. The building to which it belonged probably covered Areas 1–5. The cellar had a lower fill cg170 which included several complete pottery vessels, two copper-alloy candlesticks, a small group of glassware and several small textile fragments (see discussion and Fig. 8.35). There were also the remains of three cats, two being

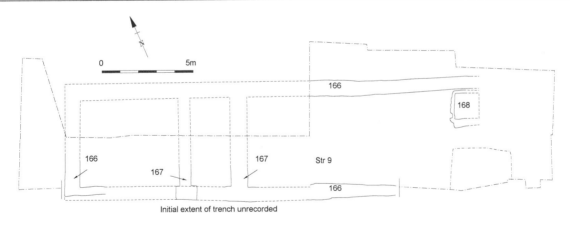

Fig. 8.20 Structure 9: LUB 42. (1:200)

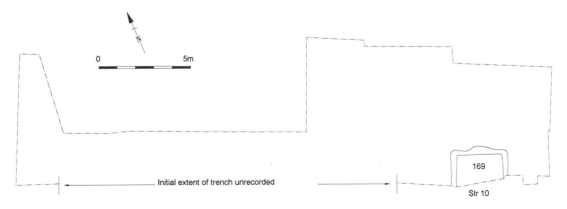

Fig. 8.21 Cellar of structure 10: LUB 44. (1:200)

relatively complete skeletons, together with a number of chicken bones, a frontal and mandible fragment of a large bird, possibly crane (*Grus sp.*) (Dobney *et al* 1994c). The pottery (57 post-Roman sherds) is tightly dated to between the late 15th to early/mid 16th centuries (Figs. 8.34); see discussion for details.

Post Medieval

Structure 10 was demolished **LUB 45** in the mid 17th century, as indicated by the glass.

Structure 11 was probably built after the demolition of Structure 10, in the mid 17th century. A soakaway **LUB 46**, the only evidence of the building to have survived, had late 17th- to early 18th-century clay tobacco pipe fragments in its fill.

LUB 45 Demolition of Structure 10 (Fig. 8.36)
The cellar was sealed by debris cg200. Debris cg200 contained a group of slightly later pottery (36 post-Roman sherds) dating the destruction of the building to sometime between the late 16th century and early to mid 17th century (Fig. 8.36); however, the glass from this debris dated the demolition of the building more clearly to the mid 17th century. For further information about finds, see Discussion.

LUB 46 Structure 11 (Fig. 8.22)
Traces of a building with a cellar were found in the form of a soakaway cg176 in Area 5; the building to which it belonged had probably covered Areas 1–5. The soakaway cg176 (four post-Roman sherds) contained pottery dating to the 17th or 18th centuries, together with several clay tobacco pipe bowls, the latest dating to *c* 1680–1720.

Modern

Structure 11 was demolished **LUB 47** between the mid 18th and 19th centuries according to the clay tobacco pipe evidence. Another building **LUB 48** was probably constructed at the turn of the 20th century.

LUB 47 Demolition of Structure 11
Structure 11 was levelled and sealed with rubble cg177. Cg177 contained three sherds of 18th- to 20th-century pottery (BS) whilst the latest clay tobacco pipes from cg177 are dated *c* 1740–1800.

LUB 48 Structure 12 (Figs. 8.23 and 8.25)
Earlier stratigraphy was truncated by a brick-lined cellar cg198 in Area 5. To the north-west of this was the cut of a drain trench cg178, in Area 3, possibly

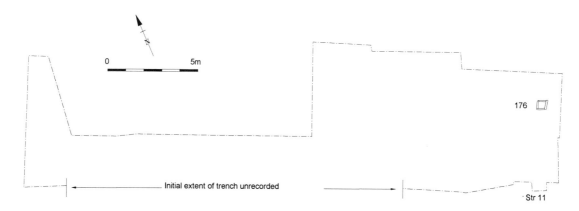

Fig. 8.22 Soakaway of structure 11: LUB 46. (1:200)

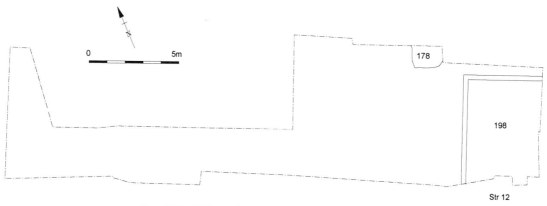

Fig. 8.23 Cellar of structure 12: LUB 48. (1:200)

for a down pipe on the north wall of the property; the building again would probably have extended across Areas 1, 2, 3, 4 and 5.

Discussion

Dating of the Roman sequence: ceramic evidence

The site is extraordinary, when compared with the other Wigford sites, because of the high incidence of 1st-century Roman pottery, in particular material dating from *c* AD 40–80. There appears to be a decline in the early 2nd and a moderate rise in the mid to late 2nd century. This perhaps reflects the hiatus between the abandonment of the legionary fortress and the development of the *colonia*. This is followed by a further decline in the early 3rd century with, in turn, a smaller peak in the mid to late 3rd century and another slight decline in the early 4th century. Apart from the latest phase of the site which tends to tail off towards the end of the 4th century, this pattern of rise and fall appears to mirror the economic cycles suggested by Christopher Going (Going 1992). He proposed that there was: a boom around *c* AD 40–90; a slump around *c* AD 90–130; a boom from *c* AD 130–200; another slump from *c* AD 200–250; followed by a boom *c* AD 250–300; a long slump from *c* AD 300–370; followed by a boom around *c* AD 370–400. These results are stimulating and point the way to further research, but there are many other factors which should be taken into consideration, including the dating generally ascribed to nationally distributed Roman wares.

Alternative interpretations: earliest phases

Slight alterations have been suggested in the interpretation of the late Iron Age to Early Roman features (Darling and Jones 1988); this has stemmed from further detailed investigation of the stratigraphic record. The best way to compare this interpretation with that already published is through the phase plans (Figs. 8.4 and 8.5 together with Darling and Jones 1988, Fig. 4). There are differences in some of the feature dimensions; the measurements used here are congruent with the published sections (Darling and Jones 1988, Fig. 3) as well as the plans (both in this volumes and those already published).

The earlier interpretation had tentatively divided the features into three possible phases, recognising that there was not strong enough stratigraphic evidence for the published Period Iab to be differentiated from Period Ibc; the published sequence of most of these two groups of features could be reversed given the paucity of evidence – the only definite relationship lay in cg12 being later than cg4. Postholes cg21 were later than cg9, but this is not clear in the published phasing. Features cg192 were not mentioned at all in the earlier publication, perhaps because they were not given context letters during excavation. Slot cg20 (LUB 3) cut cg1 (LUB 1) as did cg7 (LUB 3) and both were sealed by cg22 (LUB 3), indicating that both could have belonged to the same phase of activity. The pottery from pit cg3 (LUB 4) indicates that it was possibly slightly later in date than gully cg11 (LUB 2), and may have been created after the structure inside the gully went out of use. Pit cg49 (LUB 4) cut gully cg11.

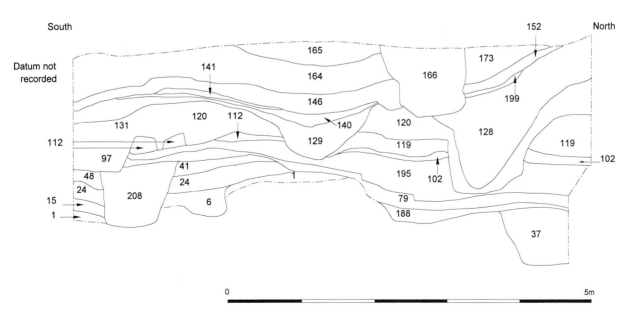

Fig. 8.24 Section to the west of Area 3 and the northern part of Area 4, illustrating the stratigraphy here, from LUB 1 to LUB 42. (1:50)

Topography

The layout of the site from LUB 2 onwards was dominated by the presence of a north–south road to the east of the site with all its commercial potential. Ditch cg9 (LUB 3) is possibly the only evidence that there was a precursor to Ermine Street, or it could be that this ditch was instead linked to conquest period activity and to the construction of the road. Contemporary activity suggests timber buildings (LUB 2) and possibly some sort of roadside activity (LUB 3). The possible timber buildings of LUBs 4–5 do not have such a clear link with the road, but Structure 4 is seen to front Ermine Street, with possible roadside activity to the east in the form of stalls or booths (LUBs 10, 14 and 17), similar to that from LUB 3. Structure 4,

probably of late 1st-century date, is best interpreted as representing early *colonia* activity outside the walls; it appears to stretch back from the road with a boundary/structural wall extending beyond the limit of excavation to the west.

The site went through a phase of industrial use (LUB 22), when a curved ditch (LUB 23) first cut around to the west of Areas 2, 3 and 4. Within the area of the ditch a circular stone-founded building, Structure 5, was constructed up against the road. This burned down, to be replaced by Structure 6, a stone-founded building fronting the road; contemporary was evidence of roadside activity (LUB 27).

The site was abandoned from the very late Roman period through to the Late Saxon period, when it was used for pitting (LUB 30); any associated

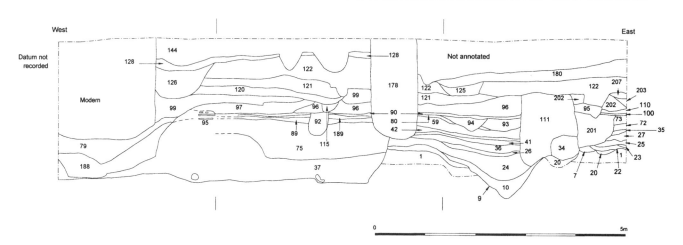

Fig. 8.25 Section to the north of Areas 3 and 5, illustrating the stratigraphy here, from LUB 1 to LUB 48. (1:73)

Fig. 8.26 Looking north at the section of ditch cg9, sealed by later floors, cut by wall cg34, robbed by trench and fill cg111.

structural features fronting the road were probably cut away by Victorian cellaring (LUB 48), but there were traces of subsequent late Saxon buildings running back from the road (LUBs 32, 33, 35 and 36) with middens between them (LUB 38).

Any early medieval building fronting the road was also cut away by Victorian cellaring (LUB 48); there were traces of a cobbled yard to the rear (LUB 40) and pitting (LUB 41). Evidence of high medieval Structure 9 (LUB 42), a stone-founded building, almost covers the entire extent of the plot on which the excavation took place. It probably fronted the road, but this part of the building was cut away by Victorian cellaring (LUB 48), and extended about 24m from it.

There was evidence in the form of cellars for subsequent buildings on the site – Structures 10, 11 and 12 (LUBs 44, 46 and 48). It would seem that this was a prime position on the High Street, occupied from the Late Saxon period onwards.

The Iron Age and Roman property boundaries

The first indication of property alignment is north–south ditch cg9 (LUB 3) of the mid 1st century, which ran parallel with, and about 5 or 6 metres from, Ermine Street. This does not seem to have survived long and there is no trace of any boundaries in LUBs 4, 5 and 6.

By the late 1st century, Structure 4 provides two very clear boundaries – that with the road (robbed north–south wall) and east–west wall cg47 to the south of the site; this wall extends for at least 26 metres to the west. These boundaries survive until sometime between the early and mid 2nd century, when Structure 4 was demolished (LUB 20). Then a curved ditch (LUB 23) was inserted, possibly a boundary around an area of industrial activity (LUB 22) in the later 2nd and early 3rd century and then around Structure 5 in the early 3rd century. The curved ditch accentuated the importance of Ermine Street to which the site had direct access, and the marginal nature of the land to the west. This pattern is abandoned and the next property, Structure 6, fronted Ermine Street with a clear boundary between it and the street; the extent of Structure 6 to the north and south lay beyond the limits of the excavation.

Fig. 8.27 Looking west at hearth cg45 abutting wall cg47 (robbed by trench cg55).

Fig. 8.28 Looking west along the robber trench cg55.

The Iron Age and Roman military-phase buildings

Although there seems to have been some sort of occupation of the site in the Late Iron Age, it is difficult to understand what exactly was happening on the site. Disturbed subsoil (LUB 1), followed by postholes, gullies, pits and a hearth in Areas 1–4 (LUB 2) and postholes and slots in Areas 4 and 5 (LUB 3), indicate some sort of structural features (Structural features 1 and 2) related to timber buildings. The north–south ditch (LUB 2) might be linked to the construction of Ermine Street. The structural elements recovered on the site may well suggest temporary encampment. Pottery from LUBs 2 and 3 dates from the late Iron Age to the Roman conquest period; it is possible, given the use and re-use of pottery, that all the activity here dates to around the Roman conquest and that here the Roman army was using native pottery. A socketed iron spearhead, possibly residual, in floor cg15 (LUB 4) is the only clearly military find to escape the Roman army's abandonment of the site. The site would have been of some strategic importance, as in the late Iron Age and early Roman period the Witham was very much wider than it is today. It is probable that the land here was on an island in the river, and it was here perhaps that the river crossing was guarded, perhaps before the construction of a bridge.

There was evidence for Early Roman occupation (between the mid to late 1st century) in Areas 1–5, in the form of pits, a gully, a slot, a posthole and possible floors (Structural features 3.1, LUB 4) suggesting timber buildings, but the evidence is not strong enough to give a clear indication about how the site was arranged. There seems to have been a period of abandonment before there were further traces of occupation in the form of an area of collapsed wallplaster and an east–west slot (Structural features 3.2, LUB 5). To the east of the site in Area 5, sealing features in LUB 3, were possible surfaces, perhaps indicating an area to the edge of Ermine Street (LUB 6).

Colonia – period buildings

The site appears to have been more formally laid out at a later date, possibly in the late 1st century. What appears to have been a "strip building", Structure 4, was then erected gable-ended on to the street (LUB 7). The change of use possibly reflects changes in the requirements of the Roman settlement. A military presence to the south of the river was no longer required, but provisioning of the city was growing more important. The change may have taken place when the *colonia* was founded (between AD 85 and AD 95). The outstanding feature of this building was the substantial east–west wall that ran from the street frontage to the west of the site, at least 26m long. This wall seems to have acted as a boundary wall with rooms built against it close to the road.

Structure 4 is discussed above in a series of LUBs; LUB 7 is the construction of the whole building; LUBs 8, 12 and 15 deal with three phases of room 4A to the west of Area 4; LUBs 9, 13 and 16 with three phases of room 4B to the east of Area 4; and

Fig. 8.29 Looking north; the slight walls of the sub-circular building can be traced to the left of the photograph; the burning of the underlying industrial area (lub 6.1) can be seen in the centre, cut by the bottom of the much later pit cg139.

LUBs 10, 14 and 17 at three phases of the roadside 4C in Area 5. Cellar Structure 13 (LUBs 11 and 18) might be part of a different structure to the north in Area 3. It is likely that there was at least one more room further west, but Area 1 was excavated by machine only and there is no record of this period.

So there were at least two (4A and 4B) or possibly three (Structure 13) rooms; there was also evidence for activity, on Ermine Street (4C), to the east of the building. It is unclear how the building was used, but there was a hearth in the rear room 4A (LUB 8); this area was later used for dumping rubbish (LUB 12) and then abandoned (LUB 15). In the middle room 4B several coins were recovered (LUB 13), indicating commercial activity; possibly this room reverted to more domestic use later (LUB 16). Postholes fronting Ermine Street in area 4C perhaps suggests the presence of stalls or similar roadside activity (LUBs 10, 14 and 17). There was also a sunken room (LUB 11), possibly used for cold storage; this was replaced by another similar feature (LUB 18).

Structure 4 had been in use from the late 1st century through to the early to mid 2nd century.

Fig. 8.30 Looking west along gulley cg128, showing the excavation of part of the western extension.

From the evidence it seems that the element closest to the road, 4C, probably presented the most commercially viable area; Ermine Street probably provided a good flow of customers. In the first phase the pottery suggests that drinks were on sale in Structure 4; in the second phase it seems that room 4B, to the rear of room 4C, was a centre of commercial activity (LUB 13). Room 4A with its hearth (LUB 8), may have formed a focus for liquid refreshment (see discussion of pottery below) in its first phase of use, and after that was filled with rubbish and abandoned (LUBs 12 and 15). The sunken room (LUB 18) contained a high proportion of pottery suggestive of storage and kitchen activities (see discussion of pottery above). Structure 4 was totally abandoned and robbed (LUB 20) in the early to mid 2nd century.

The pottery from this period deserves some comment. Taken together, the assemblages from Phase 1 of Rooms A, B, and C of Structure 4 were similar in nature, dating to the late 1st century or later. There is a sherd link between Room 4A.1 and Structure 13.1 which suggests that they could be contemporary. However, all the groups are individually very small and are largely composed of Iron Age tradition pottery. Some of this pottery was redeposited from below as attested by sherd joins. Structure 4, Phase 2, Rooms 4A.2, 4B.2 and 4C.2, assemblages are all very similar in date and content. Sherd links between 4A.2 and 4B.2 provide further evidence for their contemporary use. However, there are no sherd links between 4C.2 and any of the other rooms.

An analysis of the function of the pottery from Structure 4 demonstrates that it was probably domestic in nature but with some differences within the individual phases and structural elements. Structure 4, phase 1, produced an extraordinarily high amount of liquid holders, and a moderately high proportion of drinking vessels and amphorae, in comparison with the other phases, and there were much lower quantities of kitchen wares, table wares and kitchen to table wares. Taken together, this suggests that activity in this area concentrated on the pouring and imbibing of liquids.

Phase 2 appears to have been relatively domestic in nature. In phase 3 there is a moderately high proportion of liquid holders, drinking vessels and table wares together with a slightly lower amount of kitchen wares and a very low amount of kitchen to table wares, indicating an emphasis on dining activities. The pottery from Structure 13.2 shows a very high amount of kitchen wares together with moderate amounts of amphorae and liquid holders, but lower amounts of table and drinking wares, perhaps an indication of kitchen activities. This is accentuated in Structure 14, which has the highest amount of amphorae of the groups, a high proportion of liquid holders and where drinking and table wares are, respectively, very low in amount and virtually absent. But there is no evidence to suggest that Structure 4 was used as a warehouse for storing ceramics – for example, an abnormally high assemblage of imported pottery.

Butchery and Hornworking in the Early Roman Period
The majority of bone-producing context types consisted of floors and other occupation deposits and a single pit cg44 (LUB 12). The assemblages contain the remains of domestic animals, the larger ones apparently dominated by cattle (on the basis of total fragment counts only). One of the most interesting features about this assemblage is the consistency with which what appears to be commercial butchery waste is present in a number of contexts (cg44 and cg190 LUB 12; cg76 LUB 20 being the most obvious). Cattle scapulae appear to be a significant component of these assemblages, showing characteristic perforations of the blades where entire forelimbs or joints have been hung prior to and during butchery. In addition, metapodials and phalanges are also relatively numerous (particularly from cg76 LUB 20) and would appear to corroborate the presence of primary butchery waste. This type of noxious waste would almost certainly not have been regularly dumped within buildings or on floors, unless these buildings had been abandoned, thereby becoming convenient waste repositories. Alternatively, owing to the presence of residual pottery in the assemblages, it is possible that this material has been reworked from elsewhere, although the appearance of the assemblages suggests one of a less than mixed nature. The presence of a butchered horse scapula from layer cg28 (LUB 5) attests to the consumption of horse meat during the early Roman period (Dobney *et al* 1994c).

Other interesting information relates to additional butchery practices present in the assemblage. A number of fragments from both tightly-dated and mixed groups show characteristic splitting of long bones (usually metapodials). This was most probably linked with primary butchery practices (and is present in other assemblages from Wigford), or possibly with initial preparation of bone objects, though none had been subsequently worked (information from Rackham 1994). Fragments of long bones which had been longitudinally split, although present in reasonable numbers from mixed deposits, were almost entirely absent from more tightly-dated groups; it would appear, therefore, that this practice was only undertaken during the early Roman period (Dobney *et al* 1994c).

A few mixed contexts (but no more securely dated groups) produced cattle horncore fragments which had been chopped at their base in order to remove them from the skull. Numbers are obviously limited but it is possible that this also represents evidence for the presence of hornworkers' waste. Additional evidence for a similar craft activity comes in the form of a single, sawn, red deer antler fragment from cg24, LUB 5 (Dobney *et al* 1994c).

Mid Roman occupation

To the east of the site in Area 5, traces of commercial roadside activity were sealed by a series of pebble/

Fig. 8.31 Looking south at stone-lined cellar cg169, cutting robber trench cg111.

cobble surfaces (LUB 21), suggesting that Ermine Street had widened or shifted westwards.

The area to the west underwent a complete change of use, from the 2nd century and into the early 3rd century, to an area of industrial activity (LUB 22), bounded by a ditch (LUB 23). There was a bowl-shaped hearth, a small pit with a fill of clay, much of it burnt, a few postholes, a couple of worn hones, clay surfaces, areas of burning and extents of ash. All these suggest that some sort of industrial activity was going on, possibly smithing, given the fill of ditch cg79 (LUB 23).

Subsequently, in the early 3rd century, a circular building, Structure 5 (LUB 24), was constructed over Areas 3, 4 and 5. The ditch LUB 23 was still open while Structure 5 was in use. Structure 5 was internally plastered and had been refloored. The pottery suggests that the function of the building was the preparation of food and drink, while the ditch appears to have provided a convenient rubbish container for broken items. So perhaps the building served to provide refreshments on Ermine Street (LUB 21).

Structure 5 appears to have been destroyed by fire, which might link with its use as a kitchen, and was sealed by destruction material LUB 25. The extent of the life of the building is difficult to gauge, as the date of the pottery during use was the same as the date of the pottery in the destruction debris.

Another building, Structure 6.1 (LUB 26), was constructed in the mid 3rd century on Ermine Street, in Areas 2, 4 and 5. The remains of this building were not clear. Cobbles immediately to the west of a north–south wall, however, suggest an external surface; there were subsequent surfaces and internal room divisions indicating the continued use of Structure 6 through to the late 4th century (LUB 28). The pottery from Structure 6 suggests that it was possibly a tavern, with drinking vessels common throughout, but table wares less so in Structure 6.2 than 6.1. There was activity (LUB 27) from the mid 3rd century into the 4th, to the east of the building in Area 5, cutting the earlier road surfaces (LUB 21), and suggesting a re-emergence of the roadside stalls. Structure 6 was demolished and robbed in the very late 4th century and possibly later (LUB 29).

Roman commercial activity reflected in coin loss

The high occurrence of 1st-century coins on this site has been noted elsewhere (Mann and Reece 1983, 70; fig 69a, L2), while the concentration of coinage within levels of Structure 4, particularly within the floor and other layers within room 4B.2 (LUB 13), suggests that activity here was conducive to coin use and loss. Seven coins in all were found within room 4B.2, with two further coins from the latest phase of this part of the building (room 4B.3, LUB 16), whereas room 4A.2 produced only a single coin; those from destruction levels of Structure 4 are almost certainly redeposited from room 4B. A total of fifteen coins was recovered from Structure 4, with one further coin from Structure 13.2. Almost all are issues of Nero and Vespasian, with three very worn Claudian copies; whereas the former could have remained in use for some time, the latter appear to have passed out of circulation shortly after the

Fig. 8.32 Late 15th to early 16th century assemblage from cg170.

introduction of regular Neronian issues. It is argued elsewhere (Mann 1988a, 38) that these imply a degree of spending which, at this time, is almost certainly associated either directly or indirectly with the army.

The evidence from room 4B (above) contrasts markedly with structural features 4C (LUBs 10, 14 and 17), the area adjacent to Ermine Street, which is suggested to represent the position of possible roadside stalls, and thus a focus of commercial activity. No coins were recovered from these road-side LUBs at all, and the later roadside LUB (LUB 27) produced only a single coin – a *sestertius* of Marcus Aurelius – almost certainly redeposited. The absence of coin may indicate that accidental losses were more readily spotted and retrieved or that this area was regularly swept clean of rubbish.

The property boundaries from the Late Saxon period

In the first part of the 10th century there was no indication of property boundaries, but by the late 10th century there seem to be two separate buildings on the site, but with no clear boundary between them. In the early to mid 14th century the building (LUB 42) which was constructed seems to fit the area excavated indicating some continuity of boundaries to the present day. The extent of subsequent structures is unclear.

The Late Saxon buildings, and evidence for function and trade

To the west of the road were a number of 10th-century pits (LUBs 30 and 31). To the north (Area 3) were traces of a late 10th-century timber building, Structure 7.1 (LUB 32) possibly of timber frame construction. Replacing this building was an early 11th-century building of earth-fast construction, Structure 7.2 (LUB 33). To the south (Area 2) was evidence for a 10th-century timber post-structure, Structure 8.1 (LUB 35), with a subsequent phase, Structure 8.2 (LUB 36); Structure 8.2 contained pottery dating to the early to mid 11th century. Between the two sets of buildings there were dumps (LUB 34 and 38) containing pottery dating up to the mid 11th century. These late 10th- to early 11th-century buildings indicate settlement, probably gable-ended, on to Ermine Street and to the rear. In this period, direct access to the road was again important, but also space between the buildings was maintained, if even only for rubbish disposal.

Several finds from these structures suggest Viking influence or contacts, including a strap-end (Fig. 8.33 No 1), a bell (Fig. 8.33 No 2) and a soapstone vessel sherd from LUB 39. The copper-alloy strap-end bears crudely cast and punched ornament, possibly repre-senting formalised, confronted animal heads, with a zoomorphic terminal. It is almost parallel-sided, a form which occurs in Scandinavia, Iceland, Ireland and areas of Viking influence in England (Evison 1980, 35). The copper-alloy bell is almost identical to one from Freswick Links, Caithness; these and similar pieces from Iceland, the Isle of Man, Meols, York, and Goltho, Lincs, appear to be a distinct Viking type, and have been discussed recently by Batey (Batey 1988, 214–5). The soapstone sherd, and another (AG) <M63> from an unstratified context, may be from the same vessel (Berridge and Siddiqui, *pers comm*), although neither is large enough to determine the form; both have carbon deposits covering both internal and external surfaces, indi-cating that burning occurred after breakage. The precise source of this material cannot be determined, although soapstone outcrops near Cunningsburgh, Scotland (Hamilton 1956, 206–10) and in Norway, where a specialised industry catered for both local and international trade (Blindheim 1969, 37–8). The only other fragments to have been found in Lincoln are from excavations at Flaxengate (Mann 1982a, 20–1). Pottery might also indicate a Viking influence; pottery from the site includes imports from Andenne and Pingsdorf, as well as regional imports from Thetford and Stamford.

The nature of the Late Saxon pottery (heavy sooting, internal deposits, obvious exposure to high

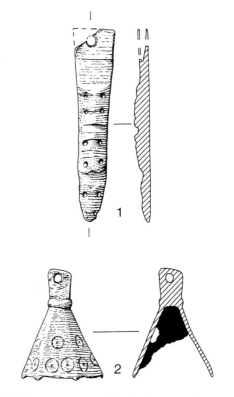

Fig. 8.33 Two registered finds from cg137: 1 Copper alloy strap-end; 2 Copper alloy bell. Scale 1:1

temperatures and the use of internal iron coating on the shell-tempered wares) indicates that much of it had a common source, an idea reinforced by joining sherds. The activity appears to have ceased by the mid 11th century as there is little ST present and there are no later LFS and ST forms. Although there are some fine wares and some of the coarse wares are unsooted, the material is heavily biased towards coarse wares used in conjunction with a fire, and vessels used, or intended to be used for liquid storage. There is not enough evidence to speculate whether this activity is likely to be domestic or industrial, or more probably some of both.

The smattering of crucible sherds from within contexts associated with Structure 7.2 (LUB 33), LUBs 34 and 37, and from the overlying dumps cg137 and cg147 (LUB 38), the possible unfinished finger-rings also from cg137, the slag (from cg137 in particular), and perhaps the ingot mould from pit cg149 LUB 39 (which may be redeposited) provide supporting evidence for some degree of 'industrial' activity here. Much of the remaining material (including the animal bone), however, represents domestic refuse, with some indication of other craft activity such as textile-working, in the form of spindlewhorls and the possible dye-pots. The nature of Late Saxon occupation is generally very similar to that at Flaxengate (Perring 1981 and Mann 1982a) – primarily domestic but with some evidence of textile – (spinning and possibly dyeing) and metalworking.

This evidence should also be set beside that of the animal bones. A large proportion of bone-bearing contexts from late Saxon deposits contained much residual pottery but those from pit cg156 (LUB 31) and dump cg144 (LUB 34) were examined. The largest of these cg144 (LUB 34) was again dominated by the remains of cattle, but pig was also present in reasonable numbers. The apparent increased importance of pig is a common occurrence at Saxon sites from this country. The representation of skeletal elements from the majority of mixed assemblages indicates either domestic refuse or a mixture of domestic and primary butchery waste. Those from the tightly-dated dump deposits, however, clearly indicate primary butchery waste, with numbers of butchered cattle horncores once more implying local hornworkers' waste. This activity appears to have continued after the Conquest. Evidence of antler was found in a number of mixed deposits (Dobney *et al* 1994c).

Medieval and Later Buildings

Any buildings that existed fronting Ermine Street between the mid 11th century and the early 14th century had been removed by subsequent construction. Hints that such buildings existed survived in the form of an area of cobbles (LUB 40), possibly indicating a yard surface and 12th-century pits (LUB 41).

In the late 13th or early to mid 14th century, an extensive stone-founded building, Structure 9, was constructed on the site (LUB 42). It probably fronted the High Street and extended at least 24m to the rear; it had a minimum of three rooms together with an internal garderobe. It was demolished (LUB 43) leaving no remains of internal flooring or other evidence of occupation. Its successor, Structure 10, was erected some time before the late 15th century; the only evidence surviving of this was a stone-lined cellar (LUB 44), but the building probably covered the whole site. This building was demolished (LUB 45) in the mid 17th century. The only evidence of the subsequent, possibly mid 17th-century building, Structure 11, was a soakaway (LUB 46). Structure 11 was demolished (LUB 47) between the mid 18th and 19th centuries. A Victorian building (LUB 48) was probably constructed at the turn of the 20th century.

From almost the 14th century to the present day, there is evidence for the importance of this site on the High Street, in the form of one structure superseded by another.

The cellar (LUBs 44 and 45) and its contents

Fill cg170 (LUB 44) contained a particularly unusual collection of complete and freshly-broken pottery vessels (Fig. 8.34). This is a tightly-dated group of late 15th- to early/mid 16th-century pottery comprising one HUM jug (Fig. 8.34 No 5) three LSW4 jugs (Fig. 8.34 Nos 3, 4 and 6) and two LLSW or LSW4 jars (Fig. 8.34 Nos 1 and 2). All of the vessels appeared to be unused and show no sign of fire damage. With the exception of the Humber ware jug, all of the vessels are likely to have been produced in Lincoln. This group must include some of the last Lincoln-produced pottery.

The other finds from cg170 (LUB 44) are consistent with this dating; the two copper-alloy candlesticks (FH) <Ae66–7> (Fig. 8.35 No 4) are of identical 'bunsen' form, of 15th-century type; X-rays suggest that originally both were plated, although little trace now remains. The glassware includes fragments of a urinal (FH) <G107,110> (Fig. 8.35 No 1), a bottle (FH) <G108–9,112> (Fig. 8.35 No 2) and a *roemer* or, less likely, a *berkemeier*, both forms of drinking-glass (Fig. 8.35 No 3). The urinal is of a type in use between the early 14th and the 17th centuries. The bottle is of late 15th- to late 16th-century type, while the *roemer/berkemeier* is of a form produced between the late 15th and the mid 17th centuries. The latter is an unusual piece, almost certainly manufactured in Germany or the Low Countries; the date of deposition of this whole group, as suggested by the

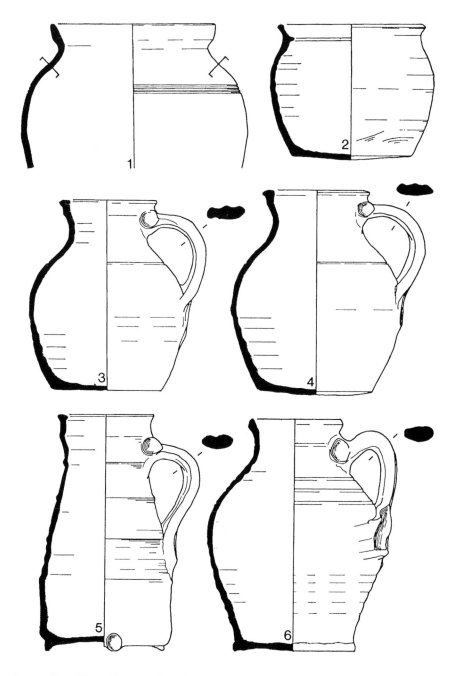

Fig. 8.34 Pottery from cellar fill cg170: 1 & 2 LLSW or LSW4 jars; 3, 4 & 6 LSW4 jugs; 5 HUM jug. Scale 1:4

pottery, places this *roemer/berkemeier* within the early part of the production of such vessels and thus suggests it to be one of the earliest to have been excavated in Britain (Adams and Henderson 1995e; Henderson forthcoming).

Debris cg200 (LUB 45) contained a group of slightly later pottery (Fig. 8.36) including CIST drinking cups (Fig. 8.36 No 1), PGE pancheons (Fig. 8.36 No 4), a LHUM jar (Fig. 8.36 No 2), an early BL mug, a MY jar (Fig. 8.36 No 3) and a nearly complete

MY chamberpot (Fig. 8.36 No 5). Most of the vessels are composed of large fragments, are freshly broken and appear to form a contemporary group. This assemblage probably dates to the destruction of the building sometime between the late 16th century and early to mid 17th century.

The debris cg200 (LUB 45) also contained several fragments of glass, one of which (FG) <G104> is a fragment from a window with painted decoration, possibly from a patterned quarry, and is likely to be

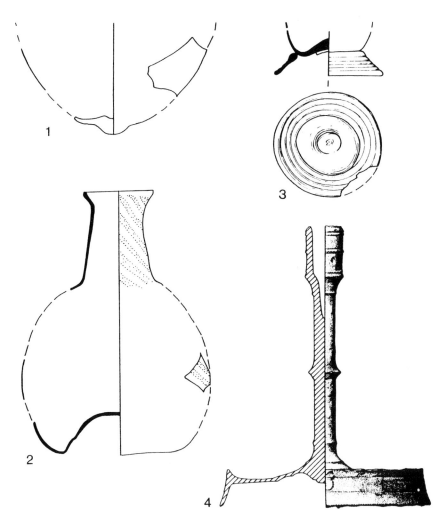

Fig. 8.35 *Finds from the cellar fill cg170. 1: glass urinal, 2: glass bottle, 3: drinking glass, 4: copper alloy candlestick. Scale 1:2.*

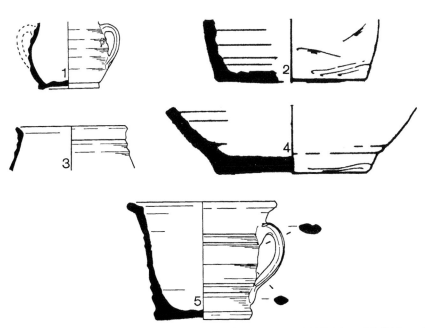

Fig. 8.36 *Pottery from demolition debris cg200: 1 CIST drinking cup; 2 LHUM jar; 3 MY jar; 4 PGE pancheon; 5 MY chamberpot. Scale 1:4*

cg/LUB	cg/LUB	cg/LUB	cg/LUB	cg/LUB	cg/LUB	cg/LUB	cg/LUB	cg/LUB	cg/LUB	cg/LUB	cg/LUB	cg/LUB	cg/LUB
1/1	16/4	31/9	46/5	61/10	76/20	91/22	106/27	121/29	136/30	151/39	166/42	181/27	196/21
2/2	17/4	32/5	47/7	62/16	77/22	92/24	107/27	122/29	137/38	152/33	167/42	182/18	197/28
3/4	18/4	33/24	48/19	63/16	78/20	93/22	108/27	123/30	138/29	153/31	168/42	183/43	198/48
4/2	19/4	34/26	49/4	64/16	79/23	94/22	109/27	124/30	139/30	154/31	169/44	184/31	199/33
5/2	20/3	35/6	50/6	65/10	80/16	95/24	110/21	125/29	140/36	155/31	170/44	185/31	200/45
6/2	21/4	36/7	51/10	66/10	81/20	96/25	111/29	126/30	141/36	156/31	171/42	186/41	201/17
7/3	22/3	37/11	52/13	67/14	82/22	97/26	112/28	127/30	142/36	157/31	172/40	187/41	202/25
8/3	23/3	38/7	53/–	68/14	83/22	98/26	113/28	128/32	143/33	158/31	173/42	188/23	203/27
9/3	24/5	39/5	54/13	69/14	84/22	99/26	114/28	129/30	144/34	159/41	174/42	189/22	204/27
10/4	25/6	40/13	55/20	70/17	85/22	100/21	115/28	130/29	145/29	160/31	175/42	190/12	205/27
11/2	26/5	41/9	56/20	71/14	86/22	101/26	116/28	131/30	146/37	161/41	176/46	191/2	206/27
12/2	27/6	42/9	57/20	72/17	87/22	102/26	117/28	132/30	147/38	162/38	177/47	192/3	207/27
13/2	28/5	43/13	58/13	73/17	88/22	103/27	118/28	133/35	148/39	163/38	178/48	193/16	208/20
14/4	29/5	44/12	59/13	74/14	89/22	104/27	119/28	134/35	149/39	164/39	179/–	194/20	209/8
15/4	30/12	45/8	60/16	75/18	90/24	105/27	120/29	135/30	150/33	165/42	180/29	195/26	

Fig. 8.37 Concordance of cg numbers with LUB numbers for hg72.

of 15th-century date (David King, *pers comm*). This would not be out of place in such a building which, as indicated by the other finds, belonged to a person of some social standing, and may reinforce the suggestion that the structure is of 15th-century date, although the possibility that this may be from another structure entirely should not be discounted. The other glassware includes fragments of a ?goblet with applied trails (FG) <G105>, and of a beaker or bottle (FG) <G106>. The former is probably of late 16th- to early 17th-century date, and may be a Wealden product, while the beaker/bottle, which was almost certainly imported from North Germany, dates to the second quarter of the 17th century (Adams and Henderson 1995e). These indicate a slightly later date for the demolition of the building than the pottery.

The occurrence of such a range of both ceramic and glass vessels, together with the candlesticks, within a cellar is of particular interest in view of the probate inventory (Johnston (ed.) 1989, no.25) of Henry Mitchell, a haberdasher who kept a range of goods including jugs, bottles, pewter vessels, chamber pots etc. in his cellar – a much wider range than most householders Another probate inventory, that of Elizabeth Manby (Johnston (ed.) 1989; no.48) indicates that she kept her linen tablecloths, sheets and pillow cases in her cellar (along with the coal). The textile fragments (FH) <SS23> from cg170 (the only organic material preserved on this site) have been identified as linen (Walton Rogers 1993).

9. Lucy Tower Street 1972 (lt72)

Introduction

Much of the Lucy Tower Street site had been occupied by a garage and part of it by an old people's day centre. These were demolished in January 1972 to make way for the construction of a multi-storey car park. Excavation work commenced in mid February and was completed in mid May 1972. The excavations were supervised by Brian Gilmour of the Lincoln Archaeological Trust, and funded by the developers, the Lincoln County Borough Council.

Initially, an area of about 7m square was investigated. A mechanical excavator was used to remove the remainder of recently demolished late 19th - century buildings as well as some of the more modern mixed topsoil. The excavation was extended until an irregular area with maximum dimensions of 18m north–south and 11m east–west was obtained (Fig. 9.14). A small area was subsequently opened west of the main trench (Fig. 9.1). The lower levels of the site proved progressively more difficult to excavate as the problems of waterlogging increased, limiting the depth of excavation; a system of sump holes and almost continuous pumping was used to facilitate work. The whole area of the site was not excavated for all periods. The earliest levels exposed in the excavation were found in an east–west trench rapidly dug across and below the line of the city wall. Interim reports were published (Gilmour 1973 and Colyer 1975, 259–266).

The excavation was carried out using feet and inches for all measurements and these have been converted to metres for ease of comparison with other reports, although all the photographs show imperial scales. Of the 130 contexts, 129 were interpreted as 75 context groups (cg1–cg76; cg65 was not used) and one was deemed unstratified. The context groups are discussed below as 26 land-use blocks, LUBs 0–25 (Fig. 9.21). The site had been subdivided into three areas for the purposes of the land-use diagram (Figs. 9.2 and 9.3); Area 1 lay to the west of the wall, Area 2 was the wall and tower and Area 3 lay to the east of the wall. In Area 1 there are natural (LUB 0), medieval (LUBs 3–4, 6–7, 10, 12–13), post-medieval to modern LUBs (LUBs 15, 20, 23 and 25). In Area 2 there are natural (LUB 0), medieval (LUBs 2–4, 6–7 and 9), post-medieval to modern LUBs (LUBs 17–18, 21–2 and 24–5). In

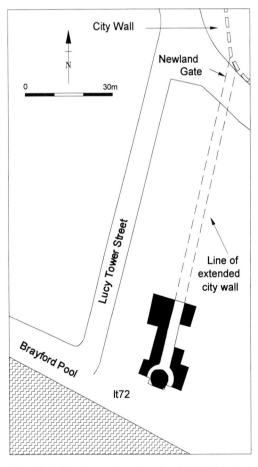

Fig. 9.1 Site location plan for lt72. (1:1,250)

Area 3 there are natural (LUB 0), Roman (LUB 1), medieval (LUBs 2–9, 11 and 14) and post-medieval to modern LUBs (LUBs 16, 19, 22, 24–5).

A total of 47 sherds of Roman and 1,230 sherds of post Roman pottery was recovered from site; much of the stratified late post-medieval and modern pottery was discarded on site without quantification. Relatively few registered finds (269) were recovered (some of these are mentioned in various archive reports – bone finds: Rackham 1994, hones: Moore 1991, other worked stone: Roe 1994), apart from a quantity of leather which had been preserved by anaerobic conditions within some of the medieval deposits and within the post-medieval fill of the town ditch (Mould 1985 and 1993). Other finds are mainly ironwork, all heavily corroded, and fragments of glass (Henderson 1984a). The damp conditions also preserved objects of wood (Gale 1992; Morris 1994). A large quantity of clay tobacco pipes (Mann 1977, 7–8) was also recovered. There was a quantity of medieval/post-medieval ceramic tile (636 fragments) from the site (although much was discarded on site), but little other building material (only 28 other fragments; stone identification: Roe 1994). An assemblage of animal bone (1,257 fragments) was recovered from this excavation, the vast majority from contexts which were of mixed origin (Dobney *et al* 1994i).

Post-excavation stratigraphic analysis was undertaken by Chris Guy and later by Kate Steane. Maggi Darling worked on the Roman pottery; Jane Young examined the post-Roman pottery. Jen Mann analysed the registered finds and Rick Kemp, the building materials. Helen Palmer Brown and Zoe Rawlings digitized the plans.

Interpretation of the sequence of events

Natural

In Areas 1, 2 and 3 of the small trench to the north of the site the earliest deposit was undated natural peat **LUB 0**.

LUB 0 Natural peat

In the east–west trench to the north of the site, which includes part of Areas 1, 2 and 3, there was a deposit of peat cg74 at the limit of excavation; however there is no dating evidence from the excavation for this.

Late Roman

In Area 3, natural (LUB 0) was cut by what has been interpreted as a Roman hardstanding **LUB 1**, dated to the mid to late 3rd century on the strength of one piece of pottery.

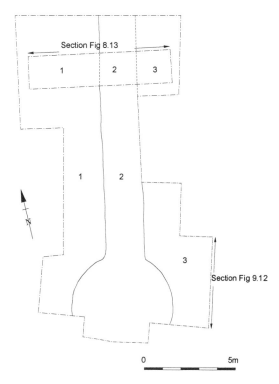

Fig. 9.2 Plan showing areas and sections for lt72. (1:200)

LUB 1 Hard-standing or foundation
(Figs. 9.4 and 9.13)

Cut into the peat cg74 (LUB 0), at a height of 2.44m OD, was a foundation aligned north–south cg1, composed of one course of rough pitched limestone blocks. Sealing the foundation was a thin layer of peat cg71 (0.025m thick), over which was a thin layer of limestone fragments and mortar cg2 (0.05m thick). Running alongside the foundation and sealing the natural peat was cg72, a low mound of redeposited peat up to 0.23m high.

This fragmentary feature has been interpreted as a hard-standing, adjacent to the contemporary edge of the Pool. The natural peat was cut into and a stone foundation cg72 laid down. It may be that the peat accumulated over the surface and was partially cleared, leading to the low mound of peat cg72 and the resurfacing of the hard-standing with limestone and mortar cg2.

A sherd of Roman pottery was found in the foundations cg1; this dated to the mid to late 3rd century. The water level in the Brayford Pool in the later Roman period has been considered to have risen, to c 4m OD, suggesting that this part of the foundation had been constructed below water level. It probably was a hard-standing, allowing access to the water. A similar late Roman surface was recovered on sb85 (LUB 4), to the east of the

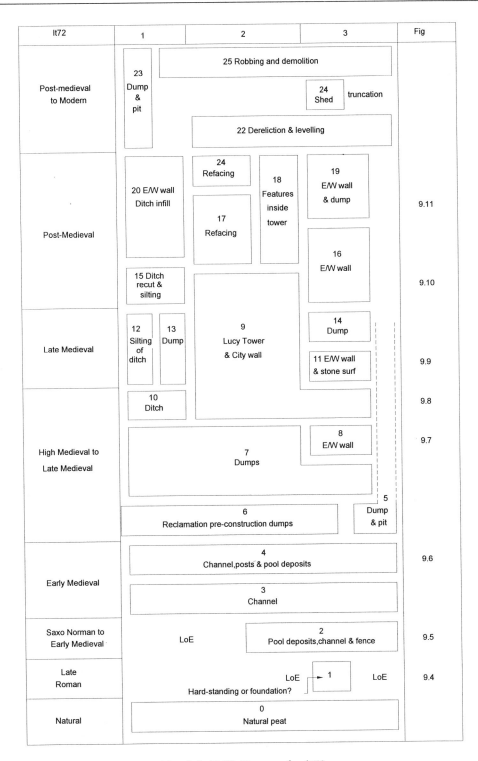

Fig. 9.3 LUB diagram for lt72.

Brayford Pool, and at Waterside North in 1989 (Donel 1990).

Saxo-Norman to Early Medieval

Waterlain deposits sealing LUB 1 were observed in Areas 2 and 3, in the trench to the north of the site;

these contained pottery dating to the 12th century. They were cut by the line of a fence **LUB 2**.

LUB 2 Pool deposits, channel and fence (Figs. 9.5 and 9.12–13)

A deposit of waterlain sand with patches of peat cg3 sealed both the foundation cg1 and the mound cg72 (both LUB 1). Within the peat were several fragments of leather (Mould 1993), four Stamford ware crucibles and three sherds of pottery probably dating to the 12th century. The surface of cg3 sloped down from east to west, suggesting that there may have been a channel aligned north–south below the limit of excavation.

Four stake-holes cg4 cut cg3 and formed a line running approximately east–west; they either mark the removal or the decay of a linear timber structure, perhaps a fence.

Early Medieval

In the trench at the north end of the site, LUB 2 was cut by a channel **LUB 3** and associated deposits contained pottery dating to the 12th century. The channel silted up, to be re-cut more than once, and wooden posts **LUB 4**. Associated pottery was only slightly later in date than LUB 3.

LUB 3 Channel (Figs. 9.12–13)
The postholes cg4 (LUB 2) were sealed by a dump of sand with pebbles and small fragments of limestone cg5 in the eastern part of the site. The dump contained several leather shoe fragments (Mould 1993), and a single crucible sherd, together with a small group of pottery (21 post-Roman sherds, including one of a PING vessel), dating to the late 12th century. The dump cg5 may have been formed through re-cutting

the north–south channel which was indicated in LUB 2, but is more definitely in this LUB with cut cg62. The limestone in dump cg5 suggests some sort of consolidation and the sand and pebble, and leather could represent waterlain material.

LUB 4 Channel, posts and pool deposits
(Figs. 9.6 and 9.12)
Sealing dump cg5 (LUB 3) to the east of the site were deposits of peat and sand cg6. Sealing the channel cg62 (LUB 3) were layers of peat and sand cg63. Both these deposits contained pottery (50 post-Roman sherds in cg6 and 21 in cg63) which was well dated to the latter half of the 12th century. A quantity of leather came from cg6 and cg63 contexts including several shoes, sole repairs and waste.

There was another channel cg7 re-cut through the deposits cg6. Peat and sand deposits cg8, accumulated within it. A further re-cut was observed cg64 through deposit cg8 and this was sealed by dumps and waterlain deposits cg9. Both deposits cg8 and cg9 contained evidence of refuse; this included pottery (three post-Roman sherds in cg8 and 41 sherds in cg9), bone and a small quantity of cobbling waste (Mould 1993). Three posts cg10, one of which was of planed wood with two chamfered edges, were probably inserted through cg9, although the site record indicates uncertainty. They may have been part of an east–west fence across the channel.

Further south, at the bottom of a small trench,

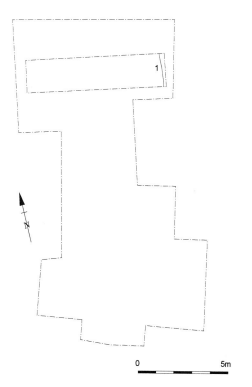

Fig. 9.4 Location of possible jetty: LUB 1. (1:200)

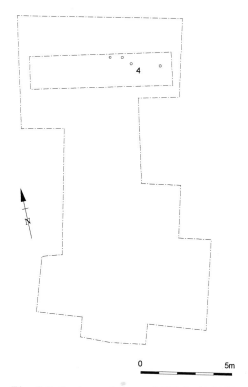

Fig. 9.5 East–west fence: LUB 2. (1:200)

was black sand and peat cg75 over which was a thin spread of mixed peat, loam and sand cg11 (five post-Roman sherds), with its surface at 2.96m OD. Four wooden posts cg12 had been broken off at the surface of cg11. The posts were found inclined at 20–30 degrees from vertical towards the southwest and formed a rough line running approximately north-west to south-east.

The posts cg10 further north were sealed by clay and peaty material c0.3m thick cg13; this contained much bone, some pottery (43 post-Roman sherds) and a few tile fragments as well as a large quantity of leather, principally shoemaking waste, together with shoe fragments (Mould 1993). There were also a few pieces of wood: parts of strips, stakes and offcuts (Morris 1994) and several iron fragments. The pottery was late 12th to early 13th century in date: the latest pottery recovered from LUB 4 is also well dated to the same period (MH3). The group includes Lincoln and local "splashed-glazed" wares as well as regional imports from Stamford, Nottingham and York. However the dating of the group of pottery from deposit cg9 within this LUB is slightly earlier, in the mid 12th century (MH2) indicating that occupation of the area had commenced by this date.

High Medieval to Late Medieval

To the east of the site was a cess pit and layer which may have dated to this period **LUB 5**. Dumps

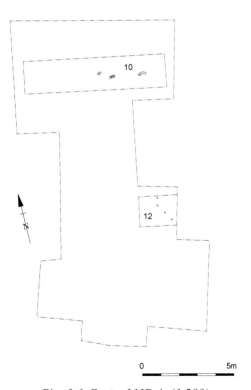

Fig. 9.6 Posts: LUB 4. (1:200)

containing twigs and straw were laid down in preparation for construction **LUB 6**; in both the northern and the southern parts of the site. Sealing LUB 5 but linked by joining sherds were dumps of sand and loam **LUB 7**; on these was a rough wall **LUB 8** possibly used to exclude the pool during construction of the tower and wall. The tower and wall were then constructed **LUB 9** and the city ditch cut **LUB 10**. The dating for the construction work comes mainly from LUBs 6,7 and 9, with pottery dating to between the 13th and 14th centuries.

LUB 5 Cess pit and layer
A cess pit cg50 on the east side of the site was filled with alternate layers of cessy and ashy material. The extent of the feature was not recorded and it is not known which contexts it cut through (unplanned). As the pottery from this pit (16 post-Roman sherds) dated from the first half of the 13th century, it seems likely that it post dated the pool deposits and posts of LUB 4, but pre-dated the construction of the city tower and wall (LUB 6). The backfill of pit cg50 included cattle horncores (four in all) which showed evidence of butchery, one at its base, the others with chops at their tips (Dobney *et al* 1994i) suggesting hornworkers' waste. Pit cg50 also contained intrusive 18th/19th-century glass. Possibly contemporary was a layer of clayey loam in the north-east part of the site, cg54 (three post-Roman sherds).

LUB 6 Reclamation pre-construction dumps (Figs. 9.12–13)
Sealing posts cg12 (LUB 4), to the south of the site were loam layers with 'manure-like' humus patches cg14 (34 post-Roman sherds); this layer contained a noticeable quantity of tile. To the east of the posts peat and sand cg75 (LUB 4) were sealed by sandy loam with patches of 'grassy' humus cg15 (20 post-Roman sherds). Layers cg14 and cg15 date to the early part of the 13th century.

Sealing both cg13 (LUB 4) to the north and cg14 to the south was a layer cg16 of twigs, straw, sand and some small pieces of limestone (about 0.2m thick); it also contained a small quantity of leather, mostly waste (Mould 1993). Over this to the south-east of the site were layers of twigs and grass interleaved with sand cg17 up to 1m thick. Dump cg16 (47 post-Roman sherds) and cg17 (27 post-Roman sherds) dated from the 13th to the earlier part of the 14th century.

A large group of pottery came from LUB 6, although it is difficult to be precise about the dating of much of it as most sherds were small and feature-less with few rims, handles or decorated pieces occurring. The pottery showed no sign of water abrasion. Cross-joins between material in these deposits and those immediately above in LUB 7 (specifically between cg14 and cg18) suggests that LUB 6 is actually the lower part of a later dumping in preparation for the construction of the city wall and tower. Although the latest may sherds date to the 14th or 15th centuries, much of the pottery dates to the 13th century. The large quantity of 13th-century material suggests that the LUB 6 dumping was largely a secondary deposit – material shifted from elsewhere used to make up the ground here. Organic material cg16 and cg17 possibly represents material laid down to give a slip-proof surface at the edge of the pool. The presence of wood chips, shavings and offcuts in LUB 6 suggests that woodworking at either a primary or secondary stage (or both) was being carried out on or near the site (Morris 1994); it is possible that this debris was created during the setting of the wooden foundations of the tower or other aspects of its construction.

LUB 7 Dumps

Sealing layer cg16 (LUB 6) at the north end of the site was a dump of gravelly sand and loam cg18 about 0.2m thick, building up to 3.88m OD; sealing layer cg17 in the south-east part of the site was a dump of sand with some limestone and loam cg19 about 0.2m thick, building up to 3.43m OD. The dumps cg18 (44 post-Roman sherds) and cg19 (57 post-Roman sherds) contained a small amount of pottery and tile. The latest sherds of pottery date to between the late 13th and the late 14th centuries.

LUB 8 East–west wall (Fig. 9.7)

A roughly-built unmortared wall cg20, aligned east–west, was constructed over the dumps cg19 (LUB 7). It was composed of reused fragments of limestone (some dressed and some burnt) and was *c* 0.56m wide, although the north face was not exposed; it was at least 2.59m long and survived to a height of 0.56m. There was a dump of rubble cg24 to the south of the wall which would have built up the ground level towards the pool, ready for the construction of the tower. This was sealed by a "matting" cg67 (no further description recorded).

The wall and rubble may have been built as an aid to the construction of the Lucy Tower, to keep some control over the flood water from the Brayford. It may be significant that it appears to run parallel with the modern Brayford North waterfront. The 'matting' cg67, may have been a waterlain deposit lying on the Brayford Pool side of wall cg20, or more 'bedding' for the stone construction. A few sherds from rubble cg24 (seven post-Roman sherds) dated to between the late 13th and 15th centuries.

LUB 9 Lucy Tower and city wall
(Figs. 9.8, 9.12, 9.15–7)

Two overlapping wooden beams aligned north–

south cg25 were set in waterlogged silty material beneath the foundations of the Lucy Tower and were left *in situ*; there is therefore no record of what the beams overlay. The wooden beams appear to have formed part of the tower foundations.

The yellow limestone foundation cg21 of the northern part of the city wall sealed dumps cg18 (LUB 7). A single course of the foundation, which was 2.5m wide, seems to have been laid to provide access to the southern part of the site. The southern-most 6.4m of the city wall and the tower had foundations of pitched limestone slabs (some possibly reused since one had a finely dressed edge), with vertical wooden piles 1m long between every second or third slab cg22. Stony loam (0.30m thick) cg27 (31 post-Roman sherds) had been built up over the pool deposit cg67 (LUB 8) and sealed the tower foundations.

Set on the foundations was the masonry of the tower and city wall cg23 (17 post-Roman sherds). The lowest course of the Lucy Tower was of roughly-dressed large blocks. Above this the outer masonry of the tower consisted of very large finely dressed ashlar blocks of limestone which had a curved outer face and fitted closely together. These blocks were bonded together with fine pale brown mortar. The ashlar blocks of the second course were chamfered, serving as a plinth to the base of the structure. The core of both tower and city wall consisted of fairly large rough blocks (up to about 0.5m in length) of limestone, laid flat in approximately level courses

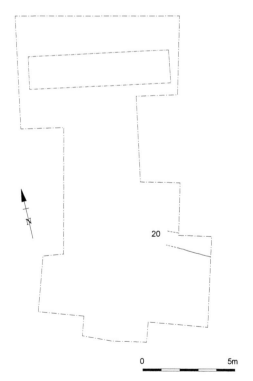

Fig. 9.7 East–west wall: LUB 8. (1:200)

and bonded with the same fine pale brown mortar in which the ashlar facing blocks were set. The tower had an external diameter of 5.6m and its wall was 0.9m thick above floor level.

The city wall was built of slightly smaller, and less well-finished, rectangular ashlar blocks of limestone set in the same fine pale brown mortar. The blocks facing the city wall had in places been neatly keyed into the ashlar tower masonry. The wall was offset one course of blocks below the chamfered plinth of the tower and it did not have a chamfered plinth. So although there was no chamfered plinth there was an offset on both sides, that on the west being at a higher level than that on the east; above the offsets the city wall was 2.02m wide.

Contemporary with the construction of the tower and city wall were dumps of loam with construction surfaces of mortar sandwiched together: cg26 (within the tower sealing cg25), cg61 (to the east of the tower sealing 'matting' cg67 LUB 8), and cg28 (east of the city wall, sealing cg23). To the east of (ie, inside) the city wall the dumps raised the ground surface to *c* 3.90m OD. The top of the dumps within the tower was at 4.74m OD.

The construction surfaces cg61 produced 69 post-Roman sherds, the latest dating from the late 13th century. There are joins to loam dump cg29 (LUB 11) sealing these deposits which seem to indicate re-working or intrusion. A few sherds from the construction deposits cg25 (five post-Roman sherds), cg26 (47 post-Roman sherds) and cg28 (six post-

Roman sherds) dated to the 13th or early 14th centuries.

LUB 10 City ditch (Fig. 9.13)
Loam cg32 was piled up against the wall cg23 (LUB 9); the pottery from this (22 post-Roman sherds) was very mixed and included intrusive material from later fills of the ditch; most of the sherds date to the 13th century and the rest were clearly residual. Sealing this dump was a layer of limestone rubble and sand cg66, possibly construction material from the building of the wall. Cutting rubble cg66 was the cut of the ditch cg58. The ditch had a steeply sloping eastern scarp and a flat base. It is likely that the ditch was cut immediately after the construction of the wall. Deposits cg18 (LUB 7) along the city wall were cut away, probably during the cutting of the city ditch cg58, just to the west of the wall.

Late Medieval

An east–west wall was constructed up against the Tower **LUB 11**; the links between the pottery and sherds from earlier LUBs suggest that this occurred not long after the tower was constructed, but the pottery from this LUB does have a later span. The city ditch proceeded to silt up **LUB 12**. There was a stony loam layer to the west of the city wall **LUB 13**. To the east of the city wall was a dump **LUB 14**. Pottery from the dump and the ditch date from the late medieval into the early post medieval periods.

LUB 11 East–west wall with stone surface (Figs. 9.9 and 9.12)
A dump of loam cg29 (0.30m thick) sealed the tower construction dumps/surfaces cg61 and cg28 (LUB 9). It contained a quantity of building debris including tile. The top of the dump was at 4.43m OD in the north of the site, sloping down towards the south. The latest pottery in dump cg29 (73 post-Roman sherds) dates to between the 14th and the late 15th centuries; there are several joins to both earlier and later LUBs. There is also intrusive 18th/19th-century glass in cg29.

Dump cg29 was sealed by an east–west wall cg30. The wall ran approximately at right angles to the city wall; it was 0.81m wide and faced with roughly dressed limestone blocks with a core of loose rubble set in clay. It was at least 1.65m long and survived to a height of 0.25m. Sealing the wall in place, both to the north and the south, was a dump of limestone rubble with some mortar. This had an overall extent north–south of 3.17m and was up to 0.2m thick. Inserted into this material and close to the north face of the wall was a wooden post 0.15m square.

That this wall was situated further to the south than earlier wall cg20 (LUB 8) suggests that the

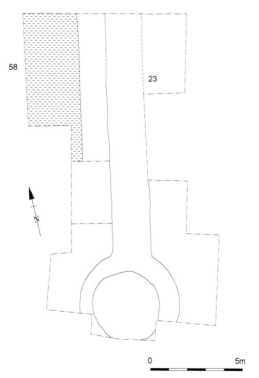

58

23

N

0   5m

Fig. 9.8 Lucy Tower and City Wall: LUB 9. (1:200)

raising of the ground level had been successful in keeping the flood waters at bay. It may conceivably represent a structure immediately behind the waterfront. Contemporary with and to the north of wall cg30 was a layer of limestone chippings and mortar which abutted the east face of the tower and city wall; this formed the make-up for a stone surface cg31 behind wall cg30 at 4.00m OD.

LUB 12 Silting of ditch
Within the city ditch there was a build-up of sand, loam and silt cg33 up to 0.58m thick. A single sherd of pottery was recovered from cg33, a LMLOC jar which dated between the late 15th and the mid 16th century.

LUB 13 Dump between ditch and wall
Between the ditch and the city wall, sealing cg66 (LUB 10), there was a layer of stony loam cg38 (0.3m thick). There were no finds.

LUB 14 Dump (Fig. 9.12)
A layer of loam cg34 (up to 0.42m thick) was dumped or accumulated above surface cg31 (LUB 11). The complete forequarters of a very immature piglet skeleton were found in this loam. The latest few sherds of pottery from cg34 (13 post-Roman sherds) date to between the late 14th and the mid 16th centuries.

Post-Medieval

The city ditch was recut, cutting through LUBs 12 and 13 in Area 1, but again silted up **LUB 15**. The pottery from the silt dates to between the early and mid 16th century. In Area 3 an east–west wall was built **LUB 16**; associated pottery dated to between the late 15th and mid 17th centuries.

In Area 2 the tower and city wall were refaced **LUB 17** with 17th-century brick, and stone features were probably inserted into the tower **LUB 18** at the same time. Another east–west wall was built in Area 3 **LUB 19**, associated with pottery dating to between the mid 17th and mid 18th centuries. In Area 1 the ditch was infilled and sealed by an east–west wall **LUB 20**; the infill contained pottery dating between the late 17th and mid 18th centuries. In Area 2 the tower was refaced again **LUB 21** with larger and later brick.

LUB 15 Ditch re-cut and silting (Fig. 9.13)
The city ditch cg58 (LUB 10), was recut cg59, through layer cg38 (LUB 13) on the same line as before but with a slightly more rounded profile. This recut ditch gradually silted up cg37; the silt contained a quantity of leather (Mould 1993) and wood.

Silt cg37 was sealed by 'matting' cg70, which in this case was a deposit of sand and organic material including bone and a small, rather mixed assemblage of leather (Mould 1993); the depositional process indicated that cg70 was waterlain. The ditch may then have slowly filled with water-deposited rubbish. The pottery from both silt cg37 (33 post-Roman sherds) and matting cg70 (31 post-Roman sherds) dates to the early to mid 16th century and includes sherds of CIST and RAER. There is also intrusive modern leather in cg70 (Mould 1993).

LUB 16 East–west wall (Figs. 9.10, 9.12 and 9.18)
Set on loam cg34 (LUB 14) was an east–west wall cg35 which was unmortared, with a rubble core; its west end would probably have originally abutted the east side of the tower although the evidence was removed by later robbing. It was 0.99m wide and at least 2.6m long. A 0.6m thick dump of loam cg68 was deposited to the north of the new wall.

Wall cg35 lay c1.50m to the north of the location of wall cg30. The dump cg68 and the wall cg35 each contained a single sherd of pottery with a general date range of between the late 15th century and the mid 17th century.

LUB 17 Refacing of tower and city wall (Fig. 9.19)
Parts of the tower and city wall cg23 (LUB 9) were refaced in brick cg39. A crack was visible running down the earlier masonry of the tower on the eastern

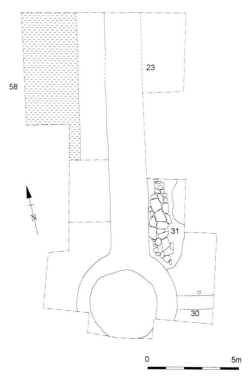

Fig. 9.9 East–west wall with stone surface, to the east of Lucy Tower: LUB 11. (1:200)

side. The foundations on this side of the tower must have subsided after the tower was built, resulting in subsidence in the south-eastern part of the structure, opening up quite large gaps between the ashlar stone blocks. The gaps were partly filled by mortar into which the brick refacing was set. The stone of the ashlar blocks next to the refacing was badly cracked and it was presumably the exfoliation of the surface of the blocks here that necessitated the partial refacing in brick. The bricks used were small (190mm long by 89mm wide by 50mm thick) and were dark red, rather irregular, and obviously handmade. On the outer (western) side, the city wall had also been refaced, using mostly the same kind of brick, but with some stone blocks. This refacing was flush with the lowermost course of larger ashlar blocks and had been built directly on top of the step in the original wall above this course. Wall cg35 may have been robbed to allow the refacing of the east side of the tower to be carried out.

The only dating evidence for this refacing is the site record description of the brick, which was probably 17th-century.

LUB 18 Stone features in tower
(Figs. 9.11 and 9.20)
Sealing the construction deposit cg26 (LUB 9), and perhaps inserted into the tower at the same time as the brick refacing cg39 (LUB 17) was carried out, were two roughly circular stone features cg41. The

bases of these were at 4.14m OD and they were 0.45m deep; sealing construction deposit cg26 was a thin layer of grey loam with charcoal cg69. The features cg41 may have been vat bases or supports for a floor. Late 17th-century material from the levels immediately overlying the features provides a probable *terminus ante quem*.

LUB 19 East–west wall with loam dump
(Figs. 9.11, 9.12 and 9.18)
The dump of loam cg68 and the wall cg35 (LUB 16) were possibly eroded away by the Pool cg60. Post-dating wall cg35 and perhaps also the brick refacing cg39 (LUB 17) of the tower was a dump of limestone rubble, mortar and tile, cg36, which filled the area cut or eroded. The small assemblage of finds from this dump is largely composed of structural debris, together with a small quantity of domestic rubbish as well as a group of pottery (70 post-Roman sherds). The latest sherds indicated a date between the mid 17th and mid 18th centuries, although much of the material dates to the 15th to early 16th centuries; included in the group was the rim of a WESER dish.

An east–west wall cg40 was set on the dump cg36; it appeared to abut the brick refacing of the tower. Wall cg40 was faced on the south side with limestone blocks mortared together and had a partly mortared rubble core; the wall was 0.70m wide and at least 2.13m long.

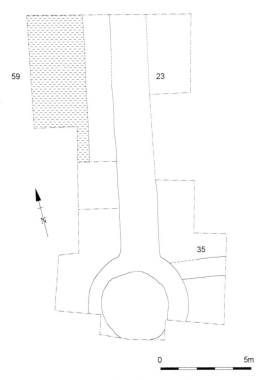

Fig. 9.10 *East–west wall to the east of Lucy Tower: LUB 16. (1:200)*

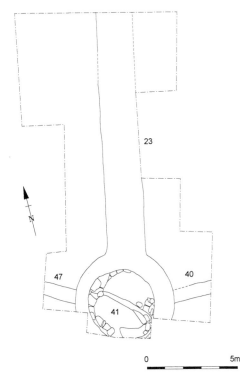

Fig. 9.11 *Features inside the Tower and east–west wall to the east of Lucy Tower together with east–west wall over infilled ditch to the west of Lucy Tower: LUBs 18, 19 and 20. (1:200)*

*LUB 20 Infilling of the ditch sealed by east–west wall
(Figs. 9.11 and 9.13)*
Over the organic layer cg70 (LUB 15) in the ditch
was a layer of loam and tile cg44 with patches of
burnt material and some leather (Mould 1993); also
in the ditch was silty cessy material cg45 and
probably loam cg46 (the exact location of cg46 is

unclear). The infill of the ditch cg44 (86 post-Roman
sherds) and cg45 (three post-Roman sherds) produced a group of pottery with a range of late medieval and post-medieval wares. The latest sherds
dated to between the late 17th and mid 18th centuries, although most of the material was of 16th-
and earlier 17th-century date.

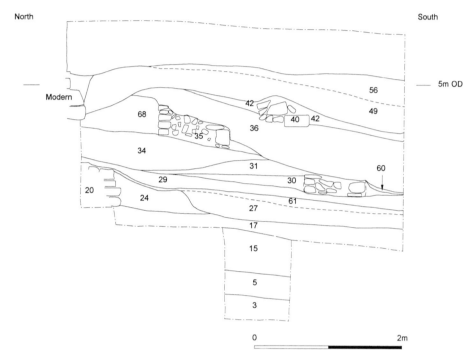

*Fig. 9.12 Section to the west of the southern part of Area 3, illustrating the stratigraphy here, from LUB 2 to LUB
25. (1:50)*

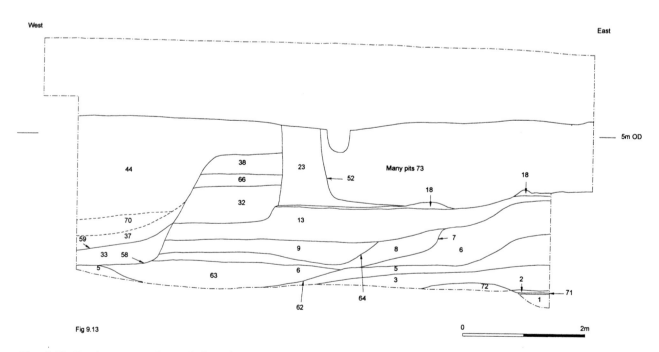

*Fig. 9.13 Section across Areas 1, 2 and 3, running from west to east towards the north of the site, illustrating the
stratigraphy here, from LUB 1 to LUB 25. (1:60)*

Over the infilling of the ditch cg45 an east–west wall cg47 was built; its east end abutted the west side of the tower. The wall was constructed mainly of limestone blocks bonded with mortar, and also some brick; it was 0.76m wide and 1.8m long. This wall could have been a defence against seasonal flooding from the Brayford.

LUB 21 Refacing of the Tower

The wall and tower were sufficiently ruinous to require further refacing in brick cg48. The refacing was of larger bricks than that used in LUB 17 and was accordingly considered to have taken place at a later date.

Post-Medieval to Modern

In Areas 2 and 3 the tower, wall and surface to the east seem to have gone out of use **LUB 22**; LUB 22 contained 18th- to 19th-century pottery and glass. There were also dumps and a pit in Area 1, dated in a similar fashion **LUB 23**. In Areas 2 and 3, over LUB 22, there were traces of a structure, possibly a shed **LUB 24**. Across Areas 1, 2 and 3 was evidence for demolition and robbing **LUB 25**; the dating evidence suggests that this took place in or after the mid 19th century.

LUB 22 Dereliction and dumps (Fig. 9.12)

Within the tower, features cg41 (LUB 18) were sealed by stony clayey loam cg43, probably associated with their demolition, and containing largely building debris (fragments of brick and tile) with a little domestic rubbish (17 post-Roman sherds). A drinking glass fragment from cg43 is of late 17th-century date (Henderson 1984b).

To the east of the city wall there were also dumps of rubble and loam cg42 which sealed wall cg40 (LUB 19); this contained building debris (tile fragments and a few pieces of window glass) and structural ironwork (mostly nails), together with a little domestic rubbish (87 post-Roman sherds). A pit filled with rubbly loam cg51 cut down into the cess pit cg50 (LUB 5). A glass jug handle from cg42 is probably of 18th-century date (Adams and Henderson 1995f). The records indicate that cg42 had contained 18th- to 19th-century pottery; this was not quantified but was discarded at the time of excavation.

Although the tower had probably been largely demolished and the area derelict, the ruins of the tower, together with the wall, would have probably remained visible in the landscape.

LUB 23 Dump and pit

Up against the south side of wall cg47 (LUB 20) there were dumps of loam with mortar and brick rubble cg53, perhaps levelling dumps to raise the ground surface. The level of the top of these dumps was not recorded. Two fragments of a late 17th- to 18th-century wine bottle were found in the dumps but the records indicate that these dumps also contained 18th- to 19th-century pottery; this was not quantified but was discarded during excavation.

Perhaps contemporary with the dump was a pit cg55, adjacent to the west side of the tower close to its junction with the city wall. The pit was *c* 1.60m in diameter and *c* 1.83m deep. It seems to have been dug to examine the foundations of the tower.

Fig. 9.14 Looking south-east at an overall view of the site, showing the cut of the north trench.

LUB 24 Structure 2 – Shed to east of tower
(Fig. 9.12)
Set on rubble dump cg42 (LUB 22) adjacent to the east side of the tower was a brick wall on a limestone foundation cg49, aligned north–south (no more description recorded). Sealing the foundation were layers cg76 which consisted of silty loam layers (about 1m thick) sealed by a layer of stones (possibly a floor inside the building) over which was a shallow layer of ash. The brick wall and layers may represent a small building, possibly a shed of some sort.

LUB 25 Robbing of city wall and tower demolition
(Figs. 9.12–13)
The northern part of the city wall was almost totally robbed away cg52. The robber trench cut through the levelling deposits above the ditch cg44 (LUB 20) and to the east of the city wall – shed cg49 (LUB 24) and dump cg51 (LUB 22). It was backfilled with loam mixed with fragments of limestone and mortar. There may have been more than one phase of robbing but the records are unclear; from the recorded section it seems that pits cg73 cut into the robber trench (Fig. 9.13).

In the southern part of the site, the levelling layer cg43 (LUB 22) within the tower and the surface to the east were sealed by dumps of rubble, brick and mortar cg56; the dumps contained a small assemblage of animal bone including cat and a component of primary butchery waste amongst others (Dobney et al 1994i).

A hearth cg57, perhaps used by the demolition contractors, cut the rubble cg56, and was sealed by debris associated with the Old People's Day Centre on the site.

Pottery associated with the robbing cg52 of the tower was dated to the 18th and 19th centuries and recorded on site before being discarded. The tower was recorded as being demolished by the mid 19th century.

Discussion of lt72

The Brayford frontage

Excavations and observations to the east of High Bridge show that in the mid Roman period the riverfront may well have lain close to the Roman city wall, and it is likely this was also the case to the west of the Bridge (Donel and Jarvis 1990; Donel 1991). Observations in 1975 immediately to the east of the Lucy Tower Street site revealed waterlain silts (see BWN75, this vol). The location of the hard-standing cg1 (LUB 1) was probably influenced by the Roman topography, set as it was to the south of the city wall.

Fig. 9.15 View of the solid wooden beams as found set under the Lucy Tower foundations.

In the early medieval period, there is evidence for a north–south channel (LUBs 2, 3 and 4). This was probably a ditch to the west of the city, which ran between the remains of the Roman walls and the Brayford Pool. This ditch can be demonstrated to have existed in the later 12th century but may have been in use earlier.

The lines of posts and postholes which ran east–west (LUBs 2 and 4) and north-west to south-east (LUB 4) may have been associated with a fishery possibly earlier than or linked with the manor of Hungate to the north-east. The medieval manor of Hungate occupied the south-western part of the old Roman lower walled town and Hill traced the lordship of the manor back to 1086. He placed the southern boundary of the manor at the Roman city wall and pointed out that the lord of the manor had a fishery on the Brayford which would have been next to the boundary where it abutted the pool (Hill 1927, 177, 187). Alternative interpretations for the posts include part of fences which may have helped to consolidate the banks of the Brayford Pool, collecting flotsam, and encouraging an adequate

Fig. 9.16 The tower and wall cg23.

Fig. 9.17 Construction layers cg26 within the tower.

depth within the Pool for the passage of boats. On the other hand, the posts perhaps formed some type of property boundary, to mark jurisdiction or ownership. In any event, they seem to have been erected close to the water's edge in the late Saxon and early medieval period.

Between the 13th and 14th centuries the land was prepared for the construction of the tower and wall (LUBs 5 and 7). Hill considered that the town wall extension was built to enclose a part of the town which consisted of reclaimed land, the suburb of Newland (Hill 1948, 157; see also below). This part of the town wall with the tower was constructed right down to the edge of the water. The watery environment to the south of the site was coped with by dumps of twigs, straw and grass over 1m thick

Fig. 9.18 East–west wall cg40 in the foreground with wall cg35 behind; east of the tower, looking north.

(LUB 6); these provided a platform from which to construct the tower. The rough wall (LUB 8) may have helped control the water during construction. Cess pit cg50 (LUB 5) may have been used during the construction of the wall, but may alternatively relate to nearby occupation predating the construction.

The earliest ground surface, as opposed to water-lain deposits, dumps and construction surfaces, was stone surface cg31 (LUB 11) at 4.00m OD. It was associated not only with the city wall (LUB 9) but also with a slightly later and less substantial east–west wall cg30 (LUB 11) which has been interpreted as a wall to restrict the impact of the seasonal flooding of the Brayford. There was a slope from north to south of the site, and the east–west wall cg30 (LUB 11) was situated at the northern edge of the Brayford Pool. There were two subsequent rises in ground level, following which a new east–west wall was re-established in broadly the same position (walls cg35 LUB 16 and cg40 LUB 19). Thus there is evidence that the northern edge of the Brayford Pool was in approximately the same position from the medieval period through to the 17th century.

A further advance of the waterfront is represented by the dump cg53 (LUB 23), seen only in the extreme south-west corner of the site. This was presumably deposited as part of the changes which were associated with the construction of Brayford Wharf North at the end of the 18th century. The robbing of the city wall and the demolition of the tower (LUB 25) in the mid 19th century marked the

end of their association with the Brayford Pool. The site was levelled and sealed by rubble brick and mortar and the edge of the Pool was shifted south.

City wall and Lucy Tower: LUB 9

Before the excavation began it was known that the east and west walls of the lower Roman town had been extended southwards to the medieval waterside and that both walls terminated in a tower. The precise location of the west tower had been the subject of debate. The Ordnance Survey maps located Lucy Tower in relation to modern features beneath the street of Brayford Wharf North, opposite the southern end of Lucy Tower Street while Marrat's map of 1817 showed the tower as still standing, inside the south-western corner of the excavation site. In this respect at least the 1817 map proved to be more accurate (Fig. 9.1).

Murage grants have been listed for this period in Lincoln (Turner 1970, 238–9) but contain no definite documentary reference to the construction of the city wall and tower cg23 (LUB 9). The archaeological evidence indicates a date between the 13th and 14th centuries. Pottery from LUBs 6–9 and 11 is difficult to interpret. The latest sherds found in LUBs 6–9 are from vessels only generally datable to between the late 13th and late 15th centuries, although much of the rest of the pottery dates directly to the 13th century. LUB 11 contains similar material, but also includes two sherds that must post-date the late 14th century. The presence of joining sherds between the

Fig. 9.19 West section of the tower showing brick rebuilding.

LUBs argues against successive dumping episodes, unless there is considerable re-working of the deposits making it difficult to date the construction deposits of the Tower. On balance the pottery seems to suggest that construction took place no earlier than the late 13th century and no later than the mid 14th century. The tower was probably not known as the Lucy Tower when it was built, but the name was probably later borrowed from the western keep of Lincoln Castle. The earliest surviving mention by name to the tower by the Brayford appears to be a corporation lease of 1611 referring to the "Leucie tower at Braford side in the west ward" (Hill 1948, 86), and it had been referred to simply as "the Tower" in 1588 (Cameron 1985, 80).

The medieval defences between Newland Gate and the Lucy Tower may have been neglected during the 16th century, as there was much stone in the loam dump immediately west of the city wall. Although the ditch to the west of the city wall on the Lucy Tower site was recut cg59 (LUB 15) in the mid 16th century, it does not appear to have been functioning as it may have been back filled or slowly silted up with waterlain deposits cg37 (LUB 15) which were then sealed by organic debris cg70 (LUB 15) by the early/mid 17th century. Speed's Lincoln map of 1610 shows the Newland Gate but not the city wall or the Lucy Tower. The excavation also confirms that the tower must have been still standing at that time but it is possible that the city wall linking the gate and tower was already ruinous. However, the excavation revealed a partial brick refacing cg39 (LUB 17) of the southern end of the city wall and the Lucy Tower which probably took place in the 17th century.

In 1722 Stukeley reported that "to the west (side of the lower town) the ditch and the foundation of the wall is still left, though many times repaired and demolished in the frequent sieges the town has sustained...at the bottom of it towards the pool is a round tower called Lucy Tower." (Stukeley 1776, 90). The Bucks' 1743 `South-West Prospect of the City of Lincoln' shows two slit-like openings on the same level about half way up the surviving tower. It also shows the partial brick refacing of the tower. The tower was still surviving to about the same height when drawn in 1768. The depiction also shows walls fronting Brayford Wharf North to either side of the tower as well as boundary walls running northwards along either side of Lucy Tower Street. The street is first recorded in 1833 as Lucy Tower Lane (Cameron 1985, 80) but the drawing shows that it was in existence prior to that date. The excavation uncovered traces of later repairs to the tower in wider brick cg48, probably dating to the mid 18th century (ie, postdating the Bucks' drawing).

By the 19th century the tower may have been incorporated into, or at least stood adjacent to, buildings of the first phase of roadside development along Brayford Wharf North. The wider brick used in the final repairs to the tower was similar to much brick found in the demolition rubble from 19th-century buildings on the site, and the tower was probably patched up when some of these buildings

Fig. 9.20 Features cg41 within the tower.

were being constructed. Although marked on Marratt's 1817 map, Lucy Tower had disappeared by the time of Padley's 1842 map. In *c* 1850 Ross records that "This tower was destroyed and completely taken down some years ago by the proprietor Mr Cuttle who built a rotund structure of like dimensions on the site. This relic has now disappeared" (Ross 1853). Thus, Lucy Tower may have survived as late as *c* 1830 but had been demolished by *c* 1840. With this disappeared the last remaining above-ground traces of the medieval extensions to the defences of the lower walled town.

Trade and Industry indicated by the refuse

The finds provide clear evidence for medieval leatherworking; the Late Saxon and medieval river or water margin seems to have been used as a convenient disposal site for the refuse. Much of the small assemblage of leather from the riverlain deposits and dumps (LUBs 2–5) is waste offcuts, both primary (from the initial cutting and sorting of hides) and secondary (from pattern cutting) – the latter probably from shoemaking. A significant proportion of the shoe fragments also show evidence of deliberate cutting-up for reuse, indicative of cobbling.

In peat and sand cg6 (LUB 4) there was a complete shoe, a one-piece drawstring ankle boot with an embroidered stripe down the centre of the vamp; this style of shoe was popular in the early/mid-12th century (Grew and De Neergaard 1988, 12),

although the folded topband of the Lucy Tower shoe, with small vertical slits to take decorative stitching is more characteristic of late 11th-century shoes (Mould 1993). There were also fragments of at least 11 heavily worn and repaired turnshoe soles, and four clump sole repairs as well as a few pieces of secondary waste and a single fragment of primary waste.

The leather from clay and peat cg13 (LUB 4) considered principally of shoemaking waste. A high proportion (97%) of the shoe fragments found had been cut to salvage reusable leather, suggesting that much of this was cobbling waste. This was especially the case in LUB 6. The only recognisable shoe style among the fragments from cg13 (LUB 4) was an ankle boot with drawstring fastening passing through vertical thonging (CY) <L108>, a style popular in London during the late 12th to mid-13th century (Mould 1993; Grew and De Neergaard 1988, 14–8).

Layer cg16 (LUB 6) contained a small quantity of leather waste and a socketed bone point, which is almost certainly a craft tool; similar objects are known from late 9th- to 11th-century contexts at Flaxengate, Lincoln (Mann 1982a, fig 32) and from Anglo-Scandinavian contexts elsewhere, as at York (MacGregor 1982, fig 51, 518–21). MacGregor suggests (MacGregor 1985, 174–5), that the occurrence of several in a leather-working shop at York may be indicative of their use as craft tools. Although the Lucy Tower tool was associated indirectly with leather waste (it was from a different context within cg16), the material was all redeposited and this association may be purely fortuitous.

Evidence for leather-working was also found in later deposits on the site. The silting of the city ditch cg37 (LUB 15) contained a small quantity of leather, mainly shoe components and (secondary) waste fragments; two complete shoes and part of a third were heavily worn and appear to represent casual discards rather than cobbling waste. One of these, a child's one-piece shoe, and part of another from cg37 have broad toes, suggesting an earlier 16th-century date. Leather from cg70 includes shoe components and fragments of straps and garments, with some secondary and a little primary waste. The leather assemblage as a whole from LUB 15 shows a variety of constructional methods (turnshoe, turn-welted and welted), perhaps supporting the suggestion that the material accumulated gradually.

The leather from the ditch infill cg44 (LUB 20) was also a small mixed assemblage, with shoe components of both turnshoe and turn-welted construction and a few pieces of waste.

Another industry which is indicated is horn-working; the few cattle horncores from the high medieval pit cg50 (LUB 5) may perhaps hint at horn-workers' waste (Dobney *et al* 1994i). There is also sparse evidence for other crafts and industry: five crucible sherds from cg3 (LUB 2) and cg5 (LUB 3)

cg/LUB	cg/LUB	cg/LUB	cg/LUB	cg/LUB	cg/LUB	cg/LUB
1/1	12/4	23/9	34/14	45/20	56/25	67/8
2/1	13/4	24/8	35/16	46/20	57/25	68/16
3/2	14/5	25/9	36/19	47/20	58/10	69/18
4/2	15/6	26/9	37/15	48/21	59/15	70/15
5/3	16/6	27/9	38/13	49/24	60/19	71/1
6/4	17/6	28/9	39/17	50/5	61/9	72/1
7/4	18/7	29/11	40/19	51/22	62/3	73/25
8/4	19/7	30/11	41/18	52/25	63/4	74/0
9/4	20/8	31/11	42/22	53/23	64/4	75/3
10/4	21/9	32/10	43/22	54/5	65/–	76/24
11/4	22/9	33/12	44/20	55/23	66/10	

Fig. 9.21 Concordance of cg numbers with LUB numbers for lt72.

indicating metal working; a woolcomb tooth <Fe43> (DM) from cg6 (LUB 4); and an elder (*Sambucus* sp.) bale pin from cg37 (LUB 15), used in the handling and packaging of raw wool (Morris 1994).

A wide range of post-medieval pottery dating from the 16th to the 18th century was found on the site in various dumps and within the ditch fills. Most of the pottery came from local or regional centres (TB, GRE and LHUM), however, a small but significant number of sherds (17) came from imported vessels (RAER, DUTR, FREC, WESER, KOLS, LANG, NITALS, SIEG, MARTI and WEST).

10 St Benedict's Square 1985 (sb85)

Introduction

In late 1985 an opportunity was available to excavate a site where the remains of Roman and Saxon waterfronts might be expected. This followed the demolition of the offices and printing works formerly occupied by the Lincolnshire Echo newspaper (Fig. 10.1). The excavation was directed by Chris Guy, of the Trust for Lincolnshire Archaeology. Funding for the excavation was in part provided by Lincoln City Council and in part by a private donation.

There was an initial watching brief during demolition work prior to the excavation. Limited time and resources, coupled with the depth of the early deposits (c 3.5m below modern ground surface), and disturbance by the foundations for the printing

presses, restricted the area it was possible to examine in detail. (Fig. 10.2.)

Trench A was excavated by machine to a height of between 4.85m and 5.00m OD, removing about 1.5m of the latest stratigraphy. The trench was stepped in and hand excavated; the lowest levels were only excavated in a small part of the north of the trench. Trench B was excavated by hand after machining. Trenches A and B were linked by an east–west machine-dug trench, Trench C, at the end of the excavation. A watching brief during the construction of foundations was carried out following the excavation allowing information to be retrieved from a wider area.

Sections were drawn of the trench sides at the end of the excavation but it was not possible to annotate

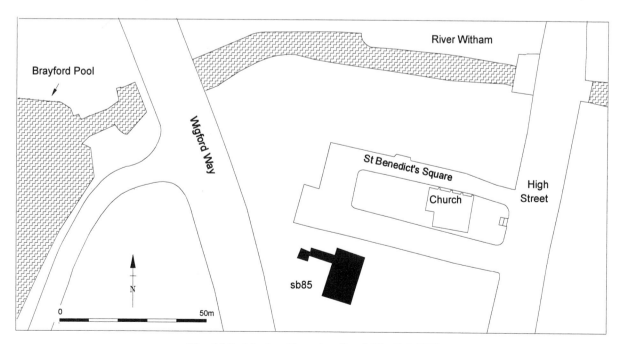

Fig. 10.1 Site location plan for sb85. (1:1,250)

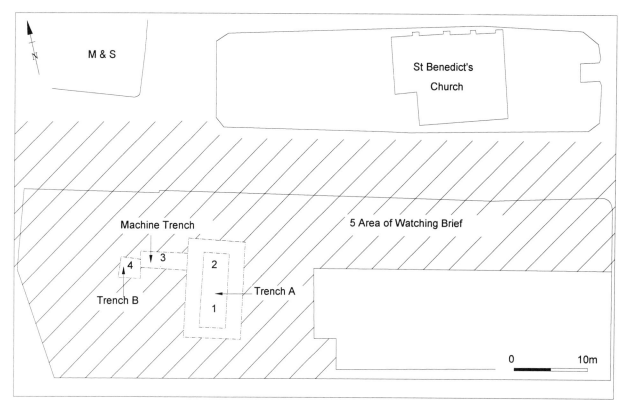

Fig. 10.2 Plan showing areas and trenches for sb85. (1:500)

them until later; the delay meant they had limited use in post-excavation analysis. A developer's plan was annotated with areas of watching brief observations, numbered I to XI, but other areas (XII to XVII) unfortunately cannot be precisely located. An interim report (Guy 1986), and a note on a runic inscription (McKinnell 1996) from a late Saxon context (see LUB 17 and discussion below), have been published.

Of the 199 contexts, 193 were interpreted as 115 context groups (cg1–cg122 but cg18, cg20, cg37, cg38, cg39, cg57 and cg113 were not used) and six were deemed unstratified. The context groups are discussed below in 25 land-use blocks, LUBs 1–25 (Fig. 10.21). The site has been subdivided into five areas for the purposes of the land-use diagram (Figs. 10.2 and 10.3); Trench A has been split into Areas 1 and 2 (southern and northern parts of Trench A); the machine trench is Area 3; Trench B is Area 4 and the extensive area of the watching brief is Area 5. The majority of the stratigraphic information from this site comes from Areas 1 and 2; there are Roman (LUBs 1–7), Ultimate Roman to late Saxon (LUB 9) and late Saxon LUBs (LUBs 10–18), Saxo-Norman (LUB 21) and modern (LUB 24). From the late Roman to late Saxon periods there is also information from Areas 3 and 4 but here material from the late Saxon period onwards had been removed by machine; there

are Roman (LUBs 5 and 8), late Saxon (LUBs 11–12 and 20) and modern LUBs (LUB 24). In Area 5 late Roman stratigraphy was observed (LUB 5) together with late Saxon to post-medieval material (LUBs 19–20, 22 and 23) as well as modern (LUBs 24–5). The Saxo-Norman, medieval and post-medieval levels were removed by machine and not recorded in Areas 1, 2 and 3, but Saxo-Norman pits were recorded in Area 2. Medieval and post-medieval stratigraphy was observed in Areas 4 and 5 and modern stratigraphy in Areas 2–5.

There were 1,522 sherds of Roman pottery and 1,821 sherds of post-Roman pottery together with 212 registered finds from this site, including some groups of leather accessioned under a single number. The relatively low number of small finds recovered is almost certainly attributable to the limited area of the site which was excavated by hand, to the predominantly wet weather, and to the general rapidity of work due to pressure on time. Some organic material was preserved by anaerobic conditions, mainly leather (Mould 1993), wood (Taylor 1987; Gale 1992; Morris 1994) and a single strand of fibre (Walton Rogers 1993); metalwork, which includes some coins (Davies 1992), is heavily corroded while other materials such as stone (Roe 1994; hones: Moore 1991), glass (Roman – Price and Cottam 1993c; post-medieval – Adams and Henderson

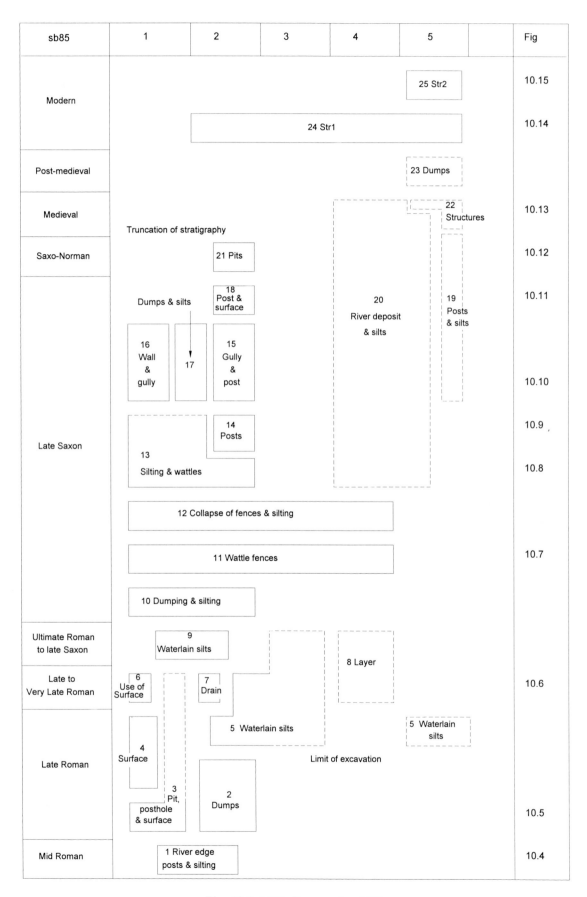

Fig. 10.3 LUB diagram for sb85.

1995b), bone and antler (Rackham 1994; McKinnell 1996) are generally well preserved. Of the building material (638 fragments) recovered from this site, most represented Roman ceramic tile (stone identification: Roe 1994). A moderately large animal bone assemblage (2,160 fragments) was recovered from the site (Dobney *et al* 1994e); the majority came from well dated contexts of the late Saxon period. A large number of samples were taken, mainly from the wattles, but included samples for botanical and molluscan analysis. Reports were produced on the land and freshwater snails (French 1987; Milles 1993) and charred plant remains (Moffett 1993).

Post-excavation stratigraphic analysis was undertaken by the excavator, Chris Guy, and later Kate Steane. Maggi Darling worked on the Roman pottery, Jane Young on the post-Roman to post-medieval pottery and Rick Kemp on the modern pottery. Jen Mann analysed the registered finds and, with Rick Kemp, the building materials; the modern bottles were examined by Rick Kemp. Pam Graves worked on the architectural stone. Helen Palmer Brown and Zoe Rawlings digitized the plans and Dave Watt drew the finds illustrations.

Interpretation of the sequence of events

Mid Roman

In Areas 1 and 2 there was evidence for river silting cut by posts, which were in turn sealed by silting **LUB 1**; the latest pottery from this LUB dates to the mid 3rd century.

LUB 1 River-edge posts and silting (Fig. 10.4)

At the bottom of Areas 1 and 2, only observed in a small sondage, were the remains of wattling cg1. These were sealed by silty sand cg2 which sloped down from south-east to north-west in Areas 1 and 2; at its highest point it was 3.15m OD. Silty sand cg2 contained a few fragments of scrap leather, rubbish from the river; the freshwater molluscan assemblage in cg2 is suggestive of quiet, slowly-flowing water conditions, possibly at the edge of a river channel, whilst terrestrial snails may have been washed in from surrounding habitats (French 1987).

Set into sand cg2, diagonally across Areas 1 and 2, were three posts cg3 which had been packed with limestone at the base; the most northerly post was squared with a flat base but the other two posts were less regular. They were apparently set at intervals of *c* 2.35m. There was no evidence of any surface associated with these posts; while it is possible they represent mooring posts, they may alternatively be evidence of another riverside activity.

Sealing the posts and sloping down to the north-west was peat layer cg4 and sandy silt with peat above cg5; these layers seem to have built up along the shallow river margins. Peat cg5 contained a little stone, a small quantity of building material and domestic rubbish. The suite of fish species from cg5 is typical of lowland river systems with a slow-flowing current and probably represents the accumulated skeletons of individuals which died naturally. It may also be due to either a pisciverous bird or mammal pelleting or defecating in the same place over a period of time. Experiments have shown (Irving 1995) that this type of bone assemblage is also associated with sand and silt deposits on British Pleistocene sites (Dobney *et al* 1994e).

From the evidence these deposits can be interpreted as being within the river or pool, but close to its edge; they show that the river was flowing north-eastwards, presumably as part of a wide curve as the river turned east.

The latest pottery from this LUB (84 sherds) suggests a mid 3rd-century date. The fine wares, MOSL, NVCC and PARC were of the the 3rd century. They include funnel-necked or plain rim beakers, folded beaker sherds, and a possible NVCC flagon sherd. Two sherds probably of DWSH occurred, and at least three wide-mouthed bowls. A rare occurrence in Lincoln is a Gallic flagon of Gose 415 form, and a sherd of NVGW from a closed form of mid 3rd-century date.

Late Roman

There were dumps **LUB 2** to the north of the site; to the south a pit and posthole were associated with a possible surface **LUB 3**. Pottery from these LUBs dated between the mid and late 3rd centuries. LUB 3 was partly sealed by a possible hardstanding **LUB**

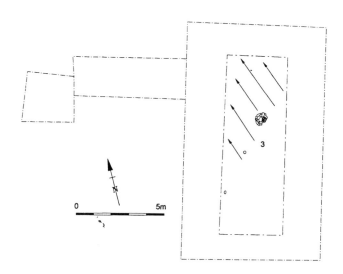

Fig. 10.4 River-edge posts: LUB 1. (1:210)

4 with pottery dating to the end of the 3rd century and into the 4th. Some of the site was sealed by dumps and waterlain silts **LUB 5** containing pottery of the early to mid 4th century.

LUB 2 Dump (Fig. 10.5)
In Area 2, building debris cg9 (up to 0.5m thick) was dumped along the river margins, sealing part of the lower river deposit cg5 (LUB 1) and building up the riverside here to 3.58m OD; this contained large fragments of burnt limestone, ceramic tile, Collyweston roof slates, nails and painted plaster together with a little domestic rubbish.

The latest pottery from this dump (total of 39 sherds) dated between the mid and late 3rd century; this date was provided by the NVCC funnel-necked, scaled folded and painted beaker sherds, a GREY wide-mouthed bowl of Rookery Lane kiln type, and a possible sherd of DWSH.

LUB 3 Pit, posthole and surface (Fig. 10.5)
In Area 1 the deepest features encountered included an irregular pit cg7; it was overlapped by a deposit of sand/clay with silt and frequent limestone fragments cg6. This only survived in a small patch and a post had at one time been set into the middle of it, leaving stone-lined posthole cg11 (which may have continued in use through to LUB 4). Within the fill of this posthole was a peculiar "glazed"' potsherd, possibly part of a crucible, or a vessel which had been used for some industrial purpose. Overlapping deposit cg6 to the south was a layer of sandy pebbles and small limestones, a possible surface cg8 at 3.88m OD.

Four sherds from the pit cg7 (total of 4 sherds) included one from a colour-coated possible flask or flagon, suggesting a mid to late 3rd-century date, and the sherds (total of 4 sherds) from the dump cg6 included a further sherd from a NAAM amphora, giving little evidence for a date beyond the 3rd century. Only two sherds were found in posthole cg11, the peculiar "glazed" sherd and a sherd from a NAAM amphora, the latter probably of 3rd-century date.

LUB 4 Surface (Fig. 10.6)
Sealing pit cg7 and surface cg8 (LUB 3) in Area 1, was a later surface cg10 at 4.05m OD; it consisted mainly of limestone fragments which covered the area to the south of posthole cg11 (LUB 3), which may have continued in use (as surface cg10 does not seal it). Within cg10 was found a small, crudely-made, perforated lead object (111) <126>, perhaps used as a net or line weight.

The surface may have represented an area of hard standing leading to the river. The pottery from cg10 (a total of 5 sherds) included DWSH and a GREY

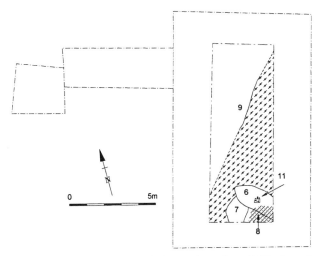

Fig. 10.5 Dump, pit, postholes and surface: LUBs 2 and 3. (1:210)

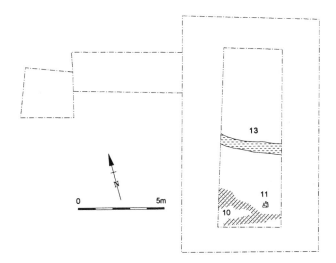

Fig. 10.6 Surface and drain: LUBs 4 and 7. (1:210)

bead and flange bowl, which can be conservatively dated to the mid to late 3rd century, but could extend into the 4th century.

LUB 5 Waterlain silts and dumps
In Area 2 the dump cg9 (LUB 2) and sand/silts cg103 in Area 3 were sealed by a series of waterlain layers interleaved with dumped material cg12 which contained some building material (*c* 4m OD).

At the limit of excavations in Area 3 there was an accumulation of sand/silts cg101 sealed by cg102 over which was cg103. The freshwater snail assemblages in cg102 and cg103 are suggestive of a mixture of water conditions, with probably slower, shallower, less open and more vegetated water conditions prevailing. Terrestrial snails may have been washed or swept in from surrounding habitats (French 1987).

Peat and sand cg97 was identified at the limit of excavation in one of the watching brief holes of Area 5. A layer of black sand and silt cg93 was recovered from the bottom of another of the watching brief holes of Area 5.

These deposits suggest that intermittent dumping took place over the area, interleaved with episodes of natural riverine accumulation. The molluscan evidence implies that the area was supporting more vegetation at this period than in LUB 1.

The pottery from layers cg12 (67 sherds) produced a SAMEG vessel of early to mid 3rd-century date, GREY vessels of Rookery Lane and Swanpool kiln types, a high beaded BB1 bead-and-flange bowl and late cooking pot, a MOSP painted mortarium, and possible NVCC open forms, all suggesting an early to mid 4th-century date. Silt cg93 in a watching brief trench contained two Swanpool SPOX vessels, a painted narrow-necked jar and a sherd from a pentice-moulded beaker. Here a date extending to the mid 4th century is applicable.

Late to very late Roman

Surface LUB 4 was used **LUB 6** into the late 4th century, as indicated by the pottery. Cutting across the silts LUB 5 was an east–west drain **LUB 7** down to the river. This was sealed by a dump or surface **LUB 8**. Pottery from both drain fill LUB 7 and layer LUB 8 dated to the very late 4th century.

LUB 6 Use of surface

Sealing the surface cg10 (LUB 4) in Area 1 were thin layers of silty sand sealed by clayey silt with charcoal cg14. Limestone fragments surrounded subsequently by clayey silt and charcoal cg15 lay over silt cg14. These layers possibly represented river silt as well as use.

The pottery from layers cg14 (14 sherds) included a GREY inturned bead-and-flange bowl and a handled collared rim jar of Swanpool type, both indicating a late 4th-century date, while the limestone fragments cg15 (8 sherds) contained a high-beaded GREY bead-and-flange bowl, a MONV mortarium and a shell-tempered double lid-seated jar, the latter indicating a more positive late 4th-century date, verging on the latest Roman dating.

LUB 7 Drain and blocking (Fig. 10.6)

About 2.5m to the north of the surface cg10 (LUB 4) there was an east–west drain cg13 to the north of Area 1 which cut cg12 (LUB 5); its depth varied from 0.18 to 0.28m and its base sloped from east (3.76m OD) to west (3.54m OD), allowing it to drain to the river.

The drain cut dump cg12 (LUB 5) indicating that it was constructed either between the early and the mid 4th century, or later. It had silted up with silty sand cg13 which also contained stone and a little building debris as well as domestic rubbish and a small quantity of bone, mainly worked fragments with some waste (see discussion).

The drain fill also contained a complete shell-tempered double lid-seated jar; the soil fill of the vessel was removed during conservation, but the only items within it were a small fragment of copper alloy and a badly degraded Constantinian coin (101) <208> of AD335–340 (the latter came from the soil level with the rim). The other vessels from the drain fill were GREY inturned bead-and-flange and necked bowls of Swanpool type, two GREY and two LCOA double lid-seated jars, NVCC bead and flange bowl (virtually complete), dish and flagon sherds, sherds from a SPOX closed form, sherds from a SPIR jar, and two OXRC necked bowls, one definitely of Young C75 type. This assemblage is typical of the latest datable Roman deposits in Lincoln, in the very late 4th century. The presence of a complete jar, near-complete vessels and other large sherds, and building debris, indicates that the drain was out of use by this date. Whether this was deliberate filling to level the site or simply a rubbish dump encroaching is impossible to determine, but the size of the sherds suggests primary dumping.

LUB 8 Layer

In Area 4, at the limit of excavation was either a dump or a surface with silt, pebble and limestone cg24, at an OD of 3.3m, suggesting that there was a slope down towards the river. This contained another fragment of bone waste similar to those from the drain silt cg13 (LUB 7). Only a few freshwater and terrestrial molluscs occurred in this deposit and it is possible that habitat conditions were unsuitable (French 1987).

The pottery from cg24 (95 sherds), as for LUB 7, included both shell-tempered and LCOA double lid-seated jars, a late NVCC bowl, a MOSP mortarium and a sherd from a SPIR jar; flanged bowl and a lid in LCOA fabric also occurred, and a rim fragment from an unusual shell-tempered jug, and all these indicate a similar very late 4th-century date for the pottery from this LUB. There was a single intrusive post-Roman sherd.

Ultimate Roman to Late Saxon

Waterlain silts **LUB 9** probably accumulated during this period; the dating is provided by the stratigraphic sequence.

LUB 9 Waterlain silts

The blocked drain cg13 (LUB 7) eventually became sealed by peat cg16 in Areas 1 and 2 which contained pottery of a very late 4th-century date; this layer probably built up on the abandonment of the site. Sealing the peat was waterlain silty sand cg17 with small fragments of tile, sandstone and a scattering of oyster shells together with a few other redeposited finds; this layer extended over both Areas 1 and 2. The presence of silty sand suggests that the source of the drain cg13 (LUB 7) was still flowing – silting was still taking place.

The Roman pottery (58 sherds) from these waterlain layers produced less conclusive evidence than earlier LUBs 7 and 8 for late 4th-century dating beyond various Swanpool types and a NVCC dish.

Late Saxon

There were dumps **LUB 10** north and south of the channel formed by the blocked drain. Covering the whole site was a network of wattle fences **LUB 11**. This collapsed **LUB 12**. Pottery from LUBs 10, 11 and 12 all dated from the early/mid to the mid 10th century.

There was silting in the channel and further evidence for wattles **LUB 13**; pottery from this LUB dated to the late 10th century. To the north of the channel, over LUB 13, were stakes and wattles **LUB 14**, replaced by a north–south gully and post **LUB 15**; to the south over LUB 13, were traces of a north–south stone wall and gully **LUB 16**. The channel, in Areas 1 and 2 over LUB 13, continued to fill through dumping and possibly silting as well **LUB 17**; in these layers were small groups of pottery dating up to the early to early/mid 11th century. It is this pottery which by association dates LUBs 15 and 16. In Area 2, over LUB 15 were layers and a post probably associated with further reclamation **LUB 18**; this LUB contained pottery dating to the early to mid/late 11th century

In Area 5 were traces of posts and silting **LUB 19**; these were associated with pottery dating from the late 10th century. Also in Area 5 and sealing LUB 12 in Area 4 were river deposits and silt **LUB 20**; the pottery was possibly intrusive.

LUB 10 Dumping and silting

Over layer cg15 (LUB 6) in Area 1 was a dump with stone cg23, and in Area 2 there was a similar dump cg22 over cg12 (LUB 5). Dump cg23, with a surface at 4.26m OD, contained a large quantity of redeposited Roman building debris, largely tile, with a small quantity of Roman residual domestic rubbish but also a copper-alloy pin with decorated polyhedral head (80) <64> of late Saxon type, and six post-Roman sherds.

A broad channel cg108 had been created by drainage through the middle of the site (along the line of the blocked Roman drain), scooping away

part of deposit cg23. The width of the channel was not clearly recorded, but it seems to have run east–west extending over most of Areas 1 and 2. There was a sequence of peat/silt deposits cg19 in the channel which sealed/cut earlier waterlain deposits cg17 (LUB 9). Deposits cg19 contained a small group of typical early/mid to mid 10th- century pottery (20 post-Roman sherds), together with a quantity of Roman tile, several fragments of bone waste (similar to those from silt cg13, LUB 7) and other residual rubbish.

Pottery from this LUB, mostly from the dumps cg22 and cg23 to the north and the south of the channel, included some fairly fresh very late 4th-century pottery (among the 495 Roman sherds), similar in composition to the pottery found in earlier deposits (LUBs 7 and 8); however, sherd links between Roman potsherds show that the material links, not with the earlier levels (LUBs 7, 8 or 9), but with similar pottery from later LUBs (LUBs 11 and 12). The inference from this is that not only was the dumping LUB 10 and wattles LUB 11 more or less contemporary but also that the dumped material was imported on to the site from very late Roman deposits.

LUB 11 Wattle fences
(Figs. 10.7, 10.16–17 and 10.22)

Set into the channel and the dumps in Areas 1 and 2, cutting cg22 and cg23 (LUB 10), were the uprights for wattle fences cg25. From the small area excavated it might be deduced that the wattles formed a north–south east–west grid, perhaps each enclosed space measuring about 7m east–west and 6m north–south. These fences would probably have originally stood upright, probably to a height of *c* 0.9m; they seem to have been supported by dumps of tile and limestone cg21, cg27 and cg34, which had later partially

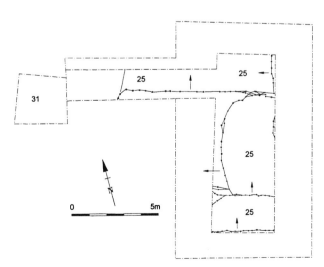

Fig. 10.7 Wattle fences: LUB 11. (1:210)

dispersed through water action. Dump cg21 overlay peat/silt deposits cg19 (LUB 10) in Areas 1 and 2; dump cg27 overlay cg23 (LUB 10) in Area 1; dump cg34 sealed cg25 in Areas 1 and 2. Snails of fresh-water, damp and drier habitat genera were present in dump cg21 (Milles 1993). The grid crossed the former channel, and here the north–south wattles can be seen to bow out to the west, possibly distorted by the flow through the underlying channel.

Silts cg26 had built up around the fences and several fragments of leather shoemaking waste and a little building debris had become trapped by the wattles cg25. A late Saxon iron knife blade (64) <41> was also found in the silts cg26.

Sections of the wattle constructions cg25 were examined in detail by Maisie Taylor. Although the species of wood used was similar to the other panels, in panel cg77 the uprights were generally larger, with less space between, but also every fourth upright was more substantial. This panel was positioned across the flow of the channel. Context 69 Sample 9 was a thin radial plank, not identified because it was heavily compressed. However, the fact that it was quite a narrow, radially split plank suggests that it was probably oak, as few woods split cleanly to make radial planks of this thickness. The position of the plank, together with the fact that there appears to have been less wattle between posts cg35 and cg33, suggests that there may have been a stile gate at this point. Stile gates are a very effective way of handling cattle and people, both of whom can step over the lower level when the bar is removed (Taylor 1987).

There was a build up of peat cg28 within the area of the channel, probably due to a diminished flow; it sealed cg21. A small quantity of leather shoemaking waste (Mould 1993) was found within peat cg28, together with a little domestic refuse and a bone skate (81) <73>, probably of late Saxon date (Rackham 1994). The moderate to large animal bone assemblage from cg28 almost certainly represents primary butchery waste (Dobney *et al* 1994e). Peat cg28 contained a good group of late Saxon pottery (115 post-Roman sherds) including LKT and LSH. The decoration and forms are typical of the early/mid to mid 10th century. There are several multi-sherd vessels indicating possible contemporary rubbish dumping. The residual Roman pottery (173 sherds) includes a sherd link back to LUB 10 and is of similar very late 4th-century date.

There was also peat cg31 to the north-west in Area 4, possibly of the same period; it sealed cg24 (LUB 8). Part of a bone flute (116) <155> probably made from a goose ulna was recovered from cg31 (Rackham 1994); similar pieces are known from late Saxon levels at Thetford (Rogerson and Dallas 1984, Fig. 194, 64–9).

The peat cg29, in Area 2, sealed dump cg22 (LUB 10); it was in turn sealed by a horizontal wattle panel cg30. The panel was similar to those of wattle constructions cg25, except that the weave was haphazard and it contained some birch; as there was no evidence of broken verticals, it is possible that it was used as a walkway (Taylor 1987).

Both the late Saxon pottery from this LUB cg28, and cg19 (LUB 10), date to the early/mid to mid 10th century. Both this LUB and LUB 10 share residual Roman pottery joins, suggesting that they were derived from the same source. It would seem that although this LUB was stratigraphically later, there was little actual time between the activities. This seems to support the interpretation that the wattle fences were being used as a framework holding dumps of stone and soil, in an attempt to hold the river bank together and resist the seasonal flooding. So the dumps in LUB 10 were there to hold the fence network and further dumps LUB 11 stabilised it. There were possibly more dumps which were subsequently washed away. The channel which continued to flow through the area was in use as a more regular dumping ground cg28; it was from here that we have the best group of contemporary pottery with multi-sherd vessels; primary butchery waste was also dumped in the channel.

LUB 12 Collapse of fences and silting
In Areas 1 and 2, some of the fences cg25 (LUB 11) had broken off and others had collapsed in one piece into peat cg32 and cg33 which had finally gathered round them. The panels had fallen either to the west, suggesting the channel flow, or to the north, following the flow of the river.

Peat cg32 sealed dump cg27 (LUB 11) in Area 1; it contained a small quantity of craft debris, including two crucible sherds and a jar sherd with a metallic deposit on its internal surface (suggesting that it may have been reused for some industrial purpose), and several pieces of leather shoemaking waste. The cattle bones from cg32 show little evidence for direct butchery, but perhaps indicate waste from hide preparation (Dobney *et al* 1994e). Peat cg33 sealed peat cg31 (LUB 11) in Area 4.

Sealing the peat in the channel was silting and debris cg35 and cg36. Silting cg35 sealed peat cg32 in Area 1; silting cg36 sealed silting cg26 (LUB 11) and peat cg32. Over cg35 and cg36 were waterlain deposits cg110 which contained residual Roman material; the level at the top of cg110 lay between 4.29 and 4.32m OD.

To the south of the channel in Area 1, sealing silt cg110, there was a drystone wall cg112 (unplanned; no further description recorded), possibly an attempt to confine the channel to the northern part of the site. Within the channel there were silts cg111 building up, sealing cg110. The channel cg109 scooped away some of the silting cg36. A thick layer of silt cg114, containing residual Roman material together with 51 post-Roman sherds, sealed the channel scoop as well as building up on both sides of the wall cg112 and sealing its remains completely.

Pottery from this LUB is similar to that from LUBs 10 and 11. Peats cg36, cg35, cg32 and cg33, with silts cg110 and cg114, provide a large group of early/mid to mid 10th-century pottery (a total of 540 post-Roman sherds). The craft debris from peat cg32 may represent contemporary rubbish.

Sherd links within the residual Roman pottery show that a proportion of the material had been reworked from LUB 11. Animal bone was recovered from cg36, cg110 and cg114, the range of which implies that much of this material was primary butchery waste (Dobney *et al* 1994e). However, both cg110 and cg114 were noted as containing a quantity of residual Roman material and it seems likely that the bone too was residual in these cases. It seems that dumps which contained quantities of Roman material (LUB 10) had been consolidated by the fence network (LUB 11), but were being "reworked"` by the processes of both the channel itself and the river to the west.

LUB 13 Silting and wattles (Fig. 10.8)
In Areas 1 and 2, the channel flow appeared to have continued to whirl around the remains of the earlier wattle framework and consequently have scooped away part of deposit cg110 (LUB 12), leaving a hollow which filled up cg43 with peat, mussel shells, silt and charcoal, together with fragments from two stave-built wooden vessels (Morris 1994) and a few pieces of leather shoemaking waste.

Sealing waterlain deposits cg114 (LUB 12) in the channel were silty sands with an area of burnt wattles with an upright stake cg105; the stake (67) <47> was a hazel (*Corylus sp*) roundwood rod with bark still adhering, probably coppiced (Morris 1994). Deposit cg105 was sealed by a deposit of dark silt containing postholes and upright stakes in silty clay associated with limestone fragments cg106. These two deposits probably together represent wattle and stakes to the north-east of the site, Area 2, which only partially survived. The remains of three upright wooden posts cg44, also in Area 2 and aligned east–west, may have formed part of the same fence; they cut deposit cg110 (LUB 12). Two of these were observed in plan and the third in the section (unpublished).

In Area 2 sealing peat cg32 (LUB 12) there was a layer of dark silt with limestone, sandy clay and silt with limestone and charcoal cg115; these layers suggest dumping of material but some silting either from the channel or the river as well. From dumped material cg115, a small group of 10th- century

pottery (29 post-Roman sherds) and a moderately-sized assemblage of animal bone, was recovered; the presence of mainly mandibles and metapodials in cg115 indicates the dumping of primary butchery waste (Dobney *et al* 1994e).

Slot/hollow cg43 contained a small group of pottery (65 post-Roman sherds) which probably dates to the late 10th century. Silts cg105 and cg106 produced a small group of pottery (15 post-Roman sherds) of types in use throughout the 10th century. The evidence suggests that at the end of the 10th century attempts to maintain this area as dry land continued with stakes cg105, cg106 and cg44 and dumping cg115 in Area 2.

LUB 14 Posts (Fig. 10.9)
The wattle and stakes cg106 (LUB 13) silted over with sand cg107 in Area 2 and in this were elongated postholes cg42; to the east of these and butting up to the line of the postholes was a dark clay/silt

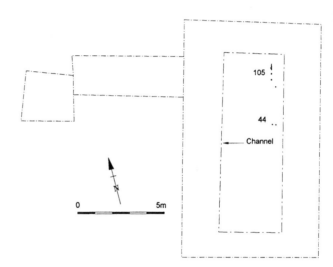

Fig. 10.8 Stakes: LUB 13. (1:210)

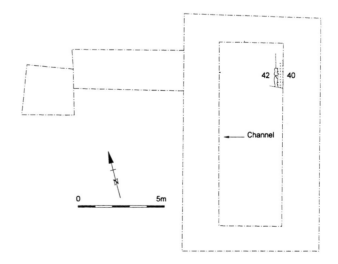

Fig. 10.9 Posts: LUB 14. (1:210)

layer cg122 enmeshed with long pieces of wood, within which was found part of a burnt micaceous sandstone ingot mould (56) <44>. Over this was a layer of clay and charcoal cg40.

The only dating evidence for this LUB consisted of sherds of undiagnostic LFS with a dating span of the late 10th to late 12th centuries.

LUB 15 Gully and post (Fig. 10.10)

Cutting into cg107 (LUB 14), in Area 2, was a gully cg121 which seemed to drain into the channel; it had silted up with very dark brown sand. Just on the eastern edge of the slot was a posthole cg48, to the east of which was a layer of sand with some compact patches cg41. The features succeeded those of LUB 14.

The contemporary pottery from this LUB had no characteristic datable features, although the high percentage of LFS indicates a date of or later than the mid/late 11th century.

LUB 16 Wall and gully (Fig. 10.10)

To the south of the channel, set into layer cg115 (LUB 13) in Area 1, there was a north–south line of limestone fragments cg46, possibly wall foundations or the remains of wattle supports. A single, very worn architectural fragment with a residual beaded moulding and hollow curve came from the wall cg46, (11) <32>, and was identified as a possible impost or cornice block of Roman date. There were also several Roman tiles. It has been noted that the optimum period of reuse of Roman stone in Lincoln and Lincolnshire was between the late 10th and 12th centuries (Stocker and Everson 1990, 86–7). The wall was abutted to the east by layers of silt, sand and limestone sealed by black sandy clay with charcoal and mortar flecks cg116 (at 4.55m OD). Cutting these layers was a gully cg45, apparently running into the channel. A small group of pottery from this LUB (54 post-Roman sherds) may date to between the late 10th century and the late 12th century, but is most likely to belong to the 11th century.

LUB 17 Silts and dumps (Fig. 10.19)

Sealing posts cg44 (LUB 13) in Areas 1 and 2, and probably contemporary with the activity to the north and south (LUBs 15 and 16), was a further build-up of material cg117 in the channel. This material consisted of dark greyish-brown sand with shell which was sealed by dark yellowish clayey sand; there were several more layers all rapidly removed by excavation with minimal recording except to note a black organic layer. It is difficult to interpret the formation processes of these layers – they may represent dumps or silting or a combination of the two. From layers cg117 was a large assemblage of animal bone which indicated the presence of pri-

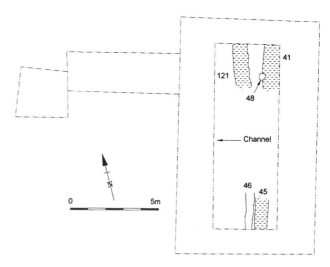

Fig. 10.10 Gully and post with wall and gulley: LUBs 15 and 16. (1:210)

mary butchery waste (Dobney et al 1994e). Layers cg117 also contained both domestic rubbish and a number of craft or industrial tools together with a fragment of animal rib bearing part of a runic inscription (29) <104> (Fig. 10.19; see discussion); and a large group of pottery (149 post-Roman sherds) with a very high proportion of residual Roman and 10th-century sherds. The latest material dates to the early to early/mid 11th century.

To south of the site in Area 1 sealing cg117 there were dumps of limestone in sand and clay cg53 (to 4.56m OD) and cg119 (to 4.74m OD); also sealing cg117 in Area 2 to the north-east were dumps cg118. Dumps cg53 and cg119 produced small groups of pottery (27 post-Roman sherds in total) dating to between the late 10th and the mid/late 11th centuries.

LUB 18 Post and surface (Figs. 10.11 and 10.20)

To the north-east of the site in Area 2, to the east of and apparently sealing posthole cg48 (LUB 15), was a dump of sand and clay with a large limestone fragment cg49. This layer was possibly cut by a further posthole cg50 which may have been associated with sandy clay cg47, which sealed cg41 (LUB 15). Over these layers, still to the north-east, was a thin layer of clay, sealed by sand and silt with stone cg51 at 4.79m OD; a stone object (39) <34> (Fig. 10.20) from this layer may have been used as a weight or even an anchor, possibly for a fish trap. (cf grooved stones found within the silting of a Norman channel in the Trent valley: (Salisbury 1991, Fig. 11.15).

To the north-west in Area 2, river deposits cg52 sealed cg121 (LUB 15). Into this foreshore material a pit cg55 had been dug and was sealed by further silting and some dumped material cg58.

These layers in Area 2 sloped west down to the river and south down to the channel. The pottery from this LUB (19 post-Roman sherds) dated to the early to mid/late 11th century.

LUB 19 *Posts and silts*

Silt deposits with posts cg98 were recorded as part of the watching brief in Area 5; they sealed cg97 (LUB 5). A small group of pottery (5 post-Roman sherds) from cg98 is only datable to between the late 10th century and the late 12th centuries.

LUB 20 *River deposits and dumps*

River deposits and dumps cg63, cg70 and cg72 were observed during the watching brief to the west of Area 5. In Area 4 layers were recorded in section while machining; sealing peat cg33 (LUB 12) were river deposits cg60, sealed by river deposits cg61 and rubble dumping cg104. There are three sherds from cg61, probably dating to the early part of the 13th century (although they may have been intrusive).

Saxo-Norman

Two pits **LUB 21** cut into the underlying stratigraphy, indicated some occupation of the site during this period. River deposits and silts LUBs 19 and 20 continued throughout.

LUB 21 *Pits (Fig. 10.12)*

In Area 2, but removed from its immediate stratigraphy by truncation, was pit cg54. Cutting this pit was another pit cg56, possibly wood-lined, which contained *prunus* stones (Moffett 1993) and a very small assemblage of animal bone which suggests that it may not have been used for rubbish disposal, but primarily as a cess-pit.

From LUB 21 there was a small group of 11th-century pottery (22 post-Roman sherds); the high number of ST and LFS sherds indicates that the material is likely to be of mid/late to late 11th-century date.

Early Medieval to High Medieval

Evidence of medieval occupation was observed in Area 5 **LUB 22**. Pottery from LUB 22 dates occupation from at least the 13th century, if not earlier.

LUB 22 *Structures: occupation and fire (Fig. 10.13)*

In the eastern part of Area 5 was a surface of limestone fragments cg82, cut by a pit cg83. A small but good group of LSW2 jugs and pipkins dating to the mid to late 13th century was recovered from pit cg83 (241 post-Roman sherds); it included two nearly-complete jugs damaged during excavation.

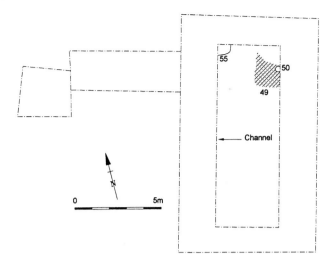

Fig. 10.11 Post and surface: LUB 18. (1:210)

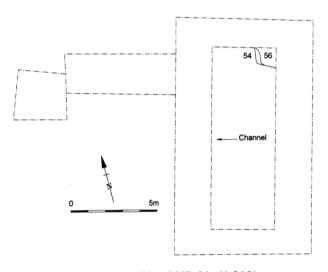

Fig. 10.12 Pits: LUB 21. (1:210)

A sequence was examined to the west of Area 5 where river silts cg63 (LUB 20) were cut by a possible pit cg64; these were sealed by sandy clay cg65. Layer cg65 produced only two sherds dating from the mid 12th to early/mid 13th centuries. Over it was a mixed layer cg66 (no further description recorded) sealed by sandy clay cg67. This was sealed by a wall cg68 aligned north–south; it was at least 4.3m long but its width is unknown. There were four rough courses of irregular limestone blocks (two of the stones were faced and probably re-used; the lowest course was offset by 0.08m and was 0.25m deep. The first and third courses above the offset were formed of large blocks *c* 0.15m thick with a single course of flat fragments 0.07m thick between. The wall had a rubble core. There was no mortar, or the mortar had broken down, as between the stones was a

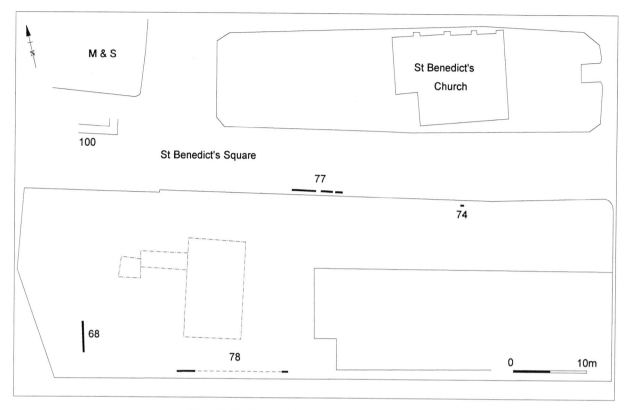

Fig. 10.13 Traces of walling: LUB 22. (1:500)

matrix of soft silty sand. The total height of the surviving wall was 0.65m. There was no sign of contemporary surfaces to the west of the wall. Wall cg68 was robbed and it was sealed by levelling dump cg69. Levelling dump cg69 produced a small group of pottery (9 post-Roman sherds) with some sherds having a possible date range of up to the mid 14th century; however, the group could date to the early to early/mid 13th century.

A wall cg78, surviving to three to four courses, ran east–west to the south of Area 5. A fragment of a possible wall cg91 was aligned north–south and was composed of limestone fragments in silt or sand (unplanned). Wall foundations cg78 and cg91 had possibly been associated with sandy silt with charcoal cg89; cg89 contained two undiagnostic sherds dating generally to between the early /mid 12th century and the early /mid 13th century.

In Area 5 at the limit of excavation there was a dump cg84 which was sealed by mortar surface cg85. Waterlain silts cg70 and cg72 (LUB 20), together with sandy silt with charcoal flecks cg89, mortar cg85 and wall cg78 were all sealed by fire debris containing charcoal, burnt brick and daub cg73. The pottery from cg73 (14 post-Roman sherds) dated between the mid/late 12th century and the

early/mid 13th century; there was also an intrusive post-medieval sherd (TB).

Several walls in Area 5 were recorded which were possibly medieval but could have been later: walls cg74, cg77, cg90, cg92, cg94 and cg100 (cg90, cg92 and cg94 were unplanned). Roughly-coursed unmortared stones cg74 at the limit of excavation were probably aligned east–west. A possible wall cg77, which had survived to two courses of squared limestone blocks at the limit of excavation was aligned east–west. Wall cg90 survived to four courses of limestone bonded with sand at the limit of excavation and was aligned east–west (unplanned). A wall cg92 of coursed limestone blocks was observed to run north–south (unplanned) at the limit of excavation. Possible north–south wall cg94 was associated with clay floor cg95 at the limit of excavation; wall cg100 at the limit of excavation was aligned east–west with a return to the north at its east end. It was about 1.15m wide and two courses of stone survived with a total height of 0.4m. There were traces of white paint or limewash on the north face of the wall.

Post Medieval

There was dated evidence for occupation in the area

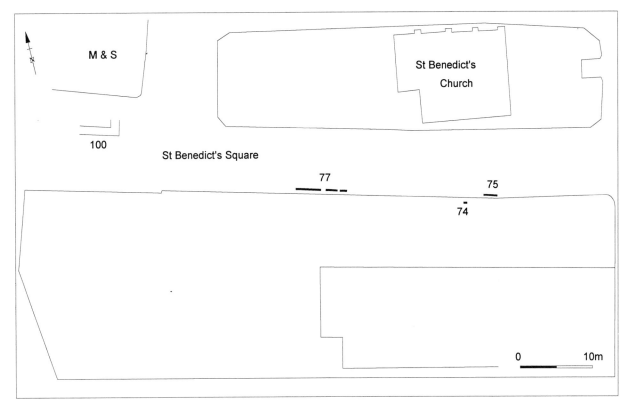

Fig. 10.14 Traces of walling: LUB 23. (1:500)

from the mid 16th century **LUB 23**. Some of the walls from LUB 22 may have belonged to or continued into this period.

LUB 23 Dumps and walls (Fig. 10.14)
In Area 5 several layers were encountered of un-certain date but possibly belonging to this period; they included rubble dumps cg79, sand dump cg87 and fire debris cg80 (all found over fire debris cg73 LUB 22), rubble dump cg86 (over surface cg85, LUB 22) and brick and stone wall foundation cg75 (which cut silt cg72, LUB 20). There was a dump cg71 which was sealed by fire debris cg120; dump cg71 produced pottery (4 post-Roman sherds) only generally datable to between the mid 16th century and the early modern period. Sealing wall cg94 and floor cg95 (both LUB 22) was a rubble dump cg96 which contained pottery (5 post-Roman sherds) which dated from the late 17th to mid 18th cen-turies.

Modern

There was evidence of a stone-founded building, Structure 1, probably associated with a well **LUB 24**, a brick-lined feature and a sewer trench in Area 5. The well had been backfilled in the mid 19th century and the sewer trench was identified as Victorian. Of a later date in Area 5 were brick and concrete foundations **LUB 25**.

LUB 24 Structure 1 (Figs. 10.15 and 10.18)
Cutting into Areas 2, 3, 4 and 5 were walls cg59; these intruded into the much earlier deposits cg117, dumps cg118 (both LUB 17) and dump cg58 (LUB 18). The pitched stone foundations had been cut from at least 6.34m OD, *c* 1.5m above the top of the excavations in Area 2. The foundations were aligned east–west and occurred towards the north end of Area 2; here they were *c* 1m wide and at least 5m long. There was an internal wall to the north between Areas 2 and 3 and a return to the north between Areas 3 and 4.

A stone-lined well cg62 was found adjacent to a wall junction (Fig. 10.18). A number of medieval architectural fragments had been reused in the construction of the stone lining of the well, together with a substantial portion of a Lincolnshire lime-stone mortar (133) <202>. The well had been back-filled and capped during the 19th century with a large quantity of rubbish including bottle glass. The presence of a Stephen Green manufactured stone-ware bottle (impressed with the name of a Lincoln ale and porter dealer, John Banks Smith) dates the

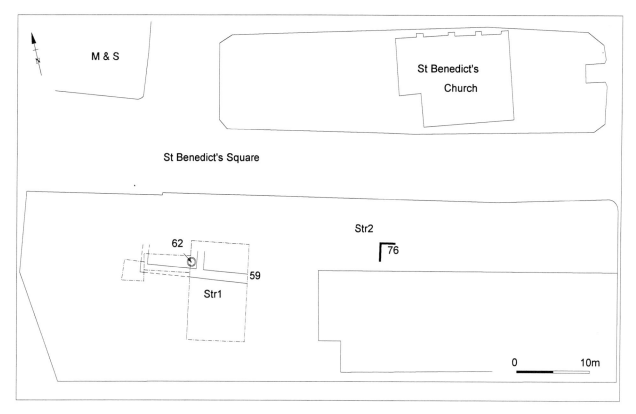

Fig. 10.15 Structures 1 and 2: LUBs 24 and 25. (1:500)

group to between 1828 and 1860, this being the period of ownership of the Lambeth factory by the former.

Two other features were recorded as part of the watching brief in Area 5: a brick-lined feature backfilled with rubbish cg88 and a Victorian sewer trench cg99.

LUB 25 Structure 2 (Fig. 10.15)
To the east of Area 5 were brick and concrete foundations cg76 which may have been associated with the printing works on the site and a pit with printing works rubbish cg81.

Discussion

Topography of the waterfront
In the mid Roman period (LUB 1) the site (its land surface around 3m OD) was probably at least partially under water and the molluscan assemblage suggests quiet, slowly-flowing water conditions. The three upright timber posts cg3 (LUB 1) may have been connected with activity related to the water margins, possibly mooring posts. The line of the river front appears to have extended from the

south-west of the site to the north-east (Fig. 10.4).

In the first part of the late Roman period, building debris dump cg9 (LUB 2) defined the river margin; there was dry land on these dumps at 3.58m OD. At this time the alignment of the river edge seems to follow the earlier one (Fig. 10.5). Subsequently in the late Roman period there were possible surfaces cg8 at 3.88m OD (LUB 3) and cg10 at 4.05m OD (LUB 4).

By a date in the 4th century waterlain layers interleaved with dumps cg12 (LUB 5) around 4m OD. These layers were cut by the east–west drain cg13 (LUB 7), which extended beyond the west of the site, suggesting that at this time the river edge lay further to the west. The reclamation of the river may indicate that it had been deepened, and that its alignment may have shifted to run north–south, if the drain was to meet the river at right angles. This might mean that the area immediately north of the site had been reclaimed from river flooding.

Any channelling of the river seems to have silted up in the immediate post-Roman period and the drain, no longer contained in a narrow channel, had overflowed to cover a broad area reaching the river about the point of the excavation (LUBs 9–13; LUB18) and not further west; this may also have been a consequence of rising river levels.

Dumping in the early/mid to mid 10th century to the north cg22 and south cg23 of the channel (LUB 10) was followed by wattle constructions over the whole area (LUB 11). There was evidence that the dumped material (LUB 10) had been imported on to the site. The wattle constructions cg25 and cg30 (LUB 11) may have represented reclamation or extension into the Brayford (cf Dorestad, Van Es and Verwers 1980); the wattle may have acted as a framework within which material had been dumped, and later much of it scoured out before the wattle collapsed (LUB 12). Evidence for dumping is suggested by the quantity of animal bone from LUBs 11 and 12; the pottery suggests that the material from LUBs 10–12 appears to be contemporary dumping. At Norwich, similar wattle fences were found together with deposits of brushwood matting (Ayers 1985); differences in the construction of fences enabled individual tenements to be identified while the brushwood was used to consolidate the beach. Here on the Brayford edge, however, there were no obvious differences between the fences and no evidence of brushwood

Fig. 10.16 Wattles cg25 under excavation, looking north-west.

Fig. 10.17 Wattles cg25 with prone fence cg30, looking south.

consolidation. But the fences were not designed as fish traps; they were interwoven where they joined and did not funnel into an enclosed basket-type structure (Salisbury 1980). It is also unlikely that the fences were set up to create enclosed pools in which fish could have been retained; there was no evidence of fish remains. It seems most likely that the wattle framework was indeed constructed to consolidate the river edge at a vulnerable location at Brayford Head.

The channel, in the mid 10th century, had silted up to between 4.29 and 4.32m OD (waterlain deposits cg110, LUB 12). The dumps and the peat deposits within the channel included domestic and some craft refuse.

Between the late 10th and 12th centuries it seems that there were further attempts to consolidate the waterfront (LUBs 13, 14, 15, 16 and 18), but this time on either side of the channel feeding into the river from the east. At the north end of the trench was one sequence of events; wattles (LUB 13) were replaced by posts (LUB 14) which in turn were replaced by a north–south gully with a post or posts to the east (LUB 15). It seems that the riverfront remained along the same line for LUBs 13–15, but then more land seems to have been reclaimed (LUB 18) and the waterfront advanced just beyond the western extent of the site; posthole cg50 may represent part of the new line, or it may lie further west. Dry land (LUB 18) in the form of a stone, sand and silt surface cg51 was at 4.79m OD.

Dumps cg116 (LUB 16) to the south of the east–west channel at 4.55m OD were cut by a north–south stone wall with a gully running parallel to the east. This may have been contemporary with LUB 15. The channel itself continued to silt (LUB 17).

Saxo-Norman pitting (LUB 21) indicates occupation of the area during the period. Sometime before the early to mid 13th century the waterfront had shifted westwards by at least 20m, probably as a result of deliberate reclamation, and possibly deepening of the river during this period. River silts cg63 (LUB 20) in Area 5 (to the southwest of Trench B) of unrecorded OD were sealed by a dry land layer cg65,

associated with two sherds of mid 12th- to early to mid 13th-century pottery; it was eventually sealed by a north–south wall cg68 (LUB 22), evidence suggesting perhaps that this area of Wigford was intensively used by the earlier part of the 13th century.

The excavation records tell us little about the late medieval and post-medieval period in the area.

By the 18th/19th centuries the ground surface was at 6.34m OD; Structure 1 (LUB 24) was cut from this level. The river lay well to the west.

Artefactual evidence for industrial activity

A small quantity of worked bone, together with some waste, was recovered from the drain silt cg13 (LUB 7); two fragments of bone from the overlying peat cg16 (LUB 9), and several other similar pieces from later levels sealing the drain (cg19, LUB 10), probably originated from the same group. Tool marks on the bone witness the use of saws, chisels and files, while the ring-and-dot motif on one piece, which may have broken during manufacture, was

Fig. 10.18 Well cg62.

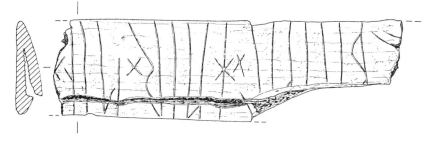

Fig. 10.19 Runic inscription from cg117. Scale 1:1.

probably produced by a bit; this implies a degree of specialised skill (Rackham 1994). The waste almost certainly represents debris from the production of small casket mounts; only one of the pieces, a trapezoidal decorated mount (101) <118> appears to be finished. Similar casket mounts were found at Richborough (Cunliffe (ed.) 1968, pl LXI, 225) in a 4th-century pit, although these were amongst re-deposited 2nd-century material. These pieces suggest that bone working activity was taking place in the late Roman period, possibly nearby in the suburb to the east.

The majority of the Roman finds lay within post-Roman dumps on the riverfront. Apart from a modelling tool (121) <182> (from cg5, LUB 1), a possible crucible sherd from cg11 (LUB 3) and the bone-working waste (see above), there was little evidence of crafts or industry among this material. No evidence was found of activities specific to the use of the water itself in either the Roman or the Late Saxon period apart from the lead weight from surface cg10 (LUB 4) – a fishing weight? – and a similar object – an anchor? – in LUB 18.

The Late Saxon dumps and peat deposits within the channel (LUB 12) contained largely domestic refuse, but also included a little leather shoemaking waste, two crucible sherds and part of another vessel which may have served an industrial purpose. From silt cg117 (LUB 17) came a quantity of both domestic and craft/industrial rubbish, including several textile-working tools, iron woolcomb fragments (16) <25> and <26>, a spindlewhorl (29) <35> and a socketed bone point (29) <28> which was almost certainly used as a craft tool, together with an iron ?drawplate (29) <19>.

Quantities of animal bone appear to represent dumping from the bank into the river. The material of this date is characteristic of primary butchery waste, with some elements of domestic refuse also present. All contexts are dominated primarily by cattle and non-meat-bearing skeletal elements. Interestingly, few elements show direct evidence of butchery, and the presence of numbers of horncore fragments may suggest possible horn working in the area. Material from cg32, although of mixed origin, has apparently similar characteristics to those more tightly-dated groups and may well be of similar date (Dobney *et al* 1994e). The Saxo-Norman period is represented by a single large assemblage of animal bones (cg117). In a number of respects its characteristics are similar to those of late Saxon date, being dominated by the remains of cattle and elements indicative of primary butchery waste. Again, splitting of both cattle and caprovid longbones has occurred. However, a wider range of species, which include dog, raven and pheasant, is present (Dobney *et al* 1994e).

Runic Inscription

The runic inscription, which seems to be in the 'Norwegian' (short-twig) version of the younger futhark, is notable because of the rarity of such pieces. It contains the first three words of an inscription in

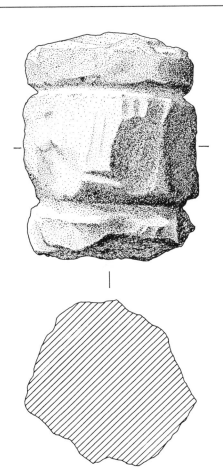

Fig. 10.20 Stone weight or anchor from cg51. Scale 1:4.

cg/LUB	cg/LUB	cg/LUB	cg/LUB	cg/LUB	cg/LUB	cg/LUB
1/1	19/10	37/–	55/18	72/20	89/22	106/13
2/1	20/–	38/–	56/21	73/22	90/22	107/14
3/1	21/11	39/–	57/–	74/22	91/22	108/10
4/1	22/10	40/14	58/18	75/23	92/22	109/12
5/1	23/10	41/15	59/24	76/25	93/5	110/12
6/3	24/8	42/14	60/20	77/22	94/22	111/12
7/3	25/11	43/13	61/20	78/22	95/23	112/12
8/3	26/11	44/13	62/24	79/23	96/23	113/–
9/2	27/11	45/16	63/20	80/23	97/5	114/12
10/4	28/11	46/16	64/22	81/25	98/19	115/13
11/3	29/11	47/18	65/22	82/22	99/24	116/16
12/5	30/11	48/15	66/22	83/22	100/22	117/17
13/7	31/11	49/18	67/22	84/22	101/5	118/17
14/6	32/12	50/18	68/22	85/22	102/5	119/17
15/6	33/12	51/18	69/22	86/23	103/5	120/23
16/9	34/11	52/18	70/20	87/23	104/20	121/15
17/9	35/12	53/17	71/23	88/24	105/13	122/14
18/–	36/12	54/21				

Fig. 10.21 Concordance of cg numbers with LUB numbers for sb85.

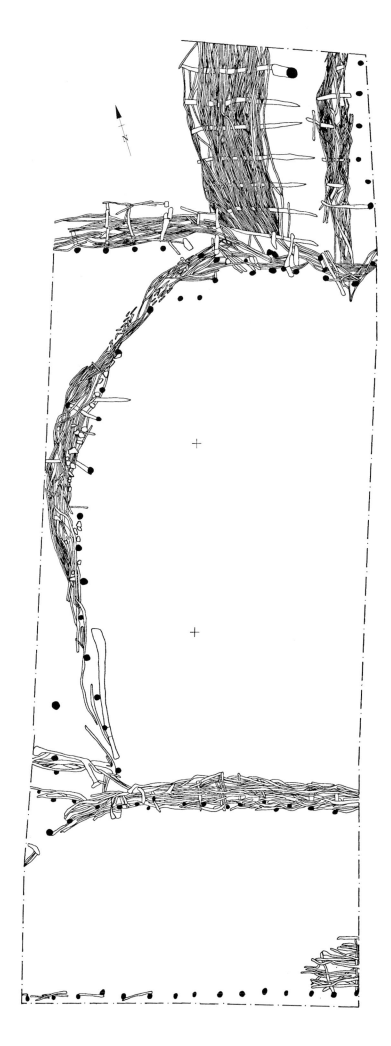

Fig. 10.22 *Drawing of Wattles. (cf Fig 10.7)*

Old Norse, but too little survives to suggest whether the carver was an inhabitant of Lincoln (which would probably suggest a 10th-century date) or a visitor, who might have brought it (eg from Norway) at any date up to the 14th century. The inscription may be compared with magical inscriptions from Bergen (Norway) and Ribe (Denmark), and may have been either a charm against fever or a kitchen charm or curse (McKinnell 1996; Holman and McKinnell forthcoming; Holman 1996, 50–1); the former now seems more likely.

Occupation of the parish of St Benedict

The mid/late 11th- to late 11th-century pits cg54 and cg56 suggest occupation which is also supported by the amount of 11th-century pottery from unstratified layers. The church of St Benedict may be of 11th-century origin. From the 12th or 13th century there are traces of stone-founded buildings in the area (LUB 21). Fire debris cg73 in the area may indicate that several buildings were burnt down between the mid 13th and the early 14th centuries. Occupation continued into the early 14th century.

There was no structural and little ceramic evidence for activity in the area from the mid 14th century possibly until the 16th century, although several unstratified finds date to this period. This minimal evidence for occupation suggests that the area was not built on during this period.

Stone fragments possibly from St Benedict's church

There were three architectural fragments reused in the foundations of Structure 1 (LUB 24); these are a polygonal colonnette capital, possibly from a window or other shafted feature <200>; a door jamb or arch voussoir with keeled roll flanked by hollows <201>; and a chamfered block <199>. The first two can be dated to the late 12th/early 13th centuries; but the third is undiagnostic, except that the tooling indicates that it dates to the late 12th century or after. The fragments may have come from St Benedict's church – the original fabric retains a very early 13th-century arcade whose inner order on the south side has a similar keeled moulding to <201>, which differs only in appearing to be slightly scrolled. The same or similar mouldings can be seen in the blocked arch at the truncated west end of the chancel, and one may surmise, on the basis of the surviving western column, that the nave arcade would have had variations on the keeled roll in its mouldings too.

A mullion or shaft with exactly the same kind of integral capital as the excavated example <200> can be seen supporting the early 13th-century *piscina* in the chancel south wall.

The nave and north aisle of St Benedict's were demolished during or after the Civil War. The parish accounts for St Benedict's record repairs to the walls between 1655 and 1677, with extensive building activity *c* 1701 (Hill 1948, 135). An account of Lincoln churches written *c* 1674 also notes that the steeple of St Benedict's fell down and had been lately rebuilt (John Ross, Scrap Books at Burton Hall, quoting MSS. Willis, 27, 40 and cited in Hill 1948, 135, n.1). The present west tower must have been rebuilt at about that time, incorporating fragments presumably from the medieval church. One might postulate that the fragments in the well also came from the church at that time, and that the well was also built in the 17th century.

Alternatively, both the keeled voussoir and the capital may have come from a domestic late 12th-century two-light window (see report for details and examples both *in situ* and excavated). This possibility rather broadens the range of possible sources for the stones, and the date of the well. However, the similarity between the *piscina* column and the well column capital raises the possibility that the *piscina* shaft is itself reset, and that it was placed there during the 17th-century repairs outlined above.

11. Waterside South 1982 (ws82)

Introduction

In 1982, in advance of the development of the C & A site on Waterside South, a new drain trench was dug by Anglian Water and was observed by Geoff Tann for the Lincoln Archaeological Trust. The project was funded by the Manpower Services Commission and the Department of the Environment. The trench ran east–west for about 100m, parallel with the river Witham to the north, with its east end on the line of Sincil Street. At the west end, the trench took a right-angle bend to reach to the river to the north; this stretch was *c* 27m long (Fig. 11.1). The trench was *c* 1m wide and up to 3.9m deep. The machining resulted in the contamination of some deposits. An interim report was published (Tann and Jones 1982).

This account of the watching brief is based on G Tann's records. Of the 39 contexts, 38 were interpreted as 13 context groups (cg1–13) and one was deemed unstratified. The context groups are discussed below as 8 land-use blocks, LUBs 1–8 (Fig. 11.5). The trench has been interpreted as one sequence of archaeology, but, as the land-use diagram indicates, some activity (LUB 3 and LUBs 5–6) only occurred to the east of the trench (Fig. 11.2).

There are 22 Roman sherds and 85 post-Roman sherds, together with 19 registered finds; the latter includes a little leather (Mould 1993) and glass. Some fragments of wood were retrieved from the trenches (Gale 1992). Some building material (239 fragments) was also recovered from the site, mostly medieval/post-medieval tile. The animal bone assemblage (261 fragments) was not considered to be worthy of further study. No samples were taken for environmental analysis. The paucity of material is doubtless due to the nature of the "excavation", and the fact that finds were retrieved mainly from the machine bucket rather than from within the trenches.

Stratigraphic analysis was carried out by Chris Guy and later by Kate Steane. Jane Young examined the post-Roman pottery. Jen Mann examined the

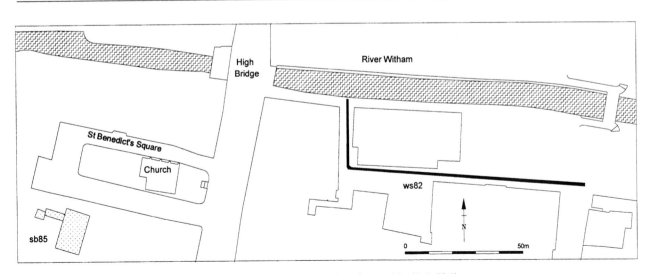

Fig. 11.1 Site location plan for ws82. (1:1,524)

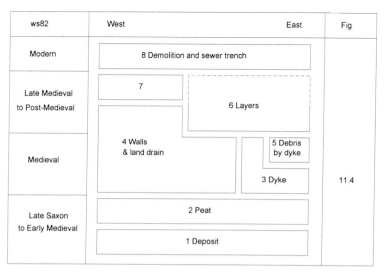

Fig. 11.2 LUB diagram for ws82.

registered finds and, with Rick Kemp, the building materials. Helen Palmer Brown and Zoe Rawlings digitized the plans.

Interpretation of the sequence of events

Late Saxon/Early Medieval

Riverine sand and clay **LUB 1** was sealed by peat **LUB 2**. Only one sherd of late 9th- to 12th-century pottery dates LUB 1; pottery from LUB 2 was mainly of 11th-century date but also included earlier and later pottery.

LUB 1 Deposit

The earliest deposit observed was compact yellow sand and clay, with a few stones cg1. This was at least 0.50m thick with its surface at *c* 2.60m OD. It was observed at the western end of the trench, in the north–south stretch, and extended at least 5m to the east of the east–west stretch.

The date of this deposit is uncertain, as is its interpretation. At a depth below 2.60m OD, the sand and clay must have been deposited into the channel of the Witham as a riverine sediment. The only find recovered was a Stamford Ware crucible sherd (26) <17>; it is of undiagnostic type and as such has a dating span of the late 9th to the 12th centuries.

LUB 2 Peat (Fig. 11.4)

The sand and clay cg1 (LUB 2) was sealed by a thick layer of peat cg2 which extended the whole length of both trenches. This was up to 2.70m thick with the top of the layer at an average of 4.15m OD.

The pottery from this deposit (17 post-Roman sherds) was mainly of 10th- and 11th-century date; however, a single medieval and a single post-medieval sherd were also present. Peat cg2 contained fragments of shell, wood and a scatter of refuse, including several pieces of vitrified glass, a small fragment of fuel-ash slag and two pieces of leather; one of the two leather fragments is a rectangular, heavily-worn piece (34) <2> which has been cut from a larger object, possibly saddlery or harness; this is more likely to be of medieval than earlier date (Mould 1993).

The predominance of 10th- and 11th-century sherds in the peat suggests that accumulation was underway during that period, but the later pottery and the leather object might suggest that the process continued into the medieval period.

Medieval

Cutting through the peat LUB 2, to the east of the site, was a large stone-lined dyke **LUB 3**, Sincil Dyke. The date of canalisation is uncertain but is likely to have been earlier than the 13th or early 14th century, the date of the pottery in its fill. The dating of the tiles suggests that the dyke clearly continued in use until at least the 15th century.

Cutting through the peat LUB 2 to the west of the site were two undated north–south walls and a land drain **LUB 4**; these were thought to be associated with medieval occupation much further to the south of the river.

Possibly contemporary with the use of dyke LUB 3 was undated debris along its edge **LUB 5**.

LUB 3 Large stone-lined dyke (Fig. 11.3–4)

To the east of the site a flat-bottomed construction

trench with a sloping western side was cut through the peat cg2 (LUB 2); it was 1.7m deep and of unknown width. Into this was built a dyke cg3, 3.2m wide (Fig. 11.4), lined with dressed stone bonded with mortar and clay; the construction trench was backfilled with a mixed sandy deposit containing stones and mid 12th-century tile.

The dyke cg3 had filled with deposits of silty sand with lenses of peat cg5. Within the silt were leather fragments: small pieces of turnshoe sole and clump repairs, with a very small quantity of secondary waste and scrap (Mould 1993). A small group of pottery (11 post-Roman sherds), the latest sherds of which date to the 13th or early 14th century, was found in the silts of the dyke cg5, and the latest tile found in this deposit dated between the early and mid/late 15th century.

From its position underlying Sincil Street, it is likely that the dyke was part of the drainage system known as Sincil Dyke. The evidence provides no support for a pre-Conquest date for the Dyke.

LUB 4 Walls and land drain (Fig. 11.3)
Cut into the peat cg2 (LUB 2), about 7m to the west of dyke cg3 was north–south wall cg6, and c 65m to the west of the dyke was north–south wall cg7, with what appeared to be a land drain cg8 about 10m further west.

Wall cg6 was constructed of irregular, but roughly rectangular, limestone blocks; it was 0.4m wide and survived to 0.65m high; the wall was set within a foundation trench 1.25m deep, and about 3m wide at the top, with sloping sides and a flattish bottom. The substantial foundation trench suggests an attempt to counteract the peaty ground at this point, perhaps indicating that here the ground was not very firm, as might be expected so near to the dyke cg3 (LUB 3).

Wall cg7 was 1m wide and survived to 2.1m in

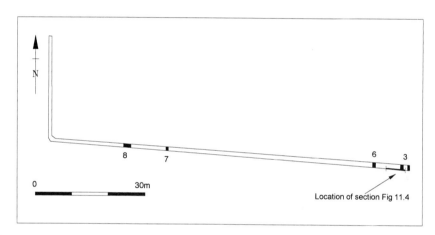

Fig. 11.3 Plan of pipe trench showing location of section, stone-lined dyke cg3 (LUB 3), walls cg6 and cg7, land drain cg8 (LUB 4) (1:1,000)

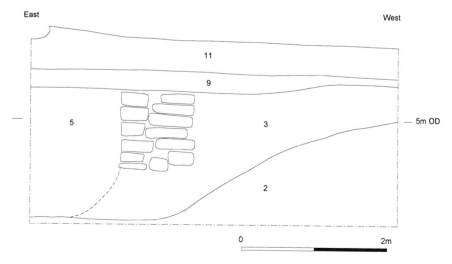

Fig. 11.4 East–west section across peat cg2 (LUB 2), the west side of stone-lined dyke cg3 and fill cg5 (LUB 3) and cutting cg9 (LUB 6) and cg11 (LUB 8); section drawn from the south side of the pipe trench. (1:50)

height; it was constructed of large irregular blocks of limestone, but there was no clear evidence of a construction trench. Drain cg8 was 1m wide and 1.8m deep with its top at *c* 4.65m OD, level with the surface of the peat cg2; it was constructed of irregular small–medium lumps of limestone with no apparent mortar; water was observed still flowing north towards the river.

The walls may represent the boundaries of properties running south from the Witham, but it is perhaps more likely that wall cg7 formed the eastern boundary of a property fronting on to the High Street, and that wall cg6 marked a property boundary just to the west of the dyke.

LUB 5 Debris by dyke
Several shallow layers of compact charcoal and burnt sand or ash, cg4 (unplanned) sealed the east side of dyke cg3. They might be fire ash from buildings to the east of the dyke. No finds were recovered.

Late Medieval to Post-Medieval

To the east of the site the dyke (LUB 3) was sealed, and walls cg7 and land drain cg8 (LUB 4) and layers cg4 (LUB 5) were sealed by further layers **LUB 6**. Pottery from LUB 6 dated between the mid 14th and mid to late 15th centuries. Wall cg6 (LUB 4) was re-used as the foundation of a brick wall **LUB 7**; there was no specific dating evidence.

LUB 6 Layers (Fig. 11.4)
Layers of clayey sand cg9, up to 2m thick, sealed deposits of peat and silt cg2 (LUB 2), the dyke fill cg5 (LUB 3), wall cg7, land drain cg8 (LUB 4) and layers cg4 (LUB 5). The layers were about 0.2m thick and faded out towards the west. The layers suggest some abandonment of the area (the silting up and sealing of the dyke) with river silting prevailing. The small group of pottery from the sand layers cg9 (19 post-Roman sherds) suggests that they were deposited between the mid 14th and mid to late 15th centuries.

LUB 7 Buildings
Wall cg6 (LUB 4) was reused as the foundation of a brick wall cg13, which was irregular in width (no further description recorded). The foundation cg13 was dated to the post-medieval period by its brick construction, and could be contemporary with the LUB 6 dump. It may have represented continuity of a property boundary.

Modern

A sewer trench, brick rubble and a feature **LUB 8** indicate modern activity. There was pottery from the 19th/20th century.

LUB 8 Demolition and sewer trench (Fig. 11.4)
Cutting layers cg9 (LUB 6) to the east of the site was a modern sewer pipe trench cg10. Brick rubble cg11 sealed cg10. To the north of the north–south trench, the underlying silts cg2 (LUB 2) were disturbed by a modern feature cg12 with a sand, brick and tile fill. Several fragments of modern bottle and window glass were recovered from this LUB; the latest pottery sherds were of 19th/20th-century glazed earthenwares.

Discussion of ws82

Waterfronts

The sand and clay deposit cg1 (LUB 1) lay below 2.6m OD, ie below the probable water level of the late Saxon period in the Brayford Pool to the west. This material probably represented silting along the channel of the River Witham and the river bank must have lain further south (over 30m south from the present bank) during this time. In the late Saxon period there may have been no recognizable waterfront as such; marshy land to the south may simply have merged gradually with the river.

The thick layer of peaty material cg2 (LUB 2) possibly accumulated below standing or running water, or in a marsh environment or even in alder carr. One might suppose, in fact, that the entire succession may have been present within the 2.70m of deposits observed in 1982, especially so since the top height of the "peat", at over 4.0m OD, was probably at or above water level in the 11th century, at which time, according to the ceramic evidence, the "peat" was still accumulating.

The High Bridge, situated to the north-west of the site, was first recorded in the mid 12th century, a date in accordance with the architectural evidence for the construction of the first stone structure in *c* 1160. The existence of the bridge may imply that the south bank of the Witham was by that time located to the north of the site, in approximately its present position. The lack of evidence for consolidation or river frontages of any kind in the north–south extent of the trench, which ran at right angles to the river across most of the Waterside South site, suggests that the construction of the bridge may have been accompanied by the canalisation of the present river channel. If so, it is worth considering the possibility that this is also the period at which the dyke, cg3, was cut through the peat.

Both the presence of a single sherd of medieval pottery in the peat, and the fact that the surface of the peat was not sealed until the late medieval period with the deposition of the cg9 dumps (LUB 6), suggest that the area was still very damp and close to the water table until at least the mid 14th century.

Sincil Dyke: LUB 3

The 1982 watching brief provides the only archaeological evidence so far for the date and earlier course of the Sincil Dyke, possibly originating in the 12th century, when both the High Bridge was erected and when Henry I (re)cut the Fossdyke. In its earliest mapped form, the Dyke formed a watercourse which branched off the Witham, ran eastwards past the later Great and Little Bargates, and then headed due north, but took a sharp turn to the east at the southern end of Sincil Street. Documentary evidence, however, indicates that the Dyke originally ran directly north along the line of Sincil Street and then re-entered the Witham. This northern branch of Sincil Dyke was still in existence in 1475 when it was used as a boundary in a deed (Gilmour and Stocker 1986, 1). By 1610, when Speed's map of Lincoln was published, the northern leg of the Dyke had ceased to exist and the eastern extension was in existence. From this watching brief it seems, in fact, that the first record of the earlier course came only just before its abandonment and backfilling. 15th-century tile was present in the dyke silt cg5 (LUB 3), and pottery from the dumps cg9 (LUB 6), which sealed the silts within the dyke,

cg/LUB	cg/LUB	cg/LUB	cg/LUB	cg/LUB	cg/LUB	cg/LUB
1/1	3/3	5/3	7/4	9/6	11/7	13/7
2/2	4/5	6/4	8/4	10/8	12/7	

Fig. 11.5 Concordance of cg numbers with LUB numbers for ws82.

dated between the mid 14th and mid to late 15th centuries.

Occupation

The traces of charcoal, sand and ash to the east of the canalised dyke, cg4 (LUB 5), are probably to be associated with the suburb of Thorngate, known otherwise only from documentary sources. Access to this suburb was not from the west, across the Dyke, but via a bridge, Thorn Bridge, spanning the Witham. Both walls cg6 and cg7 (LUB 4) were constructed on the peat cg2 (LUB 2) and were possibly property boundaries in the later medieval period; wall cg6, the more easterly of the two, appeared to have been either in continuous use or was reused in the post-medieval period (LUB 7).

The LUB 6 layers suggest that in the late medieval period this area to the south of the river was abandoned, possibly not to be reclaimed until the 19th century.

12. St Mark's Station 1986 (br85 and z86)

Introduction

The Midland Railway line, which opened in 1846 and crossed the High Street to the south of St Marks Church, was closed in 1985. Although consent for demolition of the station building had already been refused, the site became available for redevelopment.

The site of the former north siding was the first area to be made available for archaeological investigation. The Trust for Lincolnshire Archaeology (City of Lincoln office), carried out a trial excavation (br85) to assess the depth of station disturbance (Fig. 12.1). The major excavation took place in 1986 (z86), directed by Kevin Camidge (Fig. 12.1); in 1987 a small trench was excavated down to river silts (Fig. 12.2, Area 1), and also in the same year there was a watching brief on a pipe trench to the north of the station, both supervised by Malcolm Otter (Fig. 12.1).

The trial trench (br85) was funded by English Heritage, the later excavations by British Rail and the Manpower Services Commission; the watching brief on the pipe trench was funded by Anglian Water.

The main excavations of 1986 concentrated on the area between the two station platforms. The ballast along the railway lines was first removed, mechanically. An extensive east–west section across the site was provided by re-excavating the main Victorian drain. The excavation of the High Street frontage was found to be impracticable due to the existence of foundations for turn-plates, so the 1987 trench was located to the rear. The trial trench (br85) was given a separate context numbering sequence to the later excavations, while the records of both the small 1987 trench and the pipe trench were included with the area excavations of z86. As only

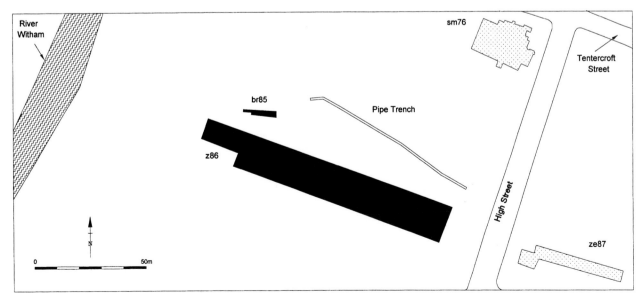

Fig. 12.1 Site location plan for z86. (1:1,623)

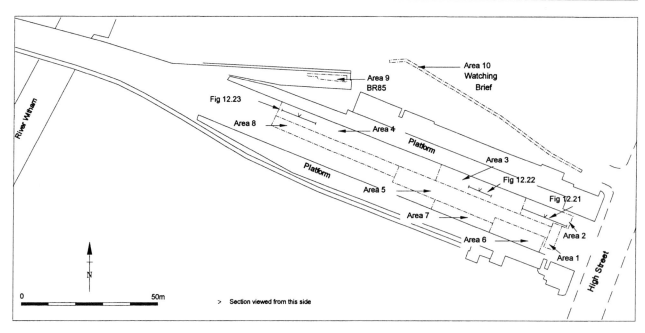

Fig. 12.2 Plan showing areas and sections for z86. (1:1,330)

a watching brief was carried out in the pipe trench, the descriptions of observed features were limited. Since excavation, interim reports have been published (Camidge 1986; Otter and Jones 1987; Otter and Jones 1988). A brief note on a copper alloy buckle plate has also been published (Cherry 1987).

The 45 contexts from br85, together with 835 contexts (of the 843, eight were unstratified) from the rest of the site (which was coded as z86) were interpreted as 408 context groups (cg1–cg417, not including cg12, cg64, cg66, cg80, cg89, cg121, cg145, cg156 and cg160 which remain unused). The context groups are discussed below in 57 land-use blocks, LUBs 1–57 (Fig. 12.37). For purposes of understanding the land-use, the site was subdivided into ten areas (Figs. 12.2 and 12.3). Area 1 was the trench excavated in 1987; it reached the natural sand in one place, having been designed to explore the Roman levels (LUBs 1–7, 9–16 and 18) on the site; some information was also gleaned on the late Saxon and medieval periods (LUBs 23–4 and 41). Area 2 lay to the north and north-west of this, including the eastern part of the Victorian drain from which information about the archaeology from the Roman period had been observed (LUBs 1, 8, 17 and 18); there had been some excavation of Saxo-Norman, medieval and post medieval features to the north-east of the drain (LUBs 22, 33, 38–40, 50, 52 and 54). Area 3 lay to the west-north-west of Area 2, and included Roman and ultimate Roman to Saxo-Norman material observed in the Victorian drain section (LUBs 18–21), an area of excavated medieval features to the north-east (LUBs 31–33, 38, 39, 40, 49, 51 and 52), and some

evidence of the post-medieval period (LUB 54). Area 4, to the west-north-west of Area 3, included part of the Victorian drain providing sections through ultimate Roman to medieval stratigraphy (LUBs 19–21 and 23); only the material from the medieval period was excavated (LUBs 23, 33 and 47). Area 5, which ran down the middle of the site contained excavated Saxo-Norman, medieval and post medieval material (LUBs 23, 25, 29, 30, 37–40, 42, 44, 48 and 55). Area 6 lay at the south-east angle of the site and here medieval features were only very partially excavated (LUBs 36, 41 and 43). Area 7 lay to the south of Area 5 and medieval features here too were partially excavated (LUBs 26–8 and 45). Area 8 lay to the west of Area 5; some medieval and post medieval material was partially excavated (LUBs 34–5 and 56). Area 9 represented the trial trench (br85), and here late Saxon material as well as medieval evidence was recovered (LUBs 19–21 and 46). Area 10 was the watching brief of the pipe trench; there were a number of medieval structures and features in Area 10, but owing to the limitations of interpretation these features have been presented in one LUB (LUB 53). It was substantially in Areas 1 and 2 that evidence for Roman activity was retrieved, with traces of riverine deposits of that period in Areas 3, 4 and 9. Late Saxon and Saxo-Norman archaeology was recovered in Areas 1, 2, 3, 4, 5 and 9, whereas medieval archaeology was recovered across the whole site (Areas 1–10). There were a few post medieval features in Areas 2, 3 and 5 which cut into the medieval levels. The insertion of the railway tracks (LUB 57) in the 19th century severely truncated the underlying stratigraphy.

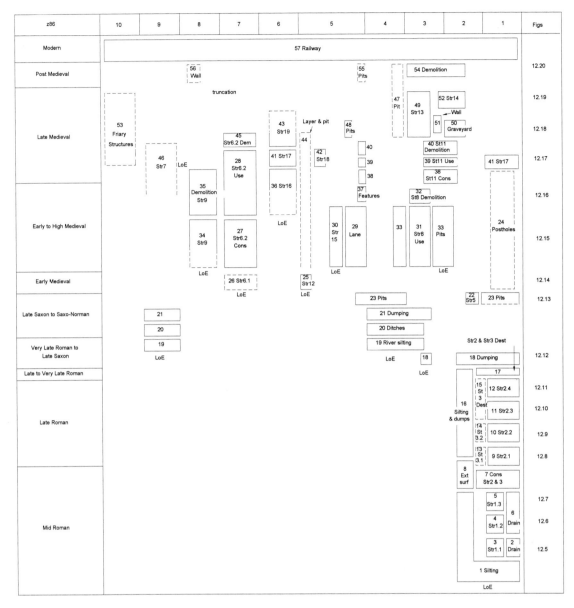

Fig. 12.3 LUB diagram for z86.

The ground level today of the pavement by St Mark's is around 7.2m OD (bench mark at 7.54m), but the top of the archaeology remaining underneath the tracks of the railway (z86) was 5.8m OD, and in the trial trench (br85) the stratigraphy had been disturbed down to 5.4m OD. The loss of well over 1m of unrecorded stratigraphy meant that there was very little evidence for activity from the 15th century onwards.

There were 4,354 sherds of Roman pottery and 3,816 sherds of post Roman pottery from the site, together with 942 registered finds. Because Area 1 was limited in size, the quantity of Roman registered finds is small and difficult to interpret. There is also a paucity of stratified medieval registered finds,

since few deposits were actually excavated. The retrieval of some categories of finds was not rigorous: this was particularly relevant in the case of metal-working debris. Because of the soil conditions, organic finds were only preserved in the fill cg19 (LUB 5) of the drain associated with the earliest levels excavated. The excavation archive holds reports on many of the finds; stone finds (Roe 1994; hones: Moore 1991; marble: Peacock and Williams 1992); bone finds (Rackham 1994); coins (Roman: Davies 1992 and 1993; Late Saxon: Blackburn 1995; medieval: Archibald 1994); glass (Roman: Price and Cottam 1993d; medieval and later vessel glass: Adams and Henderson 1995a; decorated window glass: King 1994); wood (Gale 1992; Morris 1994);

leather (Mould 1993); textile (Walton Rogers 1993). The building material (2,562 fragments) from the site mainly consisted of vast quantities of medieval and post medieval tile; there was also some Romano-British tile and some stone roof tile but only a few fragments of plaster and mortar (stone identification: Roe 1994). The animal bone assemblage (Dobney *et al* 1994h) is among the largest (7,521 fragments) of any Wigford site, but is of limited use as most of the bone bearing contexts contained relatively high proportions of residual pottery, rendering the bone of little interpretative value. There were a number of skeletal remains (Boylston and Roberts 1994), three Roman infant burials (LUBs 4 and 5) and eleven inhumations from the graveyard (LUB 45). Tony Wilkinson recorded and interpreted the soil profile in part of the Victorian drain trench (Wilkinson 1986). An assessment of charred plant remains was produced (Moffett 1993).

Post-excavation stratigraphic analysis was undertaken by Kate Steane. Maggi Darling worked on the Roman pottery and Jane Young on the post-Roman pottery. Jane Cowgill and Jen Mann analysed the registered finds and Jen Mann with Rick Kemp, the building materials; Pam Graves studied the architectural stone. Helen Palmer Brown and Zoe Rawlings digitized the plans and Dave Watt drew the finds illustrations.

Interpretation of the sequence of events

Mid Roman

In Area 1 the river silts, **LUB 1** (traces of which were found in Area 2), were cut by a drain **LUB 2** alongside of which were traces of Structure 1.1 **LUB 3**. The river silts (LUB 1) contained pottery of early 2nd century date; no dating evidence was recovered from LUB 2; samian from the mid to late 2nd century was recovered from LUB 3. Structure 1.2 **LUB 4** replaced Structure 1.1; associated pottery was mid to late 2nd century in date. Structure 1.2 was in turn replaced by Structure 1.3 **LUB 5**; the pottery was late 2nd or probably late 3rd century in date. The drain (LUB 2) was re-cut **LUB 6**; silts from it contained pottery dating to the late 2nd to 3rd century. Structures 1.1 and 1.2 appear to have been insubstantial timber buildings, probably fronting Ermine Street to the east, associated with smithing; the use of insubstantial Structure 1.3 is not clear.

Structure 1.3 (LUB 5) was demolished, the drain (LUB 6) was backfilled, and stone-founded strip buildings Structures 2 and 3 **LUB 7** were constructed in Areas 1 and 2; they represent commercial 'strip' buildings fronting on Ermine Street, with metalling **LUB 8** at the rear, down to the river. Pottery from the drain backfill dated the construction of Structures 2 and 3 to the mid 3rd century.

LUB 1 River silting (Fig. 12.21)

The earliest observed deposit, in Area 1, was a dark clayey sand, cg1, at 3.70m OD, probably deposited by the river. Over this were further river sands and silts cg2. Grey green sandy silt cg35, at the limit of excavation in Area 2 was sealed by greenish white sandy clay cg131.

Silt cg2 produced only three sherds, one of which (samian Dr18/31, from Les Martres de Veyre of *c* AD100–120) indicated an early 2nd-century date. It would appear that the river, to the west of the site, seasonally flooded possibly as far east as Ermine Street – which was presumably raised on a causeway from the early Roman period – during this period.

LUB 2 Drain (Fig. 12.4)

Cutting through river silts cg2, (LUB 1) in Area 1 was the north side of a drain or canalised watercourse, cg14. The drain indicated the possibility that the land was without natural drainage and that some trouble was being taken to make the area more habitable. This area lay just west of Ermine Street and to the south of the walled *colonia*, a prime site for development. There was no dating evidence.

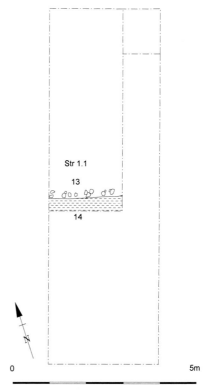

Fig. 12.4 Structure 1.1 with drain to south: LUBs 2 and 3. (1:100)

LUB 3 Structure 1.1 (Fig. 12.4)

In Area 1, along the north edge of drain cg14 (LUB 2), sealing river silts cg2 was a line of scattered limestone fragments cg13, the possible footings of an insubstantial wall. Respecting the line of the footings was a patchy layer of black mixed sand with fragments of charcoal cg3. The dating of cg3 to the mid to late 2nd century rests on a MICA B31; the bowl is dated by reference to the main period of the samian prototype.

Patchy layer cg3 was described on the context sheet as containing large fragments of charcoal, small fragments of coal, and many fragments of iron and slag; of these one iron object and 976gm of smithing slag were retrieved. The presence of spheroidal and plate hammerscale reinforces the likelihood that iron smithing was occurring close to this area, possibly within Structure 1.1. The identification of coal within well stratified smithing slag is important, and reaffirms the fact that coal (perhaps with charcoal) was used as a Roman smithing fuel.

The footings cg13 suggest that Structure 1.1 was an insubstantial building, probably of timber and with perishable roofing materials.

LUB 4 Structure 1.2 (Fig. 12.5)

Layer cg3 (LUB 3) and drain cut cg14 (LUB 2) were sealed by a dump of sand, pebbles and clay cg15,

which may have acted as a floor, as there was a stone set into it which had been burnt on the top.

Cutting dump cg15 were two postholes cg16. Separated from cg15 by the cut of a later feature (cg34, LUB 6), and possibly equivalent to it, was a dump of sand with pebbles sealed by several thin layers of silt cg4; within this material was the incomplete skeleton of an infant whose gestational age was about 36 weeks (Boylston and Roberts 1994). The layers cg4 were cut by a clay hearth cg5 in which tiles and stones had been set, including fragments of Collyweston slate roof tiles (Roe 1994) and brick; the tile and brick is considered to have been brought on to the site from elsewhere, rather than being re-used from Structure 1.1, which was insubstantial in nature.

The layers cg4 and hearth cg5 contained a small quantity of iron smithing slag (144g and 23g respectively) with iron fragments tentatively identified as nails. The significance of this small group is difficult to establish because slag was not consistently collected during excavation. If this was a smithy, it is of interest to note that only a floor-level hearth was identified; although a raised forge would be anticipated, it is possible that either no trace of this has survived or that evidence for such a hearth lay beyond the limited excavated area.

Dump cg15 had 25 sherds, giving a mid/late 2nd-century date from the residual MICA B31 and a SAMCG 18/31 of Hadrianic to early Antonine date. Spread cg4 contained only a single SAMCG31, of broad Antonine date. The hearth structure cg5 produced a SAMLM 18/31 of Trajanic date. Layer cg3 contained only three sherds; the dating to the mid to late 2nd century rests on a MICA B31, which had joining sherds with cg15.

LUB 5 Structure 1.3 (Fig. 12.6)

Sealing post-holes cg16 (LUB 4) was a makeup dump of silty sand cg21, possibly associated with the next phase of building (Structure 1.3). The southern end of Structure 1.3 was possibly indicated by a posthole cg29, which cut cg21, and the limits of a probable clay and pebble floor with ash spreads and areas of burning cg6, which sealed cg21; there were Collyweston slate fragments in cg6, and a noticeable quantity of brick. Flat stone and tile fragments in slightly burnt clay cg8 probably represented a hearth set into cg6 but could have been the remains of a later paved floor; there was a patch of burnt sand cg22 over cg6.

Two inhumations, both of infants, cg9 and cg10, had been cut into the floor cg6, as had pit cg7. Burial cg9, a 37 week old infant, was very well preserved, whereas cg10, a 38 week old infant (both gestation ages), was incomplete (Boylston and Roberts 1994) and is noted in the excavation records as very

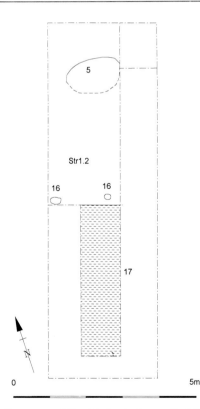

Fig. 12.5 Structure 1.2 with drain to south: LUBs 4 and 5. (1:100)

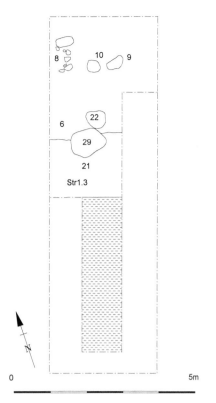

Fig. 12.6 Structure 1.3 with drain to south: LUBs 5 and 6. (1:100)

disturbed. Associated with burial cg9 were 85 body sherds of DR20 amphora dating to the late 2nd or probably 3rd century; it is possible that the burial was originally placed inside the amphora or perhaps covered with the sherds, although there is no indication of this in the original records.

Layers of brown sand with clay cg11 accumulated, possibly as a result of occupation, sealing burials cg9 and cg10 as well as possible hearth cg8. Pottery from cg11 (8 sherds) included CGBL and NVCC which indicated an early to mid 3rd-century date. Among layers cg11 was a Kentish Ragstone hone perhaps associated with the iron working; smithing activity may have continued on the site throughout the life span of Structure 1.3, but the quantity of slag is very small (46g) and perhaps residual.

LUB 6 Drain (Figs. 12.5, 12.24 and 12.35)
Cutting cg15 (LUB 4) and replacing east–west drain cg14 (LUB 2) was a re-cut cg17 of the drain; it was not fully excavated because of shifting waterlogged sand.

Oak (*Quercus sp.*) ladder fragments cg18 (663) <879> (Fig. 12.35) were found against the side of the drain (Fig. 12.24). Only a short section of a probably much longer ladder survives in the form of two upright poles and two rungs; the poles appear to

have been lengths of roundwood which were de-barked but altered very little, and are still roughly circular in cross-section. One pole still displays a slight natural curve in the wood grain between two rungs, which are made from lengths of split sections (probably greater than quarter-sections but less than half-sections); one rung still has traces of bark adhering. Three surviving rung ends were shaped into rectangular tenons to fit into similar mortice holes cut through the poles; the rungs project beyond the uprights and one rung shows that the ends were fixed to them by dowel pegs through augered holes in the poles and rungs (Morris 1994; see discussion below for parallels).

The ladder fragments were sealed by black laminated layers of peat, over which was peat cg19 containing water-washed pebbles and reed fragments, together with a small assemblage of animal bone, suggesting domestic refuse, (Dobney *et al* 1994h), and three pieces of scrap leather and pottery (46 sherds). The pottery from the drain fill cg19 included DR20 amphora body sherds, of late 2nd to 3rd century date, possibly disturbed from the infant burial cg9 (LUB 5).

Drainage of this low-lying land continued to have high priority with the re-cut of the drain.

*LUB 7 Construction of Structures 2 and 3
(Fig. 12.7 and 12.25)*
The drain cg17 (LUB 6) had been deliberately infilled with dumps of sand and pebbles cg25. Sealing layers cg11 and hearth cg22 (LUB 5) was a sandy clay dump cg23. The dumps cg25 contained 14 unidentified iron objects (40% of the total assemblage), many with hammerscale incorporated within their corrosion products suggesting that some may be unfinished objects or iron waste. There was also 1515gm of smithing slag with hammerscale, supporting the implication of the pottery that some of this dump material derived from Structures 1.1–3. Dumps cg25 contained a small battered assemblage of animal bone mostly indicating domestic rubbish; dog and butchered horse bone was also present (Dobney *et al* 1994h). The residual pottery from dump cg25 joined with sherds from LUBs 3, 4 and 5; other sherds from cg25 joined with dump cg23 suggesting contemporaneous deposition. There was also a possible sherd link between cg23 and cg11 (LUB 5). Pottery from dump cg25 (332 sherds) included DWSH and a possible NVCC flagon, which dated this activity to the mid 3rd century. Some of the pottery was complete or relatively so, suggesting that the backfill of the drain was a single operation. The dump would not only have provided makeup for the structure but also would have raised the building above the flood level of the river.

Strip building 2 was found in Area 1, and strip

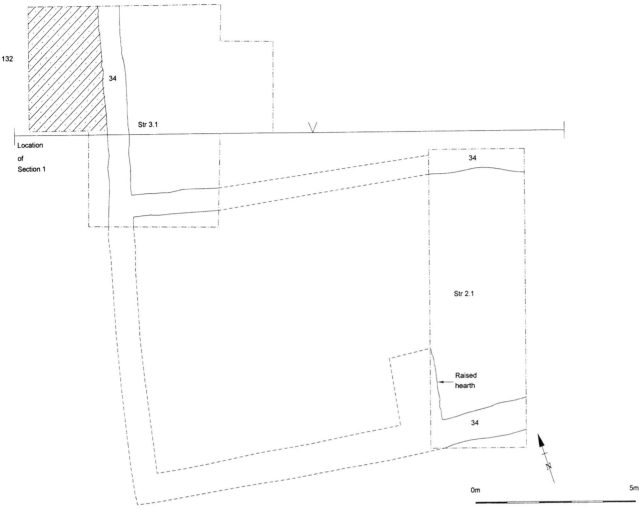

Fig. 12.7 Structures 2.1 and 3.1 with metalling to west: LUBs 8, 9 and 13. (1:114)

building 3 in Area 2. The construction of at least the north–south walls cg34 of the strip buildings 2 and 3 involved the insertion of wooden piles into foundation trenches; these trenches cut through dumps cg25 and cg23. Sealing the piles were foundations of limestone and sandstone pieces set in hard yellow mortar and sealed by mortar layers, in which was found a fragment of a Smith God pot (see discussion). The foundations were sealed by walls of well coursed limestones set in yellow mortar 0.60m wide. Structure 2 had a raised hearth (part of cg34) bonded into the south wall cg34; very little of this was excavated as it only projected slightly from the limit of excavation but the debris from its use was evident throughout the life of building phase 2.1.

Over backfill cg25 was sand, pebble and limestone cg26, which probably built up during construction. A thin layer of sandy silt cg27, probably construction trample, had accumulated over dump cg26. Patches of charcoal cg28 over dump cg23 were probably created during construction; cg28 was cut

by stake holes cg30, possibly the remains of scaffolding.

Structures 2 and 3 were probably traders' houses which fronted the west side of Ermine Street; each building would have been about 25m long. However, neither the exact location of their frontage nor the west side of the road was determined from these excavations. Had the buildings been separate properties, as proposed here, then the east–west party wall cg34 between the two was shared and the north–south wall to the rear (west) of the properties was a continuous stretch, implying that both structures were built as one operation. They have been treated as two separate buildings because of the evidence in other parts of Wigford for the narrow strip plans (eg. hg72, sm76, smg82 and ze87). Although most of these buildings were separate structures with gaps between (sm76, smg82 and ze87), there was also some evidence for a party wall at Holmes Grainwarehouse (hg72) between Structure 4 (LUBs 7–10, 12–17) and possible Structure 14

(LUB 19). The width of Structure 2 was about 7m, and that of Structure 3 at least 5.5m. The LUB was dated by pottery from dumps cg25 to the mid 3rd century (see above).

LUB 8 Surface to the rear of Structure 3 (Fig. 12.7)
In Area 2, sealing earlier river silting cg131 (LUB 1), was a metalled surface cg132 of packed stone, worn in places, which butted against the north–south back wall cg34 (LUB 7) of the strip building Structure 3. It is possible that the metalling represented a yard, or hard standing leading to the river. No finds were recovered from these contexts; but this surface probably dated to the mid 3rd century if it is assumed to have been laid down at the same time as buildings 2 and 3 were constructed.

Late Roman

The raised hearth dominated the excavated area of Structure 2.1 **LUB 9**. This went out of use and a series of floor level hearths was inserted into Structure 2.2 **LUB 10**, which was replaced at a later date by Structure 2.3 **LUB 11**. Structure 2 may have been abandoned for some time **LUB 12**. Pottery from the domestic layers of Structure 2.1 (LUB 9) dated to the mid 4th century, and pottery from LUB 11 from the mid to late 4th century. LUB 12 produced late 4th-century pottery.

In Structure 3, to the north in Area 2, there was evidence of occupation **LUB 13**, possible abandonment **LUB 14** and continued occupation **LUB 15**. Only LUB 15 produced dating evidence from the pottery, dating the sequence to the late 4th century.

To the west of Structures 2 and 3 was river silting and dumping **LUB 16**; there was no dating evidence, but LUB 16 was contemporary with the use of Structures 2 and 3.

LUB 9 Structure 2.1 (Fig. 12.7)
In Area 1, to the east of the raised hearth which was integral with the walls cg34 (LUB 7) and set into construction material associated with cg34, was a patch of stone paving cg36, over which was a thin black charcoal layer cg37. The finds from cg37 consist almost entirely of iron and 147gm of slag with associated hammerscale. This layer (124 sherds) contained residual pottery which joined with sherds from cg29 (LUB 5), cg25, cg27 and cg34 (all LUB 8), suggesting that perhaps the metal working debris was also residual.

Layer cg37 was sealed by layers of ash and clay cg38 and what may have been a hearth cg39 (un-planned). Pottery (23 sherds) from layers cg38 joined with sherds from cg37 and cg34 (LUB 8). Over hearth cg39 were layers of clay and charcoal cg40, which also contained residual pottery (joins with cg37).

The raised hearth (integral with walls, cg34 LUB 7) appears to have been repaired cg43; contemporary with its use were burnt clay and charcoal layers cg41 sealed by fine dark silty layers cg42. Pottery from layers cg42 (12 sherds) dated to the mid 4th century, on the basis of the occurrence of a MHAD flagon with disc neck (and signs of re-use, associated with metal-working?) alongside sherds from a NVCC pentice-moulded beaker, with a reddish fabric. The raised hearth was abandoned cg44. In contrast with the earlier layers, there was no ironwork from cg41 and cg42 or any joining sherds with earlier layers; cg41 and cg42 are levels contemporary with the later use of the hearth (post-repair cg43); here the finds are more representative of domestic refuse.

LUB 10 Structure 2.2 (Fig. 12.8)
Sealing layer cg42 and cg44 (LUB 9), in Area 1, was a floor of clay together with much tile and limestone cg45 (4.88–5.20m OD). Clay floor cg45 contained fifteen pieces of shell-tempered ?roofing tile, the largest concentration of this type of tile found so far in Lincoln. (Another piece of shell-tempered tile was also recovered from silty sand cg48.) At present no production source has been found in the immediate area for this type of shell-tempered tile; moreover, petrological analysis of the sherds has shown that the raw material is not local, the most probable source being the Upper Ouse area of Bedfordshire/Northants. One possibility may be that the tile was brought into the city by water (?used as ballast in a boat), and then sold to local builders. The earliest occurrence of this shell-tempered tile at Lincoln is in late 3rd to mid/late 4th century contexts. Evidence from other sites (Brown 1994) suggests production from the late 2nd to the mid 4th centuries. LUB 10 dates, from the pottery, to the mid to late 4th century. The pottery from the floor cg45 (29 sherds) is dated to the early to mid 4th century; the date comes from Swanpool kiln types, particularly a wide-mouthed bowl of D41 type, and a collared rim jar, plus more loosely a NVCC BKFB? rim fragment.

Over floor cg45 was a series of thin layers, sand with clay cg46 sealed by burnt clay cg47; next was silty sand with shell cg48, overlain by several grey/black ashy spreads cg49 and cg50. Over cg50 was an ashy layer with shell cg67 (5.31m OD), and contemporary with this were two hearths: one was a shallow depression set in cg50 and filled with burnt clay cg68, perhaps an oven, and the other was a hearth of flat tiles set in heavily burnt clay cg69, cutting cg50. Two pieces of heavily burnt limestone on the east side of this hearth cg69 perhaps represent the remains of a flue. Pottery from layers cg48, cg49 and cg67 (36 sherds) was residual. (A copper-alloy coin from cg49 is extremely corroded and illegible,

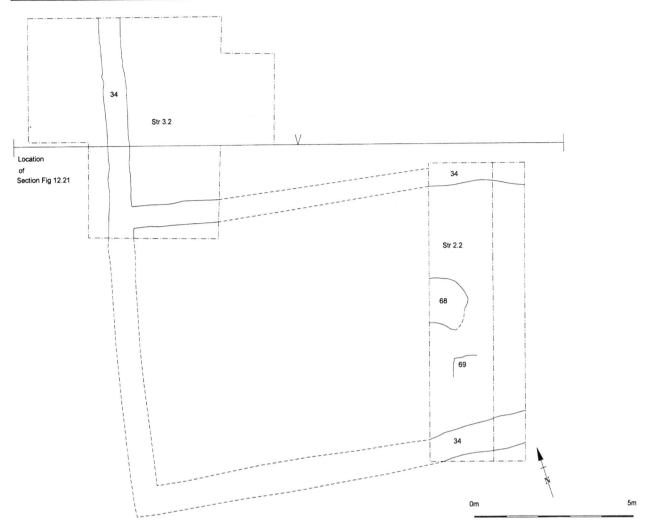

Fig. 12.8 Structures 2.2 and 3.2: LUBs 10 and 14. (1:114)

and thus no more closely datable than to within the period AD260–402.) The hearth cg69 dated to the 4th century had only two sherds of NVCC, a bowl or dish sherd and a pentice moulded beaker sherd, in reddish fabric.

LUB 11 Structure 2.3 (Fig. 12.9)
Sealing hearth cg69 and layer cg67 (LUB 10), in Area 1, was a substantial floor of clay with tile, mortar and charcoal cg70 (5.33m OD). Floor cg70 (26 sherds) dated to the mid to late 4th century; it contained a late NVCC beaker rim, a BKFB rim in a reddish fabric, a pentice-moulded beaker body sherd in a reddish fabric, a SPOX closed vessel, and a Swanpool/Rookery Lane handled jar of collared-rim type.

Layers cg71, made up of shallow layers of silt with charcoal and shell, lay over floor cg70; pottery (15 sherds) from cg71 included a BFB with notched flange, possibly related to the late BIBF type, and

an NVCC pentice-moulded beaker giving a date of the mid to late 4th century. Within layers cg71 was a *follis* of Constantine, issued AD335–40, which shows some wear.

Set on to these layers cg71 was a raised hearth or oven cg72 made of blocks of sandstone and limestone; contemporary with this was a floor of clay and ash with limestone fragments cg83. There was a pit cg76 up against the north wall cg34 (LUB 7), cutting cg71, filled with large pieces of limestone and sand; this was cut within by a long sloping pit cg79 adjacent to the wall, with a fill of burnt clay and limestone fragments, together with sherds of pottery (21 sherds) which included a late fabric NVCC BKROU, a possible SPOX footring, and a possible LCOA body sherd; these sherds had little strong dating but were probably late 4th-century in date. A hearth cg74, which was excavated as a shallow depression in cg71, had a fill of burnt clay; it was sealed by tiles set in unburnt clay cg75,

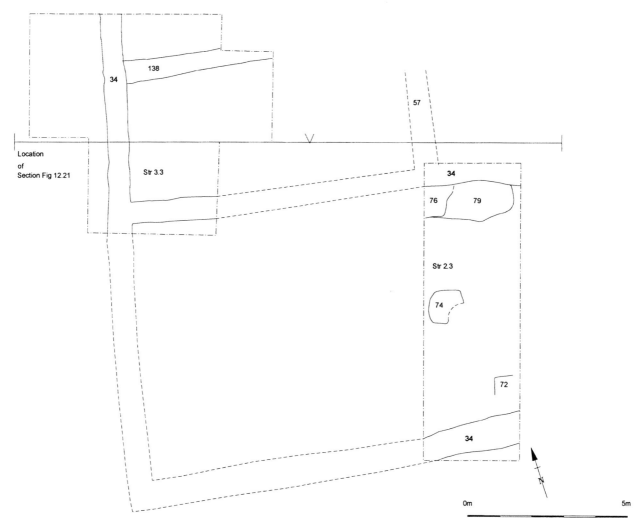

Fig. 12.9 Structures 2.3 and 3.3: LUBs 11 and 15. (1:114)

possibly the last floor surface for this phase of the building.

LUB 12 Structure 2.4 (Fig. 12.10)
Sealing cg72, cg75, cg79 and cg83 (LUB 11) in Area 1, was a dark greyish sandy silt cg82 with charcoal flecks, oyster shells, pockets of grey ash and many pebbles, and stony patches which included two large, apparently worn stones, probably representing a combination of hearth ash and floor. The finds largely represent domestic refuse; there was a small assemblage of animal bone with large bone components suggesting that cg82 also represented abandonment as well as floor and hearth ash (Dobney *et al* 1994h).

Pottery from the surface cg82 (71 sherds) included sherds of DWSH and BIBF, giving a date of the late 4th century,

LUB 13 Structure 3.1 (Figs. 12.7 and 12.21)
The internal occupation of Structure 3 was observed in an east–west section only in Area 2. There was no dating evidence or finds.

At the limit of excavation were dark 'laminated layers' cg31, sealed by a clay and pebble floor cg32, over which was a sandy ashy layer cg33. This was sealed by stony clay floor cg60.

At the limit of excavation was a yellow chalk and clay floor cg20, sealed by grey green layers of sand and clay cg24, over which was a further yellow and red chalk and clay floor cg90. Floor cg90 was sealed by dark sand cg91 and then light grey sand and clay cg92.

At the limit of excavation and apparently associated with wall cg34 (LUB 7) was an ashy layer cg137.

To the east of Area 2, sealing wall construction mortar cg34 (LUB 7) and dump cg23 (LUB 7) was sandy clay with ash cg51; over this was sand, clay and charcoal cg52, cut by stakeholes cg53. Sealing stakeholes cg53 was a red mortar with clay floor cg54, over which was a layer of charcoal cg55.

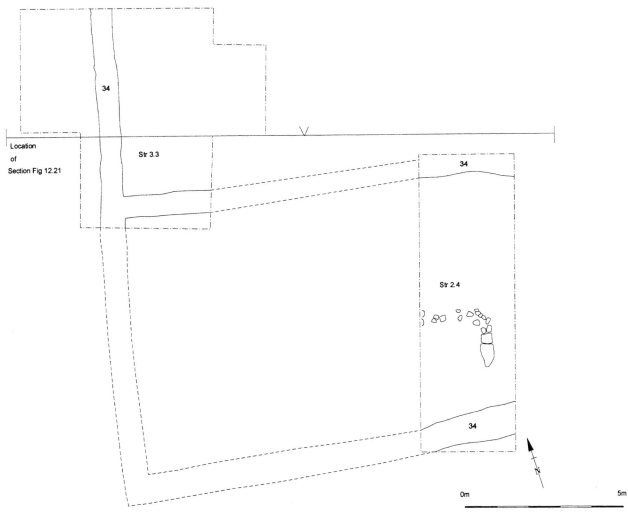

Fig. 12.10 Structures 2.4 and 3.3: LUBs 12 and 15. (1:114)

LUB 14 Structure 3.2 (Fig. 12.21)
Sealing charcoal cg55 in Area 2, was a 'fibrous layer' with grey ash and sandy clay cg56. This layer might be interpreted as a period of abandonment. There was no dating evidence or finds.

LUB 15 Structure 3.3 (Figs. 12.9 and 12.26)
In Area 2, an internal north–south wall cg57 was constructed of stone blocks on two courses of tile (the wall was only 0.30m wide), cutting the fibrous layer cg56 beneath (LUB 14). This wall was abutted by several layers, dark greyish-brown ash cg61; these layers contained pottery (11 sherds) which included a GREY FACE fragment, which could indicate a 4th-century date. Layers cg61 were sealed by a mortar and clay floor cg62, over which was charcoal cg63. Pottery from charcoal cg63 (24 sherds) included a possible LCOA rim fragment, GREY BWM and NVCC B31 and pentice-moulded beaker which gave a possible date of the late 4th century to the deposit. To the west, and possibly postdating

the construction of this wall and sealing cg60 (LUB 13), there was a layer of sand cg58, possibly make-up or flooring, partly sealed by charcoal flecks cg59, over which was a clay floor cg65.

An east–west internal wall cg138 (0.70m thick) was constructed about 3.6m to the north of the dividing wall between Structures 2 and 3; it probably divided at least part of the building down the middle, and sealed cg137 (LUB 13). The wall was of roughly-coursed limestones pieces with no apparent mortar bonding. It was sealed by an undescribed 'floor' cg139.

LUB 16 River silting and dumps (Fig. 12.21)
In Area 2, from the section (Fig. 12.21), it is possible to identify river silting cg133, which built up over metalled surface cg 132 (LUB 8), to the rear of Structure 3; over this was a sump of clay with stones cg134. There was evidence for further silting cg135, cg136 and also dumping cg141, which suggests that flooding problems continued as the river-level rose.

Further to the rear of Structure 3, but also in Area 2, there was evidence for silting; at the limit of excavation was sandy clay cg230, limestone fragments and charcoal cg231 and a greeny-brown layer with charcoal cg248; over cg231 was sand and charcoal cg232, part of which was scooped away and sealed by sand with pebble cg233. There was no dating evidence, but the stratigraphic sequence suggests that the silting and dumping was contemporary with the use of Structures 2 and 3.

Late to very late Roman

Both Structures 2 and 3 were demolished **LUB 17** and robbed in the late to very late 4th century as indicated by the pottery.

*LUB 17 Demolition and robbing
of Structures 2 and 3 (Fig. 12.21)*
The major walls cg34 (LUB 7) of Structures 2 and 3 in Areas 1 and 2 were robbed; cg73, cg81, and possibly cg144 (there was no actual record of what was immediately earlier than this) cut cg82 (LUB 12). The walls cg34 (LUB 7) were robbed down to their foundations; the internal wall cg57 (LUB 15) of Structure 3.2 was robbed by cg85, which cut cg63 (LUB 15). The internal layers (floors, etc) in Structure 3 were differentially truncated by activity during this time.

The robbing cg73 and cg81 produced 173 sherds, dated to the late to very late 4th century. The assemblage was dated by two possible LCOA body sherds possibly from JDLS, the NVCC which includes late bowl sherds, BFB, B38, BKPA/BACC, BKG43 painted and probable BKSF, together with SPOX painted, DWSH JDLS, J105, JLS and BFBH.

Very late Roman to late Saxon

Over the robbed remains of Structures 2 and 3 in Areas 1 and 2, and extending west into Area 3 (and by implication into Areas 6 and 8 too), were the remains of a massive dumping exercise **LUB 18**, bringing in rubble, ash and domestic refuse from elsewhere. The pottery suggests that this activity may have dated to the very late 4th century, or perhaps to the late Saxon period.

Between the very late Roman and the late Saxon periods, river silting continued **LUB 19** in Areas 3 and 4; there was evidence for grazing in the form of hoof marks. The only dating available was its context in the stratigraphic sequence.

*LUB 18 Dumping and building?
(Figs. 12.11, 12.21 and 12.22)*
The robber trench cg81 (LUB 17) was sealed by a dump of sand with ash and charcoal cg87, which contained late to very late 4th-century pottery. Rubble and ash cg88 were dumped on top of cg87, to a depth of about 1m (top level 5.68–5.77m OD); this dump became worm-sorted through time, leaving the larger rubble at the bottom and producing a soil profile towards the top.

A moderate to large assemblage of animal bone from cg88 suggests domestic refuse (Dobney *et al* 1994h), as does the registered finds assemblage. The fabric/form analysis of the pottery from cg88 makes it clear that the assemblage (567 sherds) contains all the ingredients of a very late 4th-century group. There is only a single probable sherd link from an earlier deposit, cg63 (LUB 15), possibly indicating that this dump of material had been brought from elsewhere on to the site, an interpretation supported by some of the other finds. The pottery shows signs of some abrasion and burning, suggesting a secondary deposit, but while sherds in the largest context are mostly medium to small, some largish sherds occur. A total of 78 post-Roman sherds was recovered from cg88, which could be interpreted either to indicate that this was essentially a late Saxon deposit, or that post-Roman pits, not recognised at the time, had contaminated an essentially late Roman sequence.

This dump was not limited to Area 1; it was seen to extend over the river silting that had built up to the west of the strip buildings in Area 2. Defining the western limit of the dump were the remains of what appeared to be a posthole cg235 in Area 3

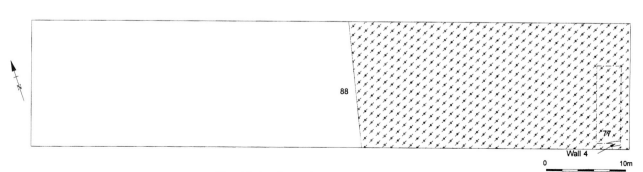

Fig. 12.11 Dumping: LUB 18. (1:461)

(identified from the north section of the Victorian drain cg120 (LUB 57); Fig. 12.22). This may have been the remains of shoring to retain the dump from the flood-waters and silty sands of the river. Only two metres away, the containment of the dumps had collapsed (south section of the drain cg120 (LUB 57); not illustrated) and the river silts cg244 and cg245 (LUB 19) had crept up over part of the slumped dump layer. However, the top of the dump remained unaffected, suggesting that the dumping had been successful in raising the ground level.

Sealing the robber trench cg73 (LUB 17) of the south wall of Structure 2 cg34 (LUB 7) in Area 1, was a further east–west wall cg77 (0.50m wide). It seems to have been of drystone construction but there is no information to indicate whether it was part of a building or a stretch of boundary wall. The wall foundations were sealed by rubble cg78 which, owing to time constraints during the excavations, was not related to other contexts.

LUB 19 River silting (Fig. 12.23)
Across both Areas 3 and 4, evidence for river silting was observed in the side of the Victorian drain which cut through this material. There was no dating evidence for any of this material. In Area 3 a scoop-shaped cut, with a fill of sandy soil sealed by fine lenses of sand cg244 with limestone fragments and pebble, cut dumps cg88 (LUB 18). Greenish-grey sandy silt layer cg245 sealed sandy soil cg244 and cg248 (LUB 16).

A layer of dark silt cg282 with charcoal flecks and some mussel shell fragments partly sealed silt cg245. It was partly sealed by dark grey sand cg288 and was cut by a scoop cg283, over which was a reddish-brown/green- brown sandy silt cg284 with charcoal and mussel shell flecks. This was cut by scoop cg285 with fill of green grey sandy silt with some mortar, charcoal and mussel shell fragments. It was sealed by sand and silt cg286. A silty sandy soil cg249 with charcoal and limestone fragments partly sealed layer cg245.

A lens, patch or remains of layer of dark brown sandy silt cg246 sealed part of cg245. Layer cg245 was cut by possible animal hoof prints cg295; these were sealed by cg253, a grey sandy layer with some silt, mortar and tile, which in turn was cut by two cuts, possible animal hoof prints cg296, and sealed by silty sand cg236.

Sand lenses with pebble cg233 (LUB 16) was sealed by a layer of dark sandy silt cg234 with charcoal and mussel shell, which also sealed sand cg236. Silt cg234 was cut by a hoof mark cg251; it was sealed by a sandy layer with mussel shell and charcoal cg211.

Partly sealing silt cg286 was sandy soil cg287, with burnt limestone chips and tile, which merged into grey silty sand towards the river. This possibly represents material dumped into the river upstream. It was cut by a scoop cg294 (0.30m deep; 1.00m east–west) partly filled with orange sand which was sealed by a layer of grey-brown silty sand cg289.

To the west of Area 4, at the limit of excavation, there was evidence for fluvial sands and interbedded silts cg297. These seem to have built up and been cut by water flow, to build up again; one of these scoops cg298 was sealed by alluvial sands and silts cg299.

Sands and silts cg297 were sealed by reddish-brown-grey sandy soil cg301 into which were animal hoof cuts cg302 (both min 0.10m deep; min 0.20m EW). They were sealed by silty sand cg303 over which was sandy loam cg304. Sealing cg299 and cg303 was silty sand cg300. This too was sealed by sandy loam cg304. Over this was river sands and silts cg305, sealed by sandy loam cg307. Cutting cg305 were two probable animal hoof marks cg306. In sandy loam cg307 were several small hollows cg308 (ranging in depth between a minimum of 0.10 and 0.25m and in width between a minimum east–west of 0.075 and 0.90m) which were possibly created by animal hooves. The presence of animals and the low-lying nature of the land suggest water meadows.

In Area 9, at the limit of excavation, was silty sand cg383.

Late Saxon to Saxo-Norman

In Areas 3 and 4 there was evidence for flood control, in the form of north–south ditches **LUB 20**, which seems to have been introduced in the 11th century (from the slight pottery evidence) and possibly as early as the 10th century (given the pitting activity to the east and the stratigraphic evidence). There was a massive dumping operation **LUB 21** in Areas 3 and 4, sealing LUB 20, which appears to have built up the ground surface above the reach of the river before the end of the 11th century. Also dating to the 11th century were traces of a timber building (Structure 5) in Area 2 **LUB 22**, possibly related to a High Street frontage structure.

To the south of Structure 5, in Area 1, were a number of pits predating, contemporary with and postdating Structure 5, cutting LUB 18; there were pits in Area 2 which cut LUB 18. There were also pits in dump LUB 20, in Areas 3 and 4. The pitting activity **LUB 23** indicates that from some time in the 10th century there was probably occupation on the High Street frontage.

LUB 20 Ditches: Limiting the river flooding
and other activity (Fig. 12.23)
In Areas 3 and 4 there were a number of north–south ditches, presumed to represent an attempt to limit the river flooding; these were identified from

the cut of the Victorian drain, the ditches being visible in the trench-sides. There was little dating evidence.

A cut cg290 (not bottomed; width not clear) in silt layer cg289 (LUB 19) was filled by silty sand; it was possibly a ditch. There was a possible re-cut cg291 of ditch cg290. It had a fill of dark clay silt.

A cut cg311 of a ditch (min 0.70m deep; min 1.00m width) in cg300 (LUB 19) had fills of layers of sandy material with charcoal and a lens of shell on top. It was cut by a re-cut cg314 (min 0.80m deep; min 1.50m width) with a fill of grey brown sand with shell and bone.

Cutting cg297 (LUB 19) was a ditch cg312 (min 1.00m deep; min 3.00m width) which was cut by re-cut cg313 (min 1.20m deep; min 1.20m width) which had a bottom fill of white sand, sealed by brown sand.

To the north, in Area 9, cutting the underlying river silting cg383 (LUB 19), was a gully cg384, possibly a ditch with a fill of sand and pebbles cg385. The cut was silted over by cg386 and cg387. Cutting this silting were two successive ditches cg397 and cg398 with fills cg388 and cg390. Only four sherds of post-Roman pottery were recovered from drain fill cg390; the latest dated to the 11th century. To the side of the ditch re-cuts silting cg389 built up.

Apart from the north–south ditches there were traces of other activity in Areas 3 and 4. Light brown sandy loam cg309 with charcoal flecks sealed possible hoof marks cg308 (LUB 19) in the river silting. It is possible that cg309 represents a levelling dump to seal the punctured surface. A cut cg310 (min 0.30m deep; min 0.50 wide) in silt layer cg300 (LUB 19) may have been a posthole. Partly sealing cg286 (LUB 19) was a sandy soil with mortar flecks cg281. Layer cg245 (LUB 19) was deliberately cut by a pit cg247 (0.70 east–west) to an unknown depth. Patches or lenses of orange, red and yellow sand cg237 sealed layer cg253 (LUB 19). There was a cut cg292 in silt layer cg289 (LUB 19).

LUB 21 Dumping (Figs. 12.22, 12.23 and 12.27)
In Areas 2, 3 and 4, there were dumps of material cg223, which overlapped the earlier dumps cg88 (LUB 18) and sealed river silts cg211, cg246, cg249, cg288, cg297, cg305, cg307 and hoof prints cg296, cg306 (LUB 19), as well as activity over the silting such as burnt sand cg237, pit cg247, mortary layer cg281, ditch cg291, cut cg292, dump cg309, cut cg310, ditch cg311, ditch cg313 and ditch cg314 (LUB 20).

Dumping cg223 built up the ground to the west of the site above the reach of river flooding; it overlapped the western edge of the earlier Roman dumping and sealed the river silting and activity further west with around a metre of material (Figs.

12.22–3). The top of the dump varied in OD height between 5.13m and 5.68m. These were not homogeneous dumps, as there was more stone and tile to the east with a greater sand content towards the river, which may reflect the source of the material; two tip lines were recognised from the north side of the section (not illustrated). Possible stone revetting cg416, which may have delimited and consolidated the western edge of the dump, was photographed to the west of the site (Fig. 12.27). There was no dating evidence from these dumps due to the fact that they were only investigated in section. It would appear that the material was deliberately laid down in order to raise the ground level to make it suitable for building. In Area 9 there were dumps cg391 (including a redeposited human skull), which sealed the earlier sequence of drains cg390 (LUB 20) to a level of 5.09m OD.

Dumps cg391 contained a small group of pottery (24 post-Roman sherds) dating up to the mid/late 11th century; it is likely that, as dumps cg391 and cg223 were similar in stratigraphic sequence and height OD, they were probably of the same date.

LUB 22 Structure 5 (Figs. 12.12 and 12.21)
In Area 2, layers of make-up, clay floors and fire ash cg125 may have represented traces of a structure sealing cg88 (LUB 18). A group of pottery (88 post-Roman sherds) was found in cg125, the latest sherds dating to the 11th century. The west wall of Structure 5 may have been robbed by cut cg123 through cg125.

Possible robber trench cg122 (LUB 23) was sealed by sand cg124; into this was a cut with a fill of ash and silty material cg143. There was an accumulation of sand with charcoal cg146 sealing this. A cut cg127 went into cg125, filled with hard sand. This was sealed by dump cg126. Dump cg126, and sand cg146 were then sealed by sand with charcoal flecks cg128; this was sealed by dump cg129.

Over part of cg146 was a stone, cg147; this was covered on one side by dark sand and charcoal cg148, and on the other was cut by a possible ditch cg149. To the west of the ditch was a posthole cg162. The possible ditch fill was sealed by dump cg151, over which was a metalled surface cg152, sealed by grey sand and silt cg153.

Cutting sand cg148 was a posthole cg150. This too was sealed by sand and silt cg153; this was cut by posthole cg154. A brown sand layer cg155 sealed these deposits, and was cut by posthole cg157. Sand and sand with clay cg158 sealed both and was itself cut by posthole cg159. Layer cg155 was cut by ash pit cg161. The sequence was truncated at this point.

The sequence of occupation layers and postholes suggests that there may have been several phases of building construction. These would probably have been associated to structures fronting the High Street, which might have been linked to some of the pitting (LUB 23). There was no pottery from most of these layers as the structure was only seen in section, but pottery from cg125 dated to the 11th century.

LUB 23 Pitting and other activity to the rear
of the High Street (Figs. 12.12, 12.21 and 12.23)
In Areas 3 and 4, in the western part of the site, dumps cg223 (LUB 21) were cut by a number of possible pits cg140, cg194, cg239, cg293, cg330, cg333, cg334 and cg335 (all unplanned). There seems to be evidence for further dumping to the west, and pit cg354 may well represent a robber trench for removing stone from bank consolidation cg416. There was no dating evidence associated with the pits in Areas 3 and 4 because they were only recorded in section, but they post-date the dumps cg88 (LUB 18), while pits cg239, cg333, cg334, cg335, cg353 and cg354 pre-date a later lane surface cg336 (LUB 29). Pottery from the site as a whole, as well as the stratigraphic evidence, indicates that the activity over the dumps, being sealed by the lane, possibly dated from the 11th to late 12th century.

In Area 1, late Roman or late Saxon dump cg88 (LUB 18) was disturbed by postholes cg86 and cut by possible slot cg93 and posthole cg97. In Area 2, pit cg130 (unplanned) with a 'sandy silt fill, cut unexcavated Roman layers; pit cg119 cut into cg136 (LUB 16), probably through dump cg88 (LUB 18) and pit cg165 probably cut through cg88 (LUB 18) but had been truncated. Pits cg163 and cg166 – both unplanned, although cg166 is shown in section (Fig. 12.21 – cut cg88 (LUB 18).

In Area 1, sandy loam cg98 sealed cg88 (LUB 18); pit cg105 cut cg98 in Area 1, and was cut by pit cg106. Pit cg105 was also cut by pit cg94 which was cut by pit cg95. Pits cg99 and cg100 cut cg98. Sandy loam cg98 was cut by pit cg101 which was cut by pit cg102. Mineralised concretions with plant material were recovered from pit cg102 (Moffett 1993). Pits cg102 and cg105 both included large assemblages of animal bone; the animal bone assemblage from pit

cg102 was very similar to that from pit cg105 in terms of the species proportions, but with a wider range of elements represented, and proportionally fewer showing evidence of butchery (Dobney *et al* 1994h). Pit cg102 also contained two iron knives (548)<694,697>.

An ash pit cg161, in Area 2, cut pits cg119 and cg130 together with layer cg155 (LUB 22). Several pits were excavated in haste as a group cg167 (unplanned) in Area 2; they cut pits cg161 and cg165. Pit cg122 cut cg88 (LUB 18) in Area 1. Pits cg228 and cg360 in Area 5 probably related to this period.

None of the pits contained large groups of pottery, and several contained only residual Roman material. Features cg106 (51 post-Roman sherds), cg130 (4 post-Roman sherds), cg86 (2 post-Roman sherds), cg93 (2 post-Roman sherds), cg97 (2 post-Roman sherds) and cg99 (3 post-Roman sherds) contained sherds that were predominantly 10th century in date. Pit cg102 contained a heavily degraded fragment of a silver coin which is tentatively identified as an Aethelred II penny, of *First Small Cross* or *First Hand* issue, dated *c* AD978–9 or *c* 979–85 (Blackburn 1995). Many of the other features contained mixed material of the late 10th to 11th century. Ash pit cg161 (29 post-Roman sherds) contained some pottery dating to the 11th century including several LFS bowls.

Later medieval and post-medieval (17th–18th century) pottery had intruded into the top of layer cg98 and pits cg100, cg106, cg167 and cg228, probably due to subsidence into the upper fills. Pit cg167 also contained a splashed glazed ridge finial dating from the mid 12th to the early 13th century. Pit cg161 included an intrusive tile disc which post-dates the mid 12th century.

Early medieval

In Area 1, cutting LUB 23, there were traces of a possible fence **LUB 24**. In Area 5 there was a lean-to structure **LUB 25** (Structure 12). In Area 7 were traces of a building **LUB 26** (Structure 6.1). LUBs 25 and 26 were associated with sherds dating between the mid 12th and early 13th century pottery.

Fig. 12.12 Pitting: LUB 23. (1:461)

LUB 24 Postholes (Fig. 12.13)
A boundary between a plot to the north of the site and one to the south may have been initially defined by a fence, recovered as an east–west line of postholes cg107 in Area 1, cutting cg101 and cg102 (both LUB 23); excavation was limited to Area 1, at the east end of the site, which meant that the full extent of the feature was not explored. The postholes cg107 cut late 10th- to late 11th-century pits and were sealed by late medieval east–west wall cg116 (LUB 41); there was no other dating evidence.

LUB 25 Structure 12 (Fig. 12.13)
A long strip of earth cg243 (in Area 5), of a different matrix from that which surrounded it, was planned but not excavated. This feature may have represented a shallow gully; other later features, similar in style and shape, were found to be gullies. Butting up to, and overlapping the south side of the strip was a spread of rough limestone rubble cg268, which contained a few mixed pottery sherds (20 post-Roman sherds), the latest dating to between the mid 12th and the early 13th century. Feature cg243 may represent the robbed foundations of an otherwise unrecorded east–west wall supporting a lean-to structure (similar to later structures LUBs 36, 41 and 43); the rough spread of limestone fragments may be the remains of the robbing, in the form of discarded stones.

LUB 26 Structure 6.1
A stone-lined pit cg254 (no record of what it cut) was cut by walls cg279 (LUB 26) of Structure 6.2. This suggests that there may have been an earlier building on the site. Stone-lining remained around three sides of pit cg254; it had a fill of sandy silt, charcoal and shell. All other structural traces of Structure 6.1 had either been removed by the construction of Structure 6.2 or were below the limit of excavation. However, pottery from the demolition of Structure 6.2 (LUB 45) included some very large unworn sherds dating between the mid 12th and early 13th century, suggesting occupation of the site from that period.

Early to High Medieval

In Area 7, replacing Structure 6.1 (LUB 26) was stone-founded structure 6.2 with at least three rooms and an integral garderobe indicating another storey **LUB 27**. The rooms contained substantial hearths **LUB 28** suggesting industrial use, confirmed by the presence of copper droplets. The pottery suggests that this building was constructed between the 12th and early 13th century and was in use throughout the 14th century.

In Area 5 there were traces of an east–west lane **LUB 29**; pottery suggests a 13th-century date. Also in Area 5, just south of the lane was a lean-to structure **LUB 30**, Structure 30. To the north of the lane was Structure 8 **LUB 31** with at least four rooms with hearths; the pottery suggests that it was in use sometime in the 13th or early 14th centuries, and was demolished **LUB 32** between the late 13th and the early to mid 14th centuries.

In Areas 2 and 3 were pits and other cut features **LUB 33** dated by pottery to the 13th century. In Area 8 was a structure with a hearth, oven or kiln **LUB 34** associated with pottery dating to the 13th or early 14th centuries; this was demolished **LUB 35** in the 14th or 15th centuries.

In Area 6 were traces of Structure 16 **LUB 36** associated with smithing; the pottery suggests activity ended in the 15th century.

In Area 5 there were features **LUB 37** which cut lane LUB 29. The pottery dating of these was inconclusive, but stratigraphically they are earlier than LUB 38.

LUB 27 Structure 6.2 construction
(Figs. 12.14 and 12.28)
Building 6, against the south section in Area 7, consisted of at least three rooms; it probably extended further to the west beyond the area investigated. Only its morthern fringe lay within the area excavated. The external walls cg279 cut stone-lined pit cg254 (LUB 26) (otherwise the excavation did not continue below the walls). The foundations cg279 were made up of pitched stones and sealed with a

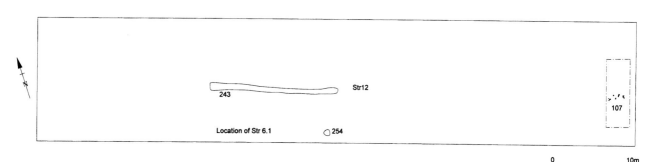

Fig. 12.13 Structures 6.1 and 12 with fence to east: LUBs 24, 25 and 26. (1:461)

clayey sand construction trench fill; the wall was made up of roughly-dressed limestone blocks. Within the wall cg279 (towards the east of the north wall), and of one build with it, was a stone-lined garderobe with a vaulted roof (Fig. 12.28); there was a lintel over the opening which was incorporated into the fabric of the wall. The garderobe extended into the interior (room 6.2A); the opening into the wall suggested that there was at least one storey above. Internal north–south wall cg259 had been completely robbed (robber trench cg276, LUB 45) and internal north–south wall cg278 survived only as footings of small limestone pieces, two courses high set in sand (0.62m wide). Possibly associated with the external wall cg279 were two short roughly-coursed north–south walls cg269 (each 0.10m wide and the two 0.70m apart; their extent north–south was 0.60m) at right angles to the wall (there was no record of what they cut); they may have formed the sides of a drain, but this was not clear. In the fill of the feature were 24 sherds of pottery; since these appear to post-date the construction of the building, the fill probably accumulated during the building's life – as normal for a drain fill.

Only a small amount of pottery was recovered from the deposits cg269 (23 post-Roman sherds) and cg279 (5 post-Roman sherds). For walls cg279 the latest pottery dates are between the 12th and early 13th centuries, but the drain fill cg269 pottery ranges in date between the 12th and 14th centuries.

LUB 28 Structure 6.2 use
(Figs. 12.15, 12.16 and 12.35)
The garderobe cg279 (LUB 27; Area 7) was sealed at ground level by a pitched tile hearth cg266. Also in room 6.2A, to the east of the vaulted roof of the garderobe, was a layer of sandy clay cg274 (no record of what it sealed); there was a stone-packed pit cg272 in the corner (no record of what it cut), possibly the base for an oven or raised hearth; to the west was a mortar floor cg265 and a small post-pad cg264. Room 6.2B had the base of a stone structure, possibly an oven cg255 (no record of

what it sealed); the burnt remains of a hearth cg261 sealed clay floor cg260 (which abutted wall cg279 LUB 27). Room 6.2C had a mortar floor cg256 (no record of what it sealed), which was sealed by a clay floor cg257 and a circular hearth of pitched tiles cg258. The tile hearth cg258 was constructed of flat roofing tiles dating to the early/mid 13th century at the earliest; it also had a ceramic kiln support built into it. Two small droplets of copper alloy were recovered from the floor cg256 and the hearth cg258. Additional copper droplets were found amongst the demolition rubble cg275 (LUB 45).

The fill of the garderobe cg279 (LUB 27) was of greyish-brown silt cg267; it contained a small assemblage of animal bone and two late 12th- or early 13th-century pottery sherds which suggested domestic refuse; none of the bone from cg267 appears to show evidence of direct ingestion (i.e., as evidenced by acid etching on the bone surface), and the fact that only bird remains are present suggests that the garderobe was also used to dispose of table refuse (Dobney *et al* 1994h).

The latest sherds from cg272 (21 post-Roman sherds) dated from the late 13th century, and those from oven cg255 (5 post-Roman sherds) from the late 14th century.

LUB 29 Lane (Fig. 12.14)
In Area 5 were the remains of a lane which sealed earlier pits cutting into the dump cg223 (LUB 21). The lane was constructed of limestone cobbles cg336 which had become worn. It sealed cuts cg334, cg239, cg335 and possibly cg333 (LUB 23). Much of it had been removed by later levelling and it only survived where it had sunk into pits; worn limestones cg96 (unplanned) in pit cg95 (LUB 23), stone layer cg164 (unplanned) in pit cg163 (LUB 23), worn cobbles cg229 in pit cg228 (LUB 23) and a patch of stones cg355 (unplanned) sealing pit cg354 (LUB 23). There is no record of what was sealed by a patch of stones cg350 (unplanned) or scatter cg382.

A small group of pottery (26 post-Roman sherds)

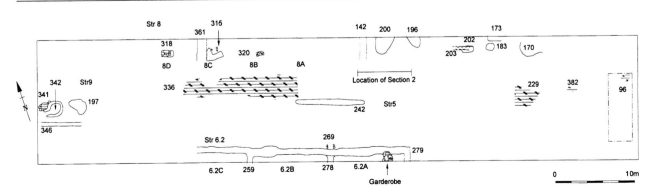

Fig. 12.14 Structures 6.2, 8, 9 and 15 with lane and pits: LUBs 27, 29, 30, 31, 33 and 34. (1:461)

was recovered from the lane, the latest dating to the 13th century. Seventeen nails were found from cg229 and cg336 (72% of total objects), and part of a horseshoe (100) <399> came from cg229.

LUB 30 Structure 15 (Figs. 12.14 and 12.29)
Gully cg242 ran east–west in Area 5 for at least 8.5m (Fig. 12.29); it was 0.28m deep and 0.80m across; it had a fill of clayey sand with silt and contained a small group of pottery (23 post-Roman sherds) ranging in date from the 10th century to the 14th century. There is no record of what the feature cut.

It seems likely that this gully represented a robbed-out east–west wall, which would have supported lean-to buildings (similar to later structures LUBs 36, 41 and 43).

LUB 31 Structure 8 – use of building (Fig. 12.14)
This building, measuring at least 26m east–west and over 3m north–south, consisted of at least four rooms, at least three with their own hearth. Room 8A, in Area 3, lay to the west of a possibly stone-founded wall cg142, which had been robbed out entirely by a robber trench cg190 (LUB 32). Room 8B straddled Areas 3 and 4 and lay to the west of room 8A; the room had a hearth of pitched tiles cg320 set to form a radiating circle; this feature had sunk into the underlying dumps cg223 (LUB 21).

In Area 4, pitched limestone with some tile cg315 (5.46m OD) had been set into dumps cg223 (LUB 21); although burning on this surface was limited to a small area, it probably formed a large hearth in room 8C. The stones were sealed in places by a white lime layer cg322, especially where it would have met the north–south (probably stone-founded) wall cg361, much of which had been totally removed by robber trench cg321 (LUB 32). The surface was cut by at least one small pit/large posthole cg317. Pit cg317, stones cg315 and lime cg322 were sealed by ash, burnt clay and charcoal cg316.

Room 8D, in Area 4, had a rectangular stone base of closely-laid, flat, irregularly-shaped, stone blocks cg318, with pitched stones edging the south side; all were bonded with sandy clay. The stones displayed an even, worn surface and showed traces of burning and wear. There was no record of what the room sealed, although it can be assumed to have been the dump material. It was recorded as itself being sealed by a thick mortar layer cg319, presumably acting as a surface (5.53m OD). The mortar surface cg319 was cut by a slot cg326.

The southern wall of Structure 8 had been cut away by the large Victorian drain, and further traces of the building removed by railway levelling. There was very little pottery (14 post-Roman sherds in total) associated with Structure 8; however, it

seems likely that the building was in use sometime in the 13th or early 14th centuries, as there were several LSW2 sherds but no LSW3. The non-local sherd (BEVO) also falls within this period.

LUB 32 Structure 8; Demolition (Figs. 12.15)
Over rooms 8A and 8B in Areas 2 and 3, was a layer cg189 which sealed cg223 (LUB 21). It consisted of sand, mortar, limestone chips, and tile; other finds included a professionally-made ?walrus ivory terminal (168) <440>. The glazed floor tile from this layer is part of a complete tile (around 180mm square?), which was scored quarterly pre-firing, then broken into quarters post-firing. This tile was made in a local fabric, most probably contemporary with the other roofing tiles from the same group, and could well be a product from a local tile kiln. It may have been part of a mosaic pavement on the site, perhaps belonging to Structure 8; such pavements suggest a high-status building, which although not consistent with much of the other evidence – except perhaps the ivory terminal – may to some extent be supported by the presence of a large amount of high quality pottery of 13th-century date recovered from the Victorian drain cutting the structure. It is of course possible that both the ivory terminal and the tile came with re-deposited rubbish from elsewhere. Layer cg189 produced a small group of pottery (39 post-Roman sherds); most of the sherds are small residual fragments. The probably contemporary material dates to the 13th century. Intrusive 14th- and late 15th-century (LSW4 LMF) sherds occur, having joins to cg270 (LUB 44).

Stone-founded wall cg361 (LUB 31) was robbed cg321; the fill consisted of dark sand with limestone rubble. The latest sherds (20 post-Roman sherds) from the demolition can only be dated generally to the 13th or early 14th centuries. Stone-founded wall cg142 (LUB 31) had been robbed out entirely by a robber trench cg190, but its fill contained sand with clay, broken limestone and mortar; the trench cut layer cg189. Layer cg189 was also cut by a large shallow scoop cg191, the interpretation of which is not clear. The scoop cg191 and the robber trench cg190 were sealed by sandy clay with limestone fragments cg192, which contained a mixed assemblage of finds, including an iron and copper-alloy barrel padlock (155) <431>, a copper-alloy mount (44) <391>, and copper-alloy sheet waste. Layer cg192 produced a small group (48 post-Roman sherds) with much residual pottery. The group also includes LLSW vessels, both wasters and used vessels, that must be intrusive from the robbing of Structure 11. The date of the latest contemporary material is probably between the late 13th and early to mid 14th century.

LUB 33 Pits and cut features (Fig. 12.14)
In Area 3, a cut cg201 (0.30m deep; min 0.35m E–W
and 1.00 N–S; unplanned) had a fill of clay, sand,
mixed mortar and crushed limestone. This was
possibly the cut remains of a pit; there is no record of
what it itself had cut. It was cut by pit cg202 which
also contained clay, sand, mortar and limestone,
together with a moderate assemblage of animal bone,
mostly domestic debris, but including cat, rat and
jackdaw (Dobney *et al* 1994h). A possible east–west
slot cg203 cut pit cg202. In Area 3, shallow pit cg196
had a sandy clay fill, while pit cg200 contained dark
sandy silt (there was no record of what they cut). In
Area 2, slot cg173 and pit cg183 had fills of silty sand
and limestone (no record of what they cut). In Area
2, pit cg168 (unplanned) cut cg88 (LUB 18) and was
sealed by an undescribed layer cg169; this was cut
by a pit cg170 with shell and limestone in its fill. Pit
cg84 (unplanned) had a fill of sandy clay, charcoal
and mortar lumps; there was no record of what it
cut, but it contained a large assemblage of animal
bone, mostly domestic debris but including cat and
wild birds (Dobney *et al* 1994h). Pit cg84 also
contained lead waste, slag, and a socketed bone point;
it also had an unusually high proportion of iron finds,
mostly nails, with some structural items.

There were two intercutting pits in Area 4 (unplanned). One, cg323, had a bottom fill of 'dark
chocolate' colour, sealed by sandy earth with charcoal
and a charcoal layer; the other pit cg324 had a fill of
sandy earth with limestone and tile.

A total of 210 post-Roman sherds was recovered
from the various features; the latest contemporary
pottery dates to the 13th century.

LUB 34 Structure 9 (Fig. 12.14)
Towards the west end of the site, in Area 8, there
were elements of another structure (Structure 9): a
clay floor cg340 (no record of what it sealed),
associated with a hearth cg341 of burnt clay and
sand, surrounded by burnt pieces of limestone (no
record of what this sealed). Cutting these was the

pit for a raised hearth, oven, or kiln cg342; stones
and clay were laid around the pit forming the base
for walls of the oven/kiln. The stoke-hole had been
cut by, or had cut, an insubstantial possible east–
west wall cg346 to the south: the relationship was
unclear. Wall cg346 was represented by a line of
limestone fragments (0.40m wide).

Hearth cg341 had only six mixed sherds associated with it, the latest dating to the 13th or early
14th centuries.

*LUB 35 Structure 9: Demolition
(Figs. 12.15 and 12.23)*
The kiln cg342 (LUB 34) was demolished and the
backfill contained charcoal, ash and limestone
rubble cg343. To the south of possible east–west
wall cg346 (LUB 34) was a scatter of stones cg345
(with no record of what they sealed), possibly
demolition debris. A possible pit cg197 (no record
of what it cut), with a fill of large pieces of limestone
cg339, may also be associated with the robbing of
Structure 9. It was sealed by a layer of clayey silt
and sand with limestone fragments cg344, also
containing tile, with a noticeable quantity of Collyweston slate (Roe 1994). It seems likely that this
layer was equivalent to a dump with much tile and
stone fragments cg356 recognised in Area 4 (Fig.
12.23).

Rubble cg343 had only eight associated mixed
sherds; the latest dated to the 13th or early 14th
centuries. The latest sherd from pit fill cg339 (8 post-
Roman sherds) was of 14th- or 15th-century date.
Deposit cg344 contained a large mixed group of
pottery (153 post-Roman sherds). The latest sherds
date to the 14th or 15th centuries. An intrusive clay
pipe stem shows that cg344 had been contaminated.

LUB 36 Structure 16 (Fig. 12.15)
In Area 6 were oblong east–west areas of light sandy
material with some limestone cg359 (0.50m wide);
these were planned but not excavated. Butting up to
the south of the westerly stretch of sandy material

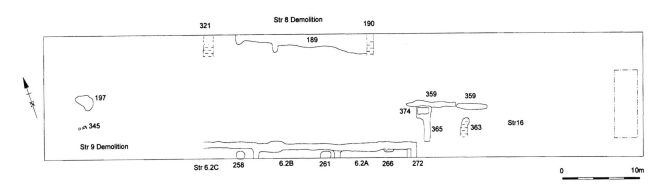

Fig. 12.15 Structures 6.2 and 16 with the demolition of 8 and 9 as well as features: LUBs 28, 32, 35, 36, 37. (1:461)

were the remains of a rectangular stone-lined pit cg374 (no record of what it cut; 0.40m north–south and 1.00m east–west) which was attached to what appeared to be the foundations of a north–south wall cg365; the wall was 0.80m wide and consisted of rough limestones bonded with brown silty clay. To the south of cg359 was a long clay-lined slot cg363 (0.45m deep; 0.70m wide; no record of what it cut).

The areas of sandy material cg359 (0.60m wide) may represent the robbed remains of east–west walls, possibly walls supporting a lean-to structure to the south. The stone-lined pit cg374 appears to have been linked with such a structure, possibly as a garderobe. Clay-lined slot cg363 (0.45m deep; about 2.40m long and 1m wide) could be described tentatively as a liquid-retaining tank; it had one fill of brown clay/sand with charcoal and ash cg209, together with iron-stained limestone and 15th-century pottery (14 post-Roman sherds). The presence of 1,868gms of iron smithing slag in cg209, with a small amount of hammerscale, coal, and four unidentified pieces of iron, suggests that perhaps the tank could have been a 'bosh', and that smithing may have occurred here. Another fill deposit of sandy clay cg377 in the stone-lined pit cg374 included 15th-century pottery (21 post-Roman sherds).

LUB 37 Features (Fig. 12.16)
In Area 5, two postholes cg240 (no record of what they cut; but probably cut LUB 29) were sealed by silty sand with limestone rubble cg241, probably construction for Structure 11. There was an oval-shaped, east–west cut cg337 through surface cg336 (LUB 29), with steep sides filled with brown silty sand and limestone rubble, possibly an empty grave. A cut cg338 through surface cg336 (LUB 29) was seen only in section (not illustrated).

Little pottery was recovered from cg241 and cg337 (a total of 26 post-Roman sherds), the latest sherds dating to between the 13th and 15th centuries.

Late Medieval

In Areas 2 and 3 large Structure 11 **LUB 38** was constructed, containing two substantial rectangular stone foundations. It post-dated LUB 32, and so dated to some time after the period between late 13th and early to mid 14th century. There was an oven within it, and a stone-lined pit to the south-west **LUB 39**. It was demolished **LUB 40**, on pottery evidence, in the 15th century.

In Areas 1 and 6 there was a lean-to, Structure 17 **LUB 41**, with hearths. In Area 5 there was another lean-to structure **LUB 42**, Structure 18. Structure 17 was superseded by Structure 19 **LUB 43**. Pottery dates LUBs 41–43 to the late 14th to 15th centuries. In Area 5, to the west (sealing LUB 25), was a layer and a pit **LUB 44**, both associated with smithing; the pottery suggested that the layer had accumulated gradually, possibly up to the 15th century.

Structure 6 was demolished **LUB 45**, the pottery indicating that this occurred in the late 15th century and that demolition was contemporary with LUB 44.

In Area 9, cutting into LUB 21, were traces of a structure, Structure 7 **LUB 46** which had been demolished by the late 15th century.

In Area 4, there was a pit cg325, which was sealed by associated levelling cg327 **LUB 47**; the pottery from pit cg325 and levelling cg327 dates the pit to the late 15th century.

There were possible mortar pits **LUB 48** in Area 5. Probably associated with pits LUB 48 in Area 3 was the construction of Structure 13 **LUB 49**, a substantial stone-founded and buttressed building, probably part of the friary church. To the east, in Area 2 and sealing LUB 40, was a graveyard **LUB 50**. Built up against Structure 13, in Area 3, was a north–south wall **LUB 51**. Cutting through the graveyard LUB 50, in Areas 2 and 3, was another substantial stone-founded and buttressed building

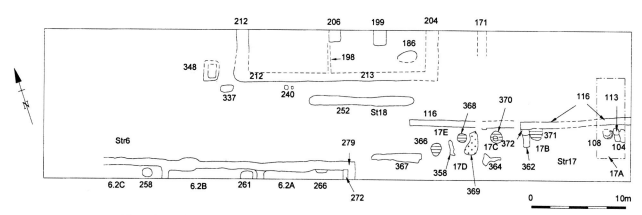

Fig. 12.16 Structures 6.2, 11, 17 and 18: LUBs 28, 39, 41 and 42. (1:385)

LUB 52 (Structure 14), possibly a chapel to the south-east of the church. None of the pottery for LUBs 48–52 post-dated the late 15th century. The evidence as a whole can be taken to suggest a major rebuilding phase in the late 15th century across much of the site.

To the north of the site, several friary buildings **LUB 53** were located in Area 10; there was no dating evidence associated with these features. Further work in this area in 1994–6 has provided much more evidence regarding the development of the Carmelite Friary.

LUB 38 Structure 11 – construction (Fig. 12.16)
Structure 11, in Areas 2 and 3, appears to have had north–south walls cg212 and cg204, with an east–west wall to the south made up of two stretches cg212 and cg213. The south wall of the western part of the building consisted of foundations cg212 (0.60–0.70m deep), which were made of large undressed limestone blocks occurring as two roughly-pitched layers; they cut into dump cg223 (LUB 21). It appeared that the wall had continued as the west wall of the building, but all traces of this part had been robbed cg193 (LUB 40). Traces of the slighter, eastern part of the south wall cg213 (0.50m at the deepest; no record of what it cut), had been removed by robber trench cg214 (LUB 40). The relationship between walls cg212 and cg213 had been lost by robbing and later cuts; there was no record of foundation widths due to both walls being sliced along their length by the Victorian drain. The change in depth of construction suggests the possibility of two phases of building; it is also possible that part of the building had deeper construction trenches in order to support a further storey. It may also be the case that the late Roman dump cg88 (LUB 18) below the shallow part of the wall cg213 was fairly compact, whereas the dump cg223 (LUB 21) under the west part of the wall cg212 was late Saxon, and probably not so stable to build over.

The east wall cg204 (sunk into slot cg203, LUB 33) was difficult to define, although there were traces of stone, but may be represented by cuts cg205 in the section of the Victorian drain (not illustrated; no record of what it cut).

Running into the north section were two rectangular stone foundations cg199 (cutting into pit cg200 LUB 33) and cg206 (c 1.80m north–south by 1.25m east–west; no record of what it cut). These may have represented the foundations for fire places, or pillar-bases. A north–south internal slot cg198 (0.16m deep; cutting pit cg200) appeared to run from the foundation cg206 possibly to the east–west wall cg213; this may represent an internal division within the building.

It is possible there was a further north–south

wall cg171 (cutting slot cg173, LUB 33) to the east of the structure; this again was seen as traces of stone, from possible robber trench cg172 (LUB 40), and glimpsed in robber trench cg174 (LUB 40). This wall may in some way have been associated with Structure 11. It was subsequently demolished along with Structure 11, cg172 and cg174 (LUB 40).

Only the southern part of structure lay within the limit of excavation and had been cut by the Victorian drain cg120 (LUB 57). Very little pottery was found (7 post-Roman sherds); the latest dates to the 13th to early 14th century.

LUB 39 Structure 11 use (Figs. 12.16 and 12.30)
Any floor remains had been levelled away, leaving an oven/hearth cg186 with pitched limestone footings isolated as it cut the underlying dump material cg223 (LUB 21). The oven/hearth appears to have been used and reused cg187, as seen by layers of burnt clay and limestone over the initial construction. To the west of Structure 11, cutting cg336 (LUB 29), there was a stone-lined pit cg348 (Fig. 12.30). The stones were bonded together with a yellow sandy mortar.

In Area 2, just to the east of Structure 11, there was a clay-lined pit cg184 (not planned) which had cut cg88 (LUB 18), and had a sandy fill cg185; this was cut by a further clay-lined pit cg178 (not planned) with a fill of sand, limestone fragments and some lumps of wall-plaster cg182. Fill cg182 contained 17 sherds dating to the 14th or 15th centuries.

LUB 40 Structure 11 demolition (Figs. 12.22)
Building 11, in Areas 2 and 3, was defined to a large extent by its robber trenches cg214 (cutting cg212 and cg213, LUB 38 along the south wall) and cg193 along the west wall cg212 (LUB 38). One of the foundation bases cg206 (LUB 38) was possibly robbed cg207, and then sealed by robbing debris cg208. Cuts cg172 (through cg171 LUB 38) and cg205 (through cg204 LUB 38), seen only in section (not illustrated), may have represented robber trenches; the backfill of cg205 included a moderately-sized assemblage of animal bone, representing domestic debris (Dobney *et al* 1994h). Hearth cg187 (LUB 39) was sealed by destruction material cg188, and stone-lined pit cg348 (LUB 39) was filled with clay, silt and rubble cg357. Tile and a few fragments of Collyweston slate were also found in the robbing cg193 and cg214.

Demolition material cg195 was levelled over the remains of Structure 11, sealing cg188 and cg193. Within it were found tile and fragments of Collyweston slate, together with a small assemblage of finds representing domestic rubbish. Wall cg171 (LUB 38) was robbed by trench cg174; this was sealed by layer cg175 and cut by robbing cg176.

Sealing the western part of the structure, over the destruction of Structure 8, was levelling cg177 (0.25m deep) of silty sand with clay and limestone chips, tile and Collyweston slate, together with domestic refuse such as shell fragments and animal bone.

The tile from the robbing cg193, cg195, and cg214 of Structure 11 dates from the early/mid 13th century, while the pottery from cg195 (45 post-Roman sherds) included some very small fragments, the latest sherds dating to the 14th or 15th centuries. The pottery from cg176 (52 post-Roman sherds) included several very large fragments; although mixed, the group dates to the 15th century. The LLSW pottery from cg176 includes wasters. A high proportion of the contemporary pottery from this group has internal white deposits, indicating that it is a mixture of both domestic and waste material. A fragment of 18th-century glass indicates some contamination.

Cg177 produced a very large group of pottery (503 post-Roman sherds). Although the deposit was mixed, the greater part of it was of contemporary 15th-century material. The deposit was unusual in containing a good part (49 sherds) of a very fragile Saxo-Norman LFS jar. Again, although this group contained waster material, there was plenty of evidence for domestic activity in the form of sooting and interior deposits. Although no cross joins were found, it seems likely that cg176 and cg177 were contemporary.

A mixed assemblage from cg177 included a ceramic kiln support (2) <945> and a complete barrel padlock (2) <465>. There was also a very large assemblage of bone, mostly domestic refuse but including chopped horncores suggesting a horn-working component (Dobney *et al* 1994h).

The most notable ceramic vessel from this LUB was a complete LLSW pipkin included in the fill cg357 of the stone-lined pit cg348.

LUB 41 Structure 17 (Fig. 12.16)
Structure 17 was a long, narrow, lean-to building (at least 24m long and about 3m wide), comprising at least five small rooms (17A–E) which were built up against the south face of a substantial east–west wall cg116 (which extended from Area 1 into Area 5). The building may have been gable-end on to the High Street or had been added to a building fronting the High Street. The rooms varied in width from about 2.8m east–west and at least 3m north–south; each room contained a substantial hearth.

At the eastern end of the site in Areas 1 and 5, east–west stone-founded wall cg116 cut cg98 (LUB 23) and sealed postholes cg107 (LUB 24). The wall foundations (0.95m wide) cg116 consisted of lime-

stone and sandstone pieces with small amounts of sand/clay, together with tile fragments packed between them; it survived in places to two courses.

To the south of this wall in Area 1 was room 17A; here pit cg103 (unplanned), with a fill of mortar with tile and limestone rubble (1.30m north–south) cut layer cg98 (LUB 23). Pit cg103 was cut in turn by a small pit cg104 (0.15m deep and 0.80m north–south), with a fill of ashy sand and charcoal. To the west, cutting pit cg102 (LUB 23), was a pitched-tile hearth cg108 with a semi-circular kerb formed of reused Millstone Grit quern fragments. The hearth cg108 was sealed by a spread of ash and charcoal cg111. To the east and butting the hearth, and sealing pit cg104, was a spread of ashy silt cg112, cut by small pit cg113. Pit cg113 was sealed by clay layer with limestone fragments cg114 and then burnt clay cg115. Further west a patch of burnt clay cg109 had sunk into pit cg101 (LUB 23), and had been sealed by a further sunken patch of clay cg110. Cutting clay cg114 of room 17A was a mortar-filled pit cg117 (unplanned), sealed by a spread of clay, tiles and broken limestone cg118.

Tiny groups of pottery (a total of 7 post-Roman sherds) were recovered from the patches of clay flooring (cg110, cg114 and cg115). The material was mixed, with the latest sherds dating to the late 14th or 15th centuries. There is a cross-join between the garderobe fill cg377 (LUB 36) and the mortar pit cg117 which only contained three sherds of LLSW, dating to the late 14th or 15th centuries. Other 15th-century sherds were recovered from cg103, cg108, cg116 and cg117.

To the west was room 17B, whose east–west dimensions were not established; it may be that 17A and 17B were part of the same room: although there was no trace of a division between them, there was a hearth in each area suggesting two rooms. A hearth of pitched tiles cg371 was positioned in the north-west corner of possible north–south wall cg372 (there was no record of what it was built on/in) and wall cg116. Possible wall cg372 was recorded as a patch of stones (0.80m wide), to the south of wall cg116; at the southern end of these stones cg372 was a linear stretch of light brown material cg362 (0.70m wide) which was not excavated. Stones cg372 and linear stretch cg362 might indicate the line of a wall.

Further west was a room 17C, about 3.80m wide; it had a hearth cg370 consisting of a circular patch of stones surrounded by ash; an internal north–south wall cg364 (0.45m wide) was suggested by traces of stone and ash with tile (there was no record of what either of these features sealed).

Further west again was a room 17D which was about 2.80m across. Traces of a wall dividing room 17C from 17D survived as a stub extending from wall cg116. Room 17D contained a hearth cg368 which consisted of pieces of limestone sealing a circular area of clay; immediately to the east and south-east lay a heap of iron-stained limestone fragments cg369.

To the west of room 17D was room 17E of unknown width; traces of clay cg358 (0.40m wide) suggest the location of a north–south wall between rooms 17D and 17E, possibly a wattle and daub internal dividing wall. In room 17E, what appeared to be a hearth cg366 was not described in the records (only planned). There was no record of what wall cg358 or hearth cg366 sealed. A stretch of hard brown soil cg367 (0.80m wide) possibly indicated the line of an east–west wattle and daub wall to the south of room 17D; it sealed part of cg209 (LUB 36), the fill of clay-lined slot cg363 (LUB 36).

LUB 42 Structure 18 (Fig. 12.16)

In Area 5, an east–west gully cg252 (0.35m deep; 0.70m north–south; 11.60m long) cut into unrecorded deposits with a fill of silty sand with charcoal flecks. Quite a large group of mixed pottery (130 post-Roman sherds) was recovered from cg252. The residual material included an early NSP spouted pitcher and 21 sherds of an AND jug which cross-join with deposit cg189 (LUB 32). The latest sherds are LLSW and date to the 15th century; the assemblage is similar to that from LUB 40. The gully may have represented robbed wall foundations of a wall against which lean-to structures were supported (similar to other structures LUBs 36, 41 and 43).

LUB 43 Structure 19 (Figs. 12.17 and 12.31)

In Area 5, wall cg116 (LUB 42) appears from the plans to have been cut and sealed by light brown strip of loam cg417 (0.50m wide).

A clay-lined slot (0.40m deep; 1.20m in length and about 0.50m wide) cg378 lay at an angle to the rest of the site; it cut wall cg116 (LUB 42) and fill cg209 (LUB 36) of the earlier clay-lined slot cg363

(LUB 36). Like cg363 (LUB 36), it could also be tentatively described as a liquid-retaining tank, perhaps a bosh with smithing close by, although there were no associated finds from its fill to confirm this interpretation.

Slot cg378 was sealed by a fill of dark yellowish-brown sandy clay cg379 with some iron-stained limestone.

The remains of possible north–south and east–west walls with stones as foundations cg373 (0.40m wide) sealed cg367 (LUB 41). A north–south stretch of light brown earth cg376 (0.50m wide), which seemed to butt against cg373 and seal cg367 (LUB 41), may have represented the line of a wattle and daub wall. To the west of cg376 was a hearth cg375 (no description recorded), which sealed wall cg365 (LUB 36). Also sealing wall cg365 (LUB 36), and possibly contemporary with the hearth, was a layer of brown sandy material with white clayey lumps cg238. To the south of wall cg373 was an area of tiles cg250; on the site plan it was described as a tiled surface; there is no further record. To the north of cg376 there was a hollow cg380 with a fill of sandy silt and charcoal cg381.

LUB 44 Layer and pit (Figs. 12.17)

In Area 5, over limestone spread cg268 (LUB 25) was a layer of greyish-brown sandy clay cg270 (unplanned). The pottery (100 post-Roman sherds) suggests that deposition started in the late 12th century, as it contained the largest group of early medieval pottery on the site. Pottery sherds join to those from the demolition of Structure 6, LUB 45, and to intrusive sherds from the demolition of Structure 8, LUB 32.

A circular pit cg271, at least 2m deep with steep sides, cut through this material; it had a fill of silty sand with charcoal cg280. There are joins with pottery from cg270, suggesting that some of the fill from the pit had spilt on to the layer.

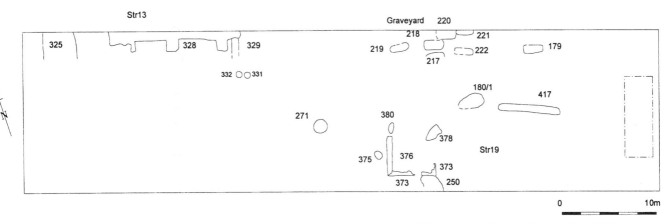

Fig. 12.17 Structures 13 and 19 graveyard and interesting pits: LUBs 43, 44, 47, 48, 49 and 50. (1:385)

Pottery from cg270 and cg280 (133 post-Roman sherds) contains waster material, as well as pottery that has sooting and interior deposits similar to that from the demolition of Structure 11, LUB 40. The presence of LSW4, LMF and the large number of Humberware vessels indicate a date of the late 15th century. Of note is a possible industrial vessel and a sherd with a moulded face-mask, possibly a product of a kiln found in 1847 or 1848 during railway construction in the parish of St Mary-Le-Wigford (ILN 1848, AI 1850 and Hobson 1903).

The majority of the registered finds from both layer cg270 and pit fill cg280 were of iron smithing waste (68% and 73% respectively), and the nature of the two assemblages suggests that they both derived from the same source at the same date. The presence of large quantities of hammerscale amongst the corrosion products suggests that there may have been a smithy nearby. The existence of only 974gm of slag is probably due to low retrieval rates. Coal was also noted amongst the corrosion and was perhaps the fuel used in the smithy. Amongst the iron finds are a lock (72) <225>, a padlock spring (72) <221> and a padlock endplate (69) <183> and twelve copper-alloy sheet offcuts, suggesting that locks may have been among the items manufactured, but the variety in shape of the remaining unidentified pieces suggests little specialisation. A complete pair of scissors was also found in layer cg270 (69) <158>, along with four hones (three of Norwegian Ragstone (69) <254> <270> <458> and one of purple phyllite (69) <441>), two of which appear to be unused.

A moderate assemblage of animal bone from pit fill cg280 indicated domestic refuse. Only a single cattle horncore, however, showed evidence of extensive butchery in the form of saw, chop and knife marks (Dobney *et al* 1994h).

LUB 45 Structure 6 demolition

In Area 7, dump cg210 sealed garderobe fill cg267 (LUB 28); hearth cg261 (LUB 28) was cut by irregular robbing cg262; cutting oven cg255 (LUB 28) was robber trench cg263. Sandy silt with limestone rubble cg273 sealed robbing cg262 and cg263 and sealed the extent of rooms 6A and 6B. There was a layer of dark clayey sand with rubble cg275, which sealed demolition cg273. It was cut by several robber trenches cg276, which removed stone from wall cg279 (LUB 27) and wall cg259 (LUB 27). These trenches cg276 were cut by a small pit cg277, which had a fill of dark clayey sand, much crushed mussel, some bone and tile.

Quite a large group of pottery was recovered from the demolition levels of Structure 6. The two largest assemblages (a total of 344 post-Roman sherds) were from cg275 and cg276 which cross-join. The material appeared to be quite fresh but was very fragmentary.

Only one LLSW jug had the major part of the vessel present, although there were several other multi-sherd vessels. Some of the LLSW vessels may be wasters; however, there was plenty of evidence for domestic activity with sooting and interior deposits. It is worth noting that some very large unworn sherds of 13th-century material were included in the group (see LUB 26). The latest material dates to the late 15th century. Similar groups were also recovered in the northern plot from the demolition deposits of Structure 11 (LUB 40), and were incorporated into the construction of Structure 13 (LUB 49). There are cross-joins between pottery from pit cg271 (LUB 44) and the latest material from layer cg270 (LUB 44), indicating that they are contemporary with the destruction of Structure 6. There was some intrusive post-medieval material in this LUB, indicating contamination.

LUB 46 Structure 7

In Area 9 (the north siding), cutting the dump cg391 (LUB 21), was the pitched rubble foundation of the south-east corner cg392 of a building (Structure 7). It was robbed cg393.

The date for the construction of the building is unknown, but it may have been demolished by the late medieval period, as suggested by a small group (25 post-Roman sherds) of pottery including the base of a DUTR pipkin from the robber trench cg393. The tile from the robber trench cg393 contained glazed ridge tile dating to the 13th century.

LUB 47 Pit (Figs. 12.17 and 12.36)

A large pit cg325 in Area 4 (1.20m deep; 2.60m east–west) cut pit cg324 (LUB 33) and had fills of mixed material which resembled tips, including sandy clay, mortar and shell. This contained building debris, including fragments of both ceramic and stone roof tile, and fourteen pieces of window glass, five with painted decoration (Fig. 12.36). There were no pieces of window came, but there was an architectural fragment, some plaster, and a few structural fittings. The remaining material was largely domestic refuse, including dress-fittings and fragments of textile (see discussion). The pit cg325 also contained a large assemblage of animal bone which suggested domestic refuse (including the remains of a swan). Four of eight caprovid scapulae showed damage to the blade consistent with hook/spike perforations (Dobney *et al* 1994h).

Pit cg325 was sealed by a dump of brown clayey sand with large pieces of limestone rubble cg327. There was a small assemblage of animal bone from cg327, domestic refuse, again including swan (Dobney *et al* 1994h).

Pit cg325 (138 post-Roman sherds) and dump cg327 (116 post-Roman sherds) produced large groups of fresh-looking contemporary pottery mixed with smaller worn sherds of residual material. Both groups include wasters and possible kiln furniture. Several multi-sherd vessels occurred and there were cross joins between the deposits. The presence of several wares (LMLOC fabric A, LSW4, LMF and RAER) put these groups in the late 15th century. With more joining sherds, there may have been several near-complete vessels between the two groups.

Pit cg325 and dump cg327 were thought to pre-date Structure 13, which must therefore have come late in the friary sequence: i.e. not before the late 15th century.

LUB 48 Pits (Fig. 12.17)
Possibly associated with the construction of Structure 13 (LUB 49) were two pits cg331 and cg332, in Area 5, originally described as mortar mixers. These were circular with fills of mortar, and apparently cut the earlier lane surface cg336 (LUB 29). The two pits cg331 and cg332 were fairly small (0.76 m diam); both had been truncated and only 0.2m of the fill of cg332 survived (the remaining depth of cg331 was unrecorded). This is described as being filled with very hard compact yellow mortar, the sides and bottom surrounded by wood, and with lime on the bottom.

LUB 49 Structure 13 (Figs. 12.17 and 12.32)
Possibly cutting levelling dump cg327 (LUB 47) was a construction trench (0.38m deep) for the south wall cg328 of Structure 13; however, it seems probable on further consideration of the evidence that it was the robber trench cg347 (LUB 54) which cut dump cg327 (LUB 47), and that in fact the construction cut levelling cg177 (LUB 40). This east–west wall cg328 (13.60m long and at least 1.20m wide – the wall was cut along its length by the railway platform), had foundations of crushed stone and mortar sealed by pitched limestone bonded with sandy clay. Of one build with the wall were three external buttresses (Fig. 12.32). The buttress situated approximately in the centre of the wall was the largest (1.30m wide, and extending about 1.00m from the wall); the buttress about 1.20m from the east end was next in size (1.20m wide and extending about 1.00m from the wall); the buttress to the west was relatively small (0.40m wide); strangely, this buttress extended 1.00m from the wall to the east, but only 0.80m from the wall to the west. It seems possible, however, that Structure 13 represents the south wall (aisle?) of the friary church, most of which lay beneath the station platform to the north, beyond the limit of excavation. Only the southern fringe of Structure 13 was therefore accessible. The small group of five pottery sherds from cg328 dated to between the late 13th and mid to late 15th centuries.

LUB 50 Graveyard (Fig. 12.17)
Levelling dump cg177 (LUB 40) was used as a graveyard in Area 2, and was cut by several inhumations cg179, cg180, cg181, cg217, cg218, cg219, cg220, cg221 and cg222. Two inhumations cg180 and cg181 may have been in the same grave, but a further two cg179, which were seen as sharing one grave cut, may have been separately buried. Cg220 had been cut by the construction trench cg225 (LUB 52) for the south wall of Structure 14 and no skeleton survived; the other inhumations were generally well preserved (Boylston and Roberts 1994).

Although the sample recovered is very small, examination of the skeletons confirmed that this graveyard is likely to have been part of the monastic cemetery (Boylston and Roberts 1994). Seven individuals were male or probably male, with six aged between 15 and 35 years; only one (cg217) was a mature adult (over 46 years), while two subadults (aged 11–14 years) may represent child-oblates. Boylston and Roberts (1994) comment that the relative youth at death contrasts with similar cemeteries (Wiggins *et al* unpublished), but point out that friars were particularly vulnerable to epidemic diseases, because they lived in cities in close contact with the population, caring for the sick (Lawrence 1989).

There was no evidence of coffins within the burials. Nails were found in four inhumations (180, cg218, cg221 and cg222), but their position within the graves was not recorded and no trace of coffin wood was noted. It is therefore possible that the nails were derived from the levelling cg177 (LUB 40).

All the graves except cg218 produced small groups of mostly residual pottery (a total of 33 post-Roman sherds). The only sherd of note was a LSW2/3 waster; similar wasters were found on the ze87 site, but do not form part of the later production there. Grave cg218 produced an unusually large group for a grave fill (33 post-Roman sherds). It appears to represent disturbed material from levelling dump cg177 (LUB 40). The vessels shared similar composition, including heavy sooting and interior deposits.

LUB 51 Wall (Fig. 12.17)
In Area 3, a north–south wall cg329, sitting on top of levelling dump cg177 (LUB 40), was built up against the south of Structure 13; very little of the wall was recovered, but it may represent a graveyard boundary wall. The wall (0.70m wide) appeared to have no foundations and was drystone, built of limestone fragments.

LUB 52 Structure 14
(Figs. 12.18, 12.33 and 12.34)
Building 14 lay to the east of Structure 13, on the same alignment; they were separated only by a gap of *c* 0.55m, suggesting that it was in some way

structually independent of Structure 13. Only part of the south wall was accessible, the rest being cut away by the station platform (the width of the foundations was over 1.20m and the length was 22m).

The construction trench for the south wall cg225 (up to 0.40m deep) cut several grave fills cg218, cg219, cg220 (LUB 50), and there were some disturbances cg216 (cutting cg206 LUB 38), and cg224 (cutting grave cg221 LUB 50). The foundations consisted of fairly small limestone fragments; the wall had three buttresses along its south face, towards the east end of the building. These were all about 1.20m wide and extended about 1.00m from the wall foundations. The most easterly was situated about 0.80m from the end of the wall foundations; the gaps between the three buttresses were each 2.80m. The existence of buttresses would suggest that more weight was being carried at the east end of the building. One idea is that it represented a bank of chapels to the south of an extended chancel.

The construction trench cg225 contained a small quantity of pottery (35 post-Roman sherds), the latest sherds dating to the 15th century.

LUB 53 Medieval stone walls and graves recorded during watching brief to the north of the station
In Area 10, a number of structures and features were only seen in the section of a pipe trench. Owing to the nature of the evidence, these features have been interpreted in one LUB. Cutting into dump cg401 (no record of what it sealed) were the stone foundations for a south-east corner whose east–west stretch of wall had a built-in garderobe cg402 (Structure 20). There were six inhumations cutting cg410, which were cg404 (two inhumations) and cg405 (four inhumations); these lay between north–south stone-founded wall cg403 (also part of Structure 20 and cutting cg401), and the north-west corner of a structure cg406 (Structure 21)

which cut cg401. To the west of the trench was a north–south stone-founded wall cg399 which cut cg401.

The building was demolished, and a dump cg407 partially sealed the wall foundations cg403 and cg406. Robber trenches cg408 cut through this dump and were sealed by construction material cg409. The north–south wall to the west was also robbed cg400 but this probably occurred later.

Construction material cg409 sealed cg408, work starting on the building of Structure 22, which consisted of a south-east corner cg410 (cutting cg401), and two north–south stone-founded walls cg411, cg412 (which cut cg409). There was a metalled surface cg413 between the corner cg410 and the north–south wall cg411.

The surface cg413 was cut by robbing cg414. The presence of a cast-iron pipe cg415 in the trench had removed any further stratigraphy.

There was no dating evidence from these structures, but it seems possible that they date to the time of the friary, i.e. sometime between the late 13th and early/mid 16th centuries.

Early post-medieval

Structures 13 and 14 in Areas 2 and 3 were demolished **LUB 54**, probably as part of the dissolution of the monasteries in the early/mid 16th century; there is no material evidence to confirm this interpretation. In Area 5 there were large pits **LUB 55** which only contained residual material, but were possibly 16th century or later in date.

At the west end of the site, in Area 8, was an east–west boundary wall **LUB 56** which probably belonged to this period; the robber trench contained 17th-century material.

LUB 54 Demolition of Structures 13 and 14
(Fig. 12.36)
Robber trench cg226 removed stone from wall cg225

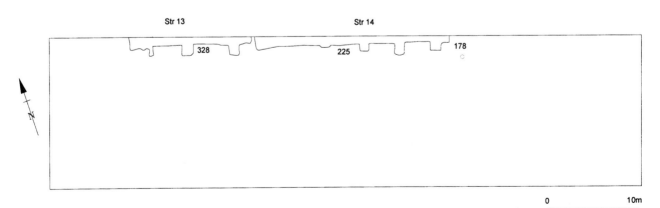

Str 13   Str 14

328   225   178

0   10m

Fig. 12.18 Structures 13 and 14: LUBs 49 and 52. (1:411)

(LUB 52); trench cg347 removed stone from cg328 (LUB 49), and over cg347 was robbing spill cg349. Robber trenches cg226 and cg349 contained residual pottery only. A quantity of window glass was recovered (Fig. 12.36; see discussion).

LUB 55 Pits (Fig. 12.19)
In Area 5, there was a large pit cg215, cutting robber trenches cg205 and cg172 (LUB 40) and probably later material, with layers of lime and sand cut by stake-holes; the backfill of this abandoned pit contained a small assemblage of animal bone indicating domestic refuse and horn working (Dobney *et al* 1994h). Pit cg215 was cut by a pit cg227 which had a fill of clayey sand, shell, limestone and charcoal, together with a moderate assemblage of animal bone indicating domestic refuse, but also including deer. Pit cg215 only contained residual Late Saxon and Saxo-Norman material.

LUB 56 Wall (Fig. 12.19)
To the west of the site, at the limit of excavation, were the robbed traces of the rough limestone foundations of an east–west stone wall cg351 (between 1.00–1.30m wide), suggesting a division of land which was not apparent further east. Wall cg351 may have been standing up to the 17th century, considering the pottery and clay tobacco pipe bowls from the fill of the robber trench cg352; the latest of these is dated *c* 1660–90.

Modern

The site was truncated by railway construction **LUB 57** in 1846 and later.

LUB 57 The railway (Fig. 12.20)
Pit cg393 (LUB 46) in Area 9 was dumped over cg394, cg396 and cut by a pit cg395. The latest pottery from the dumps cg394 and cg396 dates to the 19th/20th centuries.

The post-medieval and earlier stratigraphy had been truncated over the entire site by levelling prior to the construction of the station for the Midland Railway in 1846. The height of the site was reduced to about 6.15m OD, just over a metre lower than the surrounding area. A large east–west drain was built (cutting deeper into the stratigraphy), as well as various other features which cut down into the earlier layers. These later features cg120 very much influenced the extent of medieval features recovered.

Discussion
Topography

In the earlier part of the mid Roman period the area to the west of Ermine Street was characterised by riverine silts (LUB 1). These were drained first by east–west drain LUB 2, and later by drain LUB 6; to

Fig. 12.19 Pits and wall: LUBs 55 and 56. (1:704)

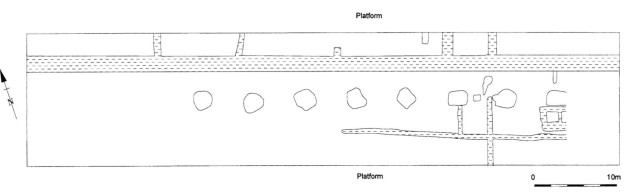

Fig. 12.20 British rail features: LUB 57. (1:441)

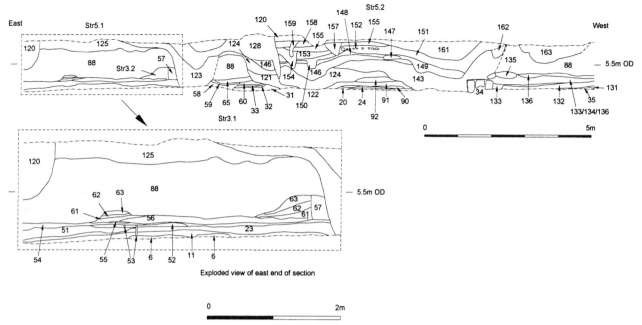

Fig. 12.21 Section from west to east, in area 1, illustrating the stratigraphy here, from LUB 6 to LUB 23, and truncation and intrusion of LUB 57. (1:110 with inset at 1:55)

the north of the drains were traces of an insubstantial timber building, Structure 1 (LUBs 3–5).

Assessing the date of the first use of the area from the pottery is problematical owing to the small quantities from early contexts. Of the twelve sherds of samian from LUBs 1 to 6, ten are dated to the early to mid 2nd century, one form 31 to the general Antonine period, but there is more positive dating from a stamp of Albucius II of *c* AD150–170 found with the cg9 (LUB 5). Two sherds of Iron Age tradition fabric occur, but the single rim would fit with types still current in the later 2nd century. The two MICA bowls do not belong with the earlier tradition, and would similarly fit a later 2nd-century date. None of the BB1 need be earlier than the mid to mid to late 2nd century, with which date the GREY flanged bowls agree. Local types loosely dated Antonine, i.e. mid to late 2nd century, occur but predominantly in LUB 7, with a deposition date in the mid 3rd century, as did the single RC beaker, where such types are residual. With the possibility that levelling material was brought to the site in the initial phases, and taking into account the evidence of the sherd links, it seems likely that primary use of the site began in the mid to late 2nd century.

In the mid 3rd century, landfill operations built up the ground and stone-founded 'strip' buildings were constructed (LUB 7), gable-ended on to Ermine Street, with a hard-standing to the rear, towards the river, which lay not far to the west of the buildings

(see bwe 82). These buildings were demolished (LUB 17) in the very late 4th century. Material was subsequently dumped (LUB 18) on to the site to prevent flooding, perhaps in the post-Roman period.

It is possible that the site was grazed by animals at some date between the late Roman period and the Late Saxon era: the river silting was punctured by possible hoof marks (LUB 19).

In the Late Saxon period the area was drained by ditches (LUB 20) and the level of the land was then raised with dumps (LUB 21). It can be presumed that there were buildings fronting the High Street during this period – traces of one of these were found (LUB 22), and there was evidence of pitting adjacent (LUB 23).

In the Early Medieval period, a lean-to building (LUB 25) stood towards the western end of the site, and another possible building, Structure 6.1 (LUB 26), along the southern fringe. It seems possible that at the beginning of the medieval period an east–west boundary running from the High Street was established initially as a fence (LUB 24).

Several buildings were constructed, associated with an east–west lane, presumably running to the riverfront (LUB 29), to the north of the location of fence LUB 24, suggesting that the boundary continued in use. These buildings included Structure 8 (LUB 31) to the north, and Structure 9 (LUB 34) at the west end. There were probably one or more buildings also fronting the High Street to the east of the site: pits (LUB 33) were noted to the east of Structure 8.

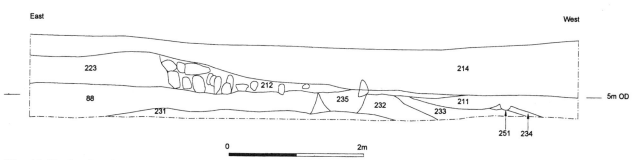

Fig. 12.22 Section from west to east, in area 3, illustrating the stratigraphy here, from LUB 17 to LUB 40. (1:55)

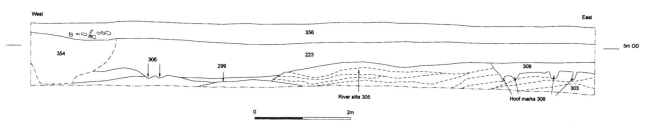

Fig. 12.23 Section from west to east, to the west of area 4, illustrating the stratigraphy here, from LUB 19 to LUB 35. (1:77)

Immediately to the south of the lane was lean-to building Structure 15 (LUB 30); further south was Structure 6.2 (LUB 27).

In the Late Medieval period Structure 6.2 continued in use; Structure 15 went out of use and Structure 16 (LUB 36) was constructed further east. The lane appears to have gone out of use, although its southern edge continued as a boundary (as indicated by the northern edge of Structure 16). Structure 9 was demolished during this period (LUB 35).

The east–west boundary at least partly continued in use, as indicated by the north wall cg116 of lean-to building Structure 17 (LUB 41). However, it seems that Structure 18 (LUB 42) may not have respected it further west. Structure 6.2, to the south, continued in use until the late 15th century when it was demolished.

Structure 11 (LUB 38) was constructed along the northern fringe of the site, within the Carmelite friary precinct. The friary occupied at least the northern part of the site and a larger area beyond – Structures 20–22 and other evidence of occupation (LUB 53), as well as Structure 7 (LUB 46) to the north-east. Structure 11 was later demolished (LUB 40) and replaced by Structure 13 (LUB 49) and graveyard (LUB 50). The graveyard was later abandoned and Structure 14 (LUB 52), immediately east of Structure 15, built over part of its site.

In the post-Dissolution period, Structures 13 and 14 were demolished and robbed (LUB 54). There was evidence for a post-medieval east–west boundary wall (LUB 56) in the western part of the site, along more or less the same line as the medieval boundaries to the east. This suggests further continuity of property boundaries. There is little other evidence of activity during the post-medieval period apart from pitting (LUB 55); it had presumably been removed by the later truncation caused by the construction of the railway (LUB 57).

River system

The river was a continuous presence to the west of the site throughout the Roman period. Early on there were large Roman drains (LUBs 2 and 6) associated with surfaces which were being used, at 4.52m OD (Structure 1.1; LUB 3) building up to 4.86m OD (Structure 1.3; LUB 6).

The ladder cg18 (LUB 5) dates to the late 2nd to 3rd century (for a description see LUB 5). There are four good parallels for the Lincoln ladder – a late Iron Age example from the lake village at Glastonbury dated to the 1st century BC (Bulleid and Gray 1911, 332, X55, Fig. 108, pl 51), a 1st century AD Roman ladder from London (Weeks 1978), a 1st/2nd-century ladder from Castleford (Morris 1998, Fig. 156, 28 and pl 44) and a 2nd-century ladder from Silchester (Fox and Hope 1901). All are rung ladders in varying states of

Fig. 12.24 *Ladder cg18 against the side of drain cg17, looking north.*

Fig. 12.25 *Oven built into wall cg34, looking west.*

preservation, and differ mainly in the species used to manufacture them, the technique of fastening the rungs into the poles and the gap between the rungs. The Lincoln, Castleford and London ladders were all made with oak poles and rungs, whereas that from Silchester had fir poles and oak rungs, and the Glastonbury ladder was made of ash. Although the ends of the rungs of the Castleford ladder were fragmentary, traces of augered holes through the poles with dowel fragments suggest that the rung tenons had been fixed in place with dowels as on the Lincoln ladder. One of the Glastonbury rungs had also been fastened by dowels passing through holes in the projecting tenons. The Silchester ladder, however, had four of its five rungs secured by wooden wedges. The rung gaps of the five ladders were 260mm (Lincoln), 350mm (Silchester), 300–430mm (Glastonbury), 440mm (Castleford) and 500mm (London). Although Roman ladders had many uses (Weeks 1978, 110–11), they rarely survive archaeologically, and then only in contexts potentially linked with their use. The Castleford and Silchester ladders were found in association with pits, and the London ladder was found in a well.

Dumps backfilled the drain for the construction of Structures 2 and 3 (LUB 7), with little actual heightening of the ground level, which later built up to 5.25m (Structure 2.3; LUB 11). Piled timbers formed part of the construction of at least the shared wall between Structures 2/3 (LUB 7), suggesting an awareness of the subsidence risk presented by the dampness of the underlying sands. Structure 3 had metalling to the rear, possibly providing access via a beach down to the river. After Structures 2 and 3 went out of use, the ground level was raised by dumping to between 5.68 and 5.77m OD (LUB 18).

In the Late Saxon period the river was controlled by a series of ditches or dykes (LUB 20) running parallel to it. This method was abandoned in favour of raising the ground level with a series of dumps (LUB 21), which overlapped the earlier dump (LUB 18) and spread down towards the river, sealing river silts and building the ground level up to between 5.13 and 5.68m OD. The 13th-century lane (LUB 29) probably did not extend as far as the river, since Structure 9 (LUB 34) was in the way. It seems

Fig. 12.26 Looking south along the back wall cg34 of the Roman strip buildings structures 2 and 3, internal dividing wall cg138 within structure 3, external surface cg132 to the right of the photograph.

that from the Late Saxon period, access to the river, at this point, was not of importance; it was more important to keep surfaces above the water level.

Street frontage

The lack of excavation along the main road, Ermine Street/High Street, has meant that the relationships between the structures recovered on the site and the road have had to be extrapolated. The Roman traders' houses (Structures 1–3; LUBs 3, 4, 5, 7, 9–12) presumably fronted on to Ermine Street. It seems most likely that buildings also fronted on to the same street in the Late Saxon and Saxo-Norman periods – the only definite example was Structure 5 (LUB 22), but pits (LUB 23) enhance the likelihood. There is no evidence for what might have fronted on to the High Street from that date, as structures were found to the rear of the road, and a lane (LUB 29) from the road appeared to have served some of these for a while. The limited nature of the excavation relating to the area fronting on to the High Street is one reason for the lack of evidence from the 12th century. The friary complex extended as far as the High Street, but may have been defined here by its precinct wall.

Roman structures

The Roman buildings 1, 2 and 3 probably devel-

oped here, along the main route outside the main walled Roman town, to serve a growing demand for various products and services. Although the extent of the 2nd-century timber Structure 1 revealed was minimal, it seems likely that either this building or one associated with it fronted on to Ermine street. Structure 1 appeared from the flimsy evidence to be a timber structure associated with iron smithing in its first two phases (LUBs 3 and 4). Residual sherds from a Smith God pot, possibly originally associated with Structure 1, were recovered in later deposits (LUBs 7 and 9). The fragments of this vessel were decorated with tongs, anvil and an axe-hammer. The Smith God vessel is unique in terms of its fabric (OX fabric), although of the same vessel type as those known from sm76 (Darling 1990).

In the mid 3rd century stone-founded buildings, Structures 2 and 3, were constructed; these buildings would have been gable-ended on to the west side of Ermine Street (similar in construction to those at other sites in Wigford). Both structures were built as one operation, implying that they may have been owned by one proprietor. An alternative interpretation is that they were both part of one large building – but the lack of evidence for large buildings in Wigford (hg72, sm76, smg82 and ze87 all contained narrow strip buildings) has favoured an interpretation of their representing separate buildings with a party wall. The buildings were

Fig. 12.27 *Looking south at the stone revetment cg416 against dump cg223. Revealed during the re-excavation of the Victorian drain (seen to the right of the photo).*

Fig. 12.28 *Looking west, along structure 6. Remains of external wall with stone vaulted garderobe cg279, sealed by pitched tiled hearth cg266.*

each about 25m long; the width of Structure 2 was about 7m, and that of Structure 3 at least 5.5m.

Very Late Roman–Late Saxon rubbish dumps: ceramic and artefactual evidence

A curious feature of this site is LUB 18 and its relationship both with the preceding pottery groups, and with the material from post-Roman contexts on the site (in particular LUB 23), both large groups of pottery between 600 and 700 sherds. LUB 18 is strongly of the later 3rd and 4th century, its peak moving from the late 3rd century (as seen in Structure 2) to the early 4th century. Although the pottery from the post-Roman LUB 23 also peaks in the early 4th century, it is at a much lower level, and the overall profile spreads back into the earlier 3rd century and is generally more similar to LUB 17 than LUB 18. It would seem likely that the material in the LUB 18 dumps came from outside, and has no relevance to the occupation of the site; this interpretation was supported by the registered finds (see below). It is possible that these dumps signify the area becoming designated (officially or unofficially) a rubbish tip, and that for some period of time it was used for the disposal of some of the city's rubbish, perhaps to help counter the effect of rising river levels.

The registered finds included a total of fifteen coins. The overall date range of the coins from cg87 is 330–40, whereas those from cg88 range from 320

to 375, suggesting that dump cg87 was earlier in date than dump cg88. Although there is only one coin datable to the Valentinianic period, the coins from cg88 may not represent a discrete group, because Constantinian issues generally had gone out of circulation by the Valentinianic period. This may be significant, and supports the contention that cg88 represents a dump of rubbish from elsewhere. The dump has the characteristics of others noted elsewhere in the city, and cannot be definitely attributed to the end of the Roman period or to a post-Roman context.

There was also vessel glass from LUB 18 (eleven vessels represented). Within dump cg88 was part of the base from a late 1st-/early 2nd-century plate or bowl (Price and Cottam 1993d); the earliest structures on this site are dated mid/late 2nd century, and unless this piece represents an 'heirloom' with a prolonged life, then it almost certainly arrived in material brought from elsewhere in the city.

The residual Roman material perhaps re-deposited from dump cg88 (LUB 18) within later undefined pits cg167 (LUB 20) included a fragment of imported marble wall veneer, *occhio di pavone pavonazzo*, from an unknown source (Peacock and Williams 1992).

Fig. 12.29 Looking east along gullies cg242 and cg252. The gullies are cut by British Rail features. The stones to the bottom right of the photograph represent the road surface cg268 and the pressure of the railway lines has distorted the surface.

This, and another fragment, possibly intrusive from dump cg88 (LUB 18) in the robber trench of Structures 2/3 (LUB 17, cg73), is a notable find because such pieces are recovered infrequently on Roman sites, and in Lincoln seem to occur mainly in association with important civic buildings or private establishments of some quality. It would seem that the source of both marble fragments was the late Roman rubbish dumping (LUB 18).

Analysis of the fabrics from LUBs 18 and 23 showed little difference between the groups, and it is only when related to vessel form and date that the contrasts can be discerned. Analysis of the functions that can be broadly attributed to the pottery showed little discernible difference between the combined LUBs from Structures 2 (LUBs 9, 10, 11 and 12) and the group from the destruction of that structure and Structure 3 (LUB 17). The group from LUB 18 dumps was distinguished by a very low percentage of drinking vessels, well below that for Structures 2 and 3 demolition deposits (LUB 17),

and it was also notably low on kitchen wares. Analysis of the pottery from the post-Roman LUB 23 was also low on drinking vessels, but otherwise relatively similar to the Structure 2 occupation and destruction assemblages (LUBs 9–12 and 16).

Late Saxon-Medieval Occupation predating the friary

The large amount of pottery attributable to the period between the late 10th and mid 12th centuries (731 sherds) indicates continuity of occupation. Much of the pottery is of a domestic nature; a few high quality Stamford ware vessels and the presence of two imported vessels (ANDE and PING) indicate that tablewares were also in use.

With the exception of the lt72 site, this is the only site in the Wigford that has more than 40 sherds datable to between the mid 12th and early/mid 13th centuries. The assemblage (*c.* 300 sherds) is highly biased towards the glazed wares (LSW1, LSW1/2, NSP and DST), and also includes several imported vessels (BLGR and BRUNS), perhaps indicating high-status use of the site before the foundation of the friary.

The Carmelite Friary

The house was founded by Odo of Kilkenny by 1269 and in this year Henry II granted the Carmelite Friars of Lincoln six beech trees for a kiln (Page 1906, 224). The reference indicates that some sort of industrial activity was taking place in the same year that the house was founded; possibly the friars were continuing an activity that was already in process. In 1280 Edward I authorised for lands adjoining the friary to be given for its enlargement (Hill 1948, 150). Before excavation, only the general location of the Carmelite Friary was known. The full extent of their property, either before 1280 or afterwards, has only been established since the subsequent excavations of 1995–6, although it was apparent that the main building of the friary stood on the site of the Midland Railway station (Hill 1948, 151).

The earliest phase of monastic occupation is not clear from the excavations. From the late 12th century the site seems to have gone through a change of use. Before that date it seems likely from the evidence that there were buildings on the High Street (LUB 22) and pits behind (LUB 23). After the late 12th century and before the mid 13th century, there was some structural activity in the western part of the site (LUB 26 Structure 6; LUB 25 Structure 12), but its full extent during this period was not recovered (see limit of excavation on LUB diagram). It seems clear, however, that the site was occupied before the founding of the friary. Pottery dating between the

Fig. 12.30 Stone-lined pit cg348, partly excavated leaving fill cg357 containing a complete LLSW pipkin. The pit was truncated by the railway lines and cut away to the north by the Victorian drain.

13th and early 14th centuries is not specific enough to tie LUBs 27 and 29–34 to the friary, and they could possibly pre-date its extension southwards.

The northern part of the site (Areas 2, 3, 4 and the north part of 5), and possibly also Area 8, appear to have belonged to the complex (by examining the extent of the later friary occupation LUBs 49–52). This suggests that at least Structure 8 (LUB 31) and pits (LUB 33) formed part of the friary. Even if not constructed by the friars, the use of these features continued into the friary period. It is possible that the east–west lane (LUB 29) represented the southern boundary of the property. Structure 9 (LUB 34) to the west of the site may or may not have become part of the friary holding, but the evidence is not clear.

There were traces of friary remains along the north side of the site in Area 10 (LUB 53), including at least three stone-founded buildings, Structures 20–22. To the north-west of the site (br85) in Area 9, another stone-founded building, Structure 7 (LUB 46), probably part of the friary precinct, was demolished in the late 15th century.

The actual constructional details of Structure 8 (LUB 31) are unclear. There were some robbed stone foundations (LUB 32), but it is possible to argue that this building was at least in part of timber-framed construction, because of the paucity of any other evidence. Structure 8 consisted of at least four rooms, at least three with their own hearths or ovens. Structure 11 (LUB 38) replaced Structure 8 and appears to have represented another stone-founded building, but with very different internal arrangements, suggesting a different function. It contained the remains of two stone foundations

cg199 and cg206, possibly to be interpreted as hearths (or pillar-bases) but only one internal division cg198. This building was replaced by Structure 13 (LUB 49), to which Structure 14 (LUB 52) was later added.

The occurrence of Collyweston slates within the building debris from the destruction or robbing of Structures 8 (cg189 LUB 32), 9 (cg344 LUB 35), 11 (cg177, cg193, cg195, cg214 LUB 40) and 14 (cg226 LUB 54), and within the fill of pit cg325 (LUB 47), suggests that at least some of the friary buildings were roofed in stone. The presence of ceramic tiles within the same contexts, however, may indicate that stone was not exclusively used.

Evidence from the buildings in the northern part of the site suggests a variety of industrial activities. In Area 3 were the large hearths of Structure 8 (LUB 31); in the demolition debris of the building (LUB 32) was copper-alloy sheet waste – possible traces of some previous activity. The pits (LUB 33) contained some domestic animal bone debris and one, cg84, some lead waste and slag. The east–west lane (LUB 29) in Area 5 probably extended from the High Street, serving Structures 8 and 9. To the west of the site (Area 8), at the end of the lane (LUB 29), there was a structure and a hearth, oven, or kiln (LUB 34); the use of this feature is unknown.

The function of Structure 11 (LUB 38), with its oven/hearth cg186/187 and possible hearth foundations, is uncertain. These internal features may not be substantial enough for it to have been the friary kitchen. There was plenty of evidence from demolition material of pottery indicating sooting and interior deposits, and large amounts of domestic

Fig. 12.31 Clay-lined slot cg378, looking north.

animal bone (LUB 40), which might support the interpretation of Structure 11 as a domestic kitchen. This material (LUB 40) also included wasters and kiln furniture, linking the friary with the kilns to the east of the High Street (ze87). Outside the building were two clay-lined pits cg184 and cg178 and one lined with stone cg348; the function of these features is not clear.

The late 15th century seems to have been a time of momentous change in the friary's layout. Pottery of that date was recovered from LUBs 40, 44, 45, 47 and 50, and suggests that radical changes affected much of the site. The friary is known to have been struck by lightning in about 1490, and the tower and dormitory were burnt down (Hill 1948, 150). A fragment of limestone, possibly from a squared architectural block (121) <599> from pit cg325 (LUB 47) was pink and blackened, possibly as a result of burning; this was the only item associated with the friary with such evidence. The fire probably affected a part of the precinct to the north, but it would appear that the functioning of the friary as a whole was affected, possibly leading to some re-organisation and rebuilding of the site. The demolition of Structure 11 and the building of Structure 13 could be seen as elements of this operation. Another aspect of the pottery from LUBs 40, 44, 45 and 47 was that these groups all contained wasters, probably from the St. Mark's kiln site across High Street to the east (ze87). These LUBs were located in Areas 3, 4, 5 and 7; so not only was the friary possibly associated with the kilns, but also the sphere of influence of the friary, at least by the end of the 15th century, may have extended to the south, at least into Areas 5 and 7, if not into Area 6 as well.

A substantial, buttressed building, Structure 13 (LUB 49), was constructed; it was the south aisle (13.60m long) of the friary church; a graveyard (LUB 50) was laid out to the east. Some of the graves were cut by a further substantial buttressed building to the east, Structure 14 (LUB 52), possibly a bank of chapels to the south of an extended chancel (22m long) or a substantial nave aisle. The building's length, as suggested by LUB 49 and LUB 52 together, was about 36m (including the gap between Structures 13 and 14); this is comparable to the length of many large churches. It is also possible that the (narrower) chancel lay beneath the station building, and that the church was even longer.

Sixty-three fragments of moulded stone were found in robber trench cg226 (LUB 54); this was robbing debris from a high-quality structure – possibly windows with flowing tracery or a piece of screenwork or panelling. The demolition team had taken away the largest, most useful pieces of the feature, and left only small scraps of the most protuberant elements. It suggests systematic post-Dissolution quarrying with the intention of retrieving good, faced masonry for reuse. Some of the fragments can be dated to the 14th century, and most probably the mid–late 14th century. Details such as miniature buttress set-offs (4) <616>, discrete miniature merlons (4) <611>, and sculpted crenellations (4) <652> suggest a piece of screenwork or decoration, such as might be found on liturgical furniture: a set of *sedilia*, an Easter Sepulchre. A case can be made for these fragments originating from the Kyme Chantry, built in the second half of the 14th century; the stones built into the conduit head at St Mary-le-Wigford may have the same origin (Stocker 1990). It is possible that Structure 14 does indeed represent a bank of chapels of which the Kyme Chantry Chapel was one; if the 14th-century date of the chapel stands, then the 15th-century pottery in LUBs 40, 49, 50 and 52 would have all to be intrusive, from the post-Dissolution robbing (LUB 54), but this seems unlikely. Other architectural fragments from robbing cg226 represent architectural features, mostly of the 14th century, including door and arch mouldings. These too might support a 14th-century date for Structures 13 and 14. In support of the idea that the 15th-century pottery was being intrusive in LUBs as early as LUBs 40 and 50, is the thoroughness of the robbing of the foundations; little stone remained in the construction trenches cutting through both these LUBs, and there was even confusion between the identity of the construction and robbing trenches (see discussion in LUB 49).

The window glass from cg325 (LUB 47) and from cg226 (LUB 54) is of particular interest, as David King (1994) comments: The relieved circles found on (5) <35> (Fig. 12.36 No 1) and (121) <352> (Fig. 12.36

Fig. 12.32 The buttressed footings cg225 of structure 13 (looking east), sealed by the railway platform with the cut of the Victorian drain to the right of the photograph.

Fig. 12.33 The buttressed footings cg225 of structure 14 (looking south) cutting inhumation cg219.

Fig. 12.34 Looking west along the buttressed footings cg225 and robber trench cg226 of structure 14, sealed by the railway platform (line of Victorian drain to left of photograph).

No 2) are similar to those found on narrow borders and edge pieces in glass from the late 13th century to the end of the 14th century, as for example, the excavated glass of *c* 1350–70 from Barton Bendish All Saints Church, Norfolk (Rogerson and Ashley 1987, Fig. 34). Another fragment (121) <353> (Fig. 12.36 No 3) appears to show drapery folds, and probably dates to *c* 1280–1330. The most interesting piece is (121) <365> (Fig. 12.36 No 4), which is probably part of a decorative window with stiff-leaf grisaille, or perhaps from the border of a medallion window. This leaf pattern is of a type known in England from the early to late 13th century and, for example, is drawn on quarry shapes in Lincoln Cathedral in the early 13th century (Morgan, N J 1983, Fig. C12), and in Westminster Abbey in the third quarter of the century (Marks 1993, Fig. 102c). (121) <365> however, is cut to the shape of the leaf, a feature seen also on unpublished excavated glass

from Ely Cathedral and in the Five Sisters window at York Minster, dated *c* 1250 (Marks 1993, Fig. 105). In the latter window, a few of the leaf forms hint at naturalism, and the painting of (121) <365> here, while still adhering to the basic stiff-leaf format, also shows a tendency towards a looser, more naturalistic drawing compared with the Lincoln, Westminster, and Ely examples cited above; this perhaps indicates a similar transitional character. The proto-naturalism of the York window, however, is unusual, and naturalistic foliage generally is not seen on English glass until the third quarter of the century; (121) <365> would therefore have to be dated to any time in the second half of the 13th century, and could thus be of similar date to the other pieces from cg325 discussed here and assigned to the 13th–14th centuries, perhaps suggesting that they are all of late 13th-century date.

The medieval pottery dating between the beginning of the 13th and the middle of the 14th century consists mainly of good-quality jugs, often highly decorated. Regionally imported material comes from several centres, including York, Beverley, Lyveden, Nottingham and Scarborough, with two imported vessels from France (SAIP) and the Low Countries (AARD). A large group of pottery of this date recovered from the Victorian drain was classed as unstratified material and has not been quantified. It is possible that it represents disturbed material from Structure 8.

The later medieval pottery, dating between the mid 14th and the late 15th century, is of a mixed nature. Very few of the jugs are decorated, and many of them have evidence of sooting and contain an internal thick white deposit. The range of vessels is wider and includes cooking pots, jars, pipkins, dripping-pans, drinking jugs and a lobed cup. Wasters occur in several deposits; LUBs 40 (Area 3), 44 (Area 5), 45 (Area 7) and 47 (Area 4), all in 15th-century deposits. Ceramic kiln supports occur on the site in LUBs 28 (Area 7) and 40 (Areas 2 and 3); other kiln furniture was located in LUBs 41 (Area 1) and 47 (Area 4).

The composition of several deposits indicates levelling of localised material, together with other material being brought on to the site (possibly from the St. Mark's kiln site (ze 87) across the High Street). The nature of the material from the two sides of the east–west lane differs until the late 15th century when several deposits (LUBs 40, 44, 45 and 47) appear to be contemporary and the first cross-lane joins are found. The presence of not only wasters on the site, but also kiln furniture, probably originating from pottery kilns nearby, may suggest that it was the friary that controlled the kiln, although there are no known parallels for this; at least a close relationship is implied.

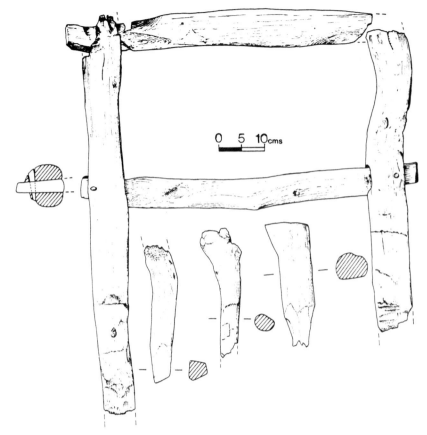

Fig. 12.35 Wooden ladder from recut drain cg17. Scale 1:8

The friary was surrendered to Richard, Bishop of Dover in February 1538–9; in 1544 the friary area was sold to John Broxholme of Lincoln (Page 1906, 224). The conduit head sited to the west of the church of St. Mary-le-Wigford is a testimony of the Dissolution; it was built in 1544 from a 14th-century chapel from the friary (Stocker 1990).

More recent excavations (in 1995–6) have taken place to the north of z86 (Trimble 1998). From the extensive but superficial remains available, it was difficult to discern distinct phases in the development of the friary over time and to define all of the structures for which evidence was recovered. However, the cloister was identified, together with its associated north-eastern ranges, and the position of the church and its graveyard to the south of the cloister were confirmed. A kitchen area, surrounded by ancillary structures, appeared in the north-western part of the site. Although the lack of phasing evidence made it difficult to build up a picture of the development of the friary from that site alone, the kitchen located to the west in 1996 represented the latest phase of the friary, while the possible kitchen (LUBs 38–9) found at z86 was earlier, its location later taken by the church and graveyard (LUB 49 and

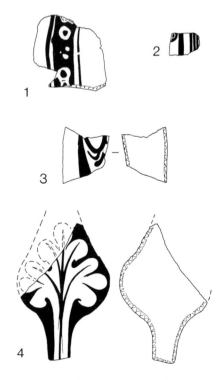

Fig. 12.36 Decorated window glass from robber trench cg225 (no 1) and pit cg325 (nos 2–4). Scale 1:2

cg/LUB	cg/LUB	cg/LUB	cg/LUB	cg/LUB	cg/LUB	cg/LUB	cg/LUB	cg/LUB	cg/LUB	cg/LUB	cg/LUB	cg/LUB	cg/LUB
1/1	31/13	61/15	91/13	121/-	151/22	181/50	211/19	241/37	271/44	301/19	331/48	360/23	389/20
2/1	32/13	62/15	92/13	122/23	152/22	182/39	212/38	242/30	272/28	302/19	332/48	361/31	390/20
3/3	33/13	63/15	93/23	123/22	153/22	183/33	213/38	243/25	273/45	303/19	333/23	362/41	391/21
4/4	34/7	64/-	94/23	124/22	154/22	184/39	214/40	244/19	274/28	304/19	334/23	363/36	392/46
5/4	35/1	65/15	95/23	125/22	155/22	185/39	215/55	245/19	275/45	305/19	335/23	364/41	393/46
6/5	36/9	66/-	96/29	126/22	156/-	186/39	216/52	246/19	276/45	306/19	336/29	365/36	394/57
7/5	37/9	67/10	97/23	127/22	157/22	187/39	217/50	247/19	277/45	307/19	337/37	366/41	395/57
8/5	38/9	68/10	98/23	128/22	158/22	188/40	218/50	248/16	278/27	308/19	338/37	367/41	396/57
9/5	39/9	69/10	99/23	129/22	159/22	189/32	219/50	249/19	279/27	309/20	339/35	368/41	397/20
10/5	40/9	70/11	100/23	130/23	160/-	190/32	220/50	250/43	280/44	310/20	340/34	369/41	398/20
11/5	41/9	71/11	101/23	131/1	161/23	191/32	221/50	251/19	281/19	311/20	341/34	370/41	399/53
12/-	42/9	72/11	102/23	132/8	162/22	192/32	222/50	252/42	282/18	312/20	342/34	371/41	400/53
13/3	43/9	73/17	103/41	133/16	163/23	193/40	223/21	253/19	283/19	313/20	343/35	372/41	401/53
14/2	44/9	74/11	104/41	134/16	164/29	194/23	224/49	254/26	284/19	314/20	344/35	373/43	402/53
15/4	45/10	75/11	105/23	135/16	165/23	195/40	225/52	255/28	285/19	315/31	345/35	374/36	403/53
16/4	46/10	76/11	106/23	136/16	166/23	196/33	226/54	256/28	286/19	316/31	346/34	375/43	404/53
17/6	47/10	77/18	107/24	137/13	167/23	197/35	227/55	257/28	287/19	317/31	347/54	376/43	405/53
18/6	48/10	78/18	108/41	138/15	168/33	198/38	228/23	258/28	288/19	318/31	348/39	377/36	406/53
19/6	49/10	79/11	109/41	139/15	169/33	199/38	229/29	259/27	289/19	319/31	349/54	378/43	407/53
20/13	50/10	80/-	110/41	140/23	170/33	200/33	230/16	260/28	290/20	320/31	350/29	379/43	408/53
21/5	51/13	81/17	111/41	141/16	171/38	201/33	231/16	261/28	291/20	321/32	351/56	380/43	409/53
22/5	52/13	82/12	112/41	142/31	172/40	202/33	232/16	262/45	292/19	322/31	352/56	381/43	410/53
23/7	53/13	83/11	113/41	143/22	173/33	203/33	233/16	263/45	293/23	323/33	353/23	382/29	411/53
24/13	54/13	84/33	114/41	144/17	174/40	204/38	234/19	264/28	294/19	324/33	354/23	383/19	412/53
25/7	55/13	85/17	115/41	145/-	175/40	205/40	235/18	265/28	295/19	325/47	355/29	384/20	413/53
26/7	56/14	86/23	116/41	146/22	176/40	206/38	236/19	266/28	296/19	326/31	356/35	385/20	414/53
27/7	57/15	87/18	117/41	147/22	177/40	207/40	237/19	267/28	297/19	327/47	357/40	386/20	415/53
28/7	58/15	88/18	118/41	148/22	178/39	208/40	238/43	268/25	298/19	328/49	358/41	387/20	416/21
29/5	59/15	89/-	119/23	149/22	179/50	209/36	239/23	269/27	299/19	329/51	359/36	388/20	417/43
30/7	60/13	90/13	120/57	150/22	180/50	210/45	240/37	270/44	300/19	330/23			

Fig. 12.37 Concordance of cg numbers with LUB numbers for z86.

50). The z86 excavations suggest a late 15th-century date for the church and graveyard (LUBs 49 and 50), and a slightly later date for the extended chancel (LUB 52), which cut the graveyard (LUB 50). A church to the south of the cloister is unusual; Trimble (1998, 77) suggests that this was possibly the case because the land on which it was built was the first acquired by the friary. However, it is just possible that the first church was originally built to the north of the cloister (beyond the northern limits of the excavations), and only relocated to the south of the cloister after the fire of around 1490.

Gold-thread garment-trimming from pit cg325 (LUB 47) by Penelope Walton Rogers

The remains of a narrow tapestry-woven band with a picotee edging (121) <329>, were recovered from pit cg325. Only the gold threads have survived from what would have been a silk-and-gold textile, and the structure has had to be described from an X-ray. The 30mm wide band has been woven tapestry-fashion, with a design of small paired discs repeated down its length. The warp, now absent, was set at 7–8 threads per cm, while the gold weft was 50 per cm.

The 'gold' thread is in fact silver-gilt strip spun in the S-direction around a core which has decayed away. The 10mm wide picotee edging has been worked in the same thread, probably by a bobbin lace technique (further details in Walton Rogers 1993).

This tapestry construction is unusual for gold-thread work. Brocading, in which the gold thread only passes over the surface of the fabric, was much more common – and more economical. The nearest parallel is a non-patterned gold braid from 17th-century Dudley Castle, West Midlands, which also has a close-set gold weft covering the warp (Walton Rogers 1992). There are, however, numerous examples of medieval gold and silver bands worked by brocading, including a 13th-century example from Swan Lane, London, which, like the Lincoln band, has a pattern of discs, although in that instance combined with rectangles and worked in silver on a silk background (Crowfoot *et al* 1992, 131 and 136).

The picotee edging along one side of the Lincoln band suggests that it was originally intended as a garment trimming. Most surviving gold bands have been recovered from ecclesiastical vestments in church burials, but Elizabethan court documents and portraiture show similar items being used as edgings on cuffs, coifs, gloves, stockings, garment panels and the front opening of dresses (Arnold 1988, 205, 207, 216–7). Whether lay or ecclesiastical, the St. Mark's example must indicate some high-status activity in the neighbourhood.

Industrial activity in the southern part of the site

The question must be asked whether activity in the southern part of the site (Areas 1, 5, 6 and 7) was associated with the friary – as suggested by the pottery wasters (see below). The nature of the pottery assemblage in this southern part of the site does, however, appear to be clearly different from that of the site of the friary until the late 15th century.

The stone-founded Structure 6.2 (LUB 27–8) was substantial, but several of the other buildings were of a lean-to nature, including Structures 15, 16, 17, 18 and 19 (LUBs 30, 36, 41, 42 and 43) in Areas 5 and 6. It seems that use of the structures covered the period from the 13th century through to the late 15th century (at which point the stratigraphic sequence was truncated). The large hearths and copper droplets might indicate some industrial use of Structure 6.2 (LUB 27). Possible lean-to buildings, Structures 12, 15 and 18 (LUBs 25, 30 and 42) have been interpreted in this way from those examples which appear either to have survived in more detail or were more thoroughly excavated and recorded, i.e. Structures 16, 17 and 19 (LUBs 36, 41 and 43). All were characterised by a substantial east–west wall against the southern side of which was a lean-to shed. Associated with Structure 16 was a clay-lined pit cg363 (a possible bosh), stone-lined pit cg374, together with quantities of smithing slag and some hammerscale, suggesting smithing (LUB 36). Structure 17 contained a number of small rooms with substantial hearths and iron-stained limestone (LUB 41). Structure 19 was also associated with a clay-lined slot (another possible bosh) and iron-stained limestone (LUB 43). To the west of Area 5 (LUB 44), just north of Structure 6.2 (LUB 28), was a quantity of iron-smithing waste, a possible dumping ground for material from some of these buildings.

Late Saxon and medieval hornworking

Evidence of hornworking appears to be represented in the vicinity of the site, sometime during both high and late medieval periods, with mainly caprovid horncores and associated skull fragments showing evidence of butchery (although two Late Saxon and late Roman contexts contained horncores which had also been chopped through their bases). This tantalising evidence may indicate the presence of hornworking nearby, certainly from the high medieval period, but perhaps originating at an earlier date (Dobney *et al* 1994h).

13. St Mark's Church 1976 (sm76)

Introduction

The Victorian church of St Mark was declared redundant in 1969, and demolished in 1972 (Fig. 13.1). Before the site was sold for redevelopment the Church Commissioners granted permission for excavation. The church sequence and part of the cemetery were investigated in a season of work from January until September 1976, and the Roman levels were excavated from April to October 1977. Overall direction was under Christina Colyer although the work on site was supervised by Michael Jones, together with Brian Gilmour from March 1976, for the Lincoln Archaeological Trust. Grants from the Manpower Services Commission and the Department of the Environment enabled the excavations to go ahead.

This was a large open area excavation (Fig. 13.2) but the area was not excavated to a uniform depth; the earliest levels were observed only in narrow slit-trenches (Fig. 13.5). Excavation of the mid Roman ditches (LUB 2) was made difficult by the fact that they were all well below the modern water-table. Roman levels were excavated in restricted areas (Fig. 13.27), partly because of the deep foundations of the later churches.

Interim reports were published (Jones *et al* 1976; Jones and Gilmour 1977; Gilmour and Jones 1978; Gilmour 1981). An interim discussion of the Roman houses was also published (Gilmour 1980). The excavation report on the post-Roman sequence, as interpreted by Brian Gilmour and David Stocker, was published in 1986 (Gilmour and Stocker 1986). Summaries of the human bone (Dawes 1986), the post-Roman pottery (Jennings and Young 1986), post-Roman registered finds (Mann 1986) and the church decorated window glass (King 1986) were published as part of the detailed publication of the church and cemetery, together with the post-Roman architectural fragments (Stocker 1986). Although only the Roman sequences remained to be published, it was decided to incorporate the post-Roman archaeological evidence into the current project's post-excavation framework in order to make the whole site available as part of the city-wide analysis. It soon become apparent that an integrated approach, linking the stratigraphic sequence with the structural aspects and the finds, allowed a new perspective on the interpretation of some aspects of the church sequence; however, the vast majority of Gilmour and Stocker's interpretations remain unchallenged.

Of the 2,794 contexts for the site, 2,726 were interpreted as 1,199 context groups and 9 were deemed unstratified. There were 555 Roman context groups (1,450 contexts) and 644 post-Roman context groups (1,276 contexts). Context group numbers from cg1–653 are mostly post-Roman with some designated as late or very late Roman (codes cg4, cg5, cg106, cg196, cg490 were not used). The Roman context groups were allocated numbers by area, the Roman site being divided into four Areas from north to south, Areas I to IV; each area was related to a building plot. The context group numbers in Area 1 cg1001–1041 are Roman (cg1012–1019 and cg1039 not used); context group numbers cg2000–2327 in Area II are Roman (cg2020, cg2223, cg2241, cg2269, cg2272, cg2285, cg2298 and cg2315 not used); in Area III context group numbers cg3000–3224 are Roman (cg3000–3025, cg3080–1, cg3099, cg3102, cg3104–5, cg3108, cg3116, cg3124, cg3135, cg3146 and cg3177 not used), and context group numbers cg4001–cg4015 in Area IV are Roman (cg4008 and cg4011–13 are not used). The context groups were interpreted as 87 LUBs (LUB 0–86) of which LUBs 1–40 were Roman and 41–86 post-Roman (Fig. 13.51). The LUB diagram for the Roman period (Fig. 13.3) has been divided into Areas I–IV, and for the post-Roman sequence (Fig. 13.4) is merely subdivided into north, central, and south. In Area I

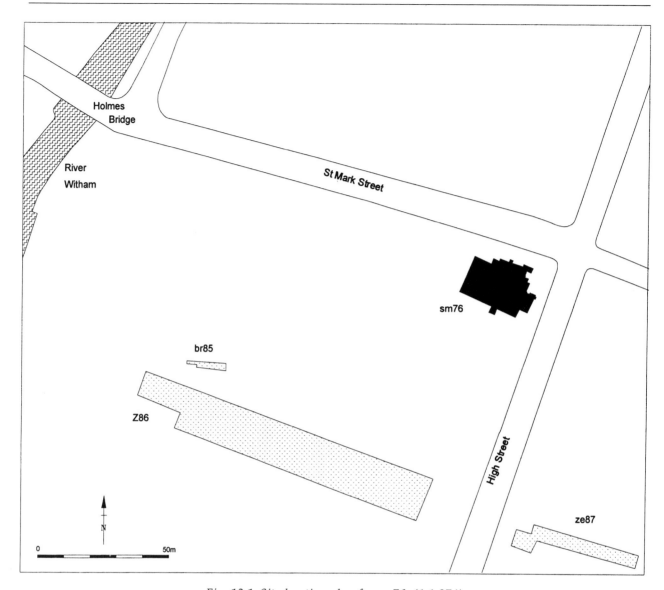

Fig. 13.1 Site location plan for sm76. (1:1,374)

there is a limited Roman sequence (LUBs 0, 1, 3, 13, 14, 31–35). In Area II Roman LUBs include natural (LUB 0), early Roman (LUB 1), mid Roman (LUBs 1–4, 6–8 and 14), late Roman (LUBs 15–23 and 35) and very late Roman LUBs (LUBs 38–39). In Area III there are early Roman (LUB 1), mid Roman (LUBs 2–5, 9–11 and 14), late Roman (LUBs 24–30 and 35) and very late Roman LUBs (LUB 40). In Area IV there is a limited Roman sequence (LUBs 12, 36 and 37). For the post-Roman period in the northern area of the site, are late Saxon to Saxo-Norman (LUBs 47–54), early medieval (LUBs 63–70), high medieval to post-medieval (LUBs 71–77) and modern LUBs (LUBs 79, 82, 84–6); in the central area of the site are late Saxon (LUBs 41–44, 46, 48 and 52), Saxo-Norman (LUBs 55–61), early medieval (LUB 63–4 and 67), high medieval to post-medieval (LUBs 68–

9 and 74), post-medieval (LUBs 75–6 and 78) and modern LUBs (LUBs 79–81, 83 and 85); and to the south of the site were late Saxon and later (LUBs 43, 45, 51 and 53) and modern LUBs (LUB 85).

There were 18,948 sherds of Roman pottery – the largest from any of the Wigford sites, and particularly important for the 3rd-century assemblage – and 2,370 sherds of post-Roman pottery from the site. A total of 3,025 registered finds was recovered. Many categories of the registered finds have been analysed by external specialists; worked bone (Rackham 1994), Roman brooches (Mackreth 1993), coins (Roman: Mann and Reece 1983; Davies 1992; Late Saxon: Blackburn *et al* 1983; medieval and later: Archibald 1994), vessel glass (Roman: Price and Cottam 1993f; medieval and later: Adams and Henderson 1995c), leather (Mould 1993), marble

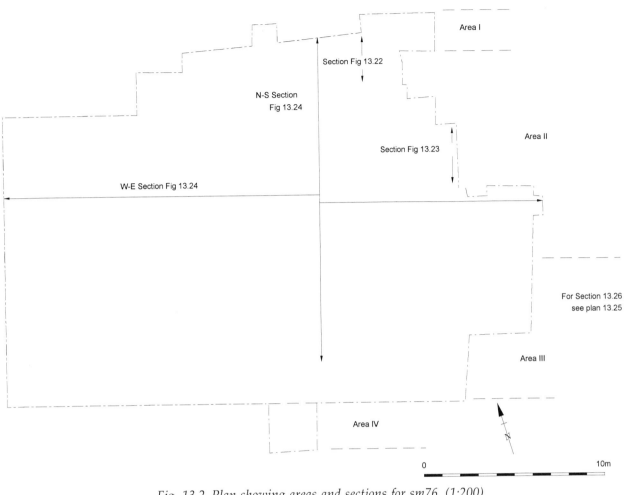

Fig. 13.2 Plan showing areas and sections for sm76. (1:200)

(Peacock and Williams 1992), precious stones (Hutchinson 1992), stone artefacts (Roe 1994; hones: Moore 1991), textile (Walton Rogers 1993) and wood (Morris 1994; Gale 1992). Unfortunately most of the nails and other coffin fittings were only briefly recorded and discarded during excavation; the presence of any early coffin elements cannot accordingly be determined. The precise location of the finds within the grave fills was not recorded, which means that it is even more difficult to determine whether an object was associated with the inhumation itself, was residual and part of the backfill, or was even intrusive. Amongst the building material (total of 10,915) from the site, there were 2,913 pieces of Roman tile, together with quantities of plaster, including Roman painted plaster (Long 1980), and some fragments of daub (stone identification: Roe 1994). Reference is also made here to architectural and sepulchral fragments from the published catalogue (Stocker 1986, 44–82): these constituted a very significant collection for the late 10th–early 11th century, by which time the

bishop's see was re-established and identified with Canterbury. It has since been further discussed, and possibly represents an expression by a booming mercantile community of identity with the Wessex Kings (Everson and Stocker, forthcoming).

The largest bone assemblage from Wigford (7,521 fragments) was recovered from this site and studied by K Dobney, A Milles, B Irving and D Jaques of the York Environmental Unit (Dobney *et al* 1994f). However, owing to the reworking of the site, a relatively small proportion of apparently well-dated Roman material, mostly that from the 3rd and 4th centuries, was available for detailed analysis. A small amount of additional material came from late Saxon and Saxo-Norman contexts. An earlier assessment of the animal bone was carried out by S Scott (Scott 1987). There were the remains of three Roman infants (Boylston and Roberts 1994). In all, 636 inhumations were recorded at the site, from the late Saxon, medieval and later cemetery; the skeletal remains were mostly studied by Jean Dawes (Dawes 1986), the rest by Boylston and Roberts (1994). The

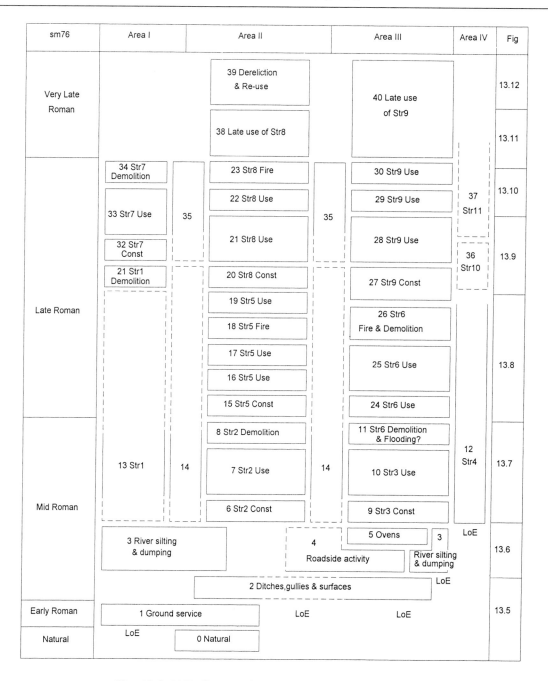

Fig. 13.3 LUB diagram for sm76 (Roman to Late Saxon).

land and freshwater snails recovered from the site have been studied (Milles 1994), as have the charred plant remains (Moffett 1993); the archive also contains an interim soil report (Taylor 1977).

The initial post-excavation stratigraphic analysis was undertaken by Brian Gilmour, who examined the Anglo-Scandinavian and later deposits (Gilmour and Stocker 1986); Kevin Camidge, having helped supervise the site recording, later analysed the Roman deposits, produced a matrix and a draft report which Paul Miles refined further. Although Kate Steane has subsequently re-examined the

Roman stratigraphy as well as the post-Roman evidence, Kevin Camidge's matrix provides the stratigraphic framework for the Roman part of the site. Jeremy Ashbee re-examined Buck's drawing of the porch. Maggi Darling worked on the Roman pottery and Jane Young on the post-Roman pottery. Jane Cowgill and Jen Mann analysed the registered finds and Jen Mann with Rick Kemp the building materials, and Pam Graves the stone. Rick Kemp, Helen Palmer Brown and Zoe Rawlings digitized the plans, and David Watt drew the finds illustrations.

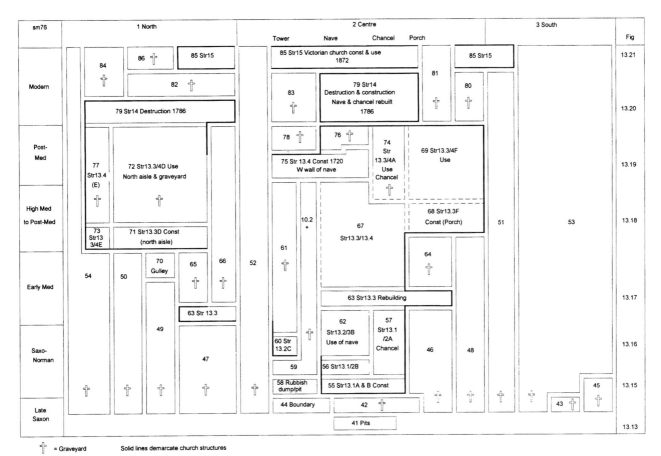

sm76	1 North	2 Centre	3 South	Fig

2 Centre headers: Tower · Nave · Chancel · Porch

Modern

84 †
86 †
85 Str15
82 †
79 Str14 Destruction 1786

85 Str15 Victorian church const & use 1872
83 †
79 Str14 Destruction & construction Nave & chancel rebuilt 1786
81
85 Str15
80 †   13.21

13.20

Post-Med

77 Str13.4 (E) †
72 Str13.3/4D Use North aisle & graveyard †

78 †
76 †
75 Str 13.4 Const 1720 W wall of nave
74 Str 13.3/4A Use Chancel †
69 Str13.3/4F Use

13.19

High Med to Post-Med

73 Str13 3/4E
71 Str13.3D Const (north aisle)

10.2 +
67 Str13.3/13.4
68 Str13.3F Const (Porch)
51
53   13.18

Early Med

54
50
70 Gulley
65 †
66
52
61 †
64 †

13.17
63 Str13.3 Rebuilding

49
63 Str 13.3

Saxo-Norman

47
60 Str 13.2C
62 Str13.2/3B Use of nave
57 Str13.1 /2A Chancel
46
48   13.16
59
56 Str13.1/2B

Late Saxon

† † † † †
58 Rubbish dump/pit
55 Str13.1A & B Const
44 Boundary
42 †
43 †
45   13.15

41 Pits   13.13

† = Graveyard   Solid lines demarcate church structures

Fig. 13.4 LUB diagram for sm76 (church).

2002

2011

2004

3054

3061   3063   3044

3063

0   10m

Fig. 13.5 Ditches, gullies and surfaces: LUBs 2. (1:200)

Interpretation of the sequence of events

Natural

Natural sand **LUB 0** was recovered at 3.1m OD.

LUB 0 Natural
Natural on the site consisted of clean light yellow
sand cg2000. This was located in many of the "slit"
trenches in Areas I and II. It lay *c* 4.0m below
modern ground level and at a height of 3.0m to
3.5m above OD.

Early Roman

There was evidence for a ground surface **LUB 1**,
possibly dating before the mid 2nd century, on the
basis of a few sherds of pottery in subsequent LUBs.

LUB 1 Ground surface
In Area I at the limit of excavation was sand and
pebbles cg1001, sealed by dumps of clay, pebbles
and ash, over which was a turf line cg1002. Pottery
from these layers (15 sherds) was undiagnostic, but
they were sealed by cg1003 (LUB 3), containing
pottery which suggests a date after the early 2nd
century.

Immediately on top of natural sand cg2000 (LUB
0) in Area II, there was a thin organic layer cg2001;
it was interpreted as "old soil profile" at the time of
excavation and probably represented a ground
surface.

Sealing natural cg2000 (LUB 0), also in Area II,
was dark grey sand layer cg2005, presumably
redeposited because it contained a fragment of a
millstone grit rotary quern (DDN) and two body
sherds which were not closely datable. It seems
likely that both the organic layer cg2001 and the
grey layer cg2005 were both part of a ground
surface. The dating of subsequent deposits (LUBs 2
and 3) suggests that the dark grey layer cg2005
dated to before the mid 2nd century.

The 17 sherds from this LUB were largely non-
diagnostic, and the dating is provided essentially
by the stratigraphic position of the LUB at the
bottom of the sequence.

Mid Roman

There were north–south ditches and gullies at the
west end of the site, and at the east end, by Ermine
Street, were metalled surfaces **LUB 2**; mid to late
2nd-century pottery was associated. The ditches
LUB 2 silted up to the west of the site **LUB 3**,
associated with late 2nd- to early 3rd-century
pottery, while roadside activity, possibly including
smithing, continued to the east **LUB 4**; a stone

volume measure was recovered from associated
layers. Pottery associated with LUB 4 dated from
the late 2nd–3rd century, with one group of the early
3rd century. Sealing LUB 3 to the south of the site
there were ovens, layers **LUB 5** which possibly
represent the remains of baking, perhaps serving
the passing custom of Ermine Street; associated
pottery was residual.

In Area II a timber, aisled 'strip' building, Structure 2, was erected **LUB 6**; there were traces of
internal surfaces, divisions and hearths **LUB 7**.
Although pottery from its construction was dated
to between the early and mid 3rd century, pottery
from its use dated to the mid 3rd century. Structure
2 was demolished **LUB 8**; the pottery from this event
dated to the mid 3rd century.

In Area III a similar building, Structure 3, was
erected **LUB 9** to the south of Structure 2. The post-
pits for this building were more substantial than
those of Structure 2 and contained pottery which
suggested a mid 3rd-century date. There were traces
of internal surfaces, divisions and ovens **LUB 10**;
some of the pottery dated to the mid 3rd century. It
was demolished **LUB 11**, and its site may have been
flooded. Over the silty deposits, there was clear
evidence of re-use of its site soon afterwards with
the construction of Structure 6 (LUB 24).

In Area IV there were layers **LUB 12**, which were
probably internal to a timber strip-building, Structure 4, to the south of Structure 3. 3rd-century
pottery indicates that these layers were of a similar
date to the buildings to the north.

In Area I, sealing the river silting LUB 3, were
traces of a building, Structure 1, with timber partitions **LUB 13**; sparse pottery suggests a mid 3rd-
century date. Between buildings 1 and 2, and
between buildings 2 and 3, were quantities of
building debris **LUB 14** which contained mid 3rd-
century pottery.

LUB 2 Ditches, gullies and surfaces
(Figs. 13.5 and 13.28)
At the limit of excavation in Area III was a layer of
ashy silt cg3043, including a stake-hole. This was
sealed by fairly extensive patches of rough limestone
cg3044; sealing cg2001 (LUB 1) in Area II was rough
limestone cg2002. These limestone patches were
located towards the eastern end of the site adjacent
to Ermine Street. Although fairly uneven in places,
cg3044 and cg2002 exhibited signs of wear, the
upper surfaces of the stones being smooth.

The ashy silt and stake-hole cg3043 may represent
traces of roadside activity. The stone surfaces cg3044
and cg2002 possibly indicate hard-standing for
roadside booths or stalls beside Ermine Street.

Further west, there were several cut features of
varying sizes aligned roughly north–south. North–

south gullies cg3045 and cg3047 (both 0.10m deep) were recorded at the limit of excavation in Area III.

Pale yellow sand with black organic material cg3049, at the limit of excavation in Area III, was sealed by dark, thick compact clay cg3050; this material was cut by ditch cg3054 (c 1.0m deep). At the limit of excavation, to the west of Area III, was a clay layer cg3060; this layer contained just six sherds of samian, closing with a Dr 37 of c AD 150– 180. About 4m west of ditch cg3054 and cutting clay cg3060 was ditch cg3063 (c 1.0m deep), with pottery from the ditch (14 sherds) possibly dating to the mid to late 2nd century. Ditch cg2011, cutting cg2005 (LUB 1) in Area II, may be the slightly narrower continuation of the same ditch. Ditch cg3063 was recut cg3064 (unplanned); pottery from recut ditch cg3064 (19 sherds) possibly dated to the mid to late 2nd century. Farthest to the west and also cutting cg3060 was ditch cg3061 (c 0.40m deep) in Area III, which continued as ditch cg2004 at the limit of excavation in Area II. An environmental sample was taken from ditch fill cg3061. Molluscs from the sample indicate that it was originally waterlogged and contained abundant freshwater snails. These finds support the suggestion that the context was a ditch with some flowing water (Milles 1994). Seeds from the sample, however, suggest a small admixture of material from human activity, in the form of fruit stones and hazel nutshell fragments, but were seeds of plants living in disturbed ground and wet habitats. Cultivated plant seeds were scarce (Moffett 1993).

The series of ditches and gullies all ran parallel to the road and the river. The ditch fills contained a small quantity of fragments from Roman leather shoes of nailed construction, together with parts of a one-piece shoe and a small quantity of primary and secondary waste from the manufacture of one-piece shoes (Mould 1993).

The 46 sherds from this LUB came from just a few context groups, cg3050, cg3060, cg3061, cg3063, cg3064; pottery from cg3060, cg3063 and cg3064 indicates that this LUB possibly dated to around the mid to late 2nd century.

LUB 3 River silting and dumping (Fig. 13.23)
In Area I, sealing turf line cg1002 (LUB 1), were interleaved layers of waterlain sand cg1003; of the three sherds of pottery from this sand, the only dating evidence was the presence of BB1, indicating a date after c AD120.

In Area II, sealing the cobbles cg2002 (LUB 2), were layers of waterlain sand cg2003 overlain by peaty silt cg2007, and further sand cg2008, suggesting that the ditches had not been effective in keeping the river at bay, and that flood levels had crept towards the road, if not over it. At the limit of excavation

were other river sand deposits cg2009 and cg2010. Ditch cg2004 was sealed by dark silty peat and sand cg2006. Over this and the fill of ditch cg2011 (LUB 2) was waterlain sand cg2012.

Undescribed layer cg1041 between Areas and I and II probably belongs to this LUB.

In Area III there was a similar pattern. Over surface cg3044 (LUB 2) and gully cg3045 (LUB 2) was a thick layer of black decomposed organic material and clayey mud cg3046. Over this and sealing gully cg3047 (LUB 2) was a thick sticky grey clay deposit with sand cg3048. Cutting into this material was a posthole cg3052 (unplanned), possibly an attempt to control the flooding; sealing cg3048 was grey clay cg3051. Sealing clay cg3051 and clay cg3050 (LUB 2) were layers of sand, black decomposed organic material and dark brown clay cg3053 which was sealed, as was ditch cg3054 (LUB 2), by sand and further deposits of organic material cg3055.

There were similar sequences in other parts of Area III. At the limit of the excavation was a peaty deposit sealed by sand, peat, sandy silt and silt cg3058. Sand cg3049 (LUB 2) was sealed by grey/ black organic material, over which was silty clay and sand cg3056 sealed by layers of silty sand cg3057. Ditch cg3061 (LUB 2) was cut by a small pit cg3062; sealing the pit and ditch cg3064 (LUB 2) was silty sand cg3065, over which was dark grey silty "slime", sandy silt and sandy clay cg3066 followed by dark grey sandy silt cg3067. Also sealing sand cg3065 was brown sand cg3068.

Soil samples from cg3046, cg3061 and cg3065 contained the remains of plants which derived partly from wet, marshy ground and partly from better-drained soils. The presence of coriander in cg3065 may possibly suggest the presence of some form of horticulture, but evidence for human intervention is otherwise sparse – suggesting that it was more likely that it represented an area of waste land (Moffett 1993).

A small quantity of leather was preserved in these waterlain deposits, reflecting the use of the river as a dump; the leather included primary and secondary shoe making waste. There were also small fragments from a sheep/goatskin one-piece shoe, fragments of a nailed bottom unit and a child's one-piece shoe (Mould 1993). Small quantities of animal bone had been washed up or dumped in the river margins; a small assemblage was recovered from dump cg2006 with horse remains, possibly from one individual; horse remains also dominated a small assemblage from mud cg3046, where there was evidence of possible butchery marks on one of the horse bones (Dobney et al 1994f).

The pottery (379 sherds) from LUB 3, was dated to around the late 2nd to early 3rd century by sherds from cg2008, cg2010 and cg3058. Slightly later sherds were present in cg3066, including a MOMH mortarium, a grey folded beaker and a NVCC folded scaled beaker sherd; there was also a sherd of the NVCC beaker from cg3067.

LUB 4 Roadside Activity
(Figs. 13.6, 13.29 and 13.50)
At the limit of excavation in Area II, to the east of the site, was dark brown ashy sand cg2013. This was cut by a posthole with stone packing cg2304 (unplanned) which was sealed by sand and gravel cg2305. Cutting this layer was a posthole cg2307 and a shallow scoop cg2306. These were in turn sealed by ashy sand and charcoal flecks cg2310. Further east, at the limit of excavation, ashy sand cg2308 was cut by pit cg2286 (only part of which survived), which in turn was cut by pit cg2309. Layer cg2310 was sealed by sand and pebbles cg2311. There was no record of what pit cg2312 cut, but, together with sand and pebbles cg2311 and pit cg2309, it was sealed by grey brown ashy silt and sand which included some cobbling cg2014, sealed by a layer of brown sand cg2313 which was possibly cut by posthole cg2314 (unplanned).

To the south, small pit cg2284 to the east of Area II (there was no record of what it cut, except that it was a sand layer) produced a small assemblage of mid to late 2nd- to early 3rd-century pottery and an illegible 3rd- or 4th-century coin. Other finds included iron slag and iron objects, including nails, an unidentified fragment and part of a T-clamp. The presence of hammerscale suggests that these objects may be associated with smithing, perhaps on site. Nearby was posthole cg2025 (no record of what it cut; unplanned).

Large pit cg2294 near to the east end of Area II may relate to this phase (there was no record of what it cut as it was truncated by a much later feature; unplanned). It contained closely-packed limestone rubble with patches of peaty material.

Sealing sand and organic deposits cg3055 (LUB 3) to the east of Area III was a layer of mixed sand, ash and silt cg3042; this, together with sandy silt cg3057 (LUB 3), was sealed by many shallow/ narrow layers cg3077 of sandy clay with ash and silt and even a mortar layer. Sitting on layers cg3077 was a curious limestone block cg3079 (Fig. 13.29). This measured *c* 1.10m x 0.40m x 0.25m and had two, different-sized cup-shaped depressions in its upper face. The most likely explanation is that this was a measure of volume – a variation on the *mensa ponderaria*, a stone table normally sited close to the forum, whose top possessed a certain number of cavities designed to serve as standard measures for the users of the market place. Such tables are known at Tivoli, Pompeii, and Nyon (Rey-Vodoz 1994).

So there was evidence for activity to the east of the site in the form of possible surfaces, pits and postholes. These features indicate a continuity of roadside activity.

Of the 220 pottery sherds from LUB 4, much was residual, but there were also sherds from cg2014, cg2294, cg2309 and cg2310 which dated from the late 2nd century into the 3rd, and pottery sherds from cg2313 which dated to the early 3rd century.

LUB 5 Oven and hearth (Figs. 13.6 and 13.30)
Towards the south side of the site, in Area III, cutting cg3068 (LUB 3), was a small circular domestic baking oven. Constructed of clay with a surviving raised outer lip cg3073, presumably the remnants of the clay dome superstructure, the flue cg3072 of the oven extended eastwards into the trench section. The oven had fallen into disuse; its surviving shell had a fill of ash silt, some burnt clay and small tile fragments cg3074. Contemporary with the oven was sand layer cg3069 (0.04m thick; no record of what it sealed); it was sealed by a sequence of layers which probably related to rakeouts from the oven – ash and charcoal mixed with silt and sand cg3070. After the oven was no longer used, yellow sand layers cg3071 sealed cg3070. Sealing layers cg3071 were layers of thick black ash and sand cg3075.

Cutting sandy silt cg3067 (LUB 3) was a clay-bonded limestone hearth base cg3076 (Fig. 13.30) with much burnt clay; there was an additional limestone side to the west, and the whole structure was sealed by red sandy clay with pebbles, possibly a collapsed superstructure.

Sandy gravel cg3178, to the south of the site, probably belongs to this LUB; set in cg3178 was an area of limestones cg3040. These layers were probably surfaces contemporary with the oven.

The oven and hearth were probably associated with a structure for which no evidence survives. The pottery (89 sherds) from this LUB was residual.

LUB 6 Construction of Structure 2 (Fig. 13.7)
The only surviving evidence for the external timber walls of Structure 2 consisted of two adjacent, stone-lined post-pits of the north wall cg2031 and cg2301, both of which cut layer cg1041 (LUB 3). A post-pipe 0.15m across and square in section was recorded in cg2031. The lines of the external walls are assumed to have followed, and their remains obliterated by, the stone walls of later structures – the later footings were relatively shallow at the point where the post-pits cg2031 survived.

Over waterlain sand cg2012 (LUB 2) was a dump of sand with small fragments of stone and tile cg2033, over which was a layer of clay, sand, silt and ash cg2034. At the limit of excavation was a posthole cg2023; both it and layer cg2034 were

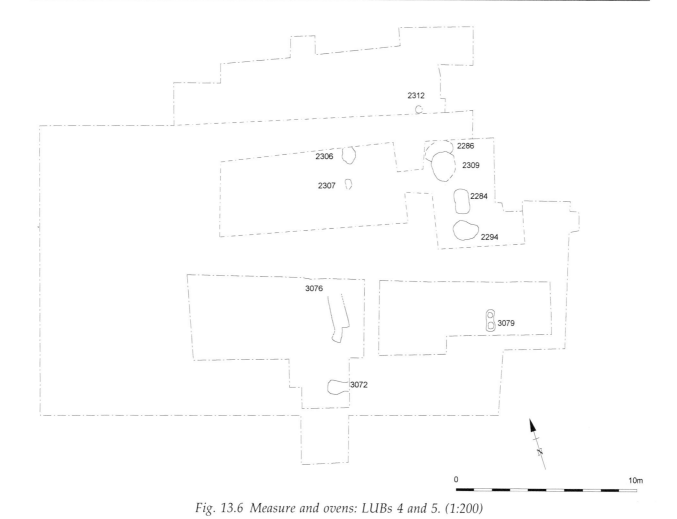

Fig. 13.6 Measure and ovens: LUBs 4 and 5. (1:200)

sealed by a thin layer of olive-brown sand cg2036, probably a construction surface. Over waterlain sand cg2008 (LUB 3) was a dump of orange sand cg2328.

Within the building, at the limit of excavation, there were traces of stone-packed postholes, cg2026, cg2288, cg2041, cg2289 and cg2290 aligned east–west in a line about 2m south of post-pits cg2031 and cg2301. About 4m to their south was another line of stone-packed postholes, cg2039, cg2299, cg2293, cg2295, cg2297, cg2302, cg2300, cg2032 and cg2037 (cg2032 is unplanned); postholes cg2039, cg2302 and cg2293 cut sand layer cg2036; posthole cg2300 cut cg2328, and posthole cg2026 probably cut sand cg2009 (LUB 3), whereas the rest of the postholes were recovered at the limit of the excavation. The two internal lines of postholes suggest an aisled timber structure. The layout of the postholes may imply more than one phase of construction, or perhaps just a series of replacements to prop up the roof.

Posthole cg2314 and sand cg2313 (both LUB 4) were sealed by a thick layer (up to 0.30m thick) of mixed burnt and unburnt clay with fragments of burnt and unburnt limestone cg2015. The thick layer of burnt and unburnt material cg2015 was probably a dump of material to build up the site above the flood level. Cutting cg2015 was a pit cg2018 (unplanned) with a fill of ashy sandy loam.

Traces of the south and west walls of the timber building were probably cut away by subsequent stone walls; the front (east) wall lay somewhere under the modern High Street.

The pottery (401 sherds) was mostly residual, but pottery sherds from construction layer cg2036 and posthole cg2039 suggest that Structure 2 may have been constructed between the early and mid 3rd century. A colour-coated triangular rim bowl from cg2033 seems more likely to be of mid 3rd-century date.

LUB 7 Occupation and internal details of Structure 2 (Figs. 13.7 and 13.23)
Sealing sand layer cg2036 (LUB 6) in Area II was a thin, compact layer of limestone chippings, clay and

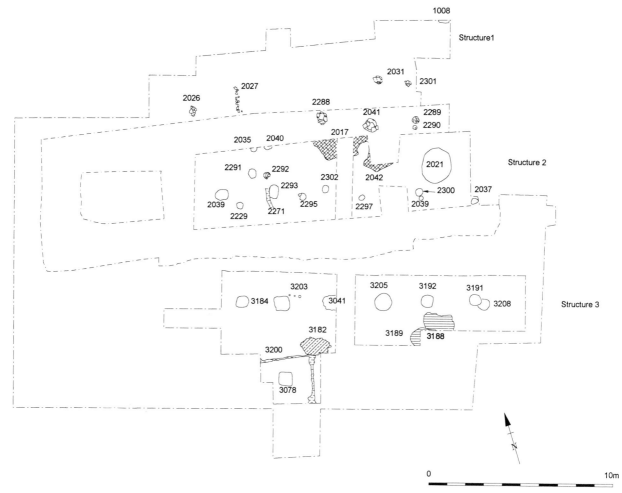

Fig. 13.7 Structures 2 and 3: LUBs 6, 7, 9 and 10. (1:200)

tile fragments cg2038, possibly an internal surface. Cutting cg2036 (LUB 6) were four stone-packed postholes cg2035, cg2040, cg2291 and cg2292. Surface cg2038 may have been cut by north–south slot cg2271 (there was no record of what this slot cut), which ran to the west of posthole cg2293 (LUB 6), and possibly up to posthole cg2292; this might suggest that there was a north–south internal division with a doorway.

Over sand cg2009 (LUB 3), in the north-west part of the building, was a north–south line of rubble cg2027, possibly the base for a timber-framed partition within Structure 2.

Pit cg2018 (LUB 6) was cut by a large pit cg2042 with a fill of packed limestone rubble set in sand, possibly the base of a central, floor-level hearth. Sealing dump cg2015 (LUB 6) and cg2042 was a thin trample layer of dark ashy sand cg2016. Over sand cg2016 (LUB 6) was an area of clean sand into which pitched stones had been set cg2017; these possibly represented the remains of a second, floor-level hearth. Sealing both pit cg2018 (LUB 6) and cg2017 was a layer of sand, pebbles and limestone chips

over which was the patchy remains of a soot layer cg2019 and cg2029. Within layer cg2019 were the remains of an infant of approximately 38 weeks gestation (Boylston and Roberts 1994). Cutting this layer was a large circular pit cg2021; flat limestones sealed the centre base of the pit and around them were stake-holes (unplanned). Pit cg2021 had a fill of limestone rubble, sand, charcoal and ash together with hammerscale and some nails. Over layer cg2019 was a patch of greenish-brown sand with ash cg2028.

Sealing both layers cg2028 and cg2029 was metalled surface cg2030 of pebbles, tiles and stones, which showed signs of wear, and in patches signs of burning. Over the east part of the building, sealing pit cg2021, was a layer of limestone rubble and tile fragments in greenish-brown sand cg2022; there were many fragments of burnt building debris together with slag. This layer was cut by a stone-packed post-pit cg2296 (unplanned).

Sealing post-pit cg2296 and earlier post-pit cg2297 (LUB 6) were the patchy remains of cobbles cg2024 in the eastern part of the building.

The majority of the accessioned finds from the building were nails. The function of the layers within the building is often unclear, and much of the material may therefore have been introduced into the building as floor make-up, a suggestion supported by the incorporation of fragments of brick and tile within many of the layers.

Much of the pottery (397 sherds in total) from LUB 7 was residual. The coarse pottery included no shell-tempered dales ware or dales ware types. From cg2019, cg2028 and cg2029 there were sherds which suggested a mid 3rd-century date; these were sherds from folded beakers in both GREY and NVCC, BB1 and GREY cooking pots which were of forms consistent with a mid 3rd-century date. There were sherds from several wide-mouthed bowls, particularly from floor cg2029, which also produced a NVCC sherd, possibly from a flagon. The first fragments of TILE vessels occurred in cg2042, but as it cut earlier levels, there is a possibility that it derived from underlying dumps of material imported on to the site.

LUB 8 Demolition and abandonment? of Structure 2
(Fig. 13.23)
Sealing the major postholes of Structure 2 and others (cg2024, cg2025, cg2035 cg2037, cg2038, cg2039, cg2040, cg2291, cg2292, cg2293, cg2295, cg2299, cg2300 and cg2302 – all LUBs 6 and 7) in Area II were layers cg2054; these consisted of a dump (0.05m–0.10m thick) of sandy loam with limestone fragments and charcoal flecks, over which was a cobbled floor.

Sealing the external postholes cg2030 and cg2031 (LUB 6) was a layer of sand sealed by a spread of smooth flat stones cg2059 (c 0.05m thick). Sealing post-pit cg2026 and slot cg2027 (both LUB 7) were dumps of sand with pebbles cg2049 (0.10m–0.20m thick), over which was a further dump cg2050.

Although there was no record of what these layers sealed, it was considered that sandy layers cg2073 (0.05m–0.10m thick) belonged to this LUB. Pale yellowish-brown compact sandy layer cg2077 may well relate to this LUB, although there was no record of what the layer sealed.

An area of light grey sandy ash and clayey charcoal cg2071 (0.24m thick), towards the west end of Structure 2, was associated with this LUB, but there was no record of what it sealed; thick layers of ash tend to suggest a period of abandonment or demolition.

The pottery (955 sherds in total) was mostly residual. There were joins back to earlier LUBs (cg2054 had links to cg2014 LUB 4, cg2033 LUB 6 and cg2036 LUB 6; cg2059 had links with cg2033 LUB 6 and cg2019 LUB 7). The residual pottery sherds also had joins between context groups (cg2054 had sherd links with cg2059); scrappy residual pottery sherds were recovered from cg2054. The latest sherds from this LUB came from context groups cg2049, cg2050, and cg2059 and dated to around the mid 3rd century.

LUB 9 Construction of Structure 3
(Figs. 13.7, 13.30)
No trace of the external walls of Structure 3 in Area III was found due to the very deep footings of the later stone building (Structure 6, LUB 24), but aisle post-pits were recovered. Along the northern side of the building was evidence for six substantial posts; two post-pits cg3184 (there was no record of what these cut; Fig. 13.30), post-pit cg3041 which cut the demolition of oven cg3076 (LUB 5), post-pit cg3205 (no record of what it cut), post-pit cg3192 which cut layers cg3077 (LUB 4) and post-pit cg3208 which also cut layers cg3077 (LUB 4), but which was replaced by post-pit cg3191 which cut it. A single post from the south aisle posts cg3078 (Fig. 13.30) was excavated; this cut layers cg3178 (LUB 5). Each post-pit had a substantial pad-stone in the base. Surviving post sockets were c 0.20m square.

The aisle posts were constructed in parallel rows, leaving a central space c 4.0m between the rows of aisle posts. It has been assumed from the relationship with Structure 2 that the aisle posts were set c 2.0m in from the outside walls. The east wall (fronting on to Ermine Street) probably lay 3m to 6m outside the excavated area. The western end of the building probably lay some 2m to 3m to the west of the excavated area, by analogy with Structure 2 to the north. The building would therefore have been c 8m wide; its length is more difficult to assess.

Sealing limestones cg3040 (LUB 5) to the south-west of the building were silty sand layers cg3179, cut by stake-hole cg3204 (unplanned) and layers of sandy silty ash cg3180, cut by a posthole cg3181 (unplanned). An assemblage of iron finds was recovered from cg3180. This consisted of a minimum of fifteen nails, three double spiked-loops including one adhering to a ?box/furniture handle and another of similar size found with it, and a smaller double spiked-loop. Perhaps these finds related to either the construction of the building or to internal fittings.

The pottery from this LUB (83 sherds in total) was mostly residual, except for a NVCC scaled folded beaker sherd dating to the mid 3rd century or later from postpit cg3184. Stratigraphically it would seem that the early to mid 3rd century was probable for this LUB; (the dating for its use – LUB 10 starts in the mid 3rd century).

LUB 10 Internal details of Structure 3
(Figs. 13.7 and 13.30)
At the west end of Structure 3 in Area III, sealing silty peat deposits cg3058 (LUB 3), was sandy silt

with limestone chips, and a greenish mortar layer cg3059, probably make-up and surface related to Structure 3. Coarse pottery from cg3059 included sherds from a GREY cooking pot of mid 3rd-century type, a GREY flagon, dales ware jar and lid-seated jar J107, sherds with burnished vertical line decoration, NVCC undecorated cornice-rimmed beaker and a basal sherd from a rouletted beaker, and a dales ware rim, all suggesting a mid 3rd-century date.

Sealing cg3180 (LUB 9) in the centre of the building, between the lines of aisle posts, was a small area of smooth flat limestones cg3182, perhaps a brazier stand probably pre-dating the insertion of the wooden partitions cg3200 (see below). Also sealing cg3180 (LUB 9) was a small patch of mixed burnt clay cg3183.

The south-western of the building was partitioned off. The partitions were indicated by two grooves or very slight beam slots cg3200 (Fig. 13.30) which cut cg3179 (LUB 9). These were only 0.10m at their widest and some 0.05m deep. They were probably no more than light timber partitions built directly on the floor. Subsequent refloorings then built up against them forming the shallow slots. The room thus formed would have been about 2.80m wide (north to south) and at least 3.0m long. How this partition functioned with aisle post cg3078 (LUB 9) in position is uncertain.

In the north of the room, compacted sand floor cg3039 was laid over the demolished remains of oven cg3076 (LUB 5). It ended in a straight line suggesting another (north-to-south) partition perhaps linking up with the north–south partition cg3200. No trace of a similar groove or small slot was found, but the sharp and straight edge to this floor probably indicates a floor-level timber partition. Cutting floor cg3039 was a series of stake-holes cg3203.

To the east of sand floor cg3039, sealing stone cg3079 (LUB 5), were layers of sand with pebbles and stone (c 0.15m thick in all) cg3185, sealed by a floor-level oven of compact clay cg3188; around it, sealing layers cg3077 (LUB 4) was an area of ash cg3186; cutting those layers was a posthole cg3207 (unplanned). The oven cg3188 had an oval, oxidised clay base c 1.0m in diameter, with limestone fragments used in the base and within the clay of the outer walls, and a narrow (0.15m) raised lip at its circumference, possibly the remains of a clay superstructure. Indications were that a short flue/stoke-hole extended westwards from the bowl of the oven. The hearth was demolished cg3187 and sealed by pieces of tile set in clay, the base for an oven of yellow clay with a circular rim cg3189. This was slightly larger in diameter (by perhaps 0.20m), and of similar construction, but without limestones in

the clay. The circular oven may have had a domed superstructure; it was also probably operated from the east but this section lay under the baulk.

Further east, with no record of what they sealed, were several layers of sand, ash and peaty debris, overlain by a limestone floor cg3190, which extended around the posts in the north-east of the building; this floor was presumably designed for heavy use, perhaps as a working surface for the ovens. There was also a posthole cg3206 (no record of what it cut; unplanned) which may have been associated with the ovens.

There were 157 sherds from this LUB. The pottery (67 sherds) from layer cg3059 dated to the mid 3rd century, although the rest of the sherds from cg3185, cg3190 and cg3203 were residual.

LUB 11 Demolition and flooding? of Structure 3
In the north-east part of Structure 3, in Area III, post-pits cg3192, cg3205 and cg3191 (LUB 9), together with postholes cg3206 and cg3207, remains of the oven cg3189 and limestone surface cg3190 (all LUB 10) were sealed by a layer of dark grey-brownish sandy silt cg3036 (c 0.10m thick); probably equivalent to greyish-brown sandy silt cg3086 (also c 0.10m thick; no record of what it sealed). In the west part of the building, over post-pits cg3078, cg3184 and cg3041 (LUB 9) partition lines cg3200, stake-holes cg3203, burnt clay cg3183 and limestone patch cg3182 (all LUB 10) was a layer of sandy silt with charcoal flecks cg3038; this was probably equivalent to grey-brown silty sand cg3094 (no record of what it sealed).

The preponderance of silt layers sealing the site suggests that perhaps the building suffered inundation, and its floors became covered with a layer of river silt.

There were 319 pottery sherds altogether from this LUB; most of the pottery (including sherds from silt cg3038 and silt cg3086) was residual from the use of Structure 3, except for one sherd of CC DPR from silt cg3036 which was probably an intrusive 4th-century sherd.

LUB 12 Structure 4 (Fig. 13.8)
At the limit of excavation in Area IV was a layer of sand cg4001, sealed by limestone rubble cg4002, possibly a make-up layer to build up the ground level. Sealing rubble cg4002 were several layers cg4003: sandy loam layers with a thin mortar spread were sealed by a thin layer of sand and clay, over which was a scatter of limestones, sealed by silty loam with charcoal flecks, over which was yellow sandy mortar. These layers probably indicate the remains of an internal floor sequence of a structure in the southern part of the site. Pottery from cg4003 (36 sherds) contained a sherd of BB1 cooking pot probably of mid 3rd-century type.

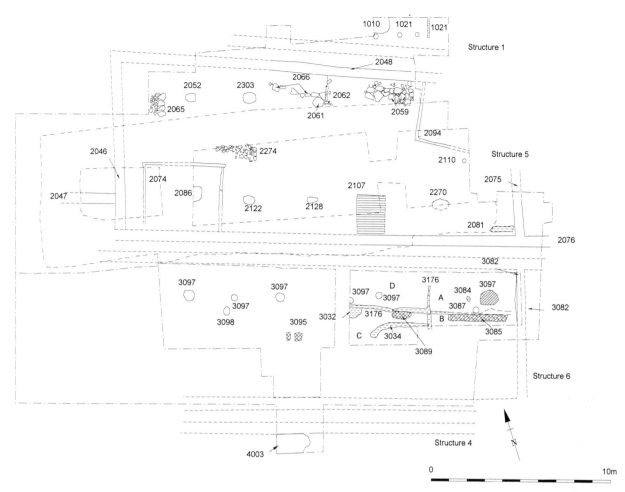

Fig. 13.8 Structures 1, 5 and 6: LUBs 13, 15, 16, 17, 18, 19, 25 and 26. (1:200)

There were 40 sherds of pottery from this LUB, 4 sherds from cg4001 and the rest from cg4003. The pottery from cg4003 could be broadly dated to the 3rd century, indicating that these layers were generally of similar date to the buildings to the north.

LUB 13 Structure 1 (Fig. 13.8)
Sealing sand cg1003 (LUB 3) were sandy layers cg1005; cut into these layers was a slight feature which contained the poorly-preserved remains of an infant of about 38 weeks gestation (unplanned; Boylston and Roberts 1994). It was sealed by a spread of clay daub in lumps cg1004; over this was a layer of sand cg1006 (0.20m thick). A folded scaled beaker sherd in cg1006 was of a later NVCC fabric; a mid 3rd-century or later date seems indicated.

Sand cg1006 was sealed by a layer of sandy yellow mortar with a greenish crust cg1007. Cutting through this was the possible slot of a timber partition cg1008, with an upper fill of burnt timber (unplanned). The slot terminated half way across the trench, perhaps indicating a doorway. It ran

parallel to and *c* 2m from the postulated external south wall, which must have occupied the same position as the later stone wall cg1025 (LUB 32).

The slot was sealed by an area of ashy grey deposit with charcoal flecks cg1009, into which were set the stones of a small hearth cg1010; around this was a spread of clay cg1011, burnt near the hearth. They were sealed by a sequence of layers cg1020: an ashy spread with crushed tile and mortar fragments, over which was a spread of sandy pale brown mortar with pebble inclusions, sealed by another sandy floor. Layers cg1020 probably represented fire ash and mortar floors.

New internal partitions cg1021 were constructed. They consisted of two beam slots *c* 0.12m wide and 0.05m deep at right-angles to each other (and three postholes which may have been associated with the beam slots). These cut the latest mortar floors cg1020, but may have been part of a contemporary structure. The east–west beam slot was right against the later stone wall cg1025 (LUB 32): if the external wall of this building lay somewhere under the position of the stone wall then this partition can have been no more than 1.0m from the wall.

Sealing partition cg1021 was a spread of burnt and collapsed timber (0.04m thick) sealed by a thin layer of ash cg1022. The burning suggests that at least part of the structure caught fire. Within the fill of beam slots cg1021 and amongst the burnt timber remains of the partitions, an ?awl (BQH) <SM77:B19> was found. The handle is made from shed antler with an almost square-sectioned piece of iron inserted. The working tip of the tool had been broken. The handle shows no sign of burning, so the object may have been used in work subsequent to the fire.

Cut through the burnt layer cg1022 were three substantial postholes cg1023, (0.25m wide and *c* 0.20m deep). These were aligned east–west, *c* 1.0m north of the supposed external wall and spaced about 1.5m apart. It seems likely that they represent an internal aisle, part of a substantial re-building.

Of the six sherds from this LUB, one undiagnostic sherd came from layers cg1005, and five sherds were found in sand cg1006, with one dating to the mid to later 3rd century.

LUB 14 Deposits between structures (Fig. 13.22)
Sealing layer cg1041 (LUB 3) in Area I, was a series of deposits cg1037 lying in the narrow (0.85m) space between the stone walls of Structures 1 and 2, (between Areas I and II); these consisted of brownish gritty loam with shell which was sealed by sandy loam, greenish in places, sand, crushed tile and burnt clay and reddish grey-brown compact loamy earth. Mid 3rd-century pottery was recovered from layer cg1037 (108 sherds), including shell-tempered dales ware, sherds from NVCC funnel-necked folded beakers, and a possible flagon or flask sherd.

Layers cg1037 were sealed by sand layer cg1038. Within cg1038 were two nails with a small amount of hammerscale and slag amongst the corrosion products, possibly churned up from underlying levels by the construction trenches for the walls.

Between Structures 5 and 6, walls cg2076 (LUB 14) and cg3082 (LUB 19), were layers cg2267. These were not described in the site record; they contained mid 3rd-century pottery.

There were 239 pottery sherds from this LUB, some of which broadly dated to the 3rd century (cg1038 – 9 sherds). Layers cg1037 and cg2267 were dated to the mid 3rd century by the pottery.

Late Roman

Subsequent to the demolition of Structure 2 (LUB 8) in Area II, another building, Structure 5, was erected on the same plan **LUB 15**; this was a stone-founded building with aisle posts, fronting on to Ermine Street. Its construction was dated by the pottery and on stratigraphic grounds to between the mid 3rd and the late 3rd century. The building contained flagstones and other floor surfaces, an oven at the north side, timber partitions including a painted plaster-lined room and possibly a shed to the rear; these features form **LUB 16**. A new partitioned room, cobbles and other surfaces, together with an oven on the south, form the redesigned plan **LUB 17**. The latest material from LUB 17 included a reworked 4th-century glass vessel and a few sherds of pottery which may date into the 4th century. Evidence was found for a fire in Structure 5 **LUB 18**, stratigraphically dating to the early 4th century, but the fire did not precipitate its demolition; it continued in use **LUB 19**. There were further internal alterations, another oven and several clay floors; LUB 19 is dated by a coin and the stratigraphic sequence to the 4th century.

Structure 5 was then replaced by Structure 8 **LUB 20**; new walls were built on the foundations of the old structure. LUB 20 dates stratigraphically to the early(?) 4th century. Internally the building had a metalled surface, a mortar floor, flagstones, the remains of a substantial oven and indications of others, a rear extension containing a pot-pit and evidence of a wall prop against the north wall; these features make up **LUB 21** which is dated by the pottery roughly to the 4th century. The north wall of Structure 8 was partially rebuilt **LUB 22** and as a result mortar and rubble were much in evidence; there was also a new oven, later replaced by another, and evidence for partitions and clay floors. The latest pottery dating evidence in LUB 22 was for the mid to late 4th century, provided by one sherd. There was evidence for a fire within the building **LUB 23** which the pottery dated to the late 4th century.

To the south, the demolition debris of Structure 3, LUB 11 in Area III, was covered by the construction of Structure 6 **LUB 24**; one sherd of pottery from this LUB dated to the mid to late 3rd century. Structure 6 was a stone-founded strip-building with aisle posts, fronting Ermine Street to the south of Structure 5. Internally the building **LUB 25** had a series of floors in the western part, including clay, cobbles and flags; to the east there was evidence of partitions – at least two rooms to begin with, one containing a pot pit; these were succeeded by a gully or drain and traces of a partition, and later were divided into four rooms. Pottery from LUB 25 dated to the mid to late 3rd century. Then there was a fire **LUB 26** at the eastern end of the building, stratigraphically within the mid to late 3rd century. Structure 6 was replaced by Structure 9 **LUB 27**, with stone walls without aisle posts, by the late 3rd century. Internally **LUB 28** there were traces of timber partitions in its eastern part, together with mainly sand and pebble floors; the southern part of the building was dominated by a large hearth associated with a mortar floor, sealed by later sand and pebble floors; to the north was evidence of timber partitions and further sand and pebble floors, as well as clay floors, and to the west were traces of more floors and further partitions. Pottery and a coin dated LUB 28 from the mid to late 3rd century into the 4th century. Subsequent internal arrangements for Structure 9 **LUB 29** included further timber partitions; the oven continued in use and another was constructed; floors were of sandy mortar or clay. Pottery dated LUB 29 to the 4th century. Later, internal arrangements for Structure 9 **LUB 30** included postholes between the central area and the front of the building, clay, mortar, pebble, cobble and flagged floors, together with traces of timber partitions; pottery dated LUB 30 to the 4th century.

Structure 1 (LUB 13) in Area I continued in use from the mid 3rd century; it was demolished **LUB 31** in the mid/late 3rd century according to the stratigraphy. In its place stone-founded Structure 7 **LUB 32** was built; pottery suggests that this might have taken place in the mid 3rd century or later. Mortar floors and traces of beam slots **LUB 33** were noted; the pottery indicates a 4th-century date for its occupation. Structure 7 was demolished **LUB 34**, probably in the later 4th century on the evidence of the pottery.

Between Structures 7 and 8, as well as between Structures 8 and 9, were rubble deposits, and also much tile between Structure 8 and 9 **LUB 35**. Pottery from these deposits date to the second part of the 4th century.

In Area IV, Structure 4 (LUB 12) probably continued in use from the mid 3rd century. It was replaced by stone-founded Structure 10 **LUB 36**; the use of this building was dated to between the mid 3rd and the 4th centuries by the pottery. Replacing Structure 10 was Structure 11 **LUB 37** which re-used the stone foundations of Structure 10; pottery associated with its use dated it to the mid 4th century.

LUB 15 Construction of Structure 5
(Fig. 13.8, 13.22 and 13.31)
Rather than levelling material being imported on to the site, the existing material (LUB 8) was used to build over in Area II.

In the northern part of Area II, cutting into sand cg2059 (LUB 8), east–west wall cg2048 was built. This was the north wall of Structure 5. There was no record of what the south wall cg2076 cut; nor was there any record of what internal north–south wall cg2075 cut, although it abutted wall cg2076; this was not the front wall of the building front of the "workshop" area, as the main south wall cg2076 was seen to continue eastwards of it. These walls were 0.45m wide; the building was at least 23m by 8m internally. The northern wall cg2048 survived to a height of four courses of masonry, consisting of

limestone blocks bonded with yellow-brown mortar. The courses were stepped or offset. The south wall cg2076 survived only three courses high. It was bonded with yellow-brown mortar and described on site as 'very poorly built', (perhaps because of limited access?). At the west end of the building was evidence of a north–south wall cg2046, which was also built of faced limestone blocks, bonded with hard yellow mortar.

A short stretch of an east–west wall cg2047 to the west of cg2046 was found, bonded with yellowish mortar (Fig. 13.31, in background); there was no record of what it had cut. This may either have been part of an internal partition, or may have represented an extension at the rear of the building, perhaps consisting of no more than a lean-to shed.

Cutting dumps cg2049 (LUB 8) was post-pit cg2303; cutting dump cg2050 (LUB 8) was post-pit cg2052. There was no record of what post-pit cg2270 cut, but around it was yellow stoney sandy mortar cg2051 (LUB 8); nor was there any record of what post-pit cg2061 cut. The post-pits were stone-lined. Layers built up around the posts in postholes cg2122, cg2128 and cg2086, obscuring the original relationships. These post-pits and postholes represented two east–west lines of aisle posts. There was no indication of the post size or section from the post-pits: the stone packing seemed to be have been disturbed, perhaps when the posts were removed; the postholes themselves offered little indication of the size of the posts.

There were 54 sherds of pottery from this LUB. The scarcity of pottery sherds can be linked to the deposit categories; wall construction, post-pits and postholes do not in general produce large quantities of pottery. Possible mid 3rd-century or later pottery (a possible slit-folded Mosel beaker with a NVCC beaker in a later fabric) was recovered from wall cg2047. Pottery sherds (from a funnel-necked scaled beaker and a dales ware type jar) from posthole cg2122 indicate a mid 3rd-century or later date; these sherds were possibly introduced into the posthole after it had gone into disuse and so cannot be used without substantiation to indicate the construction date of the building. An illegible 3rd- or 4th-century coin came from the fill of aisle post cg2128, which is inconclusive both in its own right, but also because the coin could have been deposited at any time up to LUB 21 when the pit was sealed. But it would also seem probable on stratigraphic grounds that the building was constructed in the mid to late 3rd century.

LUB 16 Occupation and alterations to Structure 5
(Fig. 13.8 and 13.31)
In the northern part of Structure 5 in Area II was an area of paved stones cg2065, bounded on the east

by four large interlocked stone flagstones (no record of what they sealed). Over one end of cg2065, and partially set into clay with ash cg2064, (no record of what it sealed) was the line of a possible partition cg2066, which consisted of a line of limestones, probably a base for a timber sill beam. A "portion of unburnt timber beam" was recorded as surviving on these stones but was not planned. Together these formed the remains of a timber partition parallel to, and about 1m south of, the north external wall of the building. Sealing partition cg2066 was an extensive layer of gravel and small pebbles cg2068.

Towards the south-western corner of the building, a fairly small room, (c 3.20m square) was created by the erection of three partition walls cg2074 (Fig. 13.31) which cut in to sandy ash cg2071 (LUB 8). These walls were sealed by clay which was coated with what appeared to be mortar on both faces and then plaster applied and painted. The total thickness of the walls was only 0.15m. The walls probably had a timber and wattle framework, but no trace survived. Aisle post cg2086 (LUB 15) lay within this room; there is no evidence that the post was no longer in place at this time – but if it was still present, then there was very little space within the room. The west wall of this new room lay parallel to the west wall of the building, and approximately 1m away. Within the room sandy ash cg2071 (LUB 8) was sealed by several thin layers of sand cg2069, which contained a small quantity of painted plaster. Sand cg2069 was sealed by an area of smooth stones and an extent of compact brownish-yellow clay cg2070, sealed by a thin layer of ash; the stones which lay at the northern end of the eastern part of partition cg2074 were thought to indicate the location of a doorway into the room. Within layers cg2070 were fragments of plaster.

To the north of Structure 5, over sand cg2059 (LUB 8) was an an area of clay (c 0.10m thick), to the east of which was a stone surface cg2316; cutting cg2059 (LUB 8) was a posthole cg2060 (unplanned). Sealing these layers was a north–south line of limestones cg2062, with clay which was burnt to a considerable depth to the east of it; the limestones stopped just short of the north wall cg2048 (LUB 15). The line of limestones and burnt clay cg2062 may have represented the western side of a flue (similar in design to that which was part of oven cg3121 (LUB 28)), with an oven to the south since removed by the deep church foundations (cg109, LUB 55). Pottery from layers cg2062 included a BB1 cooking pot likely to date to the mid to late 3rd century. The flue cg2062 was sealed by fragments of burnt and unburnt clay cg2063.

In the north-eastern part of the building were layers of ash and sand cg2058 (there was no record of what they sealed); these were sealed by burnt and unburnt clay cg2092, probably associated with flue cg2062, and equivalent to cg2063.

Sealing cg2054 (LUB 8) were layers of clay and ash cg2055, found in the vicinity of flue cg2062. Sealing layer cg2071 (LUB 8), in the centre of Area II, was a patch of smooth stones cg2274; this may have represented a brazier stand, centrally placed between the aisle posts, perhaps pre-dating the construction of partitions cg2074. Over the stones cg2274 was a series of layers cg2056 – soft sand sealed by a hard compact clay with pebbles, over which was a layer of charcoal sealed by a spread of small stones – hardcore for a compact clayish surface with patches of ash. Over layers cg2056 and cg2055 was a spread of sand cg2057. Sealing cg2077 (LUB 15) and abutting wall cg2075 (LUB 15), were layers cg2078 first of mortar, sealed by compact brown clay, over which was a layer of burnt clay and charcoal; these were situated to the east of wall cg2075.

Soft clay and ash cg2067 in the northern part of the building may have been associated with this LUB (there was no record of what they sealed). Sealing cg2071 (LUB 8) were sand layers cg2072.

In the west of Area II, sealing the construction trench of north–south wall cg2046 (LUB 15), was sandy loam sealed by sand cg2273; sherds of a GREY folded funnel-necked beaker came from cg2273.

There were 1,599 sherds of pottery from this LUB, most of which was residual; joining sherds between this and earlier LUBs indicate reworking of earlier deposits, corroborating the source of the residual material. High residuality occurred in layers cg2055; the pottery came from the earlier part of the 3rd century or earlier, and there were joins with cg2054 (LUB 8); some of the sherds were rather scrappy. Some of the pottery from this LUB dated to the mid 3rd century, including sherds from cg2056, cg2062, cg2273 and cg2275.

LUB 17 Occupation and alterations to Structure 5 (Fig. 13.8 and 13.23)
In the south-east part of Structure 5, sealing cg2077 (LUB 15) were several layers of sand cg2079, over which were other layers cg2080; cg2080 consisted of a make-up layer of crushed mortar and limestone chips sealed by a thin layer of clay; over this were thin layers of ash and sand. Cutting through these was a slot cg2081, close within the angle between walls cg2075 and cg2076 (both LUB 15); this slot was sealed by stones set in burnt clay cg2082 in the corner of the room. Around the stones were thin layers of ash and sand cg2083.

Over layer cg2092 (LUB 16), in the north-east part of the building, was a sequence of floor and hearth debris layers cg2093; there were patches of brown sand with pebbles and burnt clay sealed by ash, contemporary with a post-pad. They were sealed by sand, over which was a charcoal spread, sealed by a compact brown clay floor, over which was a spread of ash, sealed by a layer of sand, over which was another layer of ash. The various floor layers were contemporary with a partition defining a possible room at the east end of the building, indicated by a beam-slot or sill-beam impression cg2094. This ran principally east–west (obliquely to the outer walls) and had flat limestones lining its base, presumably pad-stones. Although only a relatively short length protruded from the eastern section, the feature is shown on early plans returning northwards, and is recorded as visible in the northern section. It therefore appears to have been the remains of a timber-framed partition forming a small room *c* 3.0m wide against the north wall.

Also in the northern area of the building, sealing layer cg2067 and partition cg2066 (both LUB 16), was a spread of sandy mortar and sand cg2088. Over this and sealing layer cg2063 (LUB 16), was a layer of ash cg2090 with a small assemblage of animal bone indicating domestic refuse (Dobney *et al* 1994f) and pottery (490 sherds), including a MOMH hammer-headed mortarium and a mica-coated NVCC closed vessel, which, on the evidence of its occurrence on other sites in Lincoln, appears to start in the mid 3rd century; much of the pottery from cg2090 can be dated to the mid 3rd century or later, but there is little evidence to substantiate a late 3rd-century date.

Also sealing cg2088 were ash and sand layers cg2089. Pottery from cg2089 (97 sherds) included a MOMH hammer-headed mortarium, possibly of the range 230–340, and a GREY cooking pot which could extend into the 4th century. Layers cg2089 also contained a 4th-century glass vessel base (CLH) <SM77 6159> (reworked, possibly for use as a smoother or counter). This tends to confirm a 4th-century date for deposition.

In the centre of the large "workshop" room there was a build-up of layers; sealing sand cg2057 (LUB 16) was a layer of hard compact sandy clay cg2276. Over this were several layers cg2096; pebbly sand burnt in places, sealed by pebbly clay, ash, sand, a layer of burnt clay, ash and charcoal and sand. A large quantity of pottery came from cg2096 (318 sherds); much of the pottery suggested various dates during the 3rd century, especially the late 3rd century. Sandy mortar and pebbles cg2097 probably belongs to this LUB (no record of what it sealed).

In the south-west area of the building, the plastered room was demolished and over the floor cg2070 (LUB 16) was sand, ash, daub and fallen plaster cg2084; the remains of an infant of about 37 weeks gestation (unplanned; Boylston and Roberts 1994) were recovered from cg2084. Over cg2084 was sand cg2085; similar layers cg2113 sealed layers cg2072

(LUB 16) and the wall of the room cg2074 (LUB 16). Over the demolition layers cg2084 and cg2113 were pitched cobbles set in white clay cg2087, equivalent to cobbles cg2132 which also sealed layers cg2113.

Some features in the northern part of the building – layers cg2093 and beam slot cg2094 were covered by sand cg2095, and posthole cg2061 (LUB 15) and ash cg2090 were sealed by sand cg2091, over which was a hard clay surface cg2098. Clay cg2098 also sealed layers cg2097, cg2096 and cg2089.

Sealing clay floor cg2098 were layers of sand and ash cg2099 and cg2106, and possibly similar layers cg2100 and cg2103 (there was no record of what they sealed).

During this LUB phase a hearth cg2107 was erected against the south wall of the building; no record was made of what this sealed. The evidence for this new floor-level hearth, probably rectangular in plan, consisted of a base of clay (possibly originally tiled?) with a limestone surround delimiting an area of *c* 0.5m. The excavators suggested that traces of a stoke-hole and flue could be discerned, but there was no strong evidence for these features. The hearth seems most likely to have been open, without flue or stoke-hole. Alterations were made to the hearth cg2107, the north edge of which which appears to have been repaired cg2108 with clay bounded by a line of tiles.

Sealing both sand and ash layers cg2103 and hearth cg2107 was ash cg2105. Probably equivalent to layers cg2103 were layers cg2109 and cg2111 (no record of what they sealed). Cutting layer cg2109 was a posthole cg2110.

Over sand cg2273 (LUB 16) was a layer cg2275 of sand with pieces of limestone and mortar and what was identified on site as coal; this was sealed by layers cg2053 of sandy loam sealed by loose rubble and pebbles in ashy loam. These layers were recovered in the vicinity of the rear extension wall cg2047 (LUB 15), possibly within a shed formed partly by that wall.

Layers cg2053 may belong to this LUB, but could belong either totally or partially to later LUBs (18–20); they were not sealed until LUB 21. They did, however, produce the largest pottery assemblage from this LUB (745 sherds), with an unusual quantity of sherds of shell-tempered dales ware relative to the normal GREY sherds; these layers also yielded the main concentration of sherds from TILE fabric hand-made vessels, together with a sherd from a Smith God pot, and a sherd from another vessel of the same type decorated with an applied ring. Sherds of a GREY folded funnel-necked beaker came from these layers, but most of the vessel was in sand cg2273. A MOMH mortarium with a painted flange also occurred here in cg2053, and a closed oxidized vessel, closely similar to the Swanpool fabric with a trace of painted decoration. This could suggest that the context group dated to the very end of the 3rd century.

There were 2,295 pottery sherds from this LUB (including cg2053), much of which was residual. Pottery from cg2090 and cg2096 suggests a mid 3rd-century date or later. Although layer cg2053 contained late 3rd-century pottery, its location in the sequence is not certain, so it cannot date this LUB. But pottery from cg2089 extended into the 4th century together with the reworked glass vessel base. The stratigraphy suggests that the dating of cg2089 also affects the date of surface cg2098 and layers cg2099 and cg2106.

LUB 18 Fire in Structure 5 (Figs. 13.8 and 13.23)
Set into sand cg2099 and cg2100 (both LUB 17) in the centre-east of Structure 5, near to partition cg2094 (LUB 17), were burnt timbers cg2101. These and a stake-hole cg2102 (no record of what it cut) were sealed by burnt daub and smoke-blackened plaster fragments cg2104. These may represent burnt remains of the timber partition cg2094. Debris cg2104 also included a small quantity of iron nails, together with a phallic object in TILE fabric, possibly a lid with a phallic handle, or a cult object of an upright phallus on a base.

Just to the south of where partition cg2094 (LUB 17) had stood, and sealing layers cg2111, cg2105 (both LUB 17) and cg2104 as well as posthole cg2110 (LUB 17), was a spread of burnt clay cg2114 with charcoal and ash. Fragments of heavily burnt daub, plaster, and nails were present in cg2114.

There were 171 pottery sherds from this LUB and all were possibly residual. Some pottery sherds from cg2104 were burnt, and sherds from cg2114 showed signs of much burning. The LUB may be dated stratigraphically to the early 4th century.

LUB 19 Late occupation and alterations to Structure 5 (Figs. 13.8 and 13.23)
The north–south wall cg2075 (LUB 15), at the eastern end of Structure 5 in Area III, was excavated. Cutting layer cg2083 (LUB 17), and removing stone from slot cg2082 (LUB 17), was a robber trench cg2140; this was sealed by ash layer cg2141 and a sequence of sand, ash and charcoal layers cg2143. Cutting cg2085 (LUB 17) was a posthole cg2142 which was sealed by cg2143. The removal of wall cg2075 (LUB 15) probably indicates a re-building of at least the front part of the building (see below).

Cobbles cg2087 and cg2132 (both LUB 17) continued in use, contemporary with limestone surface cg2131, as were the remains of a flagged surface cg2130 (no record of what it sealed). Ashy loam with white and burnt clay cg2133 sealed surface cg2131 and cobbles cg2132 as well as stone surface cg2130.

Sealing burnt clay cg2114 (LUB 18) was a layer of white clay cg2115; over this was a compact area of brown clay cg2118. Over layer cg2106 (LUB 17) was sand with pebbles cg2117, which was also sealed by cg2118. Clay cg2118 spread over much of the building. It was sealed by ash and sand layers cg2120 over which were layers of ash and clay cg2121. Cutting cg2120 was a posthole cg2126 which was contemporary with clay and limestone chippings cg2125 (but with no record of what it sealed), together with clay patches cg2124 and cg2123. Ash with patches of burnt white clay cg2127 sealed posthole cg2126, surface cg2125 and clay patches cg2123 and cg2124. Clay cg2127 was sealed by ash cg2129.

Clay floor cg2118 was also sealed by charcoal, clay and ash layers cg2134 and by sand in which tightly-packed cobbles were set cg2135. Sand cg2119 (no record of what it sealed), together with clay floor cg2118, was also sealed by sand, clay and ash layers cg2136; sand cg2116 (no record of what it sealed), together with sand layer cg2117, was sealed by sand, clay and ash layers cg2137. Over layers cg2137 was sand cg2138.

There were 472 sherds from this LUB, all of which were apparently residual. However, the stratigraphic sequence dates this LUB into the 4th century, as does a coin from cg2136.

LUB 20 Construction of Structure 8 (Fig. 13.9)
The walls cg2048 and cg2076 (both LUB 14) of the previous building, Structure 5 in Area II, were demolished to ground level. Flat slabs of limestone *c* 0.85m wide were then laid over the remains of these sleeper walls. The sleeper walls were only 0.45m wide: the flat limestones were laid so that their inside edges lined up with the inner faces of the sleeper walls, thus overlapping the sleeper walls considerably on the outside of the building. The main walls of the new building (cg2144 and cg2179) were then built, again with their inner faces in line with the inner faces of the old sleeper walls. Between wall cg2048 and wall cg2179 was a layer of mortary loam cg2139. A north–south wall cg2180 to the west was built on layer cg2137 (LUB 19); it was built of rough pieces of limestone and bonded with pale brown mortar. The internal dimensions of the previous building were thus exactly reproduced by the new building. The walls were of fairly evenly coursed limestone blocks bonded with yellow mortar containing pebbles.

The north wall cg2179 was found to survive to a height of seven courses. Even the remaining footing exhibited a pronounced lean towards the south. The greater width of these new walls and their much better standard of construction (even if the foun-

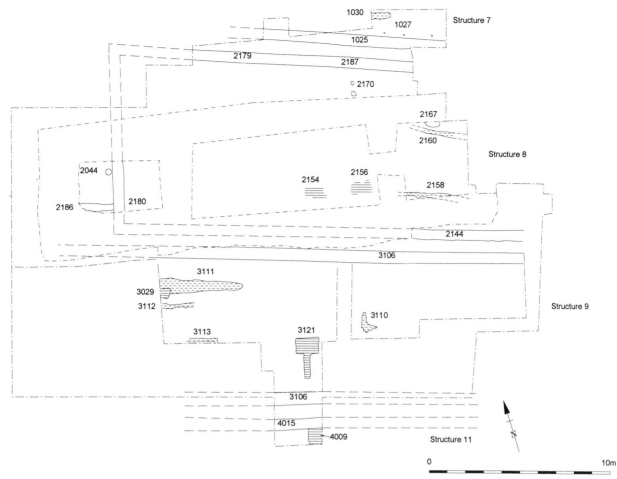

Fig. 13.9 Structures 7, 8, 9 and 10: LUBs 20, 21, 28, 29, 34, 35 and 38. (1:200)

dations were modest), taken together with the lack of aisle posts, suggests that the walls were probably entirely of stone which carried the entire weight of the building.

Pottery from this LUB (246 sherds) was probably residual as it can only be dated, stratigraphically, to the 4th century.

LUB 21 Internal details, alterations and occupation of Structure 8 (Area II; Figs. 13.9 and 13.23)
In the central and eastern parts of Structure 8, sealing post-pits cg2122 and cg2128 (both from LUB 15), together with layers cg2134, cg2129 and cg2133 (all from LUB 19), was a metalled surface of limestone chippings set in sand cg2153.

Pottery from cg2153 (142 sherds) contained residual material with links back to LUBs 17, 18, and 19; otherwise, sherds from a BB1 bead and flange bowl, a wide-mouthed bowl of Rookery Lane kiln type 38, together with NVCC beakers in late fabrics and DWSH, suggested a late 3rd-century date, possibly into the 4th.

Set on surface cg2153 was a substantial oven base cg2154; it was a platform of stone and tile set in clay on rubble and mortar foundations about 1.20m square, with a number of overlapping spreads of clay and ash extending northwards from it.

Over metalled surface cg2153 were patches of ashy loam and sand cg2155 sealed by ashy loam and sand cg2157. Sealing layer cg2155 was a base of tile and rubble sealed by a very large slab of limestone cg2156, possibly the remains of an oven base. Cutting cg2155 was an east–west slot cg2158 and posthole cg2277 (unplanned); these were sealed by a layer of sandy loam cg2159, which contained a small assemblage of animal bone representing domestic refuse (Dobney et al 1994f), together with a small pottery assemblage which included a sherd from a possible SPOX beaker, which could indicate a 4th-century date.

Layer cg2159 was cut by east–west slot cg2160 and sealed by a circular patch of burnt clay cg2161. Over burnt clay cg2161, and oven platform cg2154 were ash spreads cg2162. These were sealed by sand

and ash over which was a clay floor cg2166, burnt in patches and with green staining over its surface; the clay floor also sealed slot cg2160. Also overlying metalled surface cg2153 were the remains of a worn mortar floor cg2201; over this was a layer of mortary loam with tile and limestone fragments cg2317 and pebbles with sand cg2318.

In the northern part of the building, sealing post-pits cg2052 and cg2303 (LUB 15) was a layer of very dark greyish-brown ashy silty loam cg2112 with green staining. Partially sealing loam cg2112 was a layer of clay cg2175, sealed by an orange mortar spread into which flagstones had been laid cg2176; these flagstones sealed the offset of wall cg2179 (LUB 20).

Two postholes cg2170 cut ash layer cg2162; both were 0.20m in diameter, stone-packed and approximately 0.80m apart. It seems likely that they were part of a prop to attempt to stop wall cg2179 (LUB 20) from falling southwards.

Layer cg2112 was partially sealed by a mixed layer of dark sandy loam cg2163 and sand cg2171. Sealing layer cg2163 was a thin layer of burnt clay and loam cg2165, which in turn was sealed by cg2159 (see above). Layer cg2165 also sealed a thin layer of ash, over which was a mortar deposit cg2164 (there was no record of what these sealed). Also sealing cg2164 was a thin layer of mortar, clay and silt cg2169. Layer cg2169 could be of early 4th-century date on the basis of a BB1 bead and flange bowl; NVCC late beaker fabrics also occurred.

Sealing the top offset course of the north–south wall cg2180 (LUB 20) was a layer of yellow mortar sealed by a layer of loam and ash cg2181 and cg2182. To the west of the building, layers cg2053 (LUB 17) were sealed by dark ashy loam cg2043. The pottery from the levelling cg2043 (52 sherds) included a sherd from a BB1 high bead and flange bowl, making the layer conclusively 4th-century.

Cut into loam cg2043, a pot was placed in a pit cg2044 just big enough to contain it, against the western face of wall cg2180 (LUB 20). The pot was a broken and fragmentary large GREY jar, with only the base and walls surviving. Over this was a layer of dark brown loam flecked with charcoal and mortar patches, with some limestone cg2287.

Pottery from cg2287 (251 sherds) had residual sherd links with LUB 16 and sherd link with cg2043; the dating for this assemblage comes from a sherd from a BB1 bead-and-flange bowl of late 3rd- to early 4th-century type, fragments of late cooking pots, a fragment of a MONV mortaria, sherds from a NVCC bowl of form 31 (possibly the same in cg2043), sherds from beakers in late fabrics, and two possible SPOX sherds from a probable form 31 bowl and a closed form. There is no strong evidence to extend the date far into the 4th century, and with

sherd links to earlier contexts, some of the material is obviously residual.

Sealing layer cg2287 was brown loam, yellow mortar and tile cg2045. Ash and sand cg2183 (no record of what they sealed) and cg2045 were sealed by building rubble and debris cg2184. At the rear (western end) of the building there was some evidence of an added timber extension. Sealing rubble cg2184 was a patch of sandy grey mortar cg2185, cut by an east–west beam slot cg2186. The beam slot may have formed the remains of a timber sill-beam supporting a wooden structure against the north–south wall cg2180 (LUB 20). Pottery from the beam-slot cg2186 included a fragment of a wide-mouthed bowl of Swanpool D38 type, which suggests a 4th-century date. No other structural remains were located but the area excavated behind the rear wall was only 2.20m square. The likelihood is that this was no more than a lean-to shed on the back of the building.

Further to the west within the building, sealing layers cg2143 (LUB 19) was a layer of sand, sealed by a layer of silty loam, over which was a clay spread cg2152; a NVCC slit-folded beaker from cg2152 would indicate a 4th-century date.

Sandy silt cg2145 (no record of what it sealed) to the west of Area II was cut by a small pit cg2146 with a sandy silt fill. This was sealed by dark sandy silt cg2147, which in turn was cut by a pit cg2150 with a dark peaty fill, over which was sandy silt and mortar cg2151. Sealing cg2147 was ash cg2148 which was sealed by clayish silt, sand and loam silt cg2149; on the basis of the occurrence of sherds from a MONV mortarium, cg2149 could slip into the 4th century. Over silt cg2149 was clayey loam cg2217.

There were 1,326 sherds from this LUB and the over-riding impression is of much residual pottery with relatively sparse and evenly scattered deposition dates, most of which can only be vaguely dated to the 4th century; yet, there were no classic late vessels, no NVCC bowls or dishes etc.

LUB 22 Internal details, alterations and occupation of Structure 8 (Figs. 13.10, 13.22, 13.32)
The start of this LUB is marked by the rebuilding cg2187 of part of the north wall cg2179 (LUB 20) in Area II. The lack of deep footings appears to have caused the inevitable problems. Whether a part of the wall actually collapsed or perhaps only threatened to do so is not clear, but the eastern end of this wall was only rebuilt from the slab footings upwards. A straight joint and different mortar bonding either side of this joint, along with a difference in the level of the footings, were the main indicators of the rebuilding. It was rebuilt in the same style as the earlier wall (Fig. 13.22). Quantities of rubble were

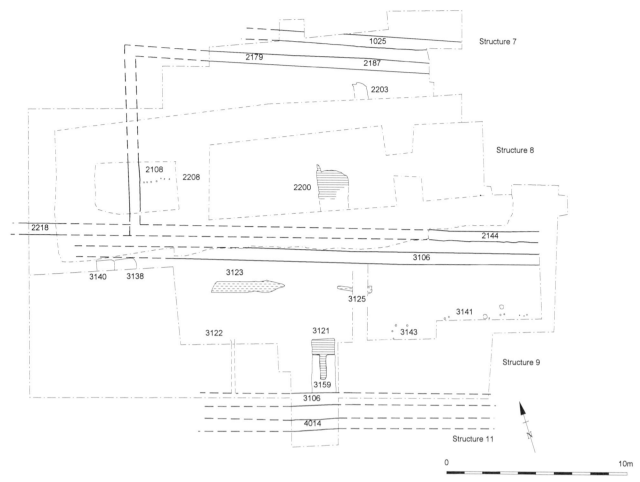

Fig. 13.10 Rebuilding of structure 8, use of structure 9 and structure 11: LUBs 22, 30 and 39. (1:200)

recovered from within the building, probably the remains of re-building. Over ash layer cg2162 (LUB 21) was a semi-circular patch of sandy mortar with pebbles and limestone rubble cg2168. Cutting clay floor cg2166 (LUB 21) was a slot filled with limestone rubble cg2167. Partially over layer cg2163 (LUB 21) was a thin spread of clay sealed by a rubbly spread cg2172 over which was a loam layer with greenish stains cg2173. Over flagstones cg2176 (LUB 21) were pieces of stone and ash cg2177 and rubble and sand cg2174. Pottery from layer cg2177 (179 sherds), contained a sherd from a BB1 bead and flange bowl, sherds from late NVCC beakers, a sherd possibly from a slit-folded beaker, and a sherd from a GREY wide-mouthed bowl of Swanpool kiln D41 type which could suggest a 4th-century date. Over cg2177 was a pile of limestone rubble with yellow mortar cg2178. Sealing layer cg2318 (LUB 21) was rubble cg2319.

To the south of wall cg2187 was a layer of limestone rubble, burnt sand, ash and clay cg2188; this layer sealed postholes cg2170 (LUB 21) and

layers cg2178 and cg2173. Pottery from layer cg2188 (243 sherds) included sherds from late beakers, two as Gillam 43, and one Gillam 48, and body sherds from a further probable pentice-moulded beaker; sherds from an oxidized shallow bowl or lid B332 first occur here; other sherds could support a 4th-century date, although those from wide-mouthed bowls were of the earlier type. Sealing cg2187 was a layer of mortar cg2190 confined to the area adjacent to the rebuilt section of wall; this mortar also sealed cg2169 (LUB 21). Sealing rubble cg2188 were layers of loam and mortar cg2189 which contained a possible NVCC bowl of form 36, probably a 4th-century vessel.

Sealing rubble layer cg2319 (above) was a layer of sand and pebbles cg2320. This was contemporary with oven cg2200 (Fig. 13.32), which was constructed over the ash spread cg2162 (LUB 21) sealing oven cg2154 (LUB 21). The ash spread cg2162 (LUB 21) had been sealed with yellow/brown clay which had five "large" flat tiles set into it cg2200. Evidence of a clay superstructure of this oven survived at the south end, to a height of almost 0.30m. This large oven measured at least 2.40m by 1.60m; the oven tiles and the surrounding clay had been burned to some depth. Pottery from the oven (10 sherds) included a DWSH possible double lid-seated jar rim fragment, a GREY beaker with the rim type near the late Gillam 43 type, and sherds from NVCC bowl of form 38 and bead and flange bowl, all of which suggest a mid to late 4th-century date, although the lateness depends upon the sherd from the double lid-seated jar. The oven was probably also associated with dark greyish brown sandy ash cg2199 (no record of what it sealed).

Over layers cg2198, cg2199, cg2320 and oven cg2200 was an ash deposit cg2202 surrounding and presumably associated with the use of the oven.

Directly sealing mortar layer cg2198 to the north were the slight remains of another oven cg2203. It was built of light yellowish-brown clay, burnt red around and beneath the flue which was filled with clay. Around the oven, sealing cg2202 was a patchy clay floor cg2204 sealed by ash cg2205. To the west of the oven was a patch of burnt cobbles cg2206 sealing cg2202, and further west, sandy loam cg2207 sealed ash cg2202 and was cut by a line of seven stake-holes cg2208, running east–west.

Sealing mortar cg2152, to the east of the building was another sandy mortar layer cg2194.

Sealing clay spread cg2152 (LUB 21) to the west, in the building was a thin layer of loam cg2210 over which was sand and charcoal patches cg2211. Over this and spreading east, sealing clay and silt cg2169, rubble cg2167 and cg2168 (all LUB 21) was a floor surface of compacted brown clay cg2212 and cg2216 (to the west) with patches of burning (see LUB 23). Pottery from floor cg2216 (214 sherds) contained a sherd from a BB1 cooking pot of late type, as Gillam 1976, no 11, dated as late 3rd to early 4th century, alongside sherds from the earlier type of wide-mouthed bowls; also a sherd from a NVCC box in a late fabric possibly of the curved-wall type. However, this group unusually contained no DWSH, a common inclusion in most of the groups.

Cutting loam cg2217 (LUB 21) was east–west stone wall cg2218, 0.57m thick and fairly well founded (footings *c* 0.60 m deep), which was added to the rear of the building, apparently continuing the line of the southern wall cg2144 (LUB 20). There may have been a similar extension of the north wall westwards. This would have lain outside the excavated area, so its extent and form could not be determined. Sealing layer cg2217 (LUB 21) was a tip of disturbed pale yellow-brown mortar cg2219, against wall cg2144 (LUB 20). Over this were thin layers of loam and charcoal cg2220 sealed by crushed mortar spread cg2221 which sealed the offset of wall cg2218.

There were 1,123 sherds of pottery from this LUB. Most of the 4th-century pottery could only be vaguely dated, except for the DWSH possible double lid-seated jar rim fragment from oven cg2200, which is the latest sherd from this LUB, dating to the mid to late 4th century. An irregular issue of Constans, of AD 335–45 (and showing some evidence of wear), may provide a *terminus post quem* for the rebuilding of the north wall cg2187, if it was genuinely from the construction of the wall, as indicated by the site record, rather than an adjacent layer.

LUB 23 Fire in Structure 8
There was evidence of a fairly severe fire within Structure 8, in the form of a layer of ash and charcoal cg2209 which covered most of the interior of the building, sealing cg2205, cg2206 and cg2208 (all LUB 22). The burning of floor surface cg2216 (LUB 22) also suggests a fire; clay floor cg2212 (LUB 22) was sealed by ash and charcoal cg2213. To the south of wall cg2179 (LUB 20) were layers of ash sealed by pieces of charred wood over which was loam and burnt clay cg2327 (there was no record of what these layers sealed). The inside face of the north wall cg2187 (LUB 22) and cg2179 (LUB 20) was scorched over much of its exposed face. The lack of similar burning on the faces of any of the other walls suggests that the fire was confined to the central-northern part of the building. The fire can be demonstrated to belong here in the sequence and not later, because the burning extends behind the masonry (cg2240 LUB 38) abutting the north wall.

There were 89 sherds of pottery from the LUB. From unclearly stratified but burnt layers cg2327, the pottery dating (77 sherds) suggests a probable late 4th-century event on the basis of two sherds from a possible head pot, a sherd from a NVCC pentice-moulded beaker, and a sherd from a DWSH plain-rimmed dish. This date fits with the stratigraphic sequence: LUB 22 has a single sherd of mid to late 4th-century pottery, and LUB 38 very late 4th-century pottery.

LUB 24 Construction of Structure 6 (Area III)
(Fig. 13.8)
The deep footings of the subsequent stone building, Structure 9, (LUB 27) had removed any trace of the external walls of Structure 6 in Area III. However, at the extreme eastern edge of the trench, north–south internal stone wall foundations cg3082 were found. These consisted of a single surviving course of limestone footings, *c* 0.50 m wide. Although only the lowest foundation course survived, the quality of construction did not seem high, and the stones had a very irregular lie to them. This wall was later robbed and some of its apparent irregularities stem from this operation. The (missing) above-ground

part of this wall can have been no wider than 0.50m. There was no record of what this wall cut.

Only postholes from the northern row of aisle posts cg3097 were found. The six post-pits were of variable size and had been packed with limestone fragments. The spacing between the posts differed more than in the timber predecessor, Structure 3 (LUB 9). Between the two most easterly posts, one post appears to be missing; either it was not there or it was not recognised by the excavators. One of the post-pits cut earlier post-pit cg3184 (LUB 9); otherwise there was no record of what the post-pits had cut. One more post, cg3098, was found, lying *c* 0.60m to the south of the line of the cg3097 posts.

Sealing layer cg3094 (LUB 11) were two small areas of closely-packed limestone cg3095. These were each about 0.45m x 0.50m and 0.30m apart, comprising a single course of limestones, positioned roughly in the centre of the building. These might represent stone bases for raised hearths.

LUB 24 produced only 23 sherds of pottery, which was generally indeterminate, apart from a sherd from an aisle post cg3097, from a wide-mouthed bowl of Rookery Lane kiln type 42, which may suggest a mid to late 3rd-century date. Although this sherd may have been deposited after the post went out of use, from the stratigraphic sequence it would seem that the construction of Structure 6 may well have taken place around the mid to late 3rd century.

LUB 25 Internal features and occupation of Structure 6 (Fig. 13.8)
Sealing cg3038 (LUB 11), to the west of Structure 6 in Area III, was a long sequence of patchy layers of sand, clay and ash and also cobbles cg3093.

Pottery from layers cg3093 (211 sherds) contained the only pottery from this LUB suggesting a late 3rd- to 4th-century date, and that only from two contexts (CVI, CVF), resting on three sherds of a NVCC plain dish which had a join with beam slot cg3111 (LUB 28). However, since cg3093 was not excavated until after the removal of oven cg3121 (LUB 28), these sherds could be intrusive. A rim from a vessel of Smith God pot type came from cg3093. The rest of the pottery broadly dating to the mid to late 3rd century.

Up against the bases cg3095 (LUB 24) were layers of clayey sand cg3096 sealed by ash and charcoal cg3223. Contemporary with layer cg3223 was an insubstantial slot cg3103 (0.04m deep; no record of what it cut; unplanned) possibly the remains of a partition; both layer and feature were sealed by silty sand cg3221. Post pit cg3098 (LUB 24) appears to have been abandoned; it was sealed by sand into which cobbles had been set cg3100. Pottery from cg3100 (165 sherds) included sherds dating from the mid to late 3rd century. Over cobbles cg3100

were large limestone slabs with ash between the stones; these seem to give a smooth flagged surface cg3101. A small assemblage of animal bone representing domestic refuse was recovered from the makeup of cg3101 (Dobney *et al* 1994f). Both flagged surface cg3101 and sand cg3221 were sealed by brown silty sand with loam cg3222.

To the east of the above sequence, sealing cg3186 (LUB 10) were layers of sand, clay and ash cg3035; contemporary with these, cutting cg3036 (LUB 11) was a posthole cg3209. Both the posthole and cg3035 were sealed by sand and ash layers cg3083 over which was a small hearth of stone and tile cg3084.

A burnt area cg3037 (no record of what it sealed), was sealed by sand and limestone over which cobbles had been set cg3088. This and a posthole cg3211 (no record of what it cut; unplanned) was sealed by an extensive layer of sand over which was a low east–west bank of compact sand with pitched limestones cg3089, probably part of east–west partitioning. Sand and ash layers cg3083 were sealed by a low east–west linear bank of sand, with upstanding limestones set into it cg3085. The raised sand feature may have indicated the position of an internal division between the north and south of the building. A small hole cg3087 was dug in layer cg3086 (LUB 24) and a complete pot was placed into it; it was a GREY cooking pot, copying a BB1 type, the rim type and haphazard latticing suggesting a mid to late 3rd-century date and the pot was covered by a stone slab, which lay just below the floor surface.

Over the entire eastern area of the building was an extent of silty clay with limestone fragments and pebbles cg3090; this sealed limestone and sand banks cg3089 and cg3085 and pot pit cg3087. Cutting this layer were a number of stake-holes cg3210. These were sealed by a sequence of sand and clay layers cg3212 and charcoal and sand layers cg3213; pottery from layers cg3213 (15 sherds) included sherds dated to the mid to late 3rd century. Contemporary with these layers was a curved gully or drain cg3034 (no record of what it cut) and a shallow east–west beam slot cg3033 (no record of what it cut; not planned). Clay ash and sand layers cg3215 sealed cg3037; silty sand cg3214 sealed cg3089.

Over the whole eastern area of the site was an area of brown sandy clay cg3091; it sealed layers cg3212, cg3213, cg3214, cg3215, as well as beam slot cg3033 and gully cg3034. Over clay cg3091, a large part of the building was sub-divided.

Subsequent timber slot partitions cg3176 divided the area to the west of wall cg3082 (LUB 24) into four smaller areas about 5m east–west (A, B, C and D on Fig. 13.8), with the two northern rooms measuring about 4m north–south. The western east–west partition survived as a charred timber plank 0.10m wide x 0.02m thick. This had been laid flat on the ground and two narrow strips of wood had been nailed to its outer edges, thus forming a 'U'-shaped timber. Traces of both of these strips survived, along with many of the nails. Several upright stakes were found still sitting in the groove thus formed, the remains of a structure incorporating wattling which would have been daubed and plastered. Concentrations of burnt daub and painted plaster were found on the north side of this partition. The north–south partition base had no surviving timberwork, but consisted of partly fired clay daub with burnt wall plaster still adhering to its eastern face. The easterly east–west partition cg3172 consisted of a burnt timber plank; some nails were found in it but no details of construction could be discerned.

Contemporary with floor cg3091 and sealing sand cg3089 was a bank of sand cg3032 up against partition cg3176, and a shallow linear feature with two stake-holes cg3174. Stake-holes cg3171 and cg3201 provided additional support for the timber partitions. Up against partition cg3172 yellow-brown sand cg3173 had been swept, creating a raised support.

There were 731 sherds of pottery from this LUB including many residual sherds. The pot from pit cg3087, together with pottery from layers cg3093, sand cg3100 and layers cg3213, dated to the mid to late 3rd century.

LUB 26 Fire and demolition Structure 6

Structure 6 in Area III suffered fire damage and was demolished. Sealing the partitions cg3176 and cg3172 (LUB 25) was an area of post-fire collapse and demolition debris cg3175. The first destruction deposit in room A consisted of sandy mortar and burnt plaster. The plaster from this deposit consisted mainly of ceiling plaster, suggesting that the ceiling fell in first. Next was general combustion debris and plaster, again mainly from the ceiling. Finally, there was another layer of heavily burnt material with more probable ceiling plaster but also wall plaster. In Room B and C was a layer of burnt daub, charcoal and ash with much wall plaster, followed by a layer of mortar, limestone rubble and more wall plaster, perhaps partly derived from the demolition of the main north sleeper wall. The first layer in room D consisted of sand and burnt daub and contained plaster fragments from the walls. This was followed by a heavily burnt layer containing charcoal and ash, as well as more wall plaster.

These layers were sealed by burnt material and more general destruction, containing a mixture of wall and ceiling plaster, which spread over the whole of the eastern end. The north–south wall cg3082 (LUB 24) was dismantled and the footings robbed out cg3092, leaving only a single course of foundations.

There were 133 sherds of pottery from this LUB;

they were all residual. The LUB was dated stratigraphically to the mid to late 3rd century. The latest date of LUB 25 was mid to late 3rd century and the earliest date of LUB 28 was also mid to late 3rd century.

LUB 27 Construction of Structure 9
(Figs. 13.9 and 13.30)

The foundation trenches for the exterior walls cg3106 of Structure 9 in Area III were dug over the site of Structure 6 (there was no record of what they cut). The footings consisted of roughly-pitched limestone bonded with yellow sand. Over the footings the wall was built in layered courses of regularly-sized limestone blocks bonded with yellow mortar. Each course of masonry was narrower than its predecessor, producing a stepped effect to the wall. The lowest course was 1.10m wide; five courses up from this it had narrowed to its final width of 0.55m.

The area inside the walls was levelled by layers of brown silty sand cg3107 up to the top of the first offset course, a depth of some 0.40m. Layers cg3107 sealed aisle posthole cg3097 (LUB 24), layer cg3222 (LUB 25), layers cg3093 (LUB 25), debris cg3175 (LUB 26) and robber trench cg3092 (LUB 26). Sand cg3107 included a quantity of tile. To the west of the building, sand was overlain with loam, stone chips and mortar cg3031, possibly debris from construction.

There were 963 sherds from this LUB, all residual. The LUB could accordingly be dated on its stratigraphical position to the mid to late 3rd century. The latest date of LUB 25 was mid to late 3rd century and the earliest date of LUB 28 was also mid to late 3rd century.

LUB 28 Occupation of Structure 9
(Figs. 13.9 and 13.33)

Sealing cg3107 (LUB 27), at the eastern end of Structure 9 in Area III, were the patchy remains of at least two successive floors cg3115; these consisted of compacted sand/stones, succeeded by a crushed sandy mortar and clay surface associated with a stake-hole. Pottery from layers cg3115 (47 sherds) included samian of c AD160–200, and large proportions of three vessels; the dating rested on dales ware and later NVCC fabric BKFO of mid to late 3rd century.

There was evidence for timber partitioning; the junction of two sill-beams cg3110 had impressed into the make-up cg3107 (LUB 28). They were partly packed with limestone, possibly originally used to level the sill-beam. Of the rest of this partitioning there was no trace, unsurprisingly as most of the floor levels did not survive in this part of the building. Butting against sill-beams cg3110 was a sequence of layers cg3114, consisting of sandy silt with limestone fragments, sealed by clay and sand, over which was in turn sand with pebbles sealed by silty ash; over the ash was sandy silt with limestone, then sandy silt, pebbles and sand; over this was sandy silt with traces of mortar; then further sandy silt with pebbles sealed by silt with traces of sand and mortar, over which was sand with pebbles sealed by silt with traces of sand and mortar; then further sand with pebbles sealed by silt with traces of charcoal and ash; then silty clay with pebbles sealed by a sandy clay floor and further sand with pebbles. Layers cg3114 might be interpreted as patchy remains of make-up layers, sand and pebble floors and fire ash spreads. Pottery from layers cg3114 (31 sherds) included a sherd from an East Gaulish, perhaps Argonne, Ludowici Vm mortarium of *c* AD 200–260 (BMG), and the only other dating came from NVCC beaker sherds of later 3rd-century fabric.

In the central part of the building, sealing sand cg3107 (LUB 27), was a sequence of make-up, floors of mortar, and fire ash spreads cg3109; sandy mortar with limestone rubble was sealed by a sandy mortar floor which survived extensively in patches. Layers cg3109 (256 sherds) contained DWSH, NVCC flagon sherds, a BB1 bead-and-flange bowl and possible later cooking pot, a wide-mouthed bowl probably of Rookery Lane kiln type and NVCC sherds consistent with a mid-late 3rd-century date; there was also a NVCC disc-necked flagon and a grey everted rim jar near a Swanpool type, both suggesting a 4th-century date.

Over layers cg3109, in the central part of the building, was a thin make-up layer of sand with rubble, sealed by sand, over which was a surface of compact sand with silt cg3217. Further to the south, mortar floor cg3109 was sealed by a further build-up in the form of sequence cg3117. It began with an ashy spread, over which was a layer of sand and pebbles, sealed by ashy silt which was cut by a posthole; the posthole was sealed by a floor of sand with mortar and pebbles, over which was ash; this was sealed by a clay floor, burnt in patches and sealed by ash; over this were compact and extensive patches of sandy clay and mortar. Sequence cg3117 can be interpreted as fire ash spreads and floor surfaces, together with a posthole. Pottery from layers cg3117 (231 sherds) dated to the mid to late 3rd century, including a high proportion of fine wares, many of which were NVCC sherds, including an unbroken plain-rimmed undecorated beaker, as well as a sherd from a stamped East Gaulish samian dish of late 2nd- to mid 3rd-century date, a sherd of 3rd-century Trier samian mortarium, sherds of DWSH and NVCC beakers of mid to late 3rd-century date, but more importantly part of an Oxfordshire red-slipped mortarium. This latter sherd seems unlikely to date much if at all before

the mid 4th century in Lincoln. Since this is the only sherd indicating a mid 4th-century date for the LUB, the possibility of intrusion must be considered. The other pottery from cg3117 included sherds from DWSH, later NVCC beakers, flagon sherds and other vessels consistent with mid to late 3rd-century dating.

In the southern of the building, sealing earlier make-up layers of sequence cg3109, was a large rectangular stone and clay hearth cg3121 with associated flue (Fig. 13.33). The front (northern) part of the oven consisted of a slightly raised rectangular flat limestone paved area, with a tile surround forming a hearth in front of the flue entrance. The structure associated with the hearth had a central flue, 0.20m wide and with a tiled base of reused *tegulae*, which sloped gently upwards from the hearth towards the south wall, but probably ended a short distance from it. The flue structure was solid, large and quite elaborate. It may have stood waist high along its full length to create a comfortable and safe working surface. The length of the flue may be connected with the distance needed to maintain the necessary draught of air, or it may simply reflect the design of the adjacent working area. The flue could have terminated in a number of ways, as a single, small hot outlet with a working surface beside it, or the heat could have been dissipated over the entire upper surface of the superstructure giving a wider hot area. If the fuel used was charcoal, the air produced would not be 'smokey' and this may explain why the flue was not heavily sooted. The activity that required this structure clearly depended on indirect heat, but the nature of that activity is otherwise not apparent. The function or even the precise form of this oven is not clear, but the fire reddening of clay and stones was extensive, and suggests that a considerable amount of heat was generated within the oven.

About 2.0m from the north wall of the building was a shallow beam slot cg3111, probably the impression of the sill-beam of a timber-based partition in make-up layers to mortar floor cg3109. Pottery from beam slot cg3111 (50 sherds) included a sherd of a NVCC plain dish indicating a 4th-century date. Over mortar floor cg3109, to the north of slot cg3111, were sand and pebble floors cg3216; these consisted of a sand and pebble floor sealed by silty sand and then ashy sand; over this was a further floor of sand with pebbles sealed by silty clay and clayey sand. A large patch of collapsed plaster found within the uppermost layer of cg3216, and ornamented with red and yellow roundels on a white ground, is interpreted (Long 1980) as collapsed ceiling plaster.

Partition cg3111 was demolished and rebuilt cg3112 further south, now more than 3m from the north wall; slot cg3112 cut layers cg3216. At the same time an east–west partition was located against the southern section of the trench: beam slot cg3113, returning towards the south wall of the building and cutting floors cg3109; cg3113 cut layers cg3217. It probably defined a room to the south-west.

To the north of slot cg3113 was an area of loamy ash with silt cg3119. Pottery from cg3119 (23 sherds) included a sherd of collared rim jar of Swanpool kiln type C41 with notched decoration, and a rim fragment from an NVCC open vessel, either a copy samian form 38 or more likely, a plain dish; these suggest a 4th-century date.

To the north of slot cg3112, sealing layers cg3216, were layers cg3118; these consisted of a compact clay floor which was sealed by black silty charcoal, over which was a mortar floor sealed by a spread of ash. Layers cg3118 (74 sherds) included 3rd-century East Gaulish samian, DWSH, late NVCC beaker fabrics and flagon sherds, all indicative of a mid to late 3rd-century date. Over layers cg3118 was a clay floor burnt in one place, possibly a floor-level hearth cg3029 comprising a single surviving heat-shattered tile set into a clay base. Sealing hearth cg3029 were layers cg3030; these consisted of ashy clay which was sealed by sooty silt and powdered charcoal; over this were floor layers of ashy clay.

At the west end of the building, cg3031 (LUB 27) was overlain by a sequence cg3120; this consisted first of a mortar floor, over which was sandy silt, sealed by another mortar floor and further silty sand in which a hearth of burnt clay had been set; over the hearth were layers of white mortary clay, sealed by ashy silt over which was burnt plaster; a thick layer of silty loam with pebbles sealed the burnt plaster, and this layer was cut by a slot filled with burnt charcoal, possibly the remains of a partition, and it was sealed by burnt plaster, ash, charcoal and more ash. Pottery from layers cg3120 (23 sherds) included both sherds of DWSH and dales ware type, and a bead-and-flange bowl fragment, indicating a mid to late 3rd-century date.

There were 686 pottery sherds from this LUB. Pottery sherds from layers cg3114, cg3115, cg3117 and cg3120 dated to the mid to late 3rd century. Pottery from slot cg3111, and layers cg3119 dated to the 4th century. A *terminus post quem* for the latest levels is provided by a copy of a *Gloria Exercitus* 1-standard issue of AD 335–45, from the fill of the slot in sequence cg3120.

LUB 29 Occupation and alterations in Structure 9 (Fig. 13.10)
Sealing layers cg3030 (LUB 28) in Area III was a dump of silty ash, sand and plaster cg3218 (0.14m thick). East–west beam-slot or sill-beam impressions cg3123 and cg3125 lay about 1.5m south of the north

wall. Slot cg3125 cut layers cg3117 (LUB 28), and slot cg3123 cut dump cg3218. Pottery from beam-slot impressions cg3123 and cg3125 (19 sherds), had little strong evidence, but beaker sherds and a sherd from a bead-and-flange bowl suggested a later 3rd-century date, possibly into the 4th century.

Cutting layer cg3119 (LUB 28), to the south of the building, was a very short length of what was probably a much longer north–south beam slot cg3122; this was probably the remains of a partition between the central area and the west.

Within the central area, the oven cg3121 (LUB 28) seems to have continued in use; the southern end of the flue was sealed by mixed burnt and unburnt clay with broken limestone and tile fragments cg3158. Over this debris, incorporating the oven cg3121 (LUB 28) but extending further south and abutting the southern wall of the building, another oven was constructed cg3159.

Between the slot cg3123 and the north wall were dumps of sandy mortar with ash, broken tile and plaster sealed by sandy silt (0.10m thick) cg3127 and cg3128. Pottery from layers cg3127 and cg3128 (124 sherds) were related by sherd links; the notable inclusions in these contexts were fragments from a face or head pot. The NVCC sherds included fragments of a plain dish, an oxidized copy samian form 38 and an everted rim bowl fragment, both possibly from the Swanpool industry, indicating a 4th-century date.

Sealing silt cg3127 was a floor of sandy mortar with pebbles cg3129, cut by a stake-hole. Over floor cg3129 and also extending into the central area, sealing cg3117 (LUB 28), was a layer 0.10m thick of dark grey silty ash sealed by a compact yellow-brown clay floor cg3130. The clay floor cg3130 near to oven cg3159 was sealed by layers cg3131, which consisted of a layer of ash and silt (0.10m thick), over which were patches of burnt and unburnt clay with silt and ash. Layers cg3159 can be interpreted as debris from the use of the oven. Sealing layers cg3117 were patches of sand and clay cg3132, the remains of floors. Layers cg3131 and cg3132 were sealed by brown sandy silt with traces of ash and charcoal cg3133.

In the eastern part of the building, sealing layers cg3114 (LUB 28), were further layers cg3126; these consisted of a dark brown sandy silt with ash and charcoal which was contemporary with a stake-hole; both were sealed by a layer of clay with patches of sand and silt, over which was compact sand sealed by dark silty loam.

To the south-east of the building were traces of internal partitions. An east to west line of nine stake-holes cg3141, and a southern return cg3143 of four stake-holes formed part of a room in the south-east corner of the building; these cut layers cg3109 and cg3114 (both LUB 28). The partitions based on these staggered lines of stake-holes must have been far from straight, and may even have been simple fence-type structures rather than walls.

To the west of the building, cutting layers cg3120 (LUB 28) was a beam slot cg3137 (unplanned) contemporary with ground level tile hearth cg3138. Sealing both the hearth and beam slot was a dump of sandy silt and loam with broken plaster cg3139 (0.13m thick). Pottery from dump cg3139 (30 sherds) included DWSH, a fragment from a NVCC bowl or dish, and beaker fragments of later NVCC fabrics, suggesting a late 3rd- or more probably 4th-century date. Into layer cg3139 a shallow tile and limestone hearth cg3140 was set.

There were 531 sherds of pottery from this LUB. Pottery from beam-slots cg3123 and cg3125, as well as dump cg3139, suggested a late 3rd-century date possibly into the 4th century. Pottery from cg3127 and cg3128 indicated a 4th-century date.

LUB 30 Late occupation and alterations in Structure 9 (Fig. 13.11)
Cutting slot cg3125 (LUB 29) in Area III was one of a north–south line of five postholes cg3142, probably a partition between the central area and the front of the building. In the east part of the building, layers cg3126 (LUB 29) were sealed by a floor of yellow clay with silt cg3136. Layers cg3133 (LUB 29) were sealed by sandy mortar with patches of silt, silty clay and burnt clay cg3145; these layers, partition cg3142 and floor cg3136 were all sealed by dark brown sandy silt cg3147. Pottery from cg3147 (5 sherds) included a sherd from a Swanpool oxidized closed form with painted decoration which suggested a 4th-century date.

Over layer cg3147 was a sequence of layers cg3148; silt and ashy charcoal was sealed by a mortar floor with pebbles, over which was an ashy layer followed by sand and limestone fragment make-up which partly sealed stake-holes cg3141 (LUB 29); over this was a floor of pebbles and limestone and tile fragments set in a sandy clay cg3148. Floor cg3148 was probably equivalent to flat limestones set in clay cg3153 which also sealed some of stake-holes cg3141 (LUB 29) further east.

Over floor cg3148 was a thin layer of dark silty sand cg3149, and some of the stones in floor cg3153 showed evidence of burning. Over sand cg3149, set in clay, along the north wall of the building were

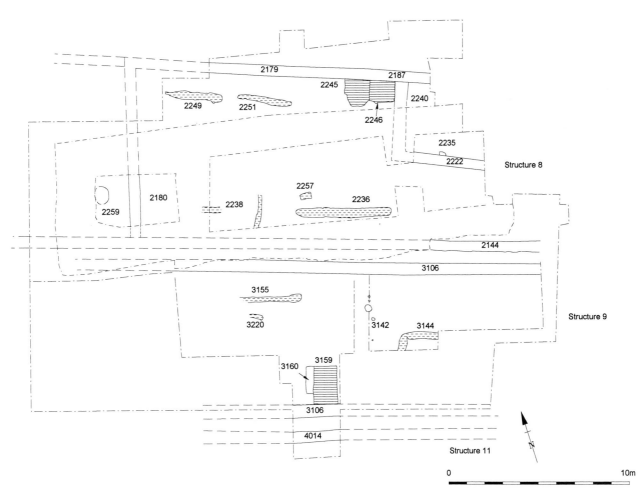

Fig. 13.11 Late occupation of structure 8 and 9: LUB 24 and 31. (1:200)

cobbles cg3150. Cutting the cobbles were two stake-holes and a posthole, sealed by a sequence of layers cg3151; these consisted of layers of sandy clay, sandy silt and several smooth limestones in the vicinity of the north wall, sealed by silty ash. Stones cg3153 were sealed by sandy silt with ash cg3194 which was contemporary with posthole cg3195 (no record of what it cut).

Sealing layers cg3151 and cg3194, together with posthole cg3195, was an extensive but patchy floor of sandy clay cg3196, burnt in places. Over this were thin layers of brown ashy silt, pebbles and clinker and silty sand cg3202. These may have been contemporary with clay layer cg3198 (no record of what it sealed).

Pottery from layers cg3148 to cg3153, together with cg3194 to cg3198 (374 sherds) included many sherds datable to the later 3rd century, but several from vessels such as a NVCC bead-and-flange bowl, late beakers including painted, probable pentice-moulded and types as Gillam 43; the presence of definite Swanpool products and mortaria sherds, and fragments of developed bead-and-flange bowls suggested a stronger 4th-century date.

Beam slot cg3144, which represented the north-west corner of a room in the south-east part of the building, replaced stake-holes cg3141 and cg3143 (both LUB 29). Pottery from beam slot cg3144 (9 sherds) included a sherd of a probable NVCC late slit-folded beaker sherd, usually only found in Lincoln in 4th-century contexts.

In the western area of the building, sealing layer cg3131 (LUB 29), was a layer of silty ash, broken tile and smooth limestone, possibly representing a metalled surface, sealed by ash cg3154. In this were the impressions of sill-beam-based partitions cg3155 and cg3220, which ran east–west. Pottery from sill-beam impression cg3155 (27 sherds) included good evidence for a 4th-century date, which rested on sherds from a high bead-and-flange bowl, late BB1 cooking pot, late painted NVCC ware and an oxidized painted hemispherical bowl.

The southern part of oven cg3159 (LUB 29) continued in use, and was abutted to the west by an extension cg3160.

There were 422 sherds of pottery from this LUB. Pottery from layers cg3147, cg3148 to cg3153 and cg3194 to cg3198, together with beam slot/sill impressions cg3144 and cg3155, all included sherds which dated to the 4th century.

LUB 31 Demolition of Structure 1 (Area I)
Structure 1 in Area I was demolished, and the postholes cg1023 (LUB 13) were sealed by earth, over which was a reddish-brown, compact, hard clayey deposit with charcoal flecks and crushed tile inclusions cg1024 (c 0.20m thick). There were 28 sherds

of residual pottery from this LUB; stratigraphically the demolition dated to the mid to late 3rd century. It was replaced by Structure 7 (LUB 32).

LUB 32 Construction of Structure 7 (Area I)
(Figs. 13.9 and 13.22)
Cutting layers cg1024 (LUB 31) and cg1037 (LUB 14) in Area I was the construction trench of wall cg1025. Pitched limestone footings were laid in a deep construction trench of the wall, then two courses were added, the second narrower than the first but wider than the wall. The wall itself consisted of evenly-sized limestone blocks bonded with pale brown mortar and was 0.55m wide. Sealing layers cg1024 (LUB 31) was a patchy deposit with crushed tile cg1026.

Construction deposits are grouped as cg1027: The area inside the building was levelled up to the bottom of the offset course with 0.20m of sand. A layer of mortar lay in a thin strip (0.45m) against the inside face of the wall. Cutting this layer there were three probable scaffolding stake-holes, evenly spaced (c 2.0m intervals); each was c 0.15m across and 0.20m deep. They were parallel to the inside face of the wall and about 0.25m north of it.

There were 71 sherds of pottery from this LUB, with no sherd links. The samian closes with a stamp of c AD 160–200. Some of the coarse ware sherds date to around the mid 3rd century. A single sherd came from wall cg1025, a GREY fragment from a face or head pot, with an eye and hair; if from a head pot, this would be more likely to be a 4th-century vessel and is probably intrusive from the robbing of the wall.

LUB 33 Occupation of Structure 7 (Fig. 13.9)
Sealing the stake-holes cg1027 (LUB 32) in Area I was a floor of sandy mortar bedded on stone chippings cg1028. This was cut by east–west beam slot cg1030 in the north-western corner of the trench. The fill of the slot contained a coin of AD 318–324; NVCC rouletted beaker sherds from the same beam slot were in a late fabric, and would substantiate the 4th-century date indicated by the coin evidence for the disuse of the slot.

Floor cg1028 was sealed by several floor layers interleaved with other deposits cg1029; a mixed deposit of charcoal and ash, over which was another mortar floor sealed by burnt organic matter and ashy loam; there was another mortar floor over stone packing. A depression in the latest mortar floor was filled with ashy loamy deposits cg1031, containing a single rim of a wide-mouthed bowl of the Swanpool kiln D39 type, suggesting a 4th-century date.

Layers cg1031 were sealed by a layer of light green ashy material cg1032, in which there was a shallow irregular gully cg1033 against the inside face of the wall. Floors cg1029 were sealed by a charcoal spread cg1035. Layer cg1032 was sealed by a floor of white clay cg1034. Pottery from cg1031 and cg1033 dated to the 4th century.

There were 79 sherds of pottery from this LUB with no sherd links.

LUB 34 Demolition of Structure 7
Sealing layers cg1035, cg1034 and gully cg1033 (LUB 33) in Area I were layers of ash and rubble cg1036, evidence of the demolition of the building. Pottery from rubble cg1036 produced evidence for mid to late 4th-century dating with sherds from three different DWSH double lid-seated jar rims, together with sherds from a wide-mouthed bowl of Swanpool kiln D39 type, a dish or lid of Swanpool kiln type G2, a Swanpool mortarium, NVCC bead-and-flange bowl and bowl or dish, a pentice-moulded beaker and a painted beaker; the presence of double lid-seated jars suggested the later 4th century.

LUB 35 Deposits between structures
Sealing the construction deposits of walls cg1025 (Structure 7; LUB 32) and cg2187 (Structure 8; LUB 22), and sealing layer cg1038 (LUB 14) in Areas I and II, were several rubbly layers cg1040; limestone rubble and chippings in sand were sealed by greenish loam, further limestone rubble with yellow mortar and roofing stone, over which was burnt building debris and rubbly loam. Pottery from cg1040 (58 sherds) contained two possible LCOA body sherds, sherds from a GREY high bead-and-flange bowl, and late beaker sherds which suggested the deposit dated to the later 4th century. These deposits were located in the gap between the stone walls of Structures 7 and 8 (Areas I and II).

Between walls cg2144 (LUB 20) and cg3106 (LUB 27) in Areas 2 and 3 was a build up of dark brown loam cg3170 with large amounts of mortar and tile (0.80m thick). Pottery from cg3170 (202 sherds) contained more BB1 than would be normal, including types of mid 3rd-century date, which ties in with some vessels more akin to Rookery Lane kiln types than Swanpool; the LCOA fabric occurred but as a lid-seated jar rather than the late type. A mid (to late) 4th-century date seems indicated by the pottery from cg3170.

Sealing the robbed remains of the south wall of Structure 8 was a dump of loam cg3179 with large chunks of mortar with tile embedded, plus very large amounts of tile (discarded).

In summary, there were 260 sherds from this LUB; those from the two context groups cg1040 and cg3170 dated to the second part of the 4th century.

LUB 36 Construction and use of Structure 10 (Area IV) (Fig. 13.9)
Sealing layers cg4003 (Structure 4, LUB 12) in Area IV was a thick deposit of brown silty sandy loam with pebble limestone chips and crushed mortar cg4004 (up to 0.50m thick). Pottery from cg4004 (80 sherds) included samian which closed with a mid–late Antonine sherd; the rest of the pottery was indeterminate and residual, the dating to the mid 3rd century resting on a sherd of GREY jar type J107.

Over layers cg4004 was a thin layer of mortar cg4005 which appeared to be similar to that in east–west stone wall cg4015. This consisted of evenly-coursed limestone blocks bonded with yellow mortar; there was no record of what it cut. Wall cg4015 formed the northern external wall of the new building.

Sealing layers cg4004 and cg4005 were several layers cg4006; first, thin layers of sandy silt, sealed by sand, then sandy clay over which was a dump (0.10m thick) of limestone and rubble, and yellow clay with limestone blocks (0.05m thick) sealed by black ash. Over these were further layers cg4007; red clay floor sealed by silty sand, over which was silt cut by a posthole; it was sealed by layers of silty sand overspread with black ash. Sealing this was an area of sand with limestone blocks, over which was burnt limestone with clay cg4009, the remains of an oven against the north wall, probably forming the base for a superstructure of clay.

Pottery from cg4006 (108 sherds) appeared to be mostly residual, dating broadly to the mid to late 3rd century, although the date of a sherd of MOMH hammerhead mortarium could extend into the 4th century. There were 203 sherds from this LUB; the only sherd links were within the group. There were only two context groups with datable pottery and these suggested that the use of this building extended from the mid 3rd century to the 4th century.

LUB 37 Structure 11: stone wall and possible construction layers (Figs. 13.10 and 13.11)
The north wall of Structure 10, cg4015 (LUB 36) in Area IV was replaced by a wall of similar construction, cg4014, built directly on top of the demolished wall. Yellowish mortar from this rebuilding partially sealed oven cg4009 (LUB 36). The oven was also sealed by layers cg4010; loam was sealed by limestone chips and stones over which was more loam and more limestone rubble, and more loam sealed by layers of sandy clay loam with limestone chips. These layers cg4010 suggest dump layers or external build-up rather than internal floors. The pottery from layers cg4010 (37 sherds) included sherds from a probable Swanpool wide-mouthed bowl, a high beaded flanged bowl, a shell-tempered

bowl or dish, and a late NVCC slit-folded beaker; a mid 4th-century date is probable.

There were 37 sherds from this LUB, all from cg4010 with sherds dating to the mid 4th century.

Very Late Roman

The shell of Structure 8, although burnt, continued to be used **LUB 38**; new stone-founded partitions created a room in the north-east corner containing a pot pit; there were clay floors, a roughly flagged surface, and substantial ovens, to the west of which was a pot pit up against the north wall and east–west slots, possibly indicating partitions. The latest pottery from LUB 38 dated to the very late 4th century.

Very late 4th-century pottery was recovered from the dereliction and re-use of Structure 8 **LUB 39**. Here rubbly layers were succeeded by a north–south wall with rough cobbles; there were pits to the south and west and later stake-holes to the west.

Structure 9 appears to have been abandoned and layers of rubble sealed LUB 30, but there was some evidence for re-use **LUB 40**; post-pits replaced the walls on the east and stake-holes were contemporary; in the centre of the site were traces of timber slots sealed by a rough flagged floor; in the southern part was an extensive hearth and small oven, and in the west was trampled rubble. The pottery for LUB 40 suggests a very late 4th-century date.

Roman or post-Roman

LUB 38 Late occupation of Structure 8
(Figs. 13.11, 13.23 and 13.34–35)
Sealing mortar cg2190 (LUB 22) in Area II was a dump of sandy loam cg2278 (0.15–.20m thick). Ash cg2213 (LUB 23) in Area II was cut by posthole cg2214 which was sealed by sandy loam and pebbles cg2215: this was equivalent to cg2278; cg2215 and cg2278 were cut by the construction trench for internal wall cg2222. The wall, constructed of irregularly-sized limestone bonded with pale brown mortar, was 0.45 – 0.50m thick. A length of just over 4.0m was exposed running east–west. It was probably of one build with north–south wall cg2240, the remains of which consisted of limestone footings. The room thus formed measured *c* 3.70m north–south by at least 4.0m east–west.

Internal to the room to the north of wall cg2222, layer cg2278 was cut by posthole cg2191 and sealed by an area of yellow sandy mortar mixed with pebbles cg2192, mortar with burnt limestone chips cg2198, and a thin mixed layer of charcoal and mortar cg2195. Cutting cg2192 was a posthole cg2193. Over layer cg2194 (LUB 22) and mortar cg2195, was rubble cg2196 sealed by loam cg2197.

This was sealed by a fine hard pebbly mortar layer cg2233, which lay up against wall cg2222. Cutting layer cg2233 was a posthole cg2234 and a small pit cg2235 which was located against the north face of wall cg2222. This pit contained a nearly complete pot, a LCOA double-lid-seated jar with a NVCC plain-rim dish apparently acting as a lid, giving a late to very late 4th-century date (Fig. 13.34). The jar was substantially complete, the only damage being some fragmentation of its rim; the dish was virtually complete although broken in two.

Outside the room, to the south of wall cg2222, sealing loam cg2215 was yellow sandy mortar cg2321, which was cut by postholes cg2224 and cg2324; layer cg2321 was sealed by a spread of charcoal cg2322; over this spread and posthole cg2224 were layers of dark sandy, ashy loam cg2323. A layer of greenish-brown ashy clay cg2325 sealed the layers cg2323 and posthole cg2324; into this cut a stake-hole cg2326, sealed by a layer of grey clay with flecks of ash, charcoal and burnt clay cg2225. Similar layers cg2226 were uncovered further south, to the north of wall cg2144, sealing cg2209 (LUB 23); they consisted of a thin layer of clayey loam, sealed by sandy loam and rubble, over which was a surface of burnt red clay, sealed by ash. Layers cg2226 included a single body sherd of SPIR, upon which the dating to the very late 4th century is based.

Over layers cg2226 was a circular patch of clay cg2227, possibly the remains of an oven structure. Sealing burnt clay cg2225 and clay layer cg2227 was a stone surface cg2229 set in silty loam cg2228; the surface consisted of flattish fragments of worn limestone pieces bonded in places by pebbly mortar. Silty loam cg2228 contained a probable 4th-century NVCC flask, but more importantly a sherd from an OXRC vessel, probably a bowl, which, together with SHEL bodysherds, should indicate a late to very late 4th-century date.

In the southern part of the building, posthole cg2230 cut layers cg2209 (LUB 23), and was sealed by greenish-yellow ashy loam cg2231, over which was a thin patchy layer of white clay cg2232. Loam cg2231 contained sherds from a NVCC pentice-moulded beaker, a probable late flask, and an OX double lid-seated jar, the basis for the late to very late 4th-century date. There was a substantial east–west beam slot cg2236 (no record of what it cut, but it was probably loam cg2231), possibly associated with beam slot cg2257 (also no record of what it cut). Pottery from beam slot cg2236 dates to the very late 4th century, on the basis of sherds from a DWSH double lid-seated jar, a GREY bowl with inturned bead and flange, a LCOA vessel, two NVCC plain rimmed dishes, and a SPIR jar rim.

To the west of the beam slots were other cut features, a posthole, a north–south and an east–west beam slot cg2238, and two postholes cg2237 which carried on the east–west alignment to the west (unplanned), to create a partition which would have reached wall cg2180; these probably all cut cg2231.

Into clay floor layer cg2212 (LUB 22) in the north-east part of Structure 8 cut a posthole cg2214 (unplanned). Also in this area, cutting the remains of oven cg2203 (LUB 22) were stake-holes cg2242; sealing oven remains was a narrow strip of lime-stone rubble cg2243 against wall cg2187 (LUB 22) sealed by rubble cg2244. Up against the north wall cg2187 (LUB 22), sealing the construction trench of wall cg2240, was an oven cg2246 (Fig. 13.35). This was constructed of limestone bonded with white clay; it appeared to consist of a chamber 1.30m square, and some of the stone facings within it had apparently been burnt. Oven cg2246 was possibly a side oven or drying chamber associated with oven cg2245 to the west. The flue of oven cg2245 (Fig. 13.35) was constructed from a square of limestone walls infilled with clay and rubble, with the flue in the centre. A noticeable quantity of tile was incorporated within platform and flue cg2245 and oven cg2246. The flue had a rectangular section and was constructed from limestone with a stone forming the base. The clay and stones were extensively burnt, and it is assumed that a large hearth or oven existed to the south (removed by the Church foundations) and generated the hot air that travelled along the flue; it seems likely that the flue was also used as a raking-out channel. Pottery from oven cg2245 included a sherd of LCOA, and a probable sherd from a MHAD hemispherical bowl, giving a very late 4th-century date.

To the west of the ovens, loam and mortar layers cg2189 (LUB 22) were sealed by grey clay over which was a dump of loam cg2247. Over this, and over cg2327 (LUB 23), was a layer of loose ash cg2248, perhaps used as the level from which post-fire repairs were carried out. A small assemblage of animal bone from layer cg2248 is consistent with domestic kitchen waste (Dobney *et al* 1994f). Pottery from layer cg2248 included sherds from three DWSH dishes, and a double lid-seated jar, supplemented by sherds from a small bowl or dish rim in LCOA of the type of Swanpool kiln type G5, a SPIR jar rim, NVCC dish and South Midlands shell-tempered jar, indicating a very late 4th-century date.

To the west of ovens cg2245 and cg2246, cutting layer cg2327 (LUB 23), were east–west beam slots cg2251 and cg2249. Pottery from beam slot cg2251 is conservatively late 4th century with sherds from a DWSH double lid-seated jar, a NVCC pentice-moulded beaker, and a Swanpool mortarium of bead-and-flange type. On dating grounds rather than stratigraphic, the beam slots might belong to an earlier phase.

Cutting layer cg2248, against the north wall cg2179 (LUB 20) was a small pit cg2253 (unplanned); this contained a complete pot, a Swanpool everted-rim bowl, complete and undamaged, which was set upright on a clay-coated stone in the bottom of the pit (perhaps used to pack up the pot to the correct height); two GREY bead-and-flange bowls, one with a high bead, were also found, together with a LCOA body sherd and a HADOX footring base, worn internally, possibly from a bowl of form 38 type; a very late 4th-century date is indicated.

To the west of the site, cutting rubble cg2184 (LUB 21), was a posthole cg2259, sealed by loam and ash cg2260 (*c* 0.20m thick). Pottery from cg2260 (134 sherds) contained Swanpool types, which included sherds from a late colour-coated mortarium, several oxidised vessels, and two bowls with Romano-Saxon decoration; other late Roman sherds included sherds from LCOA double lid-seated jars, a shell-tempered bowl or dish, an EPON bowl of form 38 and late NVCC bowls and dishes; a date after the mid 4th century is indicated. The presence of a post-Roman sherd (LKT) was probably due to contamination (from LUB 41).

There were 940 pottery sherds from LUB 38, including sherds dated to the very late 4th century from cg2236, cg2245 and cg2248. There was one intrusive Late Saxon sherd from this LUB.

LUB 39 Dereliction and reuse of Structure 8
(Figs. 13.12 and 13.23)
Sealing pot-pit cg2235, posthole cg2234, cobbles cg2229 and partition cg2222 (all LUB 38) in Structure 8, was a thick layer of silty loam cg2239 (*c* 0.20m thick) with mortar and limestone fragments. Layer cg2239 contained several vessels indicating a very late 4th-century date, including DWSH and LCOA double lid-seated jars (four of the latter fabric), LCOA triangular rim bowl, Swanpool mortaria, three NVCC bead-and-flange bowls and four plain-rimmed dishes, two possible SPCC or late NVCC plain-rimmed dishes, a probable SPIR body sherd, and a number of SPOX vessels, including three bowls of form 38, an inturned bead-and-flange bowl, a painted closed vessel, a collared rim jar and handled jar.

Sealing pot-pit cg2253 and oven cg2245 (both LUB 29), was a layer of loam and clay cg2254. Sealing beam slots cg2249 and cg2251 (both LUB 29) was limestone tumble in loam with fragments of yellow mortar cg2250; this layer included sherds of an LCOA dish dating to the very late 4th century. Sealing layer cg2248 (LUB 38) was limestone rubble cg2252. To the south of the building was a layer of sandy mortar cg2255 (there was no record of what this layer had overlain); it was sealed by sandy silt, much mortar and fragments of burnt plaster cg2256.

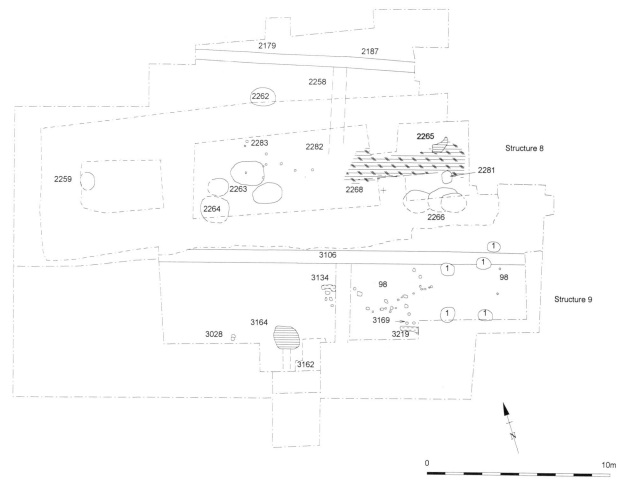

Fig. 13.12 Re-use of structures 8 and 9: LUBs 32 and 40. (1:200)

Sealing layer cg2254 were roughly-faced limestone blocks, set in mortar and greyish loam cg2258, which represented the foundation of a north–south wall abutting wall cg2187 (LUB 22), dividing up part of the building for re-use; this wall was also traced to the south cg2282. To the west of this wall, sealing limestone tumble cg2250, was a patch of red clay cg2261, and cutting it was a small pit and a stake-hole cg2262. Sealing layer cg2261 and cut features cg2262, and over the robbed north wall of Structure 8, was limestone rubble, sealed by loam ash and rubble, over which was loam cg2280. Loam cg2280 contained a range of late Roman fabrics OXRC, SPIR, LCOA, SPCC and a range of Swanpool types, late vessel forms in NVCC (270 sherds), suggesting a very late 4th-century date, as well as seven Late Saxon sherds.

Sealing layer cg2239 were rough cobbles, unevenly laid, cg2268. To the south of them was a posthole cg2281, cutting cg2239; this may have represented part of an east–west wall which would have met wall cg2282; the cobbles did not extend south of this line. Over the cobbles cg2268 was a patch of burnt clay with ash cg2265, a probable hearth. To the south of the cobbles cg2268 were three inter-cutting pits cg2266.

To the south, cutting layers cg2255 and cg2256, were three pits cg2263; pit cg2264 was probably also part of the group (there was no record of what it cut). Pit cg2264 contained one sherd of intrusive late Saxon pottery. Sealing the pits cg2263 and pit cg2264 were layers of sandy brown loam cg2279 (0.35m thick); 12 stake-holes cg2283 were found 'within' the layers cg2279. The large number of Roman sherds from cg2279 (480 sherds) all had the ingredients of a very late 4th-century group, as indicated by fabrics OXRC, SPIR, LCOA, SPCC, supplemented by a range of Swanpool types, late vessel forms in NVCC and a fragment probably from a head pot; however, there was residual material, and the sherdage was notably fragmented, suggesting that it was secondary rubbish or had been subsequently reworked (there were three intrusive Late Saxon sherds).

In all, there were 1,183 sherds of Roman pottery

from this LUB. The pottery from cg2239, cg2250, cg2280 and cg2279 all indicated a very late 4th-century date for LUB 39. There was a total of 11 Late Saxon sherds, of which seven came from cg2280. It would seem that some of these sherds were intrusive: those from cg2280 may indicate that this layer was still exposed in the late Saxon period.

LUB 40 Late use of Structure 9 (Figs. 13.12)
Layers cg3202 (LUB 30) in Area III were sealed by a thick layer of red-brown silty loam with sand cg3197 (0.13m thick). This was probably contemporary with silty loam cg3199 (no record of what it sealed). Cutting layer cg3197 were east–west slots cg3134 and cg3219, one in the north part of the building and one in the south. Sealing layer cg3197, against the north wall, was brown sandy loam with much mortar and sandy chips cg3152 (0.14m thick). Sealing ash cg3134 were further layers of ash cg3157. Sealing beam slot cg3220 (LUB 31) were layers of ashy clay and charcoal sealed by further layers of clay cg3156. Over ash cg3157 and ashy clay cg3156, was ash and sandy silt, into which smooth limestone pieces cg3163 were set, possibly part of a roughly flagged floor. Roman pottery, probably from the ash and silt into which the stone flags were set cg3163, (398 sherds), included sherds of Swanpool products including a colour-coated hemispherical painted bowl, double lid-seated jars and a dish in shell fabric, grey high bead-and-flanged bowls and the Swanpool inturned type, late NVCC beakers including painted, probable pentice-moulded vessels and types as Gillam 43; the occurrence of late types of decoration on grey vessels suggests a date towards the later 4th century. Layer cg3163 contained one sherd of Late Saxon pottery. Cut through cg3163 were two successive postholes cg3028, and over it accumulated sandy, silty loam cg3224.

Over layers cg3198 (LUB 30), cg3199, cg3152 and slots cg3134 and cg3219 was an extensive, but mostly thin, layer of silty sand with loam and limestone rubble cg3169 (0.05m thick, but up to 0.20m thick to the south). Pottery from cg3169 (378 sherds) included the fabrics and vessel types characteristic of a very late 4th-century group in Lincoln, including sherds of LCOA, SPIR, late jars and bowls of Swanpool type, Swanpool mortaria, oxidized and colour-coated vessels, late NVCC pentice-moulded beakers, Gillam 57 type and open forms, and late shell-tempered jars and open forms.

Sealing rubble cg3169 was an accumulation of dark silty loam cg644 (0.20m thick) with sandy mortary and ashy material. A large assemblage of animal bones, dominated by cattle and caprovids, was recovered from cg644; elements present suggest a mixture of commercial and domestic butchery (Dobney *et al* 1994f). Some of the Roman pottery from cg644 (from context AUL) was discarded on site, as this loam was considered during the excavation to be of post-Roman deposition. Pottery from the other context (BAD) from cg644 survived substantially complete (676 sherds), and contained a pottery assemblage of very late 4th-century date, based on 24 sherds of LCOA (17 body sherds; sherds from a bowl/dish, flange-rimmed bowl, an inturned bead and flange bowl, a double lid-seated jar, a lid-seated jar and a narrow-necked jar), together with sherds from a NVCC pentice-moulded beaker and NVCC girth beaker, a DWSH inturned bead and flange bowl and GREY inturned bead-and-flange bowls.

Stake-holes cg98 were cut within layer cg644, as were five large postholes or post-pits cg1 further to the east of the site. Two of the postholes actually cut the robbed north wall of the building; two of the stake-holes could be interpreted as an entrance to the east of the building, towards the road. They suggest possible continuity, even in the very late Roman period, of the importance of a roadside plot. The stake-holes cg98 and postholes cg1 were sealed by dark silty loam cg646. Loam cg646 was viewed as of post-Roman date during the excavation, and due to the discard policy, unexceptional Roman sherds were discarded. Only 25 Roman sherds survive from cg646, dating to the very late 4th century; they include sherds of GREY Romano-Saxon type bowl, GREY double lid-seated jar and SPIR. The post-Roman sherds (12 sherds altogether) from cg646 were of mixed date, suggesting possible intrusion (from LUBs 41 and later); the latest were sherds of LFS (late 10th century) and ST (the ST sherd is a fine ware type dating from the mid/late 11th century), while the rest dated to the late 9th to early 10th century.

The stake-holes cg98 and postholes or post-pits cg1 have been published as gravemarkers and a possible timber church (Gilmour and Stocker 1986, 15–21). An alternative interpretation of these features is explored in the discussion.

Sealing postholes cg3028 (LUB 30) and loam cg3224 (LUB 30) was rubble and lumps of mortar set in silty loam cg3027. This would appear to be rubble left after the demolition and robbing of the building, and then trampled over, as the surface stones were worn. In the rubble cg3027 was a small to moderate sized assemblage of animal bone representing domestic refuse (Dobney *et al* 1994f), together with 59 sherds of Roman pottery including sherds from at least three Swanpool mortaria, a fragment from a South Midlands shell-tempered jar (normally only occurring in later 4th-century deposits in Lincoln), and sherds of SPIR, all substantiating a late to very late 4th-century date. Rubble gh3027 included one intrusive late Saxon sherd.

Sealing rubble cg3027 was a layer of sandy loam with limestone rubble cg3168, layers of silty loam with limestone pieces and tile sealed by ashy loam cg3026 and limestone rubble cg3193. Layers cg3168 and cg3026 as well as cg3193 contained very late 4th century pottery. Pottery from cg3168 (19 sherds) included sherds from a LCOA double lid-seated jar, sherds from late Swanpool types, SPIR and late NVCC dish and bowl/dish sherds, all of which indicated a very late 4th-century date. Pottery from cg2026 (7 sherds remaining from an original 80), included a sherd from a Romano-Saxon decorated bowl, sherds from a SPIR jar and a sherd from a Swanpool oxidized handled jar and lid which suggest a very late 4th-century date. Pottery from cg3193 (21 sherds) included nine sherds probably from a single LCOA double lid-seated jar, and four sherds from a single NVCC pentice-moulded beaker, together with a NVCC bowl or dish sherd indicating a very late 4th-century date. Layer cg3168 contained one sherd of intrusive Late Saxon pottery and layer cg3026 contained three sherds, one of which was a sherd from a waster of ELSW.

Over both ovens cg3159 and cg3160 (LUB 30) was a layer of burnt and unburnt clay and limestone rubble, some of which was burnt cg3161. This was associated with traces of a further hearth cg3162.

Cutting layers cg3148 (LUB 30) and ash cg3157 was a small oven cg3164; a thick clay base (about 1.5m by 0.60m and about 0.20m thick), heavily burnt towards the top, was linked to traces of a flue leading south, towards the wall, with a brown ashy silt fill. Around the oven and flue was pink clay and sooty silt cg3165. Over this was heavily burnt clay cg3166, possibly related to the destruction of the oven. This was cut by posthole cg3167 (unplanned).

In all, there were 1,772 sherds of Roman pottery from this LUB. Pottery from cg3163, cg3169, cg644, cg3027, cg3168, cg3026 and cg3193 included sherds dating to the very late 4th century. There was a total of eighteen sherds of Late Saxon pottery, of which twelve came from cg646. These sherds are a relatively small number for such a large area and, as with LUB 39, it seems much more probable that most of these represent intrusive sherds. The presence of these sherds in cg646 might indicate that this layer was open into the late Saxon period.

Late Saxon (Anglo-Scandinavian)

To the rear of the site, pitting was in evidence **LUB 41**; pottery from these pits dated to the 10th century. Sealing LUB 41 and covering much of the area of the site was a graveyard; some of the inhumations belong entirely to this period LUBs 42–44, and others were buried during this period or later LUBs 45–54; pottery from these LUBs dated possibly as early as the late

9th, but certainly from the 10th and 11th centuries. Tombstone fragments, dated from the mid 10th century, might be a better clue to the date of the foundation of the cemetery, whether or not a church was also provided at the same time.

LUB 41 Pits (Fig. 13.13)
In the centre of the site, pit cg2 cut two pits cg2264 and cg2263 (LUB 39); a small assemblage of animal bones from pit cg2 was dominated by cattle, the most common elements consisting of horncores, mandibles and metapodials (Dobney *et al* 1994f). Pit cg2 was cut by pit cg105 and both were sealed by dark silty loam with limestone rubble cg647 (*c* 0.30m thick). Pits cg105 (four post-Roman sherds) and cg2 (six post-Roman sherds) contained pottery dating to the 10th century.

Also in the centre of the site was a dark grey silty loam cg652 with traces of mussels (there was no record of what it sealed); the north aisle cg377 (LUB 71) had cut into it (there was no record of what it sealed, although it is considered to belong to this LUB). Over the area was dark brown loam cg653 (no record of what it actually sealed); this layer contained 26 post-Roman sherds of late 9th to early 10th-century pottery. Over loam and ash cg2260 (LUB 29), at the very west end of the site, was a layer of sandy loam cg643 (*c* 0.15–0.20m thick) containing a single post-Roman sherd. Layers cg652, cg653 and cg643 were thought to represent layers probably laid down in the late Saxon period, probably overlying the very late Roman material (LUB 39). These two pits were previously interpreted as a ditch defining the west boundary of the graveyard (Gilmour and Stocker 1986, 15–16).

LUBs 42–44 Graveyard predating church Structure 13 (Figs. 13.14, 13.40)
LUB 42. Inhumations from LUB 42 cut into and reworked loam layers cg646 (LUB 40) and cg653 (LUB 41). Very few sherds were recovered from the graves, the latest being SNLS dating to the 11th century. The burials associated with LUB 42 included those graves later cut by the stone church (Structure 13.1) cg19, cg20, cg22, cg24, cg25, cg36, cg37, cg38, cg39, cg44, cg45, cg47, cg56, cg57, cg60, cg61, cg62, cg63, cg64, cg65, cg66, cg67, cg107; some cut by postholes and robber trenches to the east of the church cg40, cg41, cg42, cg43, cg46. Some of these and others were charcoal burials cg38, cg39, cg40, cg44, cg66 and cg91. Other burials from this LUB include cg8, cg11, cg16, cg17, cg41, cg42, cg43, cg46, cg80, cg82, cg83, cg84, cg85, cg90, cg92, cg95 and cg97. Charnel pit cg108 was cut by inhumation cg41. Other inhumations cg16, cg17, cg83, cg85, cg90 were dated by their radio-carbon dates roughly to the 10th century, and some earlier than an *in situ* grave stone (LUB 45) dated to

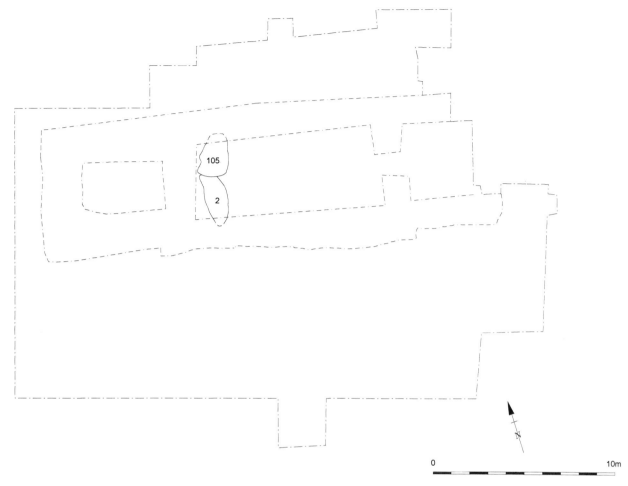

Fig. 13.13 Late Saxon pits: LUB 41. (1:200)

the late 10th to late 11th centuries: cg8, cg11, cg80, cg82, cg84, cg91, cg92, cg95, cg97. What might have been the fill cg164 of a truncated grave had been sealed by construction levels cg118 (LUB 57) of the subsequent chancel. Although some nails were found in nine of these burials, (up to a maximum of four in one grave fill (cg91)), there is no strong evidence to suggest that they were used in coffin construction. The date of the origin of the graveyard LUB 42 has been discussed in terms of burial sequences and radio-carbon dating as possibly being mid 10th century (Gilmour and Stocker 1986, 16–17). Also to be considered are the tombstone fragments (Tomb numbers 4–6,8,17,19) from this period which were re-used in the construction of the church cg109 (LUB 55); none was earlier than the mid 10th century. There was one piece of 12th-century date (Tomb number 50) but there was a question mark against the context on the original record card suggesting that it may have originated from another context. Much of the excavated area had been used as a graveyard at least from the mid-10th century. All the LUB 42 burials

were stratigraphically earlier than the first stone church on the site.

LUB 43. Inhumations in the southern area of the graveyard included those on charcoal cg50, cg99 and cg100, cist burial cg252 which also was a "charcoal burial", as well as inhumations cg81, cg101, cg102, cg103, cg104, cg175, cg178, cg179, cg248 and cg251.

Although burials extended outside the excavated area to the north, east and south, the western limit of burial, LUB 44 was found in the excavation. It may have corresponded to a break of slope which was recorded in section (Fig. 13.24; Gilmour and Stocker 1986, Fig. 66) where it can be seen that the loam cg645 (LUB 44) dropped away towards the river, away from the higher ground flanking the High Street. Loam cg645 (LUB 44) contained pottery (20 post-Roman sherds), the latest sherds of which could date to the late 10th century. The group includes wares characteristic of the late 9th or early 10th century.

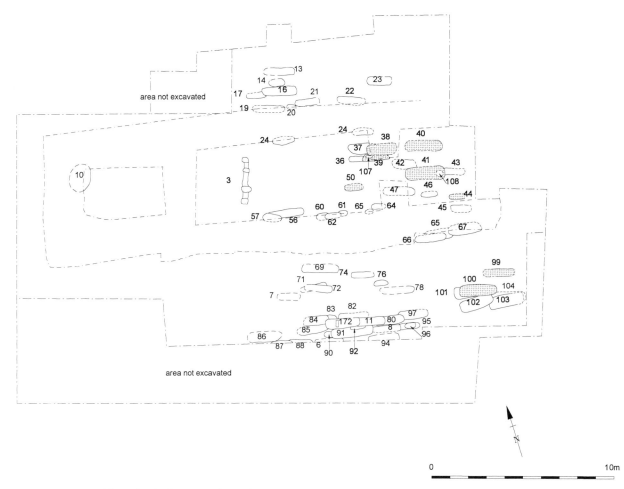

Fig. 13.14 Graveyard pre-dating stone-founded church: LUBs 42–44. (1:200)

LUBs 45–54 Graveyard (Figs. 13.41 and 13.50)
LUB 45 consists of the gravestone inhumation cg172 which cut cg11 and cg84 (both LUB 42). The grave marker which indicated the site of inhumation cg172, LUB 45 was dated between the mid 10th and the late 11th centuries (Sepulchral fragment 23; Gilmour and Stocker 1986, 67 and 73). This would mean it was either associated with the earlier graveyard or was erected when the first church was built (Structure 13.1).

LUB 46 consists of the grave yard predating the rebuilding of Structure 13.3 to the south. Inhumation cg160 and graveyard deposit cg194 were cut by inhumation cg161, over which was a spread of mortar and limestone fragments cg192 which may have represented a path and/or indicated the presence of a southern doorway in the first church. Over this mortar spread was a layer of loam cg271 and another spread of mortar and limestone fragments cg272, whose surface was sufficiently hard to suggest to the excavators that it had been a path.

This in turn was sealed by crushed mortar and limestone cg288, another possible surface. Whether it is fortuitous that the insertion of the later porch preserved these layers, or whether they were originally limited to the area outside the likely position of a south doorway, cannot be determined. Inhumation cg177 has been included in this group because of Harwell radio-carbon dating 1080±70; it cuts inhumations cg176 and cg78 (also both LUB 46). A copper-alloy bracelet ((AUY) <SM76:AE105> Fig. 13.50 No 1) was recorded as being found on the arm (possibly fortuitously) of inhumation cg78. Other inhumations belonged to LUB 46, including inhumations cg162, cg234, cg274 and cist burials cg273 and cg276. A small number of sherds dating generally to the 10th century were found in graveyard deposit cg194 (one post-Roman sherd) and inhumation fill cg161, LUB 46.

LUB 47 consists of the graveyard earlier than the rebuilding of Structure 13.3 to the north. This includes inhumations cg13, cg14, cg15, cg18, cg21, cg23, cg132, cg133, cg134, cg135, cg136, cg137, cg138, cg139, cg140, cg141, cg142, cg143, cg144, cg146, cg147, cg165, cg210, cg211, cg212, cg214, cg215, cg216, cg218, cg219, cg223, cg233 and graveyard deposit cg189. The registered finds from the burials from this part of the graveyard are either clearly residual Roman, or nails which may or may not be residual (from four burials). The pottery from LUB 47 dates to the 10th century (four post-Roman sherds each from cg133 and cg189 and single sherds from cg135, cg139, cg210 and cg211).

LUB 48 consists of the graveyard earlier than the porch Structure 13.3F; the porch directly cut several inhumations and sealed others. It includes inhumations cg7, cg70, cg73, cg86, cg159, cg166, cg167, cg168, cg170, cg256, cist inhumations cg71, cg72, cg314, cg315, cg316, cg317, cg321 and cg322, pit cg157 and pebble and limestone surface cg378. A single sherd from cg315 dates to between the mid 12th and early 13th centuries.

LUB 49 consists of the graveyard earlier than gully cg292 (LUB 70). This included inhumations cg12, cg129, cg130, cg131, cg213, cg221, cg224, cist inhumation cg222 and graveyard deposit cg296. Graveyard cg296, LUB 49, contained 11 pottery sherds the latest of which dated to the 13th century.

LUB 50 consists of the graveyard earlier than the north aisle Structure 13.3D. Included are inhumations cg145, cg220, cg225, cg226, cg227, cg229, cg230, cg231, cg232, cg293, cist inhumation cg228 and graveyard deposit cg295. A copper-alloy finger-ring was found on one finger of the skeleton in inhumation cg231 (Fig. 13.50 No 2). A quantity of nails was recovered from inhumation cg295. The latest pottery from LUB 50 (nine post-Roman sherds from cg295 and single sherds from cg227 and 293) dates to the 14th century or later.

LUB 51 consists of the south graveyard earlier than the Victorian Church Structure 15. A patch of southern graveyard loam dump cg263 was sealed by a sequence of layers, made up of mortary loam cg265, silty loam cg266, mortar with limestone fragments cg267, silty loam cg268, sandy silt with crushed mortar and limestone chips cg269 and finally another layer of mortar and limestone chips cg270; most of these possible surfaces show evidence of loamy trample. The southern area of the graveyard pre-dating the Victorian church structure included many grouped contexts; inhumations cg76, cg77, cg79, cg93, cg94, cg96, cg158, cg169, cg171, cg173, cg174, cg184, cg185, cg186, cg187, cg188, cg235, cg236, cg237, cg238, cg239, cg243, cg249, cg253, cg255, cg257, cg259, cg261, cg264, cg327, cg328, cg337, cg338, cg382, cg383, cg418, cg419, cg421, cg423, cg487 and cg488; cist

inhumations cg250, cg275, cg277, cg278, cg279, cg280, cg313, cg326, cg329, cg330, cg331, cg332, cg333, cg334, cg339, cg340, cg341, cg342, cg344, cg345, cg346, cg347, cg348, cg349, cg350, cg351, cg354, cg355, cg356, cg357, cg358, cg359, cg360, cg361 and cg381; inhumations with traces of wooden coffins cg420 and cg489; inhumations in brick shafts cg554, cg555 and cg557; charnel pits cg343, cg352 and cg353; graveyard deposit cg195, cg362, cg422 and cg513. Graveyard deposit cg195 (LUB 51) contained 10 sherds of very mixed material, some of which dated to the late 9th to early 10th century; the latest sherds date to the 13th century. The burials included in LUB 51 vary greatly in date. Four late brick shafts are included, as are a number of burials in coffins with grave furniture. Unfortunately the grips (coffin handles), nails (upholstery pins), and various escutcheon plates were all briefly recorded but then discarded shortly after the excavation, together with large numbers of iron nails. Amongst the build-up of graveyard deposits, LUB 51, was found a copper alloy pen-annular brooch and a silver penny of William 1, a *Two Sceptres* issue of AD1072–4 (Blackburn *et al* 1983, 30). These almost certainly represent earlier, casual losses rather than burial goods. A similar explanation may be given for the presence of a zoomorphic terminal in the late inhumation cg278. Small amounts of mixed post-Roman pottery were found in several graves (single sherds in; cg253, cg328, cg337, cg339, cg342 and cg354, two sherds in cg327 and cg357, three sherds in cg362, four sherds in cg332 and cg278, five sherds in cg422, six sherds in cg555 and 20 sherds in cg513).

LUB 52 consists of unstratified inhumations in the centre of the graveyard: inhumations cg9, cg26, cg27, cg28, cg30, cg31, cg32, cg33, cg34, cg35, cg48, cg49, cg51, cg52, cg53, cg54, cg55, cg58, cg59, cg148, cg149, cg150, cg151, cg152 and possible cist cg29.

LUB 53 consists of unstratified inhumations to the south of the Church. The number of generations is small, because many of these inhumations could not be tied into the stratigraphy at all, but were left "floating" within the stratigraphic sequence, since the level from which they had been cut had been disturbed by later grave-digging. These included inhumations cg6, cg68, cg74, cg75, cg87, cg88, cg89, cg163, cg180, cg181, cg182, cg183, cg240, cg241, cg242, cg244, cg245, cg246, cg247, cg258, cg260, cg262, cg335, cg336, cg549, cg552; cist burials cg69 and cg254; inhumations with traces of a wooden coffin cg548, cg550 and cg551; inhumations in brick shafts cg547 and cg553; linear feature cg193. Little post-Roman pottery was found in these burials (single sherds in cg258 and cg552, two sherds in cg68, four sherds in cg549 and six sherds in cg553).

LUB 54 consists of unstratified inhumations to the north of the Church (cg127, cg128 and cg294; cist burial cg217). There was evidence for either building debris or a path cg190 in the north part of the graveyard, sealed by further dumping or upcast cg191. Upcast cg191 contained four sherds dating to the 13th century, including one sherd from an early POTT cooking pot found nearly complete in LUB 70. A small number of post-Roman sherds were found in the burials (single sherds in cg128 and cg294 and three sherds each in cg127 and cg217).

Saxo-Norman

A stone church **LUB 55** was constructed in the graveyard; it consisted initially of a rectangular chancel (Structure 13.1A) and a nave (Structure 13.1B); pottery dates its construction to the 11th century. Traces of the early use of the nave **LUB 56** and the chancel **LUB 57** dated stratigraphically to the 11th century. Activity at the west end of the site initially appeared to be secular rubbish dumping **LUB 58**, dated by pottery to the middle part of the 11th century; this area was later absorbed into the graveyard **LUB 59**. A west tower **LUB 60** was constructed (Structure 13.2C), stratigraphically later than LUBs 58–59 and contemporary with the nave LUB 62. A grave **LUB 61** was inserted in the tower. The early phase of use of the nave LUB 56 was succeeded by **LUB 62** which was contemporary with the construction of the tower LUB 60; LUB 62 and LUB 60 were dated with the use of both stratigraphy and a coin to between the late 11th and mid 12th centuries.

LUB 55 Church construction Structure 13.1
(Figs. 13.15 and 13.36)

The construction of the first stone church cg109 was a two-cell structure consisting of a nave and a chancel. There was no evidence for the location of the external doorway. The layout of the foundations suggests that there was a narrow arch between the nave and chancel. Roman building material was incorporated in to the church construction. The remains of the church were considerably truncated by later events, and internally only two small areas of probable floor sequences survived. Four sherds of pottery were recovered from the construction deposit cg109; the latest date to the 11th century.

Nave construction (Structure 13.1B). What had previously been graveyard deposits within the area of the church was levelled and sealed cg110. Features interpreted on site as scaffolding postholes in the nave, cg111 and cg112, were not planned, but cg111 had been sealed by dump cg110, and cg112 cut into cg110 and was itself sealed by a mortar spread,

interpreted as a construction layer cg113. The construction level for the nave cg113 produced only two undatable sherds of ST, and dump cg111 a single late Saxon sherd. Sealing cg113 was the final fill of the foundation trench cg297. Three postholes cg114 in the nave cut through cg113. The postholes cg114 were filled with a brown loam which was similar in description to the overlying layer cg115, a loam floor with thin lenses of mortar (0.03m thick). This was sealed by another shallow layer cg116 (under 0.05m thick) of ash, loose grey mortar, charcoal flecks, a large quantity of molten lead (over 100 droplets), traces of copper melt and a few iron nails (with adhering droplets of non-ferrous metal). Further similar finds were found in cg114, cg115 and cg297; some of these finds were discarded. This material possibly suggests debris from leading window glass or roofing the building or some other form of lead-working; although it has already been interpreted as debris from a fire (Gilmour and Stocker 1966, 21, 41).

Internal feature of Nave (Structure 13.1B). A slot with four postholes inserted into it, cg3 probably cut deposit cg653 (LUB 39), although no written record was made of the relationship (Fig. 13.36). The feature was filled with sandy loam and loose mortar, similar to material associated with the church. The spatial relationship between the church foundations and the feature is of note. As an internal feature, possibly one that was essentially timber-framed and set in the ground, it could be interpreted as the support for a gallery (as proposed during the excavations) or perhaps a bellcote. Alternatively, cg3 may have represented the only remains of an earlier timber church. This feature cg3 was published as possibly being the remains of a north–

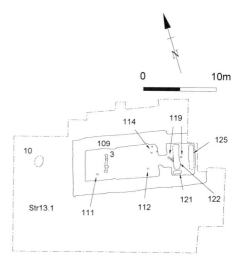

Fig. 13.15 Structure 13.1, late Saxon church: LUBs 55, 56 and 57. (1:500)

south timber fence (Gilmour and Stocker 1986, 16) located to the east of a proposed north–south ditch (which is interpreted here as two pits cg2 and cg105 pre-dating the graveyard, LUB 41).

Chancel construction (Structure 13.1A). Within the chancel a similar sequence was found. Five postholes cg119 (which were planned and may have related to the construction of the chancel arch) were found cutting the fills of earlier graves and possibly the loamy sand dump cg117 which would have filled the chancel. A large limestone block cg121 was set in the underlying loamy sand dump cg117, and has been interpreted as the base for a pillar-*piscina* or *sedile* (Gilmour and Stocker 1986, 19).

LUB 56 Use of Nave (Structure 13.1B and 13.2B)
In the western part of the nave, debris layer cg116 (LUB 55) was covered by a mortar floor or spread cg197. In the north-east corner of the nave, it was sealed by a thin patchy layer of clay cg203 with dark ash and some yellow mortar in a central depression. This may have been linked to a service of consecration where surplus ashes and water from the service might have been placed at the base of the altar, then to be sealed over by the floor of the new church. Parsons (1989, 10–12) describes the service of consecration and then notes that a pottery vessel used for wax processing, containing burnt deposits and ash with ash spread around it, had been recovered from the middle of the church floor in front of the site of the altar at Raunds in Northamptonshire .

LUB 57 Use of Chancel (in Structure 13.1A to 13.2A)
The loamy sand dump cg117 (LUB 55) was covered by a spread of pale brown mortar and limestone chips cg118. This layer may represent a mortar floor in the chancel. It was sealed by sandy silty loam cg120, which may have been associated with the robbing of what has been interpreted as the robbed remains of two successive masonry-built altars (Gilmour and Stocker 1986, 19). To the west of the chancel a rectangular pit cg122 was filled with mortary deposit cg123; at the east of the chancel was another pit cg125 with a fill of limestone rubble and mortar cg126.

LUBs 58–59 Activity west of Church
(Fig. 13.42)
Dumping cg651, LUB 58, took place over an area to the west of the church cg109 (LUB 55) sealing LUB 44; these were dumps of ash and rubbish which were probably used to level the sloping ground. The area west of the church remained for a time outside the precinct of the graveyard: a rubbish pit cg10 cut the dumps. Dumps cg651 produced a large

group of pottery (124 post-Roman sherds), the latest of which dated to the early to mid/late 11th century. Several sherds of the late 9th to early 10th century, including an overfired sherd of LSLS, are included in the group. Pottery from rubbish pit cg10 (10 post-Roman sherds) also included typical late 9th- to early 10th-century material including ELSW; the latest material again dates to the 11th century. Although the majority of the datable finds from LUB 58 were Roman, they do, however, include a triangular iron hooked tag and a green high-lead glass ring, which are likely to date to the 10th–11th centuries (Mann 1986, 41).

LUB 59 Graveyard. Grave cg155 cut the dumping cg651, but was itself cut by the later tower (LUB 60). Another inhumation cg154, to the west of the church, cut into dump cg651 and was sealed by the later demolition of the tower cg434 (LUB 75).

LUB 60 Tower construction (Structure 13.2C)
(Fig. 13.16)
The construction of the west tower cg207 cut pit cg10 (LUB 58) and inhumation (LUB 59); it may have been associated with a dump of loam cg209, thought to have been derived from upcast from the foundation trench. An arch must have been inserted into the west wall of the nave cg208 through to the tower; its base was constructed of limestone set in pink mortar. The tower is dated by its link with the nave through pink mortar, and by reason of its cutting LUBs 58–9. Construction deposit cg207 contained 27 post-Roman sherds.

LUB 61 Cist grave and an inhumation
(Fig. 13.42)
A cist grave cg153 was excavated within the area of the tower; from the lack of disturbance and careful

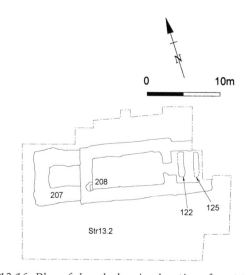

Fig. 13.16 Plan of church showing location of west tower.

alignment of the cist to the tower, it would seem likely that the tower was standing when the grave was inserted. Inhumation cg155 (LUB 59) was cut by the tower foundations. It seems unlikely, given its proximity, that the cist grave would have been so closely circumnavigated by the tower foundations without damage. It was sealed by the tower collapse cg434 (LUB 75).

LUB 62 Continued use of Nave
(Structure 13.2B and 13.3B)

In the western part of the nave, mortar cg197 (LUB 56) was sealed by a deposit of pinkish mortar with patches of burnt clay and ash cg198. This was sealed by a layer of loam cg199 over which was a mortar floor cg200, a layer of loam trample cg201 and a brown mortar floor cg202. Loam layer cg199 incorporated a small quantity of lead and copper-alloy droplets.

In the north-east part of the nave, ashy clay cg203 was covered by a patch of pinkish mortar cg204. This was sealed by a coarse mortar floor cg205 and finally a mortar floor cg206 which had decayed.

Pink mortar cg198 and cg204 may have been of the same date as the tower insertion cg208, which was bonded with similar material. The patches of burnt clay and ash in mortar cg198 may have been associated with the construction of the tower. The pinkish mortar cg204 may represent the first floor surface of the church, if ashy clay cg203 represents its consecration, suggesting that the church was not operational during the construction period of the tower.

Floor cg205 contained a fragmented silver penny of Henry I (BMC tpye XV), issued 1133–5; although this was probably lost by c 1142, a later survival is not impossible (Archibald 1994). If this coin dates floor cg205 to the middle of the 12th century, then it is likely that the pinkish mortar phase could belong to the late 11th or early 12th century, dating the construction of the tower. Two sections of what could have been late 11th-century moulded arch (Gilmour and Stocker 1986, 47–8), were re-used in the construction of the north aisle cg377 (LUB 71).

Early Medieval

The main body of the church **LUB 63** (Structure 13.3) was possibly rebuilt between after mid–late 12th century, as indicated by the date of re-used stone. Some inhumations **LUBs 64–66** can be stratigraphically dated as being later than this rebuilding. There was a sequence of floors and alterations in the nave and chancel **LUB 67**; pottery was residual and the sequence can only be dated by its place in the stratigraphic sequence, later than LUB 63 and earlier than LUB 75.

LUB 63 Re-building: Structure 13.3
(Figs. 13.17 and 13.37)

The nave and chancel of the church was rebuilt, reusing the north and west walls. The south wall of the nave and chancel was shifted south by c 1m and given two buttresses at the corners of the nave and two pilasters between them; the church was also extended to the east by c 4m. This would have involved the removal of the original south wall, together with a large part of the chancel and the roof. The previous chancel arch was removed and robbed cg312 to its foundations. The south wall was also robbed cg281, and the robber trench fill was sealed by a patchy, uneven spread of dark loam, interpreted as trample occurring during construction of the new south wall cg287. A construction trench was dug for the new wall, also providing foundations for two pilasters and the south-east buttress which were set in yellow-brown sand. The wall was roughly faced and mortar bonded. There was some evidence for a pilaster on the south-east wall of the chancel. A layer of loam with orange sand cg289 sealed the construction of the new south wall cg287; it was possibly make-up for a surface by the south entrance. South graveyard layers cg195 and cg362 (both LUB 51) were cut by the new south wall cg287 of the nave and chancel.

The foundations for a buttress at the north-west corner of the nave and two pilasters cg290 against the north wall were inserted into a long rectangular construction trench, which ran along the north of the north wall: the buttresses to the south had been erected in a similar style of trench, also there involving the rebuilding of the wall. The foundations of the buttresses to the north were irregular in width, and did not mirror those to the south, but the method of construction suggests they were built as part of the same operation at the same time. The slight

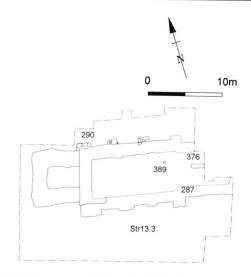

Fig. 13.17 Structure 13.3, refurbished church: LUB 63.
(1:500)

foundations of the buttresses and pilasters to the north and the south were set in yellow-brown sand. The trench for the pilasters was back-filled with a sandy loam which then formed a construction level to the north. This level was *c* 0.8m below that of the first floor of the later north aisle, suggesting grave-yard dumping had been taking place between the two periods of construction. A construction layer of pale brown sandy mortar cg300 sealed the con-struction trench fill.

The on-site interpretation of the north wall butt-resses and pilasters cg290 was re-interpreted in publication as the bases for the new arcade piers for the north aisle (Gilmour and Stocker 1986, 23–6). However, the west wall of the north aisle has a butt joint with the buttress at the north-west corner of the nave, suggesting they may not have been of the same build (Fig. 13.37).

As Gilmour and Stocker (1986, 22–3) noted, the number of 12th-century architectural fragments indicates a rebuilding in the 12th century. This interpretation is supported by the 11th-century dating of tomb-slabs incorporated into its fabric. The south wall cg287 reused stone, including 11th-century tombslabs (tombslab number 13 and two not illustrated), but there was no identifiably later material.

Re-used 12th-century stone fragments found in later walls, or picked up from the site before or during excavation, give evidence for a mid 12th-century doorway, a 12th-century string course, a 12th-century corbel table, mid/late 12th-century blind arcading and 12th-century vaulting. Sections of chevron moulding (Nos 1, 2), an abacus block (No 9) and a beakhead motif fragment (no 10) were all from a mid 12th-century doorway and were reused in the north aisle cg377 and cg406; sections of chevron moulding (Nos 3–8) were picked up before excavation. A stone moulding (No 15) from a double-chamfered string course, probably dating to the 12th century, was recovered from the des-truction of the Georgian church cg299 (LUB 79). A fragment of abacus or similar feature of 12th-century date was found in the make-up cg387 of the cobbles in the porch. Decorated corbel blocks (Nos 11–14), vault rib sections (Nos 19–33) and elements from a possible mid/late 12th-century blind arcade (Nos 40–43) were recovered before the excavations.

The presence of stone fragments might suggest that there had been vaulting; this interpretation would concur with the buttresses and pilasters along the south wall. As Gilmour and Stocker have sug-gested (1986, 22), a doorway may have been inserted, possibly to the north (it would have been demolished when the aisle was inserted). On the evidence of the rest of the architectural fragments, other refur-bishments may have included a string course, a corbel

table and some blind arcading. The date of rebuilding can be suggested as being between the mid and late 12th century, on the basis of the fragments from the doorway and the blind arcading.

The presence of large numbers of 12th-century stone moulding fragments had been explained (Gilmour and Stocker 1986, 46–52) as having been brought on to the site from other locations, alterations to the walls were dated between the early to mid 13th century based on the chancel arch, the only medieval element to have been incorporated into the Victorian church, and the steep pitch of both the nave and the aisle roofs drawn by Grimm (Gilmour and Stocker 1986, 25–6). However, it is possible that a chancel arch was inserted at a later date and re-roofing is also likely.

The graveyard contained very few pottery sherds of which a small proportion were from the 13th century. However these pottery sherds may be intrusive. The lack of definite 12th-century pottery groups may not be significant, as the total numbers of pottery sherds were so small. Although the LFS sherds are not diagnostic of the 12th century, the ware spans a wide date-range into the mid/late 12th century (a similar lack of 12th-century pottery sherds was found at St Mary's Guildhall). The robbing of the south wall cg281 produced only residual late Saxon pottery but also intrusive post-medieval material. The foundations for a buttress cg290 produced a small group of sherds, the latest dating to the 11th century. Loam/sand layer cg287, sealing the construction of the new south wall, contained a few sherds, the latest dating to the 12th century.

LUBs 64–66 Inhumations later than the rebuilding of church Structure 13.3 (Fig. 13.43)
LUB 64 consisted of inhumations cutting construction Structure 13.3 and sealed by porch Structure 13.3F. Inhumations cg318 and cg319, together with cist burials cg320, cg323 and cg325, cut loam with orange sand cg289; these inhumations were either truncated or circumscribed by the later porch. The foundations of the east wall of the porch were built leaving space for two cist burials cg324, cg325 which must have been fairly recently inhumed at the time of the subsequent porch construction.

LUB 65 consisted of the graveyard to the north of the Church, before the north aisle Structure 13.3D. Later than the buttressing, but earlier than the aisle (LUB 71), was a charnel pit cg156 and two patches of trampled graveyard upcast cg301 and cg303.

LUB 66 consisted of inhumation cg363 which cut the buttress construction cg290, but there is no record of what it was sealed by. It may have been part of the north graveyard or it may have have been one of the graves from the north aisle.

LUB 67 Floors and alterations in the Nave and Chancel 13.3 and 13.4 (Fig. 13.44)
Inside the church to the west of the nave, sealing the robber trench fill cg281 (LUB 63) to the west of the nave, was a layer of mortar with silt and small pieces of limestone rubble cg282, sealed by a sequence of layers – mortar cg283, loam cg284, mortar cg285 and mortar cg286. These layers suggest mortar floors in the west of the nave. It is possible that the loam layer cg284 represented a make-up or levelling layer.

Over these were compacted layers of loam, mortar, ash and sand cg399; at least seven different layers were observed. The ash and sand suggest alterations within the building. Layer cg399 was sealed by a mortar layer cg400 followed by four bands of silty loam cg401, possibly a mortar floor sealed by several earth floors. Sandy loam with crushed mortar and limestone cg402 was interpreted on site as the possible remains of a step from the tower-arch into the nave. If this were the case then its limited life would suggest a newly-located access to the tower, which only lasted for a short while. It was in turn sealed by loam with traces of mortar cg403. Three postholes cg426 and inhumation cg425 cut loam cg403, suggesting alterations or repairs. The postholes were sealed by a patchy mortar layer cg435 possibly equivalent to mortar cg429 which had sunk into the fill of an inhumation cg427 (which cut cg425). Cutting layer cg435 was inhumation cg428 cut by inhumation cg430, and cutting layer cg429 were inhumations cg431, cut by cg432. Mortar floors continued in use despite the insertion of inhumations at the west end of the nave. Inhumation cg430 was recorded in the context sheet as being associated with part of a slate tombstone which does not seem to have been kept.

At the east end of the nave, cutting the patchy mortar cg394, were two postholes cg395 which could be interpreted as being part of a rood screen; but it seems probable that they were connected with possible alterations in the building, as they were sealed by layers of sandy loam with thin spreads of mortar cg396. Over these mortar spreads, stone footings were set into sand cg397; these footings have been interpreted as the base of a pulpit (Gilmour and Stocker 1986, 28). Compact loam cg398 butted up against the footings. Layer cg398 was cut by a possible burial cg507 which was sealed by further compact loam cg508; the compact loam may have been levelling make-up. It was sealed by a layer of sandy loam with crushed mortar and charcoal flecks cg509; there were other layers over this, striated sandy loam with mortar layers cg510, sealed by sandy loam with mortar and charcoal cg511, and also by a layer of sandy loam with mortar flecks cg639, which

could have been equivalent to cg511. The sandy loam layers may indicate the use of flagstones set in the floor in the upper part of the nave.

Between the chancel and the nave was 0.40m of dark silty loam cg124 sealing the robbing cg123 (LUB 57). At the division between the extended nave and the new chancel, there was a limestone and rubble foundation cg298, interpreted as the footings of a later second rood screen; this cut the loam cg124. This loam may have acted as an earth floor contemporary with the screen, but it may also represent make-up for a floor since truncated. The foundations cg298 were sealed by a layer of loam cg308, possibly another truncated make-up layer (0.07m thick), and cut by a posthole cg307, indicating that the screen had been removed.

Sealing the robbing of the north chancel was a patch of mortar with limestone chips cg311 sealed by sandy mortar with small pieces of limestone rubble cg310. At the east end of the nave, near to the chancel, the construction activity was sealed by a hard fine mortar spread cg309. Over this was mortar with limestone chips cg388 which was cut by a posthole cg389. Mortar floors continued in use.

Cutting into cg396 were a further four postholes cg505, together with an inhumation cg504. Cutting fill cg126 (LUB 57) was an inhumation cg376 situated in the chancel, which contained a skeleton with a lead chalice on the left shoulder indicating that it was a priest burial (Mann 1986, 41–2, Fig. 31). The chalice is a 13th- to early 14th-century type. Postholes and inhumations were sealed by a mortar layer cg506, which in turn was sealed by mortar cg637. These may indicate actual mortar floors. Mortar layer cg637 was sealed by sandy loam cg543 which was cut by inhumation cg524. Mortar with limestone and tile cg638 sealed sandy loam layer cg511. Layers cg637 and cg638 possibly represent patches of the same spread. Cutting layer cg638 were inhumations cg641 and cg531, which were cut by another cg532 and by postholes cg640.

Sealing the mortar cg506 was a spread of sand with stone cg390; this may also indicate the use of flagstones set in the floor. Over it was a compact layer of greyish sandy loam cg391 (0.37m thick), which may represent the heightening of the chancel area. It was sealed by a thin layer of black ash with mortar over it cg392, compact sandy loam cg393 and patchy mortar cg394, possibly indicating alterations to the interior of the chancel, then a further relaying of flags, followed by more alterations.

The mortar layers probably represent floors, or they may sometimes indicate structural alterations. There is no evidence that tiles were ever set into the mortar: the mortar was not recorded as revealing any tile impressions and no floor tile was recorded from any of these layers. There is also evidence for the use of earth floors within the church. The mortar and earth floors were abandoned in favour of flagstones (as suggested by the sandy layers), at some point after inhumations were introduced into the church.

Small amounts of both residual and intrusive pottery were recovered from limestone rubble cg282 and inhumations 431 and 319. The only datable sherd was found in mortar spread cg309. This was a jug handle in a late ST fabric with an applied twisted strip decoration. Decoration of this type is usually dated to the mid/late to late 12th century (Kilmurry 1980).

High Medieval to Post-Medieval

There were alterations to the church during this period, including the construction of a porch **LUBs 68–69** (Structure 13.3F) some time possibly by the late 15th century, Its embellishment with an arcade did not predate the mid-16th century, but might have been secondary. A gully **LUB 70** along the north side of the church, containing 13th-century pottery, was sealed by the north aisle **LUBs 71–72** (Structure 13.3D), whose construction LUB 71 was associated with 14th-century pottery. Its use LUB 72 included glazed floor tiles dating to between the late 14th and the 15th century and was associated with mid 14th- to mid/late 15th-century pottery. A chapel was added to the north-east **LUB 73** (Structure 13.3/4E); documentary evidence suggests that it was in use by the early 15th century. There was evidence for inhumations and a tiled floor in the chancel **LUB 74**; the floor tiles dated to the late 14th or 15th century: the few associated sherds of pottery dated to the late 15th century.

LUB 68 Porch, Structure 13.3F
(Figs. 13.18, 13.25 and 13.38)

A substantial porch was added to the south door of the church. The foundation trenches for the two walls of the porch cg379 were wide and deep, disturbing earlier burials. The stone foundations of the west wall of the porch were built up against the south-west buttress cg287 (LUB 63). A rectangular stone-lined charnel pit had been built into these foundations (Fig. 13.25 and 13.26; Gilmour and Stocker 1986, Fig. 22); but the pit was probably only partially sealed by the porch construction (Fig. 13.26). The foundations of the east wall of the porch were built leaving space for two cist burials cg324, cg325, which must have been fairly recently inhumed at the time of porch construction. At ground level the internal sides of the entrance followed the line of the foundations. The external chamfered mouldings suggested that the outer sides of the porch stepped inward so that each wall was butt-

ressed at the southern end. A porch constructed in this way would provide a first-storey room with estimated internal dimensions of c 3.5m east–west and 2.00m north–south, if the walls of the upper storey were half as thick as below. A two-storey structure was depicted both on Speed's map of 1610 and on Buck's 1724–5 sketch (Gilmour and Stocker 1986, Fig. 4). The charnel pit which was integral with the construction of the porch was sealed with sandy loam with mortar cg649 (LUB 69).

The re-used tombstones incorporated into the foundations of the porch cg379 included a number of early 12th- to early 13th-century stones (tomb numbers 16, 24, 45, 46) but none later. 13th-century two-storey porches are very rare. It is conceivable that the development of the Cathedral, with its large Galilee porch and pointed arches and external and internal arcading, inspired the architect of St Mark's Church to produce a porch of lesser but similar type. In the drawing by Grimm there are 13th-century architectural features which would fit this theory. But it is more likely that the stones were taken from another site and that the porch is late medieval (or later), (Gilmour and Stocker 1986, 89).

The group of pottery recovered from the foundation trench for the porch cg379 included what must be viewed as intrusive material; the latest sherd is a Nottingham or Derby brown stoneware (BS), which must date to later than the late 17th century, and a few other sherds are probably also of this date (TGE, LHUM, GRE), including a copper bichrome GRE sherd (used previously to date the construction to the late 16th century). It is possible that, given the clear contamination, even the 16th-century sherd was introduced from the robbing; a similar explanation may be given for a fragment of late 17th-century bottle glass and a coffin grip of similar date. The

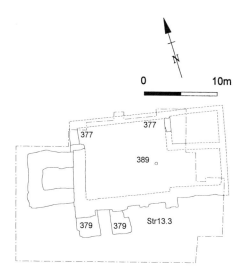

Fig. 13.18 Structure 13.3, church porch and aisle and chapel: LUBs 68, 71 and 73. (1:500)

remaining pottery (LSW2/3) dates to between the late 13th century and the early/mid 14th century. In the charnel pit fill cg649 (LUB 69) was a group of pottery sherds dating to between the late 14th century and the late 15th century; it seems likely that this pottery was introduced after the construction of the porch, as the entrance to the pit was probably not sealed by the porch construction (Fig. 13.25); as the pit continued in use, the pottery provides a guide to the construction date of the porch.

From a re-examination of Buck's drawing (Gilmour and Stocker, 1986 Fig. 4) by Jeremy Ashbee, it would appear that the arcade is structurally unrelated to the porch behind it and the difference in widths between them can only really be explained if the arcade is seen as a feature or a selection of unrelated mouldings brought in from another building and re-erected. This re-use of stone in the arcade had formerly been interpreted as contemporary with the construction of the porch, but it is also possible that the re-setting of earlier features took place after the construction of the porch: the porch itself may have been largely constructed between the late 13th and late 15th centuries, but the arcade might have been added subsequently, possibly in the mid–late 16th century, the date previously proposed for the porch construction as a whole (Gilmour and Stocker 1986, 28 and 38); the re-use of materials was generally linked to the Reformation, and a date soon after the Act of Union of Parishes in 1549 was the most likely time for the arcade to have been added to the porch (contemporary with St Mary's Conduit). However, re-setting of earlier features did take place in the medieval period; the south porch at Grantham is substantially of the 15th century but incorporates a re-set entrance of *c* 1230 (Pevsner and Harris 1989, 316).

LUB 69 Layers within porch Structure 13.3 and 13.4F (Fig. 13.39)
The charnel pit, integral with the construction of the porch cg379, was sealed by sandy loam with mortar cg649.

Sealing the construction of, and lying within, the porch cg379 was a series of layers. Mortar with limestone fragments cg380 was sealed by sandy loam with mortar patches cg384; over this was a layer with limestone chips and tile cg385, which was cut by an infant inhumation cg386 that had been buried encased (nails with adhering wood are recorded). These may represent surfaces in themselves but are more likely to be the make-up for a paving, cobble or even tile surface. The final surface in the porch was based on make-up of sand with limestone and tile fragments, into which cobbles were set in a mortar matrix cg387. These layers represent the use of the porch until its destruction.

A group of pottery sherds dating to between the late 14th century and the late 15th century came from charnel pit fill cg649. A single sherd dating to the 13th century came from mortar cg380. The latest make-up layer in the porch cg387 produced a few sherds, the latest of which dated to the 14th or 15th centuries.

LUB 70 Gully to the north of the nave
Before the addition of the north aisle, the graveyard cg296 to the north of the nave was cut by gully/soakaway cg292 (this feature was not planned). The foundations for the north aisle were later than the gully.

The gully cg292 was partly created from fragments of a near-complete early POTT cooking pot (one sherd of which joined with a sherd from cg296), with its base removed; the pot was found together with other pottery of 13th-century date.

LUB 71 Addition of North Aisle Structure 13.3D (Fig. 13.18)
The north aisle cg377 was added to the nave; one of the nave buttresses cg290 (LUB 63), at the north-west corner, was sealed by the west wall of the nave cg377, showing that the north aisle was stratigraphically later than the buttressed wall. The west wall cg377 of the aisle was *c* 1.00m thick, less substantial than the earlier buttress; the east wall was only *c* 0.80m thick – which may argue for it being an internal wall between the aisle and the chapel (LUB 73) to the east. The north wall was found to be entirely robbed, although some of it lay outside the edge of the excavations. The remains of the north aisle walls that survived showed no signs of being buttressed. Sealing the construction trench fill of the aisle cg377 was a mortar layer cg305, which, together with patches of mortar cg302, cg304, possibly indicated construction debris and floor or paving make-up associated with the construction of the aisle. There is possible evidence for a door in the east wall of the aisle: inhumation cg414 (LUB 72) cut across the line of the wall.

The aisle sealed the soakaway cg292 (which contained 13th-century pottery). There were a few sherds of pottery from the lower foundation trench fill of cg377 dating to the 14th century; pottery of a similar date was recovered from subsequent burials.

LUB 72 Burials and the use of North Aisle Structure 13.3D and 13.4D (Fig. 13.45)
Cutting construction mortar cg302 (LUB 71) was inhumation cg365, which in turn was cut by inhumation cg364. This was sealed by mortar with limestone chips cg375 and loam with several mortar lenses cg642. Cutting cg375 were three inhumations; cg369 and cg367 were cut by cg368. Striated layers of

loam, mortar and sand cg404 were sealed by mortar with sandy patches, some limestone and tile cg405. Cutting patch cg405 was what was described as a feature of uncertain purpose, a patch of sandy mortar with much rubble, limestone chips and crushed mortar cg406. It was sealed by sandy silt cg407, cut by inhumation cg408 and sealed by mortar layer 409. Sandy silt cg407 was also cut by inhumations cg413, cg414 and cg415; two fragments of glazed floor tile were recovered from inhumation cg413. Two bands of mortar cg410 had sunk into inhumation cg650 and two layers of mortar cg411, sealed by mortar cg412, were cut by inhumation cg496, which was in turn cut by cg497; a fragment of glazed floor tile was found in inhumation cg496 and several were recovered from inhumation cg497 in the north aisle. Layer cg411 was also cut by inhumation cg417 and cg371, which in turn was cut by cg416. Inhumation cg491 cut inhumations cg410 and cg409, and was sealed by a layer of silty sand with mortar patches, crushed limestone and pebbles cg495. Inhumation cg492 cut cg491; a layer of mortar cg493 had sunk into its fill. This was sealed by silty sand with limestone flecks and traces of mortar cg494.

Inhumations cg291, cut by cg498, lay in the north aisle as they were sealed by its destruction deposits cg299 (LUB 79); inhumation cg366 was sealed by mortar cg405, and inhumation cg370 was cut by inhumation cg371. However, there was no record of what they cut, although they were subsequent to the construction of the north aisle.

The interior of the north aisle may initially have been entirely covered with a mortar floor. The fragments of glazed floor tile found at the east end of the north aisle indicated differential flooring at a later date. Over the main there was still a mortar floor; the tiles lay in the vicinity of the altar.

The glazed floor tiles of Flemish type date the later floors around the altar to the late 14th or 15th century. The latest sherd from the north aisle cg377 dates to between the mid 14th century and the mid/late 15th century.

LUB 73 North-east chapel Structure 13.3E and 13.4E (Fig. 13.18)
Documentary evidence indicates that the north-east chapel was in operation by 1423 (Gilmour and Stocker 1986, 6) and was probably built either at the same time (the west, dividing wall of the chapel was narrower than the outside wall of the aisle) or later.

LUB 74 Inhumations and glazed floor tiles in the chancel Structure 13.3A and 13.4A (Fig. 13.46)
Sealing inhumation cg532 was a layer of sandy loam make-up cg533 over which was a patch of sandy loam with mortar cg535 and cg534; the second contained glazed floor tiles. These were sealed by

sandy loam with mortar cg536. Sealing layer cg535 was a sandy loam floor make-up cg525, which was cut by inhumation cg537, which in turn was cut by inhumation cg538. Sealing these and inhumation cg539 (there was no record of what it cut) was a layer of sand make-up cg540, cut by inhumation cg541 and sealed by a floor of glazed tiles set in mortar cg542. Inhumation cg541 contained a rose farthing token of Charles I (type 2f), issued in 1635/6–44, which is likely to have been lost either during or shortly after its period of issue (Archibald 1994). Also cutting layer cg525 was an inhumation cg528, which cut inhumation cg526 (no record of what cg526 cut); also cutting cg526 was another inhumation cg527, which in turn was cut by inhumations cg529 and cg530. Inhumation cg530 contained two skeletons, both encased, and included three Nurenburg jetons, all issued between 1550–86 and unlikely to have been lost much after their period of issue (Archibald 1994) and a fragment of a 17th-century clay tobacco pipe in the backfill.

In the chancel was a series of sandy loam make-up layers which would at one time have supported floor tiles; there was evidence of the red, black and yellow tiles *in situ* on the sandy make-up cg534 and cg542. The tiles had been lifted from their original positions at various times for the insertion of burials, and relaid leaving sandy make-up layers behind.

The glazed floor tile, of Flemish type, dates to the late 14th or 15th century. Two CIST sherds from mortar cg542 date to between the late 15th century and the mid 17th century. One sherd of FREC was found in mortar cg536, dating this deposit to between the mid 16th and 18th centuries; however, mortar cg536 is more closely dated by a clay tobacco pipe bowl of *c* 1660–90.

Post-Medieval

The tower collapsed in 1720 and the west end of the church was walled up **LUB 75** (Structure 13.4). There were inhumations which post-dated this event **LUBs 76–8**, in the nave, chancel and outside on the site of the demolished tower; these dated up to the late 18th century..

LUB 75 Tower collapse and west wall built Structure 13.4 (Fig. 13.19)
The tower (LUBs 60–61) collapsed and the stone was removed, robbing the tower walls to below ground level, and leaving a spread of demolition debris cg434, including a large quantity of tile. The west end of the church was rebuilt with a limestone wall cg424, and the church continued to function.

The collapse of the tower was recorded as occurring during a storm in 1720 (Gilmour and Stocker 1986, 7). The pottery consisted of mostly residual

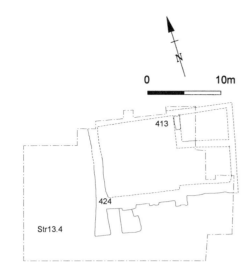

Fig. 13.19 Structure 13.4, walled up west end of church: LUB 75. (1:500)

medieval sherds, the only possible contemporary sherds being of 17th- or 18th-century TGE and SLIP wares.

LUBs 76–78 Church and Inhumations (Fig. 13.47)
LUB 76 consisted of the use of the nave after the rebuilding cg424 (LUB 75) of the west wall construction; Structure 13.4B. There was a patch of 'burnt earth', cg433 in the area (no record of what it sealed). Sealing these layers and inhumations was a layer of earth mixed with orange sand cg544 into which further inhumations cg545 and cg546 were cut.

LUB 77 consisted of inhumations in the north chapel Structure 13.4E and chancel 13.4A. In the chapel there was a brick barrel vault cg503 constructed for the Sibthorp family which contained four lead coffins and a wooden one. One of the Sibthorp coffins cg503 was inscribed "1753". A slab in brick shaft cg512 inserted into the chancel was inscribed "1779". Coffin furniture was recorded, but discarded, from both burial groups.

LUB 78 consisted of inhumations cut through the site of the robbed tower. Burials cg436, cg437, cg438, cg439, cg440, cg441 cut through the demolition debris cg434 of the tower, and some were sealed by a dump of material cg483 brought on to the site. There were further burials cg442, cg443, cg444, cg445, cg446, cg447, cg448, cg449, cg450, cg451, cg452, cg453, cg454, cg455, cg456, cg458, cg459, cg460, cg461, cg462, cg463, cg464, cg465, cg466, cg467, cg468, cg469, cg470, cg471, cg472, cg473, cg474, cg475, cg476, cg477, cg478, cg479, cg481 and two, cg457 and cg480 with traces of wooden coffins.

The burials were later sealed by the construction material cg299 (LUB 79) of the 1786 rebuilding. There was a possible sequence of ten intercutting inhumations, partly defined by the two dumps of loam cg483 and cg484 which had been brought on to the site, as they included a range of pottery sherds of an earlier date with cross-joins between the two deposits. The latest sherds date to the late 18th or earlier part of the 19th century. A sequence of ten suggests that the same grave area was being used even to the extent of digging over earlier graves to take members of the same family. Other dumps in the west area of the graveyard included dark loose loam cg482 and loam with rubble and mortar cg485. Loam cg482 sealed earlier cist inhumation cg313.

Modern

The large, much-altered church was finally demolished and a smaller Georgian church erected **LUB 79** (Structure 14) in 1786. A number of inhumations were stratigraphically later **LUBs 80–84**. The Georgian church was demolished and replaced by a Victorian church **LUB 85** (Structure 15) in 1872. Some inhumations post-dated this event **LUB 86**.

LUB 79 Small Georgian Church Structure 14 (Fig. 13.20)
The church was reduced in size; the nave remained on much the same plan but the north aisle, chapel and south porch were removed and the chancel was altered to give it a pentangular apse. The archaeological evidence for this demolition and construction work was in the form of robber trenches, foundation trenches, postholes, rubble layers and mortar spreads cg299. After the demolition of the north aisle, the walls were robbed and the area was levelled with mortar mixed with building debris; it seems that

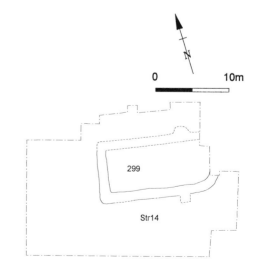

Fig. 13.20 Structure 14, Georgian church: LUB 79. (1:500)

scaffolding was used in the demolition of the building as a posthole was found. Much of this material including the posthole was sealed by levelling which was made up of loam with mortar. The construction trench for the north wall of the rebuilt church cut the levelling; this was sealed by a construction layer of yellow mortar. Two postholes probably used for scaffolding cut this.

The demolition of the north wall of the chapel was represented by mortar and limestone chips and loam, with several large pieces of stone cg299. The porch was removed, leaving mortar and rubble. To the west of the church the alterations led to a dump of loam, tile and rubble being sealed by a mortar spread; these layers sealed the underlying graves. At the east end of the church the construction trench for the apsidal end was excavated. There was no evidence of any work to the south wall of the church, suggesting that the earlier foundations were reused.

The church is recorded as having been reduced in size in 1786 (Gilmour and Stocker 1986, 7). Mortar spread cg299 contained a group of pottery sherds of mid to late 18th-century date, which agrees with the documentary evidence.

There was no evidence that the tiles from the medieval church continued to be used in the Georgian building although it is possible that this did happen. Documentary evidence exists for a new floor in 1840 (Gilmour and Stocker 1986, 31) although no archaeological evidence survives, probably due to the levelling which took place in advance of the construction of the Victorian Church.

LUBs 80–84 Inhumations around Church Structure 14 (Figs. 13.38 and 13.48)

LUB 80 consisted of inhumations which cut cg379 (the porch walls) and were cut in turn by the Victorian church. To the south of the graveyard was a deposit of 'dark earth' cg514; into this cut several inhumations. Sealing these inhumations was a graveyard loam deposit cg574 which was sealed by a tarmac path cg575. Inhumation cg558 was set in a small tile shaft and inhumation cg556 was in a brick lined shaft (Fig. 13.38). Some inhumations cg559, cg560, cg561, cg562, cg564, cg565, cg566, cg567, cg568 and cg571, together with those which retained traces of a wooden coffins cg486, cg563, cg569, cg570, belong to this LUB.

LUB 81 consisted of an inhumation, cg572 that cut cg379 (the porch walls); cg572 retained traces of a wooden coffin and contained copper pins, possibly used for a shroud.

LUB 82 consisted of inhumations north of the church, later than cg299 (LUB 79) but earlier than the Victorian Church (LUB 85). Inhumations cg501, cg515, cg516, cg517 and cg523, together with those which retain evidence of a wooden coffin cg372, cg373, cg374, cg518 and cg519 and brick shaft burial cg502 belong to this LUB.

LUB 83 consisted of inhumations west of the church, later than cg299 (LUB 79) and earlier than the Victorian Church (LUB 85). Inhumation cg573, with patterned coffin trimmings, belonged to this period: associated finds date it; stratigraphic evidence did not survive. With inhumation cg573 were two George III halfpennies, dated 1806 and 1807, the location of which was not recorded; both are comparatively unworn, suggesting deposition before *c* 1820 (Archibald 1994). Inhumations cg577, cg579, cg581, cg585, cg586, cg589, cg590, cg592, cg593, cg594, cg597, cg598, cg599, cg601, cg602, cg604, cg605, cg606, cg607, cg609, cg610, cg612, cg613, cg615, cg616, cg617, cg619 and cg623, together with those with traces of wooden coffin cg603, cg608, cg611, cg614, cg618, cg621, cg620, cg622, cg624, cg625, cg600, cg596, cg595, cg591, cg584, cg583, cg582, cg587, cg588, cg580, cg578 and cg576 and graveyard deposit cg626 belong to this LUB. Three George III halfpennies issued in 1799 and 1807, a Victorian farthing dated 1843 but probably lost (or deposited) by *c* 1860 (Archibald 1994), as well as a possible fragment of shroud were recovered from inhumation cg578. A pair of child's shoes (with straight soles) was found in child inhumation cg598. Copper pins, possibly shroud pins, were recovered from inhumations cg588 (which contained at least two skeletons), cg590 and cg600. The context sheet of inhumation cg591 describes a money purse and belt but little now remains; a once-attached buckle is now missing.

LUB 84 consisted of two inhumations cg520 and cg521 (with traces of a wooden coffin) north of the church cg299 (LUB 79).

LUB 85 Victorian Church, Structure 15 (Fig. 13.21)

The Georgian church (Structure 14) seems to have been levelled and sealed by various mortar spreads cg648 which related to the construction of the Victorian church cg627. On the north, a levelling layer of loam with a little tile was sealed by a mortar spread also with some tile. To the east, mortar with much red tile was sealed by a mortar spread. To the west was a spread of mortar with rubble and tile. The construction trenches of the Victorian church were of considerable depth (*c* 1.75m) and cut through the Georgian nave along with areas of both the west and south graveyard. This meant that much of the earlier stratigraphy of these areas was lost. The chancel and part of the Victorian nave were recovered in plan, although internal details were not recorded.

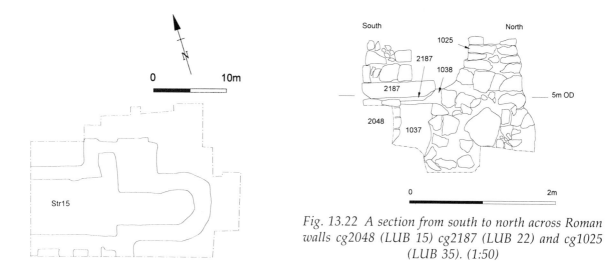

Fig. 13.22 A section from south to north across Roman walls cg2048 (LUB 15) cg2187 (LUB 22) and cg1025 (LUB 35). (1:50)

Fig. 13.21 Structure 15, Victorian church: LUB 85. (1:500)

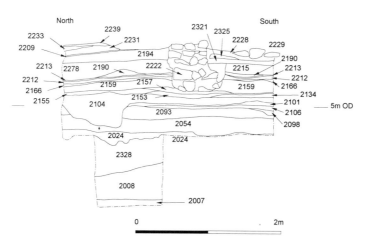

Fig. 13.23 A section from north to south across wall cg2222 (LUB 24), illustrating the stratigraphic sequence in area II, from LUBs 3 to 40. (1:50)

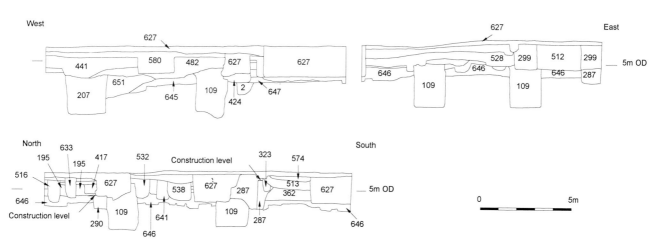

Fig. 13.24 Sections across the site, from west to east, and from north to south indicating the stratigraphy of the church from LUBs 41 to 85. (1:100)

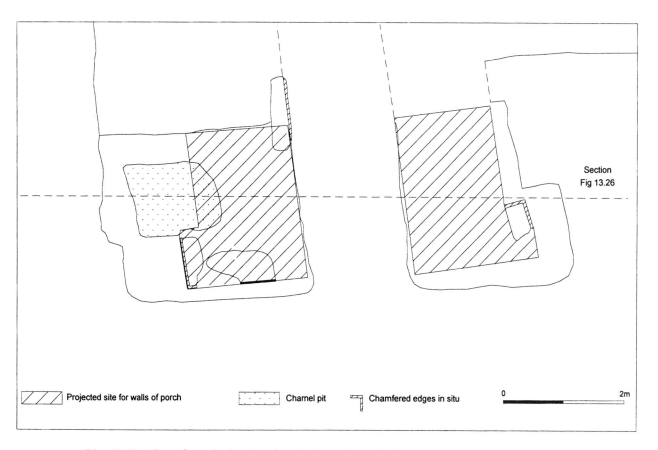

Fig. 13.25 Plan of porch showing foundations, charnel pit and the line of the walls. (1:60)

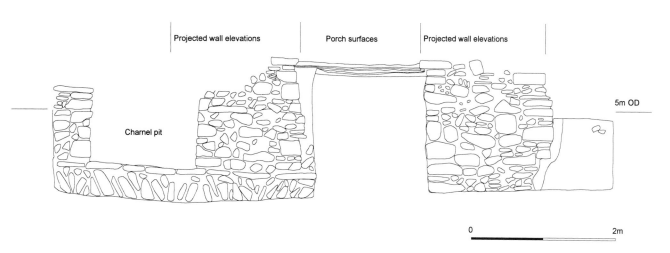

Fig. 13.26 Section through porch (see Fig 13.25), showing foundations, charnel pit, porch surfaces and projected wall elevations. (1:50)

The Georgian church was recorded as being demolished in 1871 and the Victorian one built in 1872 (Gilmour and Stocker 1986, 7). Most of the finds, including the pottery, were discarded during excavation.

LUB 86 Inhumations (Fig. 13.49)
To the north there were burials cg522, cg629, cg630, cg632, and cg636 and those with traces of timber coffins cg628, cg630, cg631 and cg633, as well as graveyard deposits of loam cg634, cg635. Sealing

destruction cg499 was loose brown loam cg500, probably grave upcast material, into which were cut several inhumations. There were fragments of cloth from two inhumations cg628 and cg630, a copper pin from cg632, one child's shoe from cg628, and from the eye socket of inhumation cg632, a very worn George III halfpenny of 1799 which had been perforated for use as a pendant.

Discussion: Roman period

Topography

Before the Roman period, the site had been part of the flood plain of the Witham which lay to the west of the site; natural riverine sand (LUB 0) was recovered at the limit of excavation. About 10m to the east of the excavation, Ermine Street was constructed by the end of the 1st century, and by the early 2nd century a ground surface (LUB 1) had developed over the site associated with sparse scattered rubbish.

By the mid to late 2nd century, the western part of the site contained north–south ditches and gullies, possibly for deliberate drainage purposes, and Ermine Street was built up with extensive metalling which extended over the eastern fringe of the site (LUB 2). The ditches silted up or were filled (LUB 3); the western half of the site was effectively a partly waterlogged wasteland between the mid and late 2nd century, accumulating leather waste and horse remains among other rubbish.

Whereas the river primarily affected the site in the early Roman period, the importance of Ermine Street to the site grew, along with the development and growth of the Roman city. Lying to the south of the walled *colonia*, the site probably contained roadside occupation from the mid 2nd century, or possibly earlier. Evidence for this included the possible traces of roadside activity and hard-standings for booths or stalls beside Ermine Street (LUB 2). There were later pits, postholes, cobbling and other possible surfaces (LUB 4) at the east of the site, suggesting further activity from the late 2nd century into the 3rd. Apparently abandoned in the early part of the 3rd century was a stone volume measure which might indicate that the site had indeed been used as a place for selling and exchanging goods. Subsequently there were structures with ovens (LUB 5) between the early to the mid 3rd century. The Roman suburb was becoming more and more developed along the Ermine Street frontage. Between the mid 2nd century and the mid 3rd, services were being provided to those travelling along the road and those living in the Roman city.

The problem of flooding was under control by the mid 3rd century: buildings were constructed over the site from that period. Fragments of brick and tile found within levels associated with the roadside occupation (LUB 4), some incorporated into the early oven in Area III (LUB 5) and within the levelling dumps prior to the construction of Structures 2 (LUB 6) and 4 (LUB 9), almost certainly represent material derived from the demolition of buildings elsewhere and brought on to this site.

It was as late as the early–mid 3rd century that the site actually became a built-up part of the commercial suburb. Three if not four timber strip buildings were constructed at this time (LUBs 6, 9, 12 and 13); contemporaneous construction suggests that the ownership of these buildings was either municipally controlled or was in the hands of a single private landlord. There was evidence for the two central building being replaced by others of a similar plan (LUBs 15 and 25) between the mid and late 3rd centuries. Further rebuilding took place across the site (LUBs 20, 28, 34 and 38) in the early 4th century. The rebuilding of four properties at the same time again may indicate a single ownership but differences in building style might suggest that, in fact, there was an owner for each plot. These buildings continue in regular use up to the late 4th century.

The importance of the road frontage meant that the buildings were all built gable-ended on to Ermine Street. Although the excavation extended over four plots, only the central two were excavated to any extent. The internal widths of the buildings within these central plots were about 8m (the northern building) and about 7m (the southern building). The gap between the walls of the two was about 0.50m. From the mid 3rd century to the late 4th, the plots retained their coverage, and the outline building plans did not appear to shift. However, the street frontage was not available for excavation. The extent the buildings covered to the west was difficult to determine; there was no clear west wall for any of the structures, since even those dug had extensions.

From the late 4th century it was the areas nearer to the street which were occupied. In the ruins of the former traders' houses, there is evidence that occupation continued or resumed (LUBs 39 and 40) close to the road.

Industrial Activity

Activity (LUB 4) between the late 2nd and 3rd centuries possibly included smithing; evidence included hammerscale. Evidence for smithing of this period has been found on other street-front sites in the southern suburb (eg, m82 and z86). So perhaps there is evidence for industrial activity within the suburb.

There is no direct artefactual evidence for any

Fig. 13.27 General view of Roman stone buildings under excavation, looking north.

Fig. 13.28 Early surface cg3044 and ditches cg3047, cg3045, cg3054, looking west.

industrial or craft activity post-dating LUB 4. However, the presence of several large hearths and ovens from the mid 3rd century through to the late 4th probably indicates activity on more than a domestic scale (Figs. 13.32–3, 13.35). Ermine Street provided

access to customers wanting services, products, or sustenance.

Building construction

Main structural elements and form (Figs. 13.29–30)
There were three main phases of Roman building construction from the early–mid 3rd century. The walls in those two properties extensively examined, in Areas II and III, were of timber (Structures 2 and 3; LUBs 6 and 9; Fig. 13.7), then a mixture of stone and timber (Structures 5 and 6; LUBs 15 and 25; Fig. 13.8) and only finally completely of stone (Structures 8 and 9; LUBs 20 and 28; Figs. 13.9–11).

Two stone-lined pits indicate an 'earth-fast' north wall for the first trader's house in Area II, Structure 2 (LUB 6). No evidence for external walls was located for Structure 3 or for the south wall of Structure 2, but the north and south walls were probably in the same position as the subsequent stone walls, as indicated by the spacing of the aisle posts. The aisle posts of Structures 2 and 3 (LUBs 6 and 9) were constructed in east–west parallel rows about 2m from the earth-fast and presumed outside walls, thus leaving a central space about 4m between the rows of aisle posts. The spacing between the posts was slightly more variable, but was normally little more than 2m. The presence of substantial aisle posts may suggest a 4m wide clerestory was incorporated. If this was the case it would have helped solve one of the major problems of this type of building, that of light. This site, in common with the others in the southern suburb, shows a marked absence of Roman window glass: only two fragments were recovered

Fig. 13.29 Carved stone feature cg3077, probably a measure.

Fig. 13.30 Looking south across the site at hearth cg3076. There are also the aisle postholes of Structure 3 cg3078 in the background and cg3203 in the foreground. Also visible are the remains of partition cg3200 and the south wall cg3106 of later stone building, Structure 9.

here. One of these came from levelling material within Structure 9 (LUB 27 cg3107), that analysis of the pottery and other finds suggests to have consisted of material brought on to the site from elsewhere. Given the successive phases of alteration, destruction (including major fires) and reconstruction of the buildings, this absence is significant, suggesting that glass may not have been used in fenestration here.

The presence of aisle posts within Structures 5 and 6 (LUBs 15 and 25) suggests that the external stone-founded walls may not have been entirely of stone. The wall foundations (0.45m wide) might have represented stone sills supporting timber-framed walls; the timber aisle posts would then have held up the roof. This might have been more likely to be true of Structure 6 than of Structure 5, because of the position of hearths/ovens around the walls of Structure 5. The spacing of the aisle posts was irregular but as with the earlier buildings, generally a little over 2m. The aisle posts also open the possibility of a clerestory throwing some light into what must have been very dark interiors.

Foundation trenches for Structure 9 (LUB 27) were cut into the underlying stratigraphy; the walls had pitched limestone foundations and were stepped, so that the foundations were 1.10m wide and the wall itself was 0.55m wide. There were no foundations for Structure 8 (LUB 20); flat slabs (some 0.85m wide) were laid over the levelled remains of the sill walls of Structure 5. The difference in construction technique between the two buildings is quite considerable and Structure 8 was not soundly based, with dire consequences: the lack of proper footings appears to have caused subsidence; part of the north wall of the building either collapsed or was in imminent danger of doing so, and had to be rebuilt (LUB 22).

Roofing

The virtual absence of ceramic tile from the demolition and levelling of Structures 2 and 3 (LUBs 8 and 11), and from contexts associated with the construction of their successors, Structures 5 and 6 (LUBs 15 and 24), suggests that they may have had roofs of perishable materials such as shingles, straw, thatch or reed. Although levels associated with the use of Structure 5 (LUB 16, cg 2053 and cg2057) contained a fair quantity of tile, it was most probably disturbed from the earlier dumps of imported material.

A quantity of ceramic tile recovered from Structure 8 (LUB 20), from within the construction levelling, from make-up material and floors, and incorporated within the foundations of the south wall, suggests that Structure 5 may have had a tiled roof. Structure 6, however, may have been roofed in perishable materials; only a few scraps of tile were recovered from the fire debris and destruction material of this building (LUB 26), and although some tile was recovered from the levelling over the internal area for the construction of its successor, Structure 9 (LUB 27, cg3107), this almost certainly represents material imported from elsewhere (as noted above).

Structure 8 may have been roofed with a mixture of ceramic tile and stone slates; a noticeable quantity of Collyweston slate was recovered from the destruction and levelling associated with the rebuilding (LUB 22), from the fire debris (LUB 23), incorporated within levels associated with the later use (LUB 38) and from the final demolition debris of the building (LUB 39). Ceramic tile was also recovered from the same contexts (but perhaps in smaller proportions than one would normally expect) and it is therefore possible that Collyweston slate was only used for part, instead of the whole roof. (Alternatively, the ceramic tile could perhaps derive from the destruction debris of some of the ovens within this building.)

There is a marked difference between Structures 8 and 9 in that there were virtually no stone slates from any of the levels associated with the Structure 9 or its destruction, and none from later levels in this part of the site; Structure 9 appears to have been roofed with ceramic tile. The use of Collyweston slate, which was imported into the city from the Stamford area about fifty miles to the south, perhaps implies a greater degree of affluence because it would have been more costly than ceramic tile, which could have been produced locally.

Interestingly, a noticeable quantity of stone slates is recorded as having been found within the floors and occupation layers associated with Structure 7 to the north, although none appears to have been found within the demolition debris of the previous building, Structure 1. This, together with the complete absence of sherd links between these groups and any others on the site, perhaps suggests that the material associated with the construction of Structure 7 was imported on to the site from elsewhere. There are too few finds, and too little of the building lay within the area excavated, however, to be certain.

During the lives of Structures 8 and 9 there were a number of east–west slots, varying between 1.5 and 2.5m from either the north or south walls. These slots may have provided additional roof support, as they were only present when aisle posts were no longer used to support the roof. But they could also define rooms and corridors. Another possible roof support included a post base in Structure 8 (LUB 21).

Fittings of the Late Roman buildings

Internal divisions
The internal space of the Roman strip buildings appears to have been normally divided up by the use of timber partitions, and later internal stone walls. The arrangement of space within the buildings changed through time, suggesting that their functions altered too.

The internal stone walls were not used in timber Structures 2 and 3, but with the later buildings. Structures 5 and 6 (LUBs 15 and 25) both had north–south walls, which lie at the east end of the site, indicating that the frontage (shop area?) of the building was divided from the rear. This indicates the possibility that the shop and the rear part might be let as two separate properties, but this would not be a normal arrangement. Later Structures 8 and 9 did not apparently possess such divisions. The rear walls of Structures 6 and 9 lay outside the area of excavation. To the rear of Structure 5 was a north–south wall, possibly representing its main west wall; it was abutted by an east–west wall (LUB 15), just over a metre north of the line of the south wall (Fig. 13.8), which is likely to be an extension added to the rear. The subsequent Structure 8 also had a north–south wall along the same line as well as an extension (LUBs 21 and 22). Other internal stone walls were inserted late in the life of Structure 8. A room, about 4m wide, was constructed in the north-east part of the main room (LUB 38; Fig. 13.11). Subsequently the room was enlarged to over 5m wide (LUB 39; Fig. 13.12). The walls need not have been entirely of stone. These rooms were in use from the late 4th century or later, the secondary one possibly not erected until Structure 8 was otherwise ruinous.

Other divisions within the buildings include small partitioned areas at the rear of Structures 3 and 5 (LUBs 10 and 16; Figs. 13.7 and 13.8) and later nearer to the eastern end of Structures 5 and 6 (LUBs 17 and 26; Figs. 13.8). These areas varied in shape and size; the earlier examples were around 3m by 4m and the latest 2.5m to 5m. Whether they actually contained aisle posts is uncertain (Structure 3, LUB 10 and Structure 5, LUB 16); it would seem more likely that the room partition itself was used to support the roof timbers.

A beam slot or sill-beam impression (LUB 17 cg2094) at the east end of Structure 5 almost certainly represented the remains of a timber-framed partition forming a small room against the north wall of the building. Unlike the remains of the partition at the west end, clear evidence of the construction of the framework of the partition was recovered from levels associated with the fire in this building (LUB 18). These deposits included a scatter of burnt timbers cg2101, probably representing part of the collapsed framework of the partition, sealed by spreads of burnt clay, daub and painted plaster cg2104, within which was a small quantity of iron nails; fragments of heavily burnt daub and plaster were also found within the charcoal and ash spread cg2114 sealing cg2104. Some of the daub fragments show clear impressions of wattle on the reverse, while several pieces also bear timber impressions, suggesting that the partition was based on a timber framework, infilled with wattle and daub. The fragments of plaster facing were mainly very small pieces which had been so heavily burnt that original colours cannot be distinguished, although one fragment shows evidence of red and yellow stripes, possibly on a white (burnt grey) ground.

There were traces of similar narrow slots in Structures 5, 8 and 9, possibly indicating internal divisions, and possibly also the remains of small rooms (LUBs 17, 21, 29, 30 and 31). In the remains of Structures 8 and 9 stake-holes were identified; it is possible that stakes indicate a light partition (LUBs 22 and 30). Other evidence for partitions from Structure 8 (LUB 22) is provided by a modest quantity (19.9 k) of burnt plaster and daub (2.5 k) from cg2231 (LUB 38), directly sealing debris from the fire (LUB 23), and lying within the southern part of Structure 8. Impressions on some of the daub suggest that it was applied to a wattled framework, formed from bundles of tied reeds used as an infill between timber uprights, almost certainly representing the remains of a partition belonging to the earlier phase of occupation (LUB 22) but destroyed in the fire.

Interior decoration

The complete absence of daub or plaster from the burnt debris of the timber partitions in Structure 1 (LUB 13, cg1008 and cg1022) could suggest that these were light wooden screens without any form of surface coating (although only a very small area of this building was excavated).

The only evidence of internal decor within Structure 2 may be that provided by a small quantity (2.3 kg) of painted plaster redeposited within the later levels of its successor, Structure 5 (LUB 16 cg2069), and incorporated within the possible threshold cg2070 at the northern end of the east partition wall in that building. All fragments are painted in a streaky yellow-ochre and pinky-red; the surface is very uneven and therefore the plaster may have come from close to the junction of wall and floor. Several pieces show evidence of redecoration and on these the streaky yellow-red appears to represent the earliest coat applied. Although damaged – many fragments comprise only the uppermost painted surface and backing layer – the colours are reasonably fresh with no evidence of burning.

One room at the west end of Structure 5 (LUB 16) was plastered and painted; the east wall is recorded as having had plaster on both faces. Within the room, part of the painted dado was preserved *in situ*,

decorated with a marbled pattern of red, black, yellow and white splashes on a flesh-coloured ground, discoloured buff to grey by burning. Some indication of the decoration on the upper parts of the walls is provided by a large quantity of plaster (more than 90 kg) from the collapse of the north and east walls (LUB 17 cg2084 and cg2113). It is impossible to determine from which wall or walls the plaster fell, although it is possible that both faces of these walls are represented. Study of the plaster (Long 1980) shows that a major component of the colour scheme comprised areas of red and yellow, which appear to have formed the basis of panelled designs. Red panels bordered by a thin yellow stripe with blobs at the corners and surrounded by white, green and black, appear to be separated by areas of white with thin vertical yellow-green lines. Yellow panels are bordered by a thin black stripe, surrounded by red and white. Some of the red-painted pieces had been well finished, possibly burnished, and several fragments were from obtuse angled mouldings, perhaps from a door (or window?) jamb.

An area at the eastern end of Structure 6 (LUB 25) was also partitioned to create four separate rooms, at least one of which was plastered and painted; a large quantity of plaster (52.4 kg) and daub (29.7 kg) was recovered from the levelled out destruction debris or robbing of the building, and the concentration of debris on the north side of the east–west partitions suggests that the use of painted plaster may have been restricted to rooms A and B. By far the largest quantity (24.5kg) of both ceiling and wallplaster came from the initial dump of destruction debris cg3175 within the eastern end of room A, and from the fill of the robber trench of the east wall cg3092 (7.7 kg). A further large quantity (12.6 kg) was found within a later spread of debris cg3175 covering rooms A and B. While extending into the two southern rooms, destruction debris cg3175 appears to have been levelled out and spread from the north, as it spilled around and respected the position of the sand "banks" within rooms C (cg3174) and D (cg3173); however, some material had intruded into sand cg3173; it contained a small quantity (3.7 kg) of painted plaster, mostly large fragments probably from a dado, and all burnt to varying degrees. An original sketch of the north–south partition shows the stump of this wall in relation to floors cg3090 and cg3091; in both cases the plaster on the east face of the wall was clearly applied prior to the laying of the earliest floor, whereas no such facing was visible on the western face of the wall; here, the floors simply butt up to the unfaced clay. This suggests that perhaps only a single room on the east side of the partition, i.e. room A, was decorated.

Although much of the plaster from rooms 6A

and 6B had been burnt, it all appears to be painted in a similar manner. Fragments painted with black, white, red, and yellow splashes on a white ground are clearly from a dado, similar to that in the western room of Structure 5. Other fragments suggest some kind of panelled scheme, as in Structure 5, but possibly of white panels with a red surround, although black and yellow stripes also occur. The most interesting plaster was white with black lines, some of the latter angled at 90 or 140 degrees and suggesting perhaps a geometric pattern of squares and octagons, such as would be used on a ceiling (Long 1980). If the room had an enclosed ceiling, then it is likely that it received no natural light at all.

Some evidence of the internal decoration within Structure 8 (LUB 22) is provided by a modest quantity (19.9 kg) of burnt plaster and daub (2.5 kg) from cg2231 (LUB 38), directly sealing debris from the fire (LUB 23), and lying within the southern part of Structure 8. The plaster mainly comprises small fragments, generally heavily burnt, so that it is difficult to distinguish the original colours. A variety of decorative motifs is still evident, however, including foliage – some stylised – and swastika whorls with curved rather than angled arms. Some of the plaster shows clear evidence of redecoration, while pigment analysis (Wilthew 1984) has provided evidence for the use of cinnabar for some of the red-painted fragments, suggesting that the materials used were relatively expensive. Several pieces with obtuse-angled mouldings are perhaps from a door or window surround.

Ovens and hearths

Floor-level hearths, raised hearths, ovens with traces of clay domes could leave different traces and be used in different ways. However, it is difficult on the surviving evidence to identify their functions and reconstruct their superstructures: food preparation and heating may have formed one element.

In timber Structure 2 there was evidence of two successive central hearths and in timber Structure 3 the remains of two ovens with clay superstructures, also central to the building (LUBs 7 and 10; Fig. 13.7). That fire was restricted to the centre of these timber buildings was essential for safety purposes. They may have had domestic functions.

However, in Structure 5 hearths and ovens were situated against the walls suggesting that perhaps the walls rose to some height in stone. The remains of a large flue were found against the north wall of Structure 5 (LUB 16); subsequently there was an open floor-level hearth against the south wall (LUB 17), which was later shifted westwards (LUB 19). Structure 6 contained the bases of raised hearths

(LUB 24) and a small hearth of stone and tile in the centre of room 6A (LUB 25).

In Structure 8 was the base of a substantial raised hearth, possibly an oven base (LUB 21), just to the south of the centre of the building. This was succeeded by two sequential large ovens with clay superstructure, and a smaller one against the north wall of the building (LUB 22). Later Structure 8 had the remains of a large oven, by the side of which was a less substantial feature, possibly the remains of a drying oven (LUB 38). In the very late 4th century a burnt clay hearth was used within the small room in the east of the building (LUB 39).

In Structure 9, near to the south wall was a large rectangular hearth with flue; there was also a small floor-level hearth and to the west a small hearth of burnt clay (LUB 28; Fig. 13.9). Later the large rectangular hearth near the south wall was extended and further west, against the north wall, a ground-level tile hearth was succeeded by a tile and limestone hearth (LUB 29). The hearth against the south wall was again altered (LUB 30). During the last years of the building it seems that a much smaller oven in this area of the building was in operation.

Function of the buildings

The fittings of the buildings suggest several functions, principally commercial. The large raised hearths or oven bases in Structure 5 (LUB 16), Structure 8 (LUBs 21, 22 and 24) and Structure 9 (LUBs 28, 29 and 30) could have been associated with preparing food on a large scale in the late Roman period. Although there was no evidence of any industrial use of the hearths and ovens, the remains of ovens and hearths dominate the site, because their clay structures have survived.

The small decorated rooms (LUBs 16 and 25) suggest privacy and entertainment. The room to the rear of Structure 5 (LUB 16) might simply have been a bedroom for the tenant, or might be associated with providing services and entertainment to clients. The four small rooms (6A decorated) in Structure 6 (LUB 25) may have fulfilled similar functions. In room 6A the location of a pot indicates the likelihood of its being part of a commercial concern. From the remains cg2104 (LUB 18) of a burnt plastered partitioned room a phallic object, possibly a lid with a phallic handle, or a cult object of an upright phallus on a base was recovered. This might be taken to support the idea of licentious activity taking place in these buildings, but could simply have been a good luck symbol (see Section on Smith-God pots, below).

It may be significant that the site produced an unusually high number (22) of quern fragments, with twelve of the fourteen pieces stratified in Roman

Fig. 13.31 Plastered partition walls cg2074 (Structure 5), looking south-west. Also earlier western extension wall cg2047 in background.

levels coming from Area II, virtually all associated with the sequence of buildings (Structures 2, 5 and 8) on this part of the site (although at least three of these, from dumps of LUBs 1 and 6, almost certainly represent material imported onto the site). These appear to be concentrated within Structure 8 (but see coins, below), and it is possible that another four fragments reused in the construction of the earliest church (LUB 55 Structure 13.1) also originated from the demolition levels of Structure 8.

Apart from the querns, the finds provide little solid evidence for the function of the buildings and any attempt at interpretation is complicated by the persistent redeposition of earlier material within later levels.

Coin loss and commercial activity

Although a notable quantity of coins was recovered from levels associated with the use and destruction of the Roman buildings, like the pottery and other finds, they had largely been redeposited in later levels. The number of base silver *denarii* found within Structures 5 and 8 was at least partially responsible for the unusually high peak in late 2nd- to early 3rd-century coinage at this site (Mann & Reece 1983, 70; Fig. 69b, L5). They may represent commercial activity within Structure 5 (those that were found within Structure 8 certainly represent earlier, redeposited material) or, just possibly, the

contents of a dispersed 'hoard', perhaps the contents of a purse that had been dropped and lost.

Three coins found within the same context in ash cg2089 (LUB 17) include a slightly worn base silver *denarius* of Julia Soaemias (AD 218–22) and two very worn *sestertii* of Marcus Aurelius and Faustina the younger (AD 161–80) that, when found, were corroded together. These clearly had changed hands many times; all three coins could perhaps represent part of a single circulation group while a fourth coin, an *as* of Hadrian (AD 117–38), is also extremely worn and could be a contemporary 3rd-century loss.

Six coins (including three base silver *denarii*) were recovered from contexts associated with the earliest (LUB 21) use of Structure 8, the 4th-century successor to Structure 5. The latest coin is a worn *antoninianus* of Elagabalus (AD 218–22) and all are likely to represent a circulation group of mid–late 3rd-century date; none would have been current at the time Structure 8 was in use. Five of these coins show an apparent clustering in the southern central part of the building, in levels associated with, or close to, the metalled surface cg2153 and oven cg2154, possibly reflecting the area where they were originally lost.

Later levels within Structure 8 (LUBs 22 and 38) produced further 3rd-century issues, including two more *denarii* of Septimius Severus; again, although levels of LUB 38 are dated to the late 4th century,

Fig. 13.33 Large hearth or oven cg3121 (Structure 9) looking south.

Fig. 13.32 Hearth cg2200 (Structure 8) looking south.

all of the associated coins are considerably earlier in date; the latest are Constantinian issues of the 330s–340s. Among the 3rd-century issues found here, however, two small clusters of exclusively 3rd-century coins are apparent. A small group of three worn base silver *antoniniani* – a Gallienus issue of 253–68 and two Postumus issues of 259–68 – were found corroded together in the northern part of the building (cg2215); like the coins found within an earlier level (ash cg2089) of Structure 5, these too could represent the contents of a 'hoard' or purse. The second group of three *antoniniani* came from the area between the stone-walled room and the south wall of Structure 8.

It may be significant that the early 3rd-century *denarii* occurred more frequently on this plot (Structures 5 and 8) rather than on that to the south (Structures 6 and 9), while, if only in terms of volume, Structure 8 appears to have been more conducive to coin use (and therefore loss) than Structure 9. There is also a visible difference in the quality of building construction, implicit in the use of Collyweston slate

for Structure 8 (and of cinnabar for the wall paintings) that reflects a higher level of expenditure here, possibly engendered by greater commercial success at this period.

Within the southernmost plot, only four coins were recovered from levels associated with the use of Structure 6, all from the eastern end of the building – perhaps significant in view of the existence of the partitioned areas, and their suggested function. The coins are *sestertii* and *asses*, the latest being an issue of Antoninus Pius (AD 154–5); all, however, are worn and could have remained in use well into the middle years of the 3rd century, contemporary with the use of this building.

It is impossible to determine the function of Structure 9, even by examining the material from later levels, because the redeposition of material within this building is complicated by the probability that the earliest levels contain material brought on to the site. Levelling cg3107, associated with the construction of Structure 9, contained a large pottery assemblage with a very high residual content; examination of this assemblage, however, showed a complete absence of cross-joins between this and any earlier levels – significant here because redeposition is otherwise a persistent feature –

prompting the suggestion that cg3107 may represent rubbish brought on to the site.

In support of this idea is the occurrence of several other finds from cg3107 that seem out of place among the rest of the material: a cast, copper-alloy disc mount (CEI) <SM77 Ae39> of a type that occurs on military sites elsewhere as at Zugmantel and Caerleon (Oldenstein 1976, taf 90, 1159), a gold finger-ring set with chalcedony (CEI) <SM77 Au1), of 2nd- or early 3rd-century date, and a fragment of cast window pane. The latter certainly seems likely to have been brought on to the site, because there is virtually no evidence for glazed windows in any of buildings here (see above). Given the probability that this material was brought on to the site, it is therefore likely that any of the material redeposited in later levels within Structure 9 could have originated from elsewhere.

A sharp peak in coin loss is apparent within the very latest levels of Structures 8 and 9: fifty-four coins were recovered from Structure 8 (LUB 39) and fifty-three from Structure 9 (LUB 40). This, however, cannot be taken as indicative of the level of commerce within the buildings, not least because, by the 4th century, the production of very low value denominations which could be used for ordinary transactions led to a correspondingly higher rate of use, and therefore loss. The peak here in any case is spurious, caused largely by the high number of coins found within the loam accumulations/dumps sealing the robbed walls of the buildings (cg653 and cg2280, LUB39: representing 74% of the coin assemblage; cg644 and cg646, LUB 40: representing 70% of the coin assemblage); in this respect, the loams show a marked similarity to the late Roman – post-Roman 'dark earth' deposits found on sites within the lower walled city (as at Flaxengate (f72) and Hungate (h83) (see *LAS 4*, forthcoming). It is possible that at least some of the material within these dumps comprises rubbish brought on to the site, and this may be the origin of a 3rd-century gold earring (BAD) <SM77 Au1>, a surprising find among the material from cg644.

Pottery vessels and industrial activity

The Roman pottery displays a number of notable features which, in advance of more detailed publication, are discussed below. These are the occurrence of Smith God pots, tile fabric pots and buried complete pots of debatable function, all of which have a bearing on the interpretation of the site.

Smith God Pots

An unusual group of vessels which may be relevant to the interpretation of the site were the so-called Smith God pots, vessels decorated with appliques of smiths' tools, anvils, tongs and hammers (Darling 1990). In view of the quantity of pottery from Lincoln as a whole, it is notable that these vessels have only been found at the two Wigford sites, probably five separate jars from sm76, and a single jar in a different fabric from z86.

At sm76, the earliest possible sherds were found in layer cg3038 (LUB 11) in Area III, but the evidence for these being from a Smith God pot rests upon the scar where an applique had broken off. The vessel form, a beaker-like small jar with a notched cordon, is that used for the Smith God pots, but also occurs with an applique ring. The main occurrence, as with the tile pots, was from Structure 5, with most sherds coming from deposits in LUBs 17 and 18, with two further sherds disturbed and re-deposited in LUBs 19 and 22.

A further sherd reflecting religious beliefs had part of the *caduceus* from a figure of Mercury, probably applied to a very similar jar as those decorated with smiths' tools (from cg2138, LUB 19). These jars may be related to the extraordinary face-pot from Area II, disturbed by the foundations for the later church tower (LUB 60), showing a heavily-bearded man with some indication of a head-dress or crown (Darling 1981). The grey fabrics are all very similar, and the association with Structure 5 seems clear.

It is probable that these vessels were connected with worship, perhaps in a household shrine, perhaps as decorative items or for the storage of substances for use in sacrifices; there is no evidence for their use as normal cooking wares. The fact that they are only found on this site and at the adjacent z86 is perhaps significant, and while metalworking debris occurs on both sites, its juxtaposition with these vessels is unclear. Possibly a shrine, whether erected by a guild of metalworkers or by an individual smith, seems to be indicated, and the tile phallic object may be interpreted as an object specifically designed to ensure safety and good will from the gods for people working in a dangerous industry.

Tile Vessels

Several Lincoln sites have occasional vessels apparently made in tile fabric, apart from lamp chimneys. The greatest concentration, 93 fragments, probably representing ten vessels, comes from sm76. The evidence is extremely fragmentary, but the sherds seem to come from large, hand-made vessels of closed form, their rims estimated at 0.24m diameter; base diameters are in the region of 0.20–24m, while body diameters may be 0.50m or more.

These are clearly outside the normal domestic

pottery range, and may be viewed as having some function related to industry in the widest sense. There are no obvious clues as to their function: traces of burning are rare and could be post-breakage, and while some have greenish deposits on the interior, these seem likely to derive from the conditions in the individual contexts.

The vessel fragments are a feature of Area II (71%), with only a few in Area III (27%), including a group with fabrics differing from the main fabric occurring only in LUBs 29–31 of Structure 9. The first occurrence of sherds of the main group is in LUB 7, Structure 2, Area II, but the bulk of the sherds came from Structure 5, the greatest concentration being in LUB 16, with re-deposited sherds in LUB 21. Apart from the discrete late group in Area III, a few sherds also come from Structure 6 levelling LUB 26, with some disturbed into the grossly residual levelling of LUB 27.

Only four fragments came from Structure 2, one from LUB 7 levelling possibly from the same vessel as in LUB 17. It is notable that sherd links of the tile vessels specifically in LUB 16 are all to later, rather than preceding, LUBs. Whatever the function of these large vessels, it seems to have commenced in Structures 2 and 3, but probably continued in Structures 5 and 6 and possibly later.

Two further objects in tile may be related. A phallic object, possibly a lid with a phallic handle, or a cult object of an upright phallus on a base, came from LUB 18, cg2104 destruction deposit, with a further fragment disturbed into LUB 21. The other is a deep circle of tile from LUB 28, cg3131, oven destruction. Similar "collars" have been found on the Flaxengate site (f72), and their function, domestic or industrial, is unknown. They show signs of burning, but not of excessive heat.

Buried complete vessels (Fig. 13.34)

The circumstances of these finds have been described in the site narrative. All except one consisted of a whole pot buried against a wall with the rim just below the contemporary ground level. In all five were found, four in Area II and one in Area III; these are catalogued by Area, in order of deposition:

LUB 21, cg2044, Area II, a broken and fragmentary large GREY jar, only the base and walls surviving. Although it contained some oyster shell and a small mammal skull, this is equivocal evidence because of the obvious later disturbance of the vessel. Location at west end of Structure 8.

LUB 38, cg2235, Area II, a LCOA double-lid-seated jar with a NVCC plain-rim dish apparently acting as a lid. The jar was substantially complete, the only damage being some fragmenting of its rim; the dish was virtually complete although broken in two.

Location at the east end of Structure 8 (late occupation).

LUB 38, cg2253, Area II, a Swanpool everted-rim bowl, complete and undamaged. Some other pottery was found with this vessel. Location east end of Structure 8 (late occupation).

LUB 39, cg2263, Area II, a broken large DWSH dales ware jar with rare scored wavy line decoration. This was found in a pit with other rubbish, and seems less likely to have been the same type of deposit as the other jars. Location in central area. Late re-use of Structure 8.

LUB 25, cg3087, Area III, a GREY cooking pot, copying a BB1 type, the rim type and haphazard latticing suggesting a mid to late 3rd-century date. Location at east end of building (Structure 6); pit dug into levelling, the pot being covered by a stone slab which lay just below the floor surface.

The broken jar from LUB 39 may be tentatively discounted as being from a different type of deposit from the other jars. The large jar from LUB 21 is also less certain, and is notably the only one located in the western area of the buildings, away from the street frontage.

The other three were all located towards the eastern end of the buildings; two had some evidence for the provision of lids, a flat stone and a dish placed upright, while the third was totally undamaged. This latter, the bowl from cg2253, differs from the other two deposits in being an open vessel form, and, since it was found with other pottery, the circumstances of its deposition may differ. Any contents have left no trace, and while totally organic

Fig. 13.34 Buried pot cg2235 (Structure 8) looking east.

Fig. 13.35 Hearths cg2245 and cg2246 (Structure 8) looking north.

deposits cannot be excluded, it seems unlikely these were ritual deposits. The provision of lids could suggest that access to the vessels was intended, and a more probable explanation would be that they formed safety deposit boxes, the contents having been safely retrieved.

Fires

The timber buildings 2 and 3 escaped any major problems with fire. The buildings were demolished after 30 to 50 years of use.

Either a fire broke out in Structure 5 (LUB 18) and was contained within the building but spread to Structure 6 (LUB 26), or Structure 5 was singed by a large and intensive fire in Structure 6. Structure 5 contained an open floor-level hearth against the south wall (LUB 17), but Structure 6 consisted of a number of small enclosed rooms (6A–D), ideal places for a fire to go out of control. This fire led to the demolition of Structure 6 (LUB 26) while Structure 5 continued in use, merely shifting its hearth westwards along the south wall (LUB 18).

Structure 8 suffered a fire within the building (LUB 23), although it subsequently was refurbished and continued in use (LUB 38).

Very late Roman occupation

It would seem that the regular use of Structure 8 (LUB 38) came to end in the late 4th century. Subsequently there may have been some sort of

squatter occupation life amongst the ruins, concentrated at the east end of the plot (LUB 39). Occupation of Structure 9 seems to have continued, with alterations to maintain the roof in the form of huge post-pits (LUB 40).

Very Late Roman roadside structure/early church and wooden grave markers?

Four of the five postholes cg1 (LUB 40) were previously interpreted (Gilmour and Stocker 1986, 15) as being part of a Late Saxon timber church associated with the earliest burials. As the postholes had cut layer cg644, and had been sealed by layer cg646, if both are to be interpreted as very late Roman layers, the timber post structure could also be associated with very late Roman use of the site (LUB 40). The presence of a fifth posthole to the north (previously dismissed as anomalous), and the spatial arrangement of the five postholes as aligned within the eastern part of Structure 9, could argue for a very late Roman date. The postholes were cut by inhumations, including charcoal burial cg99, typologically similar to others within the early graveyard, and so likely to belong to period VIII. The burials in this part of the graveyard could only be seen as being dense if the pits represented a church belonging to the earliest Late Saxon phase; if the pits are interpreted as very late Roman, then the Late Saxon burial density was much the same as on the rest of the south side of the graveyard.

Of the twenty-six stake-holes cg98 (LUB 40)

interpreted as wooden grave markers (Gilmour and Stocker 1986, 20–1), nineteen had been recorded on site as not just cutting very late Roman layer (BAD) cg644 (LUB 40), but having 'cut from within'; in other words the upper part of the accumulation appeared to seal many of the postholes. If the ashy loam layer cg644 did accumulate slowly over a period of time, it would have to allow for the stakes to rot or be removed, and for the holes to become sealed; or for the loam layer to be reworked after the stakes had been removed, so that the layer still appeared to be one. Sealing both stake-holes and layer cg644 was very late Roman dark silty loam cg646 (LUB 40). For the stake-holes to have survived at all suggests that they were not associated with the graveyard above, since this would have meant that the graves would have had to have been pierced by the stakes associated with the postholes in order to leave marks in the underlying layer (cf Gilmour and Stocker 1986, 20–21).

Discussion: Post-Roman period

Summary of published interpretation and alternatives

The published report on the church and cemetery (Gilmour and Stocker 1986) proposes that a cemetery was established in the mid 10th century, with a small timber-built structure interpreted as probably being the contemporary church (*op cit*, 15–17; discussed above). The authors suggest that this was replaced by a new stone church in the mid 11th century, and that a west tower was added, as part of a general refurbishment after a destructive fire in the early 12th century (*op cit*, 17–23). The sequence continues with a 13th-century rebuilding of the church (except the tower), when the nave and chancel were enlarged and a north aisle was added (*op cit*, 23–26). A chapel was added to the north of the chancel, in the mid or late 14th century, and the Reformation period saw the construction of a large two-storey stone porch (Gilmour and Stocker 1986, 27–29). The report also describes the physical decay of the church, the collapse of its tower in 1720, the Georgian rebuild in 1786, and the total rebuild in 1871 in neo-Gothic style, followed more recently by its redundancy, and subsequent demolition in 1972 (Gilmour and Stocker 1986, 29–33).

Much of the interpretative framework which has been provided above stands unchallenged, but the process of creating grouped contexts from the original site contexts suggested some alternative interpretations. Specific points are discussed in detail below; in summary these are briefly listed here. It seems possible that the timber structure was very late Roman or sub-Roman in date, rather than an early church. There may in any case have been a burial ground here before the first church was built in the 11th century. Charcoal burials are here all seen as predating the stone church, rather than being contemporary with it (Gilmour and Stocker 1986, 16 and 20). An alternative interpretation for the altar features of the first stone church has been suggested above. The evidence for the major fire no longer carries the same weight, or at least an alternative interpretation of the evidence is offered. The relationship of the cist burial to the west tower was uncertain, and on stratigraphic grounds the grave could be later, but the occurrence of a cist burial in such a location would be most unusual. It may have preceeded the tower's construction, but if so, probably not by many years. Rather than refurbishment in the early 12th century and re-building in the 13th century, the possibility of substantial mid to late 12th-century work on the church is seen as an alternative worth consideration. The flooring (*op cit*, 25 and 31) has been re-examined, as has the dating of the porch (*op cit*, 27–29). Further consideration has been given to the windows (*op cit*, 26). The ground level of the graveyard has been studied. In addition coffins and coffin furniture, as well as graveyard games are noted below.

Earliest Post-Roman use of the site

There is no evidence of occupation between the very late 4th century and the late 9th. There were 11 sherds of late 9th- to 10th-century pottery from LUB 39 and 18 sherds of similar and slightly later pottery from LUB 40. This pottery appears to have either intruded into, or been laid on to, very late Roman stratigraphy. Evidence of 10th-century activity was found, in the form of pitting (LUB 41); the LUB contained 37 sherds of late 9th- to 10th-century pottery. Several vessels are characteristic of this period (LSLOC fabrics A and D, LSLS and ELSW).

Boundary? Internal feature? Timber church? (LUB 55) (Figs. 13.14, 13.15 and 13.36)

Pit cg2 was cut by pit cg105 and both were sealed by dump cg647, a deposit earlier than the graveyard which sealed it (Fig. 13.24; *op cit* Fig. 66); It is still uncertain that the pits could have formed a boundary ditch, as has been suggested (Gilmour and Stocker 1986, 15); being both non-continuous and earlier than the graveyard they were meant to delimit, they were more probably part of the scatter of pits predating the graveyard.

The idea that the slot with four postholes cg3 may have formed a part of the earlier boundary (*c* 1.25m long) was proposed in the publication (*op*

Fig. 13.36 Slot and postholes cg3 and internal structure or the remains of fencing.

cit, 16). If, however, this feature can no longer can be seen to be set along the eastern edge of a ditch (see pits cg2 and cg105 above), then the interpretation is invalid. An alternative is that they belonged to a timber feature within the stone church (*ibid*, 16). The spatial setting of the feature within the church and its fill (similar to material associated with the church, rather than the loam dumping/levelling on which the church was built) makes this a possibility. The 10th/11th-century church at Raunds in Northamptonshire supported a bellcote (Parsons 1986, 11), but the features at St Mark's are not convincing evidence of a similar structure.

The likelihood of a church building in the 10th century has been stressed by Stocker; he considered that there was adequate evidence for the post-pits cg1 (LUB32) to be interpreted as the church (Gilmour and Stocker 1986, 15). However, an early church may alternatively have been located elsewhere on the site, in areas which had been truncated extensively by later activity. It is also possible that the traces of an earlier church were entirely removed by the stone foundations of the 11th-century structure. The postholes cg3 may represent the only

remains of a timber church on the site of the medieval and later buildings. Stocker would now concede that the presence of a church would not be necessary.

"Charcoal burials" (LUBs 42–3) (Fig. 13.14)

Inhumations cg38, cg39, cg40, cg41, cg44, cg66 and cg91 in LUB 42 all consisted of the corpses laid out on a charcoal bed. No pottery was found in association. As these seven burials belonged to the earliest graveyard, other charcoal burials cg50, cg99, cg100 and cg252 (all LUB 43) might be seen to reflect a shared custom. There is no stratigraphic argument against this interpretation. Burial cg50 was at the bottom of the sequence in the central area of the site, cut by inhumation cg51 (LUB 52); burial cg99 cut post-pits cg1 and was itself sealed by graveyard deposit cg195 (LUB 51); burial cg100 cut inhumations cg101, cg102, cg103, cg104 (all LUB 43) and was cut by cist burial cg351 (LUB 51); cist burial with charcoal cg252 cut inhumations cg251 and cg248 (all LUB 43), the first of which cut cg179 and cg178 (both LUB 43) and the second cg175 and cg81 (both LUB 43).

Altars? (LUB 57) (Figs. 13.15 and 13.16)

The robber pits in the chancel of the stone church (LUB 57) were previously interpreted as representing the successive positions of substantially masonry-built altars (Gilmour and Stocker 1986, 19) although there was no indication of a sequence. However, of the two robber pits, it is possible that pit cg122 indicated the location of an altar while pit cg125 represented the position of a clergy bench set at the back of the chancel, behind the altar. A similar location for a clergy bench can be seen from excavation at Raunds (Parsons 1986, 11).

Major fire? (LUB 55)

Before the erection of the tower it was suggested (Gilmour and Stocker 1986, 21) that there had been a major fire. A re-examination of the evidence suggests that these remains could rather represent the result of inserting windows. The deposits cg116, which were interpreted as the result of a fire which severely burnt the nave roof, were described as under 0.05m thick and included grey mortar; the molten lead, traces of copper and piece of heat-distorted glass do not, however, in themselves indicate roof damage. Layer cg203 possibly represented a thin layer of ashy clay floor (0.01m thick), rather than levelled burnt debris.

Burial in the Tower (LUB 61)

The relationship between the cist burial cg153 and

the tower was not clear on stratigraphical grounds. Yet, although cist burials are normally found in Lincoln in the period when the tower was standing, and in spite of the grave's apparent position against the tower's north wall, a grave in such a position would be unusual.

Rebuilding in the 12th century? (LUB 63)

A major programme of works in the mid 12th century included a large new doorway, a string course, a corbel table and some blind arcading. This interpretation is discussed in detail in the site narrative.

Flooring in Medieval church (LUBs 63, 67, 71, 74) (Figs. 13.37–9)

The flooring in the medieval nave had been truncated by later events except for two small areas, one strip at the west end of the nave and an area in the west part of the chancel. Mortar layers represent construction deposits and floor surfaces. The floors were either mortar or earth until a date after the introduction of inhumations into the body of the church, when flagstones were used. The north aisle probably had mortar floors to begin with, but two pieces of glazed tile associated with the aisle possibly indicate that its east end, at least, had been tiled from the late 14th century. Similar tiles were found set in sandy bedding in the chancel. The floors around the altars were also tiled, distinguishing this area from the rest of the church.

The glazed floor tiles recovered from these floors (and from the later inhumations that cut them) consisted of two types: the larger tiles measure 240mm x 240mm x 35mm and are glazed with either a copper/dark brown glaze or a slipped yellow glaze, while the smaller type measures 105mm x 105mm x 25mm, with a similar glaze. Although the tiles show similarities, petrological examination has identified two distinct fabric types, which could possibly signify different production centres and/or sources of materials. This mixture of large and small tiles has also been recovered from the sites of the Lincoln Greyfriars and the Lincoln Bishop's Old Palace. The tiles are of Flemish type, distinguished by their glaze, fabric and, most characteristically, the nail holes in the face.

Mortar layers were found in the Anglo-Saxon Cathedral at Sherborne (Gibb and Gem 1975, 83, 85 and 87), the earliest being interpreted as a construction surface made up of several fine layers of lime or mortar. There were also mortar floors in the early transept. In the church of St Augustine's Abbey, Canterbury, within the Anglo-Saxon tower, was evidence of a white mortar floor made up with stone chippings (Saunders 1978, 35). At All Saints, Barton Bendish in Norfolk, a 14th-century floor was of hard mortar (0.07–0.13m thick) with a level surface, and a compact layer over it (Rogerson and Ashley 1987, 14). More friable mortar was recovered from grave fills but this was not deemed to have represented a floor. Floors at Bordesley Abbey reflect an elaborate liturgy which goes through at least four changes

Fig. 13.37 The north wall with buttress additions, looking east-north-east.

between the 12th to the 15th century (Coppack 1990, 55–57). Here clay, earth and tile floors were used to differentiate various parts of the church. Another factor was that of economics – the expensive tile floors were laid on specific areas of the church (more visible or perhaps more important areas), while the rest of the flooring was composed of less expensive material.

Porch (LUB 68) (Fig. 13.38)

Given a re-examination of the pottery from the porch and its charnel pit, it is clear that it was erected at a date after the late 13th century. The arcading is, on balance, unlikely to be contemporary with the porch, although both dated after and possibly as late as the mid–late 16th century (Gil-

Fig. 13.38 The south porch cut by cg556, a brick shaft inhumation.

Fig. 13.39 The remains of the medieval church, looking north.

	LUB 42	LUB 43	LUB 44
inhums	36	10	–
charcoal	6	3	–
cist	–	1(ch)	–
shaft	–	–	–
vault	–	–	–
coffin	–	–	–
charnel pit	1	–	–
generations	5	4	–

Fig. 13.40 Burial types for LUBs 42–44

	45	46	47	48	49	50	51	52	53	54
inhums	1	8	31	11	7	10	41	24	26	3
charcoal	–	–	–	–	–	–	–	–	–	–
cist	–	2	–	8	1	1	35	1	2	1
shaft	–	–	–	–	–	–	3	–	2	–
vault	–	–	–	–	–	–	–	–	–	–
coffin	–	–	–	–	–	–	–	2	–	3	–
charnel pit	–	–	–	1	–	–	3	–	–	–
generations	1	3	6	4	3	8	8	3	4	3

Fig. 13.41 Burial types for LUBs 45–54

	LUB 58	LUB 59	LUB61
inhums	1	1	–
charcoal	–	–	–
cist	–	–	1
shaft	–	–	–
vault	–	–	–
coffin	–	–	–
charnel pit	–	–	–
generations	1	1	1

Fig. 13.42 Burial types for LUBs 58–59 and 61

	LUB 64	LUB 65	LUB 66
inhums	2	–	1
charcoal	–	–	–
cist	4	–	–
shaft	–	–	–
vault	–	–	–
coffin	–	–	–
charnel pit	–	1	–
generations	2	–	1

Fig. 13.43 Burial types for LUBs 64–66

	LUB 67
inhums	13
charcoal	–
cist	–
shaft	–
vault	–
coffin	–
charnel pit	–
generations	4

Fig. 13.44 Burial types for LUB 67

	LUB 72
inhums	20
charcoal	–
cist	–
shaft	–
vault	–
coffin	4
charnel pit	–
generations	6

Fig. 13.45 Burial types for LUB 72

	LUB 74
inhums	2
charcoal	–
cist	–
shaft	–
vault	–
coffin	7
charnel pit	–
generations	3

Fig. 13.46 Burial types for LUB 74

	LUB 76	LUB 77	LUB 78
inhums	1	–	44
charcoal	–	–	–
cist	–	–	–
shaft	–	–	–
vault	–	1	–
coffin	1	6	2
charnel pit	–	–	–
generations	1	?	10

Fig. 13.47 Burial types for LUB 76–78

	LUB 80	LUB 81	LUB 82	LUB 83	LUB 84
inhums	11	–	5	28	1
charcoal	–	–	–	–	–
cist	–	–	–	–	–
shaft	2	–	1	–	–
vault	–	–	–	–	–
coffin	4	1	5	23	1
charnel pit	–	–	–	–	–
generations	4	1	2	4	2

Fig. 13.48 Burial types for LUBs 80–84

	LUB 86
inhums	4
charcoal	–
cist	–
shaft	–
vault	–
coffin	4
charnel pit	–
generations	2

Fig. 13.49 Burial types for LUB 86

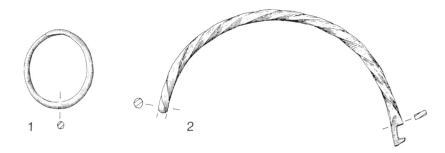

Fig. 13.50 Finds from Late Saxon inhumation burials. 1: copper alloy bracelet from cg78; 2: copper alloy finger-ring from cg231. Scale 1:1.

mour and Stocker 1986, 27–8; 89). If the arcading was secondary – since this date is quite late – but not without parallel – for a porch, the porch structure itself possibly dates somewhere in the late or or sub-Medieval period to accommodate human remains from another parish.

Late Medieval Windows

Windows of the 14th/15th century have been identified and dated from early prints (Gilmour and Stocker 1986, 26). The east end of the south wall of the nave was dated to *c* 1310–1350, the west window of the south wall of the chancel to between the mid 14th to 15th centuries, and the east window in that wall to *c* 1300. The two windows in the north aisle wall were dated to the mid 14th to 15th centuries (similar to the west window in the south wall of the chancel) as was the north-west door. The chapel windows were more difficult to date but a mid or later 14th-century date was considered most likely. Windows cannot, however, be relied on as a method of dating the wall in which they are set, as it was quite common practice to insert up-to-date replacements. The fact that there seems to have been much renovation being carried out in the mid 14th to 15th centuries makes it probable that the windows and the door of the north aisle were original to its construction, even if the windows in the south nave and chancel were later insertions.

Ground level of Graveyard

The level from which the south wall cg287 (Structure 12.1) was built was *c* 6.8m OD. In contrast, the buttresses to the north cg290 have a construction level of *c* 6m OD. Sealing the construction level was a dump of graveyard make-up which then heightened the ground level to *c* 6.8m OD. That the ground level was higher to the south suggests that the south was used more for burial; imported dumps of

graveyard make-up had to keep up with the input of inhumations.

Burials, coffins and coffin furniture

It was postulated that coffins and shrouds may have been present from the earliest use of the graveyard (Gilmour and Stocker 1986 16, 20, 23). There is, however, no evidence in the record for coffin furniture before the post-medieval period (a precise date cannot be given because of the problems with phasing the burials and the fact that the coffin furniture was discarded). There was no evidence for the early types of 'binding' found at St Paul-in-the-Bail. The few iron nails that remain are definitely nails, rather than shroud pins, and may have been redeposited from the underlying Roman structures. No definite shroud pins have been identified among the surviving material. This does not mean that coffins and shrouds were not used during these phases, only that the evidence has not survived, except perhaps in the sole instance of the charcoal burial in a wooden coffin cg38 (LUB 42) (Gilmour and Stocker 1986, 16).

There are numerous other references in the context records to inhumations associated with traces of wood from a coffin. Inhumation cg530 (LUB 74) was the earliest of these, dated to the 17th century (see above), but no coffin fittings were recovered. Graves with coffin fittings would be expected to be common from the 1660s when the fashion for elaborate furniture became more popular (Litten 1991, 99, 106–109). It is not possible to discuss the date-range or variety of fittings encountered because they were nearly all discarded on site; no detailed records were made. Copper-alloy nails (upholstery tacks) and fragments of cloth were also found in many graves suggesting the presence of a shroud or textile coffin covering, but the majority of these were also discarded. As a result the collection cannot be compared with that from St Paul-in-the-Bail.

cg/LUB	cg/LUB	cg/LUB	cg/LUB	cg/LUB	cg/LUB	cg/LUB	cg/LUB	cg/LUB	cg/LUB	cg/LUB	cg/LUB
1/40	65/42	129/49	193/53	257/51	321/48	385/69	449/78	513/51	577/83	641/67	2010/3
2/41	66/42	130/49	194/46	258/53	322/48	386/69	450/78	514/80	578/83	642/72	2011/2
3/55	67/42	131/49	195/51	259/51	323/64	387/69	451/78	515/82	579/83	643/41	2012/3
4/-	68/53	132/47	196/-	260/53	324/64	388/67	452/78	516/82	580/83	644/40	2013/4
5/-	69/53	133/47	197/56	261/51	325/64	389/67	453/78	517/82	581/83	645/44	2014/4
6/53	70/48	134/47	198/62	262/53	326/51	390/67	454/78	518/82	582/83	646/40	2015/6
7/48	71/48	135/47	199/62	263/51	327/51	391/67	455/78	519/82	583/83	647/41	2016/7
8/42	72/48	136/47	200/62	264/51	328/51	392/67	456/78	520/84	584/83	648/85	2017/7
9/52	73/48	137/47	201/62	265/51	329/51	393/67	457/78	521/84	585/83	649/69	2018/6
10/58	74/53	138/47	202/62	266/51	330/51	394/67	458/78	522/86	586/83	650/72	2019/7
11/42	75/53	139/47	203/56	267/51	331/51	395/67	459/78	523/82	587/83	651/58	2020/-
12/49	76/51	140/47	204/62	268/51	332/51	396/67	460/78	524/67	588/83	652/41	2021/7
13/47	77/51	141/47	205/62	269/51	333/51	397/67	461/78	525/74	589/83	653/41	2022/7
14/47	78/46	142/47	206/62	270/51	334/51	398/67	462/78	526/74	590/83	1001/1	2023/6
15/47	79/51	143/47	207/60	271/46	335/53	399/67	463/78	527/74	591/83	1002/1	2024/7
16/42	80/42	144/47	208/60	272/46	336/53	400/67	464/78	528/74	592/83	1003/3	2025/7
17/42	81/43	145/50	209/60	273/46	337/51	401/67	465/78	529/74	593/83	1004/13	2026/6
18/47	82/42	146/47	210/47	274/46	338/51	402/67	466/78	530/74	594/83	1005/13	2027/7
19/42	83/42	147/47	211/47	275/51	339/51	403/67	467/78	531/67	595/83	1006/13	2028/7
20/42	84/42	148/52	212/47	276/46	340/51	404/72	468/78	532/67	596/83	1007/13	2029/7
21/47	85/42	149/52	213/49	277/51	341/51	405/72	469/78	533/74	597/83	1008/13	2030/7
22/42	86/48	150/52	214/47	278/51	342/51	406/72	470/78	534/74	598/83	1009/13	2031/6
23/47	87/53	151/52	215/47	279/51	343/51	407/72	471/78	535/74	599/83	1010/13	2032/6
24/42	88/53	152/52	216/47	280/51	344/51	408/72	472/78	536/74	600/83	1011/13	2033/6
25/42	89/53	153/61	217/54	281/63	345/51	409/72	473/78	537/74	601/83	1012/-	2034/6
26/52	90/42	154/59	218/47	282/67	346/51	410/72	474/78	538/74	602/83	1013/-	2035/7
27/52	91/42	155/59	219/47	283/67	347/51	411/72	475/78	539/74	603/83	1014/-	2036/6
28/52	92/42	156/65	220/50	284/67	348/51	412/72	476/78	540/74	604/83	1015/-	2037/6
29/52	93/51	157/48	221/49	285/67	349/51	413/72	477/78	541/74	605/83	1016/-	2038/7
30/52	94/51	158/51	222/49	286/67	350/51	414/72	478/78	542/74	606/83	1017/-	2039/6
31/52	95/42	159/48	223/47	287/63	351/51	415/72	479/78	543/67	607/83	1018/-	2040/7
32/52	96/51	160/46	224/49	288/46	352/51	416/72	480/78	544/76	608/83	1019/-	2041/6
33/52	97/42	161/46	225/50	289/63	353/51	417/72	481/78	545/76	609/83	1020/13	2042/7
34/52	98/40	162/46	226/50	290/63	354/51	418/51	482/78	546/76	610/83	1021/13	2043/21
35/52	99/43	163/53	227/50	291/72	355/51	419/51	483/78	547/53	611/83	1022/13	2044/21
36/42	100/43	164/42	228/50	292/70	356/51	420/51	484/78	548/53	612/83	1023/13	2045/21
37/42	101/43	165/47	229/50	293/50	357/51	421/51	485/78	549/53	613/83	1024/31	2046/15
38/42	102/43	166/48	230/50	294/54	358/51	422/51	486/80	550/53	614/83	1025/32	2047/15
39/42	103/43	167/48	231/50	295/50	359/51	423/51	487/51	551/53	615/83	1026/32	2048/15
40/42	104/43	168/48	232/50	296/49	360/51	424/75	488/51	552/53	616/83	1027/32	2049/8
41/42	105/41	169/51	233/47	297/55	361/51	425/67	489/51	553/53	617/83	1028/33	2050/8
42/42	106/-	170/48	234/46	298/67	362/51	426/67	490/-	554/51	618/83	1029/33	2051/15
43/42	107/42	171/51	235/51	299/79	363/66	427/67	491/72	555/51	619/83	1030/33	2052/15
44/42	108/42	172/45	236/51	300/63	364/72	428/67	492/72	556/80	620/83	1031/33	2053/17
45/42	109/55	173/51	237/51	301/65	365/72	429/67	493/72	557/51	621/83	1032/33	2054/8
46/42	110/55	174/51	238/51	302/71	366/72	430/67	494/72	558/80	622/83	1033/33	2055/16
47/42	111/55	175/43	239/51	303/65	367/72	431/67	495/72	559/80	623/83	1034/33	2056/16
48/52	112/55	176/46	240/53	304/71	368/72	432/67	496/72	560/80	624/83	1035/33	2057/16
49/52	113/55	177/46	241/53	305/71	369/72	433/76	497/72	561/80	625/83	1036/34	2058/16
50/43	114/55	178/43	242/53	306/73	370/72	434/75	498/72	562/80	626/83	1037/14	2059/8
51/52	115/55	179/43	243/51	307/67	371/72	435/67	499/79	563/80	627/85	1038/14	2060/16
52/52	116/55	180/53	244/53	308/67	372/82	436/78	500/86	564/80	628/86	1039/-	2061/15
53/52	117/55	181/53	245/53	309/67	373/82	437/78	501/82	565/80	629/86	1040/35	2062/16
54/52	118/57	182/53	246/53	310/67	374/82	438/78	502/82	566/80	630/86	1041/3	2063/16
55/52	119/55	183/53	247/53	311/67	375/72	439/78	503/77	567/80	631/86	2000/0	2064/16
56/42	120/57	184/51	248/43	312/63	376/67	440/78	504/67	568/80	632/86	2001/1	2065/16
57/42	121/55	185/51	249/51	313/51	377/71	441/78	505/67	569/80	633/86	2002/2	2066/16
58/52	122/57	186/51	250/51	314/48	378/48	442/78	506/67	570/80	634/86	2003/3	2067/16
59/52	123/57	187/51	251/43	315/48	379/68	443/78	507/67	571/80	635/86	2004/2	2068/16
60/42	124/67	188/51	252/43	316/48	380/69	444/78	508/67	572/81	636/86	2005/1	2069/16
61/42	125/57	189/47	253/51	317/48	381/51	445/78	509/67	573/83	637/67	2006/3	2070/16
62/42	126/57	190/54	254/53	318/64	382/51	446/78	510/67	574/80	638/67	2007/3	2071/8
63/42	127/54	191/54	255/51	319/64	383/51	447/78	511/67	575/80	639/67	2008/3	2072/16
64/42	128/54	192/46	256/48	320/64	384/69	448/78	512/77	576/83	640/67	2009/3	2073/8

Fig. 13.51 Concordance of cg numbers with LUB numbers for sm76.

cg/LUB	cg/LUB	cg/LUB	cg/LUB	cg/LUB	cg/LUB	cg/LUB	cg/LUB	cg/LUB	cg/LUB	cg/LUB	cg/LUB
2074/16	2116/19	2158/21	2200/22	2241/–	2282/39	2323/38	3035/25	3076/5	3117/28	3158/30	3199/40
2075/15	2117/19	2159/21	2201/21	2242/38	2283/39	2324/38	3036/11	3077/4	3118/28	3159/29	3200/10
2076/15	2118/19	2160/21	2202/22	2243/38	2284/4	2325/38	3037/25	3078/9	3119/28	3160/30	3201/25
2077/8	2119/19	2161/21	2203/22	2244/38	2285/–	2326/38	3038/11	3079/4	3120/28	3161/40	3202/30
2078/16	2120/19	2162/21	2204/22	2245/38	2286/4	2327/23	3039/10	3080/–	3121/28	3162/40	3203/10
2079/17	2121/19	2163/21	2205/22	2246/38	2287/21	2328/6	3040/5	3081/–	3122/29	3163/40	3204/9
2080/17	2122/15	2164/21	2206/22	2247/38	2288/6	3000/–	3041/9	3082/24	3123/29	3164/40	3205/9
2081/17	2123/19	2165/21	2207/22	2248/38	2289/6	3001/–	3042/4	3083/25	3124/–	3165/40	3206/10
2082/17	2124/19	2166/21	2208/22	2249/38	2290/6	3002/–	3043/2	3084/25	3125/29	3166/40	3207/10
2083/17	2125/19	2167/22	2209/23	2250/39	2291/7	3003/–	3044/2	3085/25	3126/29	3167/40	3208/9
2084/17	2126/19	2168/22	2210/22	2251/38	2292/7	3004/–	3045/2	3086/11	3127/29	3168/40	3209/25
2085/17	2127/19	2169/21	2211/22	2252/39	2293/6	3005/–	3046/3	3087/25	3128/29	3169/40	3210/25
2086/15	2128/15	2170/21	2212/22	2253/38	2294/4	3006/–	3047/2	3088/25	3129/29	3170/35	3211/25
2087/17	2129/19	2171/21	2213/23	2254/39	2295/6	3007/–	3048/3	3089/25	3130/29	3171/25	3212/25
2088/17	2130/19	2172/22	2214/38	2255/39	2296/7	3008/–	3049/2	3090/25	3131/29	3172/25	3213/25
2089/17	2131/19	2173/22	2215/38	2256/39	2297/6	3009/–	3050/2	3091/25	3132/29	3173/25	3214/25
2090/17	2132/17	2174/22	2216/22	2257/38	2298/–	3010/–	3051/3	3092/26	3133/29	3174/25	3215/25
2091/17	2133/19	2175/21	2217/21	2258/39	2299/6	3011/–	3052/3	3093/25	3134/40	3175/26	3216/28
2092/16	2134/19	2176/21	2218/22	2259/38	2300/6	3012/–	3053/3	3094/11	3135/–	3176/25	3217/28
2093/17	2135/19	2177/22	2219/22	2260/38	2301/6	3013/–	3054/2	3095/24	3136/30	3177/–	3218/29
2094/17	2136/19	2178/22	2220/22	2261/39	2302/6	3014/–	3055/3	3096/25	3137/29	3178/5	3219/40
2095/17	2137/19	2179/20	2221/22	2262/39	2303/15	3015/–	3056/3	3097/24	3138/29	3179/9	3220/30
2096/17	2138/19	2180/20	2222/38	2263/39	2304/4	3016/–	3057/3	3098/24	3139/29	3180/9	3221/25
2097/17	2139/20	2181/21	2223/–	2264/39	2305/4	3017/–	3058/3	3099/–	3140/29	3181/9	3222/25
2098/17	2140/19	2182/21	2224/38	2265/39	2306/4	3018/–	3059/10	3100/25	3141/29	3182/10	3223/25
2099/17	2141/19	2183/21	2225/38	2266/39	2307/4	3019/–	3060/2	3101/25	3142/30	3183/10	3224/40
2100/17	2142/19	2184/21	2226/38	2267/14	2308/4	3020/–	3061/2	3102/–	3143/29	3184/9	4001/12
2101/18	2143/19	2185/21	2227/38	2268/39	2309/4	3021/–	3062/3	3103/25	3144/30	3185/10	4002/12
2102/18	2144/20	2186/21	2228/38	2269/–	2310/4	3022/–	3063/2	3104/–	3145/30	3186/10	4003/12
2103/17	2145/21	2187/22	2229/38	2270/15	2311/4	3023/–	3064/2	3105/–	3146/–	3187/10	4004/36
2104/18	2146/21	2188/22	2230/38	2271/7	2312/4	3024/–	3065/3	3106/27	3147/30	3188/10	4005/36
2105/17	2147/21	2189/22	2231/38	2272/–	2313/4	3025/–	3066/3	3107/27	3148/30	3189/10	4006/36
2106/17	2148/21	2190/22	2232/38	2273/17	2314/4	3026/40	3067/3	3108/–	3149/30	3190/10	4007/36
2107/17	2149/21	2191/38	2233/38	2274/16	2315/–	3027/40	3068/3	3109/28	3150/30	3191/9	4008/–
2108/17	2150/21	2192/38	2234/38	2275/17	2316/16	3028/40	3069/5	3110/28	3151/30	3192/9	4009/36
2109/17	2151/21	2193/22	2235/38	2276/17	2317/21	3029/28	3070/5	3111/28	3152/40	3193/40	4010/37
2110/17	2152/21	2194/22	2236/38	2277/21	2318/21	3030/28	3071/5	3112/28	3153/30	3194/30	4011/–
2111/17	2153/21	2195/38	2237/38	2278/38	2319/22	3031/27	3072/5	3113/28	3154/30	3195/30	4012/–
2112/21	2154/21	2196/38	2238/38	2279/39	2320/22	3032/25	3073/5	3114/28	3155/30	3196/30	4013/–
2113/17	2155/21	2197/38	2239/39	2280/39	2321/38	3033/25	3074/5	3115/28	3156/40	3197/40	4014/37
2114/18	2156/21	2198/38	2240/38	2281/40	2322/38	3034/25	3075/5	3116/–	3157/40	3198/30	4015/36
2115/19	2157/21	2199/22									

Fig. 13.51 Continued.

Other uses of the graveyard

The post-medieval graveyard and levels associated with the construction of Structures 14 and 15 (LUBs 79 and 85) contained eighteen ceramic discs, roughly chipped from sherds of 17th- and 18th-century pottery vessels, together with fragments of broken bottle-glass and clay tobacco pipes. The high quantity of ceramic discs found on this site and at the churchyard of St Paul-in-the-Bail, compared to domestic sites, suggests that the churchyard was used as an area for socialising and games playing.

Sepulchral fragments

Last but not least, the collection of gravecovers and other fragments of gravestones from the site was of exceptional importance. It has already been subjected to an exemplary detailed treatment (Stocker 1986, 55–82), but even since that date the collection has received wide attention for what it tells us of burial practice, cultural influences, and the physical nature of the graveyard (see also Everson and Stocker, 1999).

14. St Mark's Station East 1987 (ze87 and ze90)

Introduction

Excavation on the site for the new Magistrates and County Courts was undertaken between November 1987 and February 1988, prior to construction on land to the east side of High Street, across from the St Mark's Station site (z86); further work was undertaken in 1990 (Fig. 14.1). The area had been identified as one of high archaeological potential following the discoveries made at St Mark's Station. The St Mark's East site was not originally part of the 1972–87 post-excavation project, but was included at a late stage in the project, and in the absence of funding it has not been subject to full post-excavation analysis, but has been included here in outline because of its importance within the context of the Wigford sites.

Areas 1 to 4 were initially excavated mechanically to a depth of 1m–2m; the manual excavation in 1987–

88 was undertaken by staff provided through the Manpower Services Scheme supervised by Lisa Donel and Malcolm Otter, while the site recording as a whole was directed by Prince Chitwood for the then Trust for Lincolnshire Archaeology. The work was made possible by grants from the Home Office, the Manpower Services Commission, English Heritage and Lincoln City Council. The discovery of a major medieval pottery and tile kiln site extending eastwards necessitated further work in 1990 in advance of construction work on the County Court to determine the extent of archaeological deposits. The 1990 excavation was carried out by the CLAU under the direction of Prince Chitwood.

Two areas were examined during the 1987–88 season, the larger in the western part of the site, running back from the High Street (Areas 1, 2 and 3; Fig. 14.2) and one at the extreme east of the site

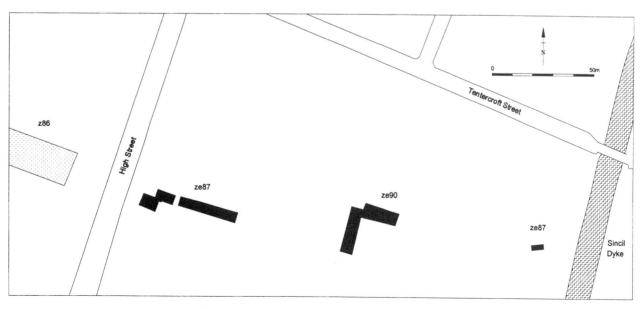

Fig. 14.1 Site location plan for ze87. (1:1,760)

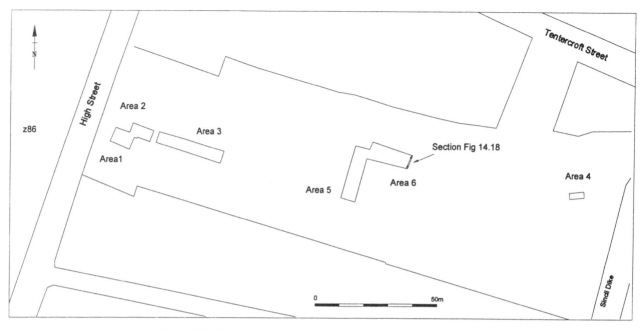

Fig. 14.2 Plan showing areas and section for ze87. (1:1,506)

adjacent to Sincil Dyke (Area 4; Fig. 14.2). In 1990 another area was opened up on the site of the proposed County Court, during the construction work on the Magistrates Court building (Areas 5 and 6; Fig. 14.2). The land-use diagram (Fig. 14.3) depicts the various investigations west–east: Areas 1, 2, 3, 5 and 6 and 4 to the east.

Single context planning was adopted for the 1987–88 season (Areas 1–4). In 1990, owing to the nature of the site and its deposits (Areas 5 and 6) and the limited time available for excavation, multi-context planning was employed; much was recorded only in section. All features and layers received an individual numerical code and descriptions were entered on standard record sheets which form the basis of the site archive for both sites.

Preliminary results have been published (Chitwood 1988 and 1990; Young *et al* 1988; Mann 1988b).

As this site was not originally part of the 1972–87 post-excavation archive, the 561 context sheets from z86 and the 135 context sheets from ze90 have not been computerised, in contrast with the other sites analysed as part of this project. This means that there is only manual access to the archive information, that description and interpretation has been more limited than has been the case with the other sites, and that there has not been the rigorous checking of the matrix and interpreted sequence of the site. The 696 contexts have been interpreted into 348 context groups (cg1–364; cg104, cg268 and cg287–300 were not used). The context groups formed 36 LUBs (LUBs 0–35; Fig. 14.21). The areas on the LUB diagram reflect the areas of the site (Fig. 14.3). In Area 1 there were

Roman (LUBs 1–9), Late Saxon (LUBs 14–15), Saxo-Norman to High medieval (LUBs 17, 25–26), post-medieval (LUB 29) and modern (LUBs 33–35). In Area 2 there were Roman (LUBs 1–3, 5–6, 8–9), Late Saxon (LUBs 14–15), Saxo-Norman to High medieval (LUBs 17, 25–26), post-medieval (LUBs 29–30) and modern (LUBs 33–35). In Area 3 there was natural (LUB 0), Roman (LUBs 1, 2, 5, 8 and 9), ultimate Roman to Late Saxon (LUBs 11–12), Late Saxon to post medieval (LUBs 13, 18–24, 27, 30 and 32) and modern LUBs (LUBs 33–34). In Area 4 to the east there was post-medieval (LUB 31) and modern LUBs (LUBs 33–34). In Areas 5 and 6 there was natural LUB (LUB 0), LUBs from the Roman period to the post-medieval periods (LUBs 10, 16 and 28) representing marsh and modern LUBs (LUBs 33–34).

Of the Roman pottery from the site, only the samian (212 samian sherds) has been archived, quantified, and reported; the coarse pottery from these excavations has not been archived, and the dating information given relies solely upon temporary viewing notes. It is therefore impossible to examine the inter-relationship of the samian and coarse wares, particularly in the light of the generally early dating of the samian when compared to other sites in the area. So far only sherds of post-Roman pottery from the site have been viewed; for the medieval and later periods, few of these have an adequate archive record beyond a basic ware-type sherd count, with limited detail of form or decoration, and material from the large waster deposits (*c* 150,000 sherds) remains unquantified. There are 478 registered finds, mostly from the three

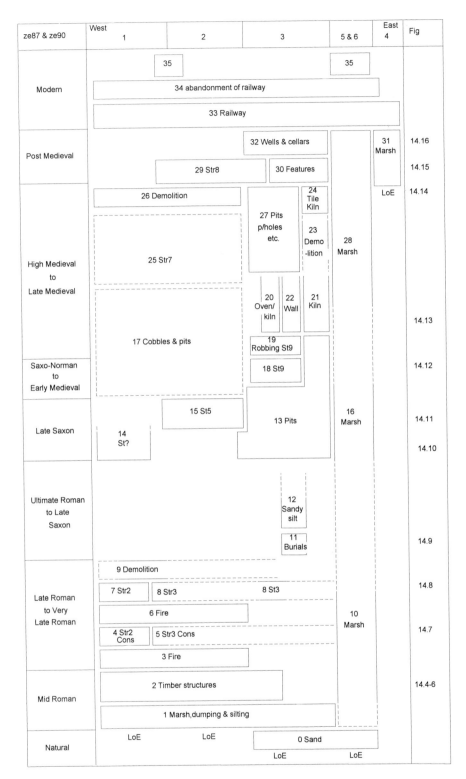

Fig. 14.3 LUB diagram for ze87.

areas to the west of the site. More than 85% of these are metal, principally heavily-corroded ironwork; a contributory factor towards the recovery of a higher than normal proportion of metalwork may have been the experimental use of a metal detector during the final season of excavation. Non-metallic finds include a fair proportion (15%) of glass, with small quantities of worked bone, ceramic and stone artefacts (including architectural fragments). The water-logged lower levels in Areas 1 and 3 had preserved a small quantity of leather; several pieces were also found within Areas 5 and 6. Other organic materials include two small groups of textile fragments and a substantial proportion of a wooden bowl, from pits in Area 3. Vast quantities of post-Roman tile were collected during excavation, as yet unquantified, but little non-ceramic building material. None of the metalwork has been cleaned apart from the coins, which were deemed to be crucial for dating purposes. Identifications have been made by examining the artefacts and their X-rays; for much of the ironwork in particular, such identifications must therefore remain tentative, and subject to confirmation or revision by investigative cleaning. Finds examined by external specialists include hones (Moore 1991); bone artefacts (Rackham 1994); coins (Roman: Davies 1992 and 1993; medieval: Archibald 1994); a Roman brooch (Mackreth 1993); wood (Gale 1992; Morris 1994); leather (Hofso 1991; Mould 1993); textile (Walton Rogers 1993). The vast quantity of building material from the site is yet to be quantified and examined. There has been no specialist assessment of the large animal bone assemblage (5,628 fragments) from the site. The remains of two Roman infant burials (LUB 7) have yet to be examined; a report on the two later burials (LUB 11) has been made (Boylston and Roberts 1994). An assessment was made of selected samples; a report on the biological remains was produced (Carrott *et al* 1994) and a sample of waterlogged wood from one sample was submitted for C14 determination (Beta Analytic Inc. 1994).

A number of people have worked on the stratigraphic material from this site. Prince Chitwood, Lisa Donel and Mike Jarvis produced the Level 2 archive for the 1987–88 excavation. Kevin Wragg worked on the Level 2 and part of the Level 3 stratigraphy for the 1990 excavation. Lisa Donel undertook the stratigraphic analysis of both sites in 1994; both she and Zoe Rawlings digitized the phase plans. Some further work on the stratigraphy has been undertaken by Kate Steane. Maggi Darling worked on the Roman pottery and Jane Young on the post-Roman pottery. Jen Mann analysed the registered finds and, with Rick Kemp, the building materials.

Further post-excavation analysis remains to be undertaken on the records of the site. This will include work on the Roman pottery, post-Roman pottery, building material, animal bone and human bone. Work on the Roman and post-Roman pottery may subsequently lead to modifications of the stratigraphic framework used here. The following interpretation of the sequence of events can therefore be only considered to be provisional, and is published here to enhance the global analysis of the Wigford sites. The site appears to have more contamination of earlier deposits than usual, possibly due to the impact of section cleaning, heavy rain, and inadequate resources.

Interpretation of the sequence of events

Natural

Sand **LUB 0** was reached, at the limit of excavation in Areas 3, and 5–6.

LUB 0 Terrace sand (Fig. 14.17)
Natural was not reached in Areas 1 and 2, but at the limit of excavation in Area 3 was a layer of yellow sand intermixed with some organic material cg269. In Area 6 there was yellow sand with numerous twigs, cg301; these layers may reflect waterlain sands and marsh debris. A C14 date of 800±70 BC was obtained from alder wood extracted from cg301 (Beta Analytic Inc. 1994). Whilst the wood may have been washed out of an earlier deposit, the absence of any evidence of human activity (eg charcoal flecks) within the residue suggests that this deposit pre-dates human occupation in the area.

Mid Roman

The marshy **LUB 1** extended right up to the line of Ermine Street with silt, sand, peat and rubbish; pottery indicates dumping activity and natural formation up to the mid 3rd century. Occupation **LUB 2** appears to have spread away from the road frontage; there were traces of timber buildings, floors and hearths; pottery indicates an early to mid 3rd century date.

LUB 1 Marsh, dumping and silting
At the limit of excavation in Area 1 were sand and pebbles cg21. Over this was a series of deposits of clay, ash and sand cg22 which were dated to the late 2nd century. Layers cg22 produced fragments of several leather shoes, one of which is of one-piece construction.

At the limit of excavation in Area 2 were layers of sand and ash cg25. Sealing dumps cg25 were layers of stoney sand cg84 and sandy silty layers cg271. Also at the limit of excavation in Area 2 was grey sand cg46 which was sealed by a layer of thick peat cg113. These layers probably represent a build up of marsh.

In Area 3, sealing sand cg269 (LUB 0), were sand and organic deposits cg143 and cg115. A little domestic refuse was found in cg143 together with fragments of six leather shoes, one of which is virtually complete (847) <332> (see Mann 1988b, Fig. 51,1, for a reconstruction). Layers cg115 were sealed by dark brown peat cg116 and sand cg121; over cg116 was a dark clayey deposit cg117 and over cg121 was blue-yellow clay cg122. Layers cg143 were sealed by layer cg142 and sandy silty layers cg267. Preliminary analysis of environmental samples from cg143 and cg267 suggests that the material was deposited in water and that it included waste possibly from stable cleanings (Carrott *et al* 1994).

The dumps from Area 3 are remarkable for the freshness of the sherds with many joining, and complete or near-complete profiles; this suggests primary dumping in the marsh. The nature of sandy, peaty, silty deposits indicates that they were also being laid down by natural processes. Most of the pottery from Area 3 dumps dates to between the mid and late 2nd century, but pottery from cg267 suggests a mid 3rd-century date. From layers cg271 a base silver *denarius* of Geta (144) <307>, issued AD 192–212, was recovered.

LUB 2 Traces of timber structures (Figs. 14.4–6)
Sealing layers cg271 (LUB 1) in Area 1 was a line of stones aligned north–south cg26 (unplanned), possibly the remains of a wall. To the west of the line of stones was sand sealed by a brown-green deposit cg270; pottery indicates an early to mid 3rd-century date. Sealing north–south stones cg26 and layer cg270 was a layer of cream coloured compact clay with mortar cg27. From cg27, an iron latchlifter (135) <301> was recovered. In Area 2, sealing sand cg84 (LUB 1) was a white mortar layer over which was firm sand cg272.

Sealing sand and ash cg113 (LUB 2), in Area 2, was compact orange sand, cg112 into which pitched stones cg47 had been set (0.60m across), possibly the foundation for a hearth or even the traces of a north–south wall. The stones cg47 were subsequently sealed by ash and sand layers cg48, cut by pit cg49 (unplanned), which was then sealed by a layer of compacted green sand cg50. Sealing layer cg50 was a black and red ashy layer cg111 and yellow and red

ashy layer cg51, burnt clay hearth cg109 and isolated stone cg52 (unplanned). Over layers cg111, hearths cg109 and cg110 and stone cg52 was sand and ash layers cg53, sealed by a hearth of flat limestones cg108 (unplanned).

Posthole cg123 cut blue-yellow clay cg122 (LUB 1) in Area 3; cutting posthole cg123 was posthole cg125 and sealing clay cg122 was a scooped hearth of reddish burnt sand cg124. Over peat cg116 (LUB 1) in Area 3 was post-pad cg119, later replaced by post-pad cg120 (unplanned); these were probably contemporary with post-pad cg118 over a clayey deposit cg117 (LUB 1).

Sealing clayey deposit cg117 (LUB 1) and post-pad cg119 was burnt sand cg137 and cutting through this was a linear feature cg136 (about 0.15m deep). Over this were layers of sand and ash cg126, followed by layers of sand, clay and ash cg131 and then a layer of limestone fragments cg132. Sealing post-pads cg118 and cg120 were layers of sand cg127, followed by peaty sand/clay cg128 and sand cg129.

Layers cg267 (LUB 1), also in Area 3 were sealed by cobbles set in sand cg144.

Late Roman to Very Late Roman

There was evidence of a fire **LUB 3** amongst the timber structures fronting Ermine Street; pottery dates this to sometime in the mid to late 3rd century. Stone 'strip' buildings (traders' houses) were erected soon afterwards: Structure 2 to the south **LUB 4** and Structure 3 to the north **LUB 5**. These too appear to have caught fire early in their lives **LUB 6**, near the street frontage. However, both Structure 2 **LUB 7** and Structure 3 **LUB 8** continued in use; pottery suggests that Structure 2 was in use to the very late 4th century, but there was no such clear evidence for Structure 3. The buildings were demolished **LUB 9**, possibly Structure 3 before Structure 2.

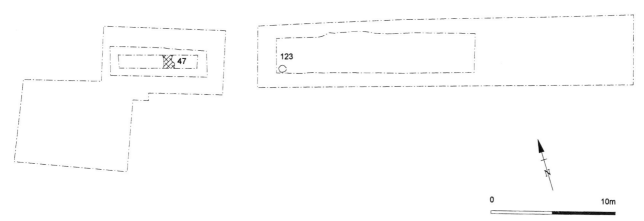

Fig. 14.4 Traces of timber structures: LUB 2. (1:291)

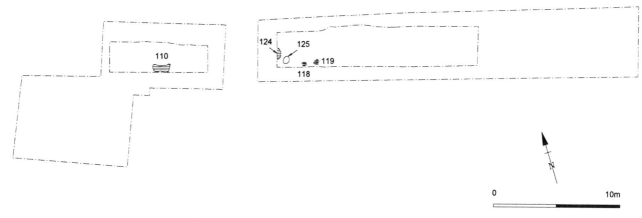

Fig. 14.5 Traces of timber structures: LUB 2. (1:291)

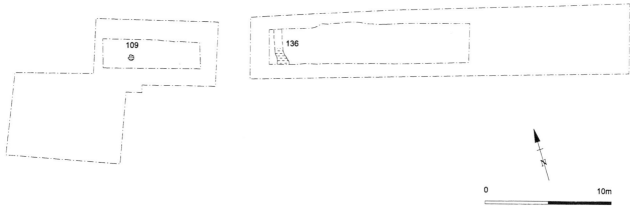

Fig. 14.6 Traces of timber structures: LUB 2. (1:291)

In Areas 5 and 6, to the east of the site, was further evidence for peat formation, **LUB 10**.

LUB 3 Fire
Sealing dumps cg22 (LUB 1) in Area 1 was a mottled heavily burnt deposit of charcoal, ash and limestone cg23. Layers cg23 were dated to the mid 3rd century or later.

A black ash layer with fragments of burnt wood and burnt sand cg54 sealed hearth cg108 (LUB 2) and extended over the whole of Area 2; it was sealed by burnt clay and sand cg57 and burnt sand and dark silt cg55. The pottery from these layers indicates a mid to late 3rd century date. At the limit of excavation in Area 2 there was evidence for an area of burnt clay and charcoal cg83. Within cg83 was a very small quantity of painted plaster, some of it burnt.

Sealing cg132, cg134 and cg135 was a thin black charcoal layer with sand cg138 and silty sand with limestone fragments cg139.

LUB 4 Construction of Structure 2 (Fig. 14.7)
At the limit of excavation in Area 1 was the construction trench (there was no record of what this trench cut) for east–west and north–south walls cg2. The walls were well built with rough foundations (0.80m wide) sealed by regularly laid and mortared limestone blocks (0.50m wide) and appear to have supported the north wall of a Roman strip building, Structure 2. From cg2 a very small group of finds was recovered, mainly ironwork including structural items. All seven sherds of pottery were residual. To the south-west of walls cg2, at the limit of excavation, was a metalled surface cg1; the excavation records note the presence of large fragments of slag, although none of this was kept. Also to the south of wall cg2, at the limit of excavation, were several layers of sand cg3.

LUB 5 Construction of Structure 3 (Fig. 14.7)
Cutting layer cg27 (LUB 2) in Area 1, was the construction trench, cg85, for the south wall cg24 of strip building, Structure 3. The wall was constructed

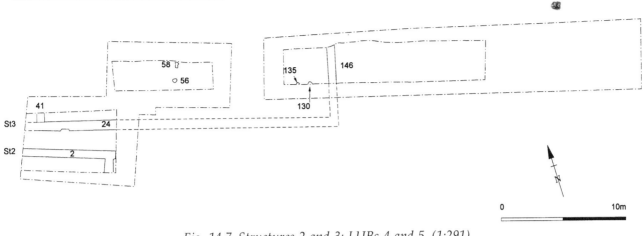

Fig. 14.7 Structures 2 and 3: LUBs 4 and 5. (1:291)

of regularly laid and mortared limestone blocks (0.50m wide). Abutting wall cg24 to the north was a similar wall cg41 (also 0.50m wide).

Up against the north of wall cg24 was a layer of sand and mortar fragments cg45, possibly construction debris. There were a number of postholes possibly related to the construction of this building: cutting layer cg45 were postholes cg43 and cg44 (unplanned) and cutting burnt layer cg55 (LUB 3) was posthole cg56, while burnt layer cg57 (LUB 3) was cut by posthole cg58.

To the west of wall cg41, at the limit of excavation, was a construction deposit of yellow mortar and small stones cg273; the bowl of an iron ladle (114) <255> was recovered from here. Sealing layers cg138 and cg139 (both LUB 3) were gritty sand with limestones cg140 and a patch of burnt sand cg141.

Layer cg129 (LUB 2) and cobbles cg144 (LUB 2) were cut by a north–south wall cg146. Wall cg146 was of rough faced limestone blocks bonded with mortar, built on pitched limestone footings (0.60m wide). It probably represented the rear wall of Structure 3. Cutting layer cg129 (LUB 2) was posthole cg130, sealed by sandy clay layer cg133. Cutting linear feature cg136, and layers cg133 and cg137 (all LUB 2) was a posthole cg135, contemporary with posthole cg134 (not planned) which cut layer cg133 (LUB 2).

This was difficult to date from the artefact assemblage: all the pottery was highly residual, while two coin fragments (119) <256, 279> were corroded together on excavation; both are extremely degraded and only datable to within the period AD 260–402 (Davies 1992).

LUB 6 Fire in Structures 2 and 3
Sealing sand cg3 (LUB 4) was a layer of burnt material cg274 south of wall cg2 (LUB 4), the north wall of Structure 2.

Over cg83 and sealing layer cg27 (both LUB 2) in Area 1 was burnt material sealed by green-brown sandy clay cg28. There was some evidence for ash deposits and burning seen on the outer face of wall cg24 (LUB 5), the south wall of Structure 3, which might indicate that there had been a fire which necessitated some rebuilding. Layer cg273 (LUB 5) in Area 1 was sealed by burnt material cg283 lying between walls cg24 and cg41 (both LUB 5). In Area 2, sand cg272 (LUB 2) was sealed by a dark brown deposit over which was a layer of burnt clay cg29. Pottery sherds from cg29 indicate an early to mid 4th-century date.

LUB 7 Post-fire activity: Structure 2 (Figs. 14.8–9)
Cutting sand cg3 (LUB 4) and probably cutting cg274 (LUB 6; although this was not recorded) in Area 1, to the south of wall cg2 (LUB 4) were infant burials cg4 and cg5. Aligned east–west with cg5 immediately to the west of cg4, the graves appeared to be relatively shallow, and close to wall cg2 (LUB 4). Grave cg5 appeared to have had a partial lining of upright stones around the sides and at the head and feet of the body, while cg4 was a simple grave; within its fill of this grave was a complete jet pin with polyhedral head (147) <346> of late 3rd–4th century type (cf. Crummy 1983, 27: type 2). Such pins are usually deemed to have been worn in the hair, but this pin was clearly not worn on the body at burial, because it was that of an infant; it was found near the feet of the skeleton.

There was a sherd join with cg25 (LUB 1) from cg4; this grave contained pottery dating to the mid to late 4th century.

Cutting burials cg4 and cg5 were pit cg7 and posthole cg6. Sealing cg7 were layers cg8; these consisted of a layer of small stones and dark brown clay, sealed by flat limestones, over which was a green sandy clay layer. Layers cg8 were

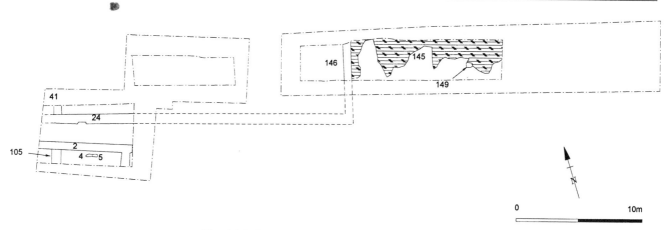

Fig. 14.8 Structures 2 and 3: LUBs 7 and 8. (1:291)

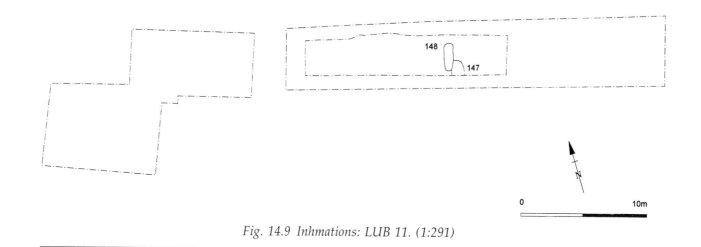

Fig. 14.9 Inhmations: LUB 11. (1:291)

subsequently sealed by layers cg9 which were made up of green-brown clay, over which was dark brown clay, both with pieces of limestone. Sealing cg9 was a north–south wall cg105 (0.70m wide), abutting wall cg2; this had been constructed of limestone. The pottery was mostly residual but with some dating between the late and very late 4th century.

LUB 8 Post-fire activity: Structure 3 (Fig. 14.8)
Over burnt material cg283 (LUB 6) was sandy clay and mortar cg284, sealed by white mortar cg285, over which was green-brown mottled sand cg286. Sealing cg142 (LUB 1) was layer cg265.

Cutting cg29 (LUB 6) in Area 1 was a north–south slot cg30 (unplanned); abutting this at right-angles were the possible robbed remains of an east–west wall cg42 (unplanned). Also cutting cg29 (LUB 6) were postholes, cg39 and cg40 (unplanned).

To the east of wall cg146 (LUB 5), sealing cobbles cg144 (LUB 2) were patches of a cobbled surface cg145 which had become well worn. Cutting cobbles cg145 was a posthole, cg149. The cobbled surfaces

are likely to have been external, to the east of Structure 3.

The pottery from this LUB was residual; there were also intrusive fragments of late medieval tile (from the kiln LUB 24).

LUB 9 Demolition of Structures 2 and 3
Sealing wall cg105 (LUB 7) was limestone wall tumble cg106. Wall cg24 (LUB 5) was cut by a small pit cg254 (unplanned). In the case of Structure 2 this operation cannot be earlier than the late to very late 4th century, on the evidence of the pottery from LUB 7.

LUB 10 Marsh: dumping, silting and draining (Fig. 14.17)
In Area 6, sealing sand and twigs cg301 (LUB 0) was a series of sand/silt layers cg302 sealed by similar layers cg303, over which was a clay layer cg307. At the limit of excavation in Area 5 was peat cg313. All these layers probably represent the remains of a semi-waterlain environment. Both cg303 and cg313 produced very small groups of finds, including structural debris. Pottery from

cg303 and cg313 was of early to mid 3rd-century date, but several 4th-century coins were recovered: cg303 and cg306 contained *Urbs Roma* and *Constantinopolis* issues of AD 330–5, while the latest of two coins from cg313 is a worn Constantinian Two Victories reverse type of AD 247–8. However, these coins may be intrusive from the 4th-century dumps sealing these layers; intrusive post medieval and modern material was also found in cg303.

Sealing cg303 in Area 6 was clayey silt and sand cg304. Cutting cg304 was a cut cg305. Cutting cg307 (LUB 2) were cuts cg308 and cg309; cg309 was cut by cut cg310. At the limit of excavation in Area 6 was sand and pebbles cg306 sealed by clayey silt with wood cg311; this also sealed cuts cg305 and cg308. Sealing cuts cg308 and cg310 was clayey silt cg312, sealed by layers sand and silt cg315, which also sealed silt cg311. Layers cg315 were sealed by sand, ash and silt cg325 and clay, sand and silt cg326. Layers cg311 were also sealed by clay sand and silt cg327 which was cut by cg359.

Sealing cg301 (LUB 0) in Area 6 were layers of peat and sand cg314, and a dump of clay and pebbles cg318. Sealing cg313 in Area 5 were layers of clayey sandy silt with wood cg316 and clayey silt cg317. Sealing cg317 and cg318 was a clay, sand and silt mix cg324. Cutting cg314 and cg324 was a linear cut cg329.

It is possible that this area of the site may have represented marginal land, regularly waterlogged. The cuts, which were only seen in section, may represent the remains of drainage ditches similar to those recognised at Chaplin Street to the south (cs73, LUBs 2, 4, 6 and 8). The pottery was mostly residual, of late 3rd- to 4th- century date but cg325 contained a sherd which dated from the mid 4th century. The few finds from this LUB consisted largely of leather (parts of two leather shoes, several waste fragments, and a piece of scrap from cg329), nails and other structural ironwork, together with several pieces of lead melt waste and the coins from cg303 and cg306, mentioned above.

Ultimate Roman to Late Saxon

Cutting the cobbles (LUB 8) in Area 3 were two burials **LUB 11**; there is no evidence other than stratigraphic for their dating. Sealing them was sandy silt, a waterlain layer **LUB 12**; although 4th-century pottery was present this was probably residual.

Further deposition, including peat formation, LUB 10 continued in the marshy ground to the east (Areas 5 and 6).

LUB 11 Burials (Fig. 14.9)
Grave cg147, a north–south adult burial, cut cobbled surface cg145 (LUB 8) and was itself subsequently cut by another north–south adult grave cg148.

Most of burial cg147 lay within the section and only the skull and several vertebrae were recovered; the burial was that of a young/middle-aged male. Burial cg148 contained parts of two individuals: the almost-complete skeleton of a 15–20 year old female, together with parts of the right arm and hand, most vertebrae and several ribs of a 25–35 year old adult, possibly male (Boylston and Roberts 1994).

LUB 12 Sandy silt
Burials cg147 and cg148 (LUB 11) were subsequently sealed by layers of sandy silt with limestone fragments cg150. There was 4th-century pottery from cg150.

Late Saxon or Saxo-Norman

In Areas 2 and 3, cutting sandy silt LUB 12 and underlying Roman stratigraphy were pits **LUB 13**; pottery from these features suggests that the LUB dates from the late Saxon period to the high medieval period.

Contemporary with some of the earliest pits were faint traces of a possible roadside timber structure **LUB 14** in Area 1; pottery suggests a 10th-century date. A later building **LUB 15**, lying back from the road was recognised in Area 2; pottery indicated an 11th-century date. Contemporary with the pits LUB 13, and these buildings LUBs 14 and 15, was further marsh activity **LUB 16** in Area 6.

LUB 13 Pits and/or postholes (Fig. 14.10)
Cutting cg28 (LUB 6), in Area 2, were two large pits, cg260 and cg261 together with postholes cg262, cg263 and cg264 (postholes unplanned).

In Area 3 were pits and postholes; cutting cg150 (LUB 12) were pits cg152 and cg153, together with posthole cg253 (unplanned) cut by pit cg151. From pit cg152 a lathe-turned wooden bowl was recovered; Carole Morris (1994) notes that bowls with rounded profiles and vertical walls, similar to that found here, include a 9th/10th-century burrwood bowl from Eastgate Street, Gloucester (Morris 1983, Fig. 118, 3), an 11th/12th-century ash bowl from Westgate Street, Gloucester (Morris 1979, Fig. 17, 17), a mid–late 12th-century alder bowl from Eastgate Street, Beverley (Morris and Evans 1992, Fig. 92, 613) and several bowls from Coppergate, York (Morris forthcoming). From pit cg153 fragments of wool textiles (775) <288–9> were recovered; one was a little finer than the other (<288> 18x10, <289> 15x8 threads per cm), but both had been woven in 2/1 twill, from a combination of Z- and S-spun yarn and both are matted on one face. One (775) <288>, had been dyed blue or green with woad (Walton

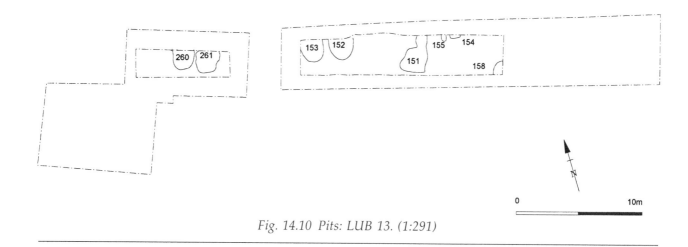

Fig. 14.10 Pits: LUB 13. (1:291)

Rogers 1993). These textiles represent the standard wool clothing fabric of the 11th to 14th centuries. There are a few 10th-century forerunners at York, London and Winchester (Walton Rogers 1996), but the general character of the Lincoln examples is more like that of the 11th century onwards.

Also cutting cg150 (LUB 12) were postholes cg154 and cg155. Cutting postholes cg253 and cg155, and pit cg154, were pit or posthole cg156 and pit cg161 (both unplanned). Sealing cg156 was dark brown sandy deposit cg157 with moderate amounts of limestone; this was later cut by pits cg158 and cg159 (not planned). Loam layer cg157 contained part of a iron horseshoe (769) <184> of mid/late 11th- to mid-13th-century type. Pit cg153 was cut by posthole cg160 (unplanned). Postholes cg158–160 were sealed by sandy silt cg162; a late 9th- to 11th-century crucible sherd (730) <403> was recovered from cg162.

The dating of all these features was positively post-Roman, but the comparatively small group of pottery ranges from the late Saxon to the post-medieval, indicating intrusion to the extent of making any precise dating of the LUB problematical. Generally it seems safe to suppose from the evidence that the LUB ranges in date from the Late Saxon to at least the high medieval period, if not beyond. In general, this part of the City appears to be re-occupied from the early–mid 10th century.

LUB 14 Possible structure? (Fig. 14.11)
In Area 1, cutting robbed wall cg42 (LUB 8) was slot cg259 running north–south; sealing cg42 (LUB 8) was a dump of light green/brown clay cg87. Sealing rubble cg106 (LUB 7) was dark brown earth cg10, cut by another north–south slot cg275 which may have been a southerly continuation of cg259 but was larger; it appeared to turn east–west at its the southern end. This was sealed by burnt sand

and wood cg276. Pottery from cg10, cg275 and cg276 dated from the 10th century. Cutting cg8 (LUB 7) was pit cg20 (unplanned). These features probably represent traces of 10th/11th-century occupation.

LUB 15 Structure 5 (Fig. 14.11)
In Area 2, sealing pits, cg260, cg261 and postholes cg262, cg263 and cg264 (all LUB 13) was sandy silt cg266. Over layer cg266 was ash and charcoal cg59. Cutting cg59 were two north–south linear features, cg66; these may represent two beam slots for a wooden structure set back from the High Street. Also cutting layer cg59 were postholes/pits cg60, cg61 (unplanned) and cg65. A small assemblage from posthole/pit cg65 includes an iron knife or shears blade (330) <129>, and a iron spike, possibly a woolcomb tooth (330) <131>. Sealing posthole/pit cg61 was ash layer cg107.

Pottery from layer cg59 indicates a mid to late 11th-century date; pottery from cg65 suggests the first half of the 11th century.

LUB 16 Marsh (Fig. 14.17)
In Area 6 a pit/posthole cg332 cut cg325 (LUB 10). Sealing cg329 (LUB 10) in Area 6 was sandy silt cg330, sealed by sand cg328 and clay cg362; sealing cg325 (LUB 10) in Area 6 was sandy ash cg333; sealing cg327 (LUB 10) was a layer of clayey silt and sand cg360. Deposit cg362 was sealed by sand cg331 and sandy silt cg363. Over cg362 was sand and pebble cg319 and then sand layers cg320, sealed by sand cg331 and sand and clay cg321. There was a cut cg322 in sand layers cg320 which was sealed by silty sand cg323. From deposit cg362 were two sherds of 10th-century pottery. The paucity of finds and pottery may suggest that this part of the site was largely unoccupied marshland.

Saxo-Norman to Early(–Late) Medieval

Subsequent to the buildings of LUBs 14 and 15 were cobbles, pits and postholes **LUB 17**; pottery indicates that this activity continued for some time, from the Saxo-Norman period through to the 14th or 15th century. To the rear of the cobbles was a substantial building, Structure 9 **LUB 18**.

Depositional activity LUB 16 continued in the marshy Areas 5 and 6, to the east.

LUB 17 Cobbles, pits and postholes (Fig. 14.12)

In Area 2, cutting pit/posthole cg60 (LUB 15), was pit cg63, cut by pit cg70 (both unplanned) and sealed by medium-to-large rough cobbles lying in sand cg64. Sealing postholes cg39 and cg40 (both LUB 6) was black burnt material cg38, sealed by dark brown sandy clay cg37; set in the clay was cobbling cg36.

Layer cg59 (LUB 15) was sealed by stone scatter cg62, possibly the remains of a stone surface and the patchy remains of cobbles, cg67. Cobbled surface cg67 was sealed by sandy clay layer cg68 cut by pit cg69 (unplanned). Two iron spikes (315) <116–7>, possibly woolcomb teeth, came from cg68.

Cutting cg64, cg68 and cg70 to the east of Area 2 were postholes cg71, cg72, cg73 and cg74 (unplanned). Sealing these postholes together with cobbling cg36 was cobbled surface cg31. A large assemblage of finds was recovered from within the makeup for, and between the stones of, the cobbled surface cg31, including a high proportion of nails and iron fragments. Sealing cg31 were layers of sand and silt cg35 and sand with shell cg103. Cg103 was cut by pit cg102 (unplanned) which was subsequently sealed by cobbles cg32 (unplanned). Cutting cobbles cg31 was an east–west slot cg33.

Stratigraphically the cobbles and some of the pits may date to the Saxo-Norman period and into the early medieval period. The pottery generally dates between the 14th and late 15th century; this may be intrusive, or may date activity on the site, increasing the date-range into the high to late medieval period.

LUB 18 Structure 9 (Fig. 14.13)

In Area 3, stone wall foundations cg176 cut cg162 (LUB 13). Also sealing cg162 (LUB 13) were buttress foundations cg175 at the west end of the building.

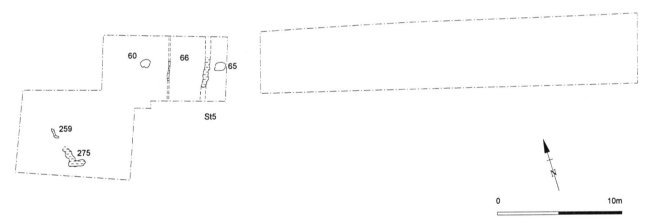

Fig. 14.11 Two timber structures?: LUBs 14 and 15. (1:291)

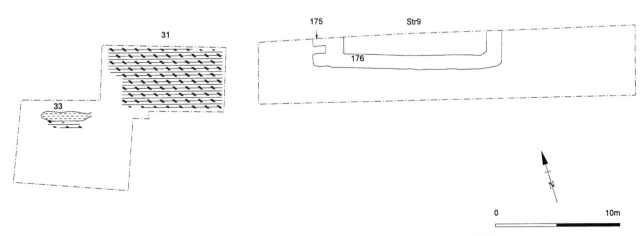

Fig. 14.12 Structure 9 and cobbling: LUBs 17 and 18. (1:291)

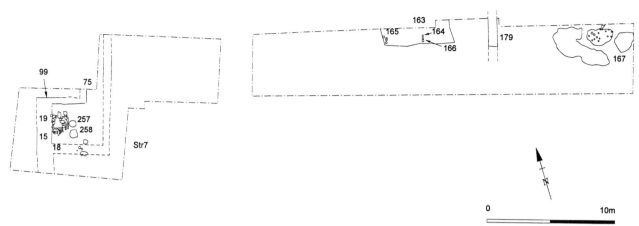

Fig. 14.13 Structure 7, pottery kilns divided by wall: LUBs 20, 21, 22 and 25. (1:291)

Although a large group of pottery was recovered from wall foundations cg176, this had probably been discarded during the extensive robbing of the structure as the sherds represent the same material as that recovered from the robbing cg178 (LUB 19). The building was probably associated with LUB 17.

High Medieval to Late Medieval

Structure 9 in Area 3 was robbed **LUB 19** and was replaced by an oven/kiln **LUB 20** and a pottery kiln **LUB 21**, with a wall between the two **LUB 22**. Pottery production in the area dated from the early 14th, peaking in the 15th century; from its relationship to the kiln, etc., the associated wall LUB 22 must date to the late 14th century. Sealing kiln LUB 20 was demolition debris **LUB 23**; this was cut by a tile kiln **LUB 24**; some of the latest forms of tile that it produced were of the late 15th century, but it may have been in production some time before that.

By the road in Areas 1 and 2 there was a building, Structure 7 **LUB 25**; only traces of this stone-founded building survived but there were large quantities of demolition debris **LUB 26**. Structure 7 can only be dated by pottery from its demolition, the latest being late 15th century.

To the rear of the site, cutting the earlier kiln activity (LUB 20), were pits, postholes and cobbles **LUB 27**. These were contemporary with the tile kiln LUB 24.

In Area 6 depositional activity **LUB 28** merges with the earlier LUB 16.

LUB 19 Robbing of Structure 9
In Area 3, wall cg176 (LUB 18) was robbed by trench cg178. The robber trench was used to dump wasters from nearby kilns, but not necessarily kilns LUBs 20 and 21.

The robbed remains of the buttressess were sealed by a thin clay layer cg177 from which a silver coin (728) <37> was recovered, a pre-Treaty penny of Edward III, minted between 1356 and 1361. The penny is corroded but is unclipped and shows little sign of wear; this suggests that it was probably lost before c 1400, and almost certainly before 1413 (Archibald 1994).

LUB 20 Oven/kiln and postholes (Fig. 14.13)
Cutting layer cg162 (LUB 13) in Area 3 was a partially preserved structure made of stone and burnt clay cg163. There was no evidence for its being a pottery kiln. Either contemporary with, or cutting, the oven/kiln were postholes cg164, cg165 and cg166.

Cutting postholes cg164, cg165 and cg166 were further postholes cg169, cg170, cg171 and cg172 and cg173 (unplanned). These postholes were sealed by sand with charcoal flecks cg252, over which was a thin black charcoal layer cg190.

LUB 21 Pottery kiln (Figs. 14.13 and 14.18)
Lying towards the north-east corner of Area 3, cutting cg162 (LUB 13) was a clay structure cg167, elements of a pottery kiln of a known late medieval type.

A small quantity (4kg) of fired clay fragments associated with this structure has been identified as packing material which was probably used, together with pottery wasters, to block the kiln flue during the final firing. They are of different fabrics, and include some shell-tempered and a few ?dung-tempered fragments; the impressions of several vessels (including that of a jug, a large jar, and at least one glazed vessel) are clearly visible on some of the pieces. One fragment of irregular oval cross-section, which is not as highly fired as the others, may have been used to plug the flue; another piece, bearing the impressions of two parallel stakes, may reflect the material used to fire the kiln.

Material directly recovered from the kiln structure cg167 has not yet been quantified; it consists entirely of kiln-type pottery. From LSW3 wasters (LUB 20), it seems that pottery production in the immediate area dated from the early 14th century; the main production period (LLSW) dated from the late 14th century.

LUB 22 North–south wall (Fig. 14.13)
Robber trench cg178 (LUB 19), in Area 3, was cut by a north–south stone wall cg179; two courses survived, the lower being of small pieces of limestone and the upper of larger limestone blocks, bonded by sandy silt and wedged with tile fragments.

LUB 23 Kiln demolition
Sealing the kiln cg167 (LUB 20) in Area 3, were clay silt layers with burnt limestone, burnt clay, ash and a large amount of pottery cg168 and burnt material, silt, tile and mortar cg174. Dumps cg174 were cut by pit cg189 (unplanned).

LUB 24 Tile kiln (Figs. 14.14 and 14.19)
Cutting dump cg168 (LUB 23) in Area 3, was tile kiln cg200. The kiln lay on an east–west orientation in the north-east corner of Area 3. Between the tiles used to build the kiln there was soft unfired clay, suggesting that perhaps it had been going through repair when it was abandoned, or that it had never been used at all.

The kiln was sealed by charcoal, ash, burnt sand and mortar, silt, rough limestone blocks, burnt tile and clay cg201. It seems likely that this fill had been derived from other kiln activity in the area.

A mixed assemblage of LLSW was recovered from both the tile kiln cg200 and the overlying dump cg201. The material has not yet been fully quantified; however, it seems to include some of the latest forms produced probably in the late 15th to mid 16th century. The roof tiles recovered from kiln cg200 and the overlying dump cg201 are mainly flat, with small applied suspension nibs, and glazed and stabbed ridge tiles; glazed louvers and finials were also found. The distinctive stabbed ridge tiles have not been found on any other site in the city: the tile awaits full quantification, and it is possible that more new types will be recognised.

LUB 25 Structure 7 (Fig. 14.13)
Cutting cobbles cg31 (LUB 17) at the west of Area 2 was a north–south wall cg75. The wall survived up to four courses high, bonded with sandy mortar. Up against wall cg75 was a large stone feature cg76 (unplanned), possibly a hearth; reused within its construction was part of a quern (5) <62>.

Sealing slot cg33 (LUB 17) were the traces of possible foundations cg100 (unplanned) on which east–west wall cg99 was built. Wall cg99 abutted wall cg75 and was itself later abutted by a possible buttress foundation cg86 (unplanned).

Over cobbles cg32 (LUB 17) were layers cg101; these consisted of blue-grey clay with lenses of sand sealed by yellow sandy clay. Layers cg101 were cut by large stones with silt and tile cg98, possibly traces of a wall.

Cutting cg10 and cg276 (both LUB 14) were postholes cg11, cg12, cg13, cg255, cg256 (all unplanned), cg257 and cg258. Also cutting cg10 (LUB 14) were limestone blocks cg17, lying up-ended and running north–south, possibly a small drain (unplanned). These were mostly sealed by dark brown sand layer cg14, but postholes cg257 and cg258 were sealed by burnt clay layer cg16 which also sealed cg14. Cutting cg16 were north–south wall cg15 and east–west wall cg18; wall cg15 was apparently of

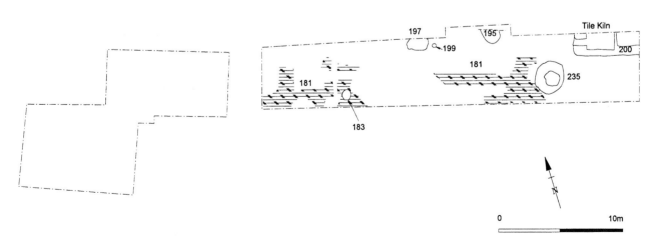

Fig. 14.14 Soakaway, pits, postholes, cobbling, and tile kiln: LUBs 24, 27 and 28. (1:291)

dry-stone construction, and wall cg18 occurred in
the form of small limestone blocks.

Sealing and incorporating the east–west wall cg24
(LUB 5) of Roman Structure 3, were the possible
remains of a stone garderobe base cg19, to the south
of wall cg15.

The latest pottery from any of these features,
other than cg19, was LLSW. Possible garderobe cg19
contained a large decorated jug as well as an
industrial jar dating to the late 15th or early 16th
century. Finds from the uppermost levels of the
garderobe fill cg19 include modern vessel and
window glass, indicating contamination, probably
from the railway construction (LUB 34). Cg249
contained two intrusive wine bottle fragments,
dated to the late 18th–early 19th century.

LUB 26 Demolition of Structure 7
Wall cg75 (LUB 25) had been levelled and sealed by
brown clay layer cg249 with sand, mortar and tile
fragments; tile from cg249 consisted of glazed floor,
ridge, flat nibbed roof and kiln furniture, all possible
products of the kiln cg200 (LUB 24). The wall
foundations cg75 were cut by robber trench cg77,
which contained a few limestone roof slates (possibly
Collyweston slate). Robber trench cg77 was subsequently sealed by layer cg78 (undescribed).

The latest pottery from this LUB was late 15th
century (LLSW).

LUB 27 Pits, postholes and cobbles (Fig. 14.14)
Sealing layer cg190 (LUB 20) in Area 3 was sandy silt
cg191; cutting layer cg191 were pits cg195 and cg197,
postholes cg199 and cg251 (the latter unplanned), as
well as stake-hole cg198 (unplanned). Postholes
cg195 and cg251 were sealed by grey-green clay
cg196. Cut features cg197, cg198 and cg199 were
sealed by silt sand and clay cg250.

Sealing wall foundations cg179 (LUB 22) was a
silty sand cg180, over which were cobbled surfaces
cg181. Surfaces cg181 were cut by posthole cg183
(on plan) and pit cg187 (unplanned). Posthole cg183
was sealed by clayey trample cg186.

Sealing cg177 (LUB 19) was sand with a small
amount of charcoal and plaster fragments cg184,
followed by layers of clayey sand cg185.

Cutting cg162 (LUB 13) was pit cg182, cut by
posthole cg188 (both unplanned).

Sealing cg189 (LUB 23) were cobbles cg192; over
these were limestone fragments, some of which were
worn cg193, cut by beam slot cg194 (unplanned).
Cutting cg194 were pits cg240 and cg234 (unplanned). Cutting pit cg240 was a well cg235, almost
entirely filled with approximately 3,850 sherds of
LLSW pottery wasters from the kilns (LUB 21 or
another kiln in the vicinity).

Small amounts of residual pottery or LLSW were

found in most deposits. A large group of kiln
material came from pit cg187. The latest pottery,
LSW4 of late 15th- or early 16th-century date, came
from dump cg180 and posthole cg195. The latest
sherds in well cg235 were 16th-century in date.

LUB 28 Marsh and dump layers (Fig. 14.17)
In Area 6, sealing layer cg363 and cg331 (LUB 16),
was silt and sand layer cg334 together with a large
quantity of kiln waste; this was sealed by sand and
ash cg336 as well as ash, sand, clay and silt layers
cg337, and was cut by cut features cg338 and cg339;
feature cg339 was cut by pit/ditch cg340. Layer cg334
produced a moderate assemblage of finds, including
dress fittings, structural fittings and window glass,
together with a small quantity of lead melt waste
and a large group of kiln waste. The presence of
post-medieval and modern material, however,
indicates that cg334 had been contaminated.

Sealing pit/posthole cg332 (LUB 16) were sand
and silt layers cg335. Sealing layers cg335, cg336,
cg337 and cuts cg338 and cg340 was black silt and
sand cg341. This was cut by an east–west boundary
wall of roughly squared limestone blocks cg343; silt
and sand cg341 was also sealed by pebble surface
cg364 probably associated with the wall. Surface
cg364 was sealed by grey-brown silty sand with
tree roots cg342. The robbed wall remains cg343
were sealed by grey black silt, sand and clay cg361,
over which was a layer of yellow chalky mortar
cg344, which also spread over cg342 as cg345. Layer
cg344 was partly sealed by black silt, sand and clay
cg348 and partly by a silty deposit cg349 with
limestone and mortar fragments. Layer cg345 was
sealed by grey-black silt sealed by sand and pebbles
cg346, and cut by a brick culvert cg347 which ran
east–west, along the same line as the underlying
wall cg343. Over layers cg348 and cg349 was silty
sand cg350, into which an upright wooden post
cg352 was set and sealed by grey-black sandy silt
cg353. Layers cg346 and cg348 as well as culvert
cg347 were sealed by sand cg351. Both post cg352
and silt cg353, as well as sand cg351, were sealed
by layers of sand, clay and silt cg354.

The date and range of pottery recovered from
these deposits indicate that they had built up from
the late medieval period. The registered finds
included some of post-medieval and modern date.

Post-Medieval

In Areas 1 and 2, replacing Structure 7, another
stone-founded frontage structure was erected **LUB
29**, Structure 8 with late 15th to early 16th century
pottery in its construction layers. To the rear were
pits, postholes and hearths **LUB 30**, dated by the
pottery to the late 15th to early 16th century or later.

Marsh deposition LUB 28 continued in Areas 5 and 6, and further east in Area 4, there was further evidence of marshy conditions **LUB 31**.

In Area 3 were wells and cellars **LUB 32**, indicating some new form of activity, probably in the form of frontage buildings, which have since been mostly removed by railway construction LUB 33. Only the deeply cut features to the rear of the site survived truncation by the railway. Pottery and other finds date from the 16th to the 18th centuries.

LUB 29 Structure 8 (Fig. 14.15)
Sealing cg249 (LUB 26) in Area 2 were dumps of clay and limestone fragments cg80 and masses of pottery waste; they appear to have been used as levelling of the waste dumps associated with the kilns. Cutting dumps cg80 and layer cg78 (LUB 26) were both pit cg81 (unplanned) and the foundations for wall cg79. Surfaces cg181 (LUB 27) were cut by east–west wall cg215 in Area 3, possibly an extension to the east of wall cg79. The wall cg79 was constructed of large roughly dressed limestone blocks and bonded with pale brown mortar. Wall cg215 was constructed of limestone blocks bonded with light brownish-yellow mortar including pottery fragments; only two courses remained, one offset above the other. A large group of finds from within the uppermost level of the dumps cg80 included kiln material that was derived from the latest production phase, possibly the late 15th century; there were also post-medieval and modern finds from both dumps cg80 and pit cg81, suggesting some contamination from rail construction (LUB 33).

In Area 2, silt and sand layer cg213 sealed cg185, cg186, cg187 and cg188 (all LUB 27). Layer cg213 was cut by north–south slot cg214 as well as posthole cg212 (unplanned).

In Area 1 stone feature cg98 (LUB 25) was sealed by sand cg95, into which had been cut limestone fragments cg94, possibly traces of wall footings. Sealing these was limestones bonded by sandy silt, traces of a wall cg93. This was levelled by a layer of mortar, silt, sand and tile cg92; layer cg92 was cut by an east–west wall cg91 of large well-dressed limestone blocks, but with no evidence of bonding material. Layer cg92 and wall cg99 (LUB 25) were also sealed by earth layer cg90, which was cut by stone feature cg89 (unplanned). Wall cg91 was repaired with a rebuild of rubble set in sandy clay cg88. Layer cg92 was cut by east–west wall cg226, which was constructed with pitched limestone footings and roughly laid limestone blocks bonded with clay.

The latest contemporary pottery (LSW4) comes from wall cg215, indicating a date after the end of the 15th or beginning of the 16th century.

LUB 30 Features to east of Structure 8 (Fig. 14.15)
Sealing cg196 and cg250 (both LUB 27) in Area 3 was a layer of grey clay sealed by burnt sand cg207; this was cut by east–west walls cg208 and cut by postholes cg206, cg209 and cg210. Sealing posthole cg210 was dark black sand cg238 sealed by a small pitched tile hearth cg237.

In Area 3, possibly cutting cg201 (LUB 24) were postholes cg202, cg203 and cg204; sealing cg201 (LUB 24) was grey clay cg205. Sealing the postholes cg202, cg203 and cg204 was a dump of ash, clay, many pottery wasters, burnt daub clay and sand cg241. Cutting cg168 (LUB 24) were stones set in clay cg242, possibly traces of a wall (unplanned).

In Area 3, layer cg213 (LUB 29) was cut by pit cg211. A burnt clay layer cg216 sealed pit cg211 and posthole cg212 (LUB 29); pit cg211 was cut by pit cg218 (unplanned). Layer cg216 was sealed by a dump of clay, limestone fragments and frequent pottery wasters cg217.

It is possible that the features represent a number

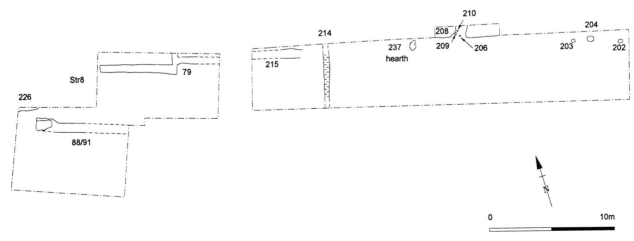

Fig. 14.15 Structure 8, pits, postholes and hearth: LUBs 30 and 31. (1:291)

of wooden outbuildings, which may have been associated with properties facing on to High Street. The latest contemporary pottery (LSW4) comes from layer cg238 and pit cg207, indicating a date after the end of the 15th or beginning of the 16th century.

LUB 31 Marsh

Observed in Area 4, this activity consisted of landfill operations to the west of the Sincil Dyke. At the limit of excavation was dark black bluey-grey clay and yellow mottled sand cg248, cut by pits cg246 and cg247. These were sealed by blue-grey clay, peaty material and more clay cg245, into which was set a line of stones cg244, possibly the foundations of a wall or jetty. These stones cg244 were subsequently sealed by clay cg243.

Dumps cg245 and cg248 produced small groups of pottery, mostly of kiln material. The latest sherds probably date to the late 15th or early 16th century.

LUB 32 Wells and cellars (Fig. 14.16)

Cutting pit cg218 (LUB 30) in Area 3, was pit cg219 (unplanned), cut by well cg220 (unplanned) with late 15th-century pottery in its fill (LLSW). Cutting cg217 (LUB 30) was well cg223 with 16th-century pottery in its fill (together with approximately 300 LLSW waster sherds), and also cutting cg217 (LUB 30) was pit cg222 (unplanned); cutting well cg223 was pit cg228 (unplanned), which included in its fill some modern pottery, intrusive from LUB 34. Pit cg218 (LUB 30) was cut by stone-lined pit cg233 (unplanned), and pit cg222 was cut by pits cg221 (unplanned); pit cg233 also contained some modern pottery; well cg220 was cut by pit cg232.

Cutting cg214 (LUB 30) in Area 3 was well cg224 with late 15th-century pottery in its fill (LLSW). Sealing wall cg226 (LUB 30) were layers of light brown sand with charcoal cg225; walls cg215 and cg226 (LUB 30) were cut by possible cellar cg227,

which contained modern pottery and finds intrusive from LUB 34. Cutting pit cg222 was well cg229 with late 15th-century pottery in its fill (LLSW). Well cg229 was in turn cut by well cg230 (unplanned) with late 15th-century pottery in its fill (LLSW).

Possibly cutting wall cg208 (LUB 30) in Area 3, was wall robbing cg239, which included pottery from the late 16th century to the mid 18th century.

Hearth cg237 (LUB 30) in Area 3, was cut by pit cg236, which contained an 18th-century wine bottle fragment.

Sealing cg100 (LUB 26) in Area 1, were traces of the foundations of an east–west wall cg97, which were sealed by a line of bricks cg96 (unplanned).

Modern

The entire site was truncated (in the west) or built up (in the east) by the construction of the railway c1850 **LUB 33**. The railway was abandoned in 1986 **LUB 34** and the site was cut by pipe trenches and a bore hole **LUB 35**.

LUB 33 Railway

In Area 3 much earlier material was truncated by the building of the railway cg231 in the mid 19th century; cg241 and cg242 (LUB 30) as well as cg222, cg225, cg228, cg230, cg232, cg233, cg234, cg235, cg236 and cg239 (all LUB 32). Other material in Area 3, cg95, cg88 and cg89 (LUB 29) was sealed by layers cg34. In Areas 5 and 6, sealing clay and silt cg354 (LUB 28) was a limestone dump cg355 (0.35m thick), probably make-up for the railway.

Over clay cg243 (LUB 31), in Area 4 was a dump of brick, stone and tile rubble cg277 as well as loam cg278. Loam cg278 was sealed by a further dump of rubble cg280 as well as a spread of mortar cg279. Over mortar cg279 and rubble cg277 was loam cg281. Over rubble cg280 was clay cg282.

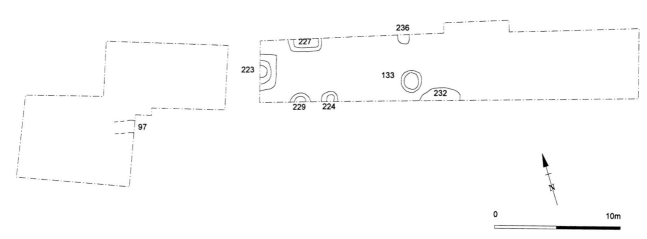

Fig. 14.16 Wells and cellars: LUB 33. (1:291)

All six areas were cut into, levelled and the railway track and buildings then built over them, from the High Street to the Sincil Dyke.

LUB 34 *Abandonment of the railway*
In 1985, the adjacent station and the railway were closed, and the track subsequently lifted; layer cg114 sealed cg231 (LUB 33).

LUB 35 *Pipe trenches and bore holes*
In Areas 1 and 2 cg249 (LUB 26) was cut by a pipe trench cg82. In Areas 5 and 6 cg354 (LUB 28) was cut by a pipe trench cg356 containing a 30mm PVC water pipe; layer cg354 (LUB 28) was also cut by boreholes cg357 and cg358.

Discussion

Topography
This part of Wigford was on low-lying ground, and most of the area excavated was marshy up to the mid to late 2nd century. The east end of the site was probably waterlogged marshland, and this may have extended even to the west of the site (LUB 1) not just in Areas 3, but also in 1 and 2, as well as in Areas 5 and 6 (LUB 10). By the Mid Roman period, however, Areas 1 and 2 were on firmer ground, and by the late Roman period Area 3 had also been rescued from the marsh, although its eastern fringe may again have become marshland before the Late Saxon period. Sandy silt (LUB 12) suggested a waterlain layer. But from the late Saxon period marshy layers only existed at the very east end of the site (Areas 4, 5 and 6; LUBs 16, 28 and 31); as these layers were truncated by the railway it seems that the eastern fringes of the site remained damp ground until the modern period.

By the early to mid 3rd century, there were timber structures in the western part of the site (Areas 1 and 2), fronting on to Ermine Street. They were replaced by stone structures (LUBs 4 and 5), possibly in the late 3rd century; these lay gable-ended on to the east side of Ermine Street. They were replaced after a fire (LUB 6) by similar buildings (LUBs 7 and 8). There was a gap (over 1m wide) between the buildings suggesting that there may have been a pathway leading to the rear of the properties.

By the Late Saxon period the importance of the street frontage was again apparent; from the 10th century there was evidence for re-occupation here (LUBs 14–15; Areas 1 and 2). The earliest post-Roman pottery dates to between the late 9th and early/mid 10th centuries. A further 200 sherds date to the 10th century, but typological work which might determine a continuous sequence has not yet commenced. During the Saxo-Norman and Early Medieval periods the area towards the High Street was extensively cobbled (LUB 17), possibly indicating the location of an industrial or commercial complex (many postholes and pits). In the early 14th century a building (Structure 7; LUB 25) was erected on the High Street in Areas 1 and 2; it was demolished and replaced in the early 16th century (Structure 8; LUB 29). Continuous occupation of the High Street frontage seems likely, as a series of wells and pits (LUB 32) was found to the rear, dating from the 16th century to the 19th century (traces of any buildings having been removed by LUB 33).

Between the frontage (Areas 1 and 2) and the marsh (Areas 5 and 6) was another area of occupation (Area 3). It was here that cobbles (LUB 8) to the east of Roman Structure 3 ran down to the marsh. Cutting the cobbles were two inhumations (LUB 11), which might date to the disturbed times of the late 4th century. They lay north–south: normally this is a

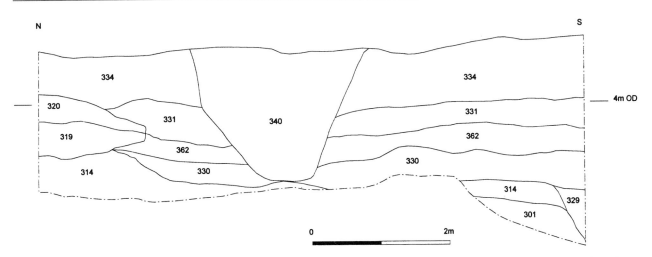

Fig. 14.17 Section from north to south illustrating the stratigraphy in area 6; LUBs 0, 10, 16 and 29. (1:53)

sign of a late Roman pagan burial. From the late Saxon to Saxo-Norman period this area was used for pitting (LUB 13). In the Early Medieval period the status of this area to the rear of the High Street seems to have become more important, the site of a substantial building, Structure 9 (LUB 18), possibly a town house or workshop (similar in location behind the frontage, period and size, to Structure 5 at Steep Hill (sh74) in the Lower City). Eventually the building was demolished and robbed (LUB 19) and in the early 14th century the rear part of the site (Area 3) became the location for pottery kilns (LUBs 20 and 21). By the late 15th century these had been replaced by a tile kiln (LUB 24), the only medieval example known within the city. The change in use of the land from the early to late medieval period may well reflect the shifting fortunes of the city. The early medieval opulence and success had produced merchants' houses in Wigford; this was followed by decline, and use for ceramic industries. From the late medieval period the rear of the High Street (Area 3) was used for pitting and outhouses (LUB 30), followed by wells and cellars (LUB 32).

Much of the post-medieval stratigraphy had been truncated over the entire site by levelling prior to the construction of the station for the Midland Railway in 1846 (LUB 33).

Roman "Strip" buildings (traders' houses)

There was evidence for timber buildings on the site from the mid Roman period. The earliest may have followed the same layout as the later buildings, but few traces survived. A fire (LUB 3), certainly affected those rooms nearer to Ermine Street.

Two Roman buildings (Structures 2 and 3; LUBs 4 and 5) were identified on the site, both gable-ended on to Ermine Street. The full dimensions of the buildings were uncertain, the gap between them being about 1m. They each had north–south internal walls, separating activity to the west fronting Ermine Street, possibly shops with workshops at the rear, perhaps also living quarters. There was no evidence for any particular activity.

Apparently during or soon after construction there appears to have been another serious fire on the street frontage affecting both buildings, at some date between the early and mid 4th century (LUB 6).

More of the extent of Structure 3 was accessible; it appears that behind the rear wall was an area of cobbling (LUB 8) leading down to the marshy ground.

The Medieval pottery and tile industry (Figs. 14.18–19)

The pottery found in cg177 and cg178 (both LUB 19) and cg189 (LUB 23) is of interest as it included waster sherds of LSW3, the principal type of Lincoln ware in production from the early 14th to the mid to late 15th century. The jugs are typified by a slightly ovoid rod handle with four distinctive finger pressings at the lower handle join. This indicates production, if not on the site, at least in the immediate area, preceding the main late medieval kiln phase. This earlier production is of a characteristic Lincoln type, whereas the later products were of a Humberware type. The early waster material was deposited after the introduction of LLSW, and joining vessels were also found in wall foundations cg176, ie, the robbing of the wall cg178 (LUB 19).

Fig. 14.18 The pottery kiln in Trench 3.

Fig. 14.19 The tile kiln in Trench 3.

Fig. 14.20 The medieval soakaway in Trench 1.

The pottery from the main late medieval production has been termed LLSW (Late Lincoln Sandy Ware) and the fine ware vessels in a white clay as LMF (Late Medieval Fine Ware). The basic flat roofing tiles are classed as type 4c. A short summary of the extremely wide range of products has been published previously (Young *et al* 1988).

Stylistically, both the pottery and the tile products are in a totally different tradition from previous Lincoln products. Distinctive differences include the lack of copper colourant in the glaze; different vessel, rim, handle and nib shapes; different decorative elements, and the use of a white firing clay for fine ware forms. The pottery does not totally replace the existing industries in the city until its final period of production at the end of the 15th century. The flat roof-tile, however, appears to dominate the tile assemblages from an earlier period.

Several of the pottery forms and decorative elements can be paralleled in the Humber and Toynton industries, while others such as the tall necked decorated jugs appear to be unique. The distinctive nibs on the flat roof tiles and the stabbing on the ridge tiles cannot as yet be paralleled.

The waster material from these sites forms an important assemblage, not only for the city but also for the understanding the surrounding area. Once it has been fully analysed we may have a better

cg/LUB	cg/LUB	cg/LUB	cg/LUB	cg/LUB	cg/LUB	cg/LUB	cg/LUB	cg/LUB	cg/LUB	cg/LUB	cg/LUB
1/4	32/17	63/17	94/29	125/2	155/13	185/27	215/29	245/31	275/14	305/10	335/28
2/4	33/32	64/17	95/29	126/2	156/13	186/27	216/30	246/31	276/14	306/10	336/28
3/4	34/33	65/15	96/32	127/2	157/13	187/27	217/30	247/31	277/32	307/10	337/28
4/7	35/17	66/15	97/32	128/2	158/13	188/27	218/30	248/31	278/32	308/10	338/28
5/7	36/17	67/17	98/25	129/2	159/13	189/23	219/32	249/26	279/32	309/10	339/28
6/7	37/17	68/17	99/25	130/2	160/13	190/20	220/32	250/27	280/32	310/10	340/28
7/7	38/17	69/17	100/25	131/2	161/13	191/27	221/32	251/27	281/32	311/10	341/28
8/7	39/8	70/17	101/25	132/2	162/13	192/27	222/32	252/20	282/32	312/10	342/28
9/7	40/8	71/17	102/17	133/2	163/20	193/27	223/32	253/13	283/6	313/10	343/28
10/14	41/5	72/17	103/17	134/2	164/20	194/27	224/32	254/9	284/8	314/10	344/28
11/25	42/8	73/17	104/–	135/2	165/20	195/27	225/32	255/25	285/8	315/10	345/28
12/25	43/5	74/17	105/7	136/2	166/20	196/27	226/29	256/25	286/8	316/10	346/28
13/25	44/5	75/25	106/9	137/2	167/21	197/27	227/32	257/25	287/–	317/10	347/28
14/25	45/5	76/25	107/15	138/3	168/23	198/27	228/32	258/25	288/–	318/10	348/28
15/25	46/1	77/26	108/2	139/3	169/20	199/27	229/32	259/14	289/–	319/16	349/28
16/25	47/2	78/26	109/2	140/5	170/20	200/24	230/32	260/13	290/–	320/16	350/28
17/25	48/2	79/29	110/2	141/5	171/20	201/24	231/33	261/13	291/–	321/16	351/28
18/25	49/2	80/29	111/2	142/1	172/20	202/30	232/32	262/13	292/–	322/16	352/28
19/25	50/2	81/29	112/2	143/1	173/20	203/30	233/32	263/13	293/–	323/16	353/28
20/14	51/2	82/35	113/1	144/2	174/23	204/30	234/27	264/13	294/–	324/10	354/28
21/1	52/2	83/3	114/34	145/8	175/18	205/30	235/27	265/8	295/–	325/10	355/33
22/1	53/2	84/1	115/1	146/5	176/18	206/30	236/32	266/15	296/–	326/10	356/35
23/5	54/3	85/5	116/1	147/11	177/19	207/30	237/30	267/1	297/–	327/10	357/35
24/5	55/3	86/25	117/1	148/11	178/19	208/30	238/30	268/–	298/–	328/16	358/35
25/1	56/5	87/14	118/2	149/8	179/22	209/30	239/32	269/0	299/–	329/10	359/10
26/2	57/3	88/29	119/2	150/12	180/27	210/30	240/27	270/2	300/–	330/16	360/16
27/2	58/5	89/29	120/2	151/13	181/27	211/30	241/30	271/1	301/0	331/16	361/28
28/6	59/15	90/29	121/1	152/13	182/27	212/29	242/30	272/2	302/10	332/16	362/16
29/6	60/15	91/29	122/1	153/13	183/27	213/29	243/31	273/5	303/10	333/16	363/16
30/8	61/15	92/29	123/2	154/13	184/27	214/29	244/31	274/6	304/10	334/28	364/28
31/17	62/17	93/29	124/2								

Fig. 14.21 Concordance of cg numbers with LUB numbers for ze87.

understanding of both its development and the complex interaction with other pre-existing industries of Lincoln glazed wares.

Apart from the material directly associated with kiln cg167 (LUB 21), fragments of kiln packing were also found dispersed within later levels of Area 3, within dumps cg201 (LUB 24) and the upper fill of pit cg187 (LUB 27), and in dump cg80 (LUB 29) in Area 2, and 'layer' cg101 (LUB 25) in Area 3. Within the fill of a pit cg81 (LUB 29) which cut dump cg80 was also found part of a possible kiln pedestal. Kiln props were found within layer cg176 (LUB 18; intrusive from the robbing cg178 LUB 19), cg181 and cg195 (both LUB 27). Without further analysis it is impossible at present to differentiate between debris from the pottery kiln cg167, and that from the tile kiln cg200 (LUB 24); there may also have been other kilns in the vicinity.

Some material that clearly derived from the pottery kiln cg167, however, was found within the uppermost level of the later dumps cg80 (LUB 29) in Area 2; this included two weights in identical fabric to that of the vessels produced. One (301) < 15> is virtually complete and pear-shaped, while the other

(301) < 17> is of somewhat irregular, triangular form; these were almost certainly produced as 'kiln fillers', and show dribbles of glaze which had almost certainly dripped from the vessels stacked within the same batch for firing. Part of a fired clay weight and a crudely shaped hand-carved chalk weight (similar to the pieces found here) were recovered from excavations at a 14th-century tilery at Grovehill, Beverley (Humberside County Council, Archaeology Unit 1987, Pl.21–2). They are suggested (Humberside County Council, Archaeology Unit 1987, 19) to have been used to secure the protective covers over external tile stacks. A similar use may have been made of the two pieces from this site, in protecting the products of the pottery kiln. Within the same context was also found a sherd from a kiln-type pottery vessel (301) < 404> with a thick internal deposit of lead glaze, and part of a conical kiln prop.

Two fragments of what appear to be a large brick or tile with finger holes pushed through to the centre, were recovered from dump cg217 (LUB 30). The fragments are in a tile fabric and have been fired. It is possible that they may have functioned as a shelf or fire-bar in the pottery kiln.

15. Discussion of Wigford and the Brayford Pool

Alan Vince and Kate Steane,
with contributions by Margaret J. Darling and Jane Young

The 1972–87 excavations in Wigford were largely confined to the northern half of the suburb (Fig. 1.2). This limit has to be borne in mind. Much of the discussion from the prehistoric period onwards has been facilitated by comparing the land use diagrams (LUB diagrams) of each site; a composite diagram gives an idea of the dated stratigraphy recovered across Wigford (Fig. 15.1). As bwn75 was so poorly dated, it has not been included in the discussion.

The Witham Gap, river terraces and riverine deposits

The suburb of Wigford lies in the glacial gap to the south and east of the River Witham as it flows through the city. The Gap contains a variety of quaternary deposits resting on Jurassic clay (not located in the 1972–1987 excavations). Evidence for a terrace at 4.8m OD was located at hg72 (LUB 1), smg82 (LUB 0), cs73 (LUB 1) and m82 (LUB 1). Over the sand was a layer of 0.2m of grey to white sand, the result of leaching of minerals, some of which formed a darker horizon between the sand and the leached horizon. The top of the terrace in the pre-Roman period must therefore have been remarkably level and would have been free-draining but, to judge by the leaching, would have supported poor soils (Fig. 15.2).

There was possibly evidence for a lower terrace around 3.5m OD, at sm76 (LUB 0), z86 (LUB 1) and ze87 (LUB 0), but the interpretation of these sands is difficult (Fig. 15.2). If we take the evidence of the St Mark's site at face value then this lower sand was at one time sufficiently above water level to allow a podsol to develop. This would imply a water table of *c* 3.0m OD or less (in contrast to the *c* 3.5m OD water table found on most sites in Wigford today). On the other hand, the survival of peat lenses and recognisable organic inclusions such as twigs in what seems to be the same deposit to the east would suggest that the water table has not been significantly lower than *c* 3.5m for an appreciable amount of time since the deposition of the sand. The alternative hypothesis is that these observations are actually of different bodies of sand, deposited at different times and under different conditions. The second hypothesis seems to be less likely but requires testing by further observations. If we follow the first hypothesis then the area occupied by the 3.5m terrace could have formed part of the Witham bed but would then have been above river level for a period long enough for podsol formation to begin. This development would have been curtailed in the mid to late 2nd century, at which time there is evidence for the deposition of organic material (which may be either natural sediments, dumping, or both) on several of the sites.

Borehole logs from a number of localities within the Witham Valley, both to the west of and in the Gap, show that the Witham lies within a deep channel now mostly filled with gravel overlain with clays, silts and peats. The eastern edge of this channel must lie somewhere to the west of the Holmes Grainwarehouse site and to the south of the Waterside South and St Benedict's Square excavations, but its exact line is complete conjecture. Riverine deposits were observed in excavations at lt72, bwn75, ws82, sb85, dm72 and bwe82; those to the north of the Brayford are undated. Analogy with similar peaty deposits exposed further east, at the Waterside Centre, suggested an Anglo-Scandinavian date, but peats recently found at a similar level to the south of the Brayford Pool have been dated by C14 determin-

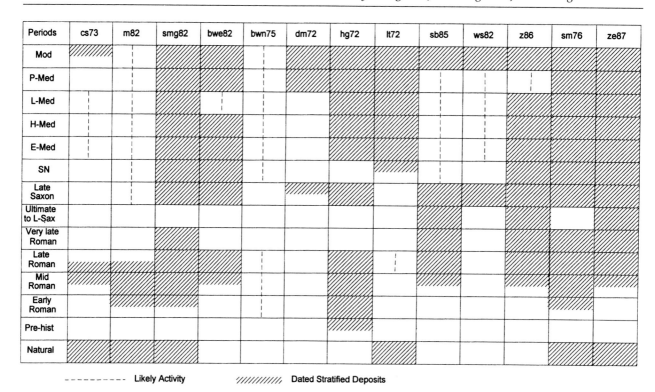

Periods	cs73	m82	smg82	bwe82	bwn75	dm72	hg72	lt72	sb85	ws82	z86	sm76	ze87
Mod													
P-Med													
L-Med													
H-Med													
E-Med													
SN													
Late Saxon													
Ultimate to L-Sax													
Very late Roman													
Late Roman													
Mid Roman													
Early Roman													
Pre-hist													
Natural													

---------- Likely Activity   ////////// Dated Stratified Deposits

Fig. 15.1 Period by period site diagram of dated stratigraphy across Wigford.

ations to the Neolithic to Bronze Age. The only datable finds associated with a rough metalling built over the peats at lt72 (maximum height 2.4m OD) were of Romano-British date (LUB 1), but they could be later.

On the south and east sides of the Brayford Pool, the sequence of deposits is extremely similar from one site to another. All dip gently from east to west, so that there is no possibility of correlation using their absolute heights. However, all contain dating evidence, mainly Roman pottery, which indicates a deposition date in the mid Roman period or later. At only one site, Brayford Wharf East, is there the possibility of earlier material, observed only in a machine-dug sondage where organic clay was observed to a depth of 0.57m OD with a top height of 1.61m OD. Similar mid-Roman dates were obtained from the earliest riverine deposits excavated at the Waterside Centre. There is therefore little doubt about both the location and character of the river channel and east bank of the Witham from the 3rd century onwards. The waterlain material of mid to late 2nd-century date, noted above, has been found at three sites: St Mark's Church, St Mark's Station and St Mark's East. The likelihood of there being a channel running east from the Brayford Pool in the early Roman period is increased by the fact that the waterlain deposits at z86 were cut by an east–west watercourse of which only the northern edge was observed (LUB 2). This could be interpreted as a culvert or canal replacing an earlier natural water-

course and itself falling out of use with the reclamation of this area.

Although the nature of the 4.8m OD terrace has been clearly established by the 1972 and later excavations, there is no such certainty about the position or history of the later river and the riverine deposits associated with it. The earliest occupation found to date, at hg72, may therefore have been on an island with the main river channel to its north and a minor channel to its south, but it is equally possible, on present evidence, that the main river channel ran to the south of the site and that the channel partially excavated between 1987 and 1990 on the site of the Waterside Centre was entirely artificial. Clearly, before the natural topography of Lincoln can be understood, a large amount of new fieldwork needs to be undertaken. In either case, the sites in Wigford with evidence for early Roman occupation would have lain on both sides of a wide area of low-lying land which, if not containing a major water channel, would at least have been so close to the water table as to make permanent settlement impossible. At this period, certainly, Wigford can have had no coherent identity.

Prehistoric Occupation

There is very little evidence from excavations in Lincoln for occupation before the Roman conquest,

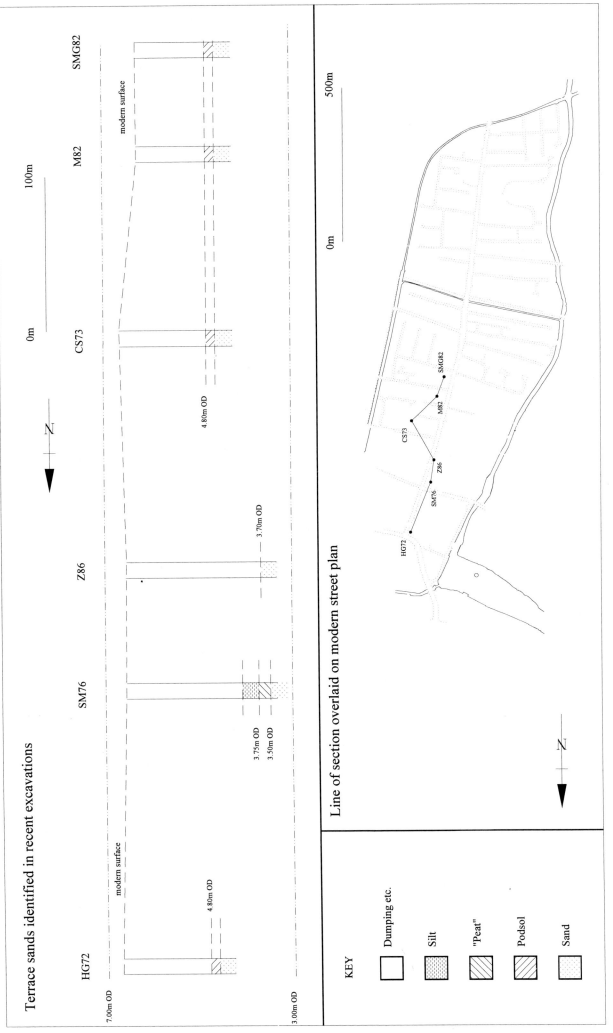

Fig. 15.2 Section of terrace sands along the centre of Wigford.

but of the two sites to produce late Iron Age pottery one lies in Wigford, hg72 (LUBs 1–3); the other site is The Lawn in the Upper City – and the material found here was less definitely pre-Roman in date. Reconstruction of the natural topography of the valley shows that the site occupied an island of terrace sand surrounded by ground which was certainly waterlogged and possibly below water. The approximate limits of this island have been defined by observations to the north and south. The western limit can also be located using dm72 and bwe82 as guides. Only the eastern limit is in doubt, but almost certainly lies somewhere between St Mary-le-Wigford church and the original line of Sincil Dyke. Both the disturbed subsoil on the Holmes Grainwarehouse site and the earliest features cutting through it contained only late Iron Age material, most of which could have been in use at the time of the Roman conquest. Reconstruction of the structures indicated by these features is impossible, but at least it is clear that the Late Iron Age activity was more than transient (Structures 1 and 2).

Early Roman Period

On most of the excavated sites no evidence for activity earlier than the later 2nd century was found, partly because the ground was too wet for settlement. What evidence we do have for this period comes from hg72, m82, and smg82.

The roads

Reconstruction of the Roman road system through Wigford suggests that two major routes, Fosse Way and Ermine Street, converged at a point less than 100m to the north of m82. The construction date of the (presumed military) roads was not recovered from the smg82 excavations, but the evidence suggests that at least the Fosse Way was constructed in the 1st century. To begin with, both roads were drained by roadside ditches and there is no evidence for the primacy of one route over the other. Excavations at both smg82 and m82 show that, later on, it was Ermine Street which gave its alignment to roadside buildings in the area, indicating that by the later 2nd century this road was perceived as being of greater importance. At this time the camber of both roads was altered and each road was provided with a central drain, as shown by the excavations at smg82 (LUBs 1 and 2). The convergence point of the two roads is thought to represent the northern limit of the 4.8m OD terrace, after which they combined to cross the low-lying ground to the island of hg72 and the line of the river Witham, presumed to have run between that

site and the later Stonebow. The alignment taken by the road is identical to that of a possibly late Iron Age or, more probably, early Roman ditch at hg72 (LUB 3), providing indirect evidence for the early date for the construction of Ermine Street.

The river, Brayford Pool and marshland

Despite the finding of mid and late Roman waterlain deposits at a number of sites along the west side of the High Street, no such deposits are known from the early Roman period. The location of the Witham at this period must have been not far to the west of the line of Ermine Street; a series of ditches running parallel with the street at sm76 had an organic fill which may have been waterlain. An indistinguishable deposit overlay these ditches, suggesting that this early attempt at drainage failed (LUB 2). Similar marshy deposits were present immediately east of this site, on the other side of Ermine Street (ze87, LUB 1). It is possible, although there is no positive evidence, that there was also a watercourse running east–west at this point with the marshy deposits to its north.

To the north of this area was another of higher ground, with evidence from hg72 for occupation. As noted above, excavations and observations to the south of Cornhill and to the west of the High Street indicate that this area was at one time under water and the excavation at sb85 (LUB 1) revealed a waterlain sand indicating fast-flowing water here.

No definite Roman deposits were found at lt72 and the excavations at bwn75 are undated. It is likely, however, that the early Roman waterfront lay much further north, close to the line of Newland/Guildhall Street/Saltergate. This conclusion is in line with discoveries made in 1987–90 on the site of the Waterside Centre (Chitwood 1989; Donel and Jarvis 1990). However, these excavations also failed to reveal any deposits earlier than the 3rd century. To the south of the Witham, east of High Street, the ws82 observation indicates that the southern side of the Witham lay much further south in the 11th century.

Military buildings?

Traces of one, or perhaps two, structures at hg72, 3A (LUB 4) and 3B (LUB 6), have been dated by associated pottery to the Neronian period, and could be contemporary with the earliest occupation of the legionary fortress. A rectilinear structure with painted wall plaster, Structure 3A.2 (LUB 5), succeeded the earlier traces; this structure is clearly aligned on Ermine Street. The paucity of Romanised wares relative to the large quantities of residual Iron Age pottery, some of which would be in contemporary use, make it impossible to define the dating more closely than mid to later 1st century, but finds of coins and samian pottery would tend to indicate official Roman rather than native use. The earliest Structures at smg82 probably belong to the *colonia* period rather than the legionary occupation, but further investigation is required.

Evidence for cemeteries

Evidence for the southern cemetery has been recorded since the 18th century, consisting primarily of tombstones and burials which indicated early burials which would, following Roman custom, lie in an area outside the city limits. Some of the finds were of legionary tombstones (see m82 text).

Cremations (LUB 4) and grave-marker slots (LUB 5) were found at m82, as well as the foundations of a stone building, perhaps a mausoleum (LUB 2). This is unlikely to represent the Mithraic temple which Stocker (1998) has proposed for this part of the city. Associated pottery was scarce but possibly indicated a late 1st-century date for the features. The possible mausoleum was demolished (LUB 6) and the cemetery abandoned at some point prior to the construction of buildings on the site in the mid to late 2nd century.

Early colonia-period buildings and other occupation

At hg72, a strip building with mortared stone foundations, Structure 4 (LUB 7), appears to date to the early *colonia* period. Its earliest phases (LUBs 8–10) may be of late 1st-century date (and have a *tpq* of AD 71 through a worn coin of Vespasian) whilst its latest phase and robbing (LUBs 15–17 and 20) are dated later than AD 120 by the presence of Dorset Black Burnished ware (BB1). Property boundaries at hg72 were not clear; Structures 4 and 13, and even 14, may have represented one property, associated with a stone-founded wall at least 26m long.

There were traces of activity between the two roads at smg72, in the form of cut features (LUBs 3 and 4) sealed by dumps of sand (LUBs 5 and 6) between the late 1st and early 2nd century.

Evidence of smithing was found at m82 (LUB 7) dating to the early to mid 2nd century and postdating the cemetery, together with a possible property boundary – a gully (LUB 7) at right-angles to Ermine Street.

Mid Roman period

The mid Roman period (the mid 2nd to the mid 3rd century) is better represented in Wigford than the earlier periods. Six sites to the west of Ermine Street (bwe82, dm72, hg72, sb85, z86 and sm76) and four

to the east (cs73, m82, smg82 and ze87) produced deposits of this date. Some sites (m82, smg82 and ze87) demonstrate a change of landuse, with buildings fronting on either side of Ermine Street, both to the north and south of the junction with the Fosse Way, as shown at smg82. The buildings laid out at m82 and smg82 took their alignment from Ermine Street, even when also fronting the Fosse Way, which is probably significant for the relative local importance of the two streets. The southern extent of the suburban development has not yet been found along either street nor, within the limited evidence available, is there any suggestion that the intensity of activity declined from north to south. Informal observations and watching briefs confirm the density of roadside activity but unfortunately throw no light on the known extent of settlement either to the north or south.

The river, marshland and Brayford Pool

Evidence for the location of the waterfront in the mid Roman period comes from two sites. At bwe82 the waterfront was marked by timber bank consolidation with river silts and peat to its west (LUBs 1 and 2), and at sb85, posts surrounded by river silt were interpreted as being set into the river bottom but close to the foreshore (LUB 1).

At z86, mid Roman river silting was observed in section only (LUB 1). It seems probable that the river flooded over the west part of sm76 (LUB 2).

To the east of the road at ze87 the marshy ground (LUB 1) was reclaimed with silt, sand, peat and rubbish; pottery indicates rubbish dumping up to the mid 3rd century.

The dumping at bwe82 could be interpreted to suggest the secondary deposition of mid to late 2nd-century debris. There is no evidence that waterside activities such as fishing were important at this period.

Drainage and gullies

At z86, the north side of what appears to have been a substantial channel was excavated (LUBs 2 and 6). It was in use up to the late 2nd–3rd century, before being backfilled in the mid 3rd century, and there is no archaeological evidence for any later replacement.

At cs73 a series of north–south ditches (LUBs 2, 4, 6 and 8) was excavated. These lay some way behind the line of Ermine Street, and may have had a drainage function. Associated pottery suggests that they were first cut at the time when occupation in Wigford intensified, in the late 2nd and early 3rd centuries.

Another series of parallel ditches was found on the west side of High Street at sm76 (LUB 2). These, however, lay much closer to the Roman road and some could be interpreted as roadside drainage ditches. They were slightly earlier in date than those at cs73 and pre-date the reclamation of this site and construction of strip buildings.

At hg72 a ditch (LUB 23) curved round Structures by the road side suggesting that there was little value to the land further west, and perhaps protecting the street frontage from river flooding to the west of the site.

Property boundaries

This period saw the development of a major commercial suburb, with landfill operations succeeded by the construction of traders' houses on either side of the street: it is uncertain whether the development was created by municipal or private enterprise.

A ditch and gully running parallel to Ermine Street at m82 before the late 2nd century was succeeded by a lane (LUB 11) dating between the late 2nd and early 3rd centuries.

The commercial suburb was divided formally into properties between the early and mid 3rd century, if not before. The evidence for this lies in the layout of the buildings at m82, smg82, sm76 and ze87; property boundaries at z86 and hg72 were unclear. At m82 the whole area seems to have undergone complete re-development in the 3rd century; the previous lane (LUB 11) was built over by a series of structures which were gable-ended to Ermine Street. Properties here were about 8m wide, to judge by Structure 3. Between Structures 2 and 3 was a lane (about 3.5m wide; LUB 17) which led off from the road between the properties.

Between the two strip buildings at smg82 was a gap (LUB 21), about 3m wide which seems to have been used as a lane and would have represented a property boundary; the building to the north (Structure 7) was about 20m long and that to the south (Structure 6) about 25m long and 10m wide.

At sm76 there is evidence for four properties and three property boundaries; the stratigraphic sequence indicates material building up in the narrow spaces (0.50m) between Structures 2 and 3 and between Structures 1 and 2 (LUB 14), but not between Structures 3 and 4. At sm76 the widths of building plots were between 8 and 9m, and while their full lengths could not be determined, one was at least 23m long. They were contained between Ermine Street to the east and the location of the river to the west. At ze87 there was a gap between Structures 2 and 3 which would have represented a property boundary; Structure 3 was at least 25m long.

At z86 and hg72 the widths of the properties were not clear. It is possible that Structures 2 and 3 at z86, with a shared dividing wall, were in fact one

building. To the rear of Structure 3 was a metalled surface, and it has been estimated that the building was about 25m long. The circular building (LUB 24) at hg72 appeared to front on to the road, but the ditch circled (LUB 23) round behind the building; it appears that the ditch defined the property at this date. There was no evidence for the use of areas not occupied by buildings or access routes.

Buildings

Six sites (m82, smg82, hg82, z86, sm76 and ze87) produced evidence for mid-Roman structures, which mostly fit the category of Roman traders' houses – long, narrow buildings gable-ended on to Ermine Street, initially built in timber and later replaced by stone-founded buildings of similar purpose. However, one building is quite different: that found at hg72 of circular plan.

The most completely excavated were at sm76 where three or four adjacent timber-aisled buildings, Structures 1 to 4, were constructed by the mid 3rd century (LUBs 6 to 13).

The evidence from smg82 is less substantial, but it seems that it too saw timber buildings erected between the 2nd and the early 3rd century (LUB 8 – Structure 5; LUB 14 – Structure 2; LUB 16 – Structure 3; and LUB 17 – Structure 4). Between the early and mid 3rd century a strip building (LUB 19 – Structure 6) fronting Ermine Street and backing on to the Fosse Way was constructed. To the north of the site another stone-founded strip building (LUB 20 – Structure 7) was built around the same time.

At z86 three phases of a probably timber-walled building were recorded (LUBs 3, 4 and 5; Structures 1.1–3). Stone-founded strip buildings Structures 2 and 3 (LUB 7) were constructed in the mid 3rd century at z86; they also represent buildings fronting on Ermine Street, with metalling (LUB 8) at the rear, down to the river.

At some date between the early and mid 3rd century, at m82, three stone-founded buildings were constructed (LUB 12 – Structure 2; LUB 13 – Structure 3; LUB 15 – Structure 4); Structure 3 was 6.5m wide internally. Occupation LUB 2 appears to have spread from the road at ze87; there were traces of timber buildings, floors and hearths from the early to mid 3rd century.

The construction of a circular building at hg72 (LUB 24 – Structure 5) succeeded industrial activity but retained the curved ditch (LUB 23). The function of this building, whose use can be dated to the early 3rd century, appears from the pottery to be linked with the preparation of food and drink – perhaps a roadside tavern. It is interesting to note that despite its very Roman ground plan the structure was decorated internally with red-painted wall plaster.

Industry

Postdating the demolition of Structure 4 at hg72 (LUB 20) was a phase of industrial activity (LUB 22) from the 2nd century into 3rd. Its exact nature was not identified. However, there was evidence of smithing at z86 (LUBs 3–4, and 5; Structures 1.1–3) from the mid 2nd century into the 3rd century.

Infant burials in Wigford

The remains of twelve infants were recovered from mainly mid Roman Structures in Wigford, five from smg82, one from hg72, three from z86 and two from sm76, with one coming from a Late Roman Structure (sm76). The infants from smg82 (LUBs 8 and 18), z86 (LUBs 4 and 5) and sm76 (LUB 13) were recovered from floor layers, that from hg72 from a destruction deposit after a fire (LUB 25), one from sm76 in a layer of soot (LUB 7), and another from demolition debris (LUB 17). They all appear to have died in the late foetal or perinatal period – which poses the question whether they were stillborn, died at birth or suffered from an acute illness in the immediate perinatal period (Boylston and Roberts 1994). Mays (1993) raised the question of possible infanticide to explain the high mortality found at many Roman sites; however, the ages of death here are evenly distributed between 37, 38 and 39 weeks, similar to the flat curve reproduced by Mays for modern stillbirths. Watts (1989) stressed that, although Roman custom proscribed burial within the city walls, an exception was made for infants dying before they were 40 days old, who were often placed beneath the floors of the houses or under the eaves. It appears that in Lincoln some stillborn infants were being buried beneath or within the floors of buildings, while others were possibly being pushed under the eaves, their remains perhaps falling to the ground after fire or demolition. The latter explanation might account for the fragmentary nature of the remains recovered from hg72 and sm76.

Late Roman

The term Late Roman is used here to refer to archaeological features dating to the second half of the 3rd century or later. The mid-3rd century was a period of transition for pottery styles and fabrics, and for coinage. It is usually therefore possible to date features containing contemporary pottery or coins, but there are likely to be deposits on most sites which are actually of late Roman date, but which cannot be identified either because they were not found associated with any pottery or coins, or because the finds were residual. Nevertheless, the main features of the Wigford area in the late Roman period are clear.

The river and the Brayford Pool

The river had been further narrowed by the late Roman period. The position of the riverfront was located at bwe82, where it was consolidated with dumps retained by timber (LUB 5); the dumps contained late 3rd-century and 4th-century pottery. By the late Roman period the waterfront had advanced to the west of sb85; at sb85 a possible hardstanding LUB 4 extended over the site (LUB 6); to the north was an east–west drain (LUB 7) leading down to the river from the higher land to the east.

At sb85, the hardstanding (LUB 4) continued in use (LUB 6) until the late 4th century as did the drain (LUB 7). At bwe82 there was evidence for late 3rd-century waterside activity in the form of stakes (LUB 3) and wattles (LUB 4), as well as contemporary river edge consolidation (LUB 5). By the mid to late 4th century silts and dumps accumulated in the river to the west of the site (LUB 6).

Wigford east of High Street

The low-lying northern part of Wigford east of the High Street is exemplified by the marsh to the east of ze87 (LUB 10). The lack of late Roman (or later) activity at cs73 may have been the result of the area being abandoned. There was little late Roman activity at m82, which it seems was also abandoned at this time, although activity continued at smg82. The Late Roman abandonment may be due to a local rise in the water table and risk of flooding, caused perhaps by the narrowing of the river channel separating Wigford from the Lower Walled City.

Property boundaries

Those boundaries from the mid Roman period at smg82, sm76 and ze87 appear to have continued in use. Similarly, there seems to have been no change at z86. At hg72 there was a radical reordering; the curved ditch was backfilled and the site re-used for a building which faced Ermine Street at right-angles. Although involving a change of use, it does not necessarily imply a change of owner. However, apart from the boundary with the road, the limits of the property lay beyond the limit of the excavation.

Buildings

At smg82 the occupation of Structures 6 and 7 (LUBs 23 and 24) continued from the mid Roman period into the mid 4th century. Structures 6 and 7 were subsequently demolished and the area seems to have gone through a period of abandonment, with the building walls robbed (LUB 25) between the mid and late 4th century.

After the demolition of Structure 5, at hg72, a rectangular strip building was constructed in its place in the mid 3rd century (LUB 26), fronting Ermine Street. It was altered in the early 4th century (LUB 28) and continued in use until the late 4th century.

At z86 the stone-founded strip buildings (LUBs 9–12 – Structure 2; LUBs 13–15 – Structure 3) continued in use through to the late 4th century.

At sm76 two stone-founded structures (LUBs 15 and 24; Structures 5 and 6) replaced earlier timber ones at the end of the 3rd century. These in turn were replaced in the early 4th century (LUBs 20 and 27; Structures 8 and 9). The building to the north (LUB 13 – Structure 1) was possibly demolished (LUB 31) in the early 4th century and stone-founded Structure 7 constructed (LUB 32). At a similar time, Structure 4 to the south (LUB 12) was replaced by stone-founded Structure 10, and later by Structure 11 (LUBs 36 and 37). The use of Structures 8 and 9 appears to continue through the late Roman period (LUBs 22–3 and 28–30), but Structures 7 and 11 were apparently not so long lived (however this impression may be misleading, since only a very limited was area investigated).

Stone strip buildings (LUB 4 – Structure 2; LUB 5 – Structure 3) at ze87 were erected between the mid and late 3rd century; Structure 2 continued in use to the very late 4th century, but there was no such clear evidence for Structure 3.

At m82 Structures 2, 3 and 4 were demolished and the area abandoned.

Very Late Roman

The section on the very late Roman period covers Roman activity in or after the late 4th century. There was evidence from a number of Wigford sites of activity during this period; smg82, sb85, z86, sm76 and ze87.

Buildings

At ze87 the strip building, Structure 2 (LUB 7), continued in use through to the very late 4th century.

Both strip buildings at z86 (LUB 16; Structures 2 and 3) were demolished and robbed in the late to very late 4th century.

The re-use of Structure 8, at sm76 (LUBs 38–9) extended into the very late 4th century, as did the re-use of Structure 9 (LUB 40).

Other Activity

In the very late 4th century, at smg82, there were a number of dumps and possible surfaces (LUB 26) over the demolished structures; these were cut by a ditch (LUB 27) over which were traces of rubble dumping (LUB 28).

Over the robbed remains of the buildings at z86 and extending westward was a massive dump of 'dark earth' (LUB 18) dated by the pottery to the very late 4th century. Three characteristics of these deposits have been examined as having a bearing on the formation processes involved: (1) the character of the pottery assemblage; (2) the ratio of animal bone to pot sherds; and (3) the presence of finds pre-dating the occupation of the sites. The pottery is characterised by fresh-looking sherds of late Roman pottery with no greater quantity of residual material than is found throughout the Wigford sequences. There is no evidence for a break in deposition between the latest pottery types found in the occupation levels below and that in the dark earth deposits, most of which can be dated to the late 4th century or later. The animal bone : potsherd ratios are quite high and this suggests both that domestic refuse (or butchery waste) was present in the dark earth and that the deposits have not been subjected to prolonged weathering (which would be the case if the deposits represented slow accumulations or had suffered through ploughing or horticulture after deposition). Artefacts of 1st- and early 2nd-century date are, however, present in these dumps in the form of coins and glass; it is unclear how this evidence should be interpreted, although it does suggest that not all of the material in the dumps could be derived from reworking of earlier deposits on the site. A few sherd links between pottery in dark earth deposits and earlier levels suggest that some reworking of earlier deposits may have contributed to the dark earth. These early finds are a very small proportion of the total assemblages and certainly do not support the notion that the dumps are composed predominantly of material dug up elsewhere in Lincoln. Most likely, they were derived from middens accumulating during the latest use of the buildings.

Waterfront and marsh

The drain into the river (LUB 7) at sb85 did not go out of use until the very late 4th century. The river seems to have been kept at bay by dumping at z86 in the very late 4th century. The marsh (LUB 10) continued in evidence to the east of ze87.

Early to mid Saxon

Although there is almost no artefactual evidence for occupation in Wigford in the later 5th–8th centuries, river silting occurred at some date between the ultimate Roman and late Saxon periods (z86, LUB 19; sb85, LUB 9), and possible animal hoof prints were found at one site (z86, LUB 19). The marsh to the east of ze87 involved a continuum between LUB 10 and LUB 16. However, cutting through Roman deposits and sealed by late Saxon stratigraphy here were two inhumations aligned north–south (LUB 11); they may belong to the uncertain times of the end of the Roman period.

The exact line of the Roman roads was not so important during the Saxon period: Ermine Street was no longer in existence but there was probably a route through Wigford based on the Fosse Way.

Apart from traces of ecclesiastical occupation in the walled city – at St. Paul in the Bail and also later at St. Peter-at-Arches, the closest early Anglo-Saxon settlement known is less than 2km away, however, on Bracebridge Heath. Mid Saxon settlement is indicated by pottery from various sites in the Upper City, but more notably from The Lawn (west of the Upper City), from Flaxengate in the Lower City, and from a site at the top of Canwick Hill, a similar location to that at Bracebridge Heath. If occupation of this period had been present in Wigford then there is no reason which it too should not have been recognised, even if only in the form of residual finds. Some Saxon pottery of MAX and GRBURN type has come to light, but in residual contexts.

Late 9th-century finds of mid Saxon type have been found at three sites in Wigford: St Mark's Station, where an ansate brooch was found in a 13th-century deposit; Monson Street; and St Mary's Guildhall. These finds suggest that there may have been some activity in Wigford in the later 9th century, although it is also possible that these artefact types continued in use into the Anglo-Scandinavian period or were brought on to the Wigford sites as a result of later dumping.

Late Saxon (Anglo-Scandinavian)

The first Anglo-Scandinavian occupation

Analysis of the pottery sequence at Flaxengate has shown that it is possible to distinguish three major phases of pottery use before the late 10th century. The earliest of these phases is characterised mainly by the presence of Lincoln Gritty ware (code LG) whilst the latest phase is marked mainly by the presence of inturned-rim bowls. In all three phases wheelthrown, shell-tempered pottery made in the town is the most common type. Small assemblages of pottery cannot therefore be distinguished unless they contain examples of the 'marker' types. There will therefore always be some uncertainty about

the date of first occupation of a site whose earliest Anglo-Scandinavian levels have probably been severely disturbed by later events. It is, however, clear that there are deposits of rubbish of early-to-mid 10th-century date at sb85 and that this dumping represents the first post-Roman activity on the site (LUB 10). Similarly, an early-to-mid-10th-century date can be assigned to the material from dumped deposits underlying the earliest cemetery at St Mark's Church (LUB 58). There, however, it is less certain that this dumping marks the first post-Roman use of the site, and there are sherds of ELSW and of LSLS incorporated into the dump. The only sherd of LG ware came from hg72. On most other sites the quality of the evidence and its nature – material from Anglo-Scandinavian pits and other features or redeposited material in later deposits – do not support any stronger statement beyond the Wigford suburb being in occupation by the early-mid 10th century, and that this period saw a re-occupation of virtually all the excavated sites.

The Waterfront

Activity at the waterside was revealed at sb85 by a network of hurdle fences (LUB 11) which in all probability were used to consolidate dumping along the water's edge (see the discussion in the site report) and at bwe82 by stakes (LUB 7) and reclamation dumps (LUB 9). There is a lack of dated evidence from Brayford North for this period, although it is quite possible that the timber stakes (LUB 17) belonged to this period. The ws82 watching brief, on the south side of the Witham, revealed evidence for peat accumulation and the deposition of domestic refuse but no waterside activity (LUB 2).

The marsh continued in evidence to the east of ze87 (LUB 16).

Property division

At sm76 the western boundary of the first graveyard was identified. It may have been marked only by a change in slope or by a ditch (LUB 44). At hg72 the buildings lay to the north and south of the site, leaving the area between for middens; they may have represented rear ranges of those fronting the street. It seems probable that the midden area constituted a boundary between the buildings.

Buildings

Structures of late Saxon date were identified at smg82 (LUB 30), hg72 (LUBs 32 and 33 – Structure 7; LUBs 35 and 36 – Structure 8), sb85 (LUBs 14 and 15 –

Structure 1; LUB 16 – Structure 2; LUB 18 – Structure 3) and at ze87 (LUBs 14 and 15 – Possible Structure? and Structure 5). The building at smg82 cut the Fosse Way, those at ze87 were situated at the High Street frontage, remains of those at hg72 lay behind the frontage (although they probably fronted on to the street; those at sb85 were situated well away from the High Street and related rather to the waterfront. The buildings at hg72 and ze87 were identified mostly from slots which might have held timber frames; the buildings at sb85 only left insubstantial traces, possibly reflecting the waterfront function.

Occupation

Dumps of material containing mainly late Roman finds deposited in the late Saxon period occurred at z86 (LUB 21), m82 (LUB 18) and cs73 (LUB 9) overlying Roman levels. There is no suggestion that these were part of a large-scale reclamation programme, and indeed that at z86 is datable to the later 10th century or later on ceramic evidence. It is more likely that plots were levelled, either by redistribution of material already on site or by the importation of material, prior to the construction of buildings as and when required.

Rubbish disposal took place by dumping into the Brayford Pool as at bwe82 (LUBs 9 and 11), sb85 (LUBs 10 and 11), in middens as at hg72 (LUB 38), or in rubbish pits, as at hg72 (LUBs 30 and 39), ze87 (LUB 13), sm76 (LUB 58), z86 (LUB 23) and smg82 (LUB 31).

The roads

There was a building encroaching on to the Fosse Way at smg82 (LUB 30) and pits cut through Ermine Street (LUB 31), which would indicate that the former Roman roads were not being used in the late Saxon period. As already noted, Ermine Street appears to have gone out of use, and the Fosse Way narrowed or shifted to the west.

Saxo-Norman

Activity dating from the late 10th century to the middle of the 12th can be dated mainly by pottery. On many sites there seems to have been some continuity from the Anglo-Scandinavian period. However, there is a lack of pottery in the 12th century at smg82 (LUB 32) and also at hg72 (between LUBs 39 and 40), suggesting either temporary abandonment of these prominent sites or truncation by later features.

Adjacent to the Brayford Pool at lt72, there were river deposits and an east–west fence (LUB 2). Little material specifically of this date was recovered from

the waterfront sites at bwe82 or the marsh in much the same form as at ze87 but both continued from the late Saxon period. Sincil Dyke may have been cut during this period (ws82).

The archaeological record is devoid of vernacular buildings for this period, but the 11th century saw the construction of the first stone church at St Mark's (LUB 55) followed by the addition of the western tower (LUB 60) sometime between the late 11th and early 12th century. There was evidence for pitting at sb85 (LUB 21), z86 (LUB 23) and ze87 (LUB 17) suggesting nearby occupation probably confined to the High Street frontage.

Early Medieval

Deposits of the mid 12th to mid 13th centuries are recognisable in Lincoln if they contain pottery with distinctive glazed wares, of local and regional origin, which first occur in this period in quantity.

The riverside, marsh and drainage

At lt72 river deposits, possibly within a defensive ditch, pre-date the Lucy Tower and City Wall (LUBs 3 and 4). The location of the Brayford waterfront at this period was established by the bwe82 excavation, where waterlain deposits and dumps of this date were revealed (LUBs 13 and 14).

The marsh to the east of ze87 (LUB 16) continued to exist.

Property division

The property boundaries of the church and graveyard at sm76 and the domestic complex at smg82 extended beyond the limit of excavation in most directions; the only boundary which was clearly recognisable was the High Street. At ze87 and z86 little can be said about the extent and nature of the properties.

Buildings

At sm76 the church may have been rebuilt (LUB 63) or embellished in the mid to late 12th century. In the late 12th century St Mary's Guildhall (smg82) was erected; substantial remains still stand (LUB 29; Stocker 1991, 17–33). The two principal ranges were disposed around what was probably an open court-yard (LUB 30; Stocker 1991, 33). It has been interpreted as being the town house built for Henry II in Wigford in 1157 (Stocker 1991, 37–41). The building underwent subsequent alterations (LUBs 31–33; Stocker 1991, 41–44).

At ze87 there was evidence for the substantial foundations of a building set back from High Street

(LUB 18) with cobbles and pits (LUB 17) between it and the road; the foundations were heavily robbed, so that little information could be obtained about this structure. There were also slight traces of 13th-century structures to the west of the High Street at z86 (LUB 25 – Structure 12; LUB 26 – Structure 6).

At hg72 (LUBs 40 and 41) pits with 12th-century pottery and a spread of cobbles are the only surviving evidence for occupation.

The road

At smg82 the main north–south artery through Wigford continued to shift further to the west of its Roman predecessor. The major domestic complex (smg82, LUB 33) encroached further on to the road. If any trace of Ermine Street survived, it only occurred further south.

High Medieval

Later 13th- and early 14th-century activity is recognisable when associated with moderate or larger assemblages of pottery, but because of truncation and machine excavation only limited deposits of this date were present in the 1972–87 Wigford excavations.

Around the Brayford Pool and along the river and the marsh

Although undated, there was probably occupation at bwe82, east of the Pool at this time; the land had been mostly reclaimed by dumping (LUBs 15 and 16). Traces of occupation were also noted during the sb85 watching brief (LUBs 19 and 22). Evidence for a possible timber wharf, constructed from part of a clinker-built boat at dm72, Area II, may also date to this period (LUB 7), succeeded by a stone-founded jetty (LUB 9). Extensive dumping was found further east at dm72 in Area I (LUB 11), associated either with activity at the waterfront or occupation behind it. The bwe82 excavation shows that the waterfront may have been advanced at this period (LUB 17). Vague traces of occupation found at ws82 on the east side of the northern branch off Sincil Dyke may be of this date since they post-date the canalisation of the Dyke (LUB 5). At ws82 Sincil Dyke was definitely constructed by the early 14th century (LUB 3) at the latest, and probably earlier. To the east of ze87 the marsh conditions persisted (LUB 29). The Lucy Tower and ditch may belong to this period (see Late Medieval period, below).

Property division

Documents form a source of evidence for this period

(see Gilmour and Stocker 1986). The church at sm76 and St Mary's Guildhall at smg82 occupied properties on either side of the High Street. At ze87 buildings fronted the High Street, but other boundaries were not apparent here. The medieval property boundaries may be reflected in modern boundaries at hg72, as structure 9 (LUB 42) covered the whole extent of the excavated site.

It would appear that during this period pressure on land was great enough for the lane (LUB 29) to be constructed at z86, opening up the land to the west of High Street frontages. Although there were a number of buildings associated with this lane, property boundaries were not clear.

The beginning of Friary occupation at z86 is not clear cut from the excavations. The Carmelite Friary (in place by 1269) covered part of z86 in the late 13th century, so while the friars may not have constructed the lane (LUB 29) they probably used it, and it may have formed a southern boundary to the expanded Friary – but this could not be proved.

Cutting through the peat (LUB 2), to the south of the river, at ws82 were two undated north–south walls and a land drain LUB 4; these were considered to be associated with medieval occupation to the south of the river, possibly boundary walls.

Buildings on and off the High Street

The church of St Mark continued in use during this period, while the major domestic complex at smg72 became the property of the Great Guild of St Mary of Lincoln in the mid 13th century – hence the name today of St Mary's Guildhall; alterations were made to the structure (LUBs 31 and 32; Stocker 1991, 41–44).

At z86, an east–west lane (LUB 29) led westwards from the High Street to service a number of 13th-century buildings which continued in use in to the 14th century (LUB 27 – Structure 6.2; LUB 30 – Structure 15; LUB 31 – Structure 8; LUB 34 – Structure 9 with kiln). While Structures 15, 8, and 9 went out of use, Structure 16 (LUB 36) associated with smithing was erected. Structure 6.2 (LUB 27) had hearths in each of its at least three rooms; Structure 8 (LUB 31) also consisted of at least four rooms with hearths. There seemed to be just the one room in Structures 9, 15 and 16 (LUB 30). It is possible that all these buildings at z86 had a stone-founded northern wall, open to the south.

Examples of buildings of high medieval date were found at two other sites, hg72 (LUB 42 – Structure 9) and traces at ze87 (LUB 25 – Structure 7). Structure 9 at hg72 was a stone-founded building about 5m wide with at least three rooms running back from the High Street.

No complete ground plans of these buildings can

be reconstructed, although that at hg72 is well-enough preserved to show that it consisted of a building aligned east–west with its gable end fronting on to the High Street.

Late Medieval

Deposits of late medieval date can be recognised in Lincoln where they contain contemporary ceramics (either pottery or tile). Late medieval occupation has been noted at a number of the 1972–87 sites, although Lincoln was undergoing some decline during this period.

At lt72 the transition between the high medieval and late medieval periods saw massive dumping (LUB 7), the temporary construction of a river wall (LUB 8), the construction of a stone wall and drum tower (LUB 9) and the cutting of the City Ditch to the west of the new wall (LUB 10). All of these events probably constituted elements of a single scheme. The construction of a new river wall butting up to the Lucy Tower, and the raising of the ground level to the east of the wall, may have been a secondary operation (LUB 11). The dating for the construction work comes from pottery dating between the late 13th and 15th centuries. Towards the end of the late medieval period the ditch was silting up (LUB 12) and there was a dump of material against the west of the wall (LUB 13) as well as to the east (LUB 14).

Between the mid 14th and late 15th centuries the dyke (LUB 3) had gone into disuse at ws82, its northern section being diverted further east.

At the ze87 site, a pottery kiln dated to the late 14th century (LUBS 20–21) was succeeded by a tile kiln (LUB 24).

St Mark's Church, St Mary's Guildhall and the building at hg72 continued in occupation on the High Street. At z86 the northern part of the site was clearly in the hands of the Carmelite Friary; there appeared to be a southern boundary to the Friary running east–west through the middle of the site (along the southern edge of the earlier lane). All graves were contained in the area to the north of this boundary. The z86 excavations as well as the more recent (1994–6) work on the friary suggest a major rebuilding in the late 15th century.

St Mark's Church was enlarged during this period, possibly during the 14th century with the construction of a north aisle and the north-east chapel (LUBs 71 and 73). A porch was added at some date after the late 13th century (LUB 68, but see the discussion of the evidence in the site report). A study of the floor tiles found in the church suggests that a new tile floor, constructed from imported Low Countries glazed earthenware tiles,

was laid out sometime between the late 14th and 15th centuries (LUB 72).

St Mary's Guildhall belonged to the guild until its dissolution in the mid 16th century. It was subsequently altered (LUBs 31 and 32), and part of the north range seems to have been let out for industrial purposes by the late medieval period (Stocker 1991, 45–49). Across the High Street and a little to the north was the fine house known as John of Gaunt's Palace, of late 14th-century date (Stocker, 1999).

At z86 the late medieval period was characterised by buildings which were clearly associated with the Carmelite Friary. There was a possible kitchen (LUBs 38–9 – Structure 11) succeeded by a probable church (LUB 49 – Structure 13) with a contemporary graveyard (LUB 50). The excavated burials were all of males. Cutting through the graveyard LUB 50, was another substantial stone-founded and buttressed building (LUB 52), likely to be an extension to the nave. To the south of the site, possibly outside the friary complex, were lean-to structures (LUB 41 – Structure 17; LUB 42 – Structure 18; LUB 43 – Structure 19), associated with smithing.

At hg72 ground-level deposits of late medieval date did not survive, but the lower fill of a cellar in Structure 10.1 shows that this stone building fronting on to the High Street was in existence by the late 15th or early 16th century (LUB 44); it contained 15th-century painted window glass in its demolition debris.

Post Medieval

At lt72 in the 16th and 17th centuries, the city ditch was recut and later silted up (LUB 15), and an east–west riverside wall was added to the east (LUB 16). The wall and tower were refaced (LUB 17), while features appeared inside the tower (LUB 18). A subsequent phase saw the raising of the ground level inside the city wall and the construction of a new river wall (LUB 19), the city ditch being finally backfilled and a river wall built across its course in the later 17th or 18th centuries (LUB 20). The tower itself, however, still stood and was repaired in brick (LUB 21).

Dumping was recorded at bwe82 (LUB 18), and at sb85 together with traces of walls (LUB 23). At dm72, sometime between the 16th and 17th centuries, Structure 4 (a warehouse?) (LUB 12) was built together with a path which led from the pool indicating unloading activity. It was replaced with Structure 5 (LUB 14) constructed sometime before the end of the 17th century, nearer the waterfront, which may also have been connected with loading and storage. The building was later demolished, and the area was sealed by dumping (LUB 15), which contained mid to late 17th-century pottery.

To the east of ze87, marshy conditions continued, LUBs 29 and 32.

The properties occupied by the church, guildhall buildings, and the stone building at hg72 continued to front on to the High Street; several medieval churches had now been demolished. To the south of the west range at smg82 there were now two 18th-century properties (Stocker 1991, 65) fronting the High Street. At this period there was clearly a southern boundary here for the guildhall. Other properties fronted the High Street at ze87 and hg72. At z86, to the far west of the site were the foundations of an east–west wall (LUB 56) which was clearly the remains of a property boundary, which appeared to echo the probable earlier friary boundary to the east of the site, further indicating a continuity of property division.

Speed's map of 1610 shows that, even at Lincoln's economic nadir, the High Street appears to have been built up along its frontage. The tower of St Mark's church collapsed in 1720 and the west end of the church was repaired (LUB 75), enabling it to continue in use. The St Mary's Guildhall buildings were acquired by the Bluecoats School in the early 17th century, although some demolition, alterations and new constructions took place here (LUB 34; Stocker 1991, 45–58). It appears that the north range continued to be used for industrial purposes; there were maltings from a date in the 18th century (LUB 36; Stocker 1991, 58–61).

An early 16th-century stone-founded structure at ze87 (LUB 30) fronted on to High Street with pits, postholes and hearths to the rear (LUB 31). Succeeding these were wells and cellars (LUB 33) indicating the probability of structures fronting the road (truncated by later disturbance); pottery and other finds date from the 16th to the 18th centuries.

A cellar (LUB 46) was the only evidence of Structure 11 at hg72, to have survived; it had late 17th- early 18th-century clay pipe remains in its fill, as well as a group of pottery.

Modern

By the 19th century the canalisation of the river meant that all the excavations were at some distance from the water. A solitary pit (LUB 19) at bwe82 is characteristic of the poor survival or limited recording of remains of this period.

Wigford was much affected by railway construction at z86 (LUB 57) and ze87 (LUB 34) in 1846 and later. This led to the truncation of deposits on z86, and the west of ze87 and the reclamation of

marshland to the east of ze87. The railways came to occupy vast areas from the south of St. Marks, including the loop line and associated sidings into Central Station from 1848.

The railways separated the northern part of the suburb from areas between the two stations, and the rest of Wigford to the south. In the north-west part was Dickinson's Mill on the Brayford, the property at hg72 fronting on the High Street, and changing patterns of development at sb85. There was also change in land-use to the north of the Brayford (lt72) as well as to the south of the river further east (ws82). Lucy Tower Street followed the line to the west of the former city ditch (lt72) down to the new edge of the Brayford Pool.

Much of the area to the south of the railways was developed with Victorian terrace housing, including the sites of cs73 and m82. A new south range (for offices) was added to St Mary's Guildhall giving a facade on to the newly created Sibthorp Street, along which Victorian terrace houses were also constructed. The buildings at St Mary's Guildhall (LUB 38) were all used for maltings (Stocker 1991, 61–65) and later as a timber yard.

At sm76, the much altered medieval church of St Mark's was finally demolished and a smaller Georgian church erected (LUB 79) in 1786. It was replaced by a Victorian church LUB 85 in 1872.

At lt72, the Lucy Tower became derelict (LUB 22), there was dumping to the west over the line of the ditch (LUB 23), and a shed was built up against the tower (LUB 24). The demolition of the City Wall and Tower occurred in the early to mid 19th century (LUB 25).

Dickinson's Flour mill (LUB 17) was erected (dm72) in the mid 19th century. At sb85 there was evidence of a stone-founded building associated with a well (LUB 24), which was backfilled in the mid 19th century. There were also traces of other buildings (LUB 25). At hg72 there were traces of a building on the frontage (LUB 48) probably constructed at the turn of the 19th/20th century. At cs73 Victorian building disturbed the earlier deposits.(LUB 12), as probably also at m82 where there were traces of wells and a cellar (LUB 19).

Summary of Roman pottery from sites in Wigford (Figs. 15.3–8)

by Margaret J Darling

There is considerable variation between the individual sites in Wigford, arising from their differing chronologies, and characters. The broad outlines of these differences in the pottery from the Wigford sites are given below.

Dating (Figs. 15.3–4)

The first chart shows all the pottery from Roman contexts (including the immediate post-Roman period) for the Wigford sites, the dating having been based on fabrics and vessel types, and spread over the period as percentages. Since the main occupation of some of the Wigford sites commenced as the importation of samian was ceasing, Fig. 15.4 is calculated on exactly the same basis, but excludes samian.

The sites to the south, m82 and the adjacent smg82, and the Brayford site hg72 show little change of profile due to the exclusion of samian, but the paucity of pre-3rd century pottery from the other sites and the 3rd–4th century emphasis are more strongly portrayed.

Both charts draw out the essential differences between the varying sites. The two adjacent southern sites, m82 and smg82, are closely similar. The Brayford sites of hg72 and bwe82 stand out as exceptional for different reasons. The late emphasis of sb85 is clear, while the differences between the adjacent sites of sm76 and z86 are more subtle.

Overview of samian dating (Figs. 15.5–6)

All samian dates have been converted to numeric dates and the quantities by sherd count spread as percentages of the total samian from the individual sites, and the results are shown in Fig. 15.5).

This makes clear the peaking of the samian from Wigford overall at *c* AD180, the bulk lying between

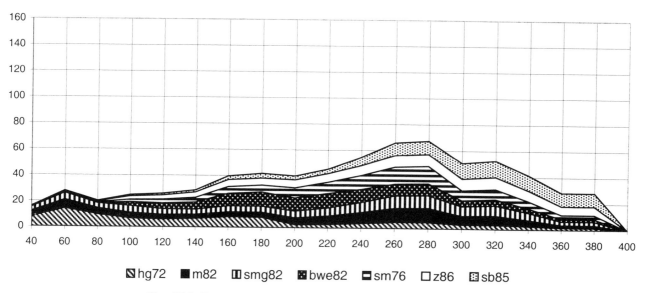

Fig. 15.3 Roman pottery chart: Wigford, all pottery, by period.

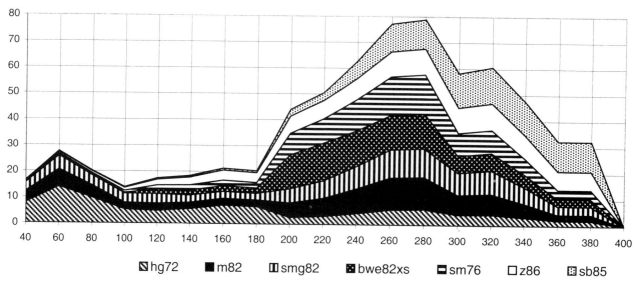

Fig. 15.4 Roman pottery chart: Wigford pottery, excluding samian.

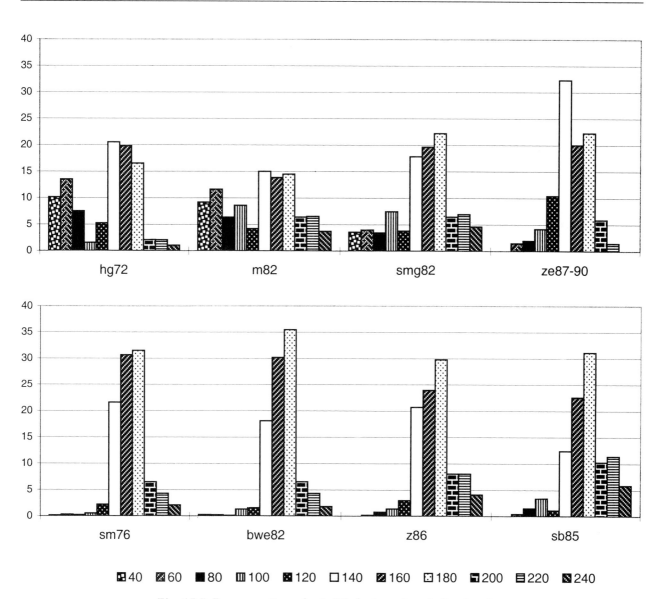

Fig. 15.5 Roman pottery chart: Wigford samian, dating by site.

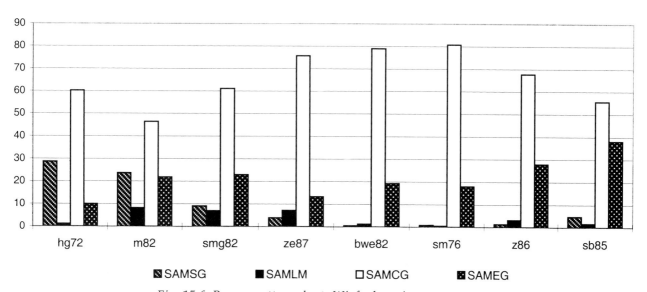

Fig. 15.6 Roman pottery chart: Wigford samian, percentages

c AD140–180, and emphasizes the small quantity of 1st century material, and its concentration in the southern sites and the Brayford site of hg72. The two sites producing most of the 1st-century samian are hg72 and m82, hg72 having the strongest early group, and declining in the later 1st century, while smg82 has significantly less 1st-century sherds. Thereafter, while m82 and smg82 have relatively similar dating profiles (although m82 is weakest in the main period *c* AD140–180), hg72 is barely represented in the late 2nd to 3rd century.

It also demonstrates, despite the peculiarity of the site, the broad similarity in the samian dating from the Brayford Wharf site bwe82 with sm76, and the earlier bias of the ze87 samian. The samian from ze87 peaks at *c* AD140, in contrast to the other sites peaking at *c* AD180; it produced small quantities for the main AD140–180 period, and very little 3rd-century material. The late bias of sb85 and the intermediate position of z86 can also be discerned. The samian from z86 contains much lower quantities for the period *c* AD140–160 than seen at sm76, but closes more strongly in the 3rd century, although below the level at sb85. The sources of the samian by site are shown in Fig. 15.6.

Overview by fabric (Fig. 15.7)

The next histogram shows the broad fabric groupings of Roman pottery, from stratified contexts including the immediate post-Roman phase, from the Wigford sites. This excludes the commonest undifferentiated GREY fabric which accounts for the remaining percentage for each site. The sites can be divided broadly into three categories: i) the early sites, hg72 by the Brayford with its Late Iron Age origin; m82, the site of the early cemetery, and the adjacent smg82; ii) the St Mark's sites of sm76 and z86, with sb85 with its later emphasis; and iii) the site of bwe82 with its extraordinary assemblage, heavily biased to samian and finewares.

The fabrics indicating pre-3rd century occupation are the Iron Age tradition wares, IASH and IAGR, and earlier oxidised fabrics, largely flagon-types, EROX. Although BB1 occurs in the 2nd century, its 3rd-century and later appearance is illustrated by its consistent share in bwe82, sm76 and z86, although the smaller quantity in sb85 suggests that this is largely confined to the 3rd century.

The main coarse fabrics characteristic of the later Roman period, broadly the mid 3rd century through

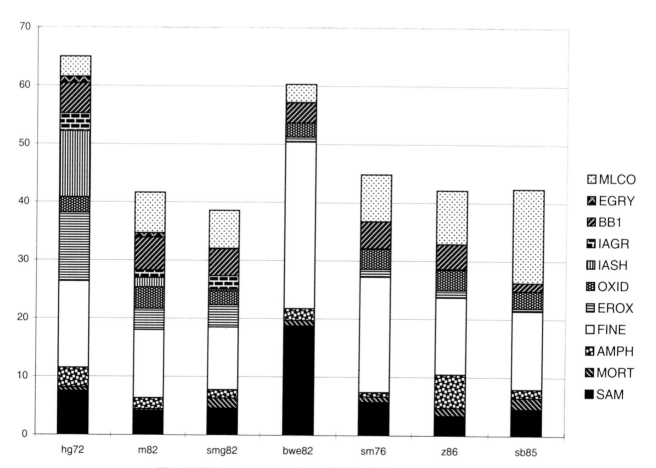

Fig. 15.7 Roman pottery chart: Wigford fabric groups by site.

the 4th, are grouped as MLCO, and comprise DWSH, LCOA, various Crambeck fabrics and South Midlands shell-tempered, the latter both rare in Lincoln. The site with the latest emphasis is sb85, although z86 has a higher proportion of late Roman pottery than the adjacent sm76.

Although many of these groups can be split between early and later Roman, the resulting categories normally yield such low percentages as to be insignificant at this level of analysis. Early fine wares, for instance, are confined to the known earlier sites, hg72 and m82, while specifically later fine wares occur on all sites, but always below 1% of the site assemblage.

Overview of sites by vessel function (Fig. 15.8)

All the vessel types in the archive database have been assigned possible functions, according to their fabric and other evidence. The total assemblages of Roman pottery from the Wigford sites have been analysed on this basis to examine the functional character of the individual sites.

The functional categories are: LH Liquid holders; DR Drinking vessels; TW Tableware; TK Table or kitchen wares; K Kitchen wares, cooking or food preparation; S Storage vessels. Other functions are also recorded, as W Writing (inkwells), I Industrial, L Lighting, and R Ritual. Inkwells were only recorded from sm76; industrial evidence only from bwe82; lighting was represented at bwe82 and smg82, and vessels possibly associated with ritual came from all sites except m82 and sb85.

The same broad groupings of sites seen in the fabric groups recur here. There are few differences

between the adjacent sites of m82 and smg82, although the significantly higher proportions of liquid holders and the smaller percentage of table-kitchen wares distinguish hg72 from these sites, as does the higher proportion of storage vessels, largely deriving from the pottery of Iron Age tradition on the site. The two sites with later Roman emphasis, primarily sb85 but also z86, are remarkably similar, and distinct from sm76, particularly in the proportions of drinking vessels. This difference is likely to be chronological. The assemblage from bwe82 continues to be exceptional, but notably only differs significantly from sm76 in the proportion of tableware, reflecting the very high samian content, which in turn depresses the proportion of kitchen vessels.

When related to other Lincoln sites, hg72 has a notably similar functional content to the Upper City sites, all with early foundations. The later site of sb85 is closely similar to the Lower City site of Hungate, also known for the late emphasis of its assemblage. Apart from bwe82, which stands alone, the other Wigford sites are most similar to sites in the Lower City, many of which have similar date ranges.

Summary of post-Roman pottery from sites in Wigford

by Jane Young

The pottery recovered from the sites discussed in this volume ranges in date from Anglo-Saxon to modern. It is difficult to make generalizations about

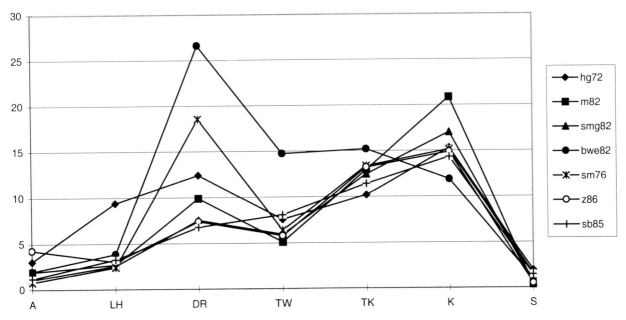

Fig. 15.8 Roman pottery chart: Wigford, functions by site.

the pottery site by site, as the character and chronological representation of each site is different. Fig. 15.9 shows the estimated percentages of pottery from each site by period.

Anglo-Saxon and mid-Saxon pottery was limited to three vessels from three different sites (smg82, m82 and lt72). None of the vessels was securely stratified in deposits that might be interpreted as being contemporary with the pottery, and it is probable that in each case the material was brought on to the site with rubbish from elsewhere.

Late Saxon pottery was present on every site, the two largest assemblages coming from sb85 (1226 sherds) and hg72 (1290 sherds). Sherds belonging to the period between the late 9th and the early/mid 10th century were found on seven sites, although the only sherd to indicate a definite late 9th-century date (a sherd of LG) came from the hg72 site. It seems probable from the pottery evidence that intensive occupation of Wigford had begun by the early/mid 10th century. It is only on the sb85 site, however, that associated groups of this date are found. The Late Saxon pottery is generally similar in character to that found on the Flaxengate site (Adams-Gilmour 1988), with most vessels being plain jars and bowls in shell-tempered fabrics. The ratio of the two main fabrics (LSH and LKT) is extremely variable from site to site and probably reflects chronological differences, as evidence from the Flaxengate site (*ibid*) suggests that LSH is more common in early/mid- to mid-10th century deposits.

Pottery from the Saxo-Norman period was also found on every site, although there is a suggestion that less activity took place on some sites (most notably on hg72 and sb85). The main ware types found in the early part of this period are reduced greywares (TORK and SNLS), superseded in the mid to late 11th century by a shell-tempered ware (LFS) and both glazed and unglazed Stamford ware (ST). Forms become more diverse, with pitchers as common as bowls by the end of the period.

Pottery of the early medieval period is poorly represented on all Wigford sites with the exception of lt72 (on the north bank of the River Witham). It is difficult to understand why so little material of this date has been found (c 591 sherds of the main ware types). Perhaps there was a decrease in population in the area for a while after the Norman conquest, deposits may have been truncated, or rubbish deposits may have lain outside the sites excavated. Vessels are mainly jugs in splashed-glaze wares, with shell-tempered cooking pots and bowls forming a minor part of any assemblage by the end of the period.

Pottery of the High-medieval period is the most common type found on only three sites (smg82, z86 and ws82). The medieval pottery was almost entirely manufactured within the city or locally. A small number of regional imports from York, Beverley, Nottingham, Scarborough, and the Lyveden kilns occur, mainly on the z86 and the lt72 sites. Only 11 continental imported sherds of this period were found in Wigford, with seven of them coming from the z86 site. Jugs are the most common occurring form, many of them highly decorated with applied and incised decoration. Several of these jugs are of shapes or have decorative techniques unique to the Wigford area, indicating perhaps local production. Other common forms include bowls, cooking pots, jars, pipkins, curfews and dripping dishes.

Late medieval pottery is not a common find on any of the Wigford sites except the ze87 kiln site. Waste material from the ze87 and z86 sites indicates at least three phases of pottery production in the area , extending from the 14th to the 16th centuries. Regional imports mainly comprised Humberwares (HUM) and Midland-purple types (MP), although they are never very common. Only a small number of imported continental sherds occur, the most notable being the Valencian Lustreware bowl from the smg82 site (Vince 1991). Jugs are still the most common form found, but the evidence from the ze87

	smg82	m82	cs73	sm76	z86	hg72	dm72	bwe82	sb85	lt72	ws82
Anglo-Saxon	0	0	0	0	0	0	0	0	0	*	0
Mid-Saxon	*	*	0	0	0	0	0	0	0	0	0
Late Saxon	29	11	23	8	15	60	31	42	67	1	16
Saxo-Norman	23	45	16	8	19	32	26	43	9	7	11
Early-Medieval	3	5	0	1	5	1.5	1	4	1.5	41	7
Medieval	29	37	20	23	47	1.5	14	7	14	18	40
Late-Medieval	2	1	10	3	11	1.5	4	2	*	5	2
Post-Medieval	2.5	2	0	34	1	3	22	1	0.5	27	9
Modern	11	0	30	22	0.5	0	0	*	7	0.5	13
Total imports	0.5	*	0	1	2	0.5	1.5	*	*	1	*

* denotes some presence but less than 0.5%

Fig. 15.9 Table showing recovered post-Roman pottery by period as percentages by site.

kiln site shows a wide range of forms available, ranging from moneyboxes to candlesticks.

Post-medieval pottery was found on every site in the Wigford except bwe82, although it accounted for more than a very minor element on only three sites (sm76, dm72 and lt72). Little of the pottery of this period is locally produced, most of the material deriving from other areas of Lincolnshire, or from the Midlands. Continental imports were scarce, with most from the (waterfront) dm72 and lt72 sites. Jugs were by this date no longer the most common form found; instead cups, jars, bowls and dishes constituted the bulk of post-medieval groups.

General Conclusions

The High Street and the water formed the two dominant elements of Wigford. In the Roman period the Fosse Way and Ermine Street converged here; to the south of the junction, Ermine Street appeared to be the dominant road, at least by the later 2nd century: the mid to late Roman buildings all fronted on to it, although some also related to the Fosse Way. Ermine Street was not apparently significant during the early and mid Saxon periods – even if it existed – but by the late Saxon period a realigned Fosse Way road was much in evidence. This route has formed the major road in Wigford to the present day.

The river was broad with a very extensive area liable to flooding in the early Roman period including much of the western and northern parts of the area. Narrowing of the river and bank consolidation was evident from the mid Roman period together with drainage of the low-lying land by the road. By the 4th century the river had been further narrowed; and it is likely that the north bank of the Brayford was being used to unload cargo. The river-front to the east of the Brayford was also exploited, as evidenced by a hardstanding, and wattles and stakes. During the Saxon period, the late Roman dumps at bwe82 and the very late Roman dumps at z86 may have kept the river at bay here, but the river encroached over the land at sb85; by the late Saxon period sb85 was the focus of land reclamation from the river. The Sincil Dyke drained the east part of Wigford by a date in the medieval period. At dm72 in the medieval period was evidence of a vertical timber wharf, replaced by a jetty. By the late medieval period at the latest, the Lucy Tower was built at the edge of the Brayford Pool, marking the limit of a stretch of City Wall and ditch extending south from the south-west corner of the Roman circuit. It was maintained well into the post-medieval period. Dumping during this period further narrowed the river and reduced the size of the Pool, which later became partly surrounded by warehouses, as at

dm72. By the 19th century the river had also been further canalised.

The 1972–87 excavations have allowed us to trace the growth and decline of the suburb from the Late Iron Age/early Roman period. The presence of stratified late Iron Age pottery (hg72) is the earliest evidence of occupation in the city. There were traces of both military and early *colonia* activity in the form of roads, buildings and cemeteries. The excavations have also provided an unprecedented insight into the mid, late and very late Roman periods. In the mid Roman period a major operation took place to drain the low-lying land, and there was much evidence of industrial activity and many associated buildings: as the suburb was developing, property boundaries were established. Occupation of the suburb continued, on several sites, into the very late Roman period, while on others there was evidence of substantial dumping.

The 1972–87 excavations confirmed an absence, to date, of definite evidence for early or middle Saxon occupation. There is no middle Saxon trading place in Wigford. If the first element is indeed *wic* then it may either mean that the suburb was named after the ford (on the site of High Bridge) leading *to* the *wic*, or that the early to mid 10th-century suburb was itself regarded as a *wic*.

There was some evidence for Late Saxon (Anglo-Scandinavian) and Saxo-Norman occupation, including the creation of several parishes. By the early medieval period, Wigford had become a place of some status and this is reflected by the substantial rebuilding of the church of St Mark and construction of the palatial complex at smg82. Although there was evidence for occupation on other sites, by contrast, it was not so impressive. The High Medieval period shows continuity and change – the church continued in use, with modifications, and the domestic complex became a guildhall; the Carmelite Friary loomed large and there was industrial activity in the form of pottery kilns. In the Late Medieval period, to the north of the Witham there is evidence of substantial waterfront defences, while industry continued, the church was enlarged and refloored, the guildhall remained in use, and the friary apparently flourished. Against a general background of decline, the archaeology suggests that some elements of the economy were still buoyant. The archaeological record has accordingly helped fill out, and to some extent contradict, the picture afforded by the historical documentation.

Unfortunately, the archaeological record for the post-medieval period is not so good as for the late medieval period (only six of the thirteen sites recorded material from these levels). The lack of precise dating for most sites and the limited number of assemblages of artefacts is unfortunate, since there is also a discontinuity in documentary sources from the late medieval to the early post-medieval period: it would have been useful to be able to compare archaeological evidence for settlement with that provided by such sources. This decline in population resulted in the union of parishes in 1549 and might also be expected to have led to the amalgamation of properties as land values fell, or to the reversion of some properties to less intensive forms of land-use, such as market gardening or orchards. It is also to be expected that these trends would have operated differentially depending on the distance of land from High Bridge and the commercial centre, and from the High Street itself.

Our knowledge of the growth of Wigford in the late 18th and 19th centuries has not been significantly increased by the excavations. This is partly because so much is known through cartographic sources and documentary evidence for this period that there is less opportunity for archaeology to make a significant contribution, and partly because for the excavations most of the record of the modern archaeology in Wigford has been slight and incidental; in many cases the modern material was removed mechanically or had already been disturbed. There are justifications for using archaeological techniques to study this period (Vince 1994), but thorough recording is a pre-requisite.

16 Suggestions for Further Work in Wigford

Alan Vince

When the project for the analysis and publication of the 1972–1987 excavations in Lincoln was proposed to English Heritage in 1991 it was stated that three main themes would be examined. These were:

Theme One: The extent of settlement in Lincoln and its suburbs through time and the development of major foci.

Theme Two: The study of spatial patterning within the town and its suburbs.

Theme Three: The examination of Lincoln's hinterland and its trading contacts and the way in which changes in their extent and shape are related to the fortunes of the town itself.

The analysis which will lead to a study of the connections between Lincoln and the wider world depends not only on the work carried out for this publication but also on work on the Upper and Lower City. The remaining two themes, however, study the overall extent of settlement and the land-use of the surrounding area and the development and influence of foci within the settlement. Both of these aspects have been considered in the previous chapter and it is now possible to revise the initial research aims as a result of this study.

Management of the Archaeological Resource

When this series of volumes was planned in 1991 it was intended to use the occasion of the ordering and interpretation of the results of two decades of archaeological activity as an opportunity to make a plea for the management of the surviving archaeological deposits in Lincoln as a resource for further study of Lincoln in particular, and of Roman and later towns in general. Since then, however, an initiative by Lincoln City Council and English

Heritage has to a certain extent overtaken this intention. In November 1994 work began on the construction of the Lincoln Urban Archaeological Database (LUAD). This is a GIS-based database which incorporates data not only from the 1972–87 excavations which are the subject of the present volumes but also earlier and more recent observations. In addition to the collection of details of all observations, the LUAD, completed in 1998, included a deposit-model which will enable town planners and archaeologists to see the extent and character of deposits of different periods. This data will provide a trend surface of the archaeological value of every part of Lincoln which can then be used to inform planning policy.

To put forward a Research Programme for the further study of Wigford's below-ground archaeological deposits would therefore now be premature. What is both timely and worthwhile, however, is to present some of the revised research objectives for the future study of Wigford. They can be set beside deposit survival, once we know it better, and can provide the future rationale for managing the resource, whether the latter means protection through mitigation or intervention through excavation.

Topography

Pre-Roman Topography

Perhaps the most interesting aspect of the pre-Roman topography to be revealed by the 1972–87 excavations is the extremely low-lying nature of the northern part of the suburb and the existence of at least one area of higher ground, revealed in the hg72 excavation. The size of this eyot needs to be established, as does the nature of the Iron Age and Conquest period occupation that took place on it. Too little excavation has yet taken place on the pre-Roman levels of any other site in Wigford to prove beyond doubt that the area to the south was unoccupied in the pre-Roman period, although this is a strong suspicion based on the complete absence of early pottery on an other excavation. Even if the lack of settlement is established the nature of the pre-Roman land-use remains to be established.

Early Roman Activity

None of the 1972–87 excavations clearly established the date of the main roads through Wigford, Fosse Way and Ermine Street. Furthermore, the nature of the river crossing, of which a tantalising glimpse is revealed by the 1878 observations of Drury, remains unclear and certainly a high priority for future research. A disappointing feature of the 1972–87 excavations was the lack of clarification of the nature of the early Roman land-use of the Wigford area. The extent of the cemetery revealed at Monson Street has not been defined, nor are the precise chronological limits of the cemetery established. It may have been founded at the same time as the fortress but could be founded within the military period. It may have continued in use after the foundation of the colonia; at present any statement about its period of use is little more than a guess. The Early Roman structures revealed at hg72 are also tantalising, in that they show that activity took place but are incapable of clear interpretation because of the small size of the excavation area and the ambiguity of the evidence from the associated finds.

Lastly, there is a suggestion from earlier observations that burials took place along the Fosse Way south of its junction with Ermine Street; early observations of burials continue as far south as the South Common. This suggestion needs to be tested by excavation.

Limit of Mid and Late Roman suburb

All the 1972–87 excavations revealed evidence for activity from the later 2nd or early 3rd century onwards, even where occupation of this period was absent, as at cs73 and sb85. The latter site seems to indicate the position of the water's edge at the point where the Brayford Pool flowed into the Witham but there is no corresponding evidence for the southern limit of the suburb, nor for whether it had any sort of physical boundary. Establishing the nature of the suburb to the south of the Fosse Way/ Ermine Street junction is therefore a priority for future research.

Late Saxon/Anglo-Scandinavian settlement

The 1972–87 excavations have clearly shown that the main period of expansion in Wigford took place in the early to mid 10th century. Historically, it would be extremely important to know under whose authority the town was at that time. This can only be determined by more precise dating, which could be provided by numismatics or by dendro-chronology.

As with the Roman suburb, there is no evidence for the location of the southern end of Wigford, nor is there any evidence for the foundation date of any of the churches which served the southern third of the area or for the existence or otherwise of a formal boundary or defence around the suburb in the pre-Conquest period.

Tenement Layout

In addition to the extent of settlement along High Street, the character of the properties lining the street is itself of considerable interest. At one or more stages in the past some central authority must have been involved in the division of land so as to obtain properties of similar width. The 1972–87 excavations have been able to examine land division directly in some instances during some periods. The subdivision and amalgamation of properties is a feature clearly capable of archaeological study and ought to reflect and add detail to our knowledge of the fluctuating demand for land. Examination of property divisions should therefore be a future research priority.

Industry

The archaeological study of industries has developed considerably since the time when most of the 1972–87 excavations were carried out and the location and nature of industries is an important element of the suburb's history, both in the Roman and later periods. For both these reasons it is important to excavate workshops and industrial complexes should the opportunity arise and to subject the residues of these industries to a wide range of analytical techniques.

Cloth

Cloth production is known from historical evidence to have been an important element in Lincoln's economy during the later 12th and 13th centuries, after which the industry declined and wool was exported to Flemish workshops. The origins of the cloth industry are not recorded in documentary sources but could be studied should the appropriate archaeological deposits be discovered. In the Wigford area the main branch of the cloth industry to be expected is dyeing and the early evidence for this craft ought to come in the form of madder-stained pots used to dye wool. Some of these have been found at sb85 in 10th-century contexts but in rubbish deposits rather than associated with the workshops where the dyeing took place. Much could be learnt about the industry through the discovery and excavation of such a workshop.

Medieval Brick and Tile industry

The extreme southeast corner of the medieval suburb of Wigford, to the southeast of St Botolph's church, has been identified through documentary sources as the site of the 'tile house' from the later 12th century onwards. The same area was the location of a brickworks in the 17th century, of which some details are known through the probate inventory of one of the brickmakers (Johnston 1989). Although brick and tile manufacturing sites have been excavated elsewhere in England the Wigford tileworks seems to offer an unrivalled potential for studying the development, or continuity, of technology through a period of at least 500 years.

Other medieval industries

Analysis of animal bones indicates that horn working was probably practised extensively, as an industry dependent on tanning and butchery for its raw material. Primary refuse deposits associated with any aspect of these industries, especially if there is an opportunity to study the workshops where the crafts were carried out as well, should be a research priority for the suburb.

Wealth and Status

A sufficiently large collection of artefacts has been recovered from mid Roman to late medieval deposits for the wealth and status of the inhabitants of the area as a whole to be studied. However, the lack of refuse deposits associated with the main period of use of St Mary's Guildhall is a disappointment and one would expect the wealth and status of the inhabitants of one of the large aristocratic complexes known from documentary sources to have existed in the area in the medieval period to differ from that of the horners, tanners or others whose tenements have been examined in detail to date. Furthermore, there is virtually no archaeological evidence for the material culture of the post-medieval or early modern inhabitants of Wigford.

Efforts should therefore be made to recover well-stratified assemblages of contemporary artefacts and other refuse of early Roman and post-medieval date and to investigate the areas on high status medieval properties which may produce similar assemblages for comparison with those already known. Since the proportion of the diet provided by small mammal, fish and bird species is likely to be an indicator of wealth and status care should be taken to ensure the recovery of these small bones through the use of sieving.

Conclusion

The list of research priorities put forward here is not exclusive and archaeological investigation is constantly producing the unexpected. Nevertheless, by combining this list with the LUAD deposit-model it should be possible to produce a Research Programme which if implemented would significantly increase our knowledge of Wigford, and be a contribution to the development of urban archaeology.

Given large enough assemblages of artefacts and clear enough stratigraphy in the Early Roman Iron Age it would be possible to correlate archaeological strata and these events but unfortunately this is not the case for any of the Wigford excavations, nor is it generally the case in the city. Therefore, deposits are assigned to the Early Roman period whilst noting any more precise dating where possible.

As with early Roman deposits, given large enough finds assemblages and clear enough strata it is possible to date late Roman deposits in Lincoln with an accuracy of 20–30 years (ie, to a quarter or third of a century). In the main, however, such dating is not possible for small assemblages. Furthermore, analysis of pottery and other finds indicates that these late Roman assemblages often contain an appreciable quantity of earlier finds. Given that the dating and taphonomy of these deposits is crucial for any further work on their finds or structural sequence, generous discussion of the likely dating of each sequence is given here. However, for the purposes of analysis all such deposits are classed together as Late Roman.

APPENDIX I
The Archiving and Analysis Projects

Alan Vince and Kate Steane

A post-excavation team was established within the newly formed City of Lincoln Archaeology Unit in early 1988 dedicated principally to the Lincoln post-excavation project, funded by English Heritage following an assessment of the backlog of work on sites investigated to the end of 1987. Alan Vince was appointed to manage this team, and other key personnel included Mickey Dore as Archives Officer.

A. The paper archive

The first element of the post-excavation project (1988–1991) involved the ordering and listing of the paper archive. The archive was divided into a number of record classes, including context cards, site notebooks, plans, sections, registers and so on. Each class was given a number and each item not physically attached to another within the class was separately numbered within its class. Thus, a three-part code was assigned to every item of which the first part is the site-code, the second a class number and the third an individual record number. Where an archive record referred to more than one excavation, for example a finds specialist report, it was sometimes copied, and copies placed in each site archive (for records of two or three pages or so in length); or alternatively, the record was either placed in the main site archive or in the archive of the first site mentioned in the report and cross-referenced in the index to the other archives.

Site Codes

All excavations carried out by the Lincoln Archaeological Trust and its successors employed a system of site codes to distinguish excavations. Each code consists of two parts, the first being a one-, two- or three-letter (mnemonic) code based on the common name of the site (e.g., hg = Holmes Grainware-house) and the second a year code. The site code is used to identify site records, finds and environmental samples. The only parts of the site archive not marked in this way are letters and administrative files (which have now been systematically sorted and catalogued by the team's record officer). Some confusion arose, however, from the practice on long-term projects of assigning a new site code at the start of each year's excavation. By and large, the system of context numbering was carried over from year to year but in some cases a new series of finds register numbers was started at the beginning of a new season. This led to a situation in which the year code is irrelevant to the management of the site stratigraphic data but crucial for registered finds. This problem has been dealt with by amalgamating multi-year excavation records under the code of the first year in which the site started.

A further problem, which only became evident as post-excavation analysis got underway, occurred where two sites excavated in different seasons and with different site codes were so closely related in terms of their results that they could only sensibly be analysed together. In the Wigford area this is the case with br85, trial excavations carried out to the north of St Mark's Station, and z86, excavations on the line of the railway tracks to the south of the station.

Categories used in the archive

Below is a conspectus of the archive system showing the number of categorized items and what each category represents.

Each item to be archived was given the site code, the category number and an item number. Thus sh74/5/10 would indicate a plan from Steep Hill and that it is the tenth plan in the archive sequence.

no. item	no. item
1 index	16 Roman pottery data
2 context sheets	17 Post Roman pottery
3 context cards	data
4 matrices	18 Other finds data
5 plans	19 interim reports
6 phase plans	20 specialist reports
7 sections	21 documentary material
8 elevations	/comparanda
9 dye-lines and	22 draft reports/final
publication plans	tyescript
10 sketches (plans and	23 miscellaneous
sections)	24 publication/public
11 black and white	relations
photographic prints	25 correspondence
12 colour slides and	26 archive reports
colour prints	27 environmental records
13 notes	28 animal bone – boxes
14 tabulated data/lists	29 human bone – records
15 survey/levels notebooks	30 administrative records

Stratigraphic Records

All early 1970s excavations in the City were recorded in site notebooks and the nature of the record was left to the discretion of the site staff. Harris/Winchester matrices were not in common use but sketch sections which recorded and explained stratigraphic relationships were often incorporated into the notebooks. Plans were multi-context and multi-phase. Section drawings were usually made of the main sides of the excavation trenches.

Stratigraphic information was often held on index cards but by the late 1970s both notebooks and card indices were superseded by A4 recording sheets modelled ultimately on those used by the Central Excavation Unit (Jefferies 1977). The layout of these sheets went through several modifications, mainly regarding the level of cross-referencing between these records and those kept for photographs, plans, sections, finds and samples but also regarding the extent to which they were intended to be updated during post-excavation work (for example by including boxes for provisional dating, interpretation, location on site matrix and so on). Despite this development in the written record, plans continued to be partly multi-context and multi-phase except part of z86 and ze87. Most of the site plans were originally drawn at 1:20 and most elevations and sections at 1:10, except for lt72 which was recorded in imperial measurements.

Monochrome Photographs

In some of the early years of the Lincoln Archaeological Trust site monochrome photographs were taken by a specialist photographer, Nicholas Hawley,

who, operating on a self-employed basis, retained ownership and possession of the negatives. Lists describing the subject of the photographs and sometimes further technical detail were probably made for all films but have often not survived. More recently, monochrome photographs were recorded by a print being attached to A4 pre-printed record cards prior to being annotated by the site staff. These are stored with the site archive while the negatives are kept together.

Colour Transparencies

In the early years of the Lincoln unit, colour slides were regarded as being an expensive and impermanent medium for an archive record. They were therefore taken with an eye to being used to a certain extent for record purposes, but primarily in publicity and lectures, and they consequently include a high proportion of general views of work in progress which are invaluable for the incidental detail they include. In more recent years, improvements in the archive quality of colour film and a reduction in the cost of colour slides relative to monochrome prints has led to slides being used as an integral part of the site archive, and the resultant production of at least two copies of every slide, one for inclusion in the site archive and the other for day-to-day use. Often, both monochrome and colour photographs were taken of a particular view, and where possible a cross-reference has been provided between the two in the archive.

Finds Records

A variety of methods was used in the recording of assemblages of bulk finds, animal bone and registered finds. There was, however, no initial index or list of finds from a deposit other than that included in the site record. There is no way to establish that the entire finds archive has been accounted for except to search through all likely repositories carrying out an audit of finds. For many of the older excavations, some categories of finds which would now be regarded as bulk materials, such as clay tobacco pipes or iron nails, were treated as registered finds. Building materials and clay tobacco pipes have been de-accessioned during the course of the project. Another difference between early practice and the present procedure is that artefacts of the same material from the same context were sometimes given a group register number, especially iron objects. These groups have been split where, for example, X-ray analysis has shown that fragments belonged to clearly distinct objects.

Two categories of material could not easily be treated in the same way as other finds – worked stone and timber. The two main collections of worked stone from Wigford excavations, sm76 and smg82, have been published (Stocker 1986; Stocker 1991) and a standard methodology employed for their archive recording (CBA 1987). Waterlogged timbers were found during several Wigford and Brayford Pool excavations, principally bwe82, dm72, lt72, sb85 and sm76. These have been examined by external specialists.

Samples

Many specialists have worked on aspects of the scientific analysis of material from excavations in Lincoln. Many of these specialists took their own samples from site and kept their own records. Attempts to trace either samples or records from excavations carried out up to 15 years previously in many cases proved to be futile but what documentation exists, either in the form of letters or reports, has been included in the archive.

Animal Bones

The animal bones from some 1972–87 Lincoln excavations were studied by T O'Connor and S Scott then based at the Environmental Archaeology Unit, University of York. (See O'Connor 1982; Dobney *et al*, 1996.) Original record sheets, draft reports and other records are deposited at the EAU rather than with the site archive.

B. Computer Archives

The computer database was created between 1988 and 1991, although much more work has been undertaken since. It was designed with three main purposes in mind: to aid site interpretation, the study of archaeological data in Lincoln on a city-wide scale, and future research.

In order to enhance analysis and interpretation of the site stratigraphy, it was necessary to allow easy retrieval of the original site records and up-grading and correction of the records without tampering with the archive record itself. Initially, only those sites with large amounts of recorded stratigraphy were fully computerised, but it was subsequently recognised that immediate access to the upgraded stratigraphic record was of value even for smaller sites. By ensuring that the same context codes were used in all computer records it has been possible to link together any two (or more) aspects of the computer database. It is worth noting that some care was needed to make this system work since the paper archive did not need consistency of case when using alphabetical context

codes (AA, AAA, etc), nor was it important in the paper record to be consistent in the use of context subdivisions (1a, 1A, 1 A and so on would all have been realised by the users to be the same context whereas the computer system demanded a single, consistent system).

For the second objective, to aid the study of archaeological data in Lincoln on a city-wide scale, one approach might take the form of a search for a particular type or date of artefact or the study of a type of deposit or feature. For example, the entire stratigraphic section of the database has been searched to retrieve deposits in which slag was noted by the site recorder, deposits in which *opus signinum* was said to have been found and for similar purposes.

It was also considered important to lay the foundations for a research archive, in order to enable future researchers to study both finds and stratigraphic data from all excavations in the city.

Four main types of computer record have been created, each with a different type of key field. The three main key fields are the site code, the site context code and the site context group number. The fourth category includes any non-stratigraphic codes.

Computer records with the site code as the key field

Information relating to the whole of an excavation is stored on computer in a directory whose name and path reflect the data type and in a file whose name includes the sitecode. Examples of this type of record are CAD drawings of site matrices and phase plans and text files containing site narratives. These are not interactive, just interpretative files.

Computer records with the site context code as the key field

The majority of data recorded in the CLAU database is stored in comma-separated variable data files, one per site, in which the first field is the site context code.

Computer records with the site context group number as the key field

Separately-recorded stratigraphic contexts have been grouped together, as described below, to create sets or groups of contexts sharing all significant stratigraphic traits. These sets are here termed 'context groups' or cgs but were formerly known internally as 'Text Sections', a jargon term used in the Museum of London archaeological archive in the mid- to late 1980s. These files include both non-interactive, interpretative files and csv data files.

Computer records with non-stratigraphic codes as the key field

There are a number of stratigraphic database tables which relate to the study or classification of finds, principally pottery, in which alphanumeric codes are used. An example would be LKT, a Late Saxon pottery fabric code. These codes are themselves key fields which link to other database tables which normally contain expansions of the code into a full name together with other data, usually relating to source, date or function. As with all aspects of the CLAU database, these tables are themselves being updated and modified in the light of research.

The evolving database

The content of the CLAU database has evolved over the duration of the archive project and new databases were being created as and when specialist studies were carried out. By controlling the structure of all research databases and stipulating and checking their contents once submitted to CLAU, it has been possible to ensure automatic interrogation of the data and leaves open the possibility of importing any or all of the CLAU data into other databases and archives.

Initial Site Interpretation

The context records for each site were computerised (csv files). During the time span 1972–1987 there were changes in the type of context sheets used. For ease of input a number of different types of computerised context input files (con74c, con74g, con88, concs73, conhg72, conlin73, conlinsi, conw73 and kevcon1), were created to mirror the different context sheets. All this material was then grouped for easy access into four files (sitecoord, sitedesc, siterel and sitexref) by site.

A stratigraphic matrix was created or, where a matrix already existed, was checked against other stratigraphic data in the archive for consistency. The paper matrix was then digitized as a multi-layer CAD file in which different types of deposit are distinguished by being on separate layers and colours. At this stage the relationships of the deposits were correct but no attempt was made to provide an absolute chronology.

In conjunction with the checking of the matrix, the contexts were grouped together as context groups (abbreviated to cg followed immediately by the number in the published volumes). Grouping contexts was most importantly an interpretative strategy: which contexts represent a single event? This would ultimately lead to a meaningful sequence of events. Context groups may have interpretative significance with regard to artefacts recovered from them. As a

side effect, the reduced number of units making up the site facilitates data manipulation, as well as enhancing inter-site analysis.

Reconstruction of the original stratigraphic events

A considerable amount of interpretation was needed at this stage since the stratigraphic record at most informs us that a series of deposits was laid down in a particular order. Deciding that a number of individually recorded contexts was actually laid down as a single event is a hypothesis which can only be tested if finds or environmental data were recovered and, even then, may well be unprovable. Recognising where the stratigraphic sequence has been truncated is often even more difficult. Often it proved to be impossible to produce single-event groupings, for example, where floor surfaces and make-up deposits could not be separated during excavation or where, as with a soil profile or a long-lived midden, the deposit was created over a period of time, perhaps even as a result of several processes. The classic example of this is the dark earth deposits on the St Mark's Station and St Mary's Guildhall sites which may incorporate destruction debris from late Roman stone-walled buildings together with deliberately dumped material of late Roman date, and later, Late Saxon (Anglo-Scandinavian) material which has been incorporated as a result of soil formation, horticulture or other mechanisms.

Facilitating finds and environmental researchers to select or exclude material for further study on taphonomic grounds

The fillings of a pit, therefore, might be grouped together in a single context group if felt to be a single-period rubbish deposit, but if they were interpreted as being rubbish fills sealed by a contemporary capping then the deposits would be grouped into two groups, since any finds and environmental evidence from the fills would have undergone different taphonomic trajectories. Determining the likely date of an assemblage of industrial waste or animal bone by looking at associated datable artefacts is clearly more likely to be reliable where the deposit is thought to be composed of contemporary refuse than where it is thought to be redeposited.

Reducing the number of units making up a site and looking to inter-site comparability

The precision with which stratigraphy was recorded on site varied from site to site and from the early excavations through to 1987. Excavations in the first five or six years of the Trust's existence used an alphabetical code, starting with AA, for recording, whereas later ones used Arabic numerals. There was also considerable variation in the degree to which minor variations in a deposit were separately recorded (i.e., in the degree to which interpretation of the stratigraphy took place on site rather than in the post-excavation phase). By introducing another number series the post-excavation team was able to reduce the number of stratigraphic units to be described, phased, interpreted and included in publications.

Context group and phasing files

Once the sequence had been divided up into stratigraphic events the CAD matrix was updated. A series of text files was created for each site, one file for each context group. Each one contained a grouped context number, a list of the contexts included and automatically extracted data from the archive about the plans, sections and photos on which the relevant contexts are represented; ideally there was also a discussion of the rationale for the contexts forming a single event, and where this grouped context sits in the matrix (its relationships). These text files were initially seen as being a hierarchical part of the site narrative.

Another set of files, one file for each site, contained a list of context numbers or deposit codes as used on site and the number of the context group to which the deposit had been assigned; internally this computer file was called *phasing*.

Relevance of artefacts to the site and the "interp" files

In parallel with the creation and analysis of the stratigraphic database, work took place on the finds archive. A multi-stage procedure was followed: first the material recovered from each site was assembled and listed. Where existing classifications were available, they were used as a basis for the CLAU system but where they were not, the listing had to go hand-in-hand with the development of fabric series, form classifications, object name thesauri, standardised notation to express dates and periods and so on. In every case the guiding principles were to allow relationships to be made between data sets and to allow for the expansion of the existing record both by CLAU team members and by external specialists. The question of pottery quantification was addressed (see Appendices 2–3). Work on registered finds proceeded more slowly owing to the greater variety of material present and the need to check all identifications of metal artefacts using X- radiography and, in some cases, investigative conservation.

One result of this series of artefact studies was the production of information about the absolute and relative date of assemblages and stratigraphic sequences. This information was given back to the stratigraphers who used it to provide provisional dates for the context groups in the form of a broad period (such as Roman, Anglo-Saxon or Medieval) and a *terminus post quem*. In the rare cases where it was possible to say that a context group was definitely earlier than a particular date, for example where it was earlier than a well-dated deposit or structure, then a *terminus ante quem* was also given. This provisional dating and phasing was held in the *interp* file; it was used to guide selection of material for further study and was sent to external specialists as a guide. Other information from the artefact specialists was added to the understanding of the depositional history.

Pottery quantification and computer files

The question of quantification was addressed. Many types of analysis require information on the amount of material present in an assemblage or site, or the relative proportion of material. Research into the theoretical basis for such studies with regard to ceramic assembly, by Orton and Tyers (1990), has suggested that the simple approach, counting the number of fragments, is invalid in situations where these fragments originate from the breakage of single artefacts. Their solution, to use Estimated Vessel Equivalents (EVEs), would have involved a very labour-intensive programme of recording and it was decided that two related records would be created (Orton *et al* 1993). The primary record would be created for all excavated material (involving in some cases the transcription of records made on site of material discarded during excavation) and would be based on simple fragment counts. The secondary record would use EVEs and weight counts to provide a more accurate measure of the quantities involved but would only cover a small subset of the total archive, chosen to provide large, well-dated assemblages with simple taphonomic characteristics (i.e., with a high possibility of reconstructing the depositional history of the assemblages).

Data was recorded which would help to assess the likely work involved in further analysis (such as the possibility and desirability of illustration and photography). Any obvious characteristics of the assemblage which might be relevant to its depositional history (abrasion or mineral coating, vivianite, calcium phosphate or mortar) were recorded. Different solutions were adopted as to how this information was stored, in an attempt to make the initial recording as straightforward as possible. The Saxon and later pottery researchers, for example, created a database table called *spotdate* in which the earliest possible date, the latest possible date and the most likely date of each deposit were recorded together with information in several fields giving the number of sherds which would require drawing for different purposes (either because of their stratigraphic context or because of their intrinsic interest), and information on the degree of difficulty involved in making the drawing. Roman pottery researchers, by contrast, recorded similar decisions in two types of comment field incorporated into their primary record. The date of an assemblage was given in a record with a dummy fabric code ZDATE and other comments were placed in a record with a dummy code of ZZZ. Both types of record are regarded by their creators as being for immediate use, as a more accurate and considered date could be given once the pottery had been examined in stratigraphic groups in the order of deposition. All the pottery records generated as part of the process of post-excavation analysis are retained within the archive.

Site narratives

The stratigraphic analysts in the team created archive narratives for Wigford which included every grouped context. It was expected that to maximise the potential for interpretation of the story, it would be necessary to be able to read the *Text sections* (a term also used initially for context groups). Each narrative began at the earliest period excavated and related the sequence of events period by period and phases within period; the dating evidence was given at the end of each phase. Each narrative included an introduction, discussion and paper sketches.

Lincoln Excavations: Analysis

Between 1988 and 1991, the team transformed the archive into what Christopher Evans in his final monitoring report for English Heritage of 3rd April 1991 termed 'the most integrated urban archive in the country, one that offers very exciting and contextually innovative publication opportunities'. During 1991 the potential of the Lincoln sites (1972–1987) was assessed and amongst many other publications a site by site presentation of site narratives for Wigford was proposed. In order to reach this point data needed to be checked and CAD illustrations produced. It was envisaged at this time that very summary site reports would be produced and that these would serve as a vehicle through which the reader could explore the computerised archive via the grouped context numbers. Although the context groups were all to be mentioned in the narrative, the report was seen at this stage as being skeletal.

The introduction of land use blocks (LUBs) in 1992 had a dramatic effect, not only on the site narrative but also on the understanding of artefacts within the site framework. The land use block (LUB) refers to an excavated area in which a particular land use was practised (for a defined period of time). In 1992 Barbara Precious (then Davies) joined the post-excavation team to work with Maggi Darling on Roman pottery. She had previously worked at the Museum of London on material from the East of Walbrook, where the sites had been divided into such land use blocks (Davies, B 1992, 30–9). It was Barbara, together with the Project Manager Alan Vince, who convinced the rest of the team of the usefulness of their application. A two-dimensional matrix or table presents the LUBs for a site (LUB diagram); the vertical axis represents time and the horizontal axis represents space. The site was divided into areas for the diagram; by and large the columns in a LUB diagram do reflect the dominant spatial arrangement of the site. The periods used for each site were standardised, so that LUB diagrams could be used to compare sites across Wigford.

All the Wigford sites were subjected to LUB analysis between 1992 and 1994. This involved providing LUB numbers in the *interp* files for each site, thereby allowing the in-house artefact specialists to look at material by LUB. The site narratives were broken into LUBs; each LUB description was followed by a section on 'Dating and Interpretation'. The stratigraphic data went through a checking process at the same time, and CAD illustrations were produced for each site.

In 1994 a site text was produced for ze87 using LUBs, together with CAD plans. Excavations at this site at the Magistrates Court had commenced in 1987 but were not completed until 1990; they were not included in the English Heritage-funded post-excavation programme and are only described here, in advance of any full post-excavation analysis, because the results have so much to offer to our understanding of that part of Wigford, east of High Street. Unlike every other site described here, there is no supporting research archive, and further post-excavation analysis is clearly required, not least since the excavation produced both a tile kiln and a pottery kiln of late medieval date.

Production of specialist studies

Having assessed the initial work on the finds 1988–1991 a programme of specialist studies was proposed and approved by English Heritage in September 1991. Some of these studies were to be carried out by CLAU staff and the remainder by external specialists. In either case the procedure was very similar. Records for all of the relevant material – usually a class of finds – were retrieved from the database and linked with the provisional dating and interpretation data. A process of selection was then carried out based on the stratigraphic context of the material, its interpretation, its dating and the ability of specialists to extract data from unstratified material. At one extreme, animal bone and soil samples, for example, material was only studied if it fulfilled rigorous criteria, whereas at the other extreme coins, pottery and Roman glass, and any other artefact classes that could be dated independently of their archaeological context, were studied even if they were totally without a stratigraphic context.

The reports on these specialist studies were added to the CLAU archive and if a database table was created as part of the study this was added and integrated with the CLAU database. In some cases specialist studies took taken place on material which had already been provisionally recorded in the first stage of analysis. For example, Samian ware was studied first by the CLAU Roman pottery researchers and then by Brenda Dickinson and/or Joanna Bird, and mortarium stamps by Kay Hartley. Similarly, Roman glass was recorded first by CLAU staff and then by Sally Cottam and Jenny Price. In both cases further detail has been added as a result of the specialist analysis, but also corrections made to the initial identifications. Similarly, as internal analysis of pottery and tile has progressed it has been necessary to re-examine and upgrade some primary records. It is important to realise that, whereas the computer database of stratigraphic data is stable and has hardly changed, if at all, from the time when it was first added to the database, the primary finds records are constantly being altered, incorporating some of the results of specialist studies. This process will presumably continue long after the post-excavation project funded by English Heritage has finished but the majority of these changes were taking place whilst the site reports were being prepared for publication.

It should be noted, for future reference, that the decision to delay specialist input until after the site narratives had been completed was probably a false economy, since feedback from some specialists has had a considerable impact on our initial interpretations, involving a large amount of alteration to the original framework. Clearly, however, some specialists' results have little impact at an individual site level, and determining which specialists' input should be sought at the site narrative phase and which later is a matter of professional judgement.

Roman pottery: Plotdate analysis

A new technique for examining Roman pottery was evolved in 1994, based upon a computer program written by Paul Tyers, which he kindly adapted for our use. This was originally designed for plotting the dated output of individual potters or kilns, and uses the same approach as that applied to samian stamps. This extracts two fields giving the earliest and latest date from a data file, and a count field. The resulting 'value' of each record is spread over its range either as the raw 'value' or converted into percentages. For example, the value or percentages for a date of 100–120 is spread over 20 years, with one-half per decade. Dates can be spread over 10, 20 or 50 year spans. The 20 year span with values converted to percentages to facilitate comparisons between groups of differing size has been used for the pottery analysis.

The pottery data from the archive is first filtered through a dating "lookup file" which covers all the fabrics and vessel types currently in the CLAU database. All have been assigned broad date ranges, the widest at present being 150 years. Dependent upon the individual site, approximately 30–35% of the pottery is used for the plotdate, the remainder being either undatable, or having too wide a date range to be useful. Clearly this leads to a "tail" of dated values beyond the date limits of the group, so that a group known to end in the late 3rd century will still have some values plotted into the 4th century arising from the presence of widely dated types or fabrics.

Effectively this means that every sherd in the database to which a date can be applied is used to define the dating content of a group. Although the technique is experimental and still evolving, the clear benefits already recognised indicate that it is a suitable tool for the examination of Roman pottery. Apart from the obvious indications it provides of residuality and mixed-date groups, it is of particular value in comparisons, whether between total site assemblages or groups within a site (see Darling in Jones M J (ed), 1999).

Plotdate analysis has been used for the Roman pottery from Wigford at varying levels to examine different aspects: comparisons between total site assemblages, examination of all the pottery from a LUB and, at the most detailed, individual context groups or sets of context groups. As with any analytical technique, its scope is limited by the size of the sample, and groups above 200 sherds have been preferred; the reliable parameters have yet to be clearly defined. In the present volume its appearance is confined to the general discussion of Roman pottery from the whole area, but detailed analyses of each site, carried out after the preliminary attempt at stratigraphic phasing, can be found in the archive.

Dates derived from post-Roman ceramic analysis

Much of the dating of the Wigford and Brayford

Pool sites derives from a study of pottery. However, since the pottery dating itself was being refined and altered throughout the period of post-excavation analysis there is a danger that a date derived from pottery studies and incorporated into the site text at the beginning of the project would be different from the date given from the same evidence towards the end of the project. The precision with which pottery assemblages can be dated also depends on the size of the assemblage and its composition. For long stretches of time there was little difference in the source or form of the most common pottery types found but larger assemblages can be dated more closely. A system was therefore required which would allow readers (including the authors themselves) to have readily available the basis of any chronological statement, whilst not interrupting the flow of the text. The solution adopted for post Roman pottery has been to use a system of Ceramic Horizon codes in the database but to translate these into absolute dates immediately before publication.

Post-Roman ceramic horizons and their suggested absolute dates

A separate table lists the date of the pottery assemblages from each context group, which is often different from the dates derived from examining individual contexts and from the date of deposition as determined by stratigraphic interpretation.

Where the sequence or deposit might have different dates depending on ones interpretation of the likelihood of intrusion or residuality, or because of uncertainty as to the identification of a potsherd or as to its date, then a discussion has been included in the text. The option of publishing a simplified statement relying on an unpublished or microfiched discussion was considered and rejected because it was suspected that very few users of the volume would actually check the unpublished sources.

Pottery analysis not only has importance for the dating of the site sequences but also for the interpretation of site formation (movement of earth, deposition of rubbish, and so on) and for the activities carried out on the site and, potentially, the status of the original users of the material. Where any statement can be made about these matters it is included in the relevant LUB text.

Pottery and registered finds in the text

The texts often have need to refer to specific pottery fabric types or forms. The fabric types both for Roman and post Roman pottery have been referred to using an internal code (see Appendices 2 and 3), because pottery fabrics quite often have no accepted common name, and would in any case often be very

long and cumbersome to use (eg. 'Lincoln Kiln Type Shelly Ware' as opposed to 'LKT'). However, pottery forms have been fully described in the text, although the codes are also used in the Roman pottery archive.

To allow registered finds to be retrieved from the Lincoln City and County Museum, the context and finds number of registered finds is given in the text.

Results of environmental analysis

The results of many of the analyses carried out on samples of soil from the Wigford and Brayford Pool sites, like those of pottery and other finds studies described above, are of three types: first, there are samples whose interpretation is site-specific; second there are samples whose study aids an overall understanding of the changing environment or plant

Horizons	Dating	Period
ASH1	5th–?E8th	Anglo-Saxon (c.450+)
ASH2	?L7th–?E8th	Middle Saxon (c.650+)
ASH3	?E8th–?M8th	
ASH4	?M8th–?L8th	
ASH5	?E9th–?M9th	
ASH6	?M9th–?L9th	
ASH7	?M/L9th–L9th	Late Saxon (c.850+)
ASH8	L9th–E10th	
ASH9	E/M10th–M10th	
ASH10	M10th–L10th	
ASH11	L10th	
ASH12	E11th–?E/M11th	Saxo-Norman (c.1000+)
ASH13	?E/M11th–M/L11th	
ASH14	L11th–E12th	
MH1	?E/M12th–M12th	Early Medieval
MH2	M12th–M/L12th	(c.1120+)
MH3	M/L12th–E13th	
MH4	E13th–E/M13th	
MH5	E/M13th–?L13th	High Medieval (c.1220+)
MH6	?L13th–?M14th	
MH7	?M14th–?L14th	Late Medieval (c.1350+)
MH8	?L14th–?E15th	
MH9	?E15th–M15th	
MH10	M15th–L15th	
PMH1	E16th–M16th	Early Post-Medieval
PMH2	M16th–M/L16th	(c.1500+)
PMH3	M/L16th–E17th	Post Medieval (c.1560+)
PMH4	E17th–M17th	
PMH5	M17th–M/L17th	
PMH6	M/L17th–L17th	
PMH7	L17th–E18th	
PMH8	E18th–M18th	Late Post-Medieval
PMH9	M18th–L18th	(c.1720+)
PMH10	L18th–E19th	
EMH	L18th–20th	Early Modern (c.1780+)

use in and around the city, but which do not add anything to the interpretation of the context in which they were found; and finally, there are those which were either not processed at all following an assessment of their archaeological context or where the botanical or molluscan content was too small for sensible interpretation. The last group is not mentioned at all in the text. Reports are available in the site archive and a table listing the samples by context and sample number is included in the CLAU database. The second group is noted using the Harvard system to cross-refer to unpublished archive reports whilst the first group is included by incorporating abbreviated sections of the specialists' reports (principally those by C A French, A Milles and L Moffett). All are listed in the Bibliography.

Animal bone analyses

A table giving fragment counts for all animal bone in a context was created as part of the computer archive and has been used as a broad check on site interpretation to compare with the distribution of other finds. A small sample of the total collection was then assessed by the Environmental Archaeology Unit, University of York, looking at the overall range of species present, the colour of the bones and their preservation.

The criteria for selection were based on both pottery residuality and type of context group, so that only assemblages of bone with low residuality (below 10%), derived from significant contexts (e.g., a pit rather than a robber trench) were fully examined. A full report on the vertebrate remains from Wigford as well as the Upper and Lower City has been published; details of the approaches to chronology and residuality were discussed therein (Dobney *et al* 1996, 18–19). The questions posed to the York Environmental Archaeology Unit with regard to these site by site volumes were – how does the animal bone contribute to the understanding of the stratigraphy or the narrative of the site? More particularly, how does the bone add to the interpretation of features and give additional understanding of the nature of the deposit and site formation processes (using preservation, angularity, fragment size and condition of bone)? Significant groups of bone needed to be examined with regard to specialised industrial or economic activity (with details of butchery where appropriate to the understanding of the stratigraphy); and the animal bone needed to be considered as an element in the assemblages (i.e., linked to other finds such as knives, etc.). Sometimes bone itself can provide broad dating evidence (certain species and butchery techniques, for example, give an indication of different periods).

Where the responses from the Environmental

Archaeology Unit at York with regard to the selected bone assemblages added significantly to the understanding of the narrative, then relevant information was included in the text. Full notes on each site can be found in site archive (Dobney *et al* 1994a-i).

Period Interpretative Structure

Previous excavation reports in Lincoln divided the stratigraphic sequence into Periods. As used in Lincoln a Period was a site-wide phase of activity whose beginning and end were defined by a stratigraphically recognisable event, such as the construction or substantial alteration of a building.

Where such recognisable events occur they provide an extremely convenient means of analysis. However, the larger the excavation, the less likelihood there is of recognising site-wide stratigraphic events. Moreover, when pottery and other finds are used as a means of correlating isolated blocks of stratigraphy to the main sequence, there is a danger of producing circular arguments and of blurring the distinction between the date when an artefact or assemblage of artefacts was discarded and the date of the stratigraphic deposit in which the artefacts were found.

The city-wide Period framework adopted here, introduced into the site narratives in 1994, can be used to analyse the stratigraphic sequence and the finds and environmental data derived from it. This Period framework is based on our ability to recognise and date phases of activity on a regular basis (there is no way that major historical events which affected the city can be used as a framework if they did not leave recognisable stratigraphic traces on a site). The Period divisions used are listed in the Introduction; the events in Wigford are discussed by Period (see discussion).

Stratigraphic Interpretative Structure: Land Use Blocks

LUB diagram Areas

Firstly, sites were divided into areas. On simple linear excavations or small trenches this presented no problems but many of the Wigford excavations had a complex development with several trenches being excavated and areas of excavation expanding and contracting at different stages. In any case, there is always some 'strain' involved in compressing a three-dimensional data set into two dimensions.

Nevertheless, by and large the columns in a LUB diagram do reflect the dominant spatial arrangement of the site. In the present volume this is mainly organised along an east-west orientation since excavations tended to examine the change of site use from the High Street (and its Roman predecessors) to the Witham or Sincil Dyke, and most development plots were themselves long, narrow and perpendicular to the High Street.

Changes in Land-use

In each area the sequence is examined to identify changes in land-use. Where a land-use in one area can be stratigraphically correlated with that in adjacent areas, then the block is enlarged to encompass both areas. The alternative, to confine each block to the same area, would have had an advantage in that we might then have been able to use this system as a link to GIS, by recording the grid reference of the centroid of each area, but the principal concern at the time was to provide as simple a structure as possible as an aid for understanding and presenting the site stratigraphy.

Where the stratigraphic sequence is unknown, for example, by the use of machine excavation or modern cellaring, or the sequence not being completely excavated, then this is shown on the LUB diagram as 'truncation of sequence' or 'limit of excavation' respectively.

Integration of data from non-archaeological sources

It is possible to identify LUBs on a site which have left no stratigraphic traces, for example, phases of abandonment or activity known from cartographic or documentary sources only. Similarly, whilst we are almost certain that a phase of abandonment existed on all of the excavated sites in Wigford from the 5th to the 9th centuries, in no case was the archaeological evidence strong enough for this phase to be enshrined in the numbering sequence. The system is therefore closely tied to the stratigraphic data in the archive rather than attempting, within the LUB structure, to reflect the entire history of land-use on a site.

This system of analysing the sites has proved to be much more flexible and useful than the system of periods and phases used previously on sites in Lincoln, and commonly used elsewhere in the UK.

Text submission and re-working

A draft of the Wigford text was first submitted to English Heritage in 1994; and a revised version in 1995. A copy of this text together with the associated *phasing* and *interp* files remain in the archive. The Reader chosen by English Heritage for the volumes of site reports was Steve Roskams, an urban stratigraphy expert based at the University of York. He made a number of radical recommendations regarding the presentation of the data, and subsequently English Heritage commissioned a programme of editorial work in line with those recommendations. This work was undertaken between 1996 and early 1999, and has set the format for the other site volumes on the Upper and Lower Cities.

The revisions have involved a more ordered presentation of the stratigraphic sequence, and a rejigging of the LUB framework. The published text is, at the time of writing, the most up to date stratigraphic tool; much of the computerised archive created during analysis is now part of the history of the project, an expression of the processes of analysis. Attention will, however, be given shortly to the digital archive: the only up to date elements are the *phasing* files and the cg and LUB number fields of the *interp* files. While the basic pottery and finds computer data files are also up to date, where there has been subsequent reflection or re-interpretation, or there is an interface between different sources of material, the changes reflect the analytical process (for example the zdates in the Roman pottery files and the tsdate files for the post Roman pottery). In due course the fully-updated archive will be passed to the Lincoln City and County Museum.

Appendix II
Roman Pottery: Vessel Type and Fabric Codes

B31	Bowl copying the samian form 31
B321	Bowl as Webster 1949, fig 14, no 72
B332	Bowl or lid as Darling 1977, fig 2, no 37
B334	Carinated bowl as Petch 1962, fig 5, nos 8–10
B38	Bowl copying the samian form 38
B393	Bowl as Darling & Jones 1988, fig 5, no 16
B411	Bowl similar to S. Yorks.type (Buckland et al 1980, fig 4, no 31)
BD	Bowl or dish
BFB	Bead-and-flange bowl
BFBH	Bead-and-flange bowl with high bead
BFBL	Bead-and-flange bowl with low bead
BG225	Bowl of the type Gillam 225
BIBF	Bead-and-flange bowl with inturned rim
BK120	Beaker with notched cordon as Darling 1990
BKBARB	Barbotine beaker body sherd/s
BKFB	Beaker with beaded funnel neck
BKFO	Folded beaker body sherd/s
BKFOC	Folded beaker with curved neck
BKFOF	Folded beaker with funnel neck
BKFOFG	Folded beaker with grooved funnel neck
BKFOS	Folded beaker with scale decoration body sherd/s
BKFOSF	Folded beaker with scale decoration and funnel neck
BKG43	Beaker of the type Gillam 43
BKPA	
BACC	Beaker sherd/s painted or with contrasting colour barbotine
BKROU	Beaker sherd/s with rouletted zone decoration
BKSF	Slit-folded beaker as RPNV 53
BTR	Bowl with triangular rim
BX308	Box of the type 308 (Hull 1958)
BWM	Wide-mouthed bowl
DFL	Flanged dish
DG225	Dish with rounded rim form as Gillam 225
DGR	Dish with grooved rim
DPR	Plain rimmed dish
DPRS	Plain rimmed dish with straight wall
DTR	Dish with triangular rim
F255	colour-coated flagon as Darling & Gurney 1995, fig 142, no 178
FACE	Face pot sherd/s
FDN	Flagon or flask with disc-neck
G43	Beaker of Gillam 43 type
J105	Lid-seated jar as Coppack 1973, fig 5, no 17
J107	Lid-seated jar as Coppack 1973, fig 7, no 48

J152	Lid-seated jar
JDLS	Jar with double lid-seated rim
JFT	Jar with flat rim-top
JLS	Lid-seated jar
JNN	Narrow-necked jar
PC16	Platter of Camulodunum type 16 (Hawkes & Hull 1947)
RPNV	
69–70	Colour-coated jar with moulded rim

Roman Fabric Codes

Code	Category	Detail
ABIV	Amph	Biv amphorae
AMPH	Amph	Miscellaneous amphorae
ARGO	Fine	Argonne ware
BAE24	Amph	Baetican Dr2–4
BAE28	Amph	Baetican Dr 28
BB1	Reduced	Black burnished 1
BB1G	Reduced	grey sandy BB1
BB2	Reduced	Black burnished 2
BLEG	Import	Black eggshell wares; North Italian or Gallic
C185	Amph	Camulodunum 185 amphorae
C186	Amph	Camulodunum 186 amphorae
C189	Amph	Camulodunum 189 carrot amphorae
CALG	Shell	Calcite tempered
CASH	Shell	Calcite/shell tempered wares
CAT24	Amph	Catalan Dr 2–4
CC	Fine	Other colour-coated wares
CGBL	Import	Rhenish; from Central Gaul
CGCC	Import	Central Gaulish colour-coated; Lezoux etc.
CGGW	Import	Central Gaulish glazed wares
CHALK	Amph	Chalk type
COAR	Reduced	Miscellaneous coarse wares
COLC	Fine	Colchester colour-coated
CR	Oxid	Cream flagon type
CRGR	Reduced	Crambeck grey wares
CRPA	Oxid	Crambeck parchment ware
CRSA	Oxid	Later Roman sandy creamish to light red-brown
DERB	Reduced	Derbyshire ware
DR20	Amph	Dr 20 amphorae
DR28	Amph	Dr 28 amphorae
DWSH	Shell	Late shell-tempered; Dales ware; lid-seated jars etc.

Code	Category	Detail
EGGS	Import?	Miscellaneous eggshell wares
EIFL	Reduced	Mayen ware; Eifelkeramik
EMED	Amph	undifferentiated East Med. amphorae
EMED24	Amph	East Medit. Dr 2–4
EPON	Import	a l'eponge ware
F148	Amph	as Fishbourne 148.3
GAU	Amph	undifferentiated Gaulish amphorae
GAU28	Amph	Gaulish Dr 28
GAU4	Amph	Gauloise 4
GAU6	Amph	Gauloise 6
GBWW	Import	Gallo-Belgic white wares
GFIN	Reduced	Miscellaneous fine grey wares
GLAZ	Import?	Other glazed wares
GMIC	Reduced	Grey fine micaceous wares
GREY	Reduced	Miscellaneous grey wares
GROG	Reduced	Grog-tempered wares
GRSA	Reduced	reduced version of OXSA
H70	Amph	Haltern 70 amphorae
HADOX	Fine	Red-surfaced Oxfordshire/Hadham variants
HUNT	Shell	Huntcliff shell-tempered wares
IAGR	Reduced	Native tradition grit-tempered wares
IAGRB	Reduced	Native trad. grit-tempered
IASA	Reduced	IA type sandy wares
IASH	Shell	Native tradition shell-tempered
IASHC	Shell	Coarse shell tempered; IA type
IASHD	Shell	Shell-tempered harder ?Romanised
IASHF	Shell	Fine shell tempered; IA type
IMMC	Import	Imported mica-dusted; beakers etc.
IT24	Amph	Italian Dr 2–4
ITAMP	Amph	Italian amphorae; undifferentiated
K117	Amph	Sandy ribbed as Kingsholm 117
KAP2	Amph	Kapitan II amphorae
KOAN	Amph	Koan/Dr 2–4 amphorae
KOLN	Import	Cologne colour-coated wares
L555	Amph	London 555 amphorae
LCOA	Reduced	Late coarse pebbly fabric
LEG	Reduced	'Legionary' cream/light grey
LOND	Reduced	London wares
LROM	Amph	Undifferentiated late Roman amphorae
LRRA	Amph	Later Roman ribbed amphorae
LRRB	Amph	Later Roman red-brown
LYON	Import	Lyon pre-Flavian colour-coats
MARB	Import	Misc. marbled wares
MHAD	Fine	Much Hadham wares
MHADR	Fine	Much Hadham reduced wares
MICA	Oxid	Mica-dusted (excluding imported beakers)
MLEZ	Import	Micaceous Lezoux ware
MOCO	Mort	Colchester mortaria
MOCR	Mort	Crambeck mortaria
MOG	Mort	Grey mortaria
MOGA	Mort	Imported Gallic mortaria
MOHA	Mort	Much Hadham mortaria
MOHX	Mort	Hadox mortaria
MOIM	Mort	Imported mortaria; source unknown
MOLO	Mort	Local mortaria
MOMD	Mort	Midlands mortaria; precise source unknown
MOMH	Mort	Mancetter-Hartshill mortaria
MONG	Mort	Gallic mortaria North Gaul
MONV	Mort	Nene Valley mortaria
MONVC	Mort	Nene Valley colour-coated mortaria
MOOX	Mort	Oxfordshire parchment ware mortaria
MOOXR	Mort	Oxfordshire red-slipped mortaria
MOOXW	Mort	Oxfordshire white-slipped mortaria
MORH	Mort	Rhenish mortaria
MORT	Mort	Mortaria; undifferentiated
MORV	Mort	Gallic mortaria Rhone Valley
MOSC	Mort	South Carlton mortaria
MOSL	Import	Rhenish; from Trier
MOSP	Mort	Swanpool mortaria
MOSPC	Mort	Swanpool colour-coated mortaria
MOTILE	Mort	Tile fabric
MOVR	Mort	Verulamium region mortaria
MRRA	Amph	Mid-Roman ribbed amphorae
NA1	Amph	North African fabric 1
NA2	Amph	North African fabric 2
NA3	Amph	North African fabric 3
NA4	Amph	North African fabric 4
NA5	Amph	North African fabric 5
NA6	Amph	North African fabric 6
NA7	Amph	North African fabric 7
NA8	Amph	North African fabric 8
NAAM	Amph	North African amphorae
NAT	Reduced	Native miscellaneous
NFCC	Fine	New Forest colour-coated
NGCR	Import	North Gaulish cream; butt-beakers etc.
NGGW	Reduced	North Gaulish grey wares
NVCC	Fine	Nene Valley colour-coated
NVGCC	Fine	Nene Valley grey colour-coated
NVGW	Reduced	Nene Valley grey ware
NVGWC	Reduced	Nene Valley grey ware coarse
NVMIC	Fine	Nene Valley colour-coated with mica overslip
NVPA	Oxid	Nene Valley parchment ware
OX	Oxid	Miscellaneous oxidized wares
OXGR	Reduced	Grog-tempered; La Tene bkr Lawn86 (45)
OXPA	Oxid	Oxfordshire parchment ware
OXRC	Fine	Oxfordshire red colour-coated
OXSA	Oxid	Early oxidized sandy
OXWS	Oxid	Oxidized with white slip
PARC	Oxid	Parchment; cream painted red; unknown source/s
PART	Reduced	Parisian type wares
PINK	Oxid	Pink micaceous flagons etc.
PRW	Import	Pompeian red ware undifferentiated
PRW1	Import	Pompeian red ware Peacock 1
PRW2	Import	Pompeian red ware Peacock 2
PRW3	Import	Pompeian red ware Peacock 3
R527	Amph	Richborough 527 amphorae
RC	Fine	Miscellaneous rough-cast colour-coated beakers
RDSL	Oxid	Early red slipped
RHOD	Amph	Rhodian amphorae
ROSAX	Reduced	Indeterminate Roman or Saxon
SACR	Import?	Sandy cream; suspected imported flagon
SAM	Samian	undifferentiated
SAMCG	Samian	Central Gaulish
SAMCG–EG	Samian	Central or East Gaulish
SAMEG	Samian	East Gaulish
SAMLM	Samian	Les Martres de Veyre
SAMMT	Samian	Montans ware
SAMSG	Samian	South Gaulish
SC	Oxid	South Carlton cream
SCCC	Fine	South Carlton colour-coated
SEAL	Amph	Amphorae seals
SHEL	Shell	Miscellaneous shell-tempered
SMSH	Shell	South Midlands shell-tempered wares
SPAA	Amph	Spanish amphorae; undifferentiated

Code	Category	Detail	Code	Category	Detail
SPCC	Fine	Swanpool colour-coated	TR	Import	Terra rubra
SPIR	Oxid	Grooved jars as Alice Holt/Farnham Class 3C; unknown source	VESIC	?Shell	Vesicular fabric
			VRW	Oxid	Verulamium region white wares
SPOX	Oxid	Swanpool oxidized wares	WHEG	Import	White eggshell wares
TILE	oxid	Tile fabric vessels	WSTO	Reduced	West Stow
TN	Import	Terra nigra			

APPENDIX III
Medieval Pottery Codes

Ware code	Description	Period	Earliest horizon	Latest horizon
AARD	LOW COUNTRIES HIGHLY DECORATED WARE	MED	MH5	MH7
ANDA	ANDALUSIAN LUSTREWARE	MED	MH5	MH9
ANDE	ANDENNE WARE	SN	ASH11	MH3
ARCH	ARCHAIC MAIOLICA	MED	MH6	MH8?
BA	BRONZE AGE	PREH	0	0
BADO	BADORF-TYPE WARE	MSAX-LSAX	ASH2	ASH8
BALT	BALTIC-TYPE WARES	LSAX-SN	ASH7?	ASH14?
BEAURP	BEAUVAIS-TYPE WARE	LSAX	ASH7?	ASH11?
BEAG	GREEN GLAZE BEAUVAIS-TYPE WARE	LMED-PMED	MH10	PMH3
BERTH	BROWN EARTHENWARES	PMED	PMH2	PMH10
BEVO	BEVERLEY ORANGE WARE	EMED-MED	MH1	MH7
BL	BLACKWARE	PMED	PMH3	EMH
BLBURN	BLACK BURNISHED WARES	MSAX	ASH3	ASH4?
BLGR	PAFFRATH-TYPE OR BLUE-GREY WARE	SN-EMED	ASH12	MH3?
BLSURF	BLACK SURFACED WARES	MSAX	ASH3	ASH4?
BORDB	BROWN GLAZED BORDER WARE	PMED	PMH3	PMH7
BORDY	YELLOW GLAZED BORDER WARE	PMED	PMH3	PMH7
BOU	BOURNE;FABRIC D	PMED	MH10	PMH4
BOUA	BOURNE;FABRICS A-C	MED	MH3	MH7
BRANS	BRANDSBY-TYPE WARE	MED	MH5	MH8
BRBURN	BROWN BURNISHED WARES	MSAX	ASH3	ASH4?
BRILL	BRILL WARES	MED	MH5	MH7
BRUNS	BRUNNSUM-TYPE FLASKS	EMED	MH2?	MH3?
BS	BROWN STONEWARE	PMED	PMH7	EMH
CEP	CHINESE EXPORT PORCELAIN	PMED	PMH6	PMH10
CHALK	UNGLAZED SANDY FABRICS WITH CHALK	SN-MED	ASH11	MH7
CHARN	CHARNWOOD FABRICS	ESAX	ASH1	ASH2
CHINS	CHINESE STONEWARE	MED-EMOD	MH4	EMH
CIST	CISTERCIAN-TYPE WARES	PMED	MH10?	PMH5
CITG	CENTRAL ITALIAN TIN-GLAZED WARE	LMED-PMED	MH9	PMH2
CMW	WHITE COAL MEASURE FABRICS	MED-PMED	MH7	PMH3
CRMWARE	CREAMWARE	EMOD	PMH9	EMH
CROW	CROWLAND ABBEY-TYPE WARE	SN	ASH12	ASH14
DERB	DERBY-TYPE WARE	LSAX	ASH10?	ASH13?
DONC	DONCASTER-HALLGATE FABRICS	EMED-MED	MH3	MH4
DST	DEVELOPED STAMFORD WARE	EMED	MH1	MH4
DUTR	LOW COUNTRIES RED EARTHENWARES	LMED-PMED	MH8	PMH5
DUTRT	LOW COUNTRIES RED EARTHENWARE-TYPES	PMED	PMH3	PMH5
EALMT	EAST ANGLIAN LMED/TRANSITIONAL WARE	LMED-PMED	MH9	PMH3

Ware code	Description	Period	Earliest horizon	Latest horizon
ECHAF	CHAFF-TEMPERED FABRICS	ESAX	ASH1	ASH2
EGSW	EARLY GERMAN STONEWARES	MED	MH5	MH6
ELFS	EARLY FINE-SHELLED WARE	MSAX	ASH6	ASH7
ELSW	EARLY GLAZED LINCOLN WARE	LSAX	ASH7	ASH8
EMED	EARLY MEDIEVAL	EMED	MH1	MH4
EMHM	EARLY MEDIEVAL HANDMADE FABRICS	EMED	MH1?	MH3?
EMLOC	EARLY MEDIEVAL LOCAL FABRICS	EMED	MH1	MH4
EMOD	EARLY MODERN	EMOD	PMH10	EMH
EMSAX	ESAX OR MSAX	ESAX-MSAX	ASH1	ASH6
EMX	EARLY MEDIEVAL NON-LOCAL FABRICS	EMED	MH1	MH4
ESAX	EARLY SAXON	ESAX	ASH1	ASH2
ESAXLOC	EARLY SAXON LOCAL FABRICS	ESAX	ASH1	ASH2
ESAXX	EARLY SAXON NON-LOCAL FABRICS	ESAX	ASH1	ASH2
ESG	YORK EARLY GLAZED WARE;TYPE 1	LSAX	ASH8	ASH12
ESGS	GREENSAND FABRICS	ESAX	ASH1	ASH2
EST	EARLY STAMFORD WARE	LSAX	ASH7	ASH11
FE	IRONSTONE ORE-TEMPERED FABRIC	ESAX	ASH1	ASH2
FERTH	FINE EARTHENWARES	PMED	PMH9	EMH
FINSP	FINE SPLASHED WARE	EMED	MH2?	MH4?
FLINT	FLINT TEMPERED FABRICS	PREH-MSAX	0	ASH3
FREC	FRECHEN/COLOGNE STONEWARE	PMED	PMH2	PMH8
FREN	FRENCH WARES (GENERAL)	MED-PMED	MH3	PMH5
GERMS	GERMAN SLIPWARES	PMED	PMH3	PMH8
GERMW	GERMAN WHITE WARES	PMED	PMH3	PMH7
GLGS	GLAZED GREENSAND FABFICS	EMED-LMED	MH2	MH10
GRBURN	GREY BURNISHED WARES	MSAX	ASH3	ASH4?
GRE	GLAZED RED EARTHENWARES	PMED	PMH3	PMH9
GRIM	GRIMSTON-TYPE WARE	MED	MH3	MH8
GS	GREY STONEWARES	EMOD	PMH5	EMH
HLKT	HORNCASTLE-TYPE LKT WARE	LSAX	ASH9?	ASH11?
HUM	HUMBERWARE	LMED-PMED	MH7	PMH2
HUMB	HUMBER BASIN GLAZED FABRICS	MED	MH1	MH10
HUY	HUY-TYPE LATE SAXON GLAZED	LSAX	ASH6	ASH12
IA	IRON AGE	PREH	0	0
IALSAX	IA OR LSAX	PREH-LSAX	0	0
IMP	UNDATED IMPORTED FABRICS	ND	ASH1	PMH7
INDUS	UNSPECIFIED INDUSTRIAL MATERIAL	ND	ASH1	EMH
IPS	IPSWICH-TYPE WARE	MSAX	ASH2?	ASH6
IS	UNIDENTIFIED IMPORTED STONEWARE	PMED	PMH1	PMH7
ISLG	ISLAMIC GLAZED WARES	SN-MED	ASH11	MH8
ITGE	IMPORTED TIN-GLAZED EARTHENWARES	LMED	MH7	MH10
KEUP	MERCIAN MUDSTONE-TEMPERED WARE	ESAX-MSAX	ASH1	ASH?
KING	KINGSTON-TYPE WARE	MED	MH5	MH6
KOLN	COLOGNE STONEWARE	PMED	PMH1	PMH2
L/LSW4	LLSW OR LSW4	LMED	MH9	PMH1
LANG	LANGERWEHE STONEWARE	LMED	MH7	PMH1
LARA	LANGERWEHE/RAEREN STONEWARE	LMED	MH8	PMH1
LEMS	LOCAL EARLY MEDIEVAL SHELLY WARE	EMED	MH1	MH4
LERTH	LATE EARTHENWARES	EMOD	PMH9	EMH
LEST	LEICESTER-TYPE WARE	LSAX	ASH7?	ASH9?
LFS	LINCOLN FINE-SHELLED WARE	SN	ASH11	MH3?
LFS/ELFS	LFS OR ELFS	MSAX-SN	ASH6	MH3?
LG	LINCOLN GRITTY WARE	LSAX	ASH7	ASH7
LG/LSLS	LG OR LSLS	LSAX	ASH7	ASH8
LHUM	LATE HUMBERWARE	PMED	PMH2	EMH

Ware code	Description	Period	Earliest horizon	Latest horizon
LIGU	LIGURIAN BERRETINO TIN-GLAZED WARE	PMED	PMH2	PMH6
LIM	OOLITE-TEMPERED FABRICS	ESAX-SN	ASH2	ASH13
LKT	LINCOLN KILN-TYPE WARE	LSAX	ASH7	ASH11
LLSW	LATE GLAZED LINCOLN WARE	LMED	MH8	MH10
LMED	LATE MEDIEVAL	LMED	MH7	MH10
LMF	LATE MEDIEVAL FINE WARES	LMED	MH9	PMH1
LMIMP	LATE MEDIEVAL IMPORTED FABRICS	LMED	MH7	MH10
LMLOC	LATE MEDIEVAL LOCAL FABRICS	LMED	MH8	PMH1
LMPM	LMED OR PMED	LMED-PMED	MH7	PMH10
LMX	LATE MEDIEVAL NON-LOCAL FABRICS	LMED	MH7	MH10
LOCC	LOCAL SPLASHED WARE	EMED	MH1	MH3?
LONS	LONDON STONEWARE	PMED	PMH7	EMH
LPM	EARLY MODERN OR MODERN	EMOD	EMH	EMH
LPMDISC	EARLY MODERN OR MODERN (DISCARDED)	EMOD	EMH	EMH
LS/SNLS	LSLS OR SNLS	LSAX-SN	ASH7	ASH13
LSAX	LATE SAXON	LSAX	ASH7	ASH11
LSCRUC	LINCOLN CRUCIBLE FABRICS	LSAX-SN	ASH7	ASH12
LSH	LINCOLN SHELLY WARE	LSAX	ASH7	ASH12?
LSIMP	LATE SAXON IMPORTED FABRICS	LSAX	ASH7	ASH11
LSLOC	LATE SAXON LOCAL FABRICS	LSAX	ASH7	ASH13
LSLS	LATE SAXON LINCOLN SANDY WARE	LSAX	ASH7	ASH8
LSMED	LSAX OR MED	LSAX-MED	ASH7	MH10
LSPLS	LIGHT-BODIED LSLS WARE	LSAX	ASH7	ASH8
LSTON	LATE STONEWARES	EMOD	PMH10	EMH
LSW	UNDATED LINCOLN FABRICS	LSAX-LMED	ASH7	MH10
LSW1	GLAZED LINCOLN WARE	EMED	MH1	MH4
LSW1/2	LSW1 OR LSW2	EMED	MH1	MH6
LSW2	GLAZED LINCOLN WARE	MED	MH4	MH6
LSW2/3	LSW2 OR LSW3	MED	MH4	MH9
LSW3	GLAZED LINCOLN WARE	LMED	MH6	MH9?
LSW4	GLAZED LINCOLN WARE	LMED	MH10	PMH1
LSWA	GLAZED LINCOLN WARE;FABRIC A	EMED-MED	MH1	MH10
LSWE/1	ELSW OR LSW1	LSAX-EMED	ASH7	MH4
LSX	LATE SAXON NON-LOCAL FABRICS	LSAX	ASH7	ASH13
MAGR	MAGREBI WARE	MED	MH5	MH7
MAMPH	ROMAN/MEDIEVAL AMPHORA	ROM-MED	0	0
MARTI	MARTINCAMP WARE;TYPE I	PMED	MH10	PMH2
MARTII	MARTINCAMP WARE;TYPE II	PMED	PMH1	PMH3
MARTIII	MARTINCAMP WARE;TYPE III	PMED	PMH3	PMH7
MAX	NORTHERN MAXEY-TYPE WARE	MSAX	ASH2	ASH6?
MAXQ	SOUTH LINCS MAXEY-TYPE WARE	MSAX	ASH2	ASH5?
MAY	MAYEN-TYPE WARES	MSAX	ASH3	ASH6?
MCRUC	MEDIEVAL CRUCIBLE FABRICS	MED	MH1	MH10
MED	MEDIEVAL	MED	MH4	MH10
MEDIT	UNGLZED MEDITERRANEAN JARS	ESAX-PMED	ASH1	PMH7
MEDLOC	MEDIEVAL LOCAL FABRICS	MED	MH4	MH10
MEDPM	MED OR PMED	MED-PMED	MH4	PMH10
MEDX	MEDIEVAL NON-LOCAL FABRICS	MED	MH4	MH10
MIMP	MEDIEVAL IMPORTED FABRICS	MED	MH4	MH10
MISC	UNDATED MISCELLANEOUS FABRICS	ND	ASH1	EMH
MLSAX	MSAX OR LSAX	MSAX-LSAX	ASH2	ASH11
MLTG	MONTELUPO POLYCHROME	PMED	MH10	PMH7
MMAX	RMAX WITH QUARTZ	MSAX	ASH2?	ASH6?
MP	MIDLAND PURPLE-TYPE WARE	LMED-PMED	MH8?	PMH3?
MSAX	MID-SAXON	MSAX	ASH2	ASH6

Ware code	Description	Period	Earliest horizon	Latest horizon
MSAXLOC	MID-SAXON LOCAL FABRICS	MSAX	ASH2	ASH6
MSAXX	MID-SAXON NON-LOCAL FABRICS	MSAX	ASH2	ASH6
MVAL	MATURE VALENTIAN LUSTREWARE	LMED	MH7	PMH3
MY	MIDLAND YELLOW-TYPE WARE	PMED	PMH2	PMH8
NCOS	NOTTINGHAM COARSE SANDY	EMED-MED	MH3	MH4
NEWG	NEWARK GLAZED SANDY WARE	MED	MH4	MH6?
NEWS	NEWARK SANDY WARE	SN	ASH11	ASH12
NFM	NORTH FRENCH MONOCHROME	MED	MH4	MH5
NFREM	NORTH FRENCH FABRICS	EMED-MED	MH3?	MH5
NFSVA	NORTH FRENCH SEINE VALLEY FABRIC A	MSAX	ASH2?	ASH4?
NHSLIP	NORTH HOLLAND SLIPWARES	PMED	PMH3	PMH7
NITALS	NORTH ITALIAN SGRAFFITO WARE	PMED	PMH3	PMH4
NLST	NORTH LINCOLNSHIRE SHELLY WARE	EMED-MED	MH1	MH8
NOTG	NOTTINGHAM GREEN-GLAZED WARE	MED	MH4?	MH7
NOTS	NOTTINGHAM WARE	LSAX	ASH9?	ASH12?
NSP	NOTTINGHAM SPLASHED GLAZED WARE	EMED	MH1	MH4?
ORP	OXIDISED RED-PAINTED FABRICS	MSAX	ASH4?	ASH6?
PBIC	LIGHT-BODIED BICHROME FABRICS	PMED	PMH2?	PMH3?
PGE	LIGHT-BODIED GLAZED EARTHENWARES	PMED	PMH3	PMH5
PING	PINGSDORF-TYPE WARE	SN-EMED	ASH7	MH3
PMCRUC	LATE AND POST MEDIEVAL CRUCIBLE FABRICS	LMED-PMED	MH10	EMH
PMED	POST-MEDIEVAL	PMED	PMH1	PMH10
PMF	POST-MED FINE WARES	PMED	PMH1	PMH7
PMIMP	POST-MED IMPORTED FABRICS	PMED	PMH1	PMH10
PMLOC	POST-MED LOCAL FABRICS	PMED	PMH2	PMH9
PMX	POST-MED NON-LOCAL FABRICS	PMED	PMH1	PMH10
PORC	PORCELAIN (GENERAL)	PMED	PMH8	EMH
PORTF	PORTUGESE TIN-GLAZED WARES	PMED	PMH3	PMH5
POTT	POTTERHANWORTH WARE	MED	MH4?	MH9?
PREH	PREHISTORIC	PREH	0	0
R	ROMAN	ROM	0	0
RAER	RAEREN STONEWARE	PMED	MH10	PMH2
RESAX	ROMAN OR ESAX	ROM-ESAX	0	0
RGRE	REDUCED GLAZED RED EARTHENWARES	PMED	PMH3	PMH9
RLG	ROMAN OR LG	ROM-LSAX	0	0
RLSAX	ROMAN OR LSAX	ROM-LSAX	0	0
RLSLS	ROMAN OR LSLS	ROM-LSAX	0	0
RMAX	SOUTHERN MAXEY-TYPE WARE	MSAX	ASH2	ASH6?
RMED	ROMAN OR MED	ROM-MED	0	0
RMSAX	ROMAN OR MSAX	ROM-MSAX	0	0
ROUEN	ROUEN-TYPE WARES	EMED-MED	MH3	MH5
RSN	ROMAN OR SN	ROM-SN	0	0
RSTON	RED STONEWARES	PMED	PMH8	PMH10
SAIG	SAINTONGE GREEN-GLAZED WARE	MED	MH5	MH6
SAIM	SAINTONGE MOTTLED WARE	MED	MH5	MH7
SAIP	SAINTONGE POLYCHROME WARE	MED	MH5	MH6
SAIPM	POST MEDIEVAL SAINTONGE	PMED	PMH1	PMH4
SAIU	UNGLAZED SAINTONGE	LMED-PMED	MH10	PMH4
SCAR	SCARBOROUGH WARE	EMED-MED	MH3	MH7
SEVIL	SEVILLE UNATTRIBUTED TYPES	?	?	?
SIEG	SIEGBURG STONEWARE	MED-LMED	MH6	PMH1
SIEB	RED SLIPPED SIEGBURG STONEWARE	LMED	MH9	PMH1
SLEMO	SOUTH LINCS EARLY MEDIEVAL OOLITIC	EMED	MH2	MH4
SLIP	SLIPWARE (GENERAL)	PMED	PMH4	EMH
SLSOF	SOUTH LINCS SHELL OOLITE AND IRON TEMPERED	EMED	MH2	MH4

Ware code	Description	Period	Earliest horizon	Latest horizon
SLST	SOUTH LINCOLNSHIRE SHELLY WARE	EMED-MED	MH1?	MH7?
SN	SAXO-NORMAN	SN	ASH7	ASH14
SNEMED	SN OR EMED	SN-EMED	ASH11	MH4
SNEOT	ST.NEOTS-TYPE WARE	SN-EMED	ASH11	MH3?
SNIMP	SAXO-NORMAN IMPORTED FABRICS	SN	ASH7	MH3
SNLOC	SAXO-NORMAN LOCAL FABRICS	SN	ASH7	MH3
SNLS	SAXO-NORMAN LINCOLN SANDY WARE	SN	ASH11	ASH13
SNTG	SOUTH NETHERLANDS TIN-GLAZED WARES	PMED	MH10	PMH1
SNX	SAXO-NORMAN NON-LOCAL FABRICS	SN	ASH7	MH3
SPAN	SPANISH UNGLAZED COARSEWARES	PMED	PMH1	EMH
SPARC	SPARRY CALCITE-TEMPERED FABRICS	ESAX-MSAX	ASH1	ASH6?
SPTG	BLUE GLAZED MEDITERRANEAN ALBARELLO	?	?	/
SRCRUC	STAMFORD OR ROMAN CRUCIBLES	ROM-SN	0	0
SST	SANDSTONE-TEMPERED FABRICS	ESAX-MSAX	ASH1	ASH6
ST	STAMFORD WARE	SN	ASH7	MH3
STANLY	STANION/LYVDEN-TYPE WARE	MED	MH5	MH7
STCRUC	STAMFORD WARE CRUCIBLES	SN	ASH7	MH3
STMO	STAFFORDSHIRE MOTTLED WARE	PMED	PMH6	PMH8
STSL	STAFFORDSHIRE SLIPWARE	PMED	PMH5	PMH8
TB	TOYNTON OR BOLINGBROKE-TYPE WARE	PMED	MH10?	PMH8
TGE	TIN-GLAZED EARTHENWARES	PMED	PMH4	PMH10
TGEM	MAIOLICA (ANGLO-NETHERLANDS)	PMED	PMH3	PMH4
THETT	THETFORD OR THETFORD-TYPE WARE	SN	ASH7	MH2
TILE	TILE FABRIC	MED	MH3	MH10
TORK	TORKSEY WARE	SN	ASH7	ASH13
TORKT	TORKSEY-TYPE WARE	SN	ASH7	ASH13
TOY	TOYNTON WARE;KILN 1 (ROSES)	MED	MH5	MH6
TOYII	TOYNTON WARE;KILN 3	LMED	MH10?	PMH1
UNGS	UNGLAZED GREENSAND	SN-MED	ASH11	MH7
VGF	VICTORIAN GARDEN FURNITURE	EMOD	PMH10	EMH
VITR	UNIDENTIFIED VITRIFIED SHERDS	ND	ASH1	EMH
WERRA	WERRA/WANFRIED WARE	PMED	PMH3	PMH4
WESER	WESER WARE	PMED	PMH3	PMH4
WEST	WESTERWALD STONEWARE	PMED	PMH4	EMH
WINC	WINCHESTER-TYPE WARE	SN	ASH10	ASH14
WS	WHITE SALT-GLAZED WARES	PMED	PMH8	PMH9
YG	YORKSHIRE-TYPE GRITTY WARES	SN	ASH13	MH3
YORK	YORK GLAZED WARE	EMED-MED	MH3	MH5?
YORKSPL	YORK-TYPE SPLASHED WARES	EMED	ASH14?	MH4?
YW	YORK WARE	LSAX	ASH6	ASH9

Bibliography

Adams Gilmour, L 1988. *Early medieval pottery from Flaxengate, Lincoln*, The Archaeology of Lincoln, **17–2**, CBA, London

Adams, P & Henderson, J 1995a. *The Vessel Glass from the Excavations at St. Mark's Station (Z86)*, Unpublished report for City Lincoln Archaeol Unit

Adams, P & Henderson, J 1995b. *The Vessel Glass from the Excavations of St. Benedict's Square (SB85)*, Unpublished report for City Lincoln Archaeol Unit

Adams, P & Henderson, J 1995c. *The Vessel Glass from the Excavations of St. Mark's Church (SM76)*, Unpublished report for City Lincoln Archaeol Unit

Adams, P & Henderson, J 1995d. *The Vessel Glass from the Excavations of St. Mark's Station East*, Unpublished report for City Lincoln Archaeol Unit

Adams, P & Henderson, J 1995e. *Vessel Glass from the Excavations at Holmes Grainwarehouse (HG72)*, Unpublished report for City Lincoln Archaeol Unit

Adams, P & Henderson, J 1995f. *Vessel Glass from the Excavations of Lucy Tower in 1972 (LT72)*, Unpublished report for City Lincoln Archaeol Unit

AI, 1850. *Memoirs, History, Antiquities of the County and City of Lincoln* Archaeological Institute Annual Meeting Lincoln 1848, **43**

Archibald, M 1994. *Lincoln Excavation Coins*, Unpublished report for City Lincoln Archaeol Unit

Arnold, J 1988. *Queen Elizabeth's Wardrobe Unlock'd*, Maney, Leeds

Ayers, B 1985. The Growth of a Saxon Port, in Herteig, A (ed), *Bergen 1983*, Conference on Waterfront Archaeology in Northern European Towns, **2**, 46–54, Historisk Museum Bergen, Bergen

Bass, W M 1987. *Human Osteology*, Missouri Archaeology Society, Columbia

Batey, C E 1988. A Viking-Age Bell from Freswick Links, Caithness, *Medieval Archaeol*, **32**, 213–6

Beta Analytic Inc 1994. *Report of Radiocarbon dating analyses*, Unpublished report for City Lincoln Archaeol Unit

Blackburn, M 1995. *Anglo-Saxon and Anglo-Norman coin finds from Lincoln excavations 1981–94*, Unpublished report for City Lincoln Archaeol Unit

Blackburn, M, Colyer, C & Dolley, M 1983. *Early Medieval coins from Lincoln and its Shire c 770–1100*, The Archaeology of Lincoln, **6–1**, CBA, London

Blindheim, C 1969. Kaupangundersokelsen avsluttet, *Viking*, **33**, 5–39

Boylston, A & Roberts, C 1994. *Excavations on the Wigford Sites 1972–1987, Interim report on the Human Skeletal Remains*, Unpublished report for City Lincoln Archaeol Unit

Brown, A 1994. A Romano-British Shell-Gritted Pottery and Tile Manufacturing Site at Harrold, Bedfordshire, *Bedford Archaeol*, **21**, 19–107

Bulleid, A & Gray, H St G 1911. *The Glastonbury Lake Village*

Cameron, K 1985. *The Place-Names of Lincolnshire. Part 1: The Place-names of the County of the City of Lincoln*, Engl Place-Name Soc, **58**

Camidge, K 1986. St Mark's Station, in Nurser, E (ed), *Archaeology in Lincolnshire 1985–1986*, Ann Rep Trust Lincolnshire Archaeol, **2**, 25–7, Lincoln

Carrott, J, Hall, A, Issitt, M, Kenward, H, Large, F & Milles, A 1994. *Assessment of biological remains from excavations at two sites in Lincoln: ze87–90 and on362*, Rep Environmental Archaeol Unit York, **94/46**

CBA 1987. *Recording Worked Stones: a practical guide*, CBA Practical Handbook, **1**

Chambers, J I & Wilson, C M 1972. Dickinson's Mill, Lincoln, *Lincs Industrial Archaeology*, **7 (2)**, 16–9.

Cherry, J 1987. Recent medieval finds from Lincoln: a Romanesque cast copper alloy buckle plate with figural scenes and a bronze buckle, *Antiq J*, **67**, 367–8

Chitwood, P 1988. St Mark's Yard East, in Nurser, E (ed), *Archaeology in Lincolnshire 1987–1988*, Ann Rep Trust Lincolnshire Archaeol, **4**, 24–6, Sleaford

Chitwood, P 1989. Waterside North, in Jones, M J (ed), *Lincoln Archaeology 1988–1989*, Ann Rep City Lincoln Archaeol Unit, **1**, 4–7

Chitwood, P 1990. St Mark's Yard East (County Court site), in Jones, M J (ed), *Lincoln Archaeology 1989–90*, Ann Rep City Lincoln Archaeol Unit, **2**, 13–5, Lincoln

Colyer, C 1975. Excavations at Lincoln 1970–72: The Western Defences of the Lower Town. An Interim Report, *Antiq J*, **55**, 227–66

Cool, H E M & Price, J 1986. *Lincoln – Holmes Grain Warehouse*, Unpublished report for Trust Lincolnshire Archaeol

Cool, H E M & Price, J 1987a. *Lincoln Dickinson's Mill (DM72)*, Unpublished report for Trust Lincolnshire Archaeol

Cool, H E M & Price, J 1987b. *The Roman Glass from Brayford Wharf East, Lincoln*, Unpublished report for Trust Lincolnshire Archaeol

Cool, H E M & Price, J 1988. Glass, in Darling, M J & Jones, M J (eds), 42–3

Coppack, G 1990. *Abbeys and Priories*, Batsford/English Heritage, London

Cowgill, J 1991. The non-ceramic finds, in Stocker, D, 72–3

Crowfoot, E, Pritchard, F & Staniland, K 1992. *Textiles and*

Clothing c.1150-c.1450, Medieval Finds from Excavations in London, **4**, HMSO, London

Crummy, N 1983. *The Roman small finds from excavations in Colchester 1971-9*, Colchester Archaeol Rep, **2**

Cunliffe, B (ed) 1968. *Fifth report on the Excavations of the Roman Fort at Richborough, Kent*, Rep Res Comm Soc Antiq London, **23**

Darling, M J 1981. A Roman face-pot from St Mark's, in Nurser, E (ed), *Lincoln Archaeological Trust 1980-81*, Ann Rep Lincoln Archaeol Trust, **9**, 27-8, Lincoln

Darling, M J 1988. The pottery, in Darling, M J & Jones, M J, 9-37

Darling, M J 1990. The blacksmiths of St Mark's and their god, in Jones, M J (ed), *Lincoln Archaeology 1989-90*, Ann Rep City Lincoln Archaeol Unit, **2**, 21-3, Lincoln

Darling, M J, 1999. Roman Pottery, in Jones, M J (ed), 52-735

Darling, M J & Jones, M J 1988. Early settlement at Lincoln, *Britannia*, **19**, 1-57

Darling, M J & Precious, B forthcoming. *A Corpus of Roman Pottery from Lincoln*, Lincoln Archaeol Stud,

Davies, B 1992. Spot dates as qualitative data?, in Steane K (ed), 30-9

Davies, J A 1987. *The coins from Lincoln*, Unpublished report for Trust Lincolnshire Archaeol

Davies, J A 1992. *Coin Catalogue*, Unpublished report for City Lincoln Archaeol Unit

Davies, J A 1993. *The Roman coins from Lincoln - an overview*, Unpublished report for City Lincoln Archaeol Unit

Dawes, J D 1986. Human bones from St Mark's, in Gilmour, B J & Stocker, D A, 33-5 and fiche Appendix IV

Dobney, K, Milles, A, Irving, B & Jaques, D 1994a. *Animal bones from bwe82*, Unpublished report for City Lincoln Archaeol Unit

Dobney, K, Milles, A, Irving, B & Jaques, D 1994b. *Animal bones from dm72*, Unpublished report for City Lincoln Archaeol Unit

Dobney, K, Milles, A, Irving, B & Jaques, D 1994c. *Animal bones from hg72*, Unpublished report for City Lincoln Archaeol Unit

Dobney, K, Milles, A, Irving, B & Jaques, D 1994d. *Animal bones from m82*, Unpublished report for City Lincoln Archaeol Unit

Dobney, K, Milles, A, Irving, B & Jaques, D 1994e. *Animal bones from sb85*, Unpublished report for City Lincoln Archaeol Unit

Dobney, K, Milles, A, Irving, B & Jaques, D 1994f. *Animal bones from sm76*, Unpublished report for City Lincoln Archaeol Unit

Dobney, K, Milles, A, Irving, B & Jaques, D 1994g. *Animal bones from smg82*, Unpublished report for City Lincoln Archaeol Unit

Dobney, K, Milles, A, Irving, B & Jaques, D 1994h. *Animal bones from z86*, Unpublished report for City Lincoln Archaeol Unit

Dobney, K, Milles, A, Irving, B & Jaques, D 1994i. *The animal bone assemblage from lt72*, Unpublished report for City Lincoln Archaeol Unit

Dobney, K M, Jaques, S D & Irving, B G 1996. *Of Butchers and Breeds. Report on vertebrate remains from various sites in the City of Lincoln*, Lincoln Archaeol Stud, **5**

Donel, L 1989. Woolworths 1989, in Jones, M J (ed), *Lincoln Archaeology 1988-1989*, Ann Rep City Lincoln Archaeol Unit, **1**, 7-8, Lincoln

Donel, L 1991. Waterside North Watching Brief, in Jones, M J (ed), *Lincoln Archaeology 1990-1991*, Ann Rep City Lincoln Archaeol Unit, **3**, 18-9, Lincoln

Donel, L & Jarvis, M 1990. Waterside North: Saltergate, in

Jones, M J (ed), *Lincoln Archaeology 1989-90*, Ann Rep City Lincoln Archaeol Unit, **2**, 6-8, Lincoln

Downey, N & Young, J 1984. A 'Delftware' tile from Dickinson's Mill, Lincoln, in Jones, M J and Nurser, E (eds), *Archaeology in Lincoln 1983-1984*, Ann Rep Lincoln Archaeol Trust, **12**, 27-9, Lincoln

Everson, P & Stocker, D A 1999. *A Corpus of Anglo-Saxon Sculpture from Lincolnshire*, Brit Acad

Evison, V I 1980. Objects of bronze and iron, in Haslam, J, A Middle Saxon iron smelting site at Ramsbury, Wiltshire, *Medieval Archaeol*, **24**, 33-41

Fox, G & Hope, W H 1901. Excavations on the site of the Roman City of Silchester, *Archaeologia*, **57**, 229-56

French, C A I 1982. *An Analysis of the Molluscs from the Roman and Saxon Waterfronts at Brayford Wharf East, Lincoln*, Unpublished report for Lincoln Archaeol Trust

French, C A I 1987. *The Molluscs from St. Benedict's Square, Lincoln*, Unpublished report for Trust Lincolnshire Archaeol

Gale, R 1992. *Wood identification: Lincoln - various sites*, Unpublished report for City Lincoln Archaeol Unit

Gejvall, N G 1981. Determination of burnt bones from Prehistoric Graves, *Ossa Letters* **2**, 1-13

Gibb, J H P & Gem, R D H 1975. The Anglo-Saxon Cathedral at Sherborne, *Archaeol J*, **132**, 71-110

Gillam, J P 1976. Coarse fumed ware in North Britain and beyond, *Glasgow Archaeol J*, **4**, 57-80

Gilmour, B J J 1973. Lucy Tower Street, in Colyer, C (ed), *Lincoln Archaeological Trust 1972-1973*, Ann Rep Lincoln Archaeol Trust **1**, 4, Lincoln

Gilmour, B J J 1980. Roman Traders' Houses at St Mark's: what trades?, in Nurser, E (ed), *Lincoln Archaeological Trust 1979-1980*, Ann Rep Lincoln Archaeol Trust, **8**, 18-22, Lincoln

Gilmour, B J J 1981. St Marks, in Jones, M J (ed), 92-101

Gilmour, B J J 1982. Brayford Wharf East, in Nurser, E (ed) *Archaeology in Lincoln 1981-82*, Ann Rep Lincoln Archaeol Trust, **10**, 20-4, Lincoln

Gilmour, B J J & Jones, M J 1978. St Marks, in Colyer, C (ed), *Lincoln Archaeological Trust 1977-1978*, Ann Rep Lincoln Archaeol Trust **6**, 13, Lincoln

Gilmour, B J J & Stocker, D A 1986. *St Mark's Church and Cemetery*, The Archaeology of Lincoln, **13-1**, CBA, London

Going, C J 1992. Economic 'Long Waves' in the Roman period? A Reconnaissance of the Romano-British Ceramic Evidence, *Oxford J Archaeol*, **11 (I)**, 93-117

Gray, H 1977. *Anatomy*, Bounty Books, New York

Grew, F & de Neergaard, M 1988. *Shoes and Pattens*, Medieval Finds from Excavations in London, **2**, HMSO, London

Guy, C J 1986. St Benedict's Square, in Nurser, E (ed), *Archaeology in Lincolnshire 1985-1986*, Ann Rep Trust Lincolnshire Archaeol, **2**, 23-5, Lincoln

Hamilton, J R C 1956. *Excavations at Jarlshof, Shetland*

Hartley, K 1973. *Dickinson's Mill 1972: Westgate 1973: Chaplin Street 1973: Mortaria report*, Unpublished report for Lincoln Archaeol Trust

Henderson, J 1984a. *Medieval and Post-Medieval glass from Lucy Tower Street*, Unpublished report for Trust Lincolnshire Archaeol

Henderson, J 1984b. *The Medieval and Post-Medieval glass from HG72*, Unpublished report for Trust Lincolnshire Archaeol

Henderson, J 1988. *Vessel fragment from DM72*, Unpublished report for City Lincoln Archaeol Unit

Henderson, J forthcoming. Medieval and Post-Medieval Glass Finewares from Lincoln: an Investigation of the Relationships between Technology, Typology and Value, *Archaeol J*

Hill, J W F 1927. The Manor of Hungate, Beaumont Fee, in the City of Lincoln, *Rep Pap Ass Architect Soc*, **38**, 175–208

Hill, J W F 1948. *Medieval Lincoln*, Cambridge Univ Press, London (reprinted with a new introduction, 1990)

Hobson, R L 1903. *Catalogue of English Pottery in the British Museum*

Hofso, T 1991. *A Roman shoe from Lincoln, England*, Stockholms Universitetet. Institutionen for antikens kultur och samhallsliv, Stockholm

Holman, K 1996. *Scandinavian Runic Inscriptions in the British Isles: Their Historical Context*, PhD thesis, Tapir, Trondheim

Holman, K & McKinnell, J forthcoming. A Magic Formula in Three Runic Inscriptions, *Saga-Book*

Humberside County Architect's Department, Archaeology Unit 1987. *The Archaeology of a Medieval Roof Tile Factory Site in Grovehill, Beverley. A description and evaluation of the results of excavations in 1986*

Hutchinson, M E 1992. *The identification of two green stones from St Mark's church, Lincoln*, Ancient Monuments Laboratory Rep, **40/92**, HBMCE

ILN, 1848. Excavations Recently Made – Chiefly for Railway Purposes in the Immediate Neighbourhood of Lincoln in the Collection of a Gentleman of the County, *Illustrated London News*, 8 April, 238

Irving, B G 1995. *Zooarchaeology and paleoecology of middle to late Pleistocene ichthyofaunas from the British Isles*, Unpublished PhD thesis, University of London

Jeffries, J S 1977. *Excavation Records: Techniques in use by the Central Excavation Unit*, Directorate Ancient Monuments & Hist Build Occas Pap, **1**

Jennings, S & Young, J 1986. The pottery, in Gilmour, B J J & Stocker, D A, 35–40

Johnston, J A (ed) 1989. *Probate Inventories of Lincoln Citizens 1661–1714*, Publ Lincoln Rec Soc, **80**, Lincoln

Jones, M J 1981. 181–3 High Street (Holmes Grainwarehouse) in Jones, M J (ed), 84–8.

Jones, M J 1982. Updating the past: Lincoln latest, *Popular Archaeology*, **4 (4)**, 14–5

Jones, M J (ed) 1981. Excavations at Lincoln, Third Interim Report: Sites outside the walled city, *Antiq J*, **61**, 83–114

Jones, M J (ed) 1999. *The Defences of the Lower City*, The Archaeology of Lincoln, **7–2**, CBA, York

Jones, M J & Gilmour, B J J 1977. St Mark's, in Jones, M J (ed), *Lincoln Archaeological Trust 1976–1977*, Ann Rep Lincoln Archaeol Trust, **5**, 5–7, Lincoln

Jones, M J, Gilmour, B J J & Colyer, C 1976. St Mark's, in Colyer, C (ed), *Lincoln Archaeological Trust 1975–1976*, Ann Rep Lincoln Archaeol Trust, **4**, 17–21, Lincoln

Jones, M J & Vince, A G forthcoming. *Lincoln: an Archaeological Synthesis*, Lincoln Archaeol Stud

Jones, R H 1973. Site of Dickinson's Mill, Brayford Wharf East, in Colyer, C (ed), *Lincoln Archaeological Trust 1972–1973*, Ann Rep Lincoln Archaeol Trust, **1**, 5, Lincoln

Jones, R H 1981c. St Mary's Guildhall: the excavation of a standing building, in Nurser, E (ed), *Lincoln Archaeological Trust 1980–81*, Ann Rep Lincoln Archaeol Trust, **9**, 14–16, Lincoln

Jones, R H 1981a. Brayford Wharf North, in Jones, M J (ed), 90–2

Jones, R H 1981b. Dickinson's Mill, in Jones, M J (ed), 88–90

Jones, R H & Jones, M J 1976. Brayford Wharf North, in Colyer, C (ed), *Lincoln Archaeological Trust 1975–1976*, Ann Rep Lincoln Archaeol Trust, **4**, 24–5, Lincoln

Kilmurry, K 1980. *The pottery industry of Stamford, Lincs, c AD 850–1250*, Brit Archaeol Rep, **84**

King, D 1986. Decorated window glass, in Gilmour, B J J & Stocker D A, 42–3

King, D 1991. The medieval window glass, in Stocker, D, 73–5

King, D 1994. *Excavated Medieval glass from St. Mark's Station, Lincoln*, Unpublished report for City Lincoln Archaeol Unit

Lawrence, C H 1989. *Medieval monasticism: forms of religious life in Western Europe in the Middle Ages*, London and New York (2nd edn)

Litten, J 1991. *The English Way of Death: The common funeral since 1450*, Robert Hale, London

Lloyd-Morgan, G 1982. *A new hand mirror from Lincoln*, Unpublished report for Lincoln Archaeol Trust

Long, C 1980. *Notes on wallplaster*, Unpublished BA Dissertation, University of Manchester

MacGregor, A 1982. *Anglo-Scandinavian finds from Lloyds Bank, Pavement, and other sites*, The Archaeology of York, **17/3**, CBA, London

MacGregor, A 1985. *Bone, antler, ivory and horn: the technology of skeletal materials since the Roman period*, Croom Helm, Beckenham

Mackreth, D F 1993. *Lincoln Brooches*, Unpublished report for City Lincoln Archaeol Unit

Magilton, J R 1982. Monson Street, in Nurser, E (ed), *Archaeology in Lincoln 1981–82*, Ann Rep Lincoln Archaeol Trust, **10**, 17–19, Lincoln

Magilton, J R 1983a. Roman houses in the southern suburbs: St Mary's Guildhall and Monson Street, *Lincolnshire Hist Archaeol*, **18**, 99–100

Magilton, J R 1983b. The Monson Street Roman cemetery, Lincoln, *Lincolnshire Hist Archaeol*, **18**, 98–9

Magilton, J R & Stocker, D A 1982. St Mary's Guildhall, in Nurser, E (ed), *Archaeology in Lincoln 1981–82*, Ann Rep Lincoln Archaeol Trust, **10**, 8–16, Lincoln

Mann, J E 1977. *Clay tobacco pipes from excavations in Lincoln 1970–74*, The Archaeology of Lincoln, **15–1**, CBA, London

Mann, J E 1982a. *Early medieval finds from Flaxengate I: Objects of antler, bone, stone, horn, ivory, amber, and jet*, The Archaeology of Lincoln, **14–1**, CBA, London

Mann, J E 1982b. Finds from St Mary's Guildhall and Monson Street, in Nurser, E (ed), *Archaeology in Lincoln 1981–82*, Ann Rep Lincoln Archaeol Trust, **10**, 30–3, Lincoln

Mann, J E 1986. Small finds, in Gilmour, B J J & Stocker, D A, 41–2

Mann, J E 1988a. Finds from excavations 1987/88, in Nurser, E (ed), *Archaeology in Lincolnshire 1987–1988*, Ann Rep Trust Lincolnshire Archaeol, **4**, 33–4, Sleaford

Mann, J E 1988b. The coins, in Darling, M J and Jones, M J (eds), 37–8

Mann, J E & Reece, R 1983. *Roman coins from Lincoln 1970–1979*, The Archaeology of Lincoln, **6–2**, CBA, London

Manning, W H 1985. *Catalogue of the Romano-British iron tools, fittings and weapons in the British Museum*, Trustees of British Mus

Marks, L 1993. *Stained Glass in England during the Middle Ages*, London

May, T 1930. *Catalogue of the Roman Pottery in the Colchester and Essex Museum*, Cambridge

Mays, S 1993. Infanticide in Roman Britain, *Antiquity*, **67**, 883–8

McKinley, J I 1989. Cremations: Expectations, methodologies and realities, in Roberts, C A, Lee, F, & Bintliff, J (eds), *Burial Archaeology*, Brit Archaeol Rep, Brit Ser, **211**, 65–76, BAR, Oxford

McKinley, J I 1993. *Romano-British Cremations from Monson Street, Lincoln*, Unpublished report for City Lincoln Archaeol Unit

McKinley, J I 1994a. Bone fragment size in British cremations and its implications for pyre technology and ritual, *J Archaeol Sci*, **21**, 339–42.

McKinley, J I 1994b. *The Anglo-Saxon cemetery at Spong Hill, North Elmham: Part VIII: The Cremations*, E Anglian Archaeol Rep, **69**, Dereham

McKinley, J I forthcoming a. *Romano-British Cremations from St Stephens Cemetery, St Albans*, St Albans Museum

McKinley, J I forthcoming b. *Romano-British Cremations from the Royston Road Cemetery (Area 15), Baldock (1991)*, The Excavations at Baldock, **4**

McKinley, J I forthcoming c. The Cremations, in Burleigh, G and Matthews, K *Wallington Road, Baldock, Hertfordshire: The excavation of a late Iron Age and Romano-British cemetery*, The Excavations at Baldock 1978–1989, **1**

McKinnell, J 1996. A Runic Fragment from Lincoln, *Nytt om Runer*, **10**, 10–11

McMinn, R M H, & Hutchings R T 1985. *A Colour Atlas of Human Anatomy*, Wolfe Medical Publications, London

Milles, A 1993. *Assessment of the land and freshwater snails recovered during excavations in Lincoln*, Unpublished report for City Lincoln Archaeol Unit

Milles, A 1994. *Molluscs from excavations at St Mark's Church, Lincoln*, Rep Environmental Archaeol Unit, York, **94/48**, York

Moffett, L 1993. *Assessment of the charred plant remains from Lincoln backlog sites*, Unpublished report for City Lincoln Archaeol Unit

Moore, D T 1991. *The petrography and provenance of the Lincoln hones*, Unpublished report for City Lincoln Archaeol Unit

Morgan, N J 1983. *The Medieval Painted Glass of Lincoln Cathedral*, Corpus Vitrearum Medii Aevi Occas Pap, **3**

Morgan, R A 1983. *Tree-Ring Analysis of Hurdle Structures from Brayford Wharf East, Lincoln*, Unpublished report for Lincoln Archaeol Trust

Morris, C A 1979. Wooden Objects, in Heighway, C M, Garrod, A P & Vince, A G, Excavations at 1 Westgate Street, Gloucester, 1975, *Medieval Archaeol*, **23**, 197–200

Morris, C A 1983. Wooden Objects, in Heighway, C M, *The East and North Gates of Gloucester and Associated Sites, Excavations 1974–81*, Western Archaeol Trust Monogr, **4**, 206–10

Morris, C A 1994. *Lincoln – Wigford sites*, Unpublished report for City Lincoln Archaeol Unit

Morris, C A 1998. The Wooden Artefacts, in Cool, H E M and Philo, C (eds), Roman Castleford Excavations 1974–85 Volume 1: the small finds, *Yorkshire Archaeol*, **4**, 335–46

Morris, C A forthcoming. *Wood and Woodworking in Anglo-Scandinavian and Medieval Coppergate*, The Archaeology of York, **17/13**, CBA, York

Morris, C A & Evans, D H 1992. The Wood, in Evans, D H & Tomlinson, D G (eds), *Excavations at 33–35 Eastgate, Beverley, 1983–6*, Sheffield Excavation Rep, 189–209

Mould, Q 1985. *Lucy Tower, Lincoln. The Leather*, Unpublished report for Trust Lincolnshire Archaeol

Mould, Q 1987. *The Leather from the excavations at Brayford Wharf East*, Unpublished report for Trust Lincolnshire Archaeol

Mould, Q 1993. *Lincoln Wigford sites*, Unpublished report for City Lincoln Archaeol Unit

Nicholson, C & Carrott, J 1993. *Parasite eggs from two Lincoln sites: Brayford Wharf East (BWE82) and Waterside Foreshore (WF89)*, Unpublished report for City Lincoln Archaeol Unit

O'Connor, 1982. *Animal bones from Flaxengate, Lincoln, c 870–1500*, The Archaeology of Lincoln, **18–1**, CBA, London

Oldenstein, J 1976. Zur Ausrustung römischer Auxiliarein-

heiten, *Bericht der Römisch-Germanischen Kommission*, **57**, 49–284

Orton, C R & Tyers, P A 1990. Statistical analysis of ceramic assemblages, *Archeologia et Calcolatori*, **1**, 81–110

Orton, C R, Tyers P A & Vince, A G 1993. *Pottery in Archaeology*, Cambridge Manuals in Archaeology, Cambridge University Press, Cambridge

Otter, M & Jones, M J 1987. St Mark's Station, in Nurser, E (ed), *Archaeology in Lincolnshire 1986–1987*, Ann Rep Trust Lincolnshire Archaeol, **3**, 27, Lincoln

Otter, M & Jones, M J 1988. St Mark's Station 1987, in Nurser, E (ed), *Archaeology in Lincolnshire 1987–1988*, Ann Rep Trust Lincolnshire Archaeol, **4**, 24, Sleaford

Page, W (ed) 1906. *Lincolnshire, II*, Victoria History of the Counties of England

Parker, H 1965. A medieval wharf at Thoresby College Courtyard, King's Lynn, *Medieval Archaeol*, **9**, 94–104

Parsons, D 1986. Sacrarium: ablution drains in early medieval churches, in Butler, L A S & Morris, R K (eds), *The Anglo-Saxon church*, CBA Res Rep, **60**, 105–20

Parsons, D 1989. *Liturgy and Architecture in the Middle Ages*, Deerhurst Lecture Ser, **3**, Friends of Deerhurst Church/ Univ Leicester Dept Adult Education

Peacock, D P S & Williams, D F 1992. *Imported Roman Marble from Lincoln*, Ancient Monuments Laboratory Rep **36/92**, English Heritage

Perring, D 1981. *Early Medieval Occupation at Flaxengate, Lincoln*, The Archaeology of Lincoln, **9–1**, CBA, London

Pevsner, N & Harris, J 1989. *Lincolnshire*, The Buildings of England, 2nd edn revised by N Antram, Penguin Books, London

Philpott, R A 1991. *Burial practices in Roman Britain: a survey of grave treatment and furnishing, AD 43–410*, Brit Archaeol Rep, Brit Ser, **219**, Oxford

Price, J & Cottam, S 1993a. *Report on the Roman glass from Chaplin Street Lincoln*, Unpublished report for City Lincoln Archaeol Unit

Price, J & Cottam, S 1993b. *Report on the Roman glass from Monson Street Lincoln*, Unpublished report for City Lincoln Archaeol Unit

Price, J & Cottam, S 1993c. *Report on the Roman glass from St. Benedict's Lincoln*, Unpublished report for City Lincoln Archaeol Unit

Price, J & Cottam, S 1993d. *Report on the Roman glass from St. Mark's Station Lincoln*, Unpublished report for City Lincoln Archaeol Unit

Price, J & Cottam, S 1993e. *Report on the Roman glass from St. Mary's Guildhall Lincoln*, Unpublished archive report, City of Lincoln Archaeology Unit

Price, J & Cottam, S 1993f. *Report on the Roman vessel and window glass from St. Mark's Church Lincoln*, Unpublished report for City Lincoln Archaeol Unit

Price, J, Cottam, S, & Worrell, S forthcoming. *Roman Glass from Excavations in Lincoln*, Lincoln Archaeol Stud,

Rackham, J 1994. *Identification of Lincoln City Archaeological bone finds*, Unpublished report for City Lincoln Archaeol Unit

Rey-Vodoz, V 1994. Mensa Ponderaria, in *Roman Museum Nyon*, **42**, Nyon

Richmond, I A 1946. The Roman city of Lincoln and the four coloniae of Roman Britain, *Archaeol J* **103**, 25–68

Roberts, N 1984. *A report on diatoms from Brayford Wharf East*, Unpublished report for City Lincoln Archaeol Unit

Roe, F 1994. *Lincoln: Wigford sites. The Worked Stone*, Unpublished report for City Lincoln Archaeol Unit

Rogerson, A & Ashley, S J 1987. The Parish Churches of Barton Bendish: the excavation of All Saints' and the architecture of St Andrew's and St Mary's, in Rogerson, A, Ashley, S J, Williams, P & Harris, A (eds), *Three Norman Churches in Norfolk*, East Anglian Archaeol, **32**, 1–66, Norfolk Archaeol Unit, Dereham

Rogerson, A & Dallas, C 1984. *Excavations in Thetford, 1948–59 and 1973–80*, East Anglian Archaeol, **22**, Norfolk Archaeol Unit, Dereham

Roskams, S 1992. Finds context and deposit status: a relational quality, in Steane K (ed), 27–9

Ross, J 1853. *Civitas Lincolniensis I*, Lincoln

Salisbury, C 1980. The Trent, the story of a river, *Curr Archaeol*, **74**, 88–91

Salisbury, C 1991. Primitive British Fishweirs, in Good, G L, Jones, R H & Ponsford, M W (eds), *Waterfront Archaeology*, CBA Res Rep, **74**, 76–87, CBA, London

Saunders, A 1978. Excavations in the Church of St Augustine's Abbey, Canterbury 1955–58, *Medieval Archaeol*, **22**, 25–63

Scott, S 1986a. *A comparative study of the Roman animal bone assemblages from Monson Street and from Roman and later deposits at St Mary's Guildhall*, Unpublished report for Trust Lincolnshire Archaeol

Scott, S 1986b. *A 16th century cattle horn core assemblage from the site of St. Mary's Guildhall, Lincoln*, Unpublished report for Trust Lincolnshire Archaeol

Scott, S 1987. *The animal bones from a series of sites in Lincoln*, Unpublished report for Trust Lincolnshire Archaeol

Scott, S 1999. Animal bones, in Jones M J (ed), 169–78, 236–46

Shepherd, L 1993. Interpreting landscapes – analysis of excavations in and around the southern bailey of Norwich Castle, in Barber J W (ed), *Interpreting Stratigraphy*, 3–10, AOC (Scotland) Ltd, Edinburgh

Speed, J 1610. Map of Lincolnshire

Steane, K (ed), 1992. *Interpretation of Stratigraphy: A review of the art, proceedings of a conference held on 18th June 1992 at Lincoln*, City Lincoln Archaeol Rep, **31**, 27–9, Lincoln

Stocker, D A 1986. The excavated stonework in Gilmour, B J J & Stocker, D A, 44–82

Stocker, D A 1990. The Archaeology of the Reformation in Lincoln, A Case Study in the Redistribution of Building Materials in the Mid Sixteenth Century, *Lincolnshire Hist Archaeol*, **25** , 18–32

Stocker, D A 1991. *St Mary's Guildhall, Lincoln*, The Archaeology of Lincoln, **12–1**, CBA, London

Stocker, D A 1998. A Hitherto Unidentified Image of the Mithraic God Arimanius at Lincoln? *Britannia* **29**, 359–363.

Stocker, D A 1999. 'A Very Goodly House Longging to Sulton...' A Reconstruction of John O'Gaunt's Palace, *Lincolnshire Hist Archaeol* 34, 5–15

Stocker, D & Everson, P 1990. Rubbish Recycled: A Study of the Re-use of Stone in Lincolnshire, in Parsons, D (ed), *Stone: Quarrying and Building in England AD 43–1525*, 83–101, Phillimore in assoc with Roy Archaeol Inst

Stukeley, W 1776. *Itinerarium Curiosum*, 2nd edn

Tann, G & Jones, M J 1982. Waterside South (C & A), in Nurser, E (ed), *Archaeology in Lincoln 1981–82*, Ann Rep Lincoln Archaeol Trust, **10**, 26–7, Lincoln

Taylor, M 1987. *St. Benedict's Square, Lincoln – wattle/hurdle structure*, Unpublished report for Trust Lincolnshire Archaeol

Taylor, T P 1977. *Lincoln – Interim soil report*, Unpublished report for Lincoln Archaeol Trust

Trimble, R 1998. *St Mark's Station, High Street, Lincoln* Unpublished report to Simons Estates Ltd May 1998, City Lincoln Archaeol Rep, **338**

Trollope, E 1860. Roman Inscriptions and Sepulchral Remains at Lincoln, *Archaeol J*, **17**, 1–21

Turner, H M 1970. *Town Defences in England and Wales: An architectural and documentary study AD 900–1500*, London

Van Beek, G C 1983. *Dental Morphology: An Illustrated Guide*, Wright, Oxford (2nd edn)

Van Es, W A & Verwers, W S 1980. *Excavations at Dorestad 1 The Harbour: Hoogstraat I*, Nederlandse Oudheden, **9**, ROB, Amersfoort

Vince, A 1991. The Valencian Lustreware Bowl, in Stocker, D A, 69–72

Vince, A (ed) 1991. *Lincoln Excavations 1972–87 Analysis and Publication Research Design*, City Lincoln Archaeol Rep, **3**

Vince, A 1994. The Archaeology of Yesterday, in Jones, M J (ed), *Lincoln Archaeology*, Ann Rep City Lincoln Archaeol Unit, **6**, 27–31, Lincoln

Vince, A (ed) 1993. *Pre-Viking Lindsey*, Lincoln Archaeol Stud, **1**, Lincoln

Walton Rogers, P 1992. *Textiles from Dudley Castle, West Midlands*, Unpublished TRA Report

Walton Rogers, P 1993. *Textiles from the City of Lincoln 1972–1989*, Unpublished report for City Lincoln Archaeol Unit

Walton Rogers, P 1996. *Textiles from The Brooks, Winchester (1987–88)*, Unpublished TRA Report on behalf of Winchester Museums Service

Watts, D J 1989. Infant Burials and Romano-British Christianity, *Archaeol J*, **146**, 372–83

Weeks, J 1978. A Roman Ladder from Queen Street, City of London, *Trans London Middlesex Archaeol Soc*, **29**, 104–12

Whitwell, J B 1992. *Roman Lincolnshire*, History of Lincolnshire, **2**, Lincoln (rev edn)

Wiggins, R, Boylston, A & Roberts, C unpublished. *Report on the Human Skeletal Material from Blackfriars, Gloucester*, unpublished report, Calvin Wells Laboratory, University of Bradford

Wilkinson, T J 1986. *St Marks Station. Sedimentary deposits at West end of site*, Unpublished report for City Lincoln Archaeol Unit

Wilthew, P 1984. *Analysis of Roman Wall Painting Pigments from St Mark's, Lincoln*, Ancient Monuments Laboratory Rep, **4316**

Young, J, Hooper, J & Wilmot, A 1988. Pottery from St Mark's East, in Nurser, E (ed), *Archaeology in Lincolnshire 1987–1988*, Ann Rep Trust Lincolnshire Archaeol, **4**, 29–32, Sleaford

Young, J & Vince, A G with Naylor, V & Kemp, R forthcoming. *A Corpus of Saxon and Medieval Pottery from Lincoln*, Lincoln Archaeol Stud

Index

*This index assumes that all readers will have read the Introduction (pages 1–10) which explains the history of the excavations and the processes of recording and reporting. This volume does not deal with finds as such, and they are referred to only cursorily in the index, as is pottery which is cited throughout the report as an indicator of the date of deposits. Pages numbers marked with an asterisk * indicate references to objects or material that has already been published elsewhere or is included in an archive report.*

Adam, mayor 3
anchor, see weight
animal bone 12*, 19*, 23*, 26*, 40*, 55*. 66*, 79*, 92*, 95,
    104*, 111, 115*, 118*, 121–2, 136*, 156*, 182*, 184, 188*,
    190*, 197*, 202, 205, 221*, 235, 252*, 290 339
antler, see bone
architectural fragments (Medieval) 39, 171, 202, 213, 219*,
    221*, 259
archive 8, 10, 331–40
awl, iron 232

Bargates 3, 177
Battle of Lincoln 3
bell 119, 130
bibliography 10, 351–6
bird bones (see also animal bones) 195
boat, clinker-built 92*, 94
bone working 158, 168–9
bone objects 12*, 18*, 39*, 66*, 92*, 104*, 136, 156*, 181*,
    220*, 290
botanical remains 19*, 66*, 92*, 156*, 163, 182*, 193, 222*,
    225
Brayford Pool 146–8, 176, 308–10, 313, 325
Brayford Wharf East 1982 (bwe82) 6, 65–80
Brayford Wharf North 1975 (bwe75) 6, 81–90
John Broxholme of Lincoln 216
buckle, copper-alloy 180*
Buck's drawings (1724 & 1743) 149, 261
building construction, Roman 269–272
buildings 100
    Roman 29, 35–6, 64, 105–10, 124, 126, 182–90, 206, 209,
        224–48, 269–74, 291, 304, 310–1, 312, 313–4
    Saxon 130, 191–3, 314–6
    Norman 37–40
    Medieval 39, 120, 131, 163–4, 193–204, 206–7, 316–7
    Post-Medieval 122

burials, see cemetery
butchery waste (animal remains) 76*, 106, 108, 120, 128,
    131, 139, 146*, 160–2, 169, 193*, 202, 225, 251

C14, see radiocarbon
candlestick 131
Carmelite Friary 3, 199, 207, 209, 211–7, 317, 318, 325
cellars
    Roman 127–8
    15/16th cent 121, 131–4, 318
    17th cent and later 97, 100, 301–2
cemetery
    Roman 19–21, 29, 31–3, 50, 213, 278–9, 283–6, 311,
    Saxon 252–4, 295
    Medieval 198, 203–4, 207, 221, 252, 254–6, 259–264,
        283–6, 318
chalice, lead 260
Chaplin Street 1973 (cs73) 6, 11–16
'charcoal burials' 253, 279–80
charnel 261
charred plant remains, see botanical remains
cg, see context groups
charcoal burials 280
church, timber 251*, 278
church, see St Mark's church
City Ditch 318, 325
city wall 148, 318, 325
coffins, coffin fittings 221, 253, 255, 262, 265, 267, 284
coins (Roman) 12*, 39*, 66*, 101–2*, 109, 115, 116, 130,
    158, 181*, 186, 187, 210, 220*, 240, 244, 274–6, 290*, 291,
    293, 295
coins (Medieval and Modern) 39, 181*, 193, 220*, 255,
    258, 263, 265, 267, 290*
colonia 1, 123, 126–7
commercial activity 62–3, 129, 150, 273–6
context groups 5–6, 335